The Celebrated Marquis

Also by John D. Bessler

Death in the Dark: Midnight Executions in America

Kiss of Death: America's Love Affair with the Death Penalty

Legacy of Violence: Lynch Mobs and Executions in Minnesota

Writing for Life: The Craft of Writing for Everyday Living

*Cruel and Unusual: The American Death Penalty and the
Founders' Eighth Amendment*

The Birth of American Law: An Italian Philosopher and the American Revolution

Against the Death Penalty (editor)

The Death Penalty as Torture: From the Dark Ages to Abolition

The Celebrated Marquis

An Italian Noble and the
Making of the Modern World

John D. Bessler

ASSOCIATE PROFESSOR OF LAW
UNIVERSITY OF BALTIMORE SCHOOL OF LAW

CAROLINA ACADEMIC PRESS
Durham, North Carolina

ISBN 978-1-61163-786-1
e-ISBN 978-1-53100-974-8

Library of Congress Cataloging-in-Publication Data

Names: Bessler, John D., author.
Title: The celebrated marquis : an Italian noble and the making of the modern
    world / John D. Bessler.
Description: Durham, North Carolina : Carolina Academic Press, [2018] |
    Includes bibliographical references and index.
Identifiers: LCCN 2017044418 | ISBN 9781611637861 (alk. paper)
Subjects: LCSH: Beccaria, Cesare, marchese di, 1738-1794. |
    Economists--Italy--Biography. | Criminologists--Italy--Biography. |
    Political science--History.
Classification: LCC HB109.B43 B47 2018 | DDC 330.092 [B] --dc23
LC record available at https://lccn.loc.gov/2017044418

Carolina Academic Press, LLC
700 Kent Street
Durham, North Carolina 27701
Telephone (919) 489-7486
Fax (919) 493-5668
www.cap-press.com

For human rights advocates and defenders everywhere

Engraving of Cesare Beccaria by Carlo Faucci, 1766

"Cesare Beccaria (1738–1794) was an Italian nobleman of Jesuit schooling whose theories were embraced by many leaders of the 'Age of Enlightenment' besides Thomas Jefferson. Beccaria's 1764 *On Crimes and Punishments* (*Dei delitti e delle pene*) was revolutionary in its time, so much so that he originally published it anonymously."

—Barbara Esposito & Lee Wood,
Prison Slavery (1982)

" 'In every human society,' says the celebrated Marquis Beccaria, 'there is an effort continually tending to confer on one part the height of power and happiness, and to reduce the other to the extreme of weakness and misery. The intent of good laws is to oppose this effort, and to diffuse their influence universally and equally.' "

—Letter of the Continental Congress to the
Inhabitants of Quebec (1774), quoting
Cesare Beccaria's *On Crimes and Punishments*

"Leopold has established a commission for the reform of the criminal code in Austrian Lombardy, and to the honour of his judgment and liberality, let it be mentioned, that he has named, as one of the members of that commission, the celebrated marquis Beccaria, so well known in the literary and political world...."

—*The American Museum* (1791)

"In the course of the last century, a very general sensation was created throughout Europe against the severity and injustice of its criminal law. In exciting this feeling, Montesquieu and Voltaire led the way with distinguished ability and success; but it was in a small state and under a despotic government, that this subject was opened to its full extent, in the celebrated work of the Marquis Beccaria."

—William Roscoe, *Observations on
Penal Jurisprudence, and the
Reformation of Criminals* (1819)

Contents

Acknowledgments

I would like to heartily thank the staff at Carolina Academic Press for their work on *The Celebrated Marquis: An Italian Noble and the Making of the Modern World*. This is the third book I have published with Carolina Academic Press, and I have been continually impressed by the responsiveness and professionalism of everyone at the press. Writing a book is hard enough, so it is a real gift to find a high-quality publisher to handle the design and production and the typesetting and marketing of the book once it is finished. A special shout out to Grace Pledger for her work on the page proofs and the cover design.

I would also like to thank my friends and colleagues at the University of Baltimore School of Law for their long-standing support of my scholarship. The law school's dean, Ron Weich, has been tremendously supportive over the years, sponsoring book events at the law school and authorizing summer grants to further my work on various writing projects, including this one. It is a real pleasure to work with such wonderful colleagues, all of whom are smart, intellectually curious, and fiercely committed to teaching the next generation of lawyers. Attorneys and judges are critical to safeguarding democratic institutions, and that is clear now more than ever. As Justice Sonia Sotomayor once advised: "I firmly believe in the rule of law as the foundation for all of our basic rights."

A special thank you is also extended to Carlo Scognamiglio Pasini, an economist and the former president of the Italian Senate who I had the honor to meet at an Aspen Institute event in Rome at a prior conference on Cesare Beccaria's life and legacy. I was there to talk about my 2014 book about Cesare Beccaria's influence on America's Founding Fathers, *The Birth of American Law: An Italian Philosopher and the American Revolution*. And he was there to talk about his own book about Beccaria's work as an economist, *L'arte della ricchezza: Cesare Beccaria economista*, published in 2014 by Mondadori Università. As I was in the final stages of working on this book, he graciously provided some important information about Beccaria—as well as some Italian-to-English translations—for incorporation into the final manuscript. He also generously gave of his time to review the entire manuscript, a courtesy for which I will be eternally grateful.

A similar thank you goes to everyone—family, friends, fellow scholars—I have spoken to over the last several years about Cesare Beccaria and his ideas. Spending time researching—and then writing about—the Enlightenment has been a real pleasure, and many people, from academic librarians to my wife, Amy, and daughter, Abigail, have indulged and facilitated my passion for the study of this endlessly interesting period of history. The people who have provided little tidbits about Cesare

Beccaria or taken an abiding interest in getting to know more about him are too numerous to mention here, but I am grateful for all of them. It is my hope that this book will expose new generations of students and scholars, as well as amateur and professional historians alike, to the life and times of Cesare Beccaria and his ideas and humanitarian impulses.

About the Author

John D. Bessler teaches at the University of Baltimore School of Law and the Georgetown University Law Center. He is also of counsel at the Minneapolis law firm of Berens & Miller, P.A., which handles complex, commercial litigation. A two-time Minnesota Book Award finalist and the winner of an *Independent Publisher* Book Award, he is the author of multiple books on the subject of capital punishment. His 2014 book about Cesare Beccaria, *The Birth of American Law: An Italian Philosopher and the American Revolution*, was the gold winner of the IndieFab Book of the Year Award for history and received the first prize in the 2015 American Association for Italian Studies Book Award contest for a work of history focused on the eighteenth and nineteenth centuries. *The Birth of American Law* also won the Scribes Book Award, an annual award given out since 1961 by the American Society of Legal Writers for "the best work of legal scholarship published during the previous year." He has also taught at the University of Minnesota Law School, The George Washington University Law School, Rutgers School of Law, and the University of Aberdeen in Scotland. In 2018 he will be a visiting scholar at the Human Rights Center of the University of Minnesota Law School.

The Celebrated Marquis

Introduction

The eighteenth-century economist and criminal-law theorist Cesare Beccaria, an aristocrat from Milan, has been called "the Italian" Adam Smith.[1] Joseph Schumpeter, the Austrian-American economist who made that pronouncement, actually characterized Smith—in a role reversal—as "the Scottish Beccaria."[2] An influential twentieth-century academic and banker who served as Austria's Finance Minister before joining Harvard University's faculty in 1932, Schumpeter thus put the two men on more or less equal footing in the history of economics.[3] Schumpeter even classed Beccaria's Milanese teaching notes—prepared in the late 1760s and early 1770s as part of Beccaria's short stint in academia but only published posthumously as *Elementi di economia pubblica* (1804)[4]—as superior to Smith's Glasgow lectures, making a favorable comparison to *An Inquiry into the Nature and Causes of the Wealth of Nations* (1776).[5] Beccaria's lectures, one commentator emphasizes, "anticipated the economic theories of Adam Smith and the theories of Thomas Malthus on population and subsistence."[6] As another source, *A History of Modern Culture*, emphasizes of the historical significance of his lectures: "Beccaria, the reformer of the criminal law, gave some lectures on *The Elements of Political Economy* (written 1769–70, published 1804) advancing new views on the relation of population to subsistence and on the division of labor and on wages. In these latter doctrines he, like so many of his contemporaries, prepared the way for the classic treatise of Adam Smith."[7]

In Peter Groenewegen's *Eighteenth-century Economics: Turgot, Beccaria and Smith and Their Contemporaries*, Beccaria is one of just three economists warranting mention in the subtitle. Beccaria, Groenewegen writes, was familiar with the work of the French economist François Quesnay (1694–1774), with "the major analytical influence on Beccaria's economics" being that of the founder of modern economics, Richard Cantillon (1680–1734), "as is apparent in the outline of his lectures which follow the content order of Cantillon's *Essai* very closely." Cantillon, the Irish-French banker and economist who, after emigrating to Paris in 1714, made millions through land speculation and his association with Scottish financier John Law (1671–1729), wrote *Essai sur la Nature du Commerce en Général* (*Essay on the Nature of Trade in General*). Cantillon's *Essai* was penned in the 1730s but it was not published until 1755, more than twenty years after his death. That essay first appeared in print in May 1755 in Paris, and it rapidly got the attention of political economists, including Quesnay, Turgot, Beccaria, Smith and Condillac. Cantillon's contemporary, John Law—the Controller General of Finances under the Duke of Orleans, regent for France's young king, Louis

XV—had previously written *Money and Trade Considered: With a Proposal for Supplying the Nation with Money* (1705) and had pioneered the use of paper money.

Schumpeter himself called Adam Smith (1723–1790), Cesare Beccaria (1738–1794), and the French physiocrat Anne-Robert-Jacques Turgot (1727–1781) the great "triumvirate" of eighteenth-century economists. A French administrator and the governor of the commune of Limoges, Turgot—part of a group of progressive economists known for their support of free trade—became known for his *Reflections on the Formation and Distribution of Wealth* (1766). Turgot, Groenewegen notes, "reached the greatest heights of his illustrious career in his position as Finance Minister (Contrôleur-général) of France from 1774 to 1776." Whereas John Law, one of Turgot's predecessors, was once sentenced to death at the Old Bailey in London for killing a man in a duel in the 1690s (a sentence later remitted to a fine) and became the architect of what came to be known as "The Mississippi Bubble" (1717–1720), one of the earliest examples of an economic bubble, Richard Cantillon coined the term *entrepreneur*. John Law—a gambler who favored paper over metallic money and who, in the words of one scholar, Joseph Salerno—"almost singlehandedly destroyed the French monetary system in the course of four short years." As the founder and head of France's national bank, the *Banque Générale*, Law also presided over the bank's collapse when rampant speculation led to panic. As values plummeted, a mad rush to convert paper money into coins led to riots, with John Law forced to flee Paris at nightfall. He later died in poverty in Venice. Richard Cantillon had helped found John Law's ill-fated Mississippi Company, but he was savvier than Law and profited handsomely as a result of his financing of speculation in the North American real estate market. Cantillon's work—considered the first treatise on economic theory—heavily influenced Beccaria, Quesnay, Turgot and Smith as the study and field of economics came into its own.[8]

While *The Wealth of Nations* turned Adam Smith into a household name and an international celebrity, Cesare Beccaria's most influential book, the now little-remembered *Dei delitti e delle pene* (1764), translated into English as *An Essay on Crimes and Punishments* (1767), came first. Published just a year before the first Stamp Act riot broke out in mid-August 1765 in Boston, Massachusetts, *Dei delitti e delle pene* openly took on the injustice of tyranny and cruelty and sought the passage of laws to further the common good. "In every human society," it proclaimed, "there is an effort continually tending to confer on one part the height of power and happiness, and to reduce the other to the extreme of weakness and misery." "The intent of good laws," it urged, "is to oppose this effort, and to diffuse their influence universally and equally.'" That central theme of Beccaria's book, a wildly popular text among Enlightenment thinkers, inspired Boston's Sons of Liberty as their discontent with King George III and the British Parliament rose to fever pitch. Even before America's Revolutionary War broke out in 1775, the American colonists (and soon-to-be American rebels and patriots) had been reading—and carefully studying—Beccaria's book, a little treatise that inspired a more egalitarian and just and civilized society.

The American Revolution, the political upheaval that led to America's independence, came about after the thirteen original colonies rejected British rule. The colonists, in the lead up to the Revolutionary War, had grown increasingly frustrated with Great Britain's oppressive monarchy, and they vehemently resisted the efforts of Britain's Parliament to tax them—and to pass oppressive laws affecting them—when the colonists had no say in their own governance. Led by General George Washington, a former British military officer who had himself been influenced by Beccaria's book, the American colonists took up arms to fight for their freedom. "The American Revolution," writes David Williams of the University of Sheffield in his book, *The Enlightenment*, "created the first modern republic, and in so doing set in train a much wider, and irreversible, process of change elsewhere, not least in France." And during that tumultuous revolution, Cesare Beccaria's much-invoked ideas—as well as his stirring prose in *Dei delitti e delle pene*, whether in the original Italian or in translation—frequently took center stage, infusing the thoughts of American revolutionaries who felt disrespected and badly mistreated by the British Empire. "In connection with the American experience, it can be said, without risking too much," Italian-American historian Adolph Caso once wrote, "that this single book found more outright application in making and shaping the new nation than is otherwise believed." "Beccaria's *Dei Delitti e Delle Pene* (On Crimes and Punishments)," Caso emphasized in *We, the People*, without much hint (or need) of hyperbole, "may have been the single most influential book of the second half of the eighteenth century, having influenced both Europeans and Americans of the Revolutionary period."[9]

A review of the historical record shows that Cesare Beccaria's impactful words appear again and again in America's founding era, including at historic moments that define U.S. history. Take, for example, the events surrounding one of America's most infamous pre-Revolutionary War episodes—a dramatic incident that would be used by American patriots, such as Samuel Adams and Paul Revere, to foment rebellion against the British monarchy and aristocracy. On March 5, 1770, British soldiers had killed five colonists in what came to be known as the Boston Massacre. "It was," as one source reports, "the culmination of tensions in the American colonies that had been growing since Royal troops first appeared in Massachusetts in October 1768 to enforce the heavy tax burden imposed by the Townshend Acts." Samuel Adams had called the killings in Boston a "bloody butchery," with his cousin John Adams—then a practicing lawyer, but later the second President of the United States of America—ultimately taking on the unenviable task of defending, along with fellow attorney Josiah Quincy, Jr., the British soldiers accused of murder. When it came time for trial, John Adams looked to Beccaria's wisdom in making his humanistic courtroom appeal. "*May it please your Honours and you Gentlemen of the Jury*," Adams said at trial, "I am for the prisoners at the bar, and shall apologize for it only in the words of the Marquis *Beccaria*: 'If I can but be the instrument of preserving one life, his blessing and tears of transport, shall be a sufficient consolation to me, for the contempt of all mankind.'" "This appeal," explains historian Richard Alan Ryerson of Adams' evocative invocation of Beccaria's words in open court, "was designed to blunt the town's rage against the British soldiers by placing the trial in its broadest legal context, to draw the jury's thoughts away from the local issue of revenge and direct them to the timeless, global question of justice, tempered by mercy."[10]

Not only did Cesare Beccaria's words shape courthouse deliberations at the Boston Massacre trial, they changed the history of the world writ large just as the American

Revolution did in the years following the first appearance of Beccaria's book. On December 16, 1773, in what came to be known as the Boston Tea Party, Massachusetts colonists disguised as Mohawk Indians destroyed a whole shipment of tea sent by the British East India Company; they were protesting the British Parliament's Tea Act of May 10, 1773, a legislative measure designed to help the financially troubled enterprise. Although the Tea Act repealed import duties on English tea to enable the British East India Company to undersell Dutch tea being smuggled into North America, the law gave the company a monopoly on the import of tea and retained the controversial Townshend duty for tea—a revenue-raiser named after Charles Townshend, the Chancellor of the Exchequer. One provision of the Townshend Acts, which raised revenue in the colonies for the salaries of governors and judges, required the payment of the unpopular duty on tea within 21 days of a ship's arrival in the American colonies. "Patriots," as one history puts it, "saw the Tea Act as a Trojan horse that would destroy liberty by seducing the settlers into accepting parliamentary sovereignty." After the colonists tossed 342 chests of tea into Boston Harbor rather than pay the loathed Townshend duty, the British responded with even more draconian measures, including a series of punitive, retaliatory laws that American patriots called the Intolerable Acts. Those acts of Parliament provided that (1) no ship was to enter or leave the port of Boston until payment was made for the destruction of the tea, worth approximately £11,000 sterling (more that $700,000 in today's dollars); (2) Massachusetts was to lose its charter and be put under the king's direct control; (3) English officers or soldiers could be taken to England for trial for acts done in the discharge of their duties in Massachusetts, making them less accountable; and (4) British troops could be quartered in houses in any American colony.[11] The Boston Tea Party thus set in motion events that would lead, inexorably, to the Revolutionary War.

It was through that political lens that Cesare Beccaria's book, *On Crimes and Punishments*, was considered by America's colonists, people desirous of liberty and anxious for new ways of looking at the world. Written by an unknown, newly minted lawyer in the Italian-speaking realm of the vast Habsburg Empire, *Dei delitti e delle pene*—denouncing tyranny, yet read by men thousands of miles away from the home of its noble author—stirred angry American colonists to agitate for freedom and self-government. "No taxation without representation" had become the rallying cry of the disgruntled and oppressed North American colonists, a slogan that—in the Age of Beccaria—soon broke into the hard-fought Revolutionary War (1775–1783).[12] As one writer, Rebecca Stefoff, notes of the crucial role that Beccaria's book played in sparking a new world order: "Copies of Beccaria's book were sold in the American colonies. Thomas Jefferson, George Washington, and John Adams all owned the book, and it appeared in several colonial newspapers. It was part of the wave of Enlightenment thought that helped mold ideas in the colonies and contributed to the Revolutionary War, the Declaration of Independence, and the U.S. Constitution." "Beccaria's work," she adds of the effect of *Dei delitti e delle pene*, "also inspired debate about the death penalty in the colonies." "Beccaria's influence in the United States, just like in Europe, was a combination of good ideas and good timing," another text has pointed out of the social change wrought by *On Crimes and Punishments*. "The late 1770s saw increasing unrest in the American colonies, which in 1775 exploded into the Revolutionary War," that source stresses.[13]

Like Montesquieu's writings and Adam Smith's *The Wealth of Nations*, Beccaria's bestseller—a product of the Italian Enlightenment—fundamentally shaped human affairs across the globe. It catalyzed the American Revolution and the French Revolution that closely followed on its heels, and it proved to be a major civilizing force in a world still mired in barbaric practices from the Dark Ages. In an era of ruthless monarchs, grotesque corporal punishments and public executions, and medieval instruments of torment, *Dei delitti e delle pene*—at first published anonymously for fear of persecution—challenged long-entrenched practices of the *Ancien Régime* by arguing for proportionality between crimes and punishments and against torture and the death penalty. In it, Beccaria spoke out against infamy and religious intolerance and in favor of jury trials and equality, with Beccaria—the young Milanese philosopher and economist, still in his mid-twenties when he wrote *Dei delitti e delle pene*—seeking clear and precise laws that would further the public good. Like his Italian mentor, the Milanese economist Pietro Verri, Beccaria wrote about maximizing people's happiness, and—following Montesquieu's advice—he railed against unjust and unnecessary punishments, calling them "tyrannical."[14] The Italian peninsula was then a hotbed of economic and philosophical inquiry, with thinkers in places such as Naples, Milan and Venice grappling with important questions of human development. For example, in 1757, the Venetian economist, mathematician and monk, Giammaria Ortes (1713–1790), also known as Giovanni Maria Ortes, had published his *Calcolo de' piaceri e de' dolori della vita umana* (*A Calculation of the Pleasures and Pains of Human Life*).[15]

By the time Cesare Beccaria penned *Dei delitti e delle pene*, the French *Encyclopédistes*—Denis Diderot (1713–1784), the writer and philosopher, and Jean le Rond d'Alembert (1717–1783), another mathematician—had already embarked on writing and editing their now famed *Encyclopédie*, a seminal work published during the Enlightenment. It was a massive, multi-decade effort, designed—as one source puts it—"as a means of diffusing" light to all of Europe and "of destroying all ancient prejudices." With inquisitorial bodies and religious persecution rampant in that era, the innovative, boundary-pushing *Encyclopédie*—at least to some—was seen as promoting godlessness and as a threat to the Catholic Church's religious doctrines and teachings. It was in 1751, in the *Preliminary Discourse* to the *Encyclopédie*, that the editors laid out their vision for what they hoped to accomplish. Published originally in French as "Discours préliminaire des editeurs" in the first volume of the work, the *Preliminary Discourse*—written by Jean Le Rond d'Alembert with ideas from his fellow scholars—has been described as "the manifesto of the French Enlightenment" and "the *locus classicus* for the French Enlightenment's self-understanding." "Its central part," *A Companion to Hume* notes, "is a potted history of intellectual progress since the Renaissance, and it is in this section that English scientists and philosophers loom large." "The story there," that resource observes, highlighting the appearance of "the immortal Chancellor of England, Francis Bacon," in d'Alembert's introduction, "has the familiar ring of Enlightenment history: of great men who rescued intellectual endeavour from the darkness and superstition imposed on it by ignorance and priestcraft."[16]

As members of a society of French writers, the *Société de Gens de lettres*, the *Encyclopédistes* promoted the advancement of science and secular thought and argued for rationality and tolerance instead of superstition and what was all-too-often religious-based brutality. The work of more than 130 contributors, the *Encyclopédie* had, as its purpose, as Diderot put it: "to collect knowledge disseminated around the globe; to set forth its general system to the men with whom we live; and transmit it to all who will come after us, so that the work of preceding centuries will not become useless to the centuries to come, and so that our offspring, becoming better instructed, will at the same time become more virtuous and happy, and that we should not die without having rendered a service to the human race." Beccaria himself had become interested in the ideas of the French *Encyclopédistes*, with the Academy of Fists—the informal salon he joined in Milan in 1762, a social academy that was said to be "the brainchild of Count Pietro Verri and his brother, Alessandro Verri"—reportedly "self-consciously modeled after the circle of the *Philosophes* of the *Encyclopédie*." Pietro Verri is said to be "the founder of the Milanese School and its chief economist," with a 2016 title emphasizing that Pietro Verri "established the *Accademia dei Pugni* (The Punching Academy) in Milan in 1761." As another source puts it, also crediting Cesare Beccaria's early participation in that informal academy: "under the intellectual influence of the brothers Alessandro and Pietro Verri, Beccaria helped to organize a society, *l'Accademia dei Pugni* (the Academy of Fists), which was committed to political and economic reform."[17]

In his own, posthumously published *Elementi di economia pubblica*, Beccaria's writings on trade and economics reflect the influence of the French physiocrats who wrote extensively about the value and importance of agriculture. "Beccaria's support of physiocratic views is particularly clearly illustrated in Part II, chapter 2, of the *Elementi*," economic historian Peter Groenewegen notes. "Beccaria's discussion of agriculture, for example, is," he explains, "largely an analysis of the causes of its decline and the policy remedies for this, an argument which is largely conducted on physiocratic lines." Among the remedies Beccaria sought: a free trade in corn, changes in taxation, and improvements in transportation to better facilitate the trade in commodities. On the subject of manufacturing, Beccaria encouraged free competition and suggested eliminating excessive taxes and restrictions or regulations on trade. In his book, *Eighteenth-century Economics*, Groenewegen surmises that portions of Beccaria's writings were "influenced by Quesnay's second article in the *Encyclopédie*, 'Grains', which Beccaria also would have read, since he had access at least to the early volumes of that work."[18] Eighteenth-century Italy produced a large number of economists, including Pietro Verri and Cesare Beccaria. As one source notes, for example, Verri wrote about "the impolicy of restrictions, especially of those restraining the freedom of the corn-trade, and of those growing out of the privileges of corporations, internal custom-houses, &c."[19]

The first seven volumes of the *Encyclopédie* were produced from 1751 to 1759, but the work was then banned in 1759 by the Catholic Church and by decree of King Louis XV. In that year, Pope Clement XII directed that Catholics have their priests burn copies of the *Encyclopédie* or face excommunication. The remaining ten volumes of the *Encyclopédie*—the last of which was not completed until 1772—were published clandestinely, with Diderot acting as the sole editor after d'Alembert, in 1758, left the ambitious, ground-breaking *Encyclopédie* even as Diderot and his printers continued their work in secret. In all, the *Encyclopédie* contained almost 72,000 articles and more than 3,000 illustrations, a feat that rivaled Samuel Johnson's nine-year effort that produced *A Dictionary of the English Language* (1755), a work that defined more than 40,000 words and that illustrated their meaning using approximately 114,000 literary quotations. Diderot and d'Alembert wrote the majority of the text of the *Encyclopédie*, but contributions also came from other leading intellectuals such as Voltaire, Rousseau and Montesquieu.[20] Despite putting himself at risk, Diderot had adamantly refused to give up the project, telling Voltaire that "to abandon the work is to turn one's back on the breach, and do what the rascals who persecute us desire." After finishing the French *Encyclopédie*, Diderot temporarily took refuge in St. Petersburg, Russia, in 1773, spending five months at the court of the enlightened czarina, Catherine II, who bought his library and provided Diderot with a pension for the rest of his life. It was the same monarch who, less than a decade earlier, after the initial, 1764 publication of *Dei delitti e delle pene*, had offered Cesare Beccaria a position in her court as a legal advisor.[21]

Dei delitti e delle pene was a game-changing text. The reform-minded French *philosophes* were immediately smitten with Beccaria's book when it first appeared in print in 1764. Voltaire—one of the most famous writers of that age—wrote a widely-reprinted commentary on it, calling Beccaria a "lover of humanity." And André Morellet, another contributor to the *Encyclopédie* who later befriended Benjamin Franklin in 1772 and who translated Thomas Jefferson's *Notes on the State of Virginia* (1785), quickly prepared a French translation of Beccaria's slender, 104-page book in late 1765.[22] Also translated into English and German and an array of other languages, *Dei delitti e delle pene* became the talk of all of Europe and the Americas, drawing attention and accolades in cities as diverse as Dublin and Paris, London and Glasgow, and Philadelphia and New York.[23] Whether openly acknowledged or not, Beccaria's cogent, clearly expressed ideas would influence the world's lawmakers for generations to come. "The celebrated Marquis Beccaria, in his 'Treatise on Crimes and Punishments,'" a writer in *The British Controversialist and Impartial Inquirer* emphasized in 1852, "attempted to reduce the proportion between offences and their penalties to the accuracy and precision of a mathematically graduated scale."[24] *On Crimes and Punishments* became a ground-breaking book against which other Enlightenment texts were measured, and it accelerated the demise of the world's torture chambers. It also hastened the curtailment of the use of the punishment of death for various felonies and—as was then the eighteenth-century custom—for minor, even trivial, offenses.

In the late eighteenth century, only a handful of books were as famous as Beccaria's treatise. In that century, a whole host of European writers produced treatises and poetry, dramas and satires, and the novel came into vogue as a literary genre. The English writer Daniel Defoe had published his wildly successful novel, *The Life and Strange Surprising Adventures of Robinson Crusoe*, in London in 1719, and a variety of French, English, Irish and Scottish works had captivated European and colonial audiences. Along with a slew of poetry collections, there was Jonathan Swift's satire, *Gulliver's Travels* (1726); Samuel Richardson's epistolary novel, *Pamela; or Virtue Re-*

warded (1740); John Cleland's erotic novel, *Memoirs of a Woman of Pleasure* (1748–1749); Voltaire's crowd-pleasing satire, *Candide, ou l'Optimisme* (1759); and Laurence Sterne's *The Life and Opinions of Tristram Shandy, Gentleman* (1759–1767), a sprawling, nine-volume comic English novel. Though *Dei delitti e delle pene* was a work of non-fiction, it moved many of its readers as much as any popular poetry collection or fashionable novel. And it was extremely accessible, even getting serialized in *The New-Haven Gazette, and the Connecticut Magazine* over the course of sixteen weeks, from February 23 to August 3, 1786, shortly before the 1787 Constitutional Convention in Philadelphia that produced the United States Constitution.[25]

On Crimes and Punishments inspired scores of reformers throughout the Americas and Europe, including America's Founding Fathers and, in Britain, leading social and penal reformers such as John Howard, Sir William Blackstone and Jeremy Bentham. Appointed the High Sheriff of Bedfordshire in 1773, the English penal reformer John Howard (1726–1790) inspected prisons throughout Europe and exposed their horrid conditions, penning *The State of the Prisons in England and Wales* (1777) in the decade after Beccaria rose to prominence. Like Bentham and Blackstone, Howard fought for penal reform and the creation of modern English penitentiaries in the wake of the publication of *On Crimes and Punishments*.[26] And in places like Tuscany, Austria and early America, Beccaria's book prompted a major overhaul of existing laws—and the existing world order—as torture and death sentences and other bodily punishments fell out of favor. In Philadelphia, *The Pennsylvania Packet*—showing the sustained popularity of *On Crimes and Punishments* after its mid-1760s release—ran this notice in September 1778: "A few Copies of the following much esteemed modern Work, may be had at Bell's Bookstore, next door to St. Paul's Church, in Third-street, Philadelphia, An Essay on Crimes and Punishments: Written by the Marquis Beccaria, of Milan. With a Commentary, attributed to Monsieur De Voltaire." Tellingly, Robert Bell—the Scottish-American printer who had, less than three years earlier, published the first edition of Thomas Paine's *Common Sense* (1776), the fiery pamphlet advocating American independence—also published an octavo edition of Beccaria's treatise in 1778 in the very midst of America's hard-fought Revolutionary War.[27]

In the advertisement for Cesare Beccaria's book, the *Pennsylvania Packet* reprinted an extended extract from the original English translator's preface. That preface, written in 1767 and summarizing the relevance of Beccaria's short treatise, helped to contextualize its importance to eighteenth-century readers. The translator's preface began: "Penal Laws, *so considerable a part of every system of legislation, and of so great importance to the happiness, peace and security of every member of society, are still so imperfect, and are attended with so many unnecessary circumstances of cruelty in all nations, that an attempt to reduce them to the standard of reason must be interesting to all mankind.*" The preface went on to describe why—and how quickly—Beccaria's criminal-law treatise had become such a public sensation: "*It is not surprising, then, that this little book hath engaged the attention of all ranks of people in every part of Europe. It is now about eighteen months since the first publication; in which time it hath passed no less than six editions in the original language; the third of which was printed within six months after its first appearance. It hath been translated into French; that translation*

hath also been several times reprinted, and perhaps no book on any subject was ever re-
ceived with more avidity, more generally read, or more universally applauded."[28]

English radicals, Italian, French, German and Scottish intellectuals, and American and Spanish revolutionaries were deeply moved by *On Crimes and Punishments* and often invoked Beccaria's name with reverence. Cesare Beccaria—as one modern academic recounts of his American impact, felt almost immediately in American state-houses, courtrooms and coffeehouses—"had great influence on Founding-era thinkers and writers." *On Crimes and Punishments* audaciously emphasized equality of treatment, clarity in lawmaking, and what that academic calls "the people's involvement in the criminal justice process." As translated into English in Robert Bell's then newly printed 1778 American edition, Beccaria spoke to America's founders in a profound way by seeking greater public accountability, better governance, and—like Montesquieu—institutional checks on power and privilege. "All trials," Beccaria wrote, arguing for transparency in the halls of justice, greater citizen participation, and clear and just written laws to guide human behavior, "should be public; that opinion which is the best or, perhaps, the only cement of society, may curb the authority of the powerful, and the passions of the judge; and that the people may say, 'We are protected by the laws; we are not slaves.'"[29] In a list of the leading authors and personalities cited by America's founders, Beccaria—per one study—ranks seventh overall in terms of frequency of citation or invocation, lagging behind only the writings of St. Paul the Apostle in the Bible, Montesquieu, Sir William Blackstone, John Locke, David Hume and Plutarch.[30]

Beccaria's book—revered by prominent intellectuals of the day but banned by the Inquisition and put on the Catholic Church's centuries-old Index of Forbidden Books—not only sought a more civilized world, it sparked a firestorm of controversy (and, ultimately, long overdue penal reform) during the Enlightenment. "The barbarity of a nation, if that concept is to be taken in its precise and philosophical sense," Beccaria believed, "is nothing but the ignorance of things useful to that nation, and of the means that are within reach in order to obtain it in a way conforming to the particular happiness of everyone." A nation should not be considered a barbarous one, Beccaria observed at a time of great cruelty and tremendous public interest in poetry, literature and philosophy, medicine and science, and the power of reason, if "knowledge and beliefs are in equilibrium with needs and the maximum happiness conceivable by anyone."[31] In reality, the Enlightenment would not have been the Enlightenment—at least not the same one—without Cesare Beccaria's perceptive vision. As John Kells Ingram, in *A History of Political Economy*, wrote in 1888 when Beccaria's name was still well-known: "Amongst the Italian economists who were most under the influence of the modern spirit, and in closest harmony with the general movement which was impelling the Western nations towards a new social order, Cesare Beccaria (1738–1794) holds a foremost place. He is best known by his celebrated treatise *Dei delitti e delle pene*, by which Voltaire said he had made himself a benefactor of all Europe, and which, we are told, has been translated into twenty-two languages."[32]

The early buyers and readers of *On Crimes and Punishments* in Europe and the Americas made it the eighteenth-century equivalent of a *New York Times* bestseller.[33] At just more than one hundred pages in length, giving it the urgency of a political pamphlet like Thomas Paine's *Common Sense*, Beccaria's book opposed tyranny, questioned long-held assumptions about the criminal law, and sought a new approach to government itself, one focused on egalitarianism and the prosperity and happiness of the people, including the poor. "If we look into history," Beccaria wrote in the introduction to *On Crimes and Punishments*, "we shall find that laws which are or ought to be conventions between men in a state of freedom have been for the most part the work of the passions of a few or the consequences of fortuitous or temporary necessity; not dictated by a cool examiner of human nature, who knew how to collect in one point the actions of a multitude and had this only end in view, *the greatest happiness of the greatest number.*" The idea of a social contract focused on the consent and contentment of people living in a state of freedom—on their individual and collective happiness—would rouse American and French (and later Italian and Spanish-speaking) revolutionaries to action. Beccaria's writings thus shaped the geopolitical map as subjects and colonists demanded equal protection of the laws, better treatment, and full-fledged citizenship. Kings and princes and feudal lords had long monopolized power, and though serfdom, slavery and debt peonage persisted in many places, exploited subjects in the Age of Beccaria were keen to become citizens of their own countries and to govern themselves according to laws that they themselves would write. In the post-*On Crimes and Punishments* era, monarchs not only had to fear royal rivals and feudal, serf and slave revolts, but kings and queens had to contend with revolutionaries demanding their freedom and a greater say in their own futures.

Liberty and happiness are innate human desires, and that was as true in the eighteenth century as it is now. "Good legislation," Beccaria wrote in one passage of *On Crimes and Punishments*, "is the art of conducting men to the maximum of happiness and to the minimum of misery, if we may apply this mathematical expression to the good and evil of life." That formulation, along with similar philosophical expressions on pleasure and pain by the likes of Francis Hutcheson (1694–1746), Claude-Adrien Helvétius (1715–1771), David Hume (1711–1776) and Joseph Priestley (1733–1804), spurred Bentham's and John Stuart Mill's utilitarianism, and inspired the writings and advocacy of scores of social reformers. While John Howard and his disciples urged much-needed reforms within monstrous, disease-ridden prisons, Jeremy Bentham devoted his life to drafting more progressive penal codes. René Descartes (1596–1650), the French philosopher and mathematician, had set the stage for the development of Western philosophy with his *Meditations on First Philosophy*, first published in Latin in 1641 and in French in 1647, and with his treatise, *Passions of the Soul*, printed in 1649. His most famous expression—"I think, therefore I am."—was contained in Descartes' *Discourse on the Method* (1637) and *Principles of Philosophy* (1644), with Beccaria adopting Descartes' introspective and deductive, scientific approach.

Seventeenth- and eighteenth-century European philosophers frequently wrote of emotions and sensations, and they debated how to incentivize virtue and suppress vice. The legendary Oxford jurist, Sir William Blackstone, specifically cited Beccaria and pushed for the creation of England's penitentiary system—one focused on the reformation, not the wholesale extermination, of offenders. While John Locke (1632–1704), in his *Essay Concerning Human Understanding* (1689), wrote that "Pleasure or Pain follows upon the application of certain Objects to us," thus effecting "our Happiness, or Misery," Beccaria associated the measurement of happiness with two concepts: (1) the distance between one's needs and the means of satisfaction for each individual, and (2) the distance between the actual distribution of happiness and the "maximal" distribution of happiness (*i.e.*, the maximal happiness "divided by the greatest possible number").[34] Across the Atlantic, Beccaria's mathematically themed ideas—some novel, many cribbed or cobbled together from others, but all packaged in a highly accessible style—were warmly embraced by many intellectuals almost as soon as they appeared. Indeed, in many locales in the Americas—as well as in the realms of more enlightened rulers—testing the efficacy of Beccaria's ideas in the wake of Isaac Newton's creation of the scientific method became a popular endeavor. Many decades after Locke and the Irish philosopher George Berkeley (1685–1753) wrote about perception and the concepts of pleasure and pain, one prominent Virginian—Edmund Randolph (1753–1813), an aide-de-camp to George Washington who became a Virginia governor—even spoke of the state's executive making "the Beccarian experiment."[35]

The American colonists, including early American lawyers like Edmund Randolph, were especially receptive to Beccaria's philosophy because they felt browbeaten by the English monarchy and the British aristocracy. Josiah Quincy, Jr.—a leading American attorney—specifically referenced Beccaria's *On Crimes and Punishments* in his commonplace book, excerpting a selection from Beccaria's treatise captioned "The Danger of Considering ye Spirit of Laws." "There is nothing more dangerous," Quincy recorded at a time when highly discretionary decisions of common-law judges were ubiquitous, than the common axiom: *the spirit of the laws is to be considered.* "To adopt it," Quincy recorded, worrying about limitless power and runaway judicial discretion, "is to give way to the torrent of opinion." Quincy himself copied an extended passage from Beccaria's treatise on the advantages of observing "the *letter* of penal laws" in preference to judges resorting to the "interpretation of them." "When ye code of laws is once fixed," Quincy wrote, cribbing from Beccaria, "it should be observed in ye *literal* sense," so that "nothing more is left to ye judge, than to determine, whether an action be, or be not conformable to the written Law." "The disorders that may arise from a vigorous observation of the *letter* of penal laws, not to be compared with those produced by ye interpretation of them," Quincy scrivened in his commonplace book, adding: "The first are temporary inconveniences which will oblige ye legislator to correct ye letter of ye law, the want of preciseness, + uncertainty of which has occasioned these disorders; and this will put a stop to the fatal liberty of explaining; the source of arbitrary + venal declarations."[36]

Beccaria's name itself became synonymous with the Enlightenment and freedom from torture and tyranny, with Beccaria's ideas frequently invoked in pre- and post-Revolutionary War texts, speeches and newspapers. For instance, in the wake of the Boston Tea Party of 1773, Josiah Quincy, Jr.—in commenting on the Boston Port Act of 1774, one of the four Intolerable Acts passed by the British Parliament that had closed the port of Boston to all shipping until compensation was paid for the tea dumped into the harbor — recited the much-invoked extract from Beccaria's book on the tendency of societies to elevate some to the pinnacle of power while reducing or assigning others to conditions of human misery. As Quincy recorded Beccaria's words in his May 1774 *Observations on the Act of Parliament Commonly Called the Boston Port-Bill; with Thoughts on Civil Society and Standing Armies*: "[I]n every society, there is an effort constantly tending to confer on one part the height of power, and to reduce the other to the extreme of weakness and misery." Right before quoting that much-beloved passage from Beccaria's treatise, Josiah Quincy, Jr. — echoing Beccaria once more — explained: "The proper object of society and civil institutions is the advancement of 'the greatest happiness of the greatest number.' "[37] Elsewhere, Quincy drew upon other tidbits of Beccaria's wisdom from a London edition of *On Crimes and Punishments* published in 1767 by the English journalist and bookseller John Almon.[38] Almon — an English printer, writer and bookseller in Piccadilly — frequently published controversial political and literary works and earned a reputation as a "firm, able, and uncompromising" opponent of "the oppressive and tyrannical proceedings of government."[39] From 1751 to 1758 Almon had apprenticed to a Liverpool printer, binder and bookseller, and after he worked as a seaman and traveled to various ports in continental Europe, he moved to London where he reestablished himself in the book business and worked as a journalist and political pamphleteer. Historian Rosamaria Loretelli observes that Almon was "a passionate political activist" who "struggled for liberty throughout his life."[40]

The quest for liberty — and the desire to be free from tyrannous monarchs, arbitrary governments, and oppressive taxes — catalyzed eighteenth- and nineteenth-century revolutions and new constitutions and declarations of rights throughout the world. Like Thomas Paine's *Common Sense, On Crimes and Punishments* not only deeply impressed the signers of America's Declaration of Independence (1776), it materially shaped the French Declaration of the Rights of Man and Citizen (1789) and the American and French Revolutions themselves. In America, John Adams and John Hancock of Massachusetts, Dr. Benjamin Rush and James Wilson of Pennsylvania, and George Washington, James Madison and Thomas Jefferson of Virginia were — among many, many others — avid readers of, and deeply affected by, Beccaria's book. Jefferson, for example, carefully studied Beccaria's writings before the American Revolution, and John Adams — a voracious reader of political philosophy and the drafter of the Massachusetts Constitution of 1780 — has been described by one historian, Richard Alan Ryerson, in this way: "he provided an explicit link to nearly every writer who became a major source for America's political and legal traditions, from Plato and Justinian, to Blackstone, Rousseau and Beccaria." Key participants in France's bloody and boisterous, at times riotous, revolution also turned to Beccaria's ideas for guidance, though French revolutionaries — eager to purge "enemies of the state" at any cost — ended up straying far afield from Beccaria's core principles as they guillotined thousands of people in a frenzied bloodlust. Among those who lost their lives: King Louis XVI, the last French monarch and a friend of America's revolutionaries who had, in the 1780s, abolished torture based on Beccaria's treatise, and who, a decade earlier, had sought to weaken the British Empire by aiding and financing the American Revolution. Mass revolts—brought on by food shortages and discontent among France's population—ultimately led to the storming of the Bastille on July 14, 1789 and to Louis XVI's execution on January 21, 1793, in the *Place de la Révolution*.[41]

Cesare Beccaria's vehement opposition to cruel and tyrannical practices proved to be contagious, forever shaping the arc of world history though Beccaria liked to stay close to home, in Milan and the surrounding Italian countryside.[42] Dr. Benjamin Rush—a Philadelphia physician and a signer of the Declaration of Independence—became a fervent Beccaria disciple and one of the first Americans to call for the abolition of capital punishment.[43] Dr. Rush's *Considerations of the Injustice and Impolicy of Punishing Murder by Death* (1792) was itself largely inspired by Beccaria's work.[44] In 1793, John Hancock, less than two decades after flamboyantly signing the Declaration of Independence, publicly sought to outlaw the non-lethal corporal punishments of "cropping and branding, as well as that of the Public Whipping Post."[45] The "peculiar institution" of slavery, with which lashing is so closely associated, also came under relentless attack, with American lawyer James Wilson—another signer of the Declaration of Independence and a major player at the 1787 convention in Philadelphia that gave birth to the U.S. Constitution—repeatedly bringing up Beccaria's ideas in his writings and law lectures.[46] Beccaria himself was regularly hailed as "benevolent," "celebrated," "learned," and "immortal," and called a "sublime philosopher" of "great genius,"[47] the kind of monikers reserved for the most revered Enlightenment writers such as Montesquieu, one of Beccaria's intellectual muses.[48] Even today, Cesare Beccaria—as one encyclopedia puts it—"is considered to be the father of the classical school of criminology." The perspective of that school of thought: people commit crimes as a result of their own free will, with Beccaria—acknowledging the rationality of human actions—positing that people behave according to how much pleasure or pain they derive or risk from their actions.[49]

The Celebrated Marquis seeks to restore Cesare Beccaria's rightful place in the pantheon of the world's most influential historical figures. Beccaria led a rich and eventful public and private life, and though he preferred the quietude of Milan and the beauty of Italy's Lake Como, his writings on equality, economics, and law and society—ones quite unexpected from a member of the aristocracy—transformed the world. But only a few discernable physical traces of his legacy remain. In Parma, Italy, where Beccaria attended a Jesuit school in his early years, the university's library still has lots of old and new editions of *Dei delitti e delle pene*—the book that Beccaria wrote while still in his mid-twenties and that catapulted him to fame. The first edition of that treatise came out just a year before the building of the Brera Observatory in Milan—one of the many European astrological observatories built by eighteenth-century Jesuits to study the stars.[50] One bound volume at the University of Parma even memorializes the building of a nineteenth-century monument to Beccaria—a marble sculpture installed in central Milan more than a hundred years after the first appearance of his small but momentous treatise. Although Giuseppe Grandi's 1871 marble statue of Beccaria was later damaged, a 1914 bronze replica still stands today in the center of the Milanese piazza named for Beccaria—a piazza just a short walk from Milan's impressive Roman Catholic cathedral, the *Duomo di Milano*. Though the precise location of Beccaria's remains is now unknown, other small reminders of Beccaria's intellectual legacy can still be found, too, if one searches carefully. In the early nineteenth century, a small Pennsylvania town was named after Beccaria, with a high school and a juvenile prison in Milan also still bearing his name.[51] Milan's public high school, Cesare Beccaria *Liceo Classico Statale*, is the oldest classical lyceum in Milan, with a rich history—what its website refers to as its "*glorioso passato*" or glorious past—dating back to 1603. The school acquired the Beccaria name—an homage to the Italian philosopher—long after its early, seventeenth-century founding at the church of St. Alexander.[52]

To be sure, Cesare Beccaria has not been totally forgotten, though much rehabilitation—especially in the United States and outside the Italian peninsula—needs to be done. Only in Italy, his birthplace, does Beccaria's formidable star still dazzle and shine brightly in an otherwise faintly lit or mostly dark night sky. Most Americans, truth be told, have no idea who Cesare Beccaria is, let alone what he did or wrote. By contrast, in 2014, colleges and universities all over Italy—in Parma, Rome, Trento, Verona and elsewhere—hosted whole symposiums to commemorate the 250th anniversary of the publication of *Dei delitti e delle pene*. Translated into all of the major European languages shortly after its initial appearance in 1764, Beccaria's book—fiercely debated since its publication—has changed hearts and minds on subjects as diverse as happiness and cruelty and human rights. In the early nineteenth century, Cesare Beccaria was still a household name throughout Europe and the Americas, with his book on many library bookshelves and in many private studies. Before Italians erected their impressive monument to Cesare Beccaria in 1871 in his native city,[53] the commission that raised the funds for it collected contributions from all over Italy—from Milan, Cremona, Pavia, Torino, Pisa and Naples, to Florence, Bologna, Caprera and San Fiorano. The commission—tapping into a deep reservoir of respect for Beccaria—also found other donors in major European cities such as London, Paris, Berlin, and Heidelberg,[54] though Beccaria's ideas (which inspired the monument) had a decidedly *global* reach, extending far beyond the borders of Europe. By railing against tyranny, *On Crimes and Punishments*—along with other Enlightenment texts such as Thomas Paine's *Common Sense* and Montesquieu's *Spirit of the Laws*—helped to ignite and spur on the American and French Revolutions, thus forever altering the course of human history.[55]

Despite the neglect of many modern historians, Beccaria's importance to world history is still evident throughout modern-day Italy and is readily apparent (if one combs the Internet or the stacks of any public library) to anyone who takes a close look at the historical record. *The 'Coterie' of Milan* (1766), a painting by Antonio Perego, depicts Cesare Beccaria and his fellow Milanese *philosophes*; John Adams owned more than one copy of Beccaria's book, once gifting a copy to his son, Thomas; and another Italian piazza, in central Florence, is also named after Beccaria, the great Italian philosopher, economist and pioneering criminologist. Beccaria's views on "equality for all before the law"—a guidebook to Florence notes of the Piazza Cesare Beccaria in that city—were "highly influential." In Philadelphia, America's cradle of liberty and the birthplace of the Declaration of Independence and the U.S. Constitution, prominent eighteenth-century booksellers—among them, William Prichard, the Quaker Joseph Crukshank, and Irish immigrants Henry and Patrick Rice, brothers of the Dublin bookseller John Rice—not only heard that city's famed Liberty Bell toll, but they regularly offered for sale copies of Beccaria's most influential book, *On Crimes and Punishments*, more than two centuries ago.[56] At the University of Pavia, where Beccaria received his law degree in 1758 before writing that seminal work on the criminal law,[57] yet another academic conference took place in 2014 in honor of that book's monumental influence—a tribute to the enduring impact of *On Crimes and Punishments* on laws and societies around the globe. It was just one of many academic gatherings held in Europe that year to celebrate the 250th anniversary of the publication of *Dei delitti e delle pene*.[58]

Although Beccaria, the economist, philosopher and long-time civil servant in Austria's Habsburg Empire, may rival Adam Smith in historical importance, it is—without question—Smith, not Beccaria, who gets the bulk of the attention these days.[59] Scores of biographies and other books have been written about the Scottish thinker,[60] while only a handful have been penned about his younger Italian counterpart.[61] In 2002, Samuel Fleischacker—a professor of philosophy at the University of Illinois, Chicago— published a lengthy article titled "Adam Smith's Reception among the American Founders, 1776–1790." "[T]here is good evidence," Fleischacker wrote in the *William and Mary Quarterly*, "that many of the founders, including Jefferson, Madison, and Wilson, were reading his work."[62] "Beccaria," though also carefully read by an array of eighteenth- and nineteenth-century intellectuals, University of Sydney historian Peter Groenewegen wrote that same year, "has been"—by contrast—"almost totally ignored" by historians of economics.[63] While Adam Smith is the equivalent of a Hall of Fame rock star in that field, Beccaria, like Smith, helped to pioneer it in eighteenth-century Europe. Almost everyone still knows Adam Smith's name, but sadly, Cesare Beccaria—for reasons that will become clear later in this book—now dwells in obscurity, a cloistered hermit in comparison to Smith's peacock-like display of global celebrity. One recent book—an examination of Smith's somewhat lesser-known work, *The Theory of Moral Sentiments* (1759)—even bears this inviting title: *How Adam Smith Can Change Your Life: An Unexpected Guide to Human Nature and Happiness*.[64]

To catapult Beccaria back into Adam Smith's stratosphere will not happen overnight; historical figures are only rarely reintroduced to the public with the glitz and rapidity associated with Lin-Manuel Miranda's blockbuster Broadway hit, *Hamilton*. Alexander Hamilton—a defender and promotor of the U.S. Constitution, the first Secretary of the Treasury, and a leader in the establishment of the Bank of the United States— was the key architect of *The Federalist Papers* and President George Washington's economic policies. While Thomas Jefferson opposed Hamilton's "implied powers" doctrine, Hamilton—a Federalist lawyer who would've been highly conversant with Beccaria's ideas and who, in fact, once questioned the frequency of executions—insisted that Article I, section 8 of the U.S. Constitution should be read to allow Congress to pass all laws "necessary and proper" for carrying out its enumerated powers. In *Federalist No. 78*, in offering a defense of the U.S. Constitution, Hamilton also argued that it was for the courts to interpret the Constitution and to decide if a branch of government had exceeded its powers. Although Hamilton expressed the view that "the judiciary is beyond comparison the weakest of the three departments of power" because while the legislative branch has "the purse" and the executive branch has "the sword," he recognized that the independence of the judiciary was of critical importance. As Hamilton wrote in *Federalist No. 78*: "The complete independence of the courts of justice is peculiarly essential in a limited Constitution. By a limited Constitution, I understand one which contains certain specified exceptions to the legislative authority; such, for instance, as that it shall pass no bills of attainder, no ex-post-facto laws, and the like. Limitations of this kind can be preserved in practice no other way than through the medium of courts of justice, whose duty it must be to declare all acts contrary to the manifest tenor of the Constitution void. Without this, all the reservations of particular rights or privileges would amount to nothing."[65]

The eighteenth century saw a profusion of economic theories tied to economic development, and scores of thinkers—from Cesare Beccaria in Italy, to Quesnay and Turgot in France, to Alexander Hamilton in America—were involved in that intellectual endeavor. As William Pencak explains in *The Philosophy of Law*: "In addition to first putting forth the theory of judicial review in the United States, Hamilton challenged the laissez-faire economics of Adam Smith's 1776 treatise, *The Wealth of Nations*, with his own 1790[s] *Report on the Manufactures* and *Report on the Public Credit*. He argued that the survival and success of the infant nation—and its infant industries—depended on active government development of the economy through tariffs, taxation, and investment (the last channeled through the Bank of the United States) to add a vigorous commercial and industrial sector to a predominantly agricultural country."[66] "[W]hile Antonio Genovesi in Naples and Cesare Beccaria in Milan proposed a set of policies that nations should follow in order to develop their manufactures and escape a situation of dependency," the *Research Handbook on Political Economy and Law* emphasizes, Alexander Hamilton "formulated the infant industry argument, later rediscovered by classical development economists in the second half of the twentieth century."[67]

Though he became best known for *On Crimes and Punishments*, Beccaria—the economist trained in mathematics who had a life-long interest in criminal justice issues—had closely studied the issues of tariffs and economic development, even resorting to the use of algebra in the 1760s to attempt to solve thorny societal problems such as smuggling. And after the publication of *Dei delitti e delle pene*, Beccaria's ideas on government were aired—and fiercely debated—by enlightened thinkers of all political stripes and persuasions as they grappled with how to best design government. For instance, in a letter written in May 1788—part of a 136-page pamphlet published in early November 1787 that was distributed by the New York Federal Republican Committee—the "Federal Farmer," in a debate over the proposed U.S. Constitution, took the position that "there is no substantial representation of the people provided for" and that "there ought to be *an increase of the number of representatives*." In that letter, the Federal Farmer wrote: "Since I advanced the idea of balancing the several orders of men in a community, in forming a genuine representation, and seen that idea considered as chimerical, I have been sensibly struck with a sentence in the marquis Beccaria's treatise: this sentence was quoted by congress in 1774, and is as follows:—'In every society there is an effort continually tending to confer on one part the height of power and happiness, and to reduce the others to the extreme of weakness and misery; the intent of good laws is to oppose this effort, and to diffuse their influence universally and equally.'"[68] From the events that inspired America's Declaration of Independence to the ratification debates over the U.S. Constitution, Beccaria's presence can be felt time and time again.

Beccaria's ideas in fact pervaded America's founding era—and the Enlightenment in general. In 1786, Dr. Benjamin Rush—the physician who had studied medicine at the University of Edinburgh in Scotland and who became one of Beccaria's biggest fans—put forward a plan to establish public schools to diffuse knowledge in Pennsylvania. Although the first official school in the U.S. was the Boston Latin School, founded in 1635, the country's creation of a public education system in the decades that followed Dr. Rush's proposal would've greatly pleased Cesare Beccaria. In emphasizing that education "promotes just ideas of laws and government," Dr. Rush actually invoked Beccaria's own words to advance his own position. "'When the clouds of ignorance are dispelled,' says the Marquis of Beccaria," Rush wrote, quoting the Italian philosopher he and so many other Americans so greatly admired, "'by the radiance of knowledge, power trembles but the authority of laws remains immovable.'" Horace Mann—a Massachusetts lawyer and politician who is often considered the father of American public education—was selected as the secretary of the Massachusetts Board of Education in 1837. He believed that a "common school" was the "birthright" of every child and would be a great equalizer. Beccaria's name, perhaps not surprisingly, shows up in early American educational journals, including in *The Common School Journal* that Mann himself edited. Here is how an 1862 article on education, published in the first volume of *The Continental Monthly*, tellingly begins: "'The most certain means,' Beccaria wrote in the preceding century, 'of rendering a people free and happy, is, to establish a perfect method of education.'"[69]

In early America, Federalists and anti-Federalists alike continually looked to Cesare Beccaria's book for guidance or wisdom. After quoting Beccaria's *On Crimes and Punishments* and Montesquieu's *Spirit of Laws*—Montesquieu had advised that "in a free state every man ... ought to be concerned in his own government"—the Federal Farmer editorialized: "It is extremely clear that these writers had in view the several orders of men in society, which we call aristocratical, democratical, merchantile, mechanic, &c. and perceived the efforts they are constantly, from interested and ambitious views, disposed to make to elevate themselves and oppress others. Each order must have a share in the business of legislation actually and efficiently." "It is deceiving a people to tell them they are electors, and can choose their legislators," the Federal Farmer concluded, "if they cannot, in the nature of things, choose men from among themselves, and genuinely like themselves." The Federal Farmer expressed the belief that "our natural aristocracy in the United States" consisted of "about four or five thousand men"—among them governors, members of Congress, "army and militia" leaders, state senators, "superior judges," "the most eminent professional men," and "men of large property." "[O]ther persons and orders in the community," the writer observed at a time when women and minorities were still systematically excluded from the social compact, "form the natural democracy." That group, the Federal

Farmer wrote, includes "the yeomanry, the subordinate officers, civil and military, the fishermen, mechanics and traders, many of the merchants and professional men." "Men of the first class," the Federal Farmer explained, referring to those with the most power, "have a high sense of honor, possess abilities, ambition, and general knowledge," while "men of the second class are not so much used to combining great objects; they possess less ambition, and a larger share of honesty; their dependence is principally on middling and small estates, industrious pursuits, and hard labour." Aristocrats and the powerful, the Federal Farmer stressed, rely "principally on the emoluments of large estates, and of the chief offices of government." In coming back to Beccaria's much-invoked maxim, the Federal Farmer then observed: "Thus, in every period of society, and in all the transactions of men, we see parties verifying the observation made by the Marquis; and those classes which have not their centinels in the government, in proportion to what they have to gain or lose, must infallibly be ruined."[70]

In America's founding period, when the British Empire's boot was on American necks, Beccaria's call for equality of treatment thus made the Italian philosopher a central figure in political and criminal justice debates, even for America's elite. At New York's ratification convention, Melancton Smith—a proponent of equality and a reader of *On Crimes and Punishments*—himself sought to ensure more middle-class participation in America's political system. After quoting Beccaria's candid assessment that every society tends to confer "the height of power" on a few while reducing others to "weakness and misery," Smith—a member of the anti-slavery New York Manumission Society along with Alexander Hamilton, John Jay and Robert R. Livingston—reiterated the importance of what he called the "middling class." A "sufficient number of the middling class," he said at New York's ratification convention, was necessary to "controul" greed and "hereditary nobility." "A representative body, composed principally of respectable yeomanry is the best possible security to liberty," Smith observed, adding: "When the interest of this part of the community is pursued, the public good is pursued; because the body of every nation consists of this class." Saying that "[a] system of corruption is known to be the system of government in Europe," Smith took the position that a "great danger" of "corruption" would result from a small number of representatives. In *On Crimes and Punishments*, Beccaria himself had advised that the laws should "favour individual men more than classes of men."[71]

The debate during the American Revolution—and over the U.S. Constitution itself—was, at its core, a debate over how best to prevent tyranny and over how far the principle of equality—the one referenced in the Declaration of Independence—would be extended in that era of slavery. In a speech at New York's ratifying convention, Alexander Hamilton specifically addressed "the objection with regard to the number of representatives as it now stands." "I am persuaded that the system, in this respect, is on a better footing than the gentleman imagine," Hamilton said. "I agree," Hamilton argued, "that there should be a broad democratic branch in the national legislature." "In free republics," he emphasized, "the will of the people makes the essential principle of the government, and the laws which control the community, receive their tone and spirit from the public wishes." "It is the fortunate situation of our country," he added, "that the minds of the people are exceedingly enlightened and refined." "Here, then," he told his fellow delegates, "we may expect the laws to be proportionably agreeable to the standard of a perfect policy, and the wisdom of public measures to consist with the most intimate conformity between the views of the representative and his constituent." "It has been observed," Hamilton said, "that a pure democracy, if it were practicable, would be the most perfect government." "Experience has proved, that no position in politics is more false than this," Hamilton emphasized in rejecting that observation, worried about what that process of unadulterated democracy might produce. As Hamilton argued, emphasizing a theme—the danger of tyranny—that Beccaria himself had warned of: "The ancient democracies, in which the people themselves deliberated, never possessed one feature of good government.—Their very character was tyranny; their figure deformity." "When they assembled, the field of debate presented an ungovernable mob," he stressed, saying such assemblies were "incapable of deliberation." "I trust that the proposed Constitution," Hamilton urged, "affords a genuine specimen of Representative and Republican government; and that it will answer, in an eminent degree, all the beneficial purposes of society."[72]

Cesare Beccaria deserves greater public recognition than he now receives. In my 2014 book, *The Birth of American Law: An Italian Philosopher and the American Revolution*, I attempted to rehabilitate Beccaria's reputation and standing by showing his substantial influence on America's founders.[73] Whereas twenty-first century Americans typically have little or no knowledge or awareness of Beccaria's life or writings, that was not at all true in the eighteenth century or even in the first half of the nineteenth century. For example, early American booksellers sold many copies of Beccaria's compact, little treatise before, during, and after the Revolutionary War and the U.S. Constitution's ratification.[74] Just as bookstores in the capitals of Europe stocked *On Crimes and Punishments*, booksellers in Boston, Philadelphia, New York and elsewhere did too. In fact, robust sales of *On Crimes and Punishments* took place throughout the Americas and Europe, in cities large and small, for many decades after the small treatise's first appearance in Tuscany.[75] In what became the United States, one Federalist lawyer, Rufus King, had himself been inspired to study law after reading *On Crimes and Punishments*—a book that would transform law itself. A signer of the U.S. Constitution, King graduated from Harvard College in 1777 and later served as George Washington's U.S. Minister to Great Britain and represented the State of New York in the U.S. Senate.[76] By the late eighteenth century, every well-read politician and civic leader—and even those who simply read newspapers or periodicals—knew Beccaria's name.[77]

Today, Cesare Beccaria—as any casual survey of Americans would reveal—dwells in such obscurity in the U.S. that, when pondering how to market *The Birth of American Law*, a nearly 700-page book about him, I decided it didn't even make sense to put his name in the book's title. American readers, the logic went, would be more intrigued to pick up a book about an "Italian philosopher" than they would be to buy or order a book with an unfamiliar name in its title.[78] I still believe that to be the case, hence (for this book) *The Celebrated Marquis* title—the moniker that the Continental Congress employed in its day, in the 1770s. In Italy, Beccaria's legacy is—as noted—still regularly celebrated, as evidenced by the Milanese statuary honoring him and the fitting series of Italian academic conferences held in 2014 on the occasion of the 250th anniversary of the publication of *Dei delitti e delle pene.*[79] In that year, Carlo Scognamiglio Pasini—a former president of the Italian Senate and an award-winning professor of applied economics—published his own 300-plus-page book about Beccaria's work as an economist, part of a renewed interest in the study of Beccaria's impact on modernity.[80] The contemporaneous headline in one Italian newspaper—"Rome Celebrates Beccaria, 250 Years after the Publication of 'On Crimes and Punishments'"—is especially revealing. In publicizing yet another Beccaria-themed seminar, one held in Rome, the Eternal City, a columnist in that paper made this observation on *Dei delitti e delle pene*: "Two hundred and fifty years have passed since the publication of that little formidable treatise that destroyed many a prejudice and fostered rights and innovative ideas that still swim in our heads. And in these two and half centuries, Cesare Beccaria himself was praised, but also neglected and misunderstood in several of his lines of thought."[81]

Because of the 250th anniversary of the publication of *Dei delitti e delle pene*, there has been a rejuvenation of interest of late in Cesare Beccaria's writings and economic lectures, although much information about Beccaria's life is still accessible only in Italian or French. A three-volume edition of Beccaria's writings, *Scritti economici*, was published in Italian in 2014,[82] though one English-language book, *History of Universities*, does helpfully highlight Beccaria's lasting contributions to the study of political economy. Along with a few older biographies, including one by the eminent historian Marcello Maestro, there are plenty of English-language sources that reveal or underscore, if only in bits and pieces or in passing, Beccaria's importance to the development of economics, the criminal law, and societal notions of happiness.[83] In fact, one still occasionally sees Beccaria's name in print in the popular press. For example, in the May 2015 issue of *The Atlantic*, one journalist included this historical reminder: "Cesare Beccaria, the jurist and philosopher, wrote a pamphlet presenting a case against harsh punishments that led to the end of state-sanctioned torture and capital punishment throughout Europe, and influenced the U.S. Constitution's prohibition against cruel and unusual punishment."[84] Likewise, in October 2015, comedian John Oliver—the host of the witty, often hilarious *Last Week Tonight*—noted that Ben Carson, then a Republican presidential candidate, had purportedly quoted Thomas Jefferson when, in fact, the words had actually come from Beccaria. Jefferson had, like Josiah Quincy, Jr. and other eighteenth-century American lawyers, simply transcribed Beccaria's words into his commonplace book.[85]

In the twenty-first century and its interconnected, global economy, Adam Smith—the Scottish economist and moral philosopher—remains nothing short of a worldwide icon, famous for *The Wealth of Nations* and its oft-cited "invisible hand" reference.[86] Frequently described as "the father" or "grandfather" of "modern economics,"[87] Smith still regularly gets cited in top-flight publications such as the *Wall Street Journal*[88] and the *New York Times*.[89] In 2017, for instance, one writer—David Siegal—wrote this in the *New York Times*: "One of capitalism's bedrock promises—one that dates back to Adam Smith—is that competition in the free market benefits society at large."[90] One can even purchase T-shirts online that depict Adam Smith's face or that contain directives like "Talk to the Invisible Hand" or "Read *The Wealth of Nations* by Adam Smith."[91] Meanwhile, the public's awareness of Beccaria's contributions to Western civilization and law and economics—which, in some cases, *pre-date* Smith's—have chiefly slipped from memory, at least in comparison to Smith's, thereby consigning Beccaria to relative obscurity. Though prominent scholars such as Richard Posner and Gary Becker have acknowledged Beccaria as a pioneer in the "economic" analysis of the criminal law,[92] Beccaria—like it or not—remains a fairly obscure historical figure throughout most of the world. "Beccaria"—explains Professor Bernard Harcourt, now at New York's Columbia Law School—"is one of those remarkable authors whose writings form the keystone of important intellectual traditions, and yet who is actually little read, especially in the United States."[93]

Adam Smith, that global celebrity, is of course hardly the only eighteenth-century personality—whether economist, military leader, scientist, jurist or philosopher—to shape the modern world. Along with prominent historical figures like William Blackstone, Jean-Jacques Rousseau, George Washington, Thomas Jefferson, Jeremy Bentham, and Montesquieu, the French jurist who inspired so many and so much (including James Madison and the separation-of-powers principle that infuses the U.S. Constitution), Smith's Italian contemporary—Cesare Beccaria—was once a central and well-known Enlightenment figure.[94] A native of Milan, and only twenty-six years of age when *Dei delitti e delle pene* first appeared in Italian more than 250 years ago, Beccaria—like Smith, Montesquieu and the others—was in fact a household name more than two and a half centuries ago.[95] Beccaria's writings were available throughout Europe and the Americas, and the widely translated and much-talked-about *Dei delitti e delle pene* was read as far and wide as Argentina, Australia, Canada and Mexico.[96] Along with works by Montesquieu, Voltaire and other social reformers, *On Crimes and Punishments* changed the global conversation and shaped the modern world in which we live. The "celebrated marquis" is thus, like Smith, a figure eminently worthy of the time and attention—and of the respect—of twenty-first century readers.

Chapter 1

A Young Nobleman

Cesare Beccaria Bonesana (chä'sä'rĕ bĕk-kä-rē'a bō-nä-sä'na), the eldest son of an Italian aristocrat, was born in Milan on March 15, 1738. Commonly known as Cesare Beccaria or by his title, the Marquis Beccaria or Marchese di (mär-kä'sĕ dĕ) Beccaria, he spent the first part of his childhood in the family's palazzo in Milan, an old house on Via Brera purchased by the family in the seventeenth century. In the summer, the family retreated to Gessate, the locale of the family's villa and country estate northeast of Milan. Beccaria's father, the Marquis Gian Saverio Beccaria Bonesana, a traditional patrician also known as Giovanni Beccaria or the Marquis Francis Xavier, was from a distinguished family, as was Beccaria's mother, Donna Maria Visconti di Saliceto (da Rho).[1] Beccaria's father's namesake, Saint Francis Xavier (1506–1552)—"Francesco Saverio" in Italian—was a Roman Catholic missionary, a co-founder of the Society of Jesus, and one of the first seven Jesuits—among them, Ignatius of Loyola—to take the vows of charity, poverty and pilgrimage (to the Holy Land) at a chapel in Paris in 1534.[2] Saint Francis Xavier, of a Spanish noble family from the kingdom of Navarre, had studied philosophy in Paris and had bound himself to a life of chastity, poverty, and obedience. After a life spent evangelizing in places like India and Japan, he had been canonized by Pope Gregory XV on March 12, 1622.[3]

"There is," as one scholar notes, "debate over Beccaria's proper title of nobility and, thus, his name." As law professor Bernard Harcourt explains of the Italian nobleman: "He is often referred to as the 'Marquis of Beccaria,' including in the *Encyclopædia Universalis* and the *Larousee*; however, recent research suggests that the title of nobility that his grandfather obtained in 1711 was for Gualdrasco and Villareggio."[4] According to Renzo Zorzi's biography of Cesare Beccaria, Cesare's grandfather, Francesco Beccaria (1669–1748) became a noble in 1711, with Holy Roman Emperor Charles VI—the father of Maria Theresa and himself the Archduke of Austria from 1711–1740—conferring the title of marquis.[5] Foreign language sources also refer to Cesare Beccaria as "Cesare Beccaria Bonesana, marquis de Gualdrasco et Villareggio" and "Cesare Bonesana-Beccarìa, marchese di Gualdrasco e di Villareggio."[6] Located south of Milan and north of Pavia, Gualdrasco and Villareggio are small towns in the region of Lombardy.[7] Both Gualdrasco and Villareggio show up in a book about the seventeenth-century economy of Spanish Lombardy, with the village of Gualdrasco listed as having "1 or more" linen weavers as of 1698. Both villages thus date back many centuries, with Villareggio also mentioned in an Italian history about the Visconti family and the fifteenth century.[8]

The title of *marquis*—below that of a *duke*—conferred hereditary privileges and prestige and was a title of nobility bestowed by monarchs, often for military service.[9]

As one compendium of Italian history describes the title's origins: "The provinces sit-uated on the confines of a kingdom were called marches, and thus the count who gov-erned and defended them from foreign invasion came to be called a *marquis*. But in process of time every prince who exercised dominion over several 'countships' came also to be called a marquis, however his dominions might be situated."[10] A marquis "is a title next below a duke," an early nineteenth-century source on heraldry stresses, further reciting: "Marquisses were antiently governors of frontier cities, or provinces, called marches."[11] According to yet another source, a mid-nineteenth-century political dictionary: "The term marquis designated originally persons who had the care of the marches of a country. The word 'marches' is the plural of 'mark,' which in its political sense sign[i]fies 'boundaries.'"[12] Per the definition found in *The New American Cy-clopædia* (1863): "MARQUIS, or MARQUESS, a title of dignity in England, France, and Italy, ranking next below that of duke. In Germany, whence it derives its origin, the corresponding title is *Markgraf*, in English margrave or lord of the marches; and the persons so called or created were originally military chieftains to whom was com-mitted the guardianship of the marches or frontiers of a kingdom."[13]

The Beccaria name itself shows up on military rosters in seventeenth-century Lom-bardy and even centuries earlier in Pavia, where two military and political men—brothers Castellino and Lancelotto Beccaria—were executed in the early fifteenth century after a power struggle.[14] In a biographical sketch of an Italian poet, Antonio Beccaria, it was noted that he "was a descendant of the noble family of Beccaria, who, from the year 1313, held the supreme authority at Pavia for forty-three years, under the protection of the Visconti." That source, taking note of the shifting alliances in those days, then observes of the ancient Beccaria family's removal from power in Pavia: "Having then transferred their alliance to the marchese of Monferrato, and Pavia being in consequence attacked by the Visconti, the inhabitants expelled them in 1357, levelled their palace, and obliged them to seek an asylum amongst strangers. In 1402 they tried to recover again their power; but being persecuted by the implacable hatred of the Visconti, and Castellino Beccaria being arrested in 1418, and murdered in prison by the duke of Milan, and Lancellotto made a prisoner at the castle of Ser-ravall[e], and hanged in the public place, the family lost every vestige of power."[15] In one book, it is stressed that Antonio Beccaria "was a popular name and several men named Antonio from or connected to the extensive and politically important Beccaria family in Pavia appear in records of the time." One Antonio Beccaria, it is noted, "ar-bitrated a family dispute in 1392 ... and acted as a procurator in a truce agreed in 1407 involving, amongst others, Castellino Beccaria, the *de facto* ruler of Pavia at the time, and his brother Lancelotto; men who were soon to be embroiled in a series of conflicts with Filippo Maria Visconti would culminate in both of their executions."[16]

In the province of Pavia, approximately thirty miles south of Milan, there is still a small town that bears the name of Montù Beccaria. That locale—a royal fief—carried with it the hereditary title of count, and it had been acquired in the seventeenth century by Carlo Belloni's grandfather, the president of the Milanese senate between 1675 and 1682.[17] Count Carlo Belloni (1706–1747) of Pavia—a man captivated by Milanese theater—is now best remembered for tutoring Maria Gaetana Agnesi (1718–

1799), one of the most prominent female mathematicians and natural philosophers of her time. Born in Milan, Agnesi—a devout Catholic—became the first woman to write a handbook on mathematics and deftly explored differential and integral calculus.[18] In Europe, some aristocratic families used the titles *marquis* and *count* (*conte* in Italian or *comte* in French) interchangeably. Often appointed by dukes or conferred by a monarch as an honorific title, counts were associated with military service or with having rendered some special service to the crown. "The title of marquis," one source stresses, "was, in theory, accorded to noblemen who owned several countships."[19] The Marquis de Lafayette—the Frenchman with that title—himself came from a wealthy family with a military background. In some sources, Cesare Beccaria is also referred to as "Count Cesare Beccaria," "conte Cesare Beccaria Bonesana," "Cesare Bonesana Count of Beccaria," or "the Marquess Beccaria of Milan."[20]

The region of Lombardy, of which Milan is the capital, came under Spanish Habsburg rule in the mid-1530s. "In Lombardy," Michael Bush writes in *The European Nobility*, "a substantial titled nobility was initially formed by the divisibility of estates and their associated titles." "[T]he higher titled nobility," he explains, "became a numerous class after the establishment of Habsburg rule in 1535, particularly with the lavish conferment of count and marquis as personal titles in the seventeenth century."[21] "Lombardy saw a similar emphasis on feudal title-holders," notes another historian, Christopher Black. "The Spanish Kings," as Black recounts, "granted 276 titles of nobility (*conti* and *marchesi*) linked to fiefs between 1554 and 1706, to which Austrian rulers added 124 more from 1707 to 1740."[22] "The Spanish Bourbons," one book observes of the history of the region, "were established in Italy by hereditary right to the duchy of Parma." As that source emphasizes: "Charles of Bourbon was the son of the first Bourbon king of Spain, Philip V, and Elisabetta Farnese of Parma. Charles ruled first as duke of Parma and Piacenza (1731–35) and then as king of Naples (1735–1759). He left Naples to become king of Spain, where he ruled as Charles III (1759–88)." "Medieval social order," another book stresses of this monarchical and aristocratic age, "was based on the idea that each person was born into a particular place in society, whether a noble or a craftsman or a serf, and everyone should stay in their place."[23]

Located in a fertile plain of the Po valley, one of Italy's most vital agricultural and industrial areas, Milan had a population of more than 120,000 inhabitants by the end of the sixteenth century. Though its population shrank to well under 100,000 by the middle of the seventeenth century, by 1750, in what has been described as "a painfully slow recovery," the population had rebounded, climbing once more to around 120,000 people. And the bustling city, pulsing with music and art and life, played an important role, both culturally and politically and as part of a trade route linking the Italian peninsula to locales north of the Alps, in the medieval and Renaissance periods. "The city's enormous wealth," Stefano D'Amico writes in *Spanish Milan: A City Within the Empire, 1535–1706*, "lay not only in the rich agriculture of its hinterland and on its role as entrepôt between the north and the south, but also on its celebrated manufactures—wool, silk, gold thread, and arms and armors." Formerly under Spanish rule, Milan came under the control of the Austrian Habsburgs in 1706—part of the powerful royal dynasty that lasted until 1918 when Charles I relinquished his throne and stepped down as Austro-Hungarian Emperor after World War I. The last Spanish Habsburg, Charles II, had died in 1700, sparking the Spanish War of Succession (1701–1713), a war that took 700,000 lives and that resulted in the Austrian Habsburgs taking control of Milan.[24] "The title of marquis," one source explains of Cesare Bonesana, the eldest son and the future Marchese di Beccaria, "was his to inherit." "He was," that book observes, "expected to be educated as a gentleman, inherit the family estate, expand it by marriage to a woman of nobility and property, and take a place in government as an official of some sort."[25]

When Cesare Beccaria was born, the Duchy of Milan was part of the Holy Roman Empire, then ruled by Charles VI (1685–1740), the Holy Roman Emperor from 1711 to 1740. Milan had been formally added to his dominion in the 1710s under the terms of the Treaty of Rastatt in March 1714. After the death of Charles II of Spain, Charles VI had declared himself King of Spain, but Philip V (1683–1746)—who later married Elisabeth Farnese, the daughter of the hereditary prince of Parma—emerged victorious in the War of Spanish Succession. The death of Charles VI in October 1740, though, set off another war—the War of Austrian Succession (1740–1748)—after power-thirsty male monarchs led by Charles Albert of Bavaria and Frederick II of Prussia challenged the legitimacy and right of Charles VI's eldest daughter, Maria Theresa, to the Habsburg dominions. As soon as he heard of Charles VI's death, the Bavarian leader ordered his minister in Vienna to protest the recognition of Maria Theresa as her father's heir. For his part, Frederick II—better known as Frederick the Great—was eager to expand his own power and territorial reach. Only twenty-three years of age when she became the Queen of Bohemia, Hungary and Croatia and the Archduchess of Austria in 1740, she served as the Holy Roman Empress from 1745 to 1765 until being succeeded by her son, Joseph II. She bore her husband, Francis I, sixteen children, among them Joseph II, the Holy Roman Emperor from 1765 to 1790, and Marie Antoinette, France's ill-fated future queen. Marie Antoinette, the Austrian princess who married King Louis XVI at age sixteen, was destined—like her husband—to be guillotined in Paris at the *Place de la Révolution* in 1793. She was just 37 years old at the time of her death.[26]

It was a tumultuous century, one replete with exploration and mapping, endless wars, royal intrigue and Machiavellian backstabbing. There was also much death, whether on the battlefield, as a result of public executions, religious persecution and judicial torture, or due to diseases such as cholera, typhus and smallpox. As one history, *Epidemics and Pandemics*, emphasizes: "In the eighteenth century, smallpox succeeded plague as the great epidemic disease of Europe. Waves of epidemic smallpox repeatedly assailed the entire continent; in the larger cities the disease was a nearly constant presence that flared in periods of higher mortality and morbidity, while less densely settled areas had periods of relative health interrupted by violent outbreaks of smallpox." "One modern estimate," that source notes, "claims that by the end of the century smallpox was claiming 400,000 European lives a year, at a time when the population of the continent numbered less than 200 million."[27] "Smallpox," a biographical sketch of the French philosopher and epistemologist Étienne Bonnot de Condillac observes, "was a scourge of even affluent society in the eighteenth century." "There was," that sketch reports, "great interest in the risks of inoculation as against its benefits, and several of Condillac's letters show his readiness to obtain information about it for his correspondents who included La Condamine and the Italian nobleman and famous jurist Beccaria."[28] Charles Marie de La Condamine, a French explorer, mathematician and geographer, spent a decade mapping the Amazon and became a contributor to the famed *Encyclopédie ou Dictionnare raisonné des sciences, des arts et des métiers*. As another source observes of the social and political turbulence that drove so much migration to the Americas in pre-Enlightenment Europe: "Roman Catholics persecuted Protestants, Protestants persecuted Roman Catholics, and different groups of Protestants persecuted each other. Not surprisingly, religious persecution in Western Europe encouraged emigration to the New World. Thus, both Protestant and Catholic forms of Christianity became established in the Americas."[29]

After the death of Charles VI in 1740 and then, a few years later, of Charles VII, Francis I officially became the Holy Roman Emperor. Formerly a prince known as Francis of Lorraine, Francis had married Maria Theresa of Austria—the eldest daughter of Emperor Charles VI and Elisabeth Christina of Brunswick-Wolfenbüttel—in 1736. Upon assuming the throne after a period of great uncertainty for the Habsburg family, Francis I served as the Holy Roman Emperor and the Archduke of Austria and Tuscany until his death in 1765, with Archduchess Maria Theresa—a Roman Catholic—serving as the only female ruler of the Habsburg dynasty. She began her reign after her father's death in 1740, and she was the sovereign of Austria, Bohemia, Hungary, Croatia, Milan and Parma, among other territories. Early in his own tenure as Holy Roman Emperor, Charles VI had, through the issuance of an edict, the Pragmatic Sanction of 1713, decreed that the Habsburg hereditary possessions could be inherited by his daughter, a conscious effort to forestall later monarchical in-fighting. That edict altered the law of succession of the Habsburg family, but Charles VI—lacking a male heir, and seeing the clear and present danger of calamitous violence should he die without one—had endeavored throughout his reign to ensure that the European sovereigns and the diets and estates in the Habsburg dominions would abide by it. In that eighteenth-century milieu, however, everything did not go as planned. After Charles VI's death, Bavaria, France, Prussia, Saxony and Spain broke their commitments and quickly contested the claims of Maria Theresa. And after the line-of-succession dispute broke out, their armed forces became enemy combatants just as Charles VI had feared.[30]

Only after a long and bitter war in which lands changed hands did a treaty end the War of Austrian Succession. Known as King George's War in the Americas because French and English forces fought over North American boundaries during the hostilities, the War of Austrian Succession claimed a half million lives. In the Treaty of Aix-la-Chapelle of 1748, which confirmed the Pragmatic Sanction and ended the war, Austria recognized Frederick II's conquest of Silesia and renounced part of its territories—including Parma—to Spain.[31] The war had began when Prussians seized the Austrian province of Silesia in 1740, and while France and Spain sided with Prussia, Austria received the support of Britain and Holland. Maria Theresa, who wanted peace and a resolution of the prolonged conflict, though she remained bitter over the loss of Silesia, ultimately sent Count Wenzel Anton Kaunitz—her trusted foreign minister—to negotiate the cessation of hostilities. After the death in 1745 of

Charles VII, the chosen Holy Roman Emperor from 1742 to 1745, Maria Theresa's husband, Francis, had assumed that lofty position, though Maria Theresa—then the head of the Habsburg dynasty—still exercised real, substantial power. The Treaty of Aix-la-Chapelle, signed in October 1748 and also called the Peace of Aachen, solidified that arrangement and resulted in the continuation of the Holy Roman Empire, with the powerful Maria Theresa ruling over Austria and the Habsburg lands.[32]

Lombardy's sovereign, Austria's Maria Theresa, reportedly had a "sprightly gait and a majestic bearing." As Count Otto Podewils, the Prussian envoy to Vienna who made that assessment, further recorded in a letter to her rival, Frederick the Great: "She has a round, full face and a bold forehead. Her pronounced eyebrows are, like her hair, blond without any touch of red. Her eyes are large, bright, and at the same time full of gentleness, all accented by their light-blue color." "No one can deny that she is a lovely person," Podewils observed, adding of her royal presence and popularity: "Full of enthusiasm, everyone stood by her and rushed to sacrifice himself for this best of all princesses. People deified her. Everybody wanted to have her picture. She never appeared in public without being greeted with applause." Described elsewhere as a "benevolent, enlightened despot prepared to tolerate a certain amount of local autonomy and opinion," Maria Theresa oversaw Lombardy during her reign, with Austrian officials—headquartered in Vienna—giving Italians, then organized into duchies or city-states, a measure of local control over their own affairs. Richer Italian residents got representation in "general congregations" and "patrimonial congregations," and in the eighteenth century the Austrian Habsburgs introduced a more equitable tax system along with a free trade in grain, allowing noble landowners to improve their properties.[33]

In Lombardy, the world revolved around agriculture, manufacturing and merchants, and the nobility, the height of Milanese high society. "Fewer than 300 noble families owned almost half of all landed property in Lombardy," Jerzy Lukowski writes in *The European Nobility in the Eighteenth Century*. "In Milan," Lukowski explains, "entry into the exclusively noble patriciate was regulated by the Collegio dei Conservatori degli Ordini (though after 1768 the nobilities of Milan and Mantua came under closer Habsburg scrutiny via the new Office of Heralds)."[34] "In Milan," another sources explains, "wealth was the means *par excellence* of social mobility and conferred per se an enviable status." "Actually," that book emphasizes, "the only absolutely indispensable requirement in order to follow the path leading to the pinnacle of Milanese society"—the aristocracy—"seems to have been wealth." Becoming a member of the College of Jurists—one path to entry, and one used by one of Cesare Beccaria's own relatives, Nicola Beccaria—was possible for the sons of merchants and tradesmen, even tailors, if one had enough money, though extreme poverty and serfdom then still plagued the continent of Europe.[35] By the eighteenth century, Milan's College of Jurists already dated back many centuries. "[T]he great juridical tradition of Milan (and Pavia)," scholar Massimo Zaggia writes in an article about Italian society and culture in Lombardy, "produced, in 1575, for example, a new edition of the statutes of the College of Jurists."[36]

The Habsburg Empire, headquartered in Vienna, had officials scattered throughout Europe. The Governor-General of Lombardy, appointed to that position in 1756, was Karl Joseph von Firmian (1716–1782), known in Milan as Carlo Giuseppe di Firmian. The brother of two Austrian bishops, Leopold Ernst and Virgilius Maria von Firmian, Karl Joseph von Firmian had served as Francis I's ambassador to Naples before being tapped to be the plenipotentiary minister to Lombardy. "In Beccaria's Milan," one historian explains, "the state of Lombardy was subject to the political and economic dominance of the enlightened Austro-Hapsburg ruler Maria Theresa." "Under Austrian rule," scholar Piers Beirne observes of the time, "various aspects of social life in Lombardy were somewhat more liberal than elsewhere in Italy." As Beirne writes: "Maria Theresa had loosened the influence of the Church with the *Giunta economale* and the 1762 Pragmatic Sanction, which required royal consent before papal letters and bulls could be entered and published. In addition, her representative in Lombardy, Count Firmian—to whom Beccaria would later be indebted for warding off attempts to prosecute him for his book—had enacted a variety of liberal inroads into social and intellectual life, including toleration of debate and discussion by re-form-minded *illuministi*." Count Firmian, Lombardy's governor, also served as the president of the *Giunta economale*, the economic authority for Milan.

An avid supporter of the arts and sciences, Count Firmian—described as a sort of "King of Milan"—was a protégé of Wenzel Anton, count of Kaunitz-Reitberg, better known simply as Kauntiz. An avid bibliophile and lover of music known for his impressive library and his financial support of musicians, Count Firmian hosted the likes of Wolfgang Amadeus Mozart and his father, Leopold, in Milan in 1770. Highly influential and a man of cultivated tastes, Count Firmian—described by one of his contemporaries, an art historian, as "one of the greatest and most learned" of aristocrats—commissioned Mozart, the young prodigy, to write an opera for a fee of 500 florins. The well-connected, politically powerful Count Firmian was a nephew of the former Archbishop of Salzburg, Leopold's first prince, and he sat atop—and nurtured and guided—Milanese high society. "Milan," one assessment of the Austrian government in Lombardy reported, "greatly benefited under the reign of the Empress Maria Theresa, and the administration of the great minister Kaunitz, and of Count Firmian, Austrian governor of Lombardy"; under Austrian rule, that source observes, "many sumptuous buildings" were built, schools were established and funded, arts and agriculture were encouraged, and "enlightened and virtuous men, like Pietro Verri, Carli, Parini, and others," were protected.[37]

Milan, long fortified by its rulers, was a cultured city and an economic engine where books, learning and intellectuals were highly valued. Gian Rinaldo Carli (1720–1795) and Pietro Verri (1728–1797), for example, were influential economists—Carli having moved to Milan in the service of the Austrian government after teaching at the University of Padua. Another Milanese resident, Giuseppe Parini (1729–1799), was a silk trader's son who copied manuscripts in Milan, entered the priesthood, and became a famous poet.[38] While Milan's Spanish Walls, built between 1546 and 1560 as part of the city's defenses, were ordered to be demolished after the city became part of the Napoleonic Empire, an historic building still stands in Milan in Piazza Mercanti known as the *Palazzo delle Scuole Palatine* (Palace of the Palatine School). That building dates back to the mid-seventeenth century, with that school of higher learning established by Giovanni Maria Visconti. That school later became the University of Milan, with the *Scuole Palatine* name originating between 1601 and 1605. The offerings at that school—according to one historian—"reached their zenith under Empress Maria Theresia's reform policies." As that source, *History of Universities*, notes: "In 1753, Maria Theresia entrusted reform of the University of Pavia and the Scuole Palatine to her chancellor, Prince Wenzel Anton Kaunitz (1711–1794), and to the Senate of Milan, which oversaw Lombardy's education policy as well as the University." "This reform," that source indicates, "was intended to train Lombardy's future administrators: in 1753 a new chair of *jus municipale e provinciale* was established, followed by a chair for *pratica criminale* in 1763, and the chair for *scienze camerali* in 1769." By 1773, the *Scuole Palatine* reportedly constituted "a quasi-university institution with fourteen chairs."[39]

Educated by tutors at home in his earliest years, Cesare Beccaria—the son of aristocrats—had two younger brothers, Francesco and Annibale, and a sister, Maddalena. While Francesco aspired to a military career but was rebuffed (and left disappointed) despite Cesare's recommendation of him to a military officer in Parma, Annibale was a skilled mechanic and technician. Annibale, like Cesare, was later involved in attempts to standardize weights and measures in Milan, with Cesare—on that occasion—obtaining the authorization to use his brother Annibale's services along with those of his older friend, the skilled mathematician Paolo Frisi. The Beccaria family's own ancestors included judges, military figures and ecclesiastics, with the respected Beccaria family once residing in—and, in the fourteenth century, actually ruling over—Pavia, a major commercial center where Cesare Beccaria himself would eventually study. "The Beccaria, once seigneurs of Pavia, in the eighteenth century received the title of marquis," an article on the social classes in Italy explains, writing of Italian *seigneurs*, or feudal lords. "Like all of the aristocratic families in Italy at that time, the Beccarias were Roman Catholics," it has been emphasized of the area's—and the Beccaria family's—long-standing religious association and tradition.[40] "All aspects of social life in eighteenth-century Catholic cities were structured around religious practices and objects," historian Massimo Mazzotti explains of that time. The diocese in Milan, he observes, "had an impressive religious infrastructure and, in the Catholic world, was second in importance only to Rome." When Cesare Beccaria was born in centuries-old Milan in 1738, Pope Clement XII headed the Catholic Church, with Benedict XIV and Clement XIII later serving in the papacy from 1740 to 1758 and from 1758 to 1769, respectively.

A history of Milan's fortifications gives a sense of the city's ancient origins. As one history reports: "The Milan city walls consisted of three separate projects, the first built in Roman times, the second during the Middle Ages, the third (the Mura Spagnole, or Spanish Walls) during the middle of the sixteenth century by the Spanish Habsburg rulers of the city." "The Spanish Walls," that source notes, "formed a massive rampart 15 feet (4.6 meters) or more in height, studded with bastions and a dozen or so large *port[e]* (gateways), stretching for about 7 miles (11 kilometers) around the city."[41] Within the confines of those walls developed a great city, its famous cathedral built of brick and marble quarried by the Visconti family. "[T]he Duomo of Milan," *The Encyclopædia Britannica* notes, "is the largest church in Europe; it covers an area of 14,000 sq. yds. and can hold 40,000 people." With its Gothic style, the interior is 486 feet long, 189 feet wide, and its nave is 157 feet high. As that encyclopedia further observes of the city's storied artistic and cultural traditions: "The city is rich in works of art, for Milan, with the introduction of the early Renaissance style by Filarete and Michelozzo after 1450, became the home of a Lombard school of sculpture, among the chief masters of which may be mentioned Giovanni Antonio Amadeo, or Omodeo, of Pavia (1447–1522), Cristoforo Solari, and, the last of them, Agostino Busti, known as Bambaia (*c.* 1480–1548), whose work may be seen in the cathedrals of Como and Milan and in the Certosa di Pavia."[42]

Catholicism, centered in Rome at St. Peter's Basilica and the Vatican, formerly part of a State covering central Italy and now a small independent city-state that has been the seat of the papacy for centuries, permeated nearly every aspect of life in eighteenth-century Milan. "Toward mid-century, the city of Milan alone," Massimo Mazzotti writes, "hosted more than two hundred churches, three hundred convents, and *pia loca* (pious places, i.e., religious and charitable institutions), including fifty female monasteries and the houses of thirty-nine religious orders." As Mazzotti emphasizes: "At least a quarter of city inhabitants were members of lay religious confraternities, some four hundred of which were still active in 1767. The con-fraternity was an extremely varied institution, built around the veneration of a sacred place or relic or promoting a particular type of devotion or religious practice." "Most confraternities," Mazzotti notes, "were small devotional companies active at the level of the parish or neighborhood." "The federation of the Companies of the Holy Cross," he adds, "was typical of Milan, each company being attached to one of the many crosses that graced the city's squares, intersections, and marketplaces. Those living in the vicinity of the cross would be grouped together, each group having its own saint protector and a common burial ground."[43] For Milanese boys and girls, including those of aristocratic families, Catholicism thus infused nearly every aspect of everyday life, from one's education to one's social life and worship. For instance, Pietro Verri—the son of a senator—was himself taught by Catholic religious orders, which had a long tradition in the secondary school system of Milan, before attending a Jesuit school for nobility in Parma.[44]

At the age of eight, Cesare Beccaria was sent to that same private, Jesuit-run school, the *Collegio Farnesiano* in Parma, to study with other young nobles. There, Beccaria picked up the nickname "Newtoncino" (little Newton) for his aptitude for mathematics, and he showed a particular talent for languages, especially French. According to one biographer, Beccaria possessed "a vivid and fertile imagination, and also a tendency to change his mood between depression and excitement for the slightest reason." Those years in Parma, from 1746 to 1754, were not ones young Cesare later remembered fondly, however. As he later confided to André Morellet, the French translator of *Dei delitti e delle pene*, his "sentiments of humanity" were "stifled by eight years of fanatical and servile education." "Beccaria, like most young men of quality in his day," one of Beccaria's biographers explains, "had been educated in an all-male secondary school; like most of the elite young of Roman Catholic lands, his instructors had been celibate members of the regular clergy." Notably, Parma—the place where he got that very strict and traditional education—had changed hands shortly before Beccaria's arrival. While the Farnese dynasty reigned at Parma until the death of the last male heir in 1731, Elizabeth Farnese—the wife of Philip V of Spain—claimed the duchy for her infant son, Don Carlos, to whom it had been bequeathed by the last duke. As one encyclopedia describes what transpired next: "The pope protested; but his protest was disregarded, and Don Carlos took possession of Parma in 1732. In the subsequent war of the Austrian succession, Parma and Piacenza were taken by the Austrians, and afterwards retaken by the Spaniards in 1745."[45]

The school in Parma, built in the time of Ottavio Farnese, the Duke of Parma, had been founded by the Jesuits in 1564 to prepare young boys for their university educations. The goal: teach pupils grammar and instruct them in the humanities. The Jesuits, under the direction of Duke Ranuccio Farnese (1569–1622), later opened the College of Nobles, which started offering classes in 1604. Its liberal arts curriculum covered everything from arithmetic and geometry to astronomy, rhetoric and music. In their teaching, it is known, the Jesuits focused on the classics, mathematics and languages. The ruthless Duke of Parma, Ranuccio Farnese, himself became known for putting down a plot against him in 1612 by overseeing the torture and execution of several area nobles. Described as "gloomy, severe, suspicious and avaricious," Ranuccio I—as he was also known—ordered a secret trial, beheadings, and the confiscation of the plotters' estates. When Cesare Beccaria arrived in Parma, though, Ranuccio I's iron-fisted reign was a matter purely for historians and the Collegio Farnese (as it was also known in that locale) was—in the words of two scholars—regarded as "the most distinguished boarding school for children of aristocratic families from the Austrian provinces of Lombardia." The curricula of the College of Nobles in Parma, another source explains, "included many of the chivalric arts"; "in Italy," it observes, "it was the upper strata who patronized the Jesuit colleges."[46] The college's chapel—per a traveler's later account—reportedly had "some good paintings by Lanfranco, Leonello Spada, Francesco Stringa, Bibiena," with its great hall containing "some very fine frescos attributed to Giovanni of Troy, in the style of Guido, his master."[47] If Beccaria was ill at ease in Parma, known today for its tasty prosciutto, its flavorful cheeses, and its university and gracious hospitality, it was an unease that Beccaria—a pupil in the all-male institution—was expected to endure as part of his childhood.

In a passage of *Dei delitti e delle pene*, Beccaria—perhaps revealing of his own feelings of discontent in Parma's Jesuit-dominated school—described colleges run by clerics as "those institutions where ardent youth is penned up and in which, as an insurmountable barrier to every other sort of interaction, all of the burgeoning natural vigour burns out in ways useless to humanity and even bring on premature old age." Beccaria's January 1766 letter to his French translator, André Morellet, scholars Mario Ricciardi and Filippo Santoni de Sio point out, shows that young Cesare was "unhappy" in Parma at the Jesuit *Collegio dei Nobili*, though "there is no evidence as to what precisely caused these feelings." Though perhaps just a bad case of homesickness, a real possibility given Cesare's shy, introspective demeanor, the words he chose in *Dei delitti e delle pene* suggest—they contend—something more extreme, "a sense of physical and mental duress, something that stifles rather than promote human flourishing." Duke Ranuccio I had reportedly "founded and endowed the university

College of Nobles with a distinguished faculty, which attracted over 3,000 students" between 1731 and 1748. But the institution was—as *Collier's Encyclopedia* puts it— "neglected," with "[b]righter prospects" only reappearing in 1768 when Ferdinand I of Bourbon used possessions and resources confiscated from the Jesuits to reinvigorate educational opportunities in Parma. Whatever drove Beccaria to dislike his time in Parma, and whatever the condition of the facilities at the time he was there, the fact that Beccaria's fellow students at the *Collegio dei Nobili* nicknamed him "Boy Newton ('Newtoncino')" in homage to the great English physicist and mathematician, Sir Isaac Newton (1643–1727), shows that Beccaria had a special felicity for math—and the respect of his peers—even if he was not the happiest lad in the world.

Though there was an eruption of interest in science in the eighteenth century, Sir Isaac Newton was, by far, the most prominent scientific figure of the age. His book, *Philosophiæ Naturalis Principia Mathematica* (1687), laid out his laws of motion and universal gravitation and is still regarded as one of the most important works in the history of science. Newton helped to lay the foundation for the scientific method itself, with the French physicist Alexis Clairaut—in 1747—identifying Newton's book (which, from the Latin, translates as *Mathematical Principles of Natural Philosophy*) as marking "the epoch of a great revolution in physics." Being compared to Newton—the brilliant Cambridge professor who pioneered calculus and modern physics, and whom American president Thomas Jefferson once called (along with Francis Bacon and John Locke) one of "the three greatest men" who had ever lived—was high praise, especially for a boy of Cesare Beccaria's tender years.[48] While Francis Bacon (1561–1626)—an English author, lawyer, philosopher and statesman—asserted that knowledge is gained by inductive reasoning from empirical data, the English philosopher and physician John Locke (1632–1704) wrote *Two Treatises on Government* (1690) and *An Essay Concerning Human Understanding* (1690), supported religious toleration (as had the Dutch in the seventeenth century), and expressed the view that human beings are motivated by self-interest, thus setting the stage for Adam Smith's *The Wealth of Nations*. Years later, when Beccaria wrote *Dei delitti e delle pene*, he acknowledged the novelty of some of his own ideas—and presciently anticipated the resistance to some of them despite all the scientific and social progress that had taken place by 1764. Tellingly, Beccaria chose this perceptive quote from the much-revered Francis Bacon to open his own little treatise, *Dei delitti e delle pene*: "In all negociations of difficulty, a man may not look to sow and reap at once, but must prepare business, and so ripen it by degrees."[49]

Around the time Beccaria was finishing his studies in Parma, yet another deadly and costly war—the tumultuous Seven Years' War (1756–1763)—broke out, throwing the society into more turmoil as European monarchs again flexed their military muscles. That war took 1.5 million lives and involved the continent's great powers, splitting Europe into two camps, one led by Great Britain and the other by France. Maria Theresa wanted Silesia back from Prussia's king, Frederick II, and when, in 1756, Prussian troops marched into Saxony, yet another long and expensive European war began. Already, the French and Indian War (1754–1763) was underway in North America, with the British Parliament increasing taxes on its colonies to help pay for the costs of an extended war. "The eighteenth-century," Shaun Regan and Frans De

Bruyn write in *The Culture of the Seven Years' War*, "has sometimes been called the second Hundred Years' War between Britain and France, with large-scale wars between the two nations marking the beginning, middle, and end of the century." The Seven Years' War, they explain, "unfolded in theatres on four continents, affecting the regions of South Asia (India), the Caribbean, Europe, the west coast of Africa, and the Philippines, along with North America." The Hundred Years' War (1337–1453) was a series of conflicts that had pitted English and French forces over the succession to the French throne. Whereas Prussia and Portugal sided with Britain in the Seven Years' War, the Austrian Habsburgs—along with Russia, Saxony, Spain and Sweden—came to the aid of French forces in that bitter and deadly conflict. Winston Churchill, in his historical account of the war in *A History of the English-Speaking Peoples*, actually called the Seven Years' War "The First World War" because of its breadth and scope and all the bloody carnage it wrought.[50]

After finishing his Jesuit education in Parma, Cesare Beccaria left that locale to attend the University of Pavia, where he studied law from 1754 to 1758, ultimately graduating with a Doctor of Laws at the age of twenty. Pavia's location near the juncture of the Ticino and Po Rivers had made that city a major commercial center, and the University of Pavia—its point of civic pride—had seen many students come and go in past decades as the city and its university experienced good times and bad. "The University of Pavia," as one source puts it, "naturally had its ups and downs with the political vicissitudes of so many centuries of invasion, war, destruction and reconstruction, until the final barbarous pillage of the French army under Lautrec, in 1527, from which the city never recovered, devastated the country." "[T]hough the country and the city did not recover their previous splendor," that source notes, referencing a history of marble palaces in that ancient metropolis, "the seat of learning remained." "After the ruin of the Spanish era," that source, a history of medical studies at Italian universities, continues, speaking of the city's long history and Pavia's road back to greatness, "it was revived by Maria Theresa, who placed in it the splendid new buildings that exist still, and started it upon a new prosperity."

Founded in 1361, making it one of the oldest universities in the world, the University of Pavia received its charter from Emperor Charles IV. Endowed by Charlemagne and Gian Galeazzo Visconti, it was the only university in the Milan region until the twentieth century and was well known for legal studies. Law had been taught at Pavia since 825 A.D., when King Lotharius established a school for training judges and notaries, so Cesare Beccaria was following in the well-trodden tracks of many Italians in going to Pavia to study that subject.[51] "Probably," Mario Ricciardi and Filippo Santoni de Sio observe of Beccaria's decision to continue his studies there, "this choice was undertaken in the hope to follow in the footsteps of his paternal uncle, Nicola Francesco Beccaria, a member of the college of Lawyers, and judge in Pavia and Milan." Nicola Francesco Beccaria (1702–1765)—or Don Nicola Beccaria—had become a member of the *Collegio dei nobili giurisperiti* (College of Noble Jurists) in 1738, the year of Cesare Beccaria's birth. He had served as a judge in Pavia from 1742 to 1745 and, later, in Milan. As those two scholars explain of what likely compelled his nephew, Cesare Beccaria, the young marquis in waiting, to enroll at the University of Pavia and to obtain his law degree in September 1758: "Despite having a title that in other European countries is frequently associated with large fortunes, the Beccaria were comfortably well off, but they did not live in luxury. We can assume, therefore, that the prospect of a legal career, or of an employment in the imperial administration, was by no means contemptible for the young man just graduated from University (and maybe also for his father on whom he depended for his livelihood)."[52]

Cesare Beccaria, away at law school in Pavia when the Seven Years' War broke out, did not participate in that war. Instead, he finished his legal studies and, once back in Milan, led what Ricciardi and Santoni de Sio describe as "the relatively carefree life of the young man of good family," taking part in "literary competitions" as a member of the *Accademia dei Trasformati*. The *Accademia dei Trasformati* (Academy of the Transformed), one of many salons and literary and reading societies of that age, was founded in 1546 and revived in 1743 by the wealthy Count Giuseppe Maria Imbonati (1688–1768). Such Italian academies had sprung up all over, "growing out of"—as one scholar notes—"pompous receptions in the palaces of cardinals or of princesses, and out of disorderly carouses at literary coffee-houses," often with names that were "allusions, riddles, jokes, or gibberish." Bologna had the Frozen Ones, Siena had the Crazed Ones, and other Italian societies went by Drunkards, Frigids and Phlegmatics. "Academies of this type, which flourished in Italy in the seventeenth and eighteenth centuries," one of Beccaria's biographers, Marcello Maestro, writes, "had witty or ludicrous names, such as the Lunatics, the Extravagant, the Drowsy, the Apathetic, the Anxious, the Confused, the Fantastic, the Ethereal."[53] Count Imbonati owned an elegant sixteenth-century palace, known as Palazzo Imbonati, which bore the markings of the Visconti-Sforza families. A set of mid-fifteenth century tarot cards commissioned by Filippo Maria Visconti (1392–1447), the one-time Duke of Milan, and by his son-in-law and successor, Francesco Sforza (1401–1466), are the oldest known surviving tarot cards. Those hand-painted cards contain heraldic insignia, evidence of their aristocratic origins.[54]

The Academy of the Transformed that met at Count Imbonati's palace—and that Beccaria joined—had taken its name from an older academy of noblemen interested in medicine and the natural sciences. The salon's new iteration admitted both men and women, and popular topics included "the defense of the Italian language and of the Milanese dialect," "[t]he need to use a natural style in literature," and "the history of local traditions." "To gain entrance to the Trasformati," writes Aaron Thomas, a translator of Beccaria's *Dei delitti e delle pene*, "Beccaria is presumed to have written a few poems, including some rather unoriginal verses on the immensely destructive Lisbon earthquake of 1755, and a piece that lampooned a hypothetical book collector, who was interested solely in the prestige he would garner through his ownership of rare volumes of Newton, Descartes, Gassendi, Voltaire, or Racine, and who couldn't be troubled to actually read the 'many books piled on high / that arrived from strange faraway lands, / from Amsterdam, Paris and England.'" The members of that socially prestigious literary society—one of the most fashionable in Milan—met at Count Imbonati's manse to enjoy one another's company, to exchange ideas on issues of the day, and to recite their compositions on various topics. The Trasformati was known as a "moderate and traditional" group; its activities characterized as "bland and prudent reformism." Though the group normally met at Count Imbonati's palace in Piazza San Fedele, in September its members also made an annual visit to the count's impressive, sixteen-bedroom villa at Cavallasca, near Lake Como. The Trasformati reportedly brought people together "from very different walks of life." While some of Milan's wealthiest residents were in the Academy of the Transformed, a commoner—a talented dialect poet—served as the Academy's permanent secretary.[55]

The membership of the moderately conservative *Accademia dei Trasformati* included Cardinal Giuseppe Pozzobonelli (1796–1783) and Padre Giovenale Sacchi (1726–1789), a mathematician, writer and musical theorist; the poets Giuseppe Parini (1729–1799), Vittorio Amedeo Cigna-Santi (1730–1795), Carlo Antonio Tanzi (1710–1768), Gian Carlo Passeroni (1713–1803), Francesco Sforzino da Carcano (1735–1794), and Domenico Balestrieri (1714–1780); the Italian thinkers and writers Giovan Mauro Mazzucchelli (1707–1765), Giuseppe Baretti (1719–1789), Remigio Fuentes (1706–1778), and Giuseppe Candido Agudio (1698–1765); a doctor, Giammaria Bicetti (1708–1778), and a leading composer of symphonies, the musician Giovanni Battista Sammartini (1700–1775); Giuseppe Cerini (1738–1779), a lawyer who took a great interest in literary matters; and another a lawyer, Count Giorgio Giulini (1714–1780), a man who served as the official historian of Milan and who studied antiquities, coins, seals, and the monuments of his native city. To facilitate his work, Count Giulini got an annual pension from Empress Maria Theresa. The Academy also included Cesare Beccaria's older friend and mentor, Pietro Verri (1728–1797), as well as Maria Gaetana Agnesi (1718–1799), the Italian mathematician and humanitarian who wrote a book on calculus and became the first woman to be offered a university appointment as a mathematics professor. "[A]s a member of the Accademia dei Trasformati," one book notes of Giovanni Battista Sammartini, a musically talented member of the group, "he fully participated in the intellectual and literary circles of Milan, a city judged to be one of the most important Italian centres for its trade, for the circulation of ideas and also for its art and music."[56]

The *Accademia dei Trasformati* admitted the rich and, occasionally, the poor, though one's artistic or literary gifts or one's status within Italian society—whether conferred by wealth or religious orders—was incredibly important to membership. The academy, for a time starting in the 1750s, published a journal, *Raccolta milanese*, and the wide-ranging topics published in that publication dealt with law, medicine, natural philosophy and social policies. As historian Massimo Mazzotti writes in *The World of Maria Gaetana Agnesi, Mathematician of God*: "A recurring theme in these academic works was the perceived decadence of Italian culture and society. War and internal feuds were the common culprits, but the traditional education system, the pre-eminence of Latin, and the way in which philosophy and theology were taught at universities and colleges were also singled out." "The academicians," Mazzotti observes, "cultivated satire, in particular, which they directed primarily at the moral and cultural degeneration of the Italian aristocracies." "Other recurrent themes in Trasformati publications," he continues, "were the scandal of the castrati, the increasing

number of women entering the cloister, and the excesses of baroque religious ceremonies." "Reform," he adds, "was recommended for all these, along the lines of enlightened Catholicism." "Thus," Mazzotti stresses of the academy's suggested solutions,
"Italian should replace Latin, more space should be given to the modern sciences and
to modern history in curricula, and textbooks should be written in a plain, natural
language, as bad style would impede the diffusion of modern knowledge." The Trasformati sought to better educate the children of non-aristocratic families, publishing a
grammar and seeking uniform instruction in reading, writing and arithmetic and in
religion and the arts. The Trasformati's emblem: a tree with branches full of apples.[57]

Giuseppe Parini—one of the Trasformati members who had become an ordained
priest, giving him a special place within Milanese society—studied philosophy and
theology and wrote a celebrated satire, "Il Giorno" ("The Day"), about the daily life
and pleasures of Milanese nobles. Said to be "wretchedly poor" and "obliged to support
himself by copying law-documents and taking pupils," Parini became a Professor of
Rhetoric at the Academy of the Brera, wrote poetry and plays, and campaigned against
the barbaric practice of castration. A *castrado*—a classical and then popular male
singing voice—was produced by castrating the singer before puberty, a sixteenth-century Italian practice that continued into the nineteenth century. Praised as "the greatest
Italian poet of his day and the most complete representative of Enlightenment literature
in the country," Parini was admitted to the prestigious academy in 1753, a few years
before Beccaria became a member. Because of his skills, Parini was a tutor to the
children of Duke and Duchess Serbelloni until 1762—and then to those of the academy's moving force, Giuseppe Maria Imbonati. Educated by Jesuits, Giuseppe Baretti—
another prominent figure in the group—published his first poems in Milan after living
in Turin and Venice, and he had been a popular teacher of the Italian language in London. Baretti's books included *Remarks on the Italian Language and Writers* (1753), *An
Introduction to the Italian Language* (1755), *The Italian Library* (1757), *A Dictionary
of English and Italian Languages* (1760), and *A Grammar of the Italian Language* (1762).[58]

The world of the Trasformati orbited around books and ideas and music, ballet
and opera. "The duchy of Lombardy," Daniel Heartz writes in *Music in European
Capitals: The Galant Style, 1720–1780*, "was a fief of the Habsburgs throughout most
of the eighteenth century, and its musical life reflected this." As Heartz explains: "The
large opera house built at Milan in 1717 was subject to remote control from Vienna,
a factor that brought several Austrian and Bohemian composers, including Mozart,
commissions to write for it. Local talents were not scarce, the greatest in the operatic
field being Giovanni Battista Lampugnani, who lived from 1706 to 1781. But Milan
imported much more than it exported in the domain of opera throughout the eighteenth century." Per Heartz's history: "Gluck, Christian Bach, Sarti, and Salieri were
among the major composers to come to Milan for a time and win either employment,
commissions, or both. During the 1770s the court theatre in Milan, like its Viennese
counterpart, became a battleground for the two great exponents of dramatic ballet,
Gasparo Angiolini and Jean-Georges Noverre." A highly cultured dancer, choreographer
and composer, the Florence-born Gasparo Angiolini (1731–1803) was married to a
beautiful dancer, Maria Teresa Fogliazzi, and the two dancers, as a couple, reportedly

"moved easily in the circles of educated society." Angiolini, who directed ballet at the Imperial Theatre in Vienna starting in 1758, became the director of the Imperial Theater in St. Petersburg, Russia, in 1766, and, in 1778, he came to Milan to direct productions at the La Scala theatre, with Angiolini corresponding with the likes of Rousseau, Beccaria and Giuseppe Parini. "By this time," Heartz stresses of the ever-changing cultural scene, "Milan had emerged as a leading center of the Enlightenment, with close ties to developments at Paris." "Literary figures such as the Verri brothers, Cesare Beccaria, and Giuseppe Parini," Heartz notes, "were in the thick of the controversies raging on many matters, including ballet and opera." As Heartz concludes: "Milan was thus a lively artistic center, notwithstanding its foreign yoke (and partly because of it). Sammartini was a friend of Parini, and like him a member of the Accademia dei Trasformati, along with Verri and Beccaria."[59]

Count Pietro Verri—a leading figure of the northern Italian Enlightenment who would study economics in Vienna, the dynastic capital of the Habsburg Empire—was an economist, public servant, and a moral and political philosopher. The son of Count Gabriele Verri, a conservative member of the Milanese Senate, Pietro Verri became fascinated by the subject of political economy during the Seven Years' War. During that war, in which Verri served as a captain in the Imperial Austrian army, he met Henry Lloyd—a Welsh soldier and later political economist—in September 1759 in fields near Bautzen. Lloyd had joined the Austrian army in 1758, and he became a lieutenant and was at battles in 1758 and 1759. The two men began a friendship, and they had many long conversations about the military and economics. As Riccardo Faucci writes of Verri's intellectual pursuits in *A History of Italian Economic Thought*, Verri "stumbled upon such authors as Farbonnais, Melon, Dutot and Hume" and "entered into an acquaintance with a noteworthy character from a military-economic background—Henry Lloyd, author of *An Essay on the Theory of Money* that came out in 1771 (the same year in which Verri published his *Meditazioni sull'economia politica*)." Verri and Lloyd, another source stresses, "shared common philosophic pursuits"; after the war, in fact, Lloyd "traveled to Italy and for some time resided with his close friend and Italian *philosophe*, Pietro Verri." Verri's *Meditazioni sulla felicità* (1763), the publication of which predates Beccaria's *Dei delitti e delle pene* by a year, translates as *Meditations on Happiness*.[60]

Henry Lloyd also developed friendships with Cesare Beccaria and Paolo Frisi (1728–1784), an Italian mathematician, physicist and astronomer. Frisi wrote a major treatise on hydraulics, *Del modo di regolare i fiumi, e i torrenti* (*A Treatise on Rivers and Torrents, 1762*), penned commentaries on the works of Galileo Galilei and Sir Isaac Newton, and belonged to many scientific societies of his day, including ones in Berlin, St. Petersburg, London and Paris. A member of the Barnabite religious order, Frisi—an ordained priest—had studied together with Pietro Verri in school, became a teacher in Milan and Pisa, and interacted with the French *philosophes*, Benjamin Franklin and David Hume in his travels abroad. The Italian and French philosophes were always eager to share their ideas with one another, though, sadly, Cesare Beccaria himself never got a chance to meet Hume during his 1766 trip to Paris. In *The Reception of David Hume in Europe*, one contributor, Paola Zanardi, notes that while Beccaria and his companion, Alessandro Verri, "attended the *salons* of d'Holbach and

Helvétius during the same period Hume enjoyed his times there," Beccaria "was not able to manage a meeting with Hume, so he gave André Morellet the job of taking him a new edition of his text."[61]

Like Cesare Beccaria, Pietro Verri and his fellow soldier, Henry Lloyd (1729–1783), shared a passion for economics and public economy. Educated at Oxford and the son of an Anglican cleric, Lloyd served as a staff officer in the Seven Years' War. While Verri published his "*Elementi del Commercio*" (1764) in *Il Caffè*, a publication Paolo Frisi helped his friend, Pietro, to edit, Lloyd—an historian and economist—published a history of the Seven Years' War, with its first volume appearing in 1766, as well as *An Essay on the English Constitution* (1770). In *An Essay on the Theory of Money* (1771), Henry Lloyd wrote of "the celebrated Montesquieu" and included a section titled "*Liberty is in proportion to the equality, and despotism to the inequality of circulation.*" As Henry began that section: "An extensive circulation will in a short time become unequal, especially in very civilized nations, where in general, hereditary successions, and testaments take place, so that in a little time circulation will be unequally divided, and the more it is so, the fewer will be the number of the rich, and the greater that of the poor. That inequality of riches, necessarily produces an inequality of power." "It is from this principle," Henry asserted, "that republics, and free governments degenerate in proportion as they grow rich, and are finally overthrown, when the riches and power which be equally divided between all those who form the legislative authority are concentered in few persons only." "In monarchies," Lloyd added, "an inequality of circulation and power is a necessary consequence of that species of government, because the monarch alone having the power of levying taxes, and of employing such as he pleases in all the different departments, it follows evidently, that none can be either rich or powerful but such as are dependant upon, and connected with the court; hence that abject slavery, intrigue and dissimulation which characterizes that class of men called, Courtiers; as they have no power nor scarce existence but what is derived from the imperial nod." A courtier was someone who attended a royal court or served as an advisor to a king or queen.

Pietro Verri and Henry Lloyd must have had many in-depth discussions about how best to structure a society. "The end of the social pact," Verri wrote in 1763 in his own book, *Meditations on Happiness*, "is the well-being of each of the individuals who join together to form society, who do so in order that this well-being becomes absorbed into the public happiness or rather the greatest possible happiness distributed with the greatest equality possible." While Milan's aristocracy, of which Pietro's father was a leading member, sought to preserve their privileges and autonomy through the Milanese Senate, younger Italian intellectuals—such as Gabriele Verri's son, Pietro, and Cesare Beccaria—were more open to change. "The contrast between Gabriele Verri (senator and civil servant, and a jealous, clever guardian of autonomy in opposition to Vienna) and his sons, Pietro in particular," the *Encyclopedia of the Enlightenment* reports, reflect the motivation of "an entire generation of intellectuals to enter the struggle against privilege." "Pietro Verri's *Meditazioni sulla felicià* (ca. 1763; Meditations on Happiness)," that source reports, "was an elaboration of an ethical system intended to be both secular and utilitarian." Henry Lloyd, writing at the inception of the field of economics, seems to have been influenced by Verri's ideas, and they no doubt influenced each other as a result of their friendship. As Lloyd writes in *An Essay on the Theory of Money* (1771): "If in a democracy, the quantity of circulation is great, and consequently unequal, the principles of the constitution will soon be corrupted. The whole power of the state will be centered in few persons, whereas it should be distributed equally, among all those who partake of the legislative authority." "In an aristocracy, where circulation is become unequal, and consequently some few families are grown too powerful," Henry added, "these must be employed in expensive employments in order to reduce them to an equality with their fellow citizens."[62]

The fields of monetary policy and economics were incredibly new at the time that Pietro Verri, Cesare Beccaria, and Henry Lloyd were writing about those topics. In writing about eighteenth-century Italian economists, one writer stresses that "[t]he major Italians" differed from the rank-and-file physiocrats "not only in considering the manufacturing sector as contributing more to the 'net product' than agriculture, but also in emphasizing the larger social and cultural forces it mobilized." "The Neapolitans and the Milanese," that writer observes, taking note of Beccaria's and Verri's perspectives in that vein, "both argued for a synergy rather than a fundamental opposition between industry and agriculture," believing investments in them "were vital to prepare for international commerce." Although pointing out that "[m]ost of the major Italian economists of the time were generally in favour of 'free trade'," that concept — as Edwin Seligman explains — did not mean then what it means today. "Free trade," Seligman observes, "denoted in those days something very different from what it signifies today." "It did not mean freedom to import goods without payment of duty," but, instead, it represented "freedom to export goods as over against the companies which possessed a monopoly of trade." Freedom of trade, Seligman stresses, thus meant "freedom of competition, not freedom or exemption from taxation of duties." "Almost all the 'Free Traders,'" he writes, noting their opposition to monopolies and privileges but their more cautious attitudes relating to foreign commerce, "were in fact what we should today call Protectionists."[63]

If Pietro Verri was a disciplined soldier, his younger friend, Cesare Beccaria, was a dreamer and more undisciplined idealist, unwilling to compromise his passions and core beliefs during his youth. In 1760 in Milan, as the Seven Years' War still raged, Beccaria fell in love with Teresa de Blasco, a sixteen-year-old girl who was the daughter of an army colonel, Domenico de Blasco, of Spanish-Sicilian origin. Both Cesare and Teresa took music lessons from Carlo Monza (1735–1801), a choirmaster and well-known operatic composer. As one source reports: "Monza ... was a composer and organist in Milan all of his life, composing opera for various theaters in Italy. He had written opera for about 10 years in 1769." "Carlo Monza," another biographical sketch reports, "was one of the most prominent and popular composers in Milan in the second half of the eighteenth century." Though Teresa lacked an elevated social position on the same plane as Cesare, she was beautiful and had a lively personality to match her good looks. After Cesare and Teresa got to know one another, the two decided to marry, but Beccaria's father vehemently opposed the match, leaving young Cesare and his betrothed in a quandary. Teresa did not have a substantial dowry, and Cesare — headstrong and head-over-heels in love but lacking his father's blessing — was still dependent on the patriarch of his family for financial support. What followed was an epic battle of wills between father and son. As one text notes: "Beccaria experienced more than his share of hardships, beginning with his father's refusal to approve his marriage to the woman of his choice."[64]

The de Blasco family had honorably served the Habsburg dynasty and had important social connections of their own. Domenico de Blasco and his brother, cartographer Michel Angelo de Blasco, had joined Habsburg troops after Charles VI invaded Sicily in 1718. Sicily was, by a 1720 treaty, given to Emperor Charles VI. "After the loss of Sicily in 1735," one source notes, "the de Blascos gave up all their properties on this island, and continued their service as part of the Habsburg army."[65] Michel Angelo de Blasco (1697–1772), for example, was a military engineer who served the Austrian monarchs and the king of Portugal, once dedicating a map of Italy to Empress Maria Theresa in 1769; he reportedly "participated in campaigns in Sicily, the Habsburg-Ottoman border on the Danube and northern Italy" and had "distinguished himself during the implementation of the Treaty of Madrid (1750)." After the birth of Maria Theresa's first son in 1741, Michel Angelo de Blasco had — in the midst of the War of Austrian Succession — even dedicated a sonnet to Maria Theresa, ending it with these lines of flattery: *Oh, our soul is happy! Oh, sublime gift! / In the great suffering, here is TERESA, / Happily showing us the SON from the Austrian Throne.* Despite the family's distinguished history of military service, Michel Angelo's brother, Domenico di Blasco — as his name is also spelled — was considered insufficiently wealthy by the Marchese Gian Saverio Beccaria Bonesana. Domenico de Blasco has been described as "a relatively impoverished military officer," a condition made worse by being from a family of much doubtful noble ancestry.[66]

Despite his father's obstinacy, Cesare Beccaria continued courting Teresa and even proposed marriage, sending her passionate letters declaring his intentions during the midst of the intra-familial, highly volatile father-son dispute. "My dear spouse," one letter began even before the couple had wed, with the love-struck Beccaria writing: "Let me call you by this sweet name which shall be my consolation through my whole life if you will remain faithful to me and if I will be able to earn your love." "I swear that when I will be your husband," Beccaria pledged in that letter, written in the fall of 1760, "all my time will be spent in serving you, pleasing you, loving you, and doing everything that will make you happy and merry." "You don't know, my love, how I suffer," he continued, observing in his letter: "I try not to show it, but I see my father and my uncle talking in secret and plotting something against you and me. Whatever they do, I am determined to marry you." As a steadfast, strong-willed Cesare ended his letter, asking for assurances from a teenage Teresa about her commitment and love for him: "My dear, have faith in me. Even if I should be jailed — it may well happen — I will never change. But I am afraid that if you or your parents hear that I may be thrown out of my house with the smallest allowance you will not stay with me, and this gives me a terrible anxiety. Please answer me on this point because I am ready to be miserable and homeless." "I swear to God," Cesare dramatically concluded, "that I am ready to die rather than leave you."

In an era when Italian fathers had extraordinary powers, Cesare Beccaria's father had his son placed under house arrest for three months in an effort to block Cesare from marrying Teresa and to make him "more leisurely reflect on his condition." "A father at that time," one book notes, "had the power to enforce his will under the doctrine of *patria potestas*, a Roman rule that gave fathers virtually unchecked power over the lives of their children." The notion of *patria potestas*—as one source puts it—originated in Roman antiquity and gave to the father "the complete control of the son's actions." "In early law," one legal historian, Barry Nicholas, wrote in *An Introduction to Roman Law*, "there was evidently little difference between son and slave, both being regarded as the property of the *pater-familias* to be disposed of as he wished." For a brief time, Cesare Beccaria's father's tactics worked and young Cesare—in spite of his early resolve—appeared to be willing to appease his father. Although Cesare had earlier appealed to Domenico de Blasco, who then spoke to Cesare's father without consequence or effect, Cesare ended up writing to Teresa to explain that, after much reflection, he had concluded that marrying someone against his father's wishes would not lead to a happy marriage. Cesare thus asked to be released from his promises to marry. But soon thereafter, Beccaria—still under the spell of love, and having second thoughts—reversed course and became as determined as ever to marry his sweetheart. In December 1760, Colonel de Blasco—himself doggedly determined to help Cesare and his own daughter—also addressed a plea to the Empress Maria Theresa to facilitate the marriage of the two young lovers. As Beccaria biographer John Hostettler writes: "Teresa's father appealed to the Empress, Maria Theresa, stressing his own nobility, the dowry he was prepared to procure for his daughter, and the suitor's warm affection for her."[67]

In February 1761, Cesare Beccaria was finally set free from his father's constraints. His final decision? He would elope. On February 14, 1761, just days after leaving his mother and father's house to get married without his parents' consent, Beccaria penned a letter to his father and had it delivered by hand. After the opening salutation, "My dear father," it began: "I don't want to leave any doubt about my true and final decision. This is why I am stating it in writing, asking your forgiveness for what I am going to tell you in all sincerity." "Please be assured that only death can destroy my resolution, and the idea of death doesn't frighten me," the letter read, adding: "I swear before God that I will not change my decision. I ask you in the name of Jesus Christ to stop putting obstacles to this marriage and to stop doing violence to my will and my conscience." "[P]lease leave me free to follow my destiny," it continued, with the letter asserting in no uncertain terms: "If the result of my decision will be bad, as you say, it will be my fault, not the fault of my parents. I did everything I could in order to please you, against my own soul, but now I cannot change anymore." As Cesare Beccaria's plaintive letter concluded: "I am ready to leave your house and to accept whatever little subsidy you will give me, but I ask you to let me do what I want. Otherwise I don't know what will happen to your poor son who has suffered all possible torments. I kiss your hand and ask for your fatherly blessing."

Cesare and Teresa's marriage ceremony took place on February 22, 1761, but despite all of the colonel's and Cesare's efforts, the blessing of Beccaria's father and family was not forthcoming. The wedding ceremony was not attended by Beccaria's parents, and the falling out between father and son—no small spat, but a bitter contest of wills—forced Beccaria to live in relative poverty on a small allowance. While Domenico de Blasco had done his best to obtain Cesare Beccaria's father's approval, Beccaria's parents—along with Beccaria's paternal uncle, Niccolò Beccaria, a cleric then living at the same house—all vehemently opposed the marriage and would not relent. By early July 1761, Cesare—accustomed to a certain lifestyle and without sufficient money to support himself and his new wife—was already writing to Count Firmian to complain about his father's denial of means to allow him and Teresa to live decently. Cesare also complained to Count Firmian about his lack of access to the Beccaria family home on Via Brera.[68] Cesare Beccaria desperately wanted to get back in the good graces of his parents and to patch things up, and Count Firmian was a man who could make things happen. "Count Firmian, the Austrian governor of Lombardy," one biographical sketch notes, "distinguished himself not only as a liberal patron of sciences and letters, but as the friend of every reform which could be grounded on solid principles."[69]

It was during this time—in 1761—that Beccaria read Montesquieu's *Persian Letters* and underwent a "philosophical conversion." Montesquieu's *Lettres persanes* (1721), as it first appeared in French, tells the story of two Persian nobles on their travels through France; the novel unites ethics, philosophy and politics with observations on Western society.[70] Through Pietro Verri, scholars Mario Ricciardi and Filippo Santoni de Sio explain, Beccaria "came into contact with a group of bright young intellectuals, which nourished literary ambitions" and led him into "a passion for the new philosophical ideas coming from France, Scotland and England." Only in 1762, the year of the birth of the newlywed's first child—their daughter, Giulia—did Cesare Beccaria and his mother and father reconcile. Born on July 21, 1762, Giulia—conceived in the midst of Cesare Beccaria's intra-familial trauma—was named after the heroine in Jean-Jacques Rousseau's extremely popular novel, *Julie, or The New Héloïse* (1761).[71] "Novels," Lynn Hunt writes in *Inventing Human Rights*, speaking of the impact of celebrated works of eighteenth-century fiction, "made the point that all people are fundamentally similar because of their inner feelings," with Hunt emphasizing that reading them "created a sense of equality and empathy through passionate involvement in the narrative."[72] "*Julie*," the editors of a modern translation emphasize, "became one of the greatest international publishing successes in the eighteenth century, with scores of editions, and the English translation itself went through fifteen editions before it withered on the vine in 1812."[73]

Italian aristocrats were part of a small, highly privileged circle, and they interacted frequently with one another. As an adult, Cesare and Teresa's first child, Giulia Beccaria (1762–1841), would go on to become a lover of Pietro Verri's younger playboy brother, Giovanni Verri (1745–1818), and, later, of the wealthy nobleman and banker, Carlo Imbonati (1753–1805), the son of Count Giuseppe Maria Imbonati, the aristocrat who hosted the meetings of the *Accademia dei Trasformati*. In her early twenties, she also became the mother of Alessandro Manzoni (1785–1873), the famous Italian poet and novelist who greatly admired the work of his maternal grandfather, Cesare Beccaria.[74] "Alessandro Manzoni's mother was Beccaria's daughter, Giulia (1762–

1841)," one book notes, emphasizing of Giulia: "Strong, beautiful, and intelligent, she had fallen in love with Verri but entered into a loveless marriage with a nobleman from Lecco." When Giulia, at age twenty, entered into a marriage with Pietro Manzoni (1736–1807), Pietro Manzoni was 46, more than twice her age. A wealthy, childless widower who lived a cloistered, conservative life with his siblings, Pietro Manzoni was an incompatible match—one that Cesare Beccaria himself had arranged in spite of the age difference and their unsuitability for one another. "After seven years in a steadily worsening relationship," *The Cambridge History of Italian Literature* observes of Giulia Beccaria's arranged marriage in 1782 to Pietro Manzoni, a much older man, "Giulia went to live with Carlo Imbonati, a wealthy merchant banker, and Alessandro was farmed out to various religious boarding schools which gave him very unpleasant memories but a good classical education."[75]

Rousseau's widely read novel, from which Cesare Beccaria's daughter got her name, was a runaway bestseller. After first appearing in Paris in February 1761, pirated editions began appearing all over France and, in all, seventy-two French editions were offered for sale between 1761 and 1800.[76] The epistolary novel—originally printed by Rousseau's Amsterdam-based publisher, Marc-Michel Rey (1720–1780), and with chapter titles such as "Love's first kiss," "The inoculation of love," "Paternal force," and "The confidence of beautiful souls"—focuses on the relationship between an aristocratic young woman, Julie, and Saint-Preux, her middle-class tutor and lover. It consists of an exchange of letters between Julie and Saint-Preux, a cousin and friend, and ultimately Baron de Wolmar, the man Julie ends up marrying. In the novel, Julie becomes pregnant after she and Saint-Preux consummate their love, but then Julie's father becomes enraged and hits her, causing a miscarriage. Along with her mother, Julie falls ill, with Julie coming down with smallpox after her sexual liaison. After Saint-Preux leaves, Julie marries the baron—the man Julie's father had always intended for her to marry—and the couple have children and live on a model estate, Clarens. Given Cesare Beccaria's painful experience with his own father, the plot of Rousseau's novel—originally titled *Lettres de deux amans habitans d'une petite ville au pied des Alps* (*Letters from Two Lovers Living in a Small Town at the Foot of the Alps*) and, later, like Voltaire's writings, put on the Roman Catholic Church's *Index Librorum Prohibitorum*—must have spoken to Beccaria in a deeply personal way. When, in the novel, Saint-Preux returns, Julie confesses her love for Saint-Preux to her husband, who then, magnanimously, invites Saint-Preux to live under his own roof as a tutor to their children as proof of his own faith and confidence in his wife and her former lover. As one Rousseau scholar describes the plot twist that then ensues: "They live together amicably for some time, but when Wolmar goes away for a while, Julie and Saint-Preux go boating on Lake Geneva and are trapped at the very spot where, years before, Saint-Preux had lain in a torment of desperate love yearning for Julie. She, however, resists his renewed declaration and seems to have overcome the intemperate passions of her youth." "Yet having contracted pneumonia after saving one of her children from drowning," that plot summary continues, taking note of Julie's tormented, fictional fate, "she confesses in her dying moments to having never ceased to love him." The novel ends with Baron de Wolmar and Saint-Preux living side-by-side on the family's estate.[77]

It was during his intense, intra-familial squabble that Cesare Beccaria befriended Pietro Verri, the Milanese aristocrat ten years his senior. They shared common interests, including in literature, economics and political economy, and through what Verri called a "coffee-house" friendship, Beccaria got introduced to other intellectuals, such as Paolo Frisi, and a wide array of Enlightenment ideas. In addition to reading Montesquieu and Voltaire, Beccaria became familiar with the writings of Bacon, Diderot, Helvétius, Hume and Rousseau. When Rousseau's book *Du Contrat Social* (*The Social Contract*) came out in 1762, Beccaria read it enthusiastically and it had a "deep influence" on him. He also read *De l'esprit* (*On Mind*), the work of Helvétius, which was first published in 1758 and which was also widely read by scores of enlightened thinkers. "In the letter to Morellet," Mario Ricciardi and Filippo Santoni de Sio write of Beccaria's post-*Dei delitti e delle pene* publication correspondence with his translator, "Beccaria reconstructs this journey of discovery through the names of the authors and the titles of the works that shaped his intellectual development: Montesquieu and his *Lettres persanes*, Helvetius and his *L'esprit*, and then Buffon, Diderot, Hume, d'Alembert, and finally Condillac, who Beccaria met during a visit in Milan."[78] "Doubtless it was his friend and mentor Pietro Verri who introduced him to Helvétius since *De l'esprit* was a book that had also greatly impressed Verri," Jonathan Israel writes of Cesare Beccaria in *Democratic Enlightenment: Philosophy, Revolution, and Human Rights, 1750–1790*. "In aspiring to become a 'philosophe,'" Israel explains, "Beccaria was motivated by his reading and by a quarrel with his family over wishing to marry a girl he loved whom his parents deemed their social inferior."[79]

Like Rousseau's novel and Montesquieu's writings, *De l'esprit* (1758), the book of philosophy by Claude Adrien Helvétius, played a central role in Cesare Beccaria's intellectual awakening. That book "wrought a revolution in me," Beccaria explained, adding: "It was he who pushed me powerfully in the direction of the truth and first awoke my attention to the blindness and misfortunes of mankind. I owe a large portion of my ideas to the reading of *De l'esprit*." That book, translated into English as *On Mind*, was condemned by the church as heretical and burned in Paris in 1759, forcing Helvétius—descended from a family of physicians, trained in finance, but charged with being an atheist after the publication of *De l'esprit*, his magnum opus—to issue three retractions. Among other things, *De l'esprit* had declared that human beings are motivated exclusively by the pursuit of pleasure and the avoidance of pain. Helvétius, who later spent time in England and in Berlin at the invitation of the Prussian king, Frederick II, weighed in on a number of subjects, and even had something to say on the topic of punishment. "[L]et us cast our eyes," he wrote, "upon a man who sacrifices all his fortune to save a relation, who is an assassin, from undergoing the severity of the law." "This man," Helvétius observed, "will certainly be considered by his family as extremely virtuous, though he is really extremely unjust." "I say extremely unjust," Helvétius continued, "because, if the hope of impunity multiplies crimes, and the certainty of punishment is absolutely necessary to preserve order in any nation, it is evident, that a pardon granted to a criminal, is injustice to the public, of which he renders himself an accomplice, who solicits for such a pardon." After serving as the farmer-general, a tax-collecting post he served in at the request of France's queen, Helvétius divided his time between his family's Parisian townhouse and their country estate, Château de Voré. Helvétius also spent his time seeking to improve agriculture and development of industries and to improving the lot of the poor.[80]

During the Enlightenment, intellectuals became obsessed with the concepts of pleasure and pain and the law's role in shaping society—and Pietro Verri and Cesare Beccaria, in Austrian Lombardy, were no different than Helvétius in that respect. In *De l'esprit*, Helvétius himself wrote: "If pleasure be the only object of a man's pursuit, we need only imitate nature, in order to inspire a love of virtue. Pleasure informs us of what she would have done, and pain what she forbids, and man will readily obey her mandates." "Why may not a legislature, armed with the same power," he asked, "produce the same effects?" "The hatred most men have for virtue," Helvétius posited, "is not then the effect of the corruption of their nature, but of the imperfection of the legislation." As Helvétius observed: "It is the legislation, if I may venture to say so, that excites us to vice, by mingling it with pleasure; the great art of the legislator is that of separating them, and making no proportion between the advantage the villain can receive from his crime, and the pain to which he exposes himself." "If among the rich men, who are often less virtuous than the indigent, we see few robbers and assassins," he added, "it is because the profit obtained by robbery is never to a rich man proportionable to the hazard of a capital punishment; but this is not the case with respect to the indigent; for the disproportion falling infinitely short of being so great with respect to him, virtue and vice, are in a manner placed in equilibrium."[81] In the eighteenth century, the death penalty was the customary punishment for both highway robbery and murder.[82]

It was in part due to Pietro Verri's concerted efforts and clever, behind-the-scenes scheming that Cesare Beccaria actually reunited with his family, thus putting an end to the painful, months' long separation with his parents. Pietro had a good relationship with Cesare Beccaria's father, and that relationship played a role in helping put Cesare back in the good graces of his father. "It took more than a year before father and son made peace—a peace achieved through the intervention of Cesare's new friend, Count Pietro Verri," historian Marcello Maestro writes. As Maestro explains Verri's ingenious approach in theater- and drama-obsessed Milan: "Knowing that nothing could be accomplished by reasonable discussion, Verri staged a melodramatic scene that produced the desired result. One day at dinner time the young couple were walking, as if by pure chance, in front of the family house on Via Brera, and Cesare asked if they might come in for a moment because Teresa had just had a fainting spell." "In the house," Maestro relays, "all rushed around Teresa who affected a slow recovery and showed with her tears that she was touched by so much care." Though Cesare Beccaria's father and mother had both obstinately opposed the match and the bride and groom's wedding, the ploy worked, with Cesare and Teresa—the young newly-weds—obtaining Cesare's parents' forgiveness and regaining access to the warmth of the family's Milanese home. "The marriage between Domenico de Blasco's daughter,

Teresa, and Cesare Beccaria," an expert on the de Blasco family writes, summing up the whole affair, "gave birth to one of the biggest scandals of the Milanese societies in the early 1760s, as Beccaria's parents refused to acknowledge this clandestine marriage until the imperial authorities in Vienna intervened in Teresa de Blasco's favour."[83]

Pietro Verri and Cesare Beccaria both grew up in a very conservative society—one in which the Roman Catholic Church and traditional religious schooling and academies were prevalent. The Roman Curia—the Holy See's administrative apparatus—is the papal court and it was formally organized in 1588 with the creation of permanent congregations. "The congregations," a Catholic encyclopedia points out, "consisted of, or were involved, in the following: the Holy Inquisition; the Signature of Grace; the erection of churches; the papal territories; the sacred rites and ceremonies; the papal navy; the Index of Forbidden Books; interpreting and advancing the decrees of the Council of Trent; aiding and relieving the ills of the States of the Church; religious orders; bishops; the maintenance of roads, bridges, and waterways; the printing press of the Vatican; and the regulation of the affairs of the temporal dominions of the Church." Milanese archives have preserved lists of poor parishioners, and "at the end of 1586," a history of Milan notes, "an *Index divitum et nobilium habitantium in Curis Mediolani qui possunt elemosinam largiri* (Index of the wealthy and noble men able to give alms living in the diocesan curia of Milan) was drawn up." Though it was a powerful organization, the Roman Curia underwent at least some modest changes in the mid-eighteenth century as Cesare Beccaria was growing up. "During the pontificate of Benedict XIV (1740–58)," Nicholas Davidson writes of Italy in *Toleration in Enlightenment Europe*, "influential figures within the Curia, such as Cardinals Angelo Maria Querini, who was Prefect of the Index, and Domenico Passionei, as well as the Pope himself, used their power to reduce the number of titles prohibited by the Church; and in 1753, Benedict altered the procedures of the Congregation so that authors were allowed an opportunity to defend their texts before a decision to ban them was made." Though books such as Rousseau's *Contrat social* and Beccaria's *Dei delitti e delle pene* still ended up on Rome's Index of Forbidden Books, by 1768 Pietro Verri felt comfortable writing of his native city and the transformation that had taken place there: "I believe that in no Italian city—nor even in any French city—is there such freedom for books as we now have in Milan."[84]

In Italy, the Arcadia—one of the most storied of the traditional academies—was formed in 1690 in Rome by 14 literati who had gathered around Queen Christina of Sweden (1626–1689), the highly-educated daughter of Swedish King Gustav II Adolf. After her father's death, she had reigned in Sweden from 1632 to 1654, but she ultimately decided not to marry, abdicated her throne in 1654, converted to Roman Catholicism, and moved to Rome at the age of twenty-eight. A patron of the arts, Christina had instituted the *Accademia Reale*, the immediate predecessor of the Arcadia society founded in her memory and honor after she passed away. The *Accademia degli Arcadi* or *Accademia dell'Arcadia*—a prominent cultural institution that lasted for the next two hundred years—promoted neoclassicist values, with its members meeting regularly to recite poetry and to hold literary competitions modeled on the Olympic games. Its members, calling themselves Arcadians, often dressed as shepherds, they honored the child Jesus as their protector, and they called their meeting place Bosco Parrasio, with their chosen objective to reform the diction of Italian poetry. An historian of Italian poetry, Giovanni Mario Crescimbeni (1663–1728), was chosen as the first president of the academy, its members chose pastoral names, and one of its members, Gian Vincenzo Gravina (1664–1718), drafted its laws in Latin, modeling them after the Twelve Tables. "Its autocratic and hierarchical order," *The Encyclopedia of Italian Literary Studies* emphasizes, "was modeled on the Roman Curia, which helps account for its cultural positions." By 1761, the Arcadia's custodian reported 56 "colonies" throughout Italy as well as one foreign outpost in Portugal, all tied to the Arcadia in Rome, which had to approve the admission of new members and which decided what would be published by its many affiliates. "Arcadia," stresses Hanns Gross in *Rome in the Age of Enlightenment*, "thus became one national cultural movement with its seat in the papal capital."[85]

In Milan, a colony of the Arcadia had naturally been set up, and it had originally met in the garden of Carlo Pertusati (1674–1755), a bibliophile and the president of Milan's senate. He had a library of approximately 24,000 books and manuscripts, which were purchased by the Congregation of the State of Lombardy in 1763. During the winter, heated greenhouses ensured that the society's meetings took place throughout the year. Yet, the attraction of the Arcadia society gradually faded. "At Milan," Vernon Lee writes in *Studies of the Eighteenth Century in Italy*, "its members themselves began to despise it." As Lee observes: "The Verris and Beccaria had set up a journal called the *Caffè*, in which, together with literary topics, they discussed whether the aristocracy would not do well to resume commerce." And they were not alone. As Lee observes of how Giuseppe Baretti, who had lived in England between 1751 and 1760 before returning to Italy, "abominated Arcadia" and chose to express his views: "In 1763 Baretti started a species of literary review, more or less on the model of *The Spectator*, to which he gave the ominous name of *La Frustra Letteraria*, the 'Literary Whip.'" Published in Venice, *The Literary Whip*—written under the pseudonym Aristarco Scannabue—provided Baretti, the critic, with an outlet for his literary judgments. Through his writings, Baretti "showered abuse on Arcadia," decried its founders as "pedantic idiots," and criticized the proliferation of mediocre novels. Baretti, however, reportedly "could not endure the Verris and Beccaria because they admired the French and set up a rival journal to his own."[86]

In their embrace of Enlightenment thought, Pietro Verri and Pietro's younger brother, Alessandro, broke away from the more staid *Accademia dei Trasformati* and, in 1761, formed their own informal society, the *Accademia dei Pugni*. In that era, literary societies and economic and social clubs were being formed throughout Europe to facilitate human progress and the advancement of agriculture, science and knowledge. English, French and Italian coffeehouses—along with printing presses and the transatlantic book trade—facilitated all manner of intellectual exchanges in the vibrant, transcontinental Republic of Letters.[87] When the Verri brothers left the prestigious *Accademia dei Trasformati*, Beccaria and their other closest friends followed, anxious to shake up societal traditions. The new club, which translates as "Academy of Fists," "Academy of Fisticuffs" or "Academy of Punches," got its fanciful name from its members' pugilistic, sometimes heated exchanges. Aside from gathering at Milanese coffeehouses, the club members met regularly at Pietro Verri's palace on Contrada del Monte, now Via Montenapoleone. Among those who joined the Verris and Beccaria: Luigi Lambertenghi, Giuseppe Visconti di Saliceto, Pietro Secco Comneno and Giambattista Biffi. The Abbott Alfonso Longo also joined the group in 1763. "An important formative point in Beccaria's career came," one criminology texts emphasizes, "when he joined with two friends, Pietro and Alessandro Verri, to form a literary club, the Academy of Fisticuffs, which met in the Verri home to discuss topics of literary and social interest."[88] Pietro Verri later described how the men shared their time together. "Our group," Pietro recounted, "would pass evenings together in the same room, each of us tormented." His brother Alessandro, he observed, giving a snapshot of the scene, would have the *History of Italy* in his hand while he (Pietro) would have "my work on political economy."[89]

The painting of the "Coterie" of Milan — one done by the Italian painter Antonio Perego — depicts the members of the Academy of Fists and shows the intellectual atmosphere in which they met. As Mario Ricciardi and Filippo Santoni de Sio describe the work of art in their article on Cesare Beccaria's life: "Seated at a table, on the left of the painting, Alessandro Verri and Cesare Beccaria sit facing each other; the first writes and the second reads (and he seems so absorbed as not [to] even notice what is happening around him). On the other side of the room Luigi Lambertenghi and Pietro Verri, also seated, are playing backgammon." As Ricciardi and Santoni de Sio describe the rest of Antonio Perego's painting, one created in the milieu of the Enlightenment: "Alfonso Longo's face is not portrayed (he is shown from the back because the painter had never seen him). Giambattista Biffi is standing behind Beccaria and Verri. Giuseppe Visconti di Saliceto, finally, reads a letter while walking in the room from the right." Pietro Verri, Jonathan Israel explains in his book, *Democratic Enlightenment*, "rose to become a high functionary in Milan" and was "the personage at the centre of the Enlightenment group dubbed the *coterie de Milan* in Paris." Antonio Perego — a popular portrait artist — also did a separate portrait of Cesare Beccaria, an engraving from a drawing by another artist, Carlo Faucci.[90] His other portraits of aristocrats include one of an elaborately dressed Countess Margherita Pallavicino Attendolo Bolognini holding a fan in her hand with a small dog on her knee, and one of a young Countess Maria Litta Castelbarco sitting on a plush red chair in a blue satin dress with a fashionable, well-coifed hairstyle adorned with ostrich feathers and a string of pearls.[91]

Members of the Verri brothers' and Beccaria's small Milanese salon were highly educated and conversant in literature, and they devoted their time to various topics, often focused on how to improve the local economy. Luigi Lambertenghi (1739–1813), the secretary of finance in the Department of Italy in Vienna from 1767 to 1774 and also later politically active in the Napoleonic regime, contributed an article to the group's *Il Caffè* journal on the postal service. Alfonso Longo (1738–1804), Beccaria's successor to the chair of political economy at the Palatine school who served in that role from 1773 to 1789, contributed a piece on watches to *Il Caffè*. Longo also wrote on trusts and spoke out, with Francesco Dalmazzo Vasco (1732–1794), on the immense and "unnatural" and "irrational" powers vested in Italian fathers. Giambattista Biffi (1736–1807), Beccaria's Cremonese friend, was a bibliophile who became enamored of the English language and gravitated to English literature. He was only in Milan for a few years before returning to his native Cremona; he later wrote a memoir, as did Pietro Verri, their older compatriot. "In the Biffi collection of the Cremona library," historian Marcello Maestro wrote in 1973 of the members of the Academy of Fists, "one can still see the notes written by these young scholars on the books that interested them." Giuseppe Visconti di Saliceto, another nobleman, was a skillful writer, while the economist Gian Rinaldo Carli (1720–1795), the oldest man in the group, was reportedly "only an occasional participant in its activities." Carli became the president of the *Supremo consiglio di economia pubblica* (Supreme Economic Council) of Milan on November 20, 1765.[92] In writing a famous essay, "Della patria degli Italiani," for *Il Caffè* in 1766, Carli mocked regional prejudices and—as one source puts it—used a common literary device at that time, writing about a stranger telling patrons of a Milan coffeehouse that the people he saw were neither Milanese nor foreigners. As the stranger stressed of the people he observed: "They are Italian … and an Italian in Italy is never a foreigner, just as a Frenchman is not a foreigner in France, an Englishman in England, a Hollander in Holland, and so forth."[93]

A close associate of the Milanese group was Carlo Sebastiano Franci (1715–1772), an economist who married the daughter of a nobleman in Milan. As a regular contributor to the group's periodically published journal, *Il Caffè*, one source emphasizes, "the Milanese *illuminista* Carlo Sebastiano Franci repeatedly extolled Empress Maria Theresa's sound judgment and exemplary moral fortitude to illustrate the characteristics of the ideal female education." Writing six articles for *Il Caffè*, Franci—a man who, like Helvétius, wanted to reduce poverty and improve the economic conditions of the people—wrote on a variety of subjects, including agriculture, politics, trade, and gold and silver. In 1771, Franci became the Inspector of the Mint of Milan—an operation that, starting in 1778, Beccaria later supervised as its provincial magistrate—though Franci died on June 20, 1772, making his administrative career (unlike Beccaria's) quite truncated.[94] Franci is now best remembered for his *Il Caffè* article, "*La difesa delle donne*" ("Defense of Women"). In that article, Franci—as one source summarizes it—"calls upon his fellow *illuministi* to recognize the practical benefits to the modern state, no less than to modern family life, of formally educating women."[95] It was an idea that had decades-old roots in Italy, as historian Rebecca Messbarger explains of earlier writings in *The Century of Women: Representations of Women in Eighteenth-Century Italian Public Discourse*: "In 1740, the cleric and *illuminista* Giovanni Bandiera published a lengthy, two-volume *Treatise on the Education of Women*. The author's radical assertions that women 'do not differ in nature from men with respect to their ability to understand the sciences,' and that their formal education is necessary for public happiness, nearly put his book on the *Index*." Following the "they can but they shouldn't" ("*possono ma non devono*") advice of Luciano Guerci, Bandiera had nonetheless advocated restricting women's education "solely to those Studies that directly benefit the family."[96]

A prominent woman, Countess Antonia della Somaglia Belgioioso (1730–1798), was in fact said to be the "muse" of the *Accademia dei pugni*. At the very bottom of his January 26, 1766 letter to André Morellet, Cesare Beccaria—in his "P.S."—noted that he was writing "this postscriptum from the house of the Countess della Somaglia, née Belgioioso, a lady of the finest qualities of mind and heart, full of virtue, sensitivity and learning." The Belgioioso—or Belgiojoso—family was a very prominent one in Milan, with Pietro Verri once writing that he had an interest "in the private affairs of the house of Belgioioso." Count Don Antonio Barbiano di Belgioioso (1693–1779) and his wife, Barbara Luigia Elisabetta D'Adda, contessa di Bronno (1707–1769), lived in the medieval castle of Belgioioso, a town just south of Milan, that had been the seat of the Belgioioso family for centuries. Count Antonio Belgioioso had served the Habsburg empress, Maria Theresa, as an imperial ambassador and councilor, and he and his wife had three children—Alberico XII (1725–1813), Lodovico (1728–1801) and their lovely daughter, Antonia. Their second son, Lodovico, also served the Habsburg family as an ambassador to Sweden from 1764 to 1769, becoming the special envoy and plenipotentiary at the Court of St. James in London in 1769 and, later, in 1783, a lieutenant field marshal of the Holy Roman Empire. "You must have met her here in Milan; in the first years of her marriage, she cut one of the most brilliant figures in Paris," Cesare Beccaria wrote in his letter to André Morellet, his French translator, of Countess della Somaglia, who had married Giovanni M. della Somaglia (1726–1790). Pietro Verri's father, Gabriele Verri, had himself married into the Somaglia family through his marriage in 1728 to his wife, Barbara Dati della Somaglia.[97] Morellet, a private tutor to the Duc de La Galaisière, had traveled in Italy in 1758 and 1759, and may have actually met Cesare Beccaria on that trip.[98]

Italian economists such as Pietro Verri and Cesare Beccaria were intent on maximizing the wealth of their society. "The key to Italy's historical success," one modern history of economic development points out, "lay in the fact that by providing Europe with manufactured goods in exchange for raw materials, it had harnessed to its advantage the differential returns to scale inherent to distinct economic activities." Antonio Serra, an influential sixteenth-century Italian economist, had—more than a century and a half before the appearance of *Dei delitte e delle pene* and Adam Smith's *The Wealth of Nations*—written about the importance of industrialization and productivity. In his 1613 book, *A Short Treatise on the Causes that Can Make Kingdoms Abound in Gold and Silver even in the Absence of Mines* (as the original title is translated into English), Serra provided this perceptive economic analysis: "In manufacturing activities it is possible to achieve a multiplication of products, and therefore of earnings. The same cannot be done with agricultural produce, which is not subject to multiplication. If a given piece of land is only large enough to sow a hundred *tomoli* of wheat, it is impossible to sow a hundred and fifty there." "In manufacturing, by contrast," Serra had written, "production can be multiplied not merely twofold but a hundredfold, and at a proportionately lower cost."[99]

In his own writings, another Italian economist, Antonio Genovesi, had spoken of the science of "political economy." That science, he contended, allowed civic leaders to "*increase the greatness, power, and wealth of the Nations, without at the same time aiming to enlarge the borders of what one possesses.*" In other words, conquests and wars were not necessary to the achievement of prosperity; what was needed were better economic policies. In 1764, the year of a review in *Giornale d'Italia* of Genovesi's translation of an English economic work, and the same year that *Dei delitti e delle pene* first appeared, Carlo Sabastiano Franci—said to be an "avid reader of Genovesi"—looked back at the economic successes of Renaissance Italy, explaining the history he saw in this way: "Around the thirteenth century the Florentines, Pisans, Amalfitans, Venetians, and Genoese began adopting a different policy for enhancing their wealth and power because they noticed that the sciences, the cultivation of land, the application of the arts and of industry, and the introduction of extensive trade could produce a large population, provide for their countless needs, sustain great luxury and gain immense riches without having to add more territories."[100] Genovesi and other Italian economists themselves had multiple influences. In 1763, Pietro Verri called David Hume the "Author of Commerce," and translations of Hume's writings were popular in Italy and read by Neapolitan and Milanese intellectuals, including Antonio Genovesi and Alessandro Verri. As a collection of writings about Hume notes of his influence on Genovesi and his devotees: "The need to renovate southern Italian society and its feudal structures, governed by the Bourbons and still burdened by a parasitic and uncultured baronial class, drove the more open-minded spirits to plan changes. Antonio Genovesi (1712–69) and his disciples cleverly blended Hume's theories with those of the other Scottish historians, entering authoritatively into the European debate on political economy."[101]

Amongst his peers and in this progressive climate of economic and literary powerhouses, Cesare Beccaria endeavored to pull his own weight and quickly became a productive member of the Academy of Fists, his newly chosen salon. In 1762, Beccaria published his first work, *Del disordine e de' rimedj dell monete nello Stato di Milano nell'anno 1762*. That monograph, which translates as *On Remedies for the Monetary Disorders of Milan in the Year 1762*, is about the need for reform of Milan's monetary system. It was written at the suggestion of Pietro Verri, who personally defended it after it came under attack following its publication. Verri had written an essay on the salt tax in 1761, and from 1762 to 1763 he was at work on a much more comprehensive work, *Considerations on the Commerce of the State of Milan*, in which he analyzed the need to revive trade through legal reform. *On Remedies for the Monetary Disorders of Milan in the Year 1762*—as one source emphasizes—showcased Beccaria's "skills as a mathematician to advocate a stable rate of exchange, in preference to Milan adopting its own currency, as the best means of facilitating trade." Many types of coins were then in circulation in Milan in Beccaria's time, and speculators had fixed arbitrary rates of exchange, thus hindering commercial transactions. For example, there was the French *old louis*; Spanish pieces and half-pieces; the French, Spanish, Roman, Milanese, Savoyard, Genoese and Florentine *doblons*; coins with the cross of the Holy Spirit or depicting St. John the Baptist; and many others of different weights and sizes. Beccaria's solution was tied to the content of gold and silver in each coin, with Beccaria attempting to compare each coin in his pamphlet, though the coins themselves varied widely in composition depending on their country of origin and the individual mint.[102]

By the time the Academy of Fisticuffs got its start, Pietro and Alessandro Verri had already established themselves in Milanese society. Pietro was a military veteran and distinguished economist, and Alessandro held the post of Protector of Prisoners in Milan, acting as an ombudsman for prisoners. Alessandro—as one source reports of his public position—"regularly traveled into the prisons," then "informed the members of the Accademia" of "what he had seen and heard on official business, and members were so incensed that Pietro Verri urged Beccaria to write about it." Though the law-trained Beccaria actually knew very little about prisons or penology when he began writing *Dei delitti e delle pene*, Pietro encouraged him and edited the book manuscript he produced. Meanwhile, Alessandro—a talented writer in his own right, then laboring over a work of history—provided valuable insights into the prison system. Alessandro even took Beccaria into some of the local prisons so that he could witness firsthand what Alessandro had seen. "Writing apparently wasn't an easy task for Beccaria," one criminology textbook emphasizes of Beccaria's struggle with the written word, with that source noting: "He would write for a short period, stop to discuss his thoughts with his colleagues in the Accademia, and then often go to sleep rather than return to his pen."[103] But it wasn't long before Beccaria's name, thanks to Beccaria's intermittent labors and the Verri brothers' encouragement and substantive and editorial help, became better known locally. Indeed, Beccaria's name soon became widely known throughout Europe and the Americas, far away from Milan, where the scandal of Cesare Beccaria's marriage to Teresa—no doubt the talk of the town—was still subsiding, if not still at white heat among the local aristocrats and gossips.

Cesare Beccaria's intellectual awakening had come about—as he would later explain in greater detail to André Morellet—from reading Montesquieu's *Lettres persanes* (1721) and other "excellent" books of European *philosophes*. Montesquieu's novel, which was translated in English as *Persian Letters* and which had attracted scores of readers, had described the experiences of two Persian noblemen as they traveled through France. Told through a series of letters, the satirical portrait of French and Persian societies was just one of the many books that inspired Beccaria to embark on a literary career of his own, of which *Dei delitti e delle pene* was just a part. As one historian notes: "Beccaria enjoyed the life of a 'literato' and philosopher, being (by his own account) converted to the new philosophy in 1761 through a reading of Montesquieu's *Lettres Persanes*. From 1764 to 1766, Beccaria contributed essays to the Italian Enlightenment journal, *Il Caffè*, founded by himself and his friends Pietro and Alessandro Verri on the model of *The Spectator*." *The Spectator*—a daily English newspaper started in 1711 and published by Joseph Addison and Richard Steele—had, as its stated aim, "to enliven morality with wit, and to temper wit with morality" and "to bring philosophy out of the closets and libraries, schools and colleges, to dwell in clubs and assemblies, at tea-tables and coffeehouses." It has been estimated that, during its life, one in every four Londoners read *The Spectator*, with one scholar noting its importance in these words: "*The Spectator* is significant in publishing history for its represents the first true outpouring of expository prose in the English language. Jonathan Swift was one of the magazine's founding writers and a major champion of the language." "During the seventeenth century," an historian emphasizes of the shift that occurred in publishing, from the traditional language of scientists to native languages, "major writers of natural philosophy still produced their works in Latin."

Conceived at a Milanese coffeehouse, *Il Caffè*—the Milanese paper—was published every ten days, far less frequently than *The Spectator*. "Explicitly modelled after the *Spectator* and the *Encyclopédie*," a scholar of the Italian Enlightenment has written, "*Il Caffè* was conceived as an open, non-academic forum for candid discussion of current issues of regional and international import." To circumvent censorship in Austrian Lombardy, the copies of *Il Caffè* were printed in Brescia, a city in northern Italy at the foot of the Alps, with Pietro and Alessandro Verri writing the bulk of the articles. Distributed from Venice and Milan, the Milanese newspaper became—as one book puts it—"the mouthpiece of the Italian Enlightenment." Beccaria contributed a total of seven articles from 1764 to 1766, and the article's titles—for example, "Il Faraone," "Frammento sugli odori," and "Tentativo analitico su i contrabbandi"—reflect their wide range, from topics as diverse as the statistical probability of winning a card game, style and the evolution of language, odors and people's sense of smell, the imagination, the function and accessibility of newspapers and magazines, and tariffs and smuggling. Beccaria's piece on smuggling is a prime example of an early effort to use mathematical methods to analyze economic matters. As law professor Bernard Harcourt—an expert on the history of law and economics—observes: "Beccaria is perhaps the first to ever have deployed mathematical modeling to analyze criminality. He published an article on smuggling in 1764—the same year he released his famous treatise—that set forth, with the use of mathematical equations and algebra, the expected relationship between tariffs, contraband, and sovereign revenue. It appeared originally as an essay in volume XV of *Il Caffè*...."[104]

Cesare Beccaria's articles reflect his intellect and his intellectual influences. For example, Beccaria's essay, "Pleasures of the Imagination," was inspired by a poem of the same name by the English poet and physician Mark Akenside (1721–1770). In that essay, Beccaria wrote: "Wise men know how brief and scarce the pleasures are that come to them in life; but through imagination these pleasures can be lengthened and made more attractive." "Men," he stressed, "strive and hurt and kill each other in order to reach the few physical pleasures that are spread here and there in the desert of human life." "But the pleasures of the imagination," he observed, "can be acquired peacefully, without any danger: they are all ours and they do not arouse any envy, since the majority of people do not know and do not appreciate them." "These pleasures," Beccaria emphasized, "may not make the soul inordinately happy, but they give it a serene joy, free from tension, from envy or malice; and they do not push continually those who possess them from hope to fear and from fear to hope." Beccaria himself was a lover of food and wine, and as a result, he put on a lot of weight over time and gradually became obese, a problem for many in the aristocratic class. "People who are able to have imaginary pleasures," Beccaria wrote in his article, "do not refuse from time to time to have some honest physical ones." As Beccaria, speaking of people and their need for physical pleasures, justified his own at times inordinate consumption of food and wine to fuel his own imagination: "They need them, after all, in order to nourish the imagination, to get, so to speak, the raw material that they will be able then to mold and tint in many shapes and colors."

Viewing serenity and happiness as life's great objects, Beccaria, in his essay on the pleasures of one's imagination, offered this advice: "Do not try to live too fast or too intensely; be as much as possible a spectator of men and do not imitate those who run blindly into each other without knowing where they go. Do what good you can to them, but stay aside and keep at a distance, so that you will not be carried away and drawn into their vortex." In setting out his philosophical approach to life, Beccaria—the sensitive young man trying to find the answers to life's most persistent questions—then added: "If you want to be left in peace, however, you must be at peace with yourself. Do not commit any crime, and be just with all the beings that surround you. Remember that even the smallest creatures, crushed by arrogant and cruel man, are endowed with a little ray of life. If you are wicked and unfair, remorse and uneasiness will be in your blood: uncertainty and fear will then push you, against your will, toward the turmoil and violence of human affairs." As Beccaria, advising his readers, wrote in his essay, written decades after Michel de Montaigne (1533–1592) penned his own ruminations on how to live: "Be a friend of blessed solitude, leave frequently the oppressive cities and go out to enjoy free nature, the oldest temple of the gods. Let the mountains echo your songs, let the roaring waves of the sea accompany your hymns." As Beccaria, praising the benefits of the natural world, ended his essay: "There you will meditate and see some important links of the eternal chain; there you will feel the smallness of our systems and enterprises. You will find everywhere the destructive traces of man, but everywhere you will see how wise nature repairs what man spoils or ruins; because man can alter, but cannot extinguish that essence of life which is a fundamental part of nature."

It was, no doubt, Beccaria's obsession with food and wine and spices and seasonings that led him to take up the topic of the sense of smell. In his "Essay on Odors," Beccaria wrote: "There is a close relationship between odors and flavors, and these two senses are friendly and faithful to each other. What seems bad to the sense of smell is almost always unpleasant to the palate, and what hurts the palate is rarely liked by the nose." Beccaria took note of society's evolution from hunters and gatherers to much more sophisticated fare, the kind of cuisine that Italians—and the French—are so known for to this day. As Beccaria observed: "We started with the simplest foods, offered by nature; we then had foods cooked in a simple way, and little by little we have arrived at the most refined and complicated dishes of the French cuisine." "But in the field of odors," Beccaria wrote, "we haven't made the slightest progress." "Wealth," he offered, "usually gives birth to new needs and new pleasures, but there is not yet a kitchen of the nose." "I may imagine living in a more refined century," Beccaria went on, using his own vivid imagination, "and seeing in the houses of rich people two cooks, one for the nose and the other for the mouth, and I would attend odorous banquets where the daintiest dishes of perfumes would be served." As Beccaria envisioned the future: "The dry odors would be symmetrically placed in little gold and silver cases, while the liquid odors would be served, as if they were drinks, in crystal phials. There would be warm odors and cold odors." "In the days dedicated to fast and abstinence," Beccaria added, "there should be a prohibition of voluptuous and sweet odors, only the chaste and bland should be permitted." "The strongest odors," he advised, "would have a place similar to that of liquors because some of them, the odor of tobacco for example, bring a momentary euphoria, even intoxication."

In eighteenth-century Italy, Milanese aristocrats knew how to entertain and consume. "[I]n the second half of the eighteenth century," one history notes of Italians, "we know that dinner and supper parties were the order of the day, though perhaps not so generally as in England and France." "In the northern provinces, especially at Milan and Turin," that source observes, "we have many references to the dinner parties of that day." As a Mrs. Piozzi wrote from Milan in November 1784: "It is surprising how very elegant, not to say magnificent, those dinners are in gentlemen's or noblemen's houses; such number of dishes at once—not large joints, but infinite variety—and I think their cooking excellent."[105] Milan's location in the Po Valley gave it access to fresh fruits and vegetables and the best wines. As one book notes: "The Po Valley is very fertile and its farms produce olives, vegetables, wheat, citrus fruits, and grapes for wine. The city of Milan became rich and politically powerful in this location during the Renaissance because it was located at the intersection of trade routes between the Alpine passes and Italy's coastal cities."[106] "In the eighteenth century," Alberto Capatti and Massimo Montanari explain in *Italian Cuisine: A Cultural History*, "Italy's Enlightenment philosophers argued the necessity of banishing strong flavors from the dinner table in favor of food characterized by refinement and lightness."[107] "There had been many Italian cookbooks since the Renaissance," another writer, John Mariani, observes in *How Italian Food Conquered the World*, "but most had been written specifically for aristocrats' kitchens, not independent chefs."[108]

All of Beccaria's articles in *Il Caffè* were signed "C." except for his "Essay on Odors," which was signed "A." As one source on eighteenth-century Italy reports of the Milanese publication's format and approach: "The formal structure of *Il Caffè* in fact suggests that the contributors meant for it to be read as a unified expression of the ideals of the *Illuminismo*. The names of the authors never appeared. Instead, one or two identifying initials usually followed an article (for example, C. for Cesare Beccaria, F. for Sebastiano Franci, X.P. for Paolo Frisi), but readers did not have a decoding key." As that source adds: "The lack of definitive attribution appears to have served the performative designs of the journal. Each article functions as a single voice within a choral exchange transpiring among this distinct assembly of *illuministi*." Beccaria himself, in one of his *Il Caffè* articles, "The Periodicals," praised newspapers and magazines as more accessible to broader segments of society than books. "We will be happy if with our articles we will make one good citizen for the country, one good husband or son in a family, or if we will be able to attract some young man to the still unfamiliar field of science," Beccaria concluded at the end of that article, adding hopefully: "We will be happy if we receive praise for our work and we will do our best to really deserve it."

Aside from Beccaria and the Verri brothers, contributors to *Il Caffè*—of which 72 total editions appeared over its short life, from June 1764 to May 1766—included François Baillou, Ruggero Boscovich, Gian Rinaldo Carli, Giuseppe Colpani, Sebastiano Franci, Paolo Frisi, Luigi Lambertenghi, Alfonso Longo, Pietro Secchi and Giuseppe Visconti. "The thirteen young patricians who collaborated in the journal's creation," one text emphasizes, "were, as Franco Venturi has described them, 'a political class *in nuce.*'" As one modern text describes the goals of *Il Caffè*: "This journal manifests the dominant aims of Italian periodical literature of the second half of the eighteenth century: to fix Italy's place in the international intellectual arena and to stimulate and direct public discourse for the promotion of practical social reforms." "The conversations of the young *caffettisti*," that text stresses, "are situated in the fictional café of the Greek national and lay political philosopher Demetrio, who provides his enlightened clientele with an ideal discursive space, a cosmopolitan *enciclopedia d'occasione*, complete with current issues of progressive Italian periodicals: 'in this shop, whoever wishes to read will find both the *Giornale enciclopedico* and the *Estratto della letteratura europea*, as well as other equally good collections of interesting narratives, which, with few exceptions, make men into Europeans who were previously Roman, Florentine, Genoese, and Lombard." "The literary frame and journal's motto, 'things not words' ('cose non parole'),'" that source adds, "signified the rejection of the elitist, socially detached academy, which fostered abstract theories impervious to praxis."

Il Caffè thus became a place for the exploration of pragmatic reform. "Inspired by the foundational theories of Montesquieu, Condillac, Helvétius, Diderot, Locke, Hume, and Rousseau," a book chapter on the *Il Caffè* notes, "the *caffettisti* joined in a self-conscious endeavor to promote among the current generation Enlightenment ideals that would give rise to a more rational and cosmopolitan Italian society." As that chapter notes of its members: "They conceived of their journal as a model of modern discourse, a primer for transparent, egalitarian, and practical exchange." "[P]rior to the publication of *Il Caffè*," that chapter stresses, "most of the journal's contributors had collaborated as members of the *Accademia de' Pugni* (*Academy of the Fists*), which may best be described as an anti-academy organized by Pietro Verri in 1761." "The Fists' defiant name," that source observes, "reflects the group's intention to challenge and subvert the esoteric conventions of the tradition academy. The *Pugni* refused official sanction, and instead gathered informally in Verri's home to discuss with candour and reason current questions of mutual concern." "After the dissolution of the journal," the book chapter reports of the periodical's principal writers in the wake of the publication's demise in May 1766, "most of *Il Caffè*'s contributors attained substantive political authority in government positions that allowed them to implement the ideas proposed in the journal." When the group of which the Verri brothers and Beccaria were members disbanded, the publication of *Il Caffè* also ceased, as the journal's final notice made clear: "The little society of friends who have written these pages has dissolved; some have gone on a trip, others are occupied by business. Necessity dictates the termination of a project that, according to plans, should not have ended so soon, and this happens at a time at which the favorable welcome of the public more than ever invited its continued existence."

Franco Venturi, in studying *Il Caffè*'s beginnings and the journal's significant impact despite its short life, called its creation and publication a pivotal time in a "generational struggle." "With this publication," it has been written, "the *caffettisti*, most of whom were in their twenties and thirties, formally declared their independence not only from their patrician fathers' authoritarian politics of entitlement but also from the rigid discursive controls and cultural canon laid down by academic elites." In a prefatory letter to its readers, Pietro Verri had promised a simple system and varied content that would appeal to a broad audience, from "tender, young minds" to the "grave magistrate" and from the "spirited maiden" to "rigorous, accomplished intellects." In reality, the journal's audience was likely more limited, though the contributors to *Il Caffè* did their best to deliver on Pietro's promise. As one historian speculates of *Il Caffè*'s readership: "[W]hile little is known about the actual demographics of the journal's subscribers, they were undoubtedly less eclectic than the ideal readership Verri describes. Given the content of the periodical and the levels of literacy in Italy at the time of its publication, it may be assumed that *Il Caffè*'s readers were well educated, from the upper classes, and predominantly male."

It was in the twenty-second issue of the *Il Caffè* journal that the then-anonymously published piece, "Defence of Women," appeared. That article sought—in the words of one scholar—"to delineate women's actual condition and social roles and to prescribe a pedagogical program to enhance their contribution to the public good." Though written by the now little-known Italian economist Carlo Sebastiano Franci (a fact not uncovered until 1993 though the discovery of an autograph), the article was not signed at the time, leading one scholar, Rebecca Messbarger, to surmise that it therefore "must not be viewed simply as the opinion of a single author." As historian Rebecca Messbarger analyzes the significance of its anonymity of authorship: "[T]he 'Defence of Women' was one of only four articles published without any attribution. While there may be more than one explanation for the article's anonymity (most obvious would be its controversial subject matter), Gianni Francioni, a foremost authority on *Il Caffè*, offers the convincing argument that anonymous articles served as editorials, implicating all of the journal's contributors." In the eighteenth century, women were denied a whole host of opportunities that were open to men. For example, historian Elisabetta Graziosi observes: "Few Italian women had the opportunity to travel in the age of the Grand Tour. If they did, they were accompanied by husbands, sons, brothers, and parents." "This," Graziosi explains, "was part of a more general impediment which kept women far from the loci of culture and from the means of procuring culture: books, travel, good instructors, and the frequenting of cultured persons in a manner not directly aimed at marriage, the objective normally allowed women who circulated in society."

The "Defence of Women" article was, in fact, an effort—in Rebecca Messbarger's words—"to curry favour with Maria Theresa." As Messbarger writes of the not-so-subtle effort of the *caffettisti* to ingratiate themselves with their female sovereign: "Aside from the subject matter itself, which presumably would have been of special interest to the monarch, the manuscript concludes with an effusive panegyric of her, with constitutes nearly 25 per cent of the total length of the article. Although the editor, Pietro Verri, cut the tribute by nearly 60 per cent, undoubtedly to render it less obsequious, it remains extravagant." In other edits, Verri deleted sections of the manuscript pertaining to "*castità*" (chastity), with all of that word's sexual connotations, and substituted in its place "*virtù*" (virtue), a much-discussed concept during the Enlightenment. In the piece, Franci—writing for the group—spoke of men's neglect in educating women and emphasized, in one passage, that "vices are of the individual and not of a sex." Though Franci's article praised Empress Maria Theresa for her "sound judgment," speaking of her toils for the populace and her efforts bringing "honour to that sex currently on the throne," Franci's vision for women of the time focused largely on the confines of the home. His article, one source notes, "is intended primarily to encourage women's domesticity and their renunciation of such worldly diversions as masquerades, the theater, and card games." But Franci—in a more progressive passage of his article—also asserted that "[i]t is not beyond the scope of the well-regulated mind of a female citizen to *manage* a workshop and to sit at an exchange table in order to *direct* the appropriate exchanges." "Sound judgment," Franci wrote, "will persuade women that the management of the household and the domestic economy is within their ability," with Franci simultaneously stressing that women also had a proper place—at least in certain occupations—in the arena of trade and commerce. At that time, up to 75 percent of those working in textile factories were women, and Franci was of the opinion that women could play supervisory roles in those facilities and that such occupations would be "compatible with women's delicacy and reserve." Not only did Franci identify women as "*cittadine*" (citizens), but "[g]iven the actual state of women's employment," Messbarger stresses, taking note of the fact that female textile workers then had no protection from guilds and mostly spun and wove in their homes or in small workshops, "Franci's proposal to assign women supervisory roles in workshops and at exchange tables is remarkable." At that time, women in rural areas worked primarily as field hands, with women in urban settings taking on mainly traditional roles such as cooks, laundresses, maids and seamstresses.[109]

Il Caffè ("The Coffeehouse"), observes one of Beccaria's biographers, "survived for some two years from 1 June 1764 to the end of May 1766." "During this time," that biographer, John Hostettler, writes of that periodical, "it introduced into Italy the enlightenment thought of French men of letters such as the indefatigable Voltaire, and Diderot who was sometimes compared with Benjamin Franklin." The first issues of *Il Caffè* were printed by Gian Maria Rizzardi in Brescia, and the latter issues of the magazine were printed by Giuseppe Galeazzi of Milan, albeit with the false designation of "in Brescia" to disguise the locale of the printing presses. Though printing had been introduced in Milan around 1469 and many beautiful books were produced there, authors always had to carefully consider the *content* of their writing before publishing them with attribution. "Beccaria"—as one historian notes, summing up his participation in Milanese social clubs—participated in "a fashionable literary academy, the Accademia dei Trasformati, where he met Giuseppe Parini and Pietro Verri; when Verri established the rival Accademia dei Pugni, Beccaria accompanied him."[110] Giuseppe Galeazzi—the Milanese publisher and bookseller who was Printer of the Royal House—was, it is known, a distributor of the *Encyclopédie*, with Galeazzi noting in one communication that he had ordered thirty-nine octavos of it and that Lombardy was already full of *Encyclopédies*.[111]

Pietro and Alessandro Verri, the Milanese brothers who shared a congenial friend-ship, had formed their own salon, the Society of Fists, to pass the time in the company of their friends. It was designed, principally, to improve the local Milanese government and economy and the quality of Italian literary works. It was Beccaria's intimate as-sociation with that group that led to Beccaria's writing of his algebraic, highly math-ematical analysis of smuggling, *Tentativo analitico su i contrabbandi*, as well as his bestseller, *Dei delitti e delle pene.* "In the summer of 1763, while he was in Gessate in a depressed mood," Mario Ricciardi and Filippo Santoni de Sio recount of that book manuscript's origins, "he wrote to Gianbattista Biffi alluding to 'new ideas' and 'philosophical views' that he hoped will help him get out of his state of procrastination." Gianbattista Biffi, a fellow noble, had studied law from 1756 to 1760, and he had met Condillac and was a friend of Giuseppe Baretti and Cesare Beccaria. Biffi would later, on Rousseau's death, proclaim: "The greatest genius of our age is dead." "My father, my guide, my master, my idol," Biffi would write of Rousseau. Beccaria's man-uscript, written between March 1763 and early 1764, was first published anonymously due to a fear of censorship and the Inquisition, an institution not to be taken lightly. It first appeared in Livorno—also known in English as Leghorn—on April 12, 1764, with the book soon translated into French as *Traité des délits et des peines* and into English as *An Essay on Crimes and Punishments.*

Not only did the Verri brothers encourage and facilitate Beccaria's writing of his book, they later publicly defended it, with *Dei delitti e delle pene* considered one of the major contributions of the Italian Enlightenment and its jocularly named Society of Fists, known for its contentious debates on issues of economics, law, philosophy and public policy.[112] The Academy of Fists sought, in Alessandro Verri's words, to avoid the "vain display of rare and delicate terms" and to write in an accessible way so as to be "understood throughout the whole world." *A History of Italy*, written by Claudia Baldoli, notes that the prose of that period "was characterized by the intro-duction of French words" and was inordinately complex, "full of subordinate clauses with the verbs at the end of sentences"; "[t]he Milanese Enlightenment thinkers of *Il Caffè*," Baldoli emphasizes, "upheld their right to invent new words and to Italianize foreign terms."[113] As Pietro Verri described the origins of *On Crimes and Punishments*—one of the most accessible works of that period—in a letter: "Beccaria was bored and a bore. In desperation, he asked for a theme, I suggested this, knowing that for a man eloquent and of lively imagination it was perfectly fit." Although Pietro explained that Beccaria "knew nothing of our criminal methods," he observed that his brother, Alessan-dro, "the *protettore dei carcerati* (the public defender of prisoners), promised him as-sistance." Alessandro was then hard at work on a history of Italy, *Saggio sulla storia d'Italia* (*Essay on the History of Italy*), but because of his position as a protector of prisoners, an honorary office which considered prisoners' needs and grievances and the possibility of pardons, he was able—and ready and willing—to assist Beccaria with his own work. At the end of July 1763, while at his family's country home in Gessate, Beccaria—struggling to overcome his writer's block—wrote to a friend of his ongoing work on *Dei delitti e delle pene*: "I will not be in Milan for another fifteen days, and I hope by then my book on punishments will be well advanced."[114]

The writing process itself was taxing for Beccaria, whom two scholars—Graeme Newman and Pietro Marongiu—once described as "lazy, timid and reclusive." As Pietro Verri's own letter about the creation of *Dei delitti e delle pene* continued, explaining Beccaria's leisurely yet arduous process, one marked by misspellings and by what another scholar describes as Beccaria's "careless" handwriting: "Beccaria began to write on pieces of paper disconnected ideas, we supported him with enthusiasm, and gave him so much encouragement that he wrote a large crowd of ideas. After lunch we went out for a walk, and there was talk of the errors of criminal jurisprudence. We disputed and questioned, and in the evening he wrote; but it is so laborious for him to write, and it costed him such an effort that after an hour he felled and he couldn't stand to go on." "Having collected the material," Pietro Verri continued of his editorial role, though he had a tendency at times to overstate his role in Cesare Beccaria's affairs, "I wrote and gave an order, and a book took shape." The resulting book, which Pietro Verri later defended from attack by a Benedictine monk, "is," Verri acknowledged, dispelling rumors of his own authorship, "of the Marquis Beccaria." "I gave him the argument, and most of the thoughts are the result of conversations that were held daily between Beccaria, Alessandro, Lambertenghi and me," Pietro explained, alluding to Luigi Lambertenghi (1739–1813), an essayist and contributor to *Il Caffè*. Newman and Marongiu—two modern translators of *On Crimes and Punishments*—conclude that "[t]he historical record" confirms "that Verri's deep intervention in Beccaria's original project was made necessary by Beccaria's personality." Beccaria, they note, was once described by one prolific nineteenth-century Italian historian, Cesare Cantù (1804–1895), as "too lazy to write" and by other historians as "moody" and prone to bouts of "melancholy."[115] In addition to Cantù's writing about Cesare Beccaria, *Il Caffè*, the history of Milan, and the struggle for Italian independence, the subjects of Cantù's many books included the Enlightenment and Machiavelli, Victor Hugo, Lord Byron and Benjamin Franklin.[116]

Il Caffè, the journal that the *Accademia dei Pugni* published periodically, was a forum for cutting-edge ideas and inspired Italians to take pride in their shared language and collective culture and heritage. It is widely considered to be the most important publication of the Italian Enlightenment or *Illuminismo*. As one scholar writes, *Il Caffè* "promoted a concept of world citizenship and connection with the general European Enlightenment" while arousing "a strong feeling of Italian, as opposed to local patriotism." As one encyclopedia summarizes its immediate and more long-lasting impact: "[I]n Milan, in the hospitable *Casa Verri*, a group of young and eager intellectuals inaugurated *Il Caffè*, a periodical which from 1764–1766 exercised real literary influence, and Cesare Beccaria wrote his great treatise on 'Crime and Punishment,'— *Dei Delitti e delle Pene*."[117] As another book, about the rise of economic societies in the eighteenth century, adds: "[T]he name *Il Caffè*—in Italian literally signifying both 'the coffee-shop' and 'the coffee'—served as a shorthand for several disparate but concatenated concepts: the group of people meeting and the imaginary place in which they met, but also for their means of communicating with the world and what they were drinking while doing so, thus embodying, as one survey of the phenomenon has asserted, 'the whole concept of the coffee-house revolution.'"[118]

The consumption of coffee in Europe—and Italy in particular—has a long history. "It is not easy to determine," one book observes, "just when the use of coffee spread from Constantinople to the western parts of Europe; but it is more than likely that the Venetians, because of their close proximity to, and their great trade with, the Levant, were first acquainted with it." "English writers of the seventeenth and eighteenth centuries were noticeably affected by coffee, and the coffee-houses of the times have been immortalized by them," that source emphasizes. While the first Italian coffeehouse is said to have opened in 1645, it is known that a coffee shop opened in Venice in 1683, with another extremely popular Venetian coffee shop, Caffè Florian, opening in 1720 under Floriono Francesconi's direction. Rome's Antico Caffè Greco, often referred to simply as Caffè Greco, opened in 1760 on Via dei Condotti and was named after its Greek owner. "It is interesting to note," William Uker's writes in *All About Coffee*, that the first European adaptation of an Oriental coffeehouse "was known as a *caffè*," with "[t]he double f" retained by Italians and thought by some writers to be derived from *coffea*. "The tea tables and coffee houses of seventeenth and eighteenth-century London, Leipzig, Milan, and Paris provided spaces for discussions of science, insurance, religion, and art," another book records of the importance of these institutions, with coffeehouses such as Caffè Greco becoming a haven for politicians, writers and artists.[119]

Though Beccaria is still best known for *Dei delitti e delle pene*, his early writings in the field of economics are also noteworthy and should not be forgotten. Those writings include his short essay, "An Attempt at an Analysis of Smuggling" (1764), in which he—in the words of one scholar—"developed a mathematical model to calculate the likely amount of goods smuggled, given the amount of goods recovered by customs officials." "Algebra," Beccaria's essay began, "is simply a precise and straightforward technique for reasoning about quantities, and it can therefore be employed not only in geometry and in other mathematical sciences but also in the analysis of anything that is capable of increasing or decreasing, and to all things which exhibit mutually comparable relationships." "Even political sciences," Beccaria offered, "can therefore make use of algebra, up to some point." "I said, 'up to some point,'" Beccaria advised, "because political phenomena are highly dependent on many isolated decisions and human passions which cannot be specified precisely." As Beccaria's analytic essay, expressing the utility of the results of his mathematical calculations for those levying tariffs on goods, stressed: "When a government imposes a duty on merchandise which enters or leaves the country it usually also decrees that merchants who attempt to avoid payment of the duty will lose their merchandise. The risk incurred by the government is then proportional to the amount of the duty, while the merchant's risk is proportional to the value of the merchandise." In his essay, Beccaria thus grappled aloud with the principle of proportionality and finding a solution "to a problem important for the budget of the State, the determination of means for dealing with the smuggling of certain goods in or out of the country."[120]

The context of Cesare Beccaria's achievements is important to recall as knowledge often develops through intellectuals standing on the shoulders of earlier intellectuals. The philosophic and scientific inquiries made in the seventeenth century by John Locke (1632–1704) and Isaac Newton (1642–1727)—along with a growing acceptance of the scientific method for the social sciences—had set the stage for advancements in the hard and social sciences.[121] In *Eighteenth-century Economics*, Peter Groenewegen specifically writes of the great triumvirate of prominent, eighteenth-century political economists. "In the history of political economy," he notes, "three figures of the Enlightenment stand out at the end of the third quarter of the century: Turgot, Beccaria and Smith." Anne-Robert-Jacques Turgot (1727–1781), a contributor to the *Encyclopédie*, not only earned honors at the Seminary of Saint-Suplice and at the University of Paris, he read and wrote on a wide variety of subjects. His "Plan for a Paper on Taxation in General" (1763) wrestled with the economic distortions caused by monopolies and with what level of taxation was optimal to prevent smuggling and the evasion of duties, the subject that Beccaria was considering around that time. "It seems that Public Finance, like a greedy monster," Turgot wrote, "has been lying in wait for the entire wealth of the people." The energetic Turgot later wrote on "Value and Money" around 1769 and became France's finance minister from 1774 to 1776, advocating for a laissez-faire economics that sought to break up cartels and unwieldy mercantilist regulation. Beccaria himself taught economics from the late 1760s into the early 1770s at the Palatine school in Milan and became known for his enlightened approach to the criminal law, while Adam Smith (1723–1790), already known for his *Theory of Moral Sentiments* (1759), went on to write his famous book, *An Inquiry into the Nature and Causes of the Wealth of Nations* (1776). "Of these three figures from the Enlightenment," Groenewegen observes, "only one, Adam Smith, has been given a prominent place in the history of economic thought." As Groenewegen writes: "Turgot has generally been given a more minor, but nevertheless relatively important place, while Beccaria has been almost totally ignored in the histories of economics."[122]

Chapter 2

The Runaway Bestseller

From the beginning of recorded history through the Middle Ages and the Renaissance, societies regularly tortured and executed people and arbitrary punishments were common.[1] "The Justinian Code, which was the basis for most European law codes," James Hitchcock writes in *History of the Catholic Church*, "prescribed the death penalty for heresy because heresy was regarded as a spiritual disease that had to be suppressed lest it kill people's souls."[2] The English "Bloody Code," the name given to England's draconian criminal laws in the eighteenth and nineteenth centuries, had—at one time—more than 200 capital offenses, punishing even minor crimes (*e.g.*, disturbing a fish pond) and disliked behavior (*e.g.*, being in the company of gypsies for a month) with death.[3] And throughout Europe, those adjudged to be witches—and there were tens of thousands found to be so—were regularly executed,[4] with criminals broken on the wheel[5] and iron-fisted monarchs making frequent use of executions for a wide array of criminal offenses—even relatively small ones (*i.e.*, shooting a rabbit, setting a cornfield on fire, etc.)—and to quash popular rebellions or religious or political dissent.[6] "In Beccaria's day," one source emphasizes of then-extant European legal codes, "laws were promulgated in Latin in much of Europe." For example, "Maria Theresa's criminal code of 1770," that textbook notes, "was drawn up in Latin" and was named the *Constitutio Criminalis Theresiana* or, simply, the *Nemesis Theresiana*.[7] That code retained torture and horrific methods of execution, infamously containing gruesome pictures showing how executioners and torturers plied their grisly craft.[8]

With the popularity of torture at its apex in the Middle Ages and into the seventeenth and eighteenth centuries, and with many adherents of the eye-for-an-eye, tooth-for-a-tooth *lex talionis* doctrine throughout Europe and the Americas in those centuries, a Massachusetts criminal code from 1641 explicitly cited Old Testament verses as authority for death sentences. Thus, then-prevailing interpretations of Deuteronomy, Exodus or Leviticus could send someone to his or her death.[9] Genesis 9:6—"Whoso sheddeth man's blood, by man shall his blood be shed"—was an especially popular verse often invoked to justify executions.[10] "In the seventeenth century," one source notes, "the dominant principles of punishment were said to be: 1. *lex talionis* is the highest justice according to the Law of God; 2. the legislator should endeavor to frighten prospective criminals by the most severe penalties; and 3. the legislator shall seek to appease the Deity by the most severe penalties." "As late as 1734," that source recalls, "the Swedish Code, 'Sveriges Rikes Lag', carried the death penalty for 68 offenses."[11] "In its pure formulation," it has been said of the life-for-life, hand-for-hand philosophy so prevalent in 1600s and 1700s, "the *lex talionis*, or law of retaliation, requires that what was done to the victim be done to the criminal."[12]

Once a universally accepted punishment for murder and many other crimes, the death penalty was often associated with political or religious offenses, whether treason, adultery, blasphemy or idolatry. Political rivals were executed, and legal codes were— across cultures—framed on the basis of the Bible or other religious texts. In the Massachusetts Bay Colony, for instance, the following twelve crimes—eleven based explicitly on Old Testament verses—were punishable by death under the 1641 legal code governing that locale: (1) adultery, (2) bestiality, (3) blasphemy, (4) conspiracy and rebellion, (5) false witness in capital cases, (6) idolatry, (7) manslaughter, (8) man stealing, (9) murder, (10) poisoning, (11) sodomy, and (12) witchcraft. "If any man after legal conviction shall have or worship any other god, but the lord god, he shall be put to death," the first capital offense in that code, the Massachusetts Body of Liberties, read. "If any man or woman be a witch, they shall be put to death," the next section provided. "If any person shall Blaspheme the name of god, the father, Son or Holy Spirit, with direct, express, presumptuous or high handed blasphemy, or shall curse god in the like manner," the third section bluntly declared, "he shall be put to death." The 1642 colonial code of Connecticut also had twelve capital crimes, with eleven of the offenses again based on scriptural passages.[13]

In the seventeenth century, executions were nearly a universally accepted form of punishment, though the practice of capital punishment varied by locale and certainly had its skeptics. For example, the Quakers—led in England by George Fox (1624– 1691), the charismatic founder of the Religious Society of Friends—favored milder punishments. An English preacher and dissenter who had been imprisoned for blasphemy, Fox wrote to judges in 1651 to protest the use of executions, and he later made an appeal against death sentences for thieves in a pamphlet *To the Parliament of the Commonwealth of England* (1659).[14] Consequently, Quaker settlements in the New World had, by design, far fewer capital crimes—at least until English authorities stepped in and insisted that criminals be treated more harshly, as they then were in England's courts. "In the Royal Charter of South Jersey (1646)," notes one scholar, "capital punishment was originally forbidden altogether, but the prohibition ended in 1691."[15] As Stuart Banner, a law professor at UCLA School of Law, summarizes early anti-gallows advocacy: "Opposition to capital punishment was not without some Anglo-American precedent. English radicals of the 1640s and 1650s argued unsuccessfully for an end to the death penalty for property crimes like robbery and burglary. Some of the Quakers went even further and advocated abolishing the death penalty for all crimes."[16]

Quakers settled in the New World after a period of great turbulence in the British Empire—indeed, after the execution of one of its unpopular kings, Charles I, a ruler who had dissolved Parliament multiple times. In 1660, King Charles II assumed the English, Scottish and Irish thrones more than ten years after the 1649 execution of his father, Charles I, outside the Banqueting House at Whitehall, London. As the heir apparent, Charles II had lived through the period of the Commonwealth of England, Scotland and Ireland and its Lord Protector, the English military and political leader Oliver Cromwell (1599–1658), and the much shorter tenure of Oliver

Cromwell's son, Richard. Cromwell and other MPs had been the ones who had Charles I put on trial for treason and executed. After taking power, Charles II had granted the colony of Pennsylvania to its founder, William Penn, in 1681, to satisfy a debt the king owed to Penn's deceased father, a "royalist" and a navy admiral who had remained loyal to Charles I. As a Quaker, Penn had himself been jailed for blasphemy in the Tower of London for his religious beliefs; as part of his "holy experiment," he permitted the death penalty in Pennsylvania only for murder and treason. Penn's *Frame of Government* for the new colony has been called "an unusually liberal document that provided for a governor, a council, and an assembly of elected freeholders." In his "Great Act of 1682," adultery, bigamy, incest, rape and sodomy were all noncapital offenses, though in 1718, the year of William Penn's death, the harsher English penal code came to Pennsylvania.[17]

During the Enlightenment, a period of intellectual awakening, eighteenth-century jurists, writers and political and religious leaders began questioning long-held assumptions about censorship, the law, and the relationship between monarchs and their subjects. In this Age of Reason, the concepts of liberty, tolerance and the separation of church and state came to the forefront. For example, in 1748, Montesquieu's enormously popular *De l'esprit des lois* (*Spirit of the Laws*) was published, with Montesquieu detailing and scrutinizing countries' penal practices and advocating for freedom of speech and separation of powers.[18] William Penn himself intended to make Pennsylvania a refuge for those facing religious persecution in Europe. Although only those professing a belief in Jesus Christ as "the Son of God and the Savior of the World" could vote or hold office in the provincial government, the colony's Frame of Government guaranteed religious freedom.[19] In America, the Continental Congress itself, focused on liberty and a division of power so as to avoid the abuse of it, later quoted these maxims of Montesquieu: "'The enjoyment of liberty, and even its support and preservation, consists in every man's being allowed to speak his thoughts, and lay open his sentiments.'" "'The power of *judging* should be exercised by persons taken from the *body of the people*, at certain times of the year, and pursuant to a form and manner prescribed by law. *There is no liberty*, if the power of *judging* be not *separated* from the *legislative* and *executive* powers.'"[20]

In his own book, *Dei delitti e delle pene*, Beccaria expressed similar sentiments, writing of religious toleration and individual liberty and "the necessity to defend the depository of public welfare against the usurpation of individuals." Not only did *Dei delitti e delle pene* advocate for jury trials and a new interpretation of the social contract, but it spoke out against infamy, then a punishment, concluding that "infamy causes infamy." "The law according to which every man should be tried by his peers is a very useful one," Beccaria wrote, "because, when a citizen's freedom and fortune are at stake, the sentiments inspired by inequality should be silenced." "A man accused of a crime, incarcerated then absolved," Beccaria continued, "should not endure any trace of public infamy." "Painful and corporal punishments," he added, "should never be applied to fanaticism; for, being founded on pride, it glories in persecution." According to the editors of one modern edition of Beccaria's treatise: "There are three master themes of the enlightenment that run through the *Treatise*. These are the idea of the social contract, the idea of science, and the belief in progress." As those editors emphasize, noting how Beccaria repackaged many ideas borrowed from others: "Beccaria has brought to bear many, perhaps all, the great ideas of the enlightenment thinkers on the problem of crime and criminal justice. In that sense, there is little in the *Treatise* that is original. Montesquieu in particular had written much about the origin and meaning of law as had Voltaire who not only wrote about the law, but also practiced it in a reformist manner." Of course, the way in which Beccaria said it was fresh and new, as was his outspoken written advocacy for the abolition of executions.[21]

During the Enlightenment, writers built on the ideas and writings of others and searched for logic and rationality wherever they could find them. For example, in *The Federalist Papers*, written to persuade New Yorkers to ratify the U.S. Constitution, James Madison — speaking of separation of powers — referred to "the celebrated Montesquieu" as "[t]he oracle who is always consulted and cited on this subject." Madison famously looked to Montesquieu for guidance in framing the U.S. Constitution and its Bill of Rights to prevent abuses of power and to safeguard individual rights.[22] The three branches of government would check each other, with Article I of the Constitution governing the legislative branch, Article II regulating executive power, and Article III setting up the judiciary — in particular, the U.S. Supreme Court. The press, serving as the Fourth Estate, would check all three branches, with the First Amendment prohibiting "an establishment of religion" and guaranteeing freedom of worship, freedom of speech and press, and "the right of the people peaceably to assemble, and to petition the Government for a redress of grievances." The right to trial by jury — and the guarantee of grand juries in cases of "capital" or "infamous" crimes — would also check governmental power, ensuring that ordinary citizens, not kings or their ministers, would remain in control of criminal prosecutions. It was the power of government that was feared, and America's founders wanted to ensure individual liberty, especially from abusive or vindictive prosecutions.[23] The first three words of the U.S. Constitution's preamble also made clear who would ultimately control and guide the ship of state: "We the People of the United States, in Order to form a more perfect Union, establish Justice, insure domestic Tranquility, provide for the common defence, promote the general Welfare, and secure the Blessings of Liberty to ourselves and our Posterity, do ordain and establish this Constitution for the United States of America."[24]

In prior centuries, the disgruntled and downtrodden *subjects* of kings had, from time to time, put their names to documents designed to check monarchical power or to demand or establish rights, freedoms, or better rules of governance. Most famously, in 1215 in the Magna Carta, King John of England was compelled to agree to a compact with a group of barons, bishops and other "loyal subjects." The charter guaranteed, among other things, that "the English Church shall be free, and shall have its rights undiminished, and its liberties unimpaired"; that heirs of earls and barons would have certain inheritance rights; that heirs could "be given in marriage, but not to someone of lower social standing"; and that "[f]or a trivial offence, a free man shall be fined only in proportion to the degree of his offence, and for a serious offence correspondingly, but not so heavily as to deprive him of his livelihood." "The barons shall elect twenty-five of their number to keep, and cause to be observed with all their might, the peace and liberties granted and confirmed by them by this charter," the Magna Carta read, setting an important precedent for representative democracy. Now more than 800 years old, the Magna Carta—the Great Charter, as it came to be known— has been celebrated by English barristers and jurists and by the American Bar Association as a "foundation of the rule of law" (even though, at the time of its promulgation, it only protected a small, privileged class of people).[25] "Thee whole constitutional history of England is little more than a commentary on the Magna Carta," William Stubbs, the Bishop of Oxford, observed in his nineteenth-century history of constitutional law. Democratic aspirations were "written in Magna Charta," President Franklin Delano Roosevelt concluded in 1941 in his Third Inaugural Address.[26]

At the heart of any social or political contract, Rousseau, Beccaria and others understood, was the consensual relinquishment of some freedoms to a ruler or magistrate or some governing body, such as the British Parliament or another group of elected officials. Thomas Hobbes (1588–1679), in *Leviathan* (1651), had written of "the nature of man," describing life in a state of nature as lacking in arts and letters, one of "continual fear and danger of violent death," and as "solitary, poor, nasty, brutish, and short."[27] But views of the ideal social compact varied widely, and they depended on the area's state of economic development and the political views of its inhabitants. Seventeenth- and eighteenth-century political theorists, including Hugo Grotius (1583– 1645) and Samuel Pufendorf (1632–1694), explored the relationship of individuals to the state but had fairly conservative views of authority. A Dutch philosopher and legal scholar, Grotius wrote of a "social pact" but believed that "rebellion is not permitted by the law of nature." Some powers, he observed, were established "for the Sake of the Governor, as that of a Master over his Slave." In 1672, Pufendorf similarly stressed: "Those persons are not to be endured who assert ... that a King when he degenerates into a tyrant, may be deprived of his crown, and brought to punishment by his people." In the sixteenth and seventeenth centuries, kings were feared for their enormous power—power that encompassed life-or-death matters, including whether someone should be put to death. The Tudor monarch, King Henry VIII, famously oversaw a slew of executions, including that of Thomas More and two of his own wives, Anne Boleyn and Catherine Howard.[28] Only when a king's gross abuses of power so displeased the populace—as with Charles I, who quarreled bitterly with Parliament, refused to accept a constitutional monarchy, and whose actions led to civil war—was a monarch actually put to death. In his case, Charles I—beheaded in 1649—had been put on trial for treason and "wicked" and "evil" practices "against the public interest, common right, liberty, justice, and peace of the people of this nation."[29]

The political theorists who wrote before the appearance of Cesare Beccaria's *Dei delitti e delle pene* had a lot to say. While Thomas Hobbes argued that individuals living in a "war of all against all" wanted, above all else, to ensure bodily security, John Locke (1632–1704) was concerned with the protection of property rights. In Locke's *Second Treatise of Government* (1689), Locke concluded that a government not based on the consent of the governed was illegitimate. A defense of the Glorious Revolution of 1688, which involved the overthrow of King James II of England by a union of English parliamentarians and the Dutch stadtholder, William III of Orange, and which famously installed William and Mary on the throne and established a constitutional monarchy with parliamentary primacy, Locke's influential book discussed "political power." It concluded that "the power of a *magistrate* over a subject may be distinguished from that of a *father* over his children, a *master* over his servant, a *husband* over his wife, and a *lord* over his slave." "*Political power*," Locke observed of the criminal-law realm, "I take to be a *right* of making laws with penalties of death, and consequently all less penalties, for the regulating and preserving of property, and of employing the force of the community, in the execution of such laws, and in the defence of the common-wealth from foreign injury; and all this only for the common good."[30] Meanwhile, Jean-Jacques Burlamaqui (1694–1748), a professor of natural and civil law in Geneva, wrote of how a sovereign gives laws to his subjects for "his own satisfaction and glory" for the purpose of "rendering his subjects happy."[31]

The Swiss diplomat, philosopher and legal expert Emer de Vattel (1714–1767), himself became known for his book, *Le Droit des gens; ou, Principes de la loi naturelle appliqués à la conduite et aux affaires des nations et des souverains* (*The Law of Nations; or, the Principles of Natural Law Applied to the Conduct and to the Affairs of Nations and of Sovereigns*, 1758). Vattel's book was first translated into English in 1760, but it was also a popular book in Italy. For example, Pietro Verri owned the first edition of *Droit des gens* and used it in 1761 and 1762 as he wrote drafts of his *Saggio della grandezza e decadenza del commercio di Milano*. "Vattel," one writer notes, "became an authoritative source for Verri's contention that trade pursued with rigour and force never develops, but it does grow as a result of kindness, justice and good laws." In a 1766 issue of *Il Caffè*, Pietro's brother, Alessandro, also praised Vattel, describing him as one of the first writers to explain "the true interests of nations." Earlier, Cesare Beccaria had also cited Vattel in *Dei delitti e delle pene* in discussing the legitimacy of punishments. Nations, Vattel believed, normally had no right to kill prisoners of war or enemy soldiers who had laid down arms. But Vattel articulated the view that a nation could execute war criminals, that is, those who violated the then-existing laws of war, as well as prisoners of war in retaliation for the killing of prisoners by the enemy. Vattel, a diplomatic envoy to Dresden, was read by many Italian thinkers and was known to the Habsburg monarchy and was even cited in correspondence to which Maria Theresa was a party.[32]

The earliest social compacts were rudimentary, sometimes created out of sheer necessity. The Mayflower Compact (1620), signed by Pilgrims aboard the *Mayflower* before they disembarked onto American soil, is often cited as evidence of early representative democracy in action. In it, the colonists vowed to "covenant and combine ourselves together in a civil body politic, for our better ordering and preservation," and to frame "such just and equal laws, ordinances, acts, constitutions, and offices from time to time, as shall be thought most convenient for the general good of the colony." The pilgrims had been bound for Virginia, where they had secured rights to property, but they had ended up in New England—off the coast of Cape Cod— after their ship had been blown off course. "The Mayflower Compact was the first written constitution in North America," one source emphasizes, noting that it "bound" the settlers "to live in a civil society according to their own laws." It would remain the fundamental law until the Plymouth colony became part of Massachusetts in the late seventeenth century.[33] As one modern source describes the two components of any social compact: (1) "the rights as well as the obligations of citizenship," including "the civil, political, and social rights that belong to each and every citizen," and (2) "a civil ethos, the principles and beliefs that support those rights and obligations under it."[34]

It was the Enlightenment that took the idea of a social compact to a whole new level, one more advanced—at least in terms of its philosophical underpinnings—than in earlier centuries. In *A Discourse on a Subject Proposed by the Academy of Dijon: What Is the Origin of Inequality Among Men, and Is It Authorised by Natural Law?*, Jean-Jacques Rousseau (1712–1778) explored those centuries' past and wrote in 1754 that, if born into an ideal society, "I should have wished then that no one within the State should be able to say he was above the law." "I should have chosen a community," he emphasized, "in which the individuals, content with sanctioning their laws, and deciding the most important public affairs in general assembly and on the motion of the rulers, had established honoured tribunals, carefully distinguished the several departments, and elected year by year some of the most capable and upright of their fellow-citizens to administer the justice and govern the State." "If we look at human society with a calm and disinterested eye," Rousseau wrote at the beginning of his essay, "it seems, at first, to show us only the violence of the powerful and the oppression of the weak." "The different forms of government," Rousseau conjectured in Part II of his essay, as he traced at length the development of inequality in societies in an attempt to win a prize being offered by the Academy of Dijon, "owe their origin to the differing degrees of inequality which existed between individuals at the time of their institution." The Academy of Dijon had been founded by Hector-Bernard Pouffier, the dean of the Parliament of Bourgogne, and it offered gold medallions as prizes. Highlighting "wise and good princes," Rousseau concluded his essay by urging that all those who "love their fellow-citizens" will "serve them with all their might" and "scrupulously obey the laws, and all those who make or administer them."[35]

Less than ten years later, those views—Rousseau's essay did not claim the prize in the competition—had evolved further and morphed into a new book that became a huge bestseller. In 1762, Jean-Jacques Rousseau's *Du Contrat Social* (*The Social Contract*) first appeared, with Rousseau opening his book in more strident language. "Man is born free, and everywhere he is in chains," Rousseau wrote.[36] Rousseau, one scholar observes, "claimed that the state of nature initially provided a pure experience for humans who lived peacefully, like animals, until competition drove humans to enslave themselves in the chains of custom and illegitimate government." "For Rousseau," that scholar, Claire Curtis, explains, "we consent to enter into the social contract, not for protection of life and property, as with Hobbes and Locke, but rather to gain 'civil freedom' and the true fulfillment of humanity." *The Social Contract* inspired social and political reform in Europe and in the Americas, and it placed the authority to govern in the people, not in ruthless monarchs. Although *The Social Contract* was not as popular as his other books, Rousseau received 2,200 *livres* in royalty payments for it and, in 1762 alone, at least eight pirated editions of the book appeared in addition to the two authorized editions that were published in Amsterdam. "After the first flurry of interest had abated," James Miller writes in *Rousseau: Dreamer of Democracy*, "new editions, mostly unauthorized, continued to pop up: two in 1763, one in 1766, one in 1775, and a cheap pocket edition in 1782."[37]

It was Enlightenment writers like Beccaria, Montesquieu and Rousseau to whom American and French revolutionaries turned as they sought intellectual firepower for the revolutionary impulses they felt. In one of his voluminous "My dearest Friend" letters to his wife Abigail, John Adams—later the second U.S. president—inquired as to whether she had read "J. J. Rousseau." "If not, read him," his 1778 letter urged. John Adams had read Rousseau's *Du contrat social* back in the 1760s, with Adams owning no fewer than three copies, a pirated French version and two copies of the first English translation. That translation, *A Treatise on the Social Compact, or the Principles of Politic Law*, was published in London in 1764, the same year *Dei delitti e delle pene* first appeared in Italian. As evidenced by a letter she later wrote in 1781, Abigail did, in fact, read Rousseau as she quoted him in that letter.[38] In 1773, John Adams—the practicing lawyer—referred to Rousseau as "a very celebrated Writer," with Adams reading Rousseau's *The Social Contract* as early at 1765 when a group of young Boston lawyers met under the tutelage of Jeremy Gridley (1701–1767). A Harvard-educated attorney, newspaper editor and colonial legislator, Gridley trained John Adams, Samuel Quincy and James Otis, among others. A distinguished counselor-at-law, Gridley became known as the "Father of the Boston Bar." As one biographical sketch reports, he was "content with moderate fees from those able to pay, and often served the poor without a fee." As that source reports of Gridley's own stated worldview: " 'Pursue the study of law,' said he, 'rather than its gain. Pursue its gain enough to keep out of the briers, but give main attention to its study.' "[39]

During the eighteenth century, Enlightenment figures, participating in an array of academies and societies and in the exchange of countless letters and ideas, also began questioning torturous acts and the necessity for bodily punishments such as the death penalty, if not for all crimes then at least for some. For example, from 1760 to 1761, inspired by Montesquieu's writings, Giuseppe Bencivenni Pelli (1729–1808) of Florence wrote an unpublished dissertation against the death penalty, which is now at the Florence State Archives. In his *Discorso della pena di morte*, he concluded that a just constitution would exclude use of the death penalty. Pelli, who had studied law in Pisa, went on to be the director of the Royal Gallery in Florence. He thought long and hard about the death penalty throughout his life, became a correspondent of Beccaria, and was, in fact, said to be "a particular admirer of Beccaria."[40] On what is now Italian soil, a pioneering female journalist in Florence, Elisabetta Caminer Turra, also argued against the death penalty for deserters. During her own life, she translated a number of French writers, including Diderot, the *Encyclopédiste*, into Italian. She once criticized an anonymous writer who, she wrote, "praises the gallows and condemns journalists because they hope that education will make gallows less necessary."[41] Enlightenment thinkers were often interested in more than one subject, frequently combining an interest in agriculture, science, medicine, music or art with a passion for pamphleteering or political philosophy. And they regularly shared an abiding concern about tyrannical acts and barbaric punishments.

Certain books made more significant impressions than others. Montesquieu's writings were a particular inspiration to countless Enlightenment-era lawmakers and intellectuals, both as to checking abusive government power in general and reforming outdated penal systems in particular. As William Schabas, a leading expert on the death penalty's long history, notes of the French thinker's views: "Montesquieu, for example, called for limitation of the death penalty to murder, attempted murder, certain types of manslaughter and some offences against property, although he did not commit himself to full abolition."[42] In *De l'esprit des lois* (1748), Montesquieu wrote that, in "moderate states," "the head of even the lowest citizen is esteemed," and "he is deprived of his life only when the homeland itself attacks it; and when the homeland attacks his life, it gives him every possible means of defending it."[43] In "moderate states," Montesquieu emphasized, "a good legislator will insist less on punishing crimes than on preventing them; he will apply himself more to giving mores than to inflicting punishments."[44] Montesquieu's book, translated into English in 1750 as *The Spirit of the Laws*, became a worldwide sensation, inspiring its European and American readers, of which there were many. It would lead to major changes in the world's constitutions and laws as lawmakers designing and implementing legal systems divvied up power so no one actor—no one king or president or lawmaker—could accumulate too much.[45]

During the Enlightenment, the topics of religious tolerance and avoiding harsh punishments were on the minds of many reform-minded aristocrats and civic leaders. In *The Spirit of the Laws*, Montesquieu wrote that "[p]enal laws must be avoided in the matter of religion."[46] He also worried aloud about "cruel punishments," something the English and American colonists had prohibited in their legal texts, though without simultaneously barring executions or barbarous corporal punishments.[47] The English Bill of Rights of 1689—the predecessor of the U.S. Constitution's Eighth Amendment, and put in place after the Glorious Revolution of 1688—explicitly prohibited "cruel and unusual punishments," while the Massachusetts Body of Liberties (1641), which contained different language prohibiting cruelty, was explicitly predicated on "the word of God." Drafted by the Reverend Nathaniel Ward, an English attorney and a Puritan pastor, the Body of Liberties provided: "For bodilie punishments we allow amongst us none that are inhumane, barbarous or cruel."[48] "In our time," Montesquieu wrote, raising questions about the death penalty's efficacy by examining past experience, "desertion has been very frequent; the death penalty has been established against deserters, yet desertion has not diminished."[49] In a section of *The Spirit of the Laws* titled "*On the just proportion between the penalties and the crime*," Montesquieu, articulating a general principle, further observed: "Among ourselves, it is a great ill that the same penalty is inflicted on the highway robber and on the one who robs and murders. For the public safety, it is evident that there must be some difference in the penalties."[50]

A baron, Charles-Louis de Secondat, Baron de La Brède et de Montesquieu (1689–1755), better known simply as Montesquieu, lived in France at a time of intense religious-based violence and atrocities. He studied law, including the changes in England that had established a constitutional monarchy in the wake of its Glorious Revolution, and he had achieved enormous literary successes with his *Lettres persanes* (*Persian Letters*, 1721) and *De l'Esprit des Lois* (*The Spirit of the Laws*, 1748). His popular writings sparked a wholesale reexamination of deeply entrenched cultural rituals by raising serious questions about the proper functioning of government and the administration of justice. As Montesquieu, enthralled with history and a man familiar with many then-existing legal systems around the world but seeking a new approach, explained in one section of *The Spirit of the Laws* on "*the nature of penalties*" and "*their proportion*": "It is the triumph of liberty when criminal laws draw each penalty from the particular nature of the crime. All arbitrariness ends; the penalty does not ensue from the legislator's capriciousness but from the nature of the thing, and man does not do violence to man."[51] Montesquieu—as one account of his views reports—"absolutely detested the intolerance, violence and inhumanity of the age." "In a humanitarian view finding such a wide resonance that it made him the most popular author in the eighteenth century," that source reports of Montesquieu, "he campaigned for practical reforms aimed at religious tolerance, the abolition of the slave trade, the humanisation of the criminal law, distributional justice and peace."[52]

Yet, while actively exploring alternatives to the brutality of death sentences, Montesquieu—a wealthy aristocrat and the product of the 1700s—saw a continued place for capital punishment, writing: "A citizen deserves death when he has violated security so far as to take or to attempt to take a life. The death penalty is the remedy, as it were, for a sick society." Death sentences and executions thus remained a grim reality in that era. Just two years after Montesquieu's death in 1755, Robert-François Damiens was put to death by drawing and quartering, the horrific punishment for regicides. A domestic servant, Damiens had attempted to kill King Louis XV of France in 1757 as the king was entering his carriage at the Palace of Versailles. Though Damiens only inflicted a small, non-fatal wound with a penknife, Damiens was tortured and sentenced to be drawn and quartered by horses at the *Place de Grève*. In his memoirs, the famous Italian, Giacoma Casanova, described Damiens as being "torn to pieces as if his crime had been consummated," with Casanova—who reported he had "the courage to watch the dreadful sight for four hours"—reporting: "I was several times obliged to turn away my face and to stop my ears as I heard his piercing shrieks, half of his body having been torn from him." Though Montesquieu was not around to witness Damiens' death, his writings had planted a seed—the notion that perhaps the death penalty was unnecessary for many crimes that were then being punished with death. "When one violates security with respect to goods," Montesquieu added, with his readers easily able to detect his own reservations about the penalty of death, "there can be reasons for the penalty to be capital; but it would perhaps be preferable, and it would be more natural, if the penalty for crimes committed against the security of goods were punished by the loss of goods."[53]

In the sixteenth and seventeenth centuries, severe bodily punishments—both lethal and non-lethal—were a routine part of life in the British Isles and in continental Europe. Executions were public affairs, and throngs of spectators were drawn to them by morbid curiosity. But writers like Montesquieu, Pelli and Beccaria—whether openly or privately—questioned the need for such spectacles (or at least some of them) in their own ways and opened a societal dialogue about these degrading acts of violence and vengeance. The stocks and the pillory were then still in use along with the scaffold, as were grotesque punishments such as ear cropping and cutting out or boring through a person's tongue.[54] "In Rome the pillories were erected on the Capitoline steps," the historian Marcello Maestro wrote of that bygone age, observing that "the faces of the culprits were daubed with honey so they would attract flies."[55] As with devices of torture, such as the thumbscrew and the rack,[56] whipping posts could also be found in many places throughout Europe and the Americas.[57] In some places, the *strappado*—also known as the *corda*—was used whereby a man's hands were tied behind his back, with the victim then suspended by a rope attached to the wrists, often resulting in dislocated shoulders. Each locale had its own rituals or specific rites, but killing, maiming or simply humiliating offenders was considered a legitimate exercise of state authority. "In the first third of the 1700s," Carl Ludwig von Bar observes of "the old punishments by mutilation" in *A History of Continental Criminal Law*, reflecting how corporal punishments remained a gruesome, bloody reality, "cutting off the hand (in certain cases) is the only remaining punishment of this character." "The numerous forms of death penalty," that source notes, "were slow to be repudiated."

At that time, religious doctrines and beliefs drove punishment practices and took center stage in many contentious societal debates. While the eighteenth century brought much soul searching about the treatment of criminal suspects and offenders and modes of punishments, as well as the death penalty's efficacy and morality, the Ten Commandments—the laws of Moses—were still first and foremost on the minds of seventeenth- and eighteenth-century Christian judges and lawmakers.[58] And in religious circles, the Fifth Commandment—"Thou shalt not kill"—was not typically read to bar the killing of criminals, though matters of interpretation of biblical passages were hotly debated.[59] Although a few early Popes, including Pope Gregory I and Pope Nicholas I, had questioned the morality of executions or urged the death penalty's abolition, centuries of religious leaders had supported the use of capital punishment. Thomas Aquinas (1225–1274), a Dominican friar and Italian Catholic priest, believed that the death penalty was necessary—that "certain individuals must be removed by death from human society" should they be "an impediment to the common good which is the concord of human society." "The ruler of a state," he argued, "executes pestiferous people justly and sinlessly in order that the peace of the state may not be disrupted." Another Italian, Niccolò Machiavelli, did not oppose all executions either, though he believed in impartial and egalitarian punishments. "[I]f you should be obliged to inflict capital punishment upon any one," Machiavelli wrote in *The Prince*, "then be sure to do so only when there is manifest cause and proper justification for it."[60]

Roman executions, whether at the Colosseum or elsewhere, were designed to instill fear, with military deserters publicly put to death without mercy or with men thrown to wild beasts for entertainment. The execution of criminals at the Colosseum often took place around noon after fights between animals or circus-style performances designed to entertain spectators. "Executions," Mauro Poma writes in *Discovering the Colosseum*, "could be of different natures: some were killed with a sword (*ad gladium*), others were thrown to wild animals (*ad bestias*), others burned alive (*crematio* or *ad flammas*), others crucified (*crucifixio*), and yet more were obliged to impersonate characters of myth destined to die." Death sentences and executions were so frequent that even Valentine's Day—February 14th—is said to be named after a third-century Roman priest, one Valentine, who was executed on that day in 270 A.D. for marrying couples in defiance of the orders of the emperor. After Valentine refused to renounce his Christian faith, he was beaten with clubs and then beheaded. Valentine was later made the Patron Saint of Lovers, and a tradition arose of men seeking the affection of women through written notes and greetings. "An embellishment of the St. Valentine's story," one source emphasizes, "involves the jailer's daughter falling in love with the condemned Valentine, who on the eve of his execution wrote her a note and signed it, 'Your Valentine.'"[61]

It was shortly after the execution of Jean Calas, a French cloth merchant, that Cesare Beccaria had penned *Dei delitti e delle pene*. In 1762, a court in Toulouse had condemned to death Jean Calas, a sixty-four-year-old Protestant, for supposedly murdering his son to prevent his conversion to Catholicism. In all likelihood, though, Jean Calas' son, Marc-Antoine, who had obtained a law degree but who was denied the ability to practice in his chosen profession because of his religious faith, had committed suicide, with his family attempting to conceal that fact so that Marc-Antoine's naked body would not be ignominiously dragged through the secrets and then hanged, as was then the prevailing custom. After Marc-Antoine's death on October 13, 1761, the Calas family had claimed he'd been murdered. But investigators found only a "livid mark" on the victim's neck and had concluded that Marc-Antoine had been "hanged whilst alive, by himself or by others." In a country that forbade Protestant worship services, suspicion fell on Marc-Antoine's family members, fueled in part by a rumor that Marc-Antoine had planned to abandon his faith. Jean Calas later said his son had killed himself, and that he had only concocted the murder story to avoid the legal consequences of a finding of suicide. But David de Beaudrigue, the prosecutor and magistrate rolled into one, had the Calas family members arrested, and Toulouse's *Parlement*—an appellate court—voted eight to five to convict and then condemned Jean Calas to death. "The sentence," a lengthy account in *The Paris Review* recently noted, "called for Calas to be questioned while tortured in two ways, then broken on the wheel, then burned."

The torture of Jean Calas, with prosecutor/magistrate David de Beaudrigue conducting the interrogation, was grotesque and excruciatingly painful. After Calas—a Huguenot, or French protestant, whose wife was a distant relative of Montesquieu—maintained his innocence, "The Question Ordinaire," as it was known, commenced. As one account reported: "With his wrists tied tightly to a bar behind him, Calas was stretched by a system of cranks and pulleys that steadily drew his arms up while an iron weight kept his feet in place." The second form of torture—"The Question Extraordinaire"—followed after Calas failed to give a confession. With Calas' mouth forced open with two sticks, a primitive form of water torture began. "His head was held low and a cloth placed over his mouth and on the cloth a funnel," one writer notes of the torture Calas endured, with that writer adding of Calas' torment: "His nose was pinched, but from time to time released, then water was slowly poured through the funnel on to the cloth which was sucked in by the suffocating man." After that did not prompt a confession either, Jean Calas was taken to the city's main square and tied to an X-shaped cross. Then, an executioner crushed Calas' bones with an iron rod, with two blows each to the upper and lower arms and the upper and lower legs. After the executioner delivered three blows to Calas' midsection, his broken and bruised body was tied to a wheel, and there Calas lay facing the sky for two hours. "I die innocent," he said before being strangled to death, his body then thrown onto a fire.

Voltaire, whose own writings had been placed on the papacy's Index of Forbidden Books, was incensed by the case after the facts of it reached him. He became obsessed with what had happened, met with Jean Calas' youngest son, Donat, and—persuaded by what he'd read, heard and discovered—organized, supported and led an exoneration campaign. As *The Paris Review*, in its recent exposé of the affair, emphasized of Voltaire's intimate involvement in that campaign: "He ghost-wrote legal documents; enlisted eminent lawyers; tapped his vast network of aristocratic acquaintances for support; and dispatched a young merchant to Toulouse, to investigate." After familiarizing himself with the French rules of criminal procedure, Voltaire was appalled by the prevailing law of proof associated with torture, satirically observing: "As there are half-proofs, that is to say, half-truths, it is clear that there are half-innocent and half-guilty persons." The Toulouse *Parlement* had kept secret the evidence used to convict Jean Calas, but in 1763 Voltaire was successful in having the case reopened by French authorities. Prints of the Calas family were sold throughout Europe to raise money for the cause, and in his advocacy, Voltaire minced no words, calling the dual prosecutor-magistrate a "scoundrel" and labeling those who sat in judgment "assassins." Ultimately, after three years, a panel of forty judges known as Masters of Requests posthumously—and unanimously—"acquitted" Jean Calas, though there was, of course, no mechanism to restore his life. As part of his advocacy, Voltaire had specifically campaigned against the religious intolerance displayed by the court. The Calas case, in a very public way, dramatically demonstrated that state authorities could make mistakes. Jeremy Bentham, the English penal reformer, later wrote of "the melancholy affair of Calas," while another writer, speaking of capital punishment, called the Calas case "the beginning of the abolition movement."[62]

Voltaire's campaign for religious tolerance—and for criminal justice reform—made its way around the globe. In a 1764 letter to Colonel Henry Bouquet (1719–1765), a British officer who was born in the Swiss Confederacy, Benjamin Franklin wrote: "I have lately receiv'd a Number of new Pamphlets from England and France, among which is a piece of Voltaire's on the Subject of Religious Toleration. I will give you a Passage of it, which being read here at a Time when we are torn to Pieces by Faction, religious and civil, shows us that while we sit for our Picture to that able Painter, 'tis no small Advantage to us that he views us at a favourable Distance: 'Mais que dirons-nous, dit il, de ces pacifiques Primitifs que l'on a nommès *Quakres* par dérision, et qui, avec des usages peut-être ridicules, ont été si vertueux, et ont enseigné inutilement la paix aux reste des hommes? Ils sont en Pensylvanie au nombre de cent mille; la Discorde, la Controverse, sont ignorées dans l'heureuse patrie qu'ils se sont faite, et le nom seul de leur ville de *Philadelphie*, qui leur rapelle a tout moment due les hommes sont frères, est l'exemple et la honte des peuples qui ne connaissent pas encore la tolérance.'" In his letter of September 30, 1764, Franklin added of Voltaire's motivation in taking up his pen: "The Occasion of his Writing this *Traité sur la Tolérance* was what he calls 'le *Meurire* de Jean Calas, *commis* dans Toulouse *avec le glaive de la Justice*, le 9me Mars 1762.'" Franklin's letter, which intermingled English and French, further observed of Voltaire's anonymously published treatise: "There is in it abundance of good Sense and sound Reasoning mixed with some of those Pleasantries that mark the Author as strongly as if he had affixed his Name." John Adam's copy of *Traité sur la Tolérance* was itself annotated in the margins in many locations.[63]

In *Dei delitti e delle pene*, Cesare Beccaria—like Montesquieu and Voltaire before him—argued for religious tolerance and proportion between crimes and punishments. In a chapter "On the Eradication of Heresies," Beccaria wrote: "If you wish to prevent a sect from toppling the state, use tolerance; and imitate the wise conduct followed today by Germany, England, and Holland. With regard to a new sect, the only choice to make in politics is to put to death, without mercy, the leaders and their followers— men, women, and children, without exception—or to tolerate them when the sect is large." "The first approach," Beccaria observed, "is that of a monster, the second of a wise man."[64] In his *Treatise on Tolerance* (1763), Voltaire himself had compared religious persecution and violence in France with the more tolerant practices in the same countries Beccaria wrote about in *Dei delitti e delle pene*. As Voltaire wrote in his book: "The fury unleashed by both the dogmatic spirit and the misuse of a poorly understood Christianity has spilt as much blood and caused as many disasters in Germany, in England, and even in Holland, as in France. However, religious differences present no problem today in those countries; the Jew, the Catholic, the Greek Orthodox, the Lutheran, the Calvinist, the Anabaptist, the Socinian, the Mennonite, the Moravian and many others, live there as brothers and contribute equally to the good of society."[65] The use of maniacal torture and executions for religious minorities—or for those not expressing belief in God—was part of what Voltaire and Beccaria were so outraged by as they penned their books. "Tolerance in Europe," one modern history points out, "originates in the struggle for freedom of religion and conscience and against the oppression and condemning to death of heretics and other religious dissidents."[66]

On the subject of punishments, Beccaria felt that "perpetual penal servitude"— in today's parlance, life imprisonment without possibility of parole—was the best and most efficacious way to deter crime. "For a punishment to be just," Beccaria wrote, "it must have only that degree of intensity that suffices to deter men from crime." "Now, there is no one who, upon reflection, would choose the total and permanent loss of his own liberty, no matter how advantageous a crime might be," Beccaria argued, emphasizing that "the intensity of perpetual penal servitude, substituted for the death penalty, has all that is necessary to deter even the most determined mind." "Indeed," Beccaria observed, "I would say that it has even more: a great many men look upon death with a calm and steady gaze, some out of fanaticism, some out of vanity (which almost always accompanies man beyond the grave), and some out of a final and desperate attempt either to live no longer or to escape from poverty." In a letter to the Italian scientist Paolo Frisi, his fellow mathematician and a correspondent of Benjamin Franklin, the French physicist and music theorist Jean-Baptiste le Rond d'Alembert said that Beccaria, in his book, had combined "philosophy, truth, logic, and precision with sentiments of humanity" that would garner Beccaria an "immortal reputation."[67] An equally impressed Voltaire later dedicated his *Relation de la mort du chevalier de La Barre* (1766), or *Account of the Death of the Chevalier de la Barre*, to Cesare Beccaria. In his *Philosophical Dictionary*, Voltaire specifically urged his own readers: "Ye sages who are scattered over the world—for some sages there are—join the philosophic Beccaria, and proclaim with all your strength that punishments ought to be proportioned to crimes."[68]

Other brutal applications of the death penalty also spurred reform efforts. A teenager, the Chevalier François Lefebvre de la Barre had been—like Jean Calas before him—judicially tortured and executed. La Barre, put on trial in Abbeville, Picardy, and convicted and then executed in 1766 at age nineteen, had been accused of blasphemy for mutilating a wooden crucifix. "In February 1766," one source notes, La Barre "was sentenced to have his right hand cut off and his tongue torn out, and to be burned alive." "With minor modifications," that source points out, that sentence "was duly carried out" on July 1, 1766—an execution that enraged Voltaire as much as the torture and execution of Jean Calas had just a few years earlier. "Almost immediately Voltaire poured out all his indignation at the horrifying event," it has been written, though Voltaire—a preface to a compilation of his eighteenth-century writings emphasizes—was "very cautious about circulating" his *Account of the Death of the Chevalier de la Barre*. At La Barre's trial, the prosecution sought to establish that La Barre had been in possession of impious and dangerous books, one of which was Voltaire's then recently published *Philosophical Dictionary* (1764), a life-long project for its author and one later expanded into two volumes. "Afraid for his own safety," one scholar, Simon Harvey, notes of Voltaire's reaction, "Voltaire fled to Switzerland for a few weeks during the summer, conceding bitterly that 'there are times when you have to know how to keep silent.'" As Voltaire later remarked: "I know only too well that there are monsters you cannot tame. Those who steeped their hands in the blood of the chevalier de La Barre are people I would only wish to meddle with if I had ten thousand armed men behind me."

In a section on "Execution" in his *Philosophical Dictionary*, Voltaire wrote: "Yes, we here repeat the observation, a man that is hanged is good for nothing; although some executioner, as much addicted to quackery as cruelty, may have persuaded the wretched simpletons in his neighborhood that the fact of a person hanged is a cure for the epilepsy." On the subject of another execution, a beheading, Voltaire further asked, "What necessity required this death?" In that chapter of his book, Voltaire raised questions about the use of executions for less serious offenders and crimes, the "mad" and for religious-based offenses, asking pointedly at one juncture whether it was "absolutely necessary" for the parliament to hang a "madman" for his crime. As Voltaire observed: "With respect to what is ordinarily called justice, that is, the practice of killing a man because he has stolen a crown from his master; or burning him, as was the case with Simon Morin, for having said that he had had conferences with the Holy Spirit; and as was the case also with a mad old Jesuit of the name of Malagrida, for having printed certain conversations which the holy virgin held with St. Anne, her mother, while in the womb—this practice, it must be acknowledged, is neither conformable to humanity or reason, and cannot possibly be of the least utility." Gabriel Malagrida (1689–1761) was an Italian Jesuit who served as a missionary in the Portuguese colony of Brazil. He had described the 1755 Lisbon earthquake as brought on by God's wrath for people's sins, and after being accused of having a role in a plot to kill King José I, he had been imprisoned in a dungeon and executed for blasphemy by the Inquisition after he had supposedly experienced visions of the anti-Christ and of the Virgin Mary. After being strangled to death by a garrote in Rossio Square in Lisbon on September 21, 1761, his body was burned on a bonfire before his ashes were thrown into a nearby river.[69]

Voltaire was relentless in his criticism, ultimately using Beccaria's treatise to make his point at the very end of his chapter. "What necessity could there be that La Barre should have his hand chopped off and his tongue cut out, that he should be put to the question ordinary and extraordinary, and be burned alive?" Voltaire queried, adding sarcastically: "Such was the sentence pronounced by the Solons and Lycurguses of Abbeville!" Solon was a reform-minded Greek lawmaker from Athens, while Lycurgus of Sparta — according to legend — sought to advance the virtue of equality among citizens. In writing of La Barre, Voltaire asked rhetorically: "What had he done? Had he assassinated his father and mother? Had people reason to apprehend that he would burn down the city?" In making his point, Voltaire spoke of La Barre's actions and the allegations actually leveled against La Barre that had led to his death sentence: "He was accused of want of reverence in some secret circumstances, which the sentence itself does not specify. He had, it was said, sung an old song, of which no one could give an account; and had seen a procession of capuchins pass at a distance without saluting it." The case against La Barre and other young men began after a crucifix was found to be mutilated on a road in Abbeville in August 1765 and another was found to be covered with excrement. After one of the suspects fled, La Barre admitted impious behavior but fingered his absent friend for mutilating the crucifix. After being interrogated and confessing to singing blasphemous songs and possessing impious books, he was sentenced to death, tortured and executed after King Louis XV refused to pardon him. In his writing, Voltaire, whose own *Portable Philosophical Dictionary* had been confiscated from La Barre, added hopefully: "Among this nation of barbarians, there are always to be found two or three thousand persons of great kindness and amiability, possessed of correct taste, and constituting excellent society. These will, at length, polish the others."

Voltaire, using Beccaria's ideas alongside his own sharp wit and intellect, sought to persuade his readers, often simply through the questions he posed, to come around to his point of view. "I should like to ask those who are so fond of erecting gibbets, piles, and scaffolds, and pouring leaden balls through the human brain," Voltaire wrote, "whether they are always laboring under the horrors of famine, and whether they kill their fellow-creatures from any apprehension that there are more of them than can be maintained?" "I was once perfectly horror-struck," he continued, "at seeing a list of deserters made out for the short period merely of eight years." Noting that they "amounted to sixty thousand," Voltaire questioned the sanity of using executions instead of proper discipline to motivate soldiers. "Here were sixty thousand co-patriots, who were to be shot through the head at the beat of drum; and with whom, if well maintained and ably commanded, a whole province might have been added to the kingdom." "I would also ask some of these subaltern Dracos," Voltaire skewered, referring to the ancient Greek lawgiver known for his brutality, "whether there are no such things wanted in their country as highways or crossways, whether there are no uncultivated lands to be broken up, and whether men who are hanged or shot can be of any service?" "I will not address them on the score of humanity, but of utility," Voltaire stressed, lamenting that those in favor of indiscriminate executions "will often attend to neither." As Voltaire, calling for hard labor instead of routine executions, concluded in his eighteenth-century voice in an age where Native Americans were regularly portrayed as "savages": "[A]lthough M. Beccaria met with the applauses of Europe for having proved that punishments ought only to be proportioned to crimes, the Iroquois soon found out an advocate, paid by a priest, who maintained that to torture, hang, rack, and burn in all cases whatsoever, was decidedly the best way."[70]

Dei delitti e delle pene thus appeared at a time when authorities were still frequently resorting to terror tactics and gruesome punishments—and when there was still great fear on the part of those who dared to question such practices or the motivations behind them. *On Crimes and Punishments* not only held up perpetual imprisonment as a viable alternative to such grisly executions, but it articulated a rationale for that position. "It is not the terrible but fleeting spectacle of a criminal's death that is the most powerful brake on liberty," Beccaria reasoned, "but the long and arduous example of a man deprived of his liberty, who, having become a beast of burden, repays the society he has offended through his toils." "It is not the intensity of the punishment that has the greatest effect on the human mind," he wrote, "but its extension, for our sensibility is more easily and firmly affected by small but repeated impressions than by a strong but fleeting action." Beccaria expressed the view that a criminal's death could be justifiable only when a ruler faced a dangerous threat of lawlessness (*i.e.,* where a prisoner "retains such connections and such power" within prison that "his very existence can provoke a dangerous revolution in the established form of government") or if death sentences could be shown to deter others from committing crimes. On the issue of deterrence, Beccaria wrote that "centuries of experience" had taught him that "the ultimate punishment has never deterred men determined to harm society."

In *On Crimes and Punishments*, Beccaria also covered other topics of importance, including the method by which criminals ought to be judged, how the law should handle suicide, and the use of jury trials and pardons. "The law according to which every man should be tried by his peers is a very useful one," Beccaria observed, adding that keeping a criminal suspect in custody before trial "is intrinsically of the nature of a punishment" so "it should last the minimum possible time and should be as lacking in severity as can be arranged." "The minimum time," he opined, "should be calculated taking into account both the length of time needed for trial and the right of those who have been held the longest to be tried first." Beccaria called laws punishing suicide "useless and unjust," emphasizing in the wake of the much-publicized Calas affair: "for even if it is a sin which God will punish, because only He can punish after death, it is not a crime before men, since the punishment, instead of falling on the malefactor, falls on his family." On pardons, Beccaria offered this advice: "As punishments become milder, clemency and pardons become less necessary." "To show men that crimes can be pardoned, and that punishment is not their inevitable consequence," Beccaria wrote, "encourages the illusion of impunity and induces the belief that, since there are pardons, those sentences which are not pardoned are violent acts of force rather than the products of justice."

Cesare Beccaria was interested in the improvement of society and in reducing recidivism and acts of criminality. In a chapter on "How to prevent crimes," Beccaria—an economist at heart who applied his keen intellect to law and the problem of criminal behavior—specifically emphasized the betterment of societal conditions, beginning with this bit of advice: "It is better to prevent crimes than to punish them. This is the principal goal of all good legislation, which is the art of guiding men to their greatest happiness, or the least unhappiness possible, taking into account all the blessings and evils of life." "Slavish men," Beccaria wrote in an era still dominated by serfdom, slavery and indentured servants, "are more debauched, more sybaritic and crueler than free men." "The latter," he wrote of free men, the members of his aristocratic circle of friends, "ponder the sciences and the interests of the nation, they envisage and aspire to great things; but the former," he wrote of slavish men, no doubt referring to the ones he had seen in Milan's prisons or on the city's streets, "are content with the present moment and seek amid the din of depravity a distraction from the emptiness of their everyday lives." "Do you want to prevent crimes?" Beccaria queried. "Then make sure that the laws are clear and simple and that the whole strength of the nation is concentrated on defending them, and that no part of it is used to destroy them." "[T]he surest but hardest way to prevent crime is to improve education," Beccaria concluded, summarizing his overall approach to punishment as follows: "*In order that punishment should not be an act of violence perpetrated by one or many upon a private citizen, it is essential that it should be public, speedy, necessary, the minimum possible in the given circumstances, proportionate to the crime, and determined by law.*"[71]

Cesare Beccaria's worldview of what was at stake—of the liberty interests of individuals—had been shaped by his own personal experiences, especially Beccaria's bitter and protracted rift with his father over his desire to marry Teresa de Blasco, the woman of his choice. If a society is "considered a union of families" instead of "a union of individuals," Beccaria wrote in *On Crimes and Punishments*, then—assuming "one hundred thousand people, divided into twenty thousand families, each composed of five persons, including the head of the family who represents it"—there will be "twenty thousand men and eighty thousand slaves." In that case, Beccaria contended, children "are subject to the whim of their fathers" and "the monarchic spirit will gradually permeate the republic itself, and its effects will be checked only by the conflict of individual interests, not by any feeling animated by liberty and equality." "In contrast," Beccaria wrote, "if the association is considered as consisting of individuals, then there will be a hundred thousand citizens and not a single slave." With no slaves in the republic "made up of individuals," Beccaria asserted, re-envisioning the nature of the social compact in his corner of the world, "the republican spirit will breathe not only in the public squares and assemblies of the nation, but also within the walls of the home, where much of man's happiness or misery is to be found."[72]

In his heavily Roman Catholic part of the world, Cesare Beccaria did not want to be taken for an atheist. Although he was excommunicated from the Catholic Church for writing *Dei delitti e delle pene*, Beccaria in fact wrote of God and divine justice in his book. However, he saw "necessity" and "common utility," not "the gravity of the sin," as the basis for punishment. While "some men have thought that the gravity of the sin plays a role in measuring the degree of criminality of an action," Beccaria wrote, he emphasized that "[t]he fallaciousness of this opinion will be obvious to an impartial student of the true relations among men, and between God and man." "The former are relations of equality," Beccaria observed, adding that "[t]he latter involves relations of dependence upon a perfect Being and Creator, Who has retained for Himself alone the right to be at the same time Lawgiver and Judge, for He alone can be both without impropriety." As Beccaria wrote in one of his chapters titled "Errors in the measuring of punishments": "The gravity of a sin depends on the inscrutable malice of the heart, which finite beings cannot know without special revelation. How, then, could it be used as a guide for the punishment of crimes? If such a thing were tried, men could punish when God pardons and pardon when God punishes."[73]

In his chapter on suicide, Cesare Beccaria's book singled out one act that had long been considered a crime as well as a sin. As Beccaria began that chapter: "Suicide is a crime which seems not to allow of being punished strictly speaking, since such a thing can only be visited either on the innocent or on a cold and insensible corpse. In the latter case, punishment would make no more impression on the living than whipping a statue. In the former case, it is unjust and tyrannical because man's political freedom presupposes that punishment be directed only at the actual culprit of a crime." "No law should be issued which cannot be enforced or which the nature of the circumstances make unenforceable," Beccaria stressed, concluding that laws attempting to punish suicide were as "useless and unjust" as laws making a nation's subjects "prisoners in their own land." As Beccaria emphasized of suicide, critiquing the law's punishment of it: "for even if it is a sin which God will punish, because only He can punish after death, it is not a crime before men, since the punishment, instead of falling on the malefactor, falls on his family. If it should be urged against me that such a punishment may nevertheless draw a man back from killing himself, I reply that one who calmly gives up the benefits of life, who so hates life herebelow as to prefer an eternity of sorrow, could hardly be prevailed upon by the less powerful and more distant thought of his children or relatives."[74]

In *Dei delitti e delle pene*, Beccaria also took aim at religious persecution and secret accusations. "The experience of every century shows that men have abused religion, that precious gift from Heaven, more than anything," Beccaria stressed. "Who can defend himself against false accusation when it is guarded by tyranny's strongest shield, *secrecy*?" Beccaria inquired, adding: "What is the political purpose of punishment? The instilling of terror in other men. But how shall we judge the secret and secluded torture which the tyranny of custom visits on guilty and innocent alike?"

Decrying superstition, secret denunciations and torture, Beccaria wrote: "Another absurd ground for torture is the purging of infamy, that is, when a man who has been attainted by the law has to confirm his own testimony by the dislocation of his bones. This abuse should not be tolerated in the eighteenth century. It presupposes that pain, which is a sensation, can purge infamy, which is a mere moral relation." Infamy—per one law dictionary—is "[t]hat state which is produced by the conviction of an infamous crime, and the loss of honor, which renders the infamous person incompetent as a witness or juror." "It seems that this practice," Beccaria offered, criticizing the tradition of torture, "derives from religious and spiritual ideas, which have had so much influence on the ideas of men in all nations and at all times." "I believe that the confession of guilt, which in some courts is a prerequisite for conviction," Beccaria continued, "has a similar origin, for, before the mysterious court of penitence, the confession of sin is an essential part of the sacrament." "But infamy," Beccaria concluded, "is a sentiment which is subject neither to the law nor to reason, but to common opinion."[75]

As a product of the Enlightenment, Beccaria's book drew particular inspiration from Voltaire's advocacy against cruelty and religious intolerance and—on multiple occasions—piggybacked off of ideas from Helvétius and Montesquieu's *The Spirit of the Laws*. A French philosopher, Claude Adrien Helvétius (1715–1771) argued in his 1758 book, *On Mind*, that the two animating principles of human activity are the pursuit of pleasure and the avoidance of pain.[76] As one source notes of the pervasive influence of Helvétius on Beccaria: "Helvétius had declared that all men seek to become despots and that tangible motives are necessary to check this tendency. Beccaria frankly admitted that he owed a large part of his ideas to Helvétius."[77] Yet another source on the history of the Enlightenment and the concept of utility emphasizes: "Beccaria echoes Voltaire's calls for more humane forms of punishment. Opening with the statement that laws should 'conduce to the greatest happiness shared among the greatest number', Beccaria set out to build a rationale for penal reform explicitly drawn from the teachings of Montesquieu and Helvétius." As that book, Emmanuelle de Champs's *Enlightenment and Utility*, writes of Beccaria: "Like Montesquieu he attacked the barbarity of despotism head on, and like Helvétius he strove to define principles that could guide enlightened reformers."[78] The concept that Beccaria used in his book—*felicità*—is often translated as "happiness" but also refers—as Pietro Verri made clear in *Discorso sulla felicità* (1763)—to both physical and psychological satisfaction or well-being.[79]

But despite its liberal borrowing from the works of other *philosophes* both near and far, Beccaria's treatise was quite novel in that it argued for the death penalty's abolition. Simultaneously railing against torture, Beccaria's book—initially brought out anonymously because of Beccaria's real and well-founded fear of persecution[80]—forthrightly asked: "Is death really a *useful* or *necessary* punishment for the security or good order of society?" "It seems absurd to me," Beccaria wrote, "that the laws, which are the expression of the public will, and which execrate and punish homicide should themselves commit one, and that to deter citizens from murder they should order a public murder." In the place of executions, Beccaria favored "penal servitude."

"The purpose of punishment," Beccaria wrote, "is none other than to prevent the criminal from doing fresh harm to fellow citizens and to deter others from doing the same." "Therefore," he emphasized, "punishments and the method of inflicting them must be chosen such that, in keeping with proportionality, they will make the most efficacious and lasting impression on the minds of men with the least torment to the body of the condemned." "[I]f I can demonstrate that the death penalty is neither useful nor necessary," the idealistic Beccaria proclaimed, "I will have won the cause of humanity."[81] Beccaria promised that any monarch who rejected executions would be embraced "with the secret affirmation of all mankind." As Beccaria put it, invoking the names of ancient Roman emperors: "a just posterity will assign him first place among the peaceful trophies of the Tituses, of the Antonines and the Trajans."[82] "For thinkers such as Montesquieu, Voltaire, and Beccaria," New York University law professor David Garland explains in *Peculiar Institution*, his award-winning book on America's death penalty, "the death penalty was emblematic of the absolutist *ancien regime* with its arbitrary use of power and crushing disregard for individual life and liberty."[83]

Though Cesare Beccaria advocated for a scale of punishments that would be finely calibrated in a proportionate manner to a corresponding scale of crimes, Beccaria's book had a strong, utilitarian streak to it. "The purpose of punishments is neither to torture a man nor to undo a crime already committed," Beccaria wrote. "The object of punishment," he emphasized of his approach that represented a solid break from the *lex talionis* approach, "is simply to prevent the criminal from injuring anew his fellow citizens and to deter others from committing similar injuries." Beccaria explicitly rejected punishing a criminal's family members for acts committed by a criminal, and he thus opposed the forfeiture of property and estates that might impoverish women and children. At that time, criminal offenders often lost their civil rights — and those committing treason forfeited their entire estates through a legal mechanism known as attainder — following felony convictions. Attainder or "corruption of blood" arose from commission of a capital crime, and resulted in the loss of one's hereditary title as well as one's life, property, and right to pass on any inheritance to one's heirs. "The application of the declaration of forfeiture constantly puts a price on the heads of those who are the most defenseless, and it subjects the innocent to punishments that are intended for criminals," Beccaria emphasized. At the same time, Beccaria wanted the criminal law to apply to all guilty parties (but not to innocents) and for there to be no areas of asylum (*e.g.*, churches shielding fugitives from the reach of secular judicial power). As Beccaria wrote: "Within the borders of a country, there must be no place that is placed above the law. The strong arm of the law should be able to follow each citizen, as the shadow follows the human body." "[A]sylums invite men to commit crimes more than punishments deter them," Beccaria observed, encouraging extradition treaties between different countries so long as the laws themselves were "better suited to human needs," that "persecuted innocence and despised virtue are protected," and "until tyranny has been banished to the vast plains of Asia by that universal reason which ever more closely unites the interests of the throne and its subjects."[84]

In *Dei delitti e delle pene*, Cesare Beccaria also argued against the arbitrary power of judges, preferring a fixed code of laws to the whim of a multitude of judges making capricious decisions. As Beccaria wrote: "When a fixed code of laws, which must be observed to the letter, leaves the judge no other task than to examine the actions of citizens and to judge whether or not they are consistent with the law as written, and when the norms defining the just or the unjust, which must guide the actions of the ignorant citizen as well as those of the philosopher-citizen, is a matter not of controversy but of fact, then subjects are no longer exposed to the petty tyrannies of many men."[85] As Beccaria warned of the dangers of unclear laws and arbitrary decisions by judges: "We see the same crimes punished in a different manner at different times in the same tribunals; the consequence of not having consulted the constant and invariable voice of the laws, but the erring instability of arbitrary judgments." As Beccaria advised: "The disorders that may arise from a rigorous observance of the letter of penal laws, are not to be compared with those produced by the interpretation of them. The first are temporary inconveniences, which will oblige the legislator to correct the letter of the law, the want of preciseness and uncertainty of which has occasioned these disorders. . . ." "When the code of laws is once fixed, it should be observed in the literal sense," Beccaria concluded, adding that, in that way, "nothing more is left to the judge than to determine, whether an action be, or be not, conformable to the written law." At the end of chapter four, Beccaria made this parting shot: "I should have every thing to fear, if tyrants were to read my book; but tyrants never read."[86]

After Thomas Jefferson bought an Italian edition of Beccaria's book, the fourth chapter from *Dei delitti e delle pene*—the one on "the interpretation of laws"—was the first one Jefferson chose to excerpt into his commonplace book. In that chapter, much of which Jefferson laboriously transcribed by hand in Italian, Beccaria wrote that judges should reason syllogistically, the major premise being the law, the minor premise being the person's conformity or opposition to the law, and then the conclusion: liberty or punishment. "There is nothing more dangerous than the common axiom: the spirit of the laws is to be considered," Beccaria had written in *On Crimes and Punishments*, adding that "[e]very man hath his own particular point of view, and at different times sees the same objects in very different lights." "The spirit of the laws," Beccaria had observed, describing the consequences of unmoored, arbitrary decision-making, "will then be the result of the good or bad logic of the judge; and this will depend on his good or bad digestion; on the violence of his passions; on the rank and condition of the accused, or on his connections with the judge; and on all those circumstances which change the appearance of objects in the fluctuating mind of man." In a letter written after he had read *Dei delitti e delle pene*, Jefferson wrote: "Punishments I know are necessary, and I would provide them, strict and inflexible, but proportioned to the crime." "Laws thus proportionate and mild should never be dispensed with," Jefferson wrote to Edmund Pendleton, a Virginia planter, politician and judge who served in the Virginia assembly before and during the Revolutionary War. As Jefferson added in his letter to Pendleton, speaking in decidedly Beccarian tones: "Let mercy be the character of the law-giver, but let the judge be a mere machine. The mercies of the law will be dispensed equally and impartially to every description of men; those of the judge, or of the executive power, will be the eccentric impulses of whimsical, capricious designing men."[87]

The first edition of Cesare Beccaria's *Dei delitti e delle pene*—published anonymously for fear of the Inquisition, "an ecclesiastical jurisdiction" established by the Holy See in Italy, Spain, Portugal and elsewhere "for the purpose of searching out and extirpating infidels, Jews, and heretics"[88]—was printed in the Italian port of Leghorn in 1764. As one history of the Inquisition notes, the fear of incurring the wrath of the Inquisition was hardly a hypothetical risk, with many writings of scientists and other Enlightenment thinkers—from those of Galileo, Hugo Grotius, Blaise Pascal, Francis Bacon and Baruch Spinoza in the seventeenth century to those of other thinkers in Beccaria's time— having been confiscated, squelched, and burned.[89] As Toby Green writes in *Inquisition: The Reign of Fear*: "As the Enlightenment—and the Inquisition's reaction against it— proceeded in the 18th century, so did the number of banned books." "Authors banned included Condorcet, Hume, Locke, Montesquieu, Pope, Rousseau, Swift and Voltaire," Green notes. Among the many works of Voltaire that had been put on *Index Librorum Prohibitorum*: *Candide* (1759) and *Traité sur la tolerance* (1763). The *Encyclopédie* of Denis Diderot and Jean le Rond d'Alembert, as well as *De l'Esprit* (1758) by Helvétius and Rousseau's novels and Rousseau's *Du contrat social* (1762), had also been banned.[90]

The final work on Beccaria's manuscript was likely done at Pietro Verri's residence in Milan after Beccaria's summer vacation, with the manuscript of *Dei delitti e delle pene* ready by early 1764. As Marcello Maestro writes in his magisterial English-language biography, *Cesare Beccaria and the Origins of Penal Reform*: "In April of 1764 Beccaria's manuscript was sent to the publisher Aubert of Leghorn who had already printed Pietro Verri's *Essay on Happiness*. The first finished copy of Beccaria's treatise—a small book of slightly more than 100 pages—was received in Milan three months later, on July 16, 1764." "Neither the name of Beccaria nor that of the printer appeared in the first edition," Maestro observes, though clearly Pietro Verri played a pivotal role in guiding and editing young Cesare's work on *Dei delitti e delle pene*. "If our friendship had not sustained me," Beccaria wrote to Pietro Verri on one occasion, "I should have abandoned my project, for by inclination I prefer obscurity." The first edition of the book, a translator's editorial note points out, "bore no bibliographical information, except the year and (in a few rare copies) an enclosed *errata corrige*."[91]

At the time, Giuseppe Aubert's Leghorn publishing house—a tiny operation, and the one that took charge of the project—was only equipped "with two presses and a 'cross-eyed typesetter.'" Variously described as a "man of letters" and "un editore illuminista," Giuseppe Aubert also published works by Count Francesco Algarotti (1712–1764)—an extremely popular Venetian philosopher, poet, essayist and art critic—between 1763 and 1765. In 1737, Algarotti published a bestseller, *Il Neutonianismo per le Dame, ovvero dialoghi sopra la luce e i colori* (*Sir Isaac Newton's Philosophy Explained for the Use of the Ladies*), a reply to Newton's critics in Italy that appeared in many translations, and in 1739, no less a figure than Frederick the Great wrote to the handsome and charming count to convey this message: "I will never be able to forget the eight days that you spent with me. Many other strangers have followed you; but no one meant as much to me as you." In 1762, Algarotti—the son of a rich merchant and a friend of Voltaire—wrote *Saggio sopra la pittura*, translated into English as *An Essay on Painting* (1764). In that work, published by Marco Coltellini in Livorno shortly before the release of *Dei delitti e delle pene*, Algarotti discussed the use by Italian painters of "the camera obscura"—a device that Johannes Vermeer may have employed to reproduce images in a highly accurate, luminous manner. Algarotti had earlier written an *Essay on Opera* (1755) in which he declared: "Of all the ways devised by man of producing delight in noble souls, perhaps the most ingenious and accomplished is opera." "It may well be claimed," Algarotti emphasized, "that the most attractive qualities of poetry, music, mime, dance, and painting all combine happily in opera to delight the emotions, to charm the heart, and sweetly to seduce the mind."

When it later became clear that Beccaria's book—on a far more controversial topic than painting or opera—was being condemned and censored by the Catholic Church, a condemnation that occurred in 1765 and that resulted in Beccaria's excommunication, Aubert nonchalantly remarked that the author should not worry about the condemnation. "Rome," he said, playing the part of the supportive publisher, "prohibits everything which is not childish and banal, and in any case the merit of a book is decided not by Rome but by the public."[92] In 1765, Pope Clement XIII—the leader of the Roman Catholic Church—placed Beccaria's book on the church's list of banned books for its "extreme rationalism" and "highly dangerous heretical" content.[93] It was something Italian intellectuals, such as grape-grower and Tuscan medical student turned American revolutionary Philip Mazzei (1730–1816), were all too familiar with in the eighteenth century. Mazzei had grown up in Tuscany in a world of rampant superstitions, and he had been a student at the Hospital of Santa Maria Nuova. He had done battle with inquisitors, and he was expelled from his medical studies "after having drunk warm water with sugar (because of a cold)." That event, along with familial disputes and contacts in more enlightened circles, convinced Mazzei to look for his future elsewhere. As Franco Venturi writes of Mazzei in *The End of the Old Regime in Europe*: "Close to the group of Antonio Cocchi and his son Raimondo, in contact with cultivated Jews in Florence, in continual conversation with artisans and doctors, he felt rise in him, also due to quarrels with his family, a desire to go out and get to know the world. On 4 March 1754, in the act of selling the farms he had inherited three years earlier, he declared to the notary that he intended to make 'some voyages to better adapt himself to his profession as a surgeon.'" After travelling through Vienna, Budapest, and the Banat, he arrived in Constantinople in 1755, then made his way to London, arriving there in March 1756. As he learned English, he taught English intellectuals Italian. Among his pupils: Doctor Matthew Maty (1718–1776), a Dutch physician and the second principal librarian of the British museum, and the historian Edward Gibbon (1737–1794), who later rose to fame for writing his six-volume history, *The History of the Decline and Fall of the Roman Empire*, published between 1776 and 1788.

Marco Coltellini (1724–1777), an Italian librettist and poet who lived in Leghorn, Vienna and Berlin (and later St. Petersburg), owned the Livorno printing shop that was directed by Giuseppe Aubert until 1770. Around the same time that *Dei delitti e delle pene* was published, Philip Mazzei—a compatriot of Marco Coltellini—had yet another run-in with the Inquisition, one that put him in danger. As part of a business that involved a trade in Italian wine and other products, Mazzei made trips to Tuscany and visited cities such as Mantova, Milan, Naples and Venice. "The principal obstacle against which he protested," historian Franco Venturi explains of Mazzei's difficulties, "was a denunciation by the Holy Office, after he had left London on 24 September 1765, which accused him of having 'loaded an immense quantity of banned books onto a ship destined for Genova, Livorno, Civitavecchia, and Messina, to supply all of Italy.'" "Pietro Molini, the well-known Livornese editor living in England," Venturi observes of Mazzei's book importing activities, "was clearly his 'right arm.'" "The list of books that Mazzei was accused of having sent to Italy," Venturi emphasizes, "included the works of La Mettrie and above all Voltaire, from the *Pucelle* to the *Philosophie de l'histoire*, besides more or less imaginary titles of libertines and deists: *The Material God, Paradise Destroyed, Hell Burned Out, Purgatory Spurned, The Saints Banished from Heaven, Priapus the Creator*, and many others of a similar nature in French, now a common language." This was no small matter for the concerned parties, as Venturi recounts: "The vicar of the Inquisition in Livorno added, for his own part, heavy accusations against the bookseller Marco Coltellini, who was in effect a friend of Mazzei's, for 'the commerce he maintained in most perilous books, giving them to anyone to read, and taking the profit of renting them out.' From Rome Cardinal Neri Corsini supported these accusations, with an invitation to Incontri, the Archbishop of Florence, to press the young Grand Duke Peter Leopold, arrived in Florence only a few months before, to take appropriate measures, or as the prelate expressed himself, to put into operation a 'remedy, as secret and prompt as it is suited, to the spiritual health of the subjects God has entrusted to him.'"

After Marco Coltellini and his associate, Giuseppe Aubert, received a warning, an exposed Philip Mazzei had to make a choice. He initially expressed a desire to go to Rome to defend himself against the accusations, but Mazzei's friends convinced him that would be a bad idea. As Franco Venturi described what Mazzei decided to do next: "He retired to Lucca, remaining there for three months, and then went to Naples, where Galiani and Tanucci defended him and acted on his behalf. The exile from Tuscany, to which he was condemned, terminated on 15 June 1766. The grand duke accorded him on that day 'return and residence in the state' and added that 'Senator Rucellai had seriously warned the Inquisitor at Pisa to abstain in the future from such hasty acts.'" Ferdinando Galiani (1728–1787) was an Italian economist who wrote a treatise on monetary theory, *Della Moneta* (*On Money*, 1751), and Bernardo Tanucci (1698–1783) was an Italian law professor. Raised in a poor family, Tanucci had been educated at the University of Pisa, became a law professor there in 1725, then became a trusted councilor and minister to the King of Naples. Serving until 1777, Tanucci worked to reduce the power of the Catholic Church and the feudal class that owned nine-tenths of area land. It was there, in Naples, that Antonio Genovesi taught political economy. Giulio Rucellai (1702–1778) was a professor at the University of Pisa before assisting Peter Leopold in transferring, at least in large measure, the responsibility for censorship from ecclesiastical authorities to state control and curtailing the level of censorship. "All over Europe, and indeed as far as America," one source notes, also referencing the later work of Italian jurist and philosopher Gaetano Filangieri (1752– 1788), "the names of Galiani and Filangieri brought repute to the Neapolitan school of economics and political theory."

Leopold II, who became the Grand Duke of Tuscany on August 18, 1765, was more enlightened than the Roman and Tuscan inquisitors of the time, though Maria Theresa—through her ambassador at the Court of St. James—quashed the idea of Mazzei serving as a representative of Peter Leopold in London because of Mazzei's "irreligious" views. In 1770, Archduke Peter Leopold of Tuscany actually named Giuseppe Aubert—the printer of *Dei delitti e delle pene*—the director of a new print- ing shop. Meanwhile, Mazzei—denied an official position for Grand Duke Leopold— ended up procuring two Franklin stoves, from Benjamin Franklin, for the grand duke. Mazzei also began exporting to Americans a whole host of goods, including anchovies, wine, oil, pasta, parmesan cheese and sausages. Marco Coltellini, who had settled in Vienna by 1763, was himself a man of great talent, and over the course of his life worked with leading composers, including Wolfgang Amadeus Mozart, Franz Joseph Haydn and Antonio Salieri. He has been described as Maria Theresa's "one-time court poet," a post he was appointed to in 1764—the same year that *Dei delitti e delle pene* first appeared. Marco Coltellini was a friend of Philip Mazzei, and Giuseppe Aubert himself later published 1,500 copies of the Leghorn folio of the *En- cyclopédie*, with Aubert persuading three wealthy patrons to put up the money for the project. By December 1770, Aubert had 600 subscribers for that project, with at least eight in Rome, twenty in Parma, twenty in France, and many in Florence and Milan. "More important," notes a history of the *Encyclopédie*, "the enlightened arch- duke of Tuscany, Peter Leopold, accepted the dedication of the work, shielded it against the pope, and even provided loans and a building for the presses."[94] As another source emphasizes of the Lucca and Leghorn editions of the *Encyclopédie*: "By 1771 the publishers finished printing the seventeen folio volumes of text and, it seems, they had sold out all or most of the edition, mainly in Italy. The Leghorn edition ap- peared later and under more favorable circumstances, for Lucca was a tiny, frail re- public, while Leghorn served as the main port of the powerful archduchy of Tuscany, and the Archduke Leopold, one of the few genuinely enlightened autocrats of the Continent, accepted the dedication of the book and protected the enterprise."[95]

Dei delitti e delle pene sold well enough that a second and third edition were pub- lished within the first twelve months of its release. As one text notes: "In March 1765 Aubert published a third and revised edition of the work, so called because a pirated second edition had been brought out in Florence in 1764 bearing the false place of origin of Mon[a]co." The second edition was printed by Andrea Bonducci (1715– 1766), a man who had translated Alexander Pope's work, with that unauthorized edition probably appearing in the fall of 1764. The second and fourth editions were both pirated and were released without the approval of either Beccaria or his mentor and editor, Pietro Verri. In addition, the third edition—released anonymously and with a falsified place of publication (*i.e.*, Lausanne)—included, for the first time, an iconic engraving, what has been described as "the famous allegorical frontispiece of

Justice turning away in horror from the instruments of torture and capital punishment and looking with favour on the symbols of hard labour." Beccaria himself provided a sketch and a written description of the intended design, and Giovanni Lapi (1720–1788) produced the copperplate engraving that appeared in the book. The frontispiece depicts a sword-wielding executioner trying to present three severed heads to *Justice*. Represented by a woman holding up her hands in protest, *Justice* looks away, focusing her attention instead on a pile of tools and chains and shackles, the symbols of prison labor. Born in Rome, Lapi was an architect, engraver, goldsmith, painter, and sculptor who lived in Livorno until his death. In *Inventing Criminology*, Piers Beirne describes the frontispiece engraving "of *Justice*, who is portrayed as combining law and wisdom in the features of Minerva," in this way: "*Justice* herself recoils from the executioner's offering of three decapitated heads, and instead gazes approvingly at various instruments of labor, of measurement, and of detention."[96] The fifth edition of *Dei delitti e delle pene* appeared in March 1766, again produced by Aubert of Livorno—and again bearing the false place of publication as Lausanne.[97] Giuseppe Aubert also published Rousseau's work, so he was clearly used to—and did not shy away from—matters of public controversy.[98]

During Cesare Beccaria's life, many different versions of *Dei delitti e delle pene* were published. As the *Encyclopedia of Italian Literary Studies* notes: "The text, which Beccaria continually edited, reorganized, and appended, underwent at least seven editions within the author's lifetime. André Morellet's fourth edition, a French translation that appeared in December of 1765 at the behest of the French Illuminists, completely reordered the book from Beccaria's first edition and left only four paragraphs unedited and in their original position." As that encyclopedia emphasizes: "Although Beccaria added a note to the fifth edition claiming that the French ordering was preferable to his own, he oversaw two later editions of the work that retained, for the most part, the original arrangement of material. Since 1958 Beccaria scholars have accepted the fifth edition, the so-called 'Harlem' edition, as the standard Italian text."[99] "[T]here has been some controversy," yet another source notes, "over which of the various editions of Beccaria's work best conforms to his final intentions." "The first modern edition to follow the fifth 'Harlem' edition of 1766, the last version of the text overseen by Beccaria personally," that Cambridge University Press title points out, "was Franco Venturi's, included in *Illuministi italiani*," a collection of Beccaria's writings published in 1958.[100] When Aaron Thomas translated *Dei delitti e delle pene* into English for the University of Toronto Press in 2008, he emphasized in his translator's note that "[i]t was only in 1958, with Franco Venturi's advocacy of the so-called Italian fifth edition of 1766, that some measure of fidelity [to Beccaria's original text] was restored, for it was, Venturi argued, the 'last edition for which there exists explicit evidence of the author's participation in the revision of the text.'"[101]

Both Verri's book, *Meditazioni sulla felicitá*, and Beccaria's treatise, *Dei delitti e delle pene*, are considered "masterpieces of the Italian Enlightenment." As those texts are described in one encyclopedia: "Pietro Verri's *Meditazioni sulla felicitá* (ca. 1763; *Meditations on Happiness*) was an elaboration of an ethical system intended to be both secular and utilitarian." "Beccaria's *Dei delitti e delle pene* (1764; *An Essay on*

Crimes and Punishments) challenged the European conscience to consider the question of justice and made the 'school of Milan' one of the true centers for cosmopolitan dialogue."[102] As scholar Bernard Harcourt, of Columbia Law School, writes of Beccaria's intellectual debt to Verri: "Beccaria drew heavily on the work of his compatriot and close colleague Pietro Verri, who articulated in his *Meditazioni sulla felicitá* (Meditations on happiness), published a year earlier in 1763, the keystone to their new philosophical approach: happiness." "The end of the social pact," Verri explained in 1763, "is the well-being of each of the individuals who join together to form society, who do so in order that this well-being becomes absorbed into the public happiness or rather the greatest possible happiness distributed with the greatest equality possible." Taking an egalitarian and utilitarian tact, Beccaria—foreshadowing Thomas Jefferson's Declaration of Independence, which famously speaks of "the pursuit of Happiness"—himself wrote in his own treatise of "the greatest happiness shared among the greater number."[103]

Cesare Beccaria—as the historical record shows—did not produce his masterpiece on his own. It is clear that Beccaria had a lot of assistance from the other members of the Academy of Fisticuffs in crafting his book, especially from Pietro and Alessandro Verri and Luigi Lambertenghi, an essayist and politician. As Pietro Verri—whom many initially suspected had actually written *Dei delitti e delle pene*—later described in a letter dated November 1, 1765, clarifying his role and definitively putting to rest rumors that he was the author: "And now I will satisfy you on the subject of the book *On Crimes and Punishments*. The book is by the Marquis Beccaria. I gave him the subject; the majority of the ideas are the result of conversation which took place everyday between Alessandro, Lambertenghi and myself." As Pietro explained the process leading to the creation of the book manuscript: "In our society we pass the evening in the same room, each of us working. Alessandro is working on the Storia d'Italia. I have my political and economic works, Beccaria was bored and bored with others. Desperately, he asked me for a subject and I suggested this to him, because I knew it was an excellent one for an eloquent and very imaginative man." In effect, Cesare Beccaria—the young man who had studied law but who then had little practical familiarity with the criminal justice system—had to begin his project with minimal concrete information as Pietro Verri made clear. "But he knew nothing about our criminal systems," Pietro reported in his letter, adding that his brother Alessandro, as the Protector of Prisoners, had "promised to help him." Alessandro kept that promise, with Alessandro (as one source describes it) taking Beccaria to visit "the horrifying dungeons of Milan."[104] As he wrote the manuscript, Beccaria dove in head first, becoming acquainted with Italian practices as well as those of other countries. Whereas Beccaria pointed out in *On Crimes and Punishments* that those falsely imprisoned in England could recover damages for the injustices done to them, he ruefully observed that "[i]n France, on the contrary, an innocent person, who has had the misfortune to be thrown into a dungeon and tortured almost to death, has no consolation, no damages to hope for, no action against any one; and to add to his misfortune, he has for ever lost his reputation."[105]

Pietro Verri's letter of November 1, 1765 specifically described how Beccaria's project came to fruition and how the final book manuscript ended up with Marco Coltellini and Giuseppe Aubert's little publishing house. As Pietro recalled: "Beccaria began to write his ideas on sheets of paper, and we encouraged him so much that he set down a great many ideas; every afternoon we took a walk and we talked of the errors in criminal law, we had discussions, questions, and then, at night, he did his writing; but it is so tiring for him to write that after an hour he cannot go on. When he had all the material collected, I wrote it down and we gave order to it, so to form a book." As Pietro's letter, alluding to the Inquisition and its threats and imminent dangers, concluded: "The difficulty was to publish such delicate matters without having trouble. I sent it to Mr. Aubert in Leghorn, who had published my *Meditazioni sulla felicità*. I sent the manuscript in April last year [1764] and we received the first copy in July 1764." While Pietro Verri definitely played a major role in putting the final manuscript of *Dei delitti e delle pene* together, it is equally clear that Pietro himself freely acknowledged Beccaria's authorship even while taking note of his own significant editorial contributions. As Graeme Newman and Pietro Marongiu, translators of Beccaria's book, observe of Pietro Verri's substantial role in editing the manuscript: "A comparative analysis of the two original documents (Beccaria's autographed manuscript, consisting of a small leather volume, assembled by Beccaria's son Giulio, now in possession of the Biblioteca Ambrosiana, in Milan), actually shows that almost every section of the document was changed; entire passages of Beccaria's text were deleted or given a different meaning and many others added. The result was the beginning of the metamorphosis of the text, which would become complete with Morellet's version...."[106]

The publication of *Dei delitti e delle pene*, quickly banned by the Catholic church and the Paris *Parlement*, is said, because of its temporal context and its advocacy against the death penalty, to be "[t]he beginning of the modern saga of reform and abolition."[107] "In Italy," historian David Williams explains, "opposition" to Beccaria's book came from "many jurists and theologians" and "was led by Ferdinando Facchinei, a Dominican cleric," whose *Notes and Observations on the Book 'On Crimes and Punishments'* (1765) "was written on behalf of the Council of Ten in Venice." The Venetian Council of Ten was an inquisitorial body, and Facchinei—the Dominican friar—has been described as "a mouthpiece" of that once-feared body. Facchinei called Beccaria a "socialist," by which he meant someone who believed—in opposition to the friar's own beliefs—that a society was formed through a contract between free and equal men. "It is absolutely certain," Facchinei emphasized in his critique of Beccaria, "that on this earth there never has been a perfect society created by the express will and choice of free man, as our author imagines, and I challenge the socialists and anyone else to find me a single example in all the histories and annals of the world of societies created in that way." Accusing Beccaria of heresy, sedition, and impiety, Facchinei labeled Beccaria "the Rousseau of the Italians" in his vitriolic January 1765 attack. Rousseau's books—*The Social Contract* and *Émile, ou De l'éducation* (*Emile, or On Education*) both published in May 1762—had been burned in Geneva and Paris and placed on the Index of Forbidden Books later that year. *Émile* is a treatise on education and the nature of man, with Rousseau outlining how best to raise a child and educate a model citizen. "A man's education begins at birth," a frontispiece to Rousseau's *Émile* proclaimed.

Facchinei's condemnation of Beccaria's book leveled six charges of sedition and twenty-three of blasphemy or irreligion. A sample of the allegations: "All sensible people have found the author of the book *On Crimes and Punishments* is an enemy of Christianity, a wicked man and a poor philosopher." "He is a declared enemy of the Supreme Being." "He refuses to consider heresy a crime against God. He affirms that heretics are victims of some linguistic subtleties." "He writes sacrilegious impostures against the Inquisition." "He considers all princes and monarchs of this century as cruel tyrants." "He affirms that the interest of the individual is more important than that of society in general or of those who represent it." "He states that a monarch has no right to inflict the death penalty." With neither the Inquisition nor capital punishment yet abolished in Austrian Lombardy and Tuscany, Beccaria had to take such charges extremely seriously. And he was — in the words of historian Marcello Maestro — "suddenly seized by fear." Though the book had been published anonymously, there was always the risk of being found out. But, as Maestro noted, "[t]he Verri brothers came to the rescue of their friend" by writing a defense of Beccaria's book in just a few days. Their response, *Apology of the book "On Crimes and Punishments,"* written in the first person so that it would appear to have come from Beccaria himself, gave a point-by-point response to Facchinei's charges. It was printed in Leghorn to help quiet the fervor over the publication of *Dei delitti e delle pene*, though it turned out that Count Carlo Firmian actually liked the book, making the defense of it unnecessary, at least in Milan. "The book," Firmian said, "seems to have been written with great love for mankind and with great imagination."[108]

Ferdinando Facchinei's strident, accusatory views represented those of the old order. As one text notes of the context of Facchinei's attack: "At the very time that Beccaria's work appeared, the Republic of Venice was occupied in a violent contest touching the Inquisitorial Council of Ten; and imagining that Beccaria's remarks about secret accusations had been directed against the procedure of their famous tribunal, whilst they attributed the work to a Venetian nobleman called Quirini, they forbade its circulation under pain of death. It was on their behalf and with this belief that the Dominican Padre Facchinei, took up his pen and wrote a book, entitled, 'Notes and Observations on the 'Dei Delitti,'' in which he argued, among other things, not only that secret accusations were the best, cheapest, and most effective method of carrying out justice, but that torture was a kind of mercy to a criminal, purging him in his death from the sin of falsehood."[109] The patrician and Venetian politician Angelo Querini (1721–1796) had been arrested in 1761 and imprisoned for two years after making calls for reform and questioning the powers of the Inquisition, sparking much public controversy.[110] "The Council of Ten, characterized as 'despotic' by enlightened critics," one historian, Larry Wolff, writes, "survived several challenges in the late eighteenth century to its power and prerogatives."[111] It was Pope Clement XIII — then at the head of the Catholic Church — who, in the mid-1760s, placed *Dei delitti e delle pene* on the Index of Prohibited Books, just months after the book's initial appearance in July 1764 in Leghorn, now known in the English-speaking world as Livorno.[112] In 1759, Pope Clement XIII — attempting to shield the public from exposure to new ideas — had also condemned the *Encyclopédie* for having "scandalous doctrines" and for "inducing scorn for religion."[113]

Though described as "an instant and dazzling success" despite attempts to censor it, *Dei delitti e delle pene* thus was not at all uniformly embraced; it would not, in fact, be officially removed from the list of forbidden books for almost two hundred years. That was the case even as the Catholic Church itself, over time, incorporated Beccarian themes into its own encyclicals and theology. "Although *Dei delitti* was received with rapture by a large majority of the philosophes, who unanimously endorsed Beccaria's humanitarianism," *The Criminology Theory Reader* stresses, "some disagreed with either the direction or extent of his specific proposals for reforming criminal law." Even the French *philosophes* did not agree with everything Cesare Beccaria had written in his treatise. "Against Beccaria's complete opposition to torture," that source notes, "Diderot and others argued that it was justified for the discovery of a guilty party's accomplices." "Others protested Beccaria's absolute opposition to capital punishment," that text further recites, noting that "among many jurists in Italy and France, *Dei delitti* immediately became an object of derision and scorn." For Melchoir Grimm (1723–1807), a German-born, French-speaking journalist and contributor to the *Encyclopédie*, Beccaria's suggested reforms were "too geometrical." As Stuart Henry and Werner Einstadter, summing up what transpired, write in *The Criminology Theory Reader*: "Beccaria's novel ideas about torture, capital punishment, and equality before the law were condemned as highly dangerous and his book was condemned for its extreme rationalism and placed on the papal *Index Prohibitorum*, where it remained for almost two centuries."[114]

The Catholic Church's *Index Librorum Prohibitorum* was created in 1559 by Pope Paul IV, and many books on science or relating to religion were placed on it. At the request of the Council of Trent, Pius V, in 1564, had — in the words of one leading encyclopedia — "established the Sacred Congregation of the Index to formalize the work of examining and judging books in accordance with the decisions and doctrine of the Holy Church." In Spain, though the Royal Council initially authorized the publication of *Dei delitti e delle pene*, the inclusion of an apology was simultaneously sought to make clear that it was only to be considered a "work of philosophy" that was not aimed at showing disrespect for existing law, which the translator praised as reflecting the judgment of "our holy mother Church." In spite of that fact, the Spanish Inquisition — like the Roman Inquisition — chose to ban the book anyway throughout Spain on the ground that it promoted "tolerationism" and was "a capricious, dense work" that would induce "an almost absolute impunity." Spanish censors even refused to authorize the book's publication in an altered state "as the propositions deserving of censure are scattered throughout the book" and because "to *reprove all capital punishment and to divulge that other sentences are more deserving punishments … is to calumniate against the conduct of God, who established it so in the old Testament of which He is the author.*" The Old Testament — as one source points out — "requires the death penalty not only for homicide, but for cursing one's parents, for blasphemy and for adultery."

Spanish censors also expressed concern about "the satirical tone with which" *Dei delitti e delle pene* "speaks of the procedures of the Holy Office, even though *it is not named*." After Beccaria's book was condemned by the Vatican in 1766, a Spaniard, Juan Antonio de las Casas, had nonetheless sought permission to publish his translation of it. Academicians had recommended its publication, albeit with the proviso that Beccaria's book simply constituted philosophical speculation and did not intend to criticize then-existing Spanish practices. But the translation was ultimately censored. As a history of Spain observes of the Spanish translation of Beccaria's book: "the volume dated 1774 was duly advertised in the *Gaceta de Madrid* of 3 January 1775" but "by February 1777, the Inquisition had censored and was ready to condemn the translation." An outright ban of the book was contained in an edict of June 20, 1777, an edict approved by Charles III. The inquisitor's main argument for the ban, in addition to seeking public tranquility: "We live at a time when freedom of thought on all matters threatens what is most sacred." As the history of Spain emphasizes: "The banning of Beccaria's text stands out because Government clashed with the Inquisition, and the Holy Office won by persuading the king that his power was under threat." The last updates to the *Index* were made in 1948, the same year in which the Universal Declaration of Human Rights was approved by the United Nations General Assembly. Only in 1966, when the *Index Librorum Prohibitorum* was finally abolished by Pope Paul VI, was Beccaria's book at long last removed from the church's centuries-old censorship list.[115]

The publication of *On Crimes and Punishments*—as evidenced by its tremendous impact in Europe and the Americas—changed the global conversation about liberty, tyranny, and the *Ancien Régime*'s torturous and draconian punishment practices. In large part, this geographically diffuse intellectual awakening was due to how widely the book was distributed and to the sheer number of people who read it, whether in the original Italian or in one of its many translations. As Ann and Michael Caesar write in *Modern Italian Literature*: "Beccaria's work was an immediate success, translated very quickly into the principal European languages, its author lionized in Paris." "Excluding pirated versions and reprintings," David Williams writes in *The Enlightenment*, "seven editions had appeared in Italy by 1774." As Williams observes, reflecting a consensus among scholars: "In 1774 an Italian version of the Morellet translation appeared, and this served as the standard Italian text until 1958, when Franco Venturi established the fifth edition (March 1766) as the authorised standard version." As another source observes of the publishing success of *Dei delitti e delle pene*: "By 1800 there had been no less than twenty three Italian editions, fourteen French editions and eleven English editions (three printed in the United States)."[116] Because it became such a runaway bestseller and was so widely discussed and debated, Beccaria's *Dei delitti e delle pene* shaped the world's constitutions and laws—and thus societies and human affairs more broadly—in a way that mirrored only a handful of other eighteenth-century texts.

There were, certainly, other eighteenth-century bestsellers, including Montesquieu's and Rousseau's landscape-changing books. Each changed the intellectual terrain in its own unique way. But what is very clear is that Beccaria's *On Crimes and Punishments*, like Rousseau's *The Social Contract* and Montesquieu's *The Spirit of the Laws*, was special—and nothing less than a literary sensation in all the major European languages. It was translated into French, English, German, Spanish, Swedish, and an array of other languages, and—in the course of just a few short years and decades—it inspired countless lawyers, jurists, and societies across the globe as eager readers sought it out in bookstores and libraries.[117] As Lynn Hunt writes of Beccaria's book in *Inventing Human Rights*, giving some indication of how hard it was to even keep track of all the editions of Beccaria's little treatise: "Some twenty-eight Italian editions, many with false imprints, and nine French ones came out before 1800, even though the book appeared on the papal Index of Forbidden Books in 1766. An English translation was published in London in 1767, and was followed by editions from Glasgow, Dublin, Edinburgh, Charleston, and Philadelphia. German, Dutch, Polish, and Spanish translations followed soon after." For example, the first German translation, prepared by Albrecht Wittenberg and based on Morellet's French translation, appeared in Hamburg in 1766; another German translation, done by Jakob Schultes, came out the following year. Yet another popular German edition—translated by Philip Jacob Flade—was released in the 1770s. *On Crimes and Punishments* was in fact regularly stocked in bookstores throughout the Americas and Europe before, during and after America's all-important—and itself game-changing—Revolutionary War.[118]

Each translation of Beccaria's book found its way into the hands of many local readers, shaping one community at a time. As Jonathan Israel writes in *Democratic Enlightenment* of Beccaria's book: "Published in English in 1767, it appeared in an influential Spanish version by Juan Antonio de las Casas in 1774 (this edition banned by the Inquisition three years later), and in German, at Ulm, in 1778, under the title *Des herrn Marquis von Beccaria unsterbliches Werk von Verbrechen und Strafen*."[119] As a fellow historian, Marcello Maestro, comments on the Polish translation, which came out in 1772: "A country where Beccaria's ideas found fertile ground was Poland, where the treatise *On Crimes and Punishments* was received with considerable interest soon after its publication."[120] "The movement for humanitarian criminal law had many powerful promotors in Poland," a history of Polish law notes, citing Sebastian Czochron, Tomasz Kuźmirski, Teodor Ostrowski, Józef Weyssenhoff, Józef Szymanowski, Teodor Waga, Stanisław Konarski, Andrzej Stanisław Załuski, Stanisław Lubomirski and Franciszek Ksawery Dmochowski. *On Crimes and Punishments*, that history further observes, "was well known to Polish representatives of the humanitarian movement" and "was also taught at our universities (in the 18th century, 18 copies of the book were in the library of the Jagiellonian University and 14 copies in the library of the University of Warsaw)."[121]

It was Teodor Waga (1739–1801), a Polish intellectual, who translated Beccaria's book into Polish in 1772. "Western treatises were known in Poland, in their original form or in French translation, from the late 1760s and early 1770s," Samuel Fiszman writes in *Constitution and Reform in Eighteenth-century Poland*, pointing out that "the most notable of these works were translated into Polish, including Cesare Beccaria's *Dei delitti e delle pene* and works by Montesquieu and William Blackstone." "Józef Weyssenhoff, the leading member of the Lithuanian codification committee, in the preserved draft of his proposal for the future code, referred to Montesquieu, Beccaria, and Franklin," Fiszman emphasizes, recognizing Beccaria's impact among an assortment of leading European and American intellectuals.[122] In the July 1, 1773 edition of *The Virginia Gazette*—whose slogan was "Open to ALL PARTIES, but influenced by NONE"—that newspaper ran a story on the King of Poland, listing Beccaria among the great writers of the age. As that newspaper wrote of the Polish king's reading habits in its profile: "From his intimacy with the great writers of antiquity, as Xenophon, Thucydides, Livy, Tacitus, Plutarch, and some of the most illustrious of these latter ages, as Sydney, Montesquieu, and Beccaria, he has strengthened the notions (before dictated by the happy temperature of his nature) on the rights of mankind in gross, of the obligations which the governing part, or Magistrates (whatever titles they bear) are under to make the welfare and prosperity of the great aggregate their principal, their only object...."[123] "Polish humanitarians of the eighteenth century," one book adds, echoing other Polish histories, "were strongly influenced by the works of Montesquieu, Brissot de Warville, and Voltaire and, still more, by the learned treatises of Beccaria and Filangieri."[124]

Throughout Europe, Beccaria's admirers and disciples—one of whom was the respected Neapolitan councilor Gaetano Filangieri (1752–1788), a correspondent of American scientist and statesman Benjamin Franklin—could be found everywhere, and they were often in high places and positions of power.[125] "In Germany," *The Encyclopedia of Law and Society* notes of *Dei delitti e delle pene*, "Karl Ferdinand Hommel (1722–1781) wrote a detailed criticism of it, giving him the moniker the 'German Beccaria.'"[126] Hommel—a member of the German *Aufklärung*, or Enlighteners— saw Beccaria as the "Socrates of our epoch." A professor in Leipzig, Hommel wrote about Beccaria's treatise in his German translation, writing that the death penalty should be retained only for treason, murder, arson and certain robberies.[127] "[T]he Catholic *Aufklärung*," *A Companion to the Catholic Enlightenment in Europe* stresses, "now found itself acting in a changed context compared to the 1750s." "Faced with the accelerating development of the Enlightenment," that source notes, "the gap between Catholicism and the new culture had become wider in the 1760s and 1770s after further condemnation of Voltaire's *Candide* (1762 and 1763), the *Traité sur la tolérance* (1766) and *Nouveaux Mélanges* (1763)." Hommel's "unbounded admiration for Beccaria," historian Marcello Maestro has aptly written, "is shown by the title he gave to his edition of the treatise: *The Immortal Work of the Marquis Beccaria on Crimes and Punishments*."[128]

Adding to the "growing alienation of Catholicism and Enlightenment," *A Companion to the Catholic Enlightenment in Europe* further emphasizes, "was the condemnation of Rousseau's *Émile* (1762) and the *Contrat social* (1766), Beccaria's *Dei delitti e delle pene* (1766), as well as the works of La Mettrie, d'Holbach and again Helvétius from 1770–1774." Having read Beccaria's book in its German translation, one most likely printed in Prague in 1765 but now lost, Joseph von Sperges (1725–1791)— writing from Vienna on November 30, 1768—chose to address Beccaria as "illustre filosofo"; Sperges specifically conveyed his pleasure that Beccaria would be teaching young Milanese pupils the "luminosi principia nelle scienze di Polizia, Finanza, Economia pubblica e Commercio."[129] As yet another historian, Richard Evans, notes in *Rituals of Retribution: Capital Punishment in Germany, 1600–1987*: "Ludwig Eugen of Württemberg, brother and heir-apparent of the reigning Duke, wrote to Beccaria early in 1766 assuring him that he would do all in his power to ensure the adoption of his ideas in his realm." Eugen would later rule Württemberg, then a duchy bordering Bavaria, from 1793 to 1795. As Evans described Beccaria's reach into the most elite of circles: "Friedrich II of Prussia read Beccaria's work and wrote to Voltaire that he considered it the last word on penal policy."[130]

In Europe, the debate surrounding Cesare Beccaria's ideas spread like a wildfire. "In six volumes entitled Mosaic Law published from 1770 to 1775," one source on the German Enlightenment reports, "Johann David Michaelis argued that Old Testament law was not an appropriate model for European legislators." "In two volumes in 1774 and 1775," that source emphasizes, Michaelis—a German scholar and professor at Göttingen[131]—"worked his way through the Decalogue, comparing the Mosaic penal law with modern legal practice at every step in an effort to show that ancient Israelite law was unsuitable for modern Europe." The Ten Commandments, also known as the Decalogue, are set forth in the Hebrew Bible, which states that God inscribed them on stone tablets and gave them to Moses on Mount Sinai. Michaelis opposed the death penalty for theft, and many of Michaelis's proposals for penal reform "echoed the famous treatise" that had been written by Beccaria. "More than ten years before Beccaria published *On Crimes and Punishments* (1764)," the author of *The Science of Culture in Enlightenment Germany* adds, the English lexicographer Samuel Johnson "wrote that 'to equate robbery with murder is to reduce murder to robbery,' commenting that 'the frequency of capital punishment rarely hinders the commission of a crime.'" European societies—having witnessed innumerable public executions and already skeptical of their morality and efficacy, especially for non-homicidal crimes such as theft—were thus primed to receive "Beccaria's little volume."[132]

Though editions in multiple European languages were produced, André Morellet's popular French translation, *Traité des délits et des peines*, came first, appearing in December 1765 and becoming popular in pre-revolutionary France the following year.[133] In spite of the Inquisition and all the book burning that took place in that era, English and Spanish translations appeared shortly thereafter, in 1767[134] and 1774 respectively.[135] *Dei delitti e delle pene* was also translated into Portuguese as *Dos Delitos e das Penas*,[136] with Beccaria's ideas quickly flowing from Europe to the Americas thanks to the active transatlantic book trade. In October 1774, on the cusp of the Revolutionary War (1775–1783), the Continental Congress—as an entire body—itself publicly invoked "the celebrated Marquis Beccaria," quoting these stirring words from Beccaria in their message to the inhabitants of Quebec: "In every human society there is an effort continually tending to confer on one part the height of power and happiness, and to reduce the other to the extreme of weakness and misery. The intent of good laws is to oppose this effort, and to diffuse their influence universally and equally."[137] And the translations of *Dei delitti e delle pene* continued to flow through the years. "By 1984," yet another source notes, "twenty-two French, sixteen English, fourteen German, nine Spanish, six Russian, five Portuguese, three Hungarian, two Greek, two Polish, two Serbo-Croatian, two Swedish, one Danish, one Dutch, one Czech and one Turkish edition were recorded, but the list is far from complete."[138]

The study of political economy has deep roots in Italy, and Beccaria was an indispensable part of that Italian tradition. As scholar Wolfgang Rother writes, Italians were the first to abandon cameralism, an Austrian and German variety of mercantilism that developed after the Thirty Years' War (1618–1648), and that is closely associated with centralizing government administration, finance and economic policies. One chair of *Cameralwissenschaft* at the University of Vienna was held by Johann H. G. von Justi; his book, *Foundations of the Power and Happiness of States* (1760–1761) was an early authoritative text on *cameralism*, named after the German royal treasure chamber, the *Kammer*, and which has been defined as "the science of state administration." Another chair at the University of Vienna was held by Joseph von Sonnenfels, the author of *Basic Principles of the Science of Administration, Business and Finance*, a three-volume treatise published between 1765 and 1776. "The 1648 Peace of Westphalia," one text notes, "recognized more than three hundred sovereign territories, ranging widely in size, wealth, and power." As that source recounts of its hodgepodge of locales: "The Holy Roman Empire, with its hundreds of kingdoms, duchies, principalities, and bishoprics, presented a staggering diversity of administrative structures, geography, and economic activities. Accordingly, cameralists filled their books with endless detail about everything from pigs and iron mines to forests and barley fields."[139] In the 1760s, one of Beccaria's "models"—as two economic historians explain—"seem to be Joseph von Sonnenfels' *Grundsätze der Polizei, Handlung und Finanzwissenschaft.*[140]

In the Habsburg dominions, the need for effective administration and governance—especially following a series of costly conflicts—was clear. A counselor to Maria Theresa and her son, Joseph II, the dynamic writer and teacher Joseph von Sonnenfels (1732–1817) had been appointed in 1763—just a year before the initial publication of *Dei delitti e delle pene*—to be the University of Vienna's first chair in the field of government science. The German name of his full professor's chair: *Lehrstuhl für Polizei und Kameralwissenschaften*. The grandson of a rabbi from Berlin, Sonnenfels and his father—living in a society in which social and economic advancement often depended upon one's faith—had converted to Christianity in 1740. Sonnenfels studied law in Vienna, was gifted at languages, and became—as one source puts it—"one of the more important and conspicuous figures of Maria Theresia's Austria." As that book notes of Sonnenfels: "His field of interest was perhaps most of all economics. Here he became virtually an apostle of centralism as a means for furthering the mercantile interests of the state. He spoke out against the myriad internal customs frontiers that still inhibited Austria's commerce. He was equally opposed to the guilds, which regulated all trade and manufacturing on the local level. He was against the economic powers of the noble landlords, and for the lightening or even abolition of the legal serfdom of the rural population." As another source emphasizes of his career: "Sonnenfels exerted considerable influence on the policies of the government of the Habsburg monarchy in the age of 'enlightened absolutism', especially under the reign of Empress Maria Theresa, in his capacity as member of various consultative committees as well as—more indirectly—teacher of several generations of students of state science who formed the main corps of civil servants of the Habsburg monarchy."[141]

As history shows, the Italian Enlightenment became known far and wide for its philosophers — and for its focus on political economy, criminal-law reform, and its efforts to maximize people's happiness.[142] Foremost among those Enlightenment era philosophers was Cesare Beccaria. Like his Italian mentor, Pietro Verri, who wrote about happiness and the concepts of pleasure and pain,[143] Beccaria strenuously opposed torture — a practice Joseph von Sonnenfels convinced Maria Theresa to abandon in 1776, the same year Thomas Jefferson drafted the Declaration of Independence.[144] Beccaria also rose to prominence as the first Enlightenment thinker to make a comprehensive case against the death penalty, though the more cautious Sonnenfels — in his time — "stopped short of repudiating the death penalty" because, in the words of one history, he sought "to keep the ear of the absolutist rulers he served" and was "eager to prove that he was not motivated by free-thinking, radical-humanitarian motives."[145] As has been written of the sea change that enlightened Italian thinkers such as Beccaria brought about in the administration of the criminal law: "Appalled by the unjust laws and brutal punishments of their times, some philosophes sought to create a new approach to justice. The most notable effort was made by an Italian philosophe, Cesare Beccaria (CHAY-zuh-ray buh-KAH-ree-uh)." "In his essay *On Crimes and Punishments*, written in 1764," that commentator further observes, "Beccaria argued that punishments should serve only as deterrents, not as exercises in brutality: 'Such punishments ... ought to be chosen as will make the strongest and most lasting impressions on the minds of others, with the least torment to the body of the criminal.'"[146]

The Italian Enlightenment, or *illuminismo*, out of which Beccaria's book arose, was centered in Naples, Florence and especially Milan, and it retained — in the words of one source — "a close contact with civil society and practical life." The *illuminismo* — Italian for illumination — thus sought to replace superstition and darkness with reason and light while considering "the social conditions out of which reason emerges." "The explicit refusal of metaphysics and of abstraction," as that text explains, "is exemplified by Antonio Genovesi (1712–69), the first person in Europe to be appointed to a chair in political economy (in 1754), and whose thought focused on the interwoven interests and aspirations of humankind, and on the struggle against privilege." Genovesi — an Italian philosopher attracted by the ideas of the English physician and philosopher John Locke (1632–1704) — was appointed to his post at the behest of Bartholomew Intieri, a Florentine benefactor.[147] While Genovesi taught at the University of Naples, penning *Lezioni di Commercio* (1765), a major Italian work on economics, the cadre of Enlightenment thinkers in Milan — then under control of the Habsburg dynasty of Austria Lombardy — focused on law reform in addition to the study of economics. As one text explains of Austrian Lombardy: "The Enlightenment philosophy of Lombardy was more oriented toward law; it also found expression in the dynamic review *Il caffé* (1764–66), and its major representatives were Pietro Verri (1728–97) and Cesare Beccaria (1738–94)." As that text continues: "The Enlightenment project for them, on the one hand, developed in the direction of a modernization of society, facilitating the individual search for happiness, and, on the other, aimed at making the correctional system more humane through the abolition of torture, by humanizing punishment, and by making judgments more clear-cut and quicker."[148] In the *Il Caffé* journal, which drew only a small readership but which had a major impact, Beccaria referred in his articles to the contributions of Isaac Newton and John Locke.[149] The publication of the short-lived journal was a project that would bear much fruit in the decades and centuries to come.

Chapter 3

Monarchs and *Philosophes*

Dei delitti e delle pene brought Cesare Beccaria considerable fame. After its publication, Beccaria sent a copy to Archduke Ferdinand of Austria along with his prior essay on the monetary problems facing Milan. "The two little books that I have the honor to present to Your Highness are the fruit of the peace and protection enjoyed by the citizens living under the merciful dominion of Her Majesty," Beccaria wrote, alluding to the reign of Maria Theresa and to Archduke Ferdinand's "wise administration." Beccaria hoped to curry favor with the Austrian Habsburg family, and Archduke Ferdinand (1754–1806) was the son of Holy Roman Empress Maria Theresa. In his letter, Beccaria wrote: "I must confess that to a forensic career I have preferred to dedicate myself to those sciences which tend to regulate the economy of a state. Your Highness will forgive me if I write that I would be very happy if I could put myself and my energies at Her Majesty's service." "I think that an honorable citizen may express this desire in the confident expectation of some favorable decision," Beccaria added, in a soft but hopeful sell, not knowing that in 1771, Ferdinand would become the governor of the Duchy of Milan following Ferdinand's marriage in 1771 to Maria Beatrice d'Este, the Duchess of Massa. Though nothing came of that particular appeal, it helped to spread the word about Beccaria's work among the Habsburg family.

Dei delitti e delle pene also caught the attention of the French *philosophes*. As Bernard Harcourt—the Columbia Law School professor who also teaches in Paris at the *Ecole des hautes etudes en sciences sociales*—notes: "André Morellet, abbé of the Sorbonne, recalls in his *Mémoires* that it was the statesman, de Malesherbes, who first showed interest in Beccaria's essay. Malesherbes had a few guests over for dinner—Turgot, at the time *Intendant* of Limoges, d'Alembert, the philosopher and co-editor with Diderot of the *Encyclopédie*, Morellet and a few others—and, having just received Beccaria's tract from Italy, discussed the new work with his guests." While Turgot was a French economist who had written about paper money, Guillaume-Chrétien de Lamoignon de Malesherbes (1721–1794), often referred to simply as Malesherbes, was a lawyer—and the son of another highly prominent one—who was appointed president of the *cour des aides* in the Paris *parlement* after his father became chancellor. He was in regular contact with Diderot, the co-editor of the *Encyclopédie*, and he was instrumental in allowing it to be published. "Try to translate this, de Malesherbes told me," Morellet recalled of how he came to know about *Dei delitti e delle pene*. As Morellet's account noted of his first exposure to Beccaria's treatise at the home of Malesherbes: "I went into his library, and returned with a translation of the first passage. It seemed satisfactory, and I was encouraged to continue. I took the book with me and published it in French six weeks later." D'Alembert also urged Morellet—an economist—to translate Beccaria's book into French, with Beccaria's friend, the Italian mathematician Paolo Frisi, having sent a copy of *Dei delitte e delle pene* to D'Alembert in the first few months of 1765. Voltaire called Morellet, a man educated by Jesuits in Lyon and at the Sorbonne, "*L'Abbé Mords-les*" ("Father Bite them") for his sardonic, biting wit.

The unauthorized French translation of *Dei delitti e delle pene* appeared in December 1765, and it was only after that, in early 1766, that André Morellet (1727–1819) sent Beccaria the news, writing to him in a letter in the days before translators worried about copyrights: "Sir, without having the honor of being known to you, I take the liberty of sending you a copy of my translation of your book *On Crimes and Punishments*." The 1710 Statute of Anne, promulgated in Britain during the reign of Queen Anne, gave publishers rights for a fixed period of fourteen years, but pirated editions of authors were then still common throughout Europe. "Men of letters," Morellet praised his correspondent, "belong to all nations and to the whole world; they are united by links stronger than those which exist among the citizens of one country, the inhabitants of one city, the members of one family." "For this reason," he continued, "I hope that you will not refuse to have with me an exchange of ideas and sentiments that I will treasure very highly." "It was M. Malesherbes, with whom I have the honor to be connected," Morellet relayed, "who suggested to me the translation of your work into our language." "My translation," he wrote, noting that D'Alembert had given him a copy of *Dei delitti e delle pene* back in June, "appeared eight days ago." "I did not write you sooner because I wanted to tell you about the reception that your book would have here," Morellet stressed, adding that "the general feeling toward the author couldn't be more flattering." As Morellet's January 3, 1766, letter to Beccaria, which included the new translation and asked some questions about Beccaria's background, emphasized: "I dare assure you, Sir, that its success is universal." "In truth, Sir, if your affairs and your situation allow you to travel to France," Morellet added, "you really must come here and receive the thanks and the marks of esteem which you have deserved."

In his letter, the highly-sophisticated Frenchman let the younger Cesare Beccaria know just how much the French *philosophes* and their compatriots had appreciated his book. "I have been asked," André Morellet conveyed, "to transmit to you the compliments and the grateful expressions of M. Diderot, M. Helvétius, and M. de Buffon." After noting that he had also given a copy of Beccaria's book to Rousseau, who had "stopped in Paris on his way to England," Morellet added: "Mr. Hume, who has been living in Paris in recent years, has also asked me to send you his best regards. I don't need to mention M. D'Alembert who must have written to you already." Morellet's French translation of *Dei delitti e delle pene*, Ian Davidson writes in *Voltaire in Exile*, "was even more successful than the original Italian version; in the first six months, seven editions were published." Voltaire, born in Paris, forced into exile in England for insulting a powerful nobleman, and now buried in that city's Pantheon, was an outspoken voice for civil liberties and for the separation of church and state. As a young man, Voltaire had been imprisoned in the Bastille from 1717 to 1718, and he became attracted to the philosophy of John Locke and the ideas of Sir Isaac Newton.

He had been forced to take refuge for his searing critiques of the French government, and while in England he studied its constitutional monarchy. His plays and essays became famous throughout Europe, with Voltaire himself praising English customs and Morellet—a fellow satirist—for Morellet's written criticism of the Inquisition in 1761. In 1778, Voltaire had made what one encyclopedia calls "a triumphant return to Paris," with Voltaire being greeted by chants of "Calas man!" After being denied a Christian burial, Voltaire was ultimately interred in the Pantheon in 1791 before a crowd of 200,000 people.

André Morellet, the subject of Voltaire's praise, was a highly productive writer and translator. In February 1767, just months after converting Beccaria's prose into French, Morellet translated an essay of Benjamin Franklin on the price of corn and on how best to lift the poor out of poverty. That translated essay actually first appeared in *Ephémérides du citoyen*, a publication of the French physiocrats. Morellet would not meet Franklin until the spring of 1772 when Morellet was sent on a commercial mission to England and the two met at Lord Shelburne's estate at High Wycombe. Morellet, however, was closely following intellectual discourse and debates over economics—as well as the unfolding food crisis in Europe—in the 1760s. In 1766, the wheat crop in most of Europe had been a failure, and in other places, such as Great Britain, it had been below average. "In consequence," *The Papers of Benjamin Franklin* emphasize, "the price of wheat and flour had shot up on the Continent, and English producers, millers, and dealers were naturally tempted to ship much of their supplies to these profitable foreign markets." When wheat prices and the cost of foodstuffs began to rise in England, reports of mob violence and demonstrations—directed against millers and exporters—began appearing in English newspapers. The British king and his ministers imposed an embargo on the export of wheat and flour to avert the threat of a famine, and rising food prices led Franklin—described by the editors of his papers as "a city-dwelling colonial now temporarily living in the British metropolis"—to enter the debate about how the situation should be handled, with Franklin defending the interests of British farmers.

In that essay on European economics, originally printed in November 1766 in *The London Chronicle*, Benjamin Franklin—using the penname "Arator" and posing as a farmer—wrote: "I am one of that class of people that feeds you all, and at present is abus'd by you all; in short I am a *Farmer*." After noting "that God had sent a very short harvest to some other countries of Europe," he wrote that "the wisdom of Government forbad the exportation" of grain, which—Franklin said—would have brought "in millions among us" and made "us flow in money." Writing of the influence of "the mob" on the market for corn, and of the treatment of farmers versus manufacturers (and how manufacturers were "favour'd"), Franklin put forward his own ideas on how best to eliminate poverty. As Franklin advised in his editorial he penned using a pseudonym: "I think the best way of doing good to the poor, is not making them easy *in* poverty, but leading or driving them *out* of it. In my youth I travelled much, and I observed in different countries, that the more public provisions were made for the poor, the less they provided for themselves, and of course became poorer. And, on the contrary, the less was done for them, the more they did for themselves, and became richer." Seeking to incentivize "industry, frugality, and sobriety," and wanting to eliminate "idle, dissolute, drunken, and insolent" behavior among "the poor," Franklin called for people to adhere to "one of the old commandments long treated as out of date—that is, "Six *days shalt thou labour*"—so that "industry will increase, and with it plenty among the lower people; their circumstances will mend, and more will be done for their happiness by inuring them to provide for themselves, than could be done by dividing all your estates among them." The Abbé Morellet would later befriend not only Benjamin Franklin but other American revolutionaries such as Thomas Jefferson. "Typical of Abbé Morellet," one history reports of the witty French translator, "was a drinking song he once wrote accusing Franklin of instigating the American Revolution mainly to replace English tea with the French wines he liked so well."[1]

Because of André Morellet's prominence, it was a great honor for Cesare Beccaria to be translated by Abbé Morellet. In his own heart-felt reply to Morellet's letter, Beccaria—writing on January 26, 1766—was both gracious and wildly enthusiastic about the appearance of the new French translation of *Dei delitti e delle pene*. As Beccaria wrote: "Your delightful letter has produced in me deep feelings of friendship and gratitude. I cannot tell you how honored I feel in seeing my work translated into the language of a nation which is the guide and illuminator of Europe." "I myself owe everything to French books," Beccaria confessed, explaining: "They first developed in my soul feelings of humanity which had been stifled by eight years of a fanatical education. I already admired you for the excellent articles that you wrote for the great *Encyclopédie* and it was for me the most pleasant surprise to see that a famous man like you was willing to translate my treatise." Though Beccaria never ended up changing the order of his chapters in future Italian editions of *Dei delitti e delle pene*, he added in his self-deprecating letter to Morellet: "I thank you with all my heart and I really think that by your translation you have improved on the original. Also the order that you gave to the chapters is more natural and I will follow it myself for future editions." "I was," Beccaria continued, "very touched by the words of those illustrious men mentioned in your letter: D'Alembert, Diderot, Helvétius, Buffon, Hume, names which no one can hear without emotion." "Their immortal works," Beccaria explained of those more established writers, "are the object of my continual study, of my occupation by day and of my meditation in the silence of night." "I feel that I have been compensated beyond all my hopes by receiving praises from these great men," Beccaria relayed, clearly having learned how to accept a compliment with humility and grace.

In responding to Morellet's inquiries about his background, Cesare Beccaria gave a short sketch of himself and his family. "I am very flattered by your curiosity about myself," Beccaria wrote to Morellet in his January 26, 1766 letter, adding: "My family has some wealth, and I am the oldest son; but certain circumstances, some unavoidable and some determined by the will of someone else, did not make my life easy. I have a father whose old age and prejudices I must respect." As Beccaria's sketch of his family and home life continued: "I am married to a young and sensitive woman, eager to improve her spiritual education, to whom I am attached by a tender affection. As for me, my main interest is to study philosophy in peace and thus to satisfy three very strong feelings of mine: love of literary fame, love of freedom, and compassion for the misfortunes of men, slaves of so many errors." "My conversion to philosophy," Beccaria stressed, "dates back only five years, and I owe it to my reading of the *Persian Letters*." "The second work that made a great impression on my soul," he wrote, "was that of Helvétius." As Beccaria lauded Helvétius: "He led me on the path of truth and revealed to me the blindness and the pitfalls of mankind; to his *Esprit* I owe many of my ideas." After Helvétius had published *De l'Esprit* (*On the Mind*) it was condemned by the Jesuits, the bishops and French officials, which only served to give it more publicity and a wider audience.

To understand Beccaria, one must read Helvétius. In *De l'Esprit*, Helvétius wrote: "It is the legislation, if I may venture to say so, that excites us to vice, by mingling it with pleasure; the great art of the legislator is that of separating them, and making no proportion between the advantage the villain can receive from his crime, and the pain to which he exposes himself. If among the rich men, who are often less virtuous than the indigent, we see few robbers and assassins, it is because the profit obtained by robbery is never to a rich man proportionable to the hazard of a capital punishment: but this is not the case with respect to the indigent; for the disproportion falling infinitely short of being so great with respect to him, virtue and vice are in a manner placed in an equilibrium." "Death," Helvétius wrote, "is always preceded by pain, and life always accompanied with some pleasures. We are then attached to life by the fear of pain, and the love of pleasure; the happier life is, the more are we afraid to lose it; and from thence proceeds the horror felt by those who live in plenty at the approach of death." "[T]he true end of the legislative office," Helvétius observed, "is the general happiness," with Helvétius emphasizing: "If we are under a necessity of pursuing happiness wherever we discern it, we are at least at liberty in making choice of the means for procuring our happiness." Helvétius articulated the "simple principle" of "public utility" — "or, that of the greatest number of men, subject to the same form of government."[2]

In his letter to Morellet, Beccaria offered praise for many writers and philosophers. "The sublime work of Buffon," he emphasized of the Jesuit- and law-trained French botanist who published the 36-volume natural history, *Histoire Naturelle*, from 1749 to 1789, "opened to me the sanctuary of nature, and I was impressed by all the writings of Diderot." "My spirit was enthralled and enlightened," he continued, "by the profound metaphysics of Hume, by the truth and novelty of his views; I read recently with infinite pleasure the eighteen volumes of his history and I saw in him a political writer, a philosopher and a historian of the highest order." Daivd Hume, an empiricist, became known for his essays and systematically explored the influence of passion on human behavior. "As to M. D'Alembert," Beccaria gushed, "I have enough knowledge of mathematics to regard him as the greatest geometer of our century." In discussing *Dei delitti e delle pene*, Beccaria — in commenting on the style and prose of his own book — offered this candid self-assessment that revealed his fear of persecution: "It is true that, having in mind what happened to Machiavelli, to Galilei and Giannone, I have been obscure in some passages of my book, but the fact is that I wanted to defend humanity without becoming a martyr. It was also a question of inexperience,

perhaps forgivable in an author who is now but twenty-eight and who started writing
only five years ago."

With respect to André Morellet's invitation, Cesare Beccaria wanted to seize upon
the opportunity, though Beccaria had no desire to be persecuted for his writings. "I
would rush to Paris if I had the means to do so," Beccaria wrote in response to Morellet's
enticing invitation, adding of his then-existing situation in Milan that made an immediate departure impossible but also conveying his desired future prospects in this
way: "I hope, however, that the situation will change and that this delay will enable
me to become worthier of your company and of that of your illustrious friends." "In
the meantime," he relayed, "please consider me your correspondent in Italy for anything
you may need, and I will be glad to do the same for all your friends." "I will tell Count
Firmian all the things you have asked me to," Beccaria pledged, saying this of Count
Firmian: "He has protected my book and I owe to him my present serenity." It was
thanks in large part to Count Firmian that Beccaria avoided the fate of Machiavelli,
Galilei and Giannone. Niccolò Machiavelli (1469–1527) had been imprisoned and
tortured on the charge of treason before being exiled to his family's farm outside of
Florence; Galileo Galilei (1564–1642) was condemned to house arrest on the charge
of heresy by the Inquisition; Pietro Giannone (1676–1748) was an Italian historian
who grappled with the question of church and state and who was excommunicated
and forced into exile for his writings, which were put on the Index of Forbidden Books.[3]

On the subject of friendship and life in Italy, Cesare Beccaria was also particularly
forthcoming in his letter to Morellet. As Beccaria told his correspondent: "I lead a
tranquil and solitary life if we can call solitude a small society of friends whose souls
and hearts are in continuous motion. We share the same studies and the same pleasures. This activity prevents me from feeling like an exile in my own country." "This
city," Beccaria wrote of Milan, "is still buried under the prejudices left by its old masters." "The Milanese," he explained, "do not forgive those who would like to make
them live in the eighteenth century." "In this capital city of 120,000 people," he stressed,
"there are no more than twenty persons who would like to increase their knowledge
and who love truth and virtue." "Our group of friends, convinced of the educational
possibilities of periodical publications," Beccaria wrote of his social circle, the Academy
of Fists, clearly alluding to its Italian language magazine, *Il Caffè*, "has been printing
one that has as its model the English *Spectator*." "I will send you a collection of the
issues we have published," Beccaria promised, telling Morellet that those editions of
Il Caffè included his own articles. As Beccaria went on to explain of *Il Caffè* and his
relationship with Pietro Verri: "Some of the articles are by Pietro Verri, my best friend,
a superior man for his qualities of heart and mind. He encouraged me to write and
I owe it to him that I didn't throw the manuscript of my *Crimes and Punishments* in
the fire; he himself copied it for me with his own hand."[4]

For his proposals for reform and his efforts to set aside obsolete societal customs,
Pietro Verri, as the journal's founder, has been called "the soul" of *Il Caffè*, with Beccaria once describing the Academy of Fists and its leading contributors as "not a
society based on a fixed and determined plan" but as "a clique."[5] The years from 1758
to 1774 have been described by Franco Venturi of the University of Turin as marking

"the springtime of the Italian Enlightenment." This period, he observes, "was that of the greatest tension between the Catholic church and the Italian states and of the most incisive reforms in the relationship between civil and religious society." "It was the period," he continues, "that included the expulsion of the Jesuits and the transformation of the schools, as well as the debate on mortmain, on the regular orders, on papal power, on the Inquisition, on censorship, and so on." "Beccaria and his Milanese friends," Venturi writes of intellectuals who produced *Dei delitti e delle pene* and *Il Caffè*, "considered themselves a sort of colony of Parisian 'encyclopédistes' in Lombardy. As Beccaria wrote in French to Morellet on January 26, 1766: "Croyez, monsieur, que les philosophes francais ont dans cette Amérique une colonie et que nous sommes leurs disciples, parce que nous sommes disciples de la raison." A rough translation: "Believe me, sir, that the French philosophers have in this America a colony, and that we are their disciples, because we are disciples of reason."[6]

In fact, acclaim for *Dei delitti e delle pene* came from many quarters, not just from the pen of Beccaria's translator. "Beccaria," the Marquis de Condorcet, the French scientist and political philosopher, concluded, "refuted in Italy the barbarous maxims of French jurisprudence," with Morellet explicitly writing to Beccaria about *Dei delitti e delle pene* in February 1766: "I am especially enjoined to send you the thanks and compliments of M. Diderot, M. Helvetius, M. de Buffon.... I have submitted your book to M. Rousseau." In that same February 1766 letter, Morellet added: "M. Hume, who has been staying with me for some time, commands me to tell you a thousand things on his part.... M. d'Alembert is going to write to you." By then, David Hume (1711–1776), a Scottish philosopher, was a well-known figure, having written important works such as *An Enquiry Concerning Human Understanding* (1748), *An Enquiry Concerning the Principles of Morals* (1751), and his six-volume *The History of England* (1754–62). He was central to the Scottish Enlightenment.

Cesare Beccaria's book was widely read by enlightened French intellectuals and Scottish thinkers like Hume and the painter Allan Ramsay. In *The History of England*, Hume had traced human history from Julius Caesar's time through the Glorious Revolution of 1688—the revolution that overthrew King James II of England (James VII of Scotland) and installed the Dutch stadtholder William III of Orange on the throne. The Glorious Revolution, fueled by English Parliamentarians and brought to fruition by William III's successful armed invasion of England, produced the English Bill of Rights of 1689, an act of Parliament that set forth various civil rights and that constrained the monarch's power. Among other things, that legal instrument—a statutory restatement of an earlier declaration of rights presented in February 1689 to William and his wife, Mary, proclaiming them king and queen for life—expressly forbade "cruel and unusual punishments." Beccaria's treatise, above all else, changed the frame of the conversation. In *Scotland and France in the Enlightenment*, Ferenc Hörcher points out: "Although there are those who think that the young Milanese's little book did not achieve much more than to assemble the available radical opinions about the most urgent tasks that needed to be done if contemporary criminal law were to become less outrageous and barbaric, Beccaria's concepts were so radical, and his arguments so daring, that the *Treatise* instantly provoked a debate throughout Europe on the possible directions of criminal law reform."

On Crimes and Punishments was read by Allan Ramsay and Lord Kames, though Ramsay felt that Beccaria's ideas were too untethered from real-life questions of morality and justice. With respect to *On Crimes and Punishments*, Ramsay complained that "it is useless to treat penal questions abstractly, as if they were questions of geometry and arithmetic." Worried about the revolutionary impulses in Beccaria's book, Ramsey wrote a letter to Denis Diderot in which he took a critical view. Finding Beccaria's book to be too utopian, Ramsay found Beccaria's application of the social contract to be a "metaphysical idea which was never the source of any real transaction, whether in England or elsewhere." In particular, Ramsay asserted that "those who propose, in governments of a certain nature, to suppress torture, the wheel, impalement, the rack ... tend to deprive themselves of the best means of security, and would abandon the administration of the state to the discretion of the first armed rebels who like better to command than obey." Lord Kames also wrestled mightily with Beccaria's ideas, though he, too, did not agree with everything Beccaria had to say. Other thinkers, however, were much more receptive to Beccaria's approach to law and society. Hörcher adds that the French economist and lawyer Mathieu-Antoine Bouchaud — the translator for Lord Kames, a Scotsman once called "Beccaria's brother" by Morellet — said this: "Mr. Beccaria is a philosopher who deals with his subject from the most useful point of view for humanity." A leading figure of the Scottish Enlightenment and a founding member of the Philosophical Society of Edinburgh, Henry Home (1696–1782) — a man better known as Lord Kames — was a judge, philosopher and advocate admired by James Boswell, David Hume and Adam Smith. In *The Memoirs of the Life and Writings of Lord Kames*, Beccaria's name appears multiple times.[7]

Some of the first readers of *Dei delitti e delle pene* were thus superstars of the Enlightenment. Denis Diderot (1713–1784), a graduate of the University of Paris, was a French writer and art critic whose literary fame skyrocketed with the publication of the *Encyclopédie*, which he co-edited with Jean-Baptiste le Rond d'Alembert. Claude Adrien Helvétius (1715–1771), a French philosopher and freemason, was part of a family of prominent physicians; his father, for example, was the doctor to the queen of France. Madame Helvétius, his wife, maintained a popular salon regularly attended by leading figures of the Enlightenment while Helvétius himself spoke in egalitarian and utilitarian terms and, in his retirement, worked to alleviate the conditions of the poor. Georges-Louis Leclerc, Comte de Buffon (1707–1788), known simply as Buffon, was a French mathematician and naturalist who published works of natural history, while Jean-Jacques Rousseau (1712–1778) — a Francophone born in the Republic of Geneva — would later by interred, like Voltaire, in the Panthéon of Paris for his intellectual contributions. David Hume (1711–1776), the Scottish philosopher, historian and economist who spent time in France before retiring to Edinburgh, became friends with many of the leading intellectuals of his day, including Adam Smith and Benjamin Franklin. And the handsome, but slightly younger, Jean-Baptiste le Rond d'Alembert (1717–1783) was — like Condorcet — a skilled mathematician and philosopher who, in addition to co-editing the *Encyclopédie* and writing scores of entries for it, had been elected to various scientific societies. At that time, salons and economic, literary, philosophical and scientific societies were all the rage.

Even before Beccaria's authorship of *Dei delitti e delle pene* became known, the Patriotic Society of Berne took notice of it, choosing to award a gold medal to "a citizen who dared to raise his voice in favor of humanity against the most deeply ingrained prejudices." And it wasn't long before the success of the book cascaded throughout Europe and the New World. *On Crimes and Punishments* was avidly read by European penal reformers like Voltaire, Sir William Blackstone, and Jeremy Bentham, as well as by leading American revolutionaries such as Dr. Benjamin Rush, John Hancock, John Adams, and Thomas Jefferson.[8] Inspired by Beccaria's utilitarian approach, Voltaire concluded: "It hath long since been observed, that a man after he is hanged is good for nothing, and that punishments invented for the good of society ought to be useful to society." Striking a very Beccarian chord, Voltaire observed: "It is evident, that a score of stout robbers condemned for life to some public work would serve the state in their punishment and that hanging them is a benefit to nobody but the executioner."[9] In Britain, William Blackstone's *Commentaries on the Laws of England* called Beccaria "an ingenious writer, who seems to have well studied the springs of human action, that crimes are more effectually prevented by the certainty, than by the severity, of punishment."[10] The English reformer, John Cartwright (1740–1824), also quoted Beccaria in a 1776 political essay, *Take Your Choice!* In that essay, Cartwright raised this question: "Are not our sanguinary statutes, by which we year by year spill rivers of blood, a reproach to the political knowledge, to the humanity, to the religion of our island?"[11]

Cesare Beccaria's book was advertised in England and its colonies before the Revolutionary War.[12] Joseph Priestley, in *An Essay on the First Principles of Government, and on the Nature of Political, Civil, and Religious Liberty* (1768) included this excerpt from—and revealing editorializing on—Cesare Beccaria's work: "'The fear of the laws,' says the admirable author of the *Essay on crimes and punishments*, 'is salutary, but the fear of man is a fruitful and fatal source of crimes.'" The other words from Beccaria's treatise that Priestley chose to quote: "Men enslaved are more voluptuous, more debauched, and more cruel than those who are in a state of freedom. These study the sciences, and the interests of nations. They have great objects before their eyes, and imitate them. But those whose views are confined to the present moment, endeavour, amidst the distraction of riot and debauchery, to forget their situation. Accustomed to the uncertainty of all events, the consequences of their crimes become problematical; which gives an additional force to the strength of their passions."[13] Thomas Jefferson, in later recommending important books to one correspondent, used these words of praise for his favorite thinkers in writing about "the system of principles" upon which "an organization should be founded, according to the rights of nature": "I should recommend Locke on Government, Sidney, Priestley's Essay on the first Principles of Government, Chipman's Principles of Government, and the Federalist. Adding, perhaps, Beccaria on crimes and punishments, because of the demonstrative manner in which he has treated that branch of the subject." "If your views of political inquiry go further, to the subjects of money and commerce," Jefferson added, "Smith's Wealth of Nations is the best book to be read, unless Say's Political

Economy can be had which treats the same subjects on the same principles, but in a shorter compass and more lucid manner."

Beccaria's book was thus held in high esteem alongside classics such as John Locke's *Two Treatises on Government* (London 1689), Algernon Sydney's *Discourses Concerning Government* (1763), Joseph Priestley's *Essay on the First Principles of Government* (London, 1768), Nathaniel Chipman's *Sketches of the Principles of Government* (Rutland, Vt., 1793), Jean-Baptiste Say's *Traité d'économie politique* (*A Treatise on Political Economy*, 1803), and the two-volume collection, *The Federalist: A Collection of Essays* (New York, 1788). Not only did Priestley's book favorably cite Beccaria's treatise, but Chipman—a federal judge in Vermont—invoked "[t]he Marquis Beccaria" in his book. Chipman discussed Beccaria's ideas in two separate sections of his text: "Of the Coincidence between Natural and Civil Liberty" and "Of the Right of Punishment." "The revolution in America has opened new avenues to the science of government," Chipman wrote in the first of those sections, referring to Locke and Beccaria. Chipman said "we venerate them as men, who have extended and improved the most important science, the science of government," before articulating his own views on that subject. In an introduction to Jean-Baptiste Say's *A Treatise on Political Economy*, Clement C. Biddle—a member of the American Philosophical Society—had this to say about Cesare Beccaria, Pietro Verri and Adam Smith: "*Beccaria*, in a course of public lectures at Milan, first analysed the true functions of productive capital. The Count de *Verri*, the countryman and friend of Beccaria and worthy of being so, both a man of business and an accomplished scholar, in his *Meditazione sull' Economia politica*, published in 1771, approached nearer than any other writer, before Dr. Smith, to the real laws which regulate the production and consumption of wealth." In a footnote to that English-language translation of the French text, it was also pointed out that Beccaria, in a 1769 public lecture in Milan "before the publication of Smith's work," had taken note of "the favourable influence of the division of labour upon the multiplication of products."[14]

The Patriotic Society of Milan, of which Pietro Verri was an active and influential member, actually donated books to the American Philosophical Society in the 1780s. According to a list of donations, the American Philosophical Society received books from the Milanese society by L' Abbé Spallanzani and about mathematics, agriculture, nature and plants and animals. Lazzaro Spallanzani, an Italian Catholic priest, was a biologist who studied animal reproduction and physiology. He became the chair of natural history at the University of Pavia, and he was also a member of various scientific societies, including the Royal Swedish Academy of Sciences. At the August 15, 1788, meeting of the American Philosophical Society, with Benjamin Franklin presiding, it was noted in the minutes that "Franklin presented books, &c., from the Patriotic Society at Milan, sent him by its Secretary, Carlo Amoretti, for the purpose:—Spallanzani's Opuscules; Experiences.... Generation;.... sur la Digestion; lettres à Lucchesini." "Through some mistake, or derangement with respect to conveyances, the books and papers from Milan were not received 'till very lately, although sent ... two years ago, from Italy," those minutes state. Dr. Franklin himself was a foreign member of the Patriotic Society of Milan, established in 1776.

The American Philosophical Society's response to the delayed receipt of those items from Milan, per the society's minutes: "Secretaries ordered 'to take the earliest opportunity' to return thanks and explain; and a copy of Vol. II Trans. of the American Philosophical Society to the S. P. Milan, through Dr. Rush." In Milan, Carlo Amoretti (1741–1816)—a naturalist and geographer—was described by one person, Arthur Young, as "agreeable, well-informed, and interesting." Amoretti wrote a biography of Leonardo da Vinci, translated Sonnenfels' "Essay on the Abolition of Torture," and was elected secretary of the Società Patriotica of Milan in 1783, an office he held for fifteen years. Meanwhile, in Philadelphia, the Milanese aristocrats, Count Paolo Andreani and Count Luigi Castiglioni, were both elected as members of the American Philosophical Society, and early catalogues of the American Philosophical Society's library list a 1785 London edition of Beccaria's *On Crimes and Punishments* as well as *Atti della Società Patriotica di Milano* (1783). The latter publication lists the membership of Milan's Società Patriotica as including, among many others, "Conte Pietro Verri," "Marchese Cesare Beccaria Bonesana," and Cesare Beccaria's brother, "Don Annibale Beccaria."[15]

Everywhere, intellectuals were talking about Beccaria and his book, *On Crimes and Punishments*. In *A Fragment on Government* (1776), Jeremy Bentham tellingly gushed: "When Beccaria came, he was received by the intelligent as an Angel from heaven would be by the faithful."[16] After reading *On Crimes and Punishments*, Bentham—recognizing that Beccaria was not just describing the law as it stood (as many legal commentators had), but wanted to *change* it—called Beccaria "the father of Censorial Jurisprudence."[17] Beccaria's book got quoted and cited in William Eden's *Principles of Penal Law* (1771),[18] and in Dublin, Henry Dagge, in *Considerations on Criminal Law* (1772), specifically observed: "Several Authors of great abilities, who have wrote on the subject of Criminal Laws, agree that the Penal Codes of most nations are very defective; particularly with regard to capital punishments. Among others, the Marquis of *Beccaria*, seems to have considered this subject with great attention."[19] In 1772, the same year Dagge's book appeared, the illustrious Swiss scientist and Alpine explorer Horace-Bénédict de Saussure (1740–1799) and his wife traveled to Italy and got to know Beccaria himself.[20] Taking note of the first English translation of Beccaria's book that appeared in London in 1767, historian Marcello Maestro—in the first full-length, English-language biography of Cesare Beccaria—emphasized decades ago of *Dei delitti e delle pene*'s monumental influence: "German, Dutch, Polish, and Spanish translations were published at the time of the first English edition or soon after. Some years later Beccaria's book appeared in Greek and Russian, as well as in other languages, so that the total number of editions before the end of the century had already climbed to about sixty."[21]

The famed Scottish economist Adam Smith, author of *The Wealth of Nations*, had traveled extensively in continental Europe, and he himself owned works by both Cesare Beccaria and Beccaria's mentor, Pietro Verri.[22] *A Catalogue of the Library of Adam Smith* lists Beccaria's *Traité des délits et des peines*, a 1766 French edition identified as being published in "*Lausanne*" and as "Translated from the Italian by the Abbé André Morellet." That catalogue of Smith's library also lists two copies—one from 1771 and one from 1772, both published in Livorno—of Pietro Verri's *Meditazioni sulla Economia Politica*, as well as economic writings of the Abbé Morellet.[23]

Though Adam Smith cited neither Beccaria nor Pietro Verri's work on economics in *The Wealth of Nations*, Verri's well-received book on political economy—as well as Beccaria's inaugural lecture on the subject, translated into both French and English—in fact preceded the publication of Adam Smith's *The Wealth of Nations*. Smith did take note of "the dutchy of Milan" in *The Wealth of Nations*, with Smith noting that Milan was "divided into six provinces, in each of which there is a different system of taxation with regard to several different sorts of consumable goods." "Under such absurd management," Smith wrote of Milan and Parma, which was also subdivided into smaller territories, "nothing, but the great fertility of the soil and happiness of the climate, could preserve such countries from soon relapsing into the lowest state of poverty and barbarism." Smith also complained about "various and complicated revenue laws."[24]

Adam Smith began writing *The Wealth of Nations* in the first half of 1764, during a stay in Toulouse, and it was sent to the presses in the second half of 1775, with André Morellet—who, by then, already knew Adam Smith—among the first people to receive a copy of Smith's book.[25] Smith had risen to prominence with the publication of *Theory of Moral Sentiments* (1759), then became Vice Rector of the University of Glasgow in 1761. Smith's mentor had been Francis Hutcheson at the University of Glasgow, and *The Theory of Moral Sentiments* opened with this sentence on the topics of sympathy, self-interest and people's charitable nature: "How selfish soever man may be, there are evidently some principles in his nature, which interest him in the fortune of others, and render their happiness necessary to him, though he derives nothing from it except the pleasure of seeing it." In 1763, Smith had resigned his chair to become a tutor of the Duke of Buccleugh, and he had then spent time in Paris and Toulouse. Just as the prominent French economist, A. R. J. Turgot, had visited the much-esteemed Voltaire at his estate in Ferney, outside of Geneva, Switzerland, in 1760, Adam Smith had similarly paid the great Voltaire a visit in 1764—the same year that Beccaria's *Dei delitti e delle pene* first appeared. Although Smith did not acknowledge the work of Beccaria in *The Wealth of Nations*, several handwritten copies of Beccaria's economic lectures—made by students taking Beccaria's course in Milan—were in existence long before Smith's book was sent to the presses.[26]

Adam Smith, who toured continental Europe between February 1764 and October 1766, was an admirer of Voltaire. "[D]uring this trip," one history recounts of Smith's grand tour, "he met a number of the most prominent *philosophes*, including Voltaire, Diderot, d'Alembert, Helvétius, and the Baron d'Holbach (who had earlier supervised a French translation of *The Theory of Moral Sentiments*)." "[T]here was nothing but mutual admiration between Voltaire and Smith, who met on five or six different occasions at Ferney in 1765," that source notes, pointing out that Smith had declared Voltaire to be "the most universal genius perhaps which France has ever produced." "This Smith," Voltaire returned the compliment, "is an excellent man!" "We have nothing to compare with him, and I am embarrassed for my dear compatriots," Voltaire said of Smith. As that history, *The Problems and Promise of Commercial Society*, observes of Adam Smith's time in France in the City of Light: "Smith met the other *philosophes*, as well as *économistes* such as Turgot, Quesnay, and Mirabeau, regularly in the salons of Paris in 1766, where his reputation, breadth of knowledge, and amiable absent-mindedness—as well as his friendship with Hume, affectionately known there as *le bon David*—made him almost universally respected by his hosts despite his poor spoken French. Victor Riqueti (1715–1789), the marquis of Mirabeau, was a French economist who had published *L'ami des hommes, ou Traité de la population* (*The Friend of Man, or Treatise on Population*, 1756–1758). It was an incredibly successful book that went through more than forty editions—and many translations—in a few years; it was essentially a commentary on Richard Cantillon's *Essay*, a much-admired source on economics that Beccaria himself had read and appears to have studied carefully. Cantillon's name was not included in the varied list of economists later mentioned in Beccaria's economic lectures, and Beccaria (who looked to Francis Bacon, Gian Rinaldo Carli, François Forbonnais, Antonio Genovesi, Antoine Goguet, David Hume, John Locke, Jean-François Melon, Montesquieu, Pompeo Neri, Bernardo de Ulloa, Gerónimo de Ustáriz, Vauban as he grappled with economic issues) ended up departing from Cantillon's ideas in various respects. Whereas Cantillon saw *land* as the original and most important source of wealth, Beccaria and Adam Smith focused on *labor* as the critical source of wealth creation.[27]

Though *Dei delitti e delle pene* would, with great rapidity, cause a great stir of excitement in Europe, all—especially society's more tradition-bound, conservative members—were not so pleased with it. As scholar Bernard Harcourt notes of the initial, not-so-uniformly-positive reception of Beccaria's book: "It was met at first with mixed reviews. It was panned in the Parisian *Gazette littéraire de l'Europe* as a simple restatement of Rousseau's *Social Contract* and attacked in Italy as the work of a '*socialista*'—some historians contend that this was the first use of the term 'socialist.'" The French jurist Pierre-François Muyart de Vouglans, Harcourt emphasizes, attacked Beccaria's book as "a pleading in favor of that miserable portion of the human species, that is its curse and scourge, that dishonors it, and sometimes even seeks to destroy it." In particular, Muyart de Vouglans warned potential readers of Beccaria's book of "all the dangers of the potential consequences, especially with regard to the government, the mores, and the religion of this country." In condemning Beccaria's book, Muyart de Vouglans was especially taken aback by Beccaria's call for equality of punishments. As he indignantly maligned Beccaria and his ideas in a 1767 refutation: "The author claims that the status of the victim of the crime should no longer influence the infliction of the punishment, and the only reason he gives for this is that everyone is dependent chiefly on the social body to which he belongs. For the same reason he wishes that those of the highest rank be punished like the lowest of the people. The danger and absurdity of such a principle is self-evident."[28]

In that period, nobles were regularly treated differently and punished in a different manner than common laborers or serfs. For instance, the Abbé Emmanuel Joseph Sieyès (1748–1836) once asked: "Why do members of the privileged orders, after the most appalling crimes, almost always avoid punishment, thus depriving law and order of its most effective exemplary deterrents?" "The law," Sieyès emphasized, "prescribes different punishments for someone who is privileged than for someone who is not. It seems to show a fondness towards the noble criminal, honoring him to the very scaffold." As Sieyès, aware that nobles often escaped severe punishments altogether or were even executed in a different manner than others when they were put to death, continued: "In addition to this abominable distinction that, at bottom, must be thought to be worth preserving only by those projecting some sort of crime, there is then, as is well known, attached a further punishment, namely, that of infamy for the entire family of the unfortunate wretch executed without the benefit of privilege." "It is the law itself," Sieyès stressed, "that is guilty of this atrocity, but there are those who would refuse to reform it!" "The *duty*," he said, "is the same for everyone; the *crime* is the same; why then should the *punishment* be different?" As Sieyès asked rhetorically: "Why do the toadies of the judicial system and the police tremble in carrying out their functions on a member of the privileged orders, even when someone has been caught red-handed, while they show so much brutality towards a poor man who has merely been accused?"[29]

In some places, *Dei delitti e delle pene* was banned altogether for the ideas it expressed. As Margaret Plant's history of then-Inquisition-obsessed Venice emphasizes: "The Venetian inquisitors took umbrage at the section 'Secret Accusations', although Beccaria had been careful to note that he was not discussing any specific government. Yet the lion's mouths set up expressly to receive anonymous accusations were a conspicuous feature of Venice, and Beccaria had spelt out his views that weakness of constitution went with 'tyrannical' government in the use of such practices: secrecy is 'tyranny's strongest shield', he declared." "[T]he Lion's Mouth," as one source stresses, was the "official receptacle" for "denunciations" during the Venetian Inquisition. Citizens could accuse fellow citizens of a crime by writing down the accusation and slipping it through specially placed *Bocca di Leone* ("Lion's Mouth") slots in the walls of the Palazzo Ducale. In August 1764, immediately after its publication, the Venetian Inquisition blocked the importation of *Dei delitti e delle pene* into Venice. Copies of Beccaria's treatise—as just one example of the chilling of free speech that occurred in Venice—were actually recalled from Giambattista Pasquali, a prominent publisher and bookseller. "Since Beccaria's treatise followed closely on Angelo Querini's imprisonment by the Inquisition—Pasquali was a known friend—it was thought that the work had close Venetian connections."

Ferdinando Facchinei—the Italian monk who became a satirist and agricultural reformer—also came out with his scathing attack of *Dei delitti e delle pene* in 1765, just months after the release of Beccaria's book. He emphatically contended that the book had not proven "that the death penalty and torture are useless," and—in the words of one modern source—Beccaria's "egalitarian and utilitarian philosophy" was simply too much for Facchinei, though Facchinei was the author of a life of Isaac Newton. "It is absolutely certain," Facchinei asserted, "that on this earth there never has been a perfect society created by the express will and choice of free men, as our author imagines, and I challenge the socialists and anyone else to find me a single example in all the histories and annals of the world of societies created in that way." Facchinei, one biographical sketch points out, calling him "a defender of the old order" despite having authored a *Life of Newton* (1749 or 1751), offered "the first substantial criticism" of *On Crimes and Punishments*, "directed at the tendency in Beccaria's political thought to exclude religious considerations." Facchinei's venom was not, certainly, the only criticism directed at Beccaria and his rationalistic book, not by a long shot. But it must have stung Beccaria to be called "an enemy of Christianity, a wicked man and a poor philosopher" and "a declared enemy of the Supreme Being."[30] Another critic, Immanuel Kant, preferring an-eye-for-an-eye approach, called Beccaria's argument against capital punishment "pure sophistry."[31]

Though Beccaria's book was the subject of scorn or ridicule in some quarters, the French *philosophes* saw the greatness of it. Beccaria had published other works on discrete subjects—*Del Disordine e de' rimedi delle Monete nello stato di Milano nell'anno 1762* (*On Remedies for the Monetary Disorders of Milan in the Year 1762*, 1762) and *Tentativo Analitico sui Contrabbandi* (*An Attempt at an Analysis of Smuggling*, 1764), but *Dei delitti e delle pene*—they recognized almost immediately—was something different and far more ambitious and important.[32] In January 1766, André Morellet—its French translator—thus happily and enthusiastically invited Beccaria to Paris to be toasted by the city's intelligentsia and its leading literary lights. As Bernard Harcourt puts it: "By January 1766, Morellet sent the young Beccaria the compliments of Diderot and d'Alembert, the philosopher Helvétius, the naturalist de Buffon, the baron d'Holbach, as well as David Hume who was at the time living in Paris—all of whom, Morellet wrote, had read and greatly enjoyed the translation." Morellet had, as the translator of *Dei delitti e delle pene*, taken the liberty of changing Beccaria's manuscript without the author's permission. It was something that Morellet was criticized for by the *philosophe* Melchoir Grimm in his 1765 *Examen de la traduction du Traité des Délits et des Peines de Beccaria par Morellet*. Grateful to have had his writings translated into French by a leading intellectual, Beccaria himself seemed little troubled by the reworking—and substantial reordering—of his book, one that his friend Pietro Verri had already polished. "My work," Beccaria assured Morellet in January 1766, "has lost none of its force in your translation, except in those places where the essential character of one or the other language has imparted some difference between your expression and mine." As Beccaria emphasized in his letter: "I find quite without foundation the objection that your changing the order of my text resulted in a loss of its force. The force consists in the choice of expressions and the *rapprochement* of ideas, neither of which has been harmed."[33]

Intrigued and smitten by *Dei delitti e delle pene*, the French *philosophes* were anxious to meet Cesare Beccaria in person. And Beccaria's fortunes improved as *Dei delitti e delle pene* garnered more and more attention, with Beccaria, after a months' long wait, setting off from Milan for Paris with Alessandro Verri on October 2, 1766.[34] Although the invitation to Beccaria—as well as to his friend, Pietro Verri—had come in January of that year, it took some time before Beccaria, dependent on his father, was able to make arrangements for the trip. Beccaria's father gradually became convinced that it would be useful for his son, Cesare, to travel to Paris to become acquainted with France's intellectual leaders. Plans were thus made for an extended, six-month trip. "Beccaria's father, having little cash available," Marcello Maestro notes, "went so far as to borrow a substantial amount of money for his son's expensive trip." "Equally generous," Maestro writes, "was Alessandro Verri's father," with Maestro explaining that because Pietro Verri was, by then, a government official—a member of the Supreme Economic Council of Milan—he had little time for travel, at least for a prolonged period, and thus declined the invitation. Pietro Verri, Maestro speculates, also "may have been a little too proud to go with Beccaria as a less famous man than his former protégé." For that latter reason, Maestro concludes, "Pietro Verri thought that this brother Alessandro, a little younger than Beccaria, was the man to go to Paris."

Cesare and Alessandro's departure for Paris also spelled the end of the Academy of Fists and its lively periodical. As has been noted, *Il Caffè* ceased to be published in June 1766 as its contributors became involved in official government business or traveled or planned to do so—Alfonso Longo went to Rome, Paolo Frisi had gone to Paris, and Pietro Verri was busy with other important work. Another plausible reason why Pietro Verri may have chosen to stay behind in Milan was because of his personal interest in Cesare Beccaria's wife, Teresa. Several letters of Pietro Verri to his brother, Alessandro, show that, in the 1766 to 1767 period, there was an ongoing relationship between Pietro Verri and Cesare Beccaria's wife, Teresa. That relationship—one that made Cesare Beccaria jealous, and that explains his desire to stay away from Milan for as short a time as possible—lasted until Teresa started another relationship with the richer and younger Marquis Bartolomeo Calderari. It was only after Pietro Verri's liaison with Teresa ended that he turned to Cesare Beccaria's sister, Maddalena, for love. "Of the old Accademia dei Pugni," Maestro explains of the group's demise, one driven by jealousies, the press of business and travel, and the need to move on, "only the name remained, and the last blow came when Beccaria was able finally to accept the invitation of the French group of writers and to start on his trip to Paris."[35]

Alessandro Verri, like his older brother Pietro, was an accomplished writer, but it was understood by all (or at least it should have been) that Beccaria—because of the popularity of his new book—would be the major focus of the French *philosophes'* admiration and attention. Cesare and Alessandro, whom Beccaria described in his first post-departure letter to his wife Teresa, sent from Novara on October 2nd, as "Alessandrino," was said by Cesare to be "very gay" as the two began the more than 500-mile journey from Milan to Paris. From the first day of the trip, it became clear that Beccaria would sorely miss his wife, sending her letter after letter after he left Milan's city limits. On the very day of his departure, Beccaria—longing to stay with his wife but knowing he had to go to Paris and fulfill his commitments—wrote to his "dear spouse and friend": "My heart knows how much I love you, and Alessandro knows it also. I will not talk of my melancholy in order not to increase yours. I will always love you and I swear that in six months, in exactly 182 days, I will be back in Milan and will be in your arms." "Whatever happens," Beccaria assured her, "you will always find in me a true friend and a good husband." "[I]n order to cheer me up," Beccaria wrote of Alessandro, who enjoyed the company of his older brother Pietro, "he tries not to show that he misses his brother." Their coachman, Celestino, Beccaria wrote to his wife, Teresa, that first day, "goes at good pace, is good-natured and well-behaved, and does not have some of those Milanese traits that are so unpleasant." He is "a good man, better than any other Milanese coachman, past, present, or future," Beccaria wrote, trying to remain as upbeat as possible.

The rocky, two-week overland voyage to Paris was, itself, an eventful one, though Beccaria profoundly regretted leaving his young wife, Teresa, from the get-go. In Vercelli, Cesare and Alessandro saw two churches, one of Gothic architecture and one in the Romanesque style, with Beccaria taking note that the city's clocks were "on French time." In Turin, Beccaria was impressed that all the streets were "regularly laid out, all the houses placed at right angles, of the same height and similar palatial architecture," and that "there are majestic squares and a royal palace worthy of the greatest monarch." "We went to the comic opera, very poor performance in a small but very neat theater," Cesare reported to Teresa on October 4th. After crossing the Alps, Beccaria reported from Aiguebelle that he was "well protected against the cold" but that he missed Teresa badly. "The last two days," he wrote on October 7th, "I have felt so depressed being far from you that I was ready to go back if I hadn't thought of how ridiculous my act would have been judged for the rest of my life." As Cesare wrote: "I didn't know that I loved you so much; you are my happiness. I will certainly return earlier if this depression continues." "Give my regards to my father and my mother, greetings to my brothers," he wrote before signing off, referencing his aristocratic parents and his two younger brothers, Francesco and Annibale.

There were lots of new sights to see along the way, though Cesare Beccaria's glum mood must have put a damper on the trip. On October 12th, from Lyons, Beccaria did take note of that city's beauty and said he and Alessandro went to the theater to see a performance of *Tancrède*. He passed along to his wife, Teresa, that the actor who played the lead "was even better than Prevost who, you will remember, had that role in Milan." "My soul, my dearest, I still haven't received any news from you and I feel very depressed," Beccaria added, writing ominously and foreshadowing what was to come, "I am sorry I ever left Milan; it will be difficult for me to stay away even a month or two. If I will not be able to stay at all, I will give the excuse of my health in order to return in an honorable manner. I tell you this, so that you may start saying at home that this air is not good for me." "I think I will see you soon because I am afraid there is no other remedy for my sadness," Beccaria wrote in his letter, sending his greetings "to everyone" with "two kisses to my dear little daughters, especially to Giulietta who is old enough to understand."

Cesare Beccaria's first letter from Paris—the radiant City of Light—was sent on October 19th. "At last I arrived last night in Paris, very tired from the trip," Cesare told Teresa in his letter, adding: "The city is immense; the number of people, the beauty of the streets, everything is very impressive." Beccaria's letter was written after lunch on the 19th, and it shows that he and Alessandro started mingling with the French *philosophes* almost immediately after their arrival. As Beccaria's letter reported: "I have seen Frisi, D'Alembert, Morellet, Diderot, and Baron d'Holbach at whose house I had lunch today. You have no idea of the reception, the courtesies, the praises, the demonstrations of friendship and esteem that they all had for me and my friend Alessandro. I am particularly fond of Diderot, d'Holbach and D'Alembert." "I don't miss anything except you, my dear," Beccaria assured Teresa, telling his wife: "I am staying in a nice little apartment in the center of the city, near all the people we know. Helvétius and Buffon are still in the country. Morellet is always very kind and thoughtful, a real friend who tries to please us in everything. Remember that I love you tenderly, that to Paris and its attractions I prefer my dear wife, my family, and my friends in Milan, but you above all." "This is the truth, my joy, you know that I never lie," he stressed.[36]

In Paris, Cesare and Alessandro most likely just missed the opportunity to meet the Scottish economist Adam Smith, as Professor Peter Groenewegen explains in *Eighteenth-century Economics*. In November 1766, Turgot was just completing the writing of his most important work of economics, *Reflections on the Production and Distribution of Wealth* (1769), the same month that Beccaria "was feted by D'Alembert, Diderot, d'Holbach and Helvétius" on his October to December 1766 trip to France. As Groenewegen emphasizes of Beccaria, Smith, and Turgot, the great triumvirate of eighteenth-century economists who were all in Paris in the same year: "It would be tempting, from the fact that all three were in Paris in 1766, to deduce therefore that they may have met. This is, however, very unlikely." In *Eighteenth-century Economics*, Groenewegen points out: "Beccaria did not arrive in Paris till 18 October. Smith left Paris at the end of October." While "[t]he possibility of a meeting between Turgot, Beccaria and Smith," Groenewegen stresses, "arises from their mutual friendship with Morellet and their known presence at the house of Baron d'Holbach during this year," he notes that Smith's last letter from Paris—one to Lady Frances Scott—is dated October 19, 1766, just the day after Beccaria's arrival, and that "Turgot's correspondence provides no evidence for his presence in Paris in October 1766." It is known that André Morellet later sent Cesare Beccaria Morellet's *Prospectus for an Economic Dictionary* (1769), which contains a long article on money and value that Turgot himself may have authored, so the two definitely stayed in touch after Morellet's work came out. Smith himself was very familiar with the writings of both Italian economists and the French physiocrats, with the physiocrats and their many followers advocating an eighteenth-century version of *laissez-faire* economics. Morellet's *Prospectus for an Economic Dictionary* also ended up in Adam Smith's library, probably sent to Smith by Morellet at Hume's urging.[37]

There was a major focus on economic thought in the second half of the eighteenth century. "The physiocratic school," Marcello Maestro writes in his compact biography of Cesare Beccaria, "had been founded by the Frenchmen François Quesnay and Jean de Gournay." "The members of the group called themselves *les économistes*, until P.S. Dupont de Nemours proposed to call them by the more specific appellation of *physiocrates*," Maestro notes. With their motto—"laissez faire, laissez passer"—and their philosophy about non-intervention by the government in the economic sphere, the physiocrats inspired enlightened reformers to think about increased trade and economic development. "To be sure," Maestro writes of the economic theory that Beccaria and Pietro Verri embraced in part, "there were limitations in the liberalism of the physiocrats: agriculture was for them the fundamental activity of man, and their theory of free trade applied principally to the basic agricultural products." "In the agricultural field itself," Maestro adds, "the physiocratic doctrine did not have a universal character, but allowed for restrictions and barriers at the borders of one's country." Though Beccaria also attached great importance to industrial pursuits as they were a major and growing component of Milan's economy, he did not envision unrestricted free trade between nations, likely because — as Maestro speculates — "the Austrian empire was a very large unit." Both Pietro Verri and Beccaria were pragmatic and thus accepted — as many long had — the necessity of duties. "[A]s long as other countries put restrictions on our goods," Pietro Verri wrote, "we must do the same toward theirs." But Verri — drawn, like Beccaria, to physiocratic principles — saw that another economic system (one that, in effect, anticipated modern globalization) was possible. As Verri wrote: "If all nations could abolish their customs duties, this would certainly be of great reciprocal advantage. Nations would be nearer to each other, commerce would increase, industry would be spurred to greater production, and people would enjoy greater comforts."[38]

In those days, the salons of Paris — like those of London, Rome and Milan — were abuzz with intellectual curiosity and debate, and celebrity guests were warmly welcomed at — and often at the heart of — such gatherings. As Antoine Lilti writes in a new book, *The World of the Salons: Sociability and Worldliness in Eighteenth-century Paris*: "Direct invitation was the decision of the host to invite someone who enjoyed a certain celebrity or whom he or she had encountered at other salons. A successful book or play could provide entrée, but even then, common friends guaranteed the politeness and the amiability of the author." "Famous in France for his book on penal reform," Lilti explains, "Cesare Beccaria was introduced by Morellet, his translator, into intellectual circles and more worldly ones." "Ten years earlier," Lilti observes of another earlier entry into this world of conversation and sociability, "Morellet had been presented to Madame Geoffrin by Trudaine de Montigny, then to Madame Boufflers by Turgot." Because many Parisians left the city during the summer, Morellet had urged Beccaria to come during the winter as it would be easier to help Beccaria make "agreeable and useful acquaintances." "A disciple of Gournay and a close friend of Turgot," Lilti writes of Abbé Morellet, referencing the French economist Jacques Claude Marie Vincent de Gournay (1712–1759), "he spent his entire life preparing a dictionary of commerce, only the prospectus for which was published."[39] Gournay, like Turgot, was a physiocrat, and he helped to spread throughout France the ideas and economic theories of Richard Cantillon — the Irish-French economist whose writings influenced Turgot and many other physiocrats. Pietro Verri himself — as economic historian Peter Groenewegen notes — "shared a number of Turgot's more intimate friends, including Morellet, Trudaine and Condorcet, the first of whom sent him his prospectus for an economic dictionary while the third corresponded with Verri on price theory."[40]

In French and Italian salons, women and men intermingled freely and there was dancing, reading, music and singing, as well as card playing and chess.[41] "The French salon," one source notes, "was primarily a literary circle, open to educated men and women of different social levels: thus it was both a microcosm of polite society and a venue for female emancipation." As that source, *Schubert's Vienna*, characterizes such gatherings: "The French slogan *savoir et savoir vivre* (to be informed and know how to live) nicely characterizes the tone of the French salon. The widely varied subjects discussed both educated and amused the members of the salon; topics embraced philosophy, literature, science, theater, opera, and music, among other things." "Yet the focus of the salon," that source adds, "was conversation itself: speaking and discussing became an art of its own, demonstrating the elegant way of life and *bon goût* (good taste)." With "the lady of the house" said to be at "[t]he heart of every salon," French aristocratic salons, once formed, took place regularly once or twice a week, always on the same day of the week and at the same time.[42] "Italian city coteries of the eighteenth century were," another source reports, "much less concerned with politics than French salons, especially in states where 'foreign' salons (that is, salons hosted by foreign residents in Italy) could be inaccessible to the Italian nobility because of a law prohibiting their association with foreign political and military representatives."[43]

Salons gave intellectuals a chance to exchange ideas, for people from different cultures to interact, and for women to express themselves. In *Political Ideas of Enlightenment Women*, one scholar, Marianna D'Ezio, makes this illustrative note on European salons and the kind of people—and perhaps the kind of ideas being exchanged—at them: "Giuseppina di Lorena Carignano (1753–1794), wife of Vittorio Amedeo of Savoy, was a frequent guest of Piedmontese and French intellectual circles that gathered in the salons of Milan, Turin, and Paris, and was a friend of Pietro Verri, Cesare Beccaria, Rousseau, and Voltaire. In 1771 she wrote *Les Aventures d'Amélie* (1771), a political novel on a utopian female community established on an island, where the exclusively female inhabitants institute a government and a code of laws to guarantee future prosperity—laws that radically challenge any male dominion over life on the island and decree total equality between men and women, give the mother's surname to children, allow women to inherit, and provide education to all women."[44] The daughter of Louis Charles of Lorraine and the wife of Amadeus of Carignan, Giuseppina di Lorena—a princess—was an Italian woman who often resided in Turin but who usually wrote in French. She did not actually publish her writings, although among her unpublished works was *Les Aventures d'Amélie* (*The Adventures of Amelia*)— part of *Un Recueil de mes Rêveries* (*A Collection of My Reveries*)—in which Amelia is captured on a voyage to the Orient when a ship is attacked by pirates.

The plot line of *Les Aventures d'Amélie* shows—in the words of another scholar, Karen Green—that Giuseppina di Lorena Carignano had demonstrated that "the popular conception of a 'natural code of laws', when developed by a woman, could take a very different turn to that developed by a man, such as Rousseau." As Green writes of the plot of *Les Aventures d'Amélie*: Amelia, after her capture, was "[d]estined for the king of Persia's harem" but "Amelia assures him that as a noble, she cannot allow herself to be enslaved, and will kill herself rather than submit to his wishes." "Rather improbably," Green continues of the plot line, "this demonstration of pride results in the king falling in love with her," whereupon he asks Amelia to become his wife, which she, in time, accepts on the condition that he free the women in his harem. After the Persian Empire is reformed, Amelia becomes widowed and is, as a result of an insurrection, forced to flee with her daughter. As Green describes the plot twist that follows: "Once again captured at sea, by Turks, she and the five hundred women accompanied by their children, with whom she had fled, appear to be destined for slavery, when a providential storm shipwrecks their vessel on an uninhabited, but fertile island. Led by Amelia, the women massacre the surviving Turks and set up a new utopian community." In the novel, the new code of laws contained nine articles—including equality before the law, equal education for girls and boys, the abolition of luxury, and an equal role for women and men in educating children. The island was to be governed by eight male and female magistrates, with excess wealth to be distributed equally among the inhabitants of "the happy isle" so as to avoid the growth of inequality, said to be the origin of most crime.[45]

Arriving in Paris in the same month that they set off from Milan, the two young Italians, Cesare Beccaria and Alessandro Verri, met a who's who of French *philosophes*. In addition to many of those Morellet had written of, Beccaria gained entry to prominent figures such as Trudaine de Montigny, the Marquis de Chastellux, and courtesans and high-society hostesses, including Madame Geoffrin and Madame Necker, the wife of Jacques Necker, a future finance minister. "In 1766," one source notes, "the Paris of the Enlightenment welcomed the Milanese political philosopher Cesare Beccaria with both reverence and curiosity." This immediately put Beccaria at the very upper-echelon of French society, a rarified atmosphere he may have been accustomed to in Milan, but not in unfamiliar Parisian circles. Madame Geoffrin, eager to hobnob with famous writers and other figures of importance, deliberately sought out high-profile visitors to her salon, considered "the headquarters of the *Encyclopédie*," including Cesare Beccaria and diplomats such as Ferdinando Galiani and Charles-Henri de Gleichen. "Some of these visitors," one source notes, "recorded their impressions, including Beccaria who expressed great appreciation for the invitations." "Like many travellers to new places," that source observes, "he welcomed the opportunity to make new friends," apparently registering just one complaint. As historian Nancy Collins writes: "Beccaria noted that his fellow countryman Galiani ... was usually invited to supper on the same dates. While he conceded his wit, Beccaria complained that the Neapolitan usually dominated the conversation and rarely paused to listen to other guests." "Galiani," for his part, Collins stresses, "did not record grumblings about the Milanese marquis, but rather wrote of great affection for the meals that he enjoyed in the homes of Goeffrin and others, writing there are no dinner parties in Naples like the ones he had experienced in Paris."[46]

The Neapolitan Abbé Ferdinando Galiani (1728–1787)—a man known for his refined intelligence and sense of humor—was a popular figure in Parisian circles. "I love this abbé to distraction," Denis Diderot confessed to Sophie Volland, sending story after story to his mistress about Galiani's wit and pithy stories. "Round and plump," Galiani was said to be, radiating—in one exemplary assessment—"a contagious *joie de vivre*." "In came abbé Galiani," Diderot reported on one occasion, saying Galiani brought "gaiety, imagination, *esprit*, madness, and everything that makes one forget the afflictions of life." As an account of Galiani's time in Paris observes: "Along with Diderot, d'Alembert, Grimm, Marmontel, Saint-Lambert, Raynal, and Duclos—to mention only the most famous names—Galiani became a regular guest of Madame Geoffrin (Mondays and Wednesdays), Julie de Lespinasse (Tuesdays), Monsieur and Madame Helvétius (Thursdays), the Neckers (Fridays), Madame d'Epinay (Saturdays), and Baron d'Holbach (Sundays)." "[H]is *bon mots*, his anecdotes, his paradoxes," that account emphasizes, "became famous in Paris and Versailles and in time reached the most distant courts of Europe." Beccaria and Galiani both liked to eat, so they shared that trait along with their impressive intellects.[47]

While Galiani did not always make a favorable impression on Cesare Beccaria, and while Alessandro Verri became bitter that Beccaria got the lion's share of the attention, Beccaria made a favorable impression on his new Parisian friends. In her memoirs, Amélie Suard—the wife of the publisher of the *Gazette littéraire de l'Europe* who attended a dinner with Beccaria—was certainly won over by Beccaria. She later had this to say in her reflections: "The marquis Beccaria must have been quite pleased with the way he was received in Paris. He was made the object of the most enthusiastic praises and marks of esteem and admiration. He was rather small in stature, but he had a face that one could never forget; he had regular features and his eyes, of exceptional beauty, seemed to shine with the flame of genius." "He was very proud and at the same time he had the sweetest and most sensitive soul," Suard emphasized of the Italian she got to know through her social interaction with him. Although Alessandro Verri complained to his brother, Pietro, that Beccaria "was interested only in himself," and that he (Alessandro) therefore got little attention, Baron Paul-Henri d'Holbach—after Cesare Beccaria was back in Milan—wrote to Cesare, his new friend, in early 1767, making clear that Beccaria had been well-received by his Parisian hosts. As Baron d'Holbach wrote to Beccaria: "I received your dear letter of January 20 and I was happy seeing that you have not forgotten the poor Parisians who you cruelly abandoned when they were hoping to enjoy your pleasant company during the whole winter. Be assured that they all hope to be worthy of your friendship and that they admire and love you." "These are the feelings of our whole group; all have asked me to be their spokesman and to send you their greetings," d'Holbach stressed.

Even Alessandro Verri, despite his bitterness and seemingly boundless jealousy of Beccaria's literary success, recognized during their visit together to Paris that Beccaria was well-liked by his hosts and hostesses. "Only Beccaria shone and was listened to," Alessandro wrote to his brother, "since Beccaria was in fashion in true Parisian style, because they always go to extremes—all or nothing; and poor Verri was silent in a corner, neglected." "After dinner Beccaria was feeling gay, having drunk some glasses of good wine (I know only too well how he likes it!), and couldn't care less about me." "He was there, intoxicated by his glory," Alessandro fumed, "full of brilliant conversation, determined not to let me open my mouth, talking forever." Approximately two centuries later, Beccaria's biographer, Marcello Maestro, painted Alessandro as a prototypical unreliable narrator, writing: "Returning to Paris from London in February of 1767, Alessandro wrote to Pietro that Beccaria had left a dubious reputation in the French capital; but by now we can put very little faith in what Alessandro says. The truth is that the letters sent to Beccaria by his French friends show only respect and affection for him, despite the undoubted attempts of Alessandro to put him in a bad light."

While Alessandro Verri and Cesare Beccaria were together in Paris for a few weeks, Alessandro sought the counsel of his brother, Pietro, on how to handle his private falling out with Beccaria. Alessandro's letter of November 21, 1766, written from Paris to Pietro, gives some sense of Alessandro's scheming and desperate mood. "You are right, I shouldn't say anything in public against Beccaria," Alessandro wrote, observing that "it would only harm me in the eyes of his friends, who are all enthusiastic about him." As Alessandro stressed of Beccaria's public persona and of Beccaria's many new French friends while complaining bitterly about the way he felt Beccaria was mistreating him: "He seems to all so kind, so good-hearted, and they will consider anything critical of him as a malicious lie. And yet this man who seems so good is full of bitterness, of jealousy, of ingratitude." As Alessandro's letter went on to describe his tempestuous relationship with Beccaria during their days together in Paris: "We go to the theater almost every day; it starts at half past five. Then, at half past eight, after the theater, we usually go to dinner at Baron d'Holbach's house or to a party at Mademoiselle Lespinasse's. Sometimes I prefer to go home, and this annoys our friend, who would like me to stay for his convenience, not because he cares if I stay or not. He is perfectly at home in these groups without me, and yet he is angry if I don't want to stay." The charming and refined Jeanne Julie Éléonore de Lespinasse (1732–1776) ran a popular salon in Paris and became a close friend of Jean le Rond d'Alembert and other writers for the *Encyclopédie*.

Although Beccaria and the Verri brothers grew apart over Cesare and Alessandro's weeks together in Paris, Beccaria's Parisian hosts were part of a close-knit group of intellectuals. Years earlier, Morellet—the respected French economist and translator—had himself become a major player in high society, having been invited to Trudaine's country house. The gatherings of Trudaine—a man committed to scientific progress and to whom David Hume had shown his own writings—were said to serve as a kind of "council" for intellectuals. Beccaria's own translator, the Abbé André Morellet, a man much interested in societal reforms, actually got a little supplemental income from leading French intellectuals such as Trudaine for literary work (*i.e.*, the uncompleted preparation of *Dictionnaire de commerce*).[48] Morellet himself took on many literary and translation projects, including translating portions of a large, canon law text, *Directorium inquisitorum*, that had been written in the fourteenth century by Nicholas Eymerich. Morellet had encountered that book in 1758 while he was staying in Rome, and he had been appalled by the inquisitorial procedures he found in it. In 1762, much to the satisfaction of his fellow French *philosophes*, he published a selection of what he considered to be "the most revolting" passages in the fourteenth-century text. D'Alembert called *Directorium inquisitorum* a "monument of atrocity and ridiculousness, which renders humanity at once so odious and so pitiful," and Voltaire—in turn—told a correspondent, "I am reading with edification the manual of the Inquisition, and I am very angry that Candide killed only one inquisitor."[49]

A visit to Madame Geoffrin's salon, one frequented by writers, diplomats and aristocrats, itself conferred considerable social standing and reputation, with the ambitious Madame Geoffrin—according to her own daughter—having a "passion for celebrity" and "a jealousy for anything that might diminish her éclat." As Antoine Lilti writes of Madame Geoffrin: "She took care to keep up a correspondence with Catherine II and Stanisław II August Poniatowski, and she was so delighted to welcome the two sons of the King of Sweden that Galiani, who was fond of her but rarely missed an opportunity to tease her, claimed that if Voltaire were to rewrite *Candide*, he should situate the dinner of six kings at Madame Geoffrin's." "Madame Geoffrin's successful reputation," Lilti writes, "rested on two things: the presence of men of letters, scholars, and artists at her gatherings, and her ties with aristocrats and European royalty." "The peak of Madame Geoffrin's career," Lilti notes, "was her journey in 1766 to visit the king of Poland, Stanisław August Poniatowski, whom she had had as a guest in her house when he was a young man visiting Paris."[50] "Certain *salons*," another source observes, "became associated with foreigners," with that book pointing out that Madame de Geoffrin's salon also received Hume and Kaunitz and "was a rallying-point for those Poles who clustered around Count Stanisław Poniatowski before he became king of Poland in 1764."[51] The last king of Poland and the Grand Duke of Lithuania, Stanisław II August Poniatowski (1732–1798) reigned from September 7, 1764 to January 7, 1795, and was known as a lover of books, a patron of the arts, and a supporter of reforms. The writings of Montesquieu and Beccaria, of course, were part of the intellectual mix in Poland just as they were elsewhere in Europe. And the Polish king was himself an admirer of Beccaria's work.[52]

Ferdinando Galiani (1728–1787), an Italian economist from Naples, attained fame through his books on money and grain but also by writing about the role of the *cicisbeo* in Neapolitan society and by penning what he called "a poetic joke—a funeral oration on the death of our then recently deceased hangman, the celebrated Domenico Iannacone." In Italian aristocratic circles, including in Cesare Beccaria's Milanese high society, it was—according to one telling description—"absolutely required that every gentleman who had any pretension of belonging to it should be the faithful and de-voted servant of some lady—any lady save his own wife." The *cicisbeo* was the name given to that lady's escort—a nobleman who attended to the lady's everyday needs and who was expected to comport himself with the proper etiquette. He would see to it that the lady's carriage and horses were ready; serve her coffee and make sure she got served her favorite dishes, and pass the time with her by playing tric trac, a form of backgammon. As Giuseppe Baretti wrote, for example, of what was expected of a dutiful cicisbeo while attending church, another of his many duties: "A Cisisbeo who takes his lady to church is bound to precede her by a few paces, to lift up the door-curtain, dip his finger in the holy water, and offer it to the lady, who takes it with a slight curtsey, and crosses herself. The church-beadles then present chairs to the lady and her Cicisbeo." "When mass is over," Baretti continued of the formal and elaborate etiquette expected at that time for, and as regards, an aristocratic woman and her escort, "she gives her prayer-book to the footman or the Cicisbeo, takes her fan, rises, crosses herself, bows to the high alter, and walks out, preceded by the Ci-cisbeo, who again gives her the holy water, and offers her his arm to return home."

All of the old and sometimes stuffy traditions of Italian society—from noblemen wearing perfectly coifed powdered wigs to women appearing in public in elaborate dresses and hairstyles—gave young Italian writers plenty of fodder to poke fun at if they chose to do so. "The dress of the period," historian T. Adolphus Trollope ex-plains of eighteenth-century Italian customs, "seemed to have been invented with the scope of impeding as much as possible every movement of the body, and of re-quiring as much time as possible in the putting it on and the getting it off again";

women "wore silks and brocades nearly as solid and massive as boards, and of exceeding richness" and "[t]he dressing of the hair, for both men and women, was perhaps the most important part of the whole business of the toilette, as it was certainly that which consumed the most time." As Trollope explains: "The use of powder was universal, and the importance attached to success in causing it to fall with the utmost possible lightness on the elaborately arranged hair, and to the perfectly equal distribution of it, was such that no means of attaining the end in view was thought sufficiently efficacious save imitating the fall of the snow from heaven. An apartment was, therefore, provided in well-ordered palaces specially destined and adapted to this operation." As Trollope's description continues: "The patient entered, covered from neck to foot with a large sheet; a floury shower began to fall, and in a few minutes he emerged more than half smothered by the dust-laden atmosphere, but with the exquisite architecture of his curls powdered *à ravir*, and not a hair displaced from its artistically ordained position."

Pietro Verri, for instance, once published "An Account of a Prodigious Comet observed at Milan in the Year 1763," the meteor in question said to be "the hair of a noble lady who appeared in society adorned by such a *chef-d'œuvre* of hair-dressing art." As one source likewise writes of Ferdinando Galiani's own rise to fame through jocularly addressing his audience on a much different topic: "The young Galiani was a precocious, classically educated scholar with a love for satire. At the age of nineteen he published *Componimenti varii per la morte di Domenico Jannacone* (1748), a series of imaginary obituaries in honour of the public hangman in the pompous style of a number of local notables." In *A Wicked Company: The Forgotten Radicalism of the European Enlightenment*, historian Philipp Blom emphasizes of the writer who skyrocketed to literary fame on Italian soil before Beccaria: "Born in the Italian town of Chieti in the Abruzzi region, Galiani had shown his brilliance early, and when he took the lower orders to become an *abbé* at the age of twenty-two, he had already published books that made him famous in the two areas that would establish his reputation: an economical treatise, *Della moneta* (*On Money*), and a satirical one, *Raccolta in morte del boia* (*Eulogies on the Death of a Hangman*)." "In 1759, at age thirty-one," that source notes of his assignment as a diplomat from 1759 to 1769 at the Neapolitan embassy in Paris, "the *abbé* took up his diplomatic appointment, and soon he was found regularly at some of the leading salons, including Holbach's, whose intellectual range and frankness attracted him." Galiani wrote in both Italian and French, and his correspondents included Voltaire, Diderot, Turgot and Morellet.[53]

Cesare Beccaria, the young, newly discovered talent from Milan, did not feel entirely comfortable in the environs of Paris and its high-powered salons—the ones frequented by Galiani. Many of his hosts were older and, truth be told, far more accomplished at that point, and Beccaria—suddenly thrust into the limelight—felt depressed and ill at ease without his wife by his side. Wine served as a good social lubricant. But Beccaria, whether out of that sadness or discomfort, his ego or the jealousy of his own friends, or perhaps simply because he drank a bit too much, managed to alienate himself from the Verri brothers over the course of his short Parisian trip. The friendship between Pietro Verri and Beccaria, Roberto Bizzocchi writes, summarizing extensive 1766 correspondence between Pietro and Alessandro Verri, "was deteriorating" during Cesare and Alessandro's long trip to Paris. As Bizzocchi explains of what caused the rift: "The Verri brothers did not like the way in which Beccaria, in the Parisian *conversazioni*, pretended to forget the role they were convinced they had played in the conception of *On Crimes and Punishments*. Moreover, they found it ridiculous and detrimental that he should yearn to return to Milan as soon as possible, which in fact he did, in order to be near to his young wife." There may, in fact, have been more than a kernel of truth in the Verri brothers' frequent complaints, as Beccaria's book was written — and edited and published — with considerable assistance and ideas from others, including from the Verri brothers. "Cesare Beccaria," a book on Italian literature emphasizes, "probably owes much of his fame to Pietro, for without the continual encouragement and practical help of the energetic friend, on whom he leant almost entirely in his early life, it is highly improbable that the nervous, retiring mathematician would ever have brought himself to write his famous 'Dei delitti e delle pene.' " As that source adds of Beccaria's book: "This work produced as important results in the world as any that has ever been published. It may be true that its author is indebted to the French humanitarians for many of his ideas. He always declared that the reading of Montesquieu's 'Lettres persanes' marked the turning-point in his life. But his little book, written in two months in the Palazzo Verri, largely as the result of the conversations of the 'Pugni,' made the first definite appeal for the abolition of torture and reform in criminal legislation."[54]

In a letter dated November 3, 1766, Pietro gave his brother, Alessandro, his by-then quite jaded assessment of not only Cesare Beccaria but of the liaisons and dalliances of his wife, Teresa, back in Italy, where, while Cesare was away, she was making the rounds at villas in the Lombard countryside owned by Bartolomeo Calderara. A wealthy aristocrat, Calderara served for years as Teresa's aristocratic male escort or — in the language of the day — her *cavalier servente*. "This was the custom," one Italian historian writes, "by which married ladies were accompanied in all their social appearances by a cavalier servente or a cicisbeo who was not their husband — a husband who in his turn could be the cicisbeo of another lady." A *cavalier servente* or *cicisbeo* — the prevalent eighteenth- and nineteenth-century Italian tradition, one based in contract that piqued the interest and sarcasm of the poet Giuseppe Parini and the curiosity of many Englishmen and other foreigner observers — has been variously defined or described as "[a] gentleman that chaperones married ladies"; "a lover of an Italian married lady, one who dangles after a married lady"; or "the professed gallant or dangler of a married female."[55] Whether described as a *cavalier servente* or a *cicisbeo*, the novelty of Italian male escorts led to shock and much speculation about adultery amidst often loveless, arranged marriages.[56]

A man of letters, Pietro Verri was extremely sensitive about being slighted, and he really let loose about all things Beccaria in his correspondence with his brother, Alessandro. As Pietro Verri, who felt hurt and slighted, mocked Cesare Beccaria and his younger wife Teresa — a woman Pietro labeled a "*testina*," or "an empty little head" — in his November 1766 letter to his brother:

What impression will our friend make after such cowardly and ridiculous behaviour? And for whom? For his wife, who goes enjoying herself to the Costa,
to Turano, in good company, and who the very day of his departure enjoyed
herself very happily!... She is well, very well, and I assure you that she never
enjoyed herself so much in the autumn as now. His father, the Marquis, finds
that in this way she is not giving her husband the proof of love he deserves,
but with her he pretends and will continue to do so. He told me that a moment
after your departure he entered her room and, seeing her in tears, began to
console her telling her that after all her husband was well and would be returning soon; to which do you know what she replied? 'I'm not crying because
I doubt this, I'm crying because I won't be able to see Paris'.

Except for the summer, when Cesare and his wife, Teresa, escaped from Milan to the
surrounding countryside, they lived with their small children at Cesare's parents'
house in the city—a not uncommon practice for young couples centuries ago.[57] As
Marcello Maestro describes this time period: "Cesare's relationship with his father
was now fairly normal. There was, to be sure, a divergence of views and temperament
between them, but they lived together without too much trouble in the family house
on Via Brera, and in the summer they all spent some time at the country estate of
Gessate, not far from the city."

Notably, Pietro Verri's account differed markedly from the bleak account that
Teresa herself was painting and giving to her husband, Cesare, while he was away in
France. "[I]n her shaky and picturesque Tuscan-Milanese," Roberto Bizzocchi writes
of a letter Teresa sent to her husband, Cesare, Teresa gave this report of her travel
and activities and her self-described depressed mood:

I have been to the Costa at Ello, on Lake Como at Domaso, as far as the
Griggioni, now I am in Milan for a day and then I'm going to Pizzigetone
and Turano, but I have to tell you, my dear joy, that nothing gives me pleasure, on the contrary everything makes me sad and my sadness is written on
my face, all the more so because Calderara at times, with his hardly gracious
replies, doesn't stop needling me, to which I can't sufficiently give vent by
crying, but I try to be patient and think of his other good qualities which
cancel these. Dear little [Mar]quis, don't say anything, when you reply, about
this comment on Calderara, as he wants to see all your letters and I wouldn't
like us to make a mess [*scarpiatola*] of things.

As Teresa, eager to hear about the places that Cesare was experiencing, wrote to her
husband on October 11 before he reached Paris: "My dear Chesino, please, please
write me at every opportunity; even one day of delay makes me desperate and I think
I may die." As historian Marcello Maestro wrote of the pet names Teresa and Cesare
employed in their letters: "Chesino was short for Marchesino, little Marchese. Beccaria
sometimes also called his wife Chesina."

Cesare Beccaria—"perhaps because of his shy and confidential nature, perhaps
also because he did not fit in with the other enlightened intellectuals," as another source
reports—did not stay away from Milan for the six months that had been planned. As

Bernard Harcourt, who has studied Beccaria's trip, writes: "Beccaria began to attend salons, but his stay in Paris was abbreviated. He fled Parisian society in less than two months—perceived by many in Paris as a simpleton." As another commentator, Justice Dominic Massaro, an Italian-American who served on the Supreme Court of New York, adds of Beccaria's time to Paris in his own biographical sketch after examining the historical record: "Escorted from salon to salon, he was honored as mankind's benefactor. But he cared little for society and was not up to the attention." Though Beccaria's reformism "was warmly applauded" by the French *philosophes*, historian Jonathan Israel stresses in his book, *Democratic Enlightenment*, the "shy and uneasy" Beccaria was reportedly "taciturn and made a poor impression," though the assessments vary widely depending upon the commentator. Ultimately, Cesare ended up quarreling with Alessandro, thus poisoning his relationship with the Verri brothers and leading Cesare and Alessandro to prematurely part ways. Beccaria, for his part, drew inward amidst the spotlight and all of the glare, secretly planning an early return to Milan and putting his trust about his sudden change of plans in his wife, Teresa, and Bartolomeo Calderara, her *cavalier servente*. As Beccaria wrote to Teresa on October 12, 1766: "I confide in you totally, and you must be privy to everything because nothing must be hidden between us, but don't tell anyone except Calderara."

The real reason behind the tension and dramatics between the Verri brothers and Beccaria during the 1766 trip to Paris becomes apparent from a review of correspondence between Pietro and Alessandro Verri. After learning from Alessandro, via a letter dated November 3, 1766, that André Morellet had declined to translate Alessandro's *Il Caffé* articles into French, and after later learning that Morellet had no interest in Pietro Verri's manuscripts on Lombardy and that a fifth reprinting of Cesare Beccaria's *Dei delitti e delle pene* would be released in French, the Verri brothers realized that the French *philosophes* and *Encyclopédistes* had little to no interest in their work, but were only interested in Beccaria's. Both Italian and French aristocrats and intellectuals could be incredibly proud—and they liked to argue, sometimes if only for the sake of argument. In Dominique-Joseph Garat's *Mémoires*, he recalled that when Morellet and Pietro Verri did meet, that "although the conformity of their principles made dispute almost impossible, these conversations would have felt like an eternity to them without the resource of dispute." As Morellet wrote of his own approach in his own *Mémoires*: "I was ... violent in dispute, but my antagonist could never reproach me for the least insult. My warmth was only for my opinion, and never against my adversary; and I sometimes spit blood after a dispute in which I had not let escape a single personal remark."

In *The Republic of Letters: A Cultural History of the French Enlightenment*, Dena Goodman explains that the French writer Dominique-Joseph Garat (1749–1833) "wrote that the editorial team of Suard and Jean-François Arnaud 'conceived and executed under two successive titles, the *Journal étranger* and the *Gazette littéraire*, the project of making known to France, either by analytical extracts or by complete translations, all that would appear in Europe in the arts, in the sciences, in letters, no matter what their success, their *éclat*, or simply the noise they made.'" "Two periodical works," Garat explained of the collaborative relationship that developed between

French and Italian intellectuals, "contributed powerfully to the opening of new literary and philosophical communications" between them. The *Journal étranger* and *Il Caffé* — the latter, Garat wrote, "edited in Milan with no less success by the marquis de Beccaria, the marquis de Véry, and ... their collaborators" — provided for a regular exchange of views, at least for those intellectuals who had their work translated in the other language. As Garat explained: "Articles from the *Journal étranger* often went into *le Cafè*, those of *le Cafè* into the *Journal étranger*. Never have new ideas had such rapid circulation at long distance."[58]

Before Cesare Beccaria returned home to Milan in early December, his letters to Teresa reflected sullen loneliness and distance-driven heartache. Though he had confessed to a friend only three years earlier that his passion for his wife had "changed into sincere regard, a true friendship and an inexpressible tenderness," his letters from Paris suggested a renewed infatuation and unquenchable longing for nearness and news of Teresa's activities. "I have finally received your letter of the 11th," Cesare wrote to Teresa on October 25th, concocting his plan to leave Paris earlier than planned: "I will tell you very confidentially that my health is good, but you must say the opposite, so that I have a good excuse for leaving." "I am returning to Milan; please help me in this decision," Cesare urged Teresa, asking her to be complicit in his plan. "To my parents," he confided to his wife, "I am writing about my health, not as it is, but as it is useful for my purpose." "It is hard for me to lie and pretend," Cesare reassured his wife, still deeply depressed but trying to maintain his honor and having carefully weighed and considered his options, "but there is no other way; and in this case I am doing something good for myself without harming anyone." Alessandro Verri, in a letter to his brother Pietro, himself took note of Beccaria's unhappiness — all brought about by Beccaria's separation from his wife. "I thought at moments that he would lose his mind," Alessandro wrote to Pietro, saying Beccaria — with his vivid imagination — was "absolutely sure that his wife would die." "I will never travel again with men who have too much imagination," Alessandro wrote, adding: "Here in Paris Beccaria is received with much adoration. I am only a satellite." "I suppose that this is how it should be, I am not envious," Alessandro wrote with, it must be said, more than a hint of envy.

"My dear, my soul," one of Beccaria's translated, representative letters read, "I still haven't received your news." "I'm in the deepest melancholy," he wrote, adding: "you must know that, if it weren't for the sake of reason and the fear of making a fool of myself for ever, I wanted to come back as quickly as possible without reaching Paris and fly back into your arms." "I didn't think I loved you so much, I see that you are necessary for me," Beccaria declared, sounding much more like his younger self, the one who had — setting aside all familial protocol — so voraciously taken on his father's obstinacy. In another letter, Beccaria plaintively asked his wife to be in Milan — at their home — for his earlier-than-planned return. As Cesare wrote to Teresa on November 16, 1766, knowing that his wife was traveling extensively in his absence: "Dearest and most beloved wife, I have received all your letters. I thank you for your love for me. You have done well to enjoy yourself and go on your trips; I have also tried to enjoy myself, but in vain; my sadness is incurable, and all the causes make me want to return to Milan." "Dear joy," Beccaria's letter continued, using another pet name for her, "because of your love for me, be in Milan to meet me, it would be very unpleasant for me if in that happy moment you were elsewhere."

Even a letter from Pietro Verri—and a letter from Cesare Beccaria's own wife, Teresa, one that Pietro Verri had engineered and urged her to write—could not convince Beccaria to stay in Paris longer than he did. In a long letter dated October 26, 1766, Pietro wrote to his friend, Cesare, with a futile plea after Pietro got wind of Beccaria's plan to cut his trip short: "Your intention, as described in your letter, has saddened me very much." "Some people," Pietro counseled, "will ascribe your hurried return to an infantile weakness, and even the most reasonable persons will say that you can rise to a high level with the pen and that you sink to a very low one when you stop writing." In an attempt to guilt Beccaria into staying longer, Pietro emphasized: "I am saying this only because I feel the fear of your shame, the fear that you will be despised for the rest of your life." On the subject of Beccaria's family, Pietro added these words of assurance: "Your wife is in good health and if she were in Paris instead of you she would not have your worries; your daughters are well also and do not need you. Your good father would certainly be sorry if the money he gave you served not to bring praise for you and help to find you a good position, but to make you a laughing-stock and to show that you don't know how to behave in life." "I tell you all this," Pietro wrote, afraid of the consequences of Beccaria's immaturity, "as a friend who knows that your good qualities more than compensate for your faults ... a friend who asks you to have some pity on yourself and on your reputation." Teresa's letter—following Pietro's line of argument— had a similar theme, if softer tone, with Teresa writing to her husband: "Perhaps some people will say that you were not well received in Paris if you come back now; and also I think that if you stay longer you may find something good for your career."

Because he was so anxious to get back to Milan to reunite with his wife, Beccaria did not heed the advice and actually passed up the chance to meet Voltaire near his château, Château Ferney, outside of Geneva, Switzerland. Morellet had visited Voltaire in Ferney in June 1766, with Voltaire's *Commentaire sur le livre des délits et des peine* written after Morellet's visit.[59] Voltaire himself had first been exposed to *Dei delitti e delle pene* when he got an Italian language version of Beccaria's book from James Macdonald, a young Scotsman who had just returned from Italy, a popular destination on Grand Tours for those touring continental Europe from the British Isles. Voltaire—as he told a friend—wanted to greet Beccaria face to face, with Voltaire immediately calling Beccaria "a brother" who had produced a work of "good philosophy." "Voltaire's writing of the *Commentary*," historian Marcello Maestro observes, "started a relationship between the two men characterized by mutual admiration and the friendliest feelings." As Maestro explains: "Beccaria had instructed his bookseller, Chirol of Geneva, to send him all of Voltaire's publications as soon as they appeared, and there still exist copies of Voltaire's books with Beccaria's marginal notes." Barthélemy Chirol is known to have written to Beccaria in French, promising—on one occasion—to send him a poem written by Voltaire. "Voltaire," for his part, Maestro continued, "praised Beccaria at every turn, calling him 'a beneficent genius whose excellent book has educated Europe.'"

But despite their mutual admiration for one another, Voltaire and Beccaria's relationship was one that developed only through letters. "In spite of Voltaire's desire to see Beccaria, the two men never met," Marcello Maestro wrote in his biography, *Cesare Beccaria and the Origins of Penal Reform*. As Maestro reported of later events: "Although Beccaria planned a trip to Ferney in 1767, he never made it, probably on account of his reluctance to travel, especially after his trip to Paris." One of Voltaire's letters to Beccaria, dated May 30, 1768, also indicates that a visit never materialized, with Voltaire writing: "Why couldn't I have the honor of seeing you, of embracing you and, may I say, of crying with you!" In July 1766, François-Jean de la Barre—a young French nobleman—had, much to Voltaire and Beccaria's chagrin, been tortured and beheaded and had his body burnt on a pyre for blasphemy and sacrilege for mocking a religious procession, and Voltaire and other *philosophes* were still in mourning. "Voltaire's powerful *Account of the Death of the Chevalier de La Barre*," one English-language edition of Voltaire's writings (the first to translate and reprint Voltaire's account of La Barre's death), published in 2000, emphasizes, was "composed in 1766 and dedicated to the marquis de Beccaria." "At least I have the consolation of telling you how much I esteem you, and how much I love and respect you," Voltaire's May 30, 1768 letter to Beccaria read.[60]

The intensity of eighteenth-century public interest in Cesare Beccaria's *Dei delitti e delle pene* cannot be understated. The story of the first English language translation of Beccaria's book—told by historian Rosamaria Loretelli in a 2017 article in which she observes how quickly Beccaria's book became a bestseller—is revealing. In her article, she takes note, in particular, of the intersecting roles of Pietro Molini, a prominent London publisher and bookseller who had a home and shop on Bridge Street and who lived there with his brother Jacopo; of Filippo Mazzei, an enthusiastic reader of Beccaria's work who, in 1765, had been accused of smuggling banned books into Italy and who later played an important role in the American Revolution; of John Almon, the publisher of the first English translation of *Dei delitti e delle pene*, a one-time journalist for the Whig newspaper *Gazetteer*, and a fierce critic of George III's administration; and of John Wilkes, a friend of John Almon's who, with Almon, "fought battles against arbitrary arrest and the concentration of power in the hands of the executive" and who favored freedom of the press and the right of newspapers to publish parliamentary debates verbatim. Pietro Molini imported books for his affluent English clients and, in 1765, he had offered—in Loretelli's words—"a very rich catalogue of Latin, French and Italian books for sale." In a letter sent from London to the Congregazione del S. Offizio that same year, Mazzei had been accused of shipping books to Italy without their front pages and of bringing the front pages through a different route. "In this operation, said the letter," Loretelli reports of Mazzei's activities, "his 'right arm' was Pietro Molini."

Shortly before the first English translation of *Dei delitti e delle pene* appeared, Alessandro Verri wrote to his brother Pietro on January 15, 1767: "Beccaria's book is being translated into English for the first time and my host Molini is involved in this operation. I will bring a copy of it with me to Paris because it will see the light in a few days." On February 8, 1767, Pietro wrote back: "I have informed Beccaria that his work has been translated into English and will be published in a few days." On February 26, 1767, ten days after Alessandro had departed for Calais, Pietro Verri again wrote to his brother with further instructions: "By way of Frisi send me a copy of the English edition of *Dei delitti* and any reviews it has received." As Loretelli notes of the prominence of the Milanese scientist Pietro Verri referenced in his letter: "Paolo Frisi was an Italian philosopher and mathematician. He was at that time already a member of the Paris Academy of Sciences, of the Royal Society, of the Imperial Academy of Saint Petersburg, and of the Berlin and Stockholm Academies."

In unpacking the mystery of how the English translation of *Dei delitti e delle pene* came about and the key players behind it, Rosamaria Loretelli surmises that Pietro Molini "was involved in some forms of collaboration either with the publisher Almon or with the unknown translator" and "might have provided the Italian text, or supplied information about its publishing history for the translator's preface, or helped with the actual translation." John Almon had started his own printing shop in Piccadilly in 1763 after resigning from the *Gazetteer*, and he became—as Loretelli writes— "the most distinguished bookseller of the Whig party, and his shop turned into the official seat of the opposition club *The Coterie*." Almon was a frequent correspondent of John Wilkes, a well-known politician who opposed the use of general warrants (which specified the offense but not the alleged offender). In a seditious libel case that is now remembered as *The North Briton: Issue No. 45* affair, Almon asserted the illegality of general warrants through a journalistic campaign. After participating in a duel Wilkes was forced into exile in France, where he stayed with his daughter, Polly, from 1763 until 1768, except for a long trip to Italy in early 1765 and two surreptitious trips to England in hopes of securing a pardon. All the while, Wilkes had stayed in touch with Almon across the English Channel even as Parliament, in 1766, banned the use of general warrants—legal instruments once used by English officials to arrest the authors, printers or publishers of seditious libels without naming those to be arrested. As Loretelli recounts of Wilkes' period of exile: "During those years, Almon kept Wilkes constantly informed about the vicissitudes of English politics and of what Whig politicians thought of him. He also regularly sent Wilkes pamphlets, books, newspapers and all the printed materials he requested."

Both John Wilkes and John Almon supported the American Revolution, which was unfolding during the years of their correspondence. "The year 1767," Loretelli explains, "was crucial to Almon's publishing house." As Loretelli recounts: "Besides printing *An Essay on Crimes and Punishments* in February, in May they issued the first number of the *Political Register* and, during the summer, the first English edition of *The Examination of Doctor Benjamin Franklin, Relative to the Repeal of the American Stamp Act*, an account of Franklin's testimony of 13 February 1766 before the House of Commons." "Wilkes," Loretelli adds of Almon's promotion of Wilkes and his causes and of Almon's own printing activities, "was soon well-known in the American colonies, and from 1775 to 1784 Almon published a monthly report of American news, titled *The Remembrancer*." The personal connections between men living in Milan, Paris, and London—as well as those living in the American colonies—proved to be a powerful combination, and one that bore much intellectual and revolutionary fruit. When Almon started to promote the American cause, Mazzei was in London and Pietro Molini—the man identified as Mazzei's "right arm"—came into contact with Alessandro Verri. In fact, Alessandro Verri, who got to know Benjamin Franklin in London, stayed at Molini's house from December 1766 to February 1767. "[I]n Paris," Loretelli observes, Wilkes reconnected "with a former friend from his university days in Leiden, Baron Paul Henri Thiry d'Holbach, who conducted what was probably the most lively intellectual *salon* in Paris, a meeting place for the French *philosophes* and foreign intellectuals visiting the city." "Renewing a friendship which had been very warm twenty years before," Loretelli writes of the strong Wilkes-d'Holbach connection, "Wilkes regularly attended d'Holbach's *salon*, meeting his many Parisian guests and foreign visitors." "Among D'Holbach's most intimate English friends," one scholar has noted, "were Hume, Garrick, Wilkes, Sterne, Gibbon, Horace Walpole, Adam Smith, Franklin, Priestley, James McDonald."

Both John Wilkes and d'Holbach, like many thinkers of that era, opposed despotism. They had both been involved in dissemination of Nicolas Antoine Boulanger's *Recherches sur l'origine du despotisme oriental*; Wilkes, in fact, had translated Boulanger's work into English as *The Origin and Progress of Despotism, in the Oriental, and other Empires of Africa, Europe, and America* (1763). After Wilkes spent five months in Italy in 1765 (with stops in Milan, Florence, Bologna and Naples) with an Italian mistress, he had returned to Paris on July 2nd of that year—and it was in Paris that Wilkes built relationships with Alessandro Verri and Cesare Beccaria. As Loretelli explains of the background: "Until August 22, 1765, Beccaria's friends of the Accademia dei pugni (*Academy of the Fisticuffs*)—among them, Pietro and Alessandro Verri— discussed with Beccaria the revision of the third edition of *Dei delitti e delle pene* to be printed as fifth edition. On the 24th, Beccaria sent everything to d'Alembert. At that time, Wilkes had been in Paris, back from his Italian tour, for almost two months, and was very likely acquainted at d'Holbach's with the new edition and Morellet's translation being both prepared." "The British Library," Loretelli stressed, "holds a manuscript letter in English from d'Holbach to Wilkes," from late 1766, she notes, "where Beccaria is mentioned as a person Wilkes was well acquainted with." In that letter, Baron d'Holbach observed that "Marquis Beccaria is going to leave us very soon being obliged to return to Milan; count Veri [sic] will set out for England at the same time." November 1766 letters from Alessandro Verri to his brother, Pietro, which describe "Mr. Wilkes" as "among my friends," also confirm that Cesare Beccaria and Alessandro Verri met Wilkes in Paris, with meetings taking place both at d'Holbach's *salon* and at Wilkes' home. Alessandro called Wilkes a "famous man" of "infinite esprit and high erudition, infinitely amiable," with Wilkes inviting both Cesare Beccaria and Alessandro Verri to dine at his home on November 22, 1766.

In describing what led to the English translation of *Dei delitti e delle pene*, Rosamaria Loretelli writes that "[a] powerful thrust must have come from Wilkes' direction, given his beliefs in enlightenment principles and his admiration for the 'great friend of man, the *Marquis Beccaria*." In explaining in detail how the English translation of Beccaria's book was transformed from earlier Italian editions (just as Morellet's French translation had itself transformed the structure of Beccaria's Italian manuscript), Loretelli further emphasizes: "In the English translation, the Italian preface, entitled 'A chi legge' [*To the reader*] and the 'Avviso' [*Notice*] (one or two, according to the different printings) have disappeared, together with De Soria's *Guidizio* and Verri's *Risposta* to Facchinei, which brought the number of pages in the Italian fifth and sixth editions to more than three hundred. The English edition, instead, has 179 pages of the *Essay on Crimes*, plus 79 pages of Voltaire's *Commentary*." As Loretelli's perceptive analysis of the English translation continues: "The translation of Beccaria's text begins with his 'Introduction', and contains all the expansions which were inserted into the fifth Italian edition for the first time. This was the last edition for which explicit evidence exists of the author revising it. The text of this edition was reproduced in the two sixth editions."

Rosamaria Loretelli's conclusion: "Therefore, when Beccaria's book was translated into English, there were three editions of the same text, a fifth and two sixth editions. John Almon's *An Essay on Crimes and Punishments* was based on one of them. However, if we collate the translation with the Italian original carefully, we see that the translator had no doubt Morellet's French translation on his desk as well, since there are passages whose structure and very wording follow the lesson of the French version." The first two sentences of the English translation of Beccaria's introduction, in fact, come directly from Morellet's version of the text. In noting that Beccaria's book "galvanized the attention of European intellectuals and sovereigns" and "challenged contemporary criminal justice systems, placing the subject in a broad philosophical and social perspective," Loretelli gives this assessment after her artful sleuthing into the creation of the first English translation: "The fact that Voltaire's and Beccaria's works appeared together in Almon's 1767 edition for the first time, and that Voltaire is named as author of the anonymous *Commentaire* at such an early date, is evidence enough of the fact that the people involved in this publication were well acquainted with the French intellectual world and knew it from the inside."[61]

Chapter 4

Pride and Privilege — and Political Economy

Cesare Beccaria's 1766 trip to Paris did not proceed in the way it had originally been planned. A homesick Beccaria, desperately missing his wife, Teresa, and incredibly anxious to reunite with her, thus returned to Milan after staying in Paris for only a short time, from October to early December of 1766.[1] There may, in fact, have been unstated reasons—or even paranoia or pressing ulterior motives—for why Beccaria was so keen to cut his trip short. He may have been suspicious or jealous of another man—or, perhaps, of more than one man—catering to his young wife's affections. Even worse, there was the prospect of the birth of a child by Teresa that would not square with Cesare's time away from her while Cesare was in the City of Light. Beccaria got back to Milan on December 12, 1766, and Teresa gave birth to a child—a little boy—on August 20, 1767. "In this case," Roberto Bizzocchi writes, taking note of the usual nine-month period for a pregnancy, "the calculations about the time were made, not without a trace of ill will, by the implacable Pietro Verri, as he informed his brother Alessandro of the progress of Teresa Blasco's pregnancy." "The first announcement, on 30 March 1767," Bizzocchi explains of the relations of Teresa's cicisbeo, "also hints at the bad mood of the young Bartolomeo's staid relatives." According to Pietro Verri's March 30, 1767 letter:

> The little Marquise is so pregnant that it is visible: she cannot be more than three and a half months, calculating her husband's return, but in terms of size it seems a longer period; all the Litta and Calderari group, all those who are hostile to her ostentation and bad manners have an almanac to hand, ready to calculate this birth, which, fixing her husband's return on 12 December, should occur towards mid-September, and yet it is expected at the beginning of August.

Alessandro Verri, as historian Marcello Maestro notes, was the first of the Verri brothers "to show hostility toward Beccaria, partly because of differences in their temperaments and partly because Alessandro had resented the secondary position in which he had found himself in Paris." Though Alessandro Verri and Cesare Beccaria had quarreled and failed to get along in the environs of Paris, it was Pietro Verri, Maestro observes, "who soon became even more vindictive and implacable toward his old friend." Both Verri brothers—to use Maestro's words—"developed a real hatred toward their old friend," something that may reflect the egos and fierce pride felt by Italian aristocrats of that age. At the start, Pietro appears to have just habitually taken the side of his younger brother, with Pietro not able to assess first-hand who was behaving badly in Paris. "What can I say to you?" Pietro had written to Alessandro in Paris, adding: "I see from your letter that you are completely right and Beccaria is completely wrong; your heart is ulcerated by his conduct, and so is mine." As Maestro then summarizes Pietro's extensive correspondence with his brother, Alessandro: "In every letter to his brother, Pietro now showed feelings of increasing enmity toward Beccaria which at first are not easily explained." After Beccaria's return to Milan, Pietro saw him the day after he got back. "Beccaria arrived yesterday, received with the greatest sweetness by his dear spouse," Pietro wrote to Alessandro before penning these words in that letter: "I saw him today and he told me frankly that nobody is dearer to him than his wife.... He didn't say a word to show that anyone in Paris knows of my existence.... You see that he treats me as he treated you."

To say that Pietro Verri's ego was bruised would be a gross understatement, and Pietro and Alessandro fed upon each other's disdain for their once close friend. A few days after Beccaria's return to Milan, where Beccaria would continue to live on a modest allowance from his father, Pietro again wrote to his brother, Alessandro, to reinforce their now mutual dislike—indeed, loathing—of Beccaria. "There are more and more reasons for the coolness in my friendship with Beccaria," Pietro relayed. "He will try," Pietro wrote of Beccaria, "to come back to me once the Parisian aura has evaporated, but the pure flame that I had for his glory will not be there and he will not have my heart anymore.... Europe has declared that he is greater than I; my own conscience says the opposite." In another letter to Alessandro, Pietro announced that he would no longer have a friendship with Beccaria. "I really have no animosity toward him, nor can I reproach him for anything," Pietro wrote, speaking of Beccaria as Pietro openly wrestled with his own conscience and feelings: "He never lied to me, he never was disrespectful toward me." "He is not able to deceive," Pietro continued of Beccaria, saying it "would be too tiring for him; he enjoys the pleasures that men give him, and since the greatest pleasures come from his friends, he enjoys friendship very much." "Now," Pietro continued of his former friend, "he wants to enjoy his good luck and the superiority that the public has given him over his friends; his friends resent his attitude, this resentment is painful to Beccaria, and therefore he avoids his friends."

Shortly thereafter, Pietro had another update for his brother as the awkwardness between the Verri brothers and Beccaria spiraled out of control. As Pietro wrote: "I saw Carli and Countess Somaglia, and they both think that Beccaria has changed very much since his return, that he now smiles with an air of superiority and gives the impression that he is there to protect the unhappy human species." "As long as Beccaria needed a friend," Pietro lamented, "he found it in me; now his needs have changed, and he is looking for satellites and protégés." Pietro reported that Beccaria "forgets that men are capricious and in a few years he may not have all this admiration; and he forgets that if we two really wanted it, we could destroy his reputation." "In a month," Pietro confided to Alessandro, making a private threat, "I could find in Montesquieu, in Voltaire and in Grevius many passages similar to his, so that he would look like a plagiarist." "I will not do this," Pietro assured his brother, "but I am satisfied that I could do it if I wanted to." Johann Georg Grevius (1632–1703)—often spelled Grævius—was a German scholar.[2] In yet another letter, sent by Pietro to Alessandro on August 8, 1767, Pietro privately skewered Beccaria yet again, getting even more personal and making reference to a gift exchange between Alessandro and Cesare on their late 1766 trip to Paris. As Pietro wrote to his brother: "You would do well to give Beccaria back his clock quickly. He and his wife foresee that a child of eight months should be born and they talk about it and make arrangements as if it were a calculated matter. This messiah is expected this month."

In some people's eyes, the discord between Alessandro Verri and Cesare Beccaria was entirely foreseeable, maybe even inevitable. As Alfonso Longo, who knew both men, wrote to Pietro Verri after getting word about the rift between Beccaria and the Verris: "I see from what you have written me that you have almost broken with Beccaria. Since I have known him for a long time, you didn't need to give me any information about his character. I agree with you that he is not always the most sociable and obliging person in the world; that is why you had your little fights and why he had frequent ones with Alessandro." "When they left together on their trip," Alfonso wrote about Alessandro and Cesare's departure from Milan for Paris, "I thought that the difference in their temperaments might well produce some hot discussions." "But this has nothing to do with your friendship," Alfonso counseled Pietro Verri, writing in disbelief and hoping that the relationship could be mended: "I am unable to understand how Beccaria can be contemptuous toward you, how he can make you feel the weight of his glory, how he can be ungrateful to you, who have done so much for him, have always encouraged and defended him." "Permit me not to believe yet that he is capable of such baseness," Alfonso added.

"[Y]ou must admit this yourself," Alfonso urged his friend, Pietro, "Beccaria has a good and sensitive heart, and this is why you judged him worthy of your friendship." As Alfonso concluded, looking for a solution: "I simply can't believe that Beccaria is capable of such a change. Please tell me it isn't so, that your friendship has been renewed; or (what can I say?) explain to me how Beccaria, worthy of esteem for so many reasons, has turned out to be the most ungrateful of men." "Please be assured that I believe what you have written me," Alfonso confided, dutifully pledging his allegiance and loyalty to Pietro, though he expressed surprise "by what has happened." "[L]et us forget his faults, let us not consider him any longer an intimate friend, but let us not push our vengeance to the point of hating him," Alfonso wrote, trying to salvage the situation and looking forward to a further effort to repair the damaged friendship with these words: "We will talk about all this; in the meantime try to moderate your resentment toward him, even if it is justified." Ultimately, as the Verri brothers disparaged Beccaria in their private correspondence, Beccaria—unaware of the extent and vitriol of their personal attacks—maintained (as Marcello Maestro put it) "a dignified silence."

The act of adultery, which was implied by Pietro Verri's letter about Cesare Beccaria's wife to his younger brother, Alessandro, was then a crime, though one little discussed in polite society. In *Dei delitti e delle pene*, Beccaria—in a chapter called "Crimes difficult to prove"—had himself written about adultery as well as sodomy, saying both "are hard crimes to prove" yet "are precisely those in which, according to the received views, the tyrannical presumptions of the *nearly proofs* and *half-proofs* are admitted (as if a man could be *half-innocent* or *half-guilty*, that is, *half-punishable* or *half-acquittable*), and where, according to the cold and iniquitous teaching of some learned men who presume to offer norms and rules to the judiciary, torture exercises its cruel prerogatives on the body of the accused, the witnesses and even the whole family of the unfortunate." "Adultery," Beccaria wrote, "is a crime which, viewed politically, is motivated and directed by two factors: the fluctuating laws of men and that very powerful attraction which urges one sex toward the other." Likening sexual attraction to "the gravitational forces that move the universe," Beccaria observed in *On Crimes and Punishments*, the book he'd authored before his trip to Paris: "Like gravity, it diminishes with distance, and, if the one rules all bodily movements, the other, so long as it lasts, rules all the movements of the soul." "But sexual attraction," Beccaria clarified in his book, "differs from gravity in that gravity is counterbalanced by obstacles, whereas sex gathers strength and keenness the more obstacles are placed in its way." Writing at a time when Italian fathers still dictated the approval and terms of marriages, Beccaria emphasized: "Conjugal fidelity is always proportional to the number and freeness of marriages. Where they are held together by ancestral prejudices, where they are welded and sundered by domestic power, there gallantry will stealthily break their bonds despite common morality, whose role it is to decry the effects and excuse the causes."

Beccaria's treatment of then-existing laws punishing sodomy is, the *Encyclopedia of Homosexuality* points out, "limited to a single paragraph in the chapter entitled 'Delitti di prova difficile' (Crimes Difficult to Prove); in some editions it is Chapter XXXI, in others XXXVI." As that source observes: "He introduces the subject as 'Attic love, so severely punished by the laws, and so easily subjected to the tortures that overcome innocence,' which implies that suspects were cruelly tortured to exact confessions of guilt. He goes on to reject the notion that satiation with pleasure is the cause of this passion, but ascribes it to the practice of educating the youth at the moment when their sexual drive is mounting in seminaries that isolated them from the opposite sex." After discussing adultery, homosexuality and infanticide, Beccaria's chapter—penned in the 1760s at a time of rampant oppression and overt discrimination and when the children of nobles were educated in all-male boarding schools—ended with these words: "I do not mean to belittle the just revulsion which these crimes deserve. But, having pointed out their sources, I think I am allowed to draw a general conclusion, which is that one cannot say that a punishment for a crime is exactly just (meaning necessary) until the law has instituted the best possible means in a given nation's circumstances for preventing such a crime."[3] Though the entry about Beccaria in the *Encyclopedia of Homosexuality* states that he "had no notion of the modern concept of homosexuality," that source suggests of his utilitarian reluctance to find any punishment to be just or necessary: "Had the principles of the treatise *On Crimes and Punishments* been followed, all the laws prohibiting consensual homosexual behavior in private would have been stricken from the books in the first decade after the adoption of the Bill of Rights—as they were in France in 1791."

In discussing Beccaria's impact on U.S. law, that source further stresses: "[T]he greatest influence of Beccaria by far was on the Bill of Rights, as the part of it which refers to criminal law and procedure cannot be understood apart from Beccaria's demands for reform. The Fifth, Sixth, and Eighth Amendments to the American Constitution may be called the Lex Beccaria, since they guarantee the rights of the accused in a criminal proceeding, provide that no person 'shall be compelled in any criminal case to be a witness against himself,' and prohibit 'excessive fines' and 'cruel and unusual punishments.'"[4] In taking note of Beccaria's influence on the U.S. Bill of Rights, another source adds: "The Sixth Amendment, in its requirement of speedy and public trials, speaks to Beccaria's concern for the administration of justice in a manner most likely to have a deterrent value." "More directly, Beccaria's thought is reflected in the Fifth Amendment. That Amendment begins: 'No person shall be held to answer for a capital or otherwise infamous crime, unless on a presentment or indictment of a Grand Jury ...' Obviously, here is a reference to the civil law's institution of infamy, which Beccaria had vigorously criticized as being regulated neither by the laws, nor by reason, but entirely by opinion."[5] The Enlightenment sought to separate the concepts of crime and sin and to make punishments more rational, and Cesare Beccaria's ideas shaped the protections that criminal suspects and offenders would be afforded before they were subjected to punishments.

After Cesare Beccaria's return to Milan, the Beccaria family intrigue—and the mere thought of infidelity by Cesare's wife—was just too juicy for Pietro Verri to resist commenting on. Yet another letter from Pietro Verri to his brother Alessandro—one dated August 26, 1767—later reported on the birth of Teresa's child, though that letter—as Roberto Bizzocchi points out—contained a small error, about the date of Beccaria's return to Milan after his trip to Paris. (In his letter, Pietro was one day off about the date of Beccaria's return to Milan.) As Pietro wrote in his August 26th letter, making reference to the "Marquise" and Teresa and Cesare's newborn:

> In my last letter, I forgot to tell you about the baby boy born to Beccaria on 20th of this month. See if he hasn't been a prophet: the birth had to take place in August! He returned as you know on 13 December. He announced the news to his father, who replied 'I am glad about your consolations'; following this cold compliment, he added that really the little Marquise had anticipated the birth; *a great deal*, replied the Marquise and so ended the scene. Calderari immediately came to congratulate the Marquis; this is enough to judge his character. He, guilty of having compromised a mistress, of having dishonoured a friend, of having stolen Giulietta's inheritance, at the moment can silence his remorse or not feel it; I regard this as a demonstration of his bad character.[6]

A baby boy was seen as a particular blessing in eighteenth-century Italian society, because property—as well as a man's title—was bequeathed from father to son. If the newborn's paternity could be traced to Teresa's *cicisbeo*, it might cause all kinds of rumors and gossip, not to mention legal claims and protracted litigation, potentially jeopardizing little Giulia's inheritance down the line. But the baby boy died just a day after his birth.

Although Cesare Beccaria had rushed back to Milan, Beccaria's travelling companion, Alessandro Verri, had gone in a different direction. Taken aback by the Parisian *encyclopédistes'* often strident irreligion, Alessandro had headed across the

English Channel, though he still stayed in touch with his brother, Pietro, by letter. Unlike Cesare, to whom he would remain estranged for years to come, Alessandro continued on to England, which he visited from 1766 to 1767 after his sojourn in Paris had ended. There, he would meet with prominent figures the likes of Benjamin Franklin, whom Alessandro called the "Newton of electricity." In exchanging letters with his brother, Pietro Verri asked Alessandro, then in London, to produce "Locke's laws for America and those of Penn for Pennsylvania"—potential models for Pietro Verri's beloved Lombardy and which also would have been of great interest to Beccaria himself.[7] But despite its truncated duration—just weeks instead of months—and the stress and strain it put on his personal relationships, Beccaria's trip to Paris brought heightened attention to the ideas in *Dei delitti e delle pene* in what was then seen as one of the great capitals of Europe. As Beccaria, in one of his many love letters to his wife, Teresa, himself reported from Paris before his departure back to Milan:

> Dear wife, I pray you to reflect on how great is my love for you. I'm in the midst of adoration, the most flattering praise, considered a companion and colleague of the greatest men of Europe, regarded with admiration and curiosity, people compete to invite me for lunch, for dinner, in the capital of pleasures, in the midst of three theatres, one of which (namely the Comédie Française) presents the most interesting repertoire in the world, etc.; and yet I'm unhappy and discontented, because I'm far from you.

The trip to Paris soured the friendship of Cesare Beccaria and the Verri brothers, pushing it past the breaking point. But in the months and years that followed, booksellers—despite that falling out—continued to sell copies of *Dei delitti e delle pene* at a brisk pace in places such as England, France, Ireland and Scotland. Before the trip, the Verri brothers had high hopes for Alessandro and Cesare's journey, with their expensive, long-planned trip to be documented in letters for posterity's sake. When Beccaria and Alessandro experienced what has been described as a "difficult cohabitation" in Paris, and especially when Beccaria decided to abandon Alessandro altogether, it was seen as a personal affront and a betrayal. And Beccaria, at least in the Verri brothers' eyes, became an "*imbecille.*" Both Pietro and Alessandro Verri, desperately wanting to network and ingratiate themselves with the leading European *philosophes*, became obsessed with Beccaria's behavior; and Beccaria's perceived slights, as one scholar puts it of the fate of the friendships fostered by the short-lived Academy of Fists, led to "the breakup of the *Caffettisti*'s intellectual alliance." "Of the sixty letters exchanged by the two brothers during Alessandro's stays in Paris and London," one scholar, Lidia De Michelis, writes, "Beccaria goes unmentioned only on six occasions." "Like an aching phantom digit," Beccaria's absence, De Michelis notes, "frames and defines Alessandro's own understanding of London." As De Michelis emphasizes: "Alessandro's London journal (and even his lodgings, belonging to the publisher Molini) is haunted almost literally by Beccaria when, like a textual ghost, the first anonymous English translation of the *Essay on Crimes and Punishments* is announced: '*Il libro di Beccaria si traduce in Inghilterra per la prima volta, ed è interessato nella stampa il mio ospite Molini. No porterò meco una copia a Parigi perché esce tra pochi giorni* (January 15, 1767)." While his brother Alessandro had been on route to Paris with Beccaria, Pietro Verri had suggested that their Parisian trip would build "a bridge" between Milan and the rest of Europe. Beccaria's refusal to stay in Paris with Alessandro and complete their planned European trip was seen as a devastating blow, putting everything—all their hopes and dreams—in jeopardy.[8]

The Molini family—representatives of which were spread out throughout Europe—was engaged in the book trade in Italy, France and England, and that family became leading booksellers, selling many books, including the first English-language translation of Beccaria's *Dei delitti e delle pene*. "The founder of the Molini firm," *The Bodleian Library Record* notes, was Romualdo Molini "who began as a bookseller in Florence, but gradually expanded his business by opening branches in Paris and London." Pietro (Peter) Molini (1730–1806), according to the *British Book Trades Index*, was a "bookseller in London from 1765–1798, trading in 1795 as P & G Molini and as Molini, Polidori, Molini & Co." Pietro Molini reportedly undertook, at his own expense, to have Beccaria's *Dei delitti e delle pene* translated into English, while his brother Giovanni handled operations in Paris. Another source specifically notes that, in 1766, the publisher Giovanni Claudio Molini (1724–1812)—Pietro Molini's brother, and in partnership with him—produced a "virtually identical 'French' version, called the sixth (*edizione sesta di nuovo corretta e accresciuta*), bearing the indication of *Harlem* and *A Paris*." A native of Florence, Gian Claudio—as he was also known—did an apprenticeship in Paris starting in May 1763 and was in business as early as 1765 in time to bring *Dei delitti e delle pene* to a French audience.

The Molini family's book business had establishments in Florence, London and Paris, and it flourished and grew into a large enterprise. In *Travellers in Northern Italy*, under the heading "Booksellers," one encounters this entry for Romualdo's son, Giuseppe, in Florence: "Mr. Molini in the Via degli Arquebsieri, who is a partner in the London House of the same name, is one of the most extensive and best informed booksellers in Florence: all French and English works may be obtained at his shop, Guide Books, &c. Mr. Molini, formerly librarian to the Grand Duke, speaks English well, and travellers will find him and his son most obliging in giving information about masters and books, &c." "At his establishment," a guidebook for European travelers emphasized of the Molini family business that was built up, "a very large collection of English books are always on sale." As that 1841 source notes of the thriving Florence business and its proprietor at that time: "Books are also obtained from London and Paris. Mr. Molini speaks English and is extremely obliging."[9]

Aristocrats—possessed of great privilege and accustomed to proper decorum—could be caddy, and Pietro and Alessandro Verri were no exception. On April 29, 1767, after Beccaria had been back in Milan for four full months, Pietro snarkily (and without apparent irony) wrote to his brother Alessandro about their mutual subject of choice: "No one talks about Beccaria any more." "[H]e is," Pietro stressed of Beccaria, their now estranged friend, "restricted to the company of his wife, Calderari, Visconti and his two brothers and Odazzi: these six people are his mankind, from which you can see how much he must be enjoying himself!" Cesare Beccaria's mother was a Visconti—a distinguished Italian family with centuries-old roots on Italian soil. "The Visconti family was to become the rulers of Milan," one source notes of that family, pointing out that Pope Gregory X was a Visconti and Ottone Visconti (1207–1295) had been appointed archbishop of Milan and that "[t]he Visconti family claimed descent from Adalberto, king of Italy, who was a direct descendant of Charlemagne." In 1499, citing a Visconti grandmother, Louis XII of France (1462–1515) had once laid claim to the Duchy of Milan, sending an army in an attempt to conquer it. As one guidebook put it, Louis XII found vibrant Milan to be a "tempting plum." As that guidebook emphasized of Milan even centuries before Cesare Beccaria's birth: "The bountiful, well-irrigated, low-lying fields, manufacturing, and thriving trade with the rich lands over the Alps, all made the duchy of Milan Italy's wealthiest state." Milan's famed Duomo was a church founded in 1386 under the rule of a member of the Visconti family, Gian Galeazzo Visconti. And in the centuries of meticulous, painstaking construction yet to come, leading Visconti architects from that influential Italian family would help to build it, constructing a durable architectural masterpiece.[10]

The Beccaria and Verri families—part of Milan's tight-knit Italian aristocracy—were closely connected to one another, and the two families would continue to be entangled, in more ways than one, even after the falling out that arose out of Cesare and Alessandro's 1766 trip to Paris. After Cesare and his chosen bride, Teresa, had gotten married in 1761, it was none other than Pietro Verri, through his clever maneuvering, who had helped to get the young couple back in Cesare's parents' good graces. And the couple's first child, Cesare and Teresa's daughter Giulia, born on July 21, 1762, was—later in life—the lover of Pietro and Alessandro Verri's playboy brother, Giovanni, as well as the mother of Alessandro Manzoni, whose real father was most likely Giovanni Verri, not Giulia's much older husband, Pietro Manzoni. In 1766, the year of Beccaria's trip to Paris, Cesare and Teresa had a second daughter, Maria, who was born with severe neurological problems and died years before her father's death. And in 1767, with Beccaria still reliant on his own father for financial support, the couple's third child—Giovanni Annibale, the one whose paternity was questioned by Pietro Verri in his letters—was born, though little Giovanni Annibale—as noted—sadly died shortly after childbirth. It was a difficult time for Cesare and Teresa, and Cesare "was not happy about his continued dependence on his parents and had tried earnestly to find a government position in which he could use his best talents," historian Marcello Maestro explains. Eventually, however, Cesare's trip to Paris did bear fruit, with Cesare landing a teaching job in Milan in the late 1760s even as Cesare and Teresa continued trying to expand their family. The couple's fourth and final child, Margherita, was not born until 1772, though in an age of only rudimentary health care that newborn died too, surviving only for a few days. Teresa and Cesare's first child, their daughter, Giulia, would be the only of their children to survive into mature adulthood.[11]

Not long after the birth and death of little Margherita, Cesare's heart-broken and ill wife, Teresa, died too, her life ending on March 14, 1774. Teresa's health had been precarious before she died, with one source noting that "her constant fever and gradual weakening were symptoms of a consumptive fever." With Teresa, in the lead up to her death, staying in the countryside "where the air was purer," that source stresses, Cesare wrote to her at one point in 1773: "Please get better soon. I wish that that cursed fever would disappear; the sooner I see you, the better I will feel." Though Cesare had loved Teresa dearly, for the Italian aristocrat his period of mourning was— even for that time—remarkably short. Shortly after Teresa's death, Pietro Verri wrote to his brother to reflect on the then-existing state of affairs: "Beccaria now lives in Calderara's home. He says that sorrow doesn't do any good; this is true, but in this case it shows that his sensibility is limited. I am sure that not six months will pass before we will see him married again: he cannot survive without a support." In fact, Cesare's time as a widower was even shorter than that. Just weeks after Teresa's death, Beccaria scandalously chose to remarry another woman, Anna Barbò, the daughter of Count Barnaba Barbò, a wealthy property owner. Anna's surviving letters, sent in early May 1774, show that Cesare and Anna's romance was ardent and developed very quickly. "Your warm letter," Anna wrote on May 3rd, "arouses in me a very strong love and I cannot tell you how happy I am when I hear your voice or I see in writing your sweet words." As Anna wrote in that letter: "I want then to speed up the accomplishment of our happiness and to be soon in possession of your dear person, the sole object of my desire. The ardor that I feel for you fills me so completely that I am unable to describe it; you see that it is not my fault if I am so confused, for you are the cause of it." "I can only offer you again my heart, of which you are the only owner," Anna wrote, concluding: "My dear joy, I embrace you and tonight I will give you the fifty caresses I promised you."[12]

Cesare Beccaria's marriage to Anna Barbò took place on June 4, 1774, but she signed her letter "Your lover and spouse" on May 3, 1774, indicating a close relationship— indeed, a familiar intimacy—before their nuptials. Just two days later, on May 5th, she wrote yet another affectionate letter to Cesare that delivered a similar message. "My handsome and beloved Cesarino, remember that I am your very faithful spouse. When you come this afternoon please bring with you the key to the theater box; it may be that this will make my mother decide to go to the theater, and this would please me immensely because I would then be able to enjoy in peace the company of my treasure." Milan's then-existing *Regio Ducal Teatro*, or Royal Ducal Theater, regularly hosted opera and ballet performances such as *The Fable of Psyche* and *The Amsterdam Fair*. That theater burned down in 1776, a couple of years after Beccaria's second marriage, with the theater to be replaced by Milan's now world-famous *Teatro alla Scala*, or La Scala, which opened on August 3, 1778. The performances at the Royal Ducal Theater were incredibly extended affairs, a fact that would have given Anna and Cesare plenty of leisure time together in the event that Anna's mother chose to attend the theater. For example, Mozart's opera, *Mitridate*, performed at Milan's *Regio Ducal Teatro* in December 1770, was part of a series of operatic and ballet performances that lasted for hours; Wolfgang Amadeus Mozart's father, Leopold, actually complained the performances lasted so long that it obliged the family to delay their supper, most likely until after midnight. According to one source, Mozart's father laid the blame "on the three accompanying ballets rather than on Wolfgang's *opera seria* which, with its playing time of four hours for the three acts, was unusually prolix even by the standards of that day."

Cesare and Anna's courtship was a short but passionate one. In another letter written on May 7, 1774, it was Cesare and Anna's turn to enjoy a night out on the town.

As Anna wrote to Cesare: "I see that you kissed my letter and that you would have preferred to do that to the one who wrote it. I am sure that this is true, since I have had enough proofs not to doubt it." "I enjoy the thought," Anna added, "that tonight we will go to the theater and that our hearts will be together in our little corner."[13] Although the upper echelon of Milanese society may have been miffed or scandalized by how quickly Beccaria remarried, it was generally agreed that Cesare and Anna, the new couple, made a good match—and that their marriage was a successful one. A year after they tied the knot, Pietro Verri himself wrote to his brother Alessandro using these words: "Beccaria has been lucky, he married a good young woman, wise and affectionate; she knows how to keep peace and goodwill in the home, and everybody likes her." By 1778, the year the La Scala opened its doors, Beccaria turned forty; Cesare and Anna's first and only child, their son, Giulio, was three; and Cesare's daughter, Giulia, from his first marriage, was eighteen and finishing her own education. Cesare had sent Giulia to the monastery of San Paolo, an institution that—as one source puts it—"withered away" over the course of the eighteenth century, "its income and its population shrinking along with that of most Milanese nunneries." "In truth," that source notes, pointing out that Napoleon's bureaucrats dissolved the San Paolo convent in 1810, "the enclosed convents had mostly outlived their usefulness; the single women of the elite now had many other lives to lead." The San Paolo Converso was a Roman Catholic church in Milan built between 1546 and 1580 for the convent of the Order of the Angeliche—an order that was suppressed in 1806.[14]

While Cesare Beccaria's marriage to Anna was a successful one, there is some controversy regarding the circumstances of Cesare's marriage to Teresa as well as the cause of her death, with one article in the *Italian Journal* describing Cesare's first wife, Teresa, as "a flighty woman whose loose lifestyle led to an early and horrible death from venereal disease."[15] Cesare Beccaria's friend, Alfonso Longo, called Teresa a beautiful wife, and Italian historian Cesare Cantù—an expert on the Enlightenment and Beccaria himself—found that Beccaria dearly loved Teresa and that she fully reciprocated that love. But C.A. Vianello, another commentator, called into question Teresa's faithfulness. Indeed, in *A Lady's Man: The Cicisbei, Private Morals and National Identity in Italy*, historian Roberto Bizzocchi, taking note of the circumstances of Teresa's life and death, writes: "Cesare Beccaria had allowed his wife, Teresa Blasco, a great deal of freedom of which she had taken advantage so imprudently as to die, less than 30 years old, of a venereal disease. Teresa had, among other things, been the mistress of Pietro Verri, but not in a period that could be linked with the conception of Giulia." Beccaria's biographer, Marcello Maestro, observes that Teresa died one day before Cesare's thirty-sixth birthday and that Teresa's health had grown "progressively worse" before her death. Teresa, another source states, was "a lovely but scandalous lady who caused discord between Cesare and his family and friends and who finally died of venereal disease."

Cesare Beccaria's second marriage, to Anna Barbò, was certainly a far less turbulent one, though the quickness of it came as a surprise—and, to many of his fellow aristocrats, as a shock, though not to the aristocrats who knew him best. As one of Beccaria's biographers contextualized the marriage of Cesare and Anna: "It was as if he could not bear to be alone. Shortly before he had been appointed not only a councillor of state but also a magistrate and he was soon to serve on various commissions of inquiry, so he was not exactly idle." Beccaria's friend, Luigi Lambertenghi, who had conversed and exchanged ideas with Beccaria as he wrote *Dei delitti e delle pene*, attributed Cesare's quick remarriage to Cesare's hatred of solitude. But Pietro Verri—the frequent, if sometimes suspect, chronicler of Beccaria's activities—described Cesare's courtship of (and infatuation with) Anna and gave this assessment to his brother: "Beccaria is now a languishing suitor, shamefully in love." Beccaria's biographer, Marcello Maestro, takes a more middling path, writing: "We cannot exclude the possibility, despite the affection Beccaria showed toward Teresa all through her illness, that his feelings for her had weakened with the passing of time; but the fact remains that the relationship between Beccaria and Anna Barbò started very soon after Teresa's death." "Certainly Teresa's brother, Michele, who in that period was on a trip abroad," Maestro editorialized, "must have felt quite a shock when he received at the same time the news of his sister's death and of his brother-in-law's new marriage." Michele, however, took the news of Beccaria's nuptials to Anna in stride, expressing great sorrow at the news of his sister's death but writing, in the same letter, to congratulate Beccaria "for having proceeded to a second marriage which I hope will be gladdened by a thousand happinesses and satisfactions."

"Please do not think," Michele de Blasco assured Cesare in the more forgiving and less judgmental Age of Enlightenment, "that I disapprove of your prompt resolution; on the contrary, I would have condemned the opposite if, in order to conform to some old and ridiculous opinions, you had postponed the carrying out of your decision." Recognizing Beccaria's workload as a public councilor and the tragedy in his brother-in-law's private life, Michele added with gracious understanding: "I fully realize that your occupations and your studies do not give you the possibility of applying to family affairs those cares that you so successfully devote to the well-being of your country and of mankind. This is what I think, and certainly I will never ascribe to your decision a motive less worthy than your character." By then, Cesare was hard at work and less dependent on his father for financial support. Cesare Beccaria's father would live until the age of eighty-five, dying in 1782 and leaving the bulk of his estate—as well as his title—to his first-born son, Cesare. That inheritance, valued at approximately 60,000 *lire*, included the family house on Via Brera, the family's country estate in Gessate, and a variety of other assets. "I will always feel honored to be your brother-in-law and to have your continuous friendship, as well as that of your new, respected wife," Michele wrote. Cesare Beccaria and Michele de Blasco remained friends for life, with Beccaria's daughter, Giulia, continuing to correspond with her uncle, Michele, long after Cesare Beccaria's death in 1794, two full decades after marrying Anna Barbò.

Beccaria's professional career was a rewarding one. After having taught a two-year course in economics at the Palatine School of Milan, Cesare Beccaria had been selected in 1771 to serve on Lombardy's Supreme Economic Council—a body set up in 1765 to reform economic and social policies. It was a position he actively sought, having written to the Austrian chancellor, Kaunitz, to express his desire to join that consultative body. Teaching was a challenging and important job, but Beccaria ended up using it as a stepping stone to get the position he really coveted, one on the Supreme

Economic Council. "Although only two years have elapsed since I began to fulfill to the best of my ability the duties entrusted to me as an instructor of public economy," Beccaria had informed Kaunitz, seeking the new position as an economist, "I think I may rely on your generous feelings and express to you my great and constant desire to put myself and my knowledge of political and economic matters more directly and completely at Her Majesty's service." "For this reason," Beccaria had stressed in his letter, wanting to aid Empress Maria Theresa in a new capacity, "I take the liberty of asking Your Highness to take into consideration my wish to enter the Supreme Economic Council of this city when a vacancy should occur, since the purpose and functions of the said council are in direct line with my principal studies." "As regards the selection of another person to succeed me in the chair of public economy," Beccaria had advised Kaunitz, "I beg to inform Your Highness that in these two years I have trained more than one pupil who, with the help of my notes—which need only a little polishing to be printed—and of my direct assistance, would be able to take over the teaching until Her Majesty may decide otherwise."

Although Beccaria recommended one of his former pupils, Giuseppe Biumi (1749–1838), to be his teaching replacement, the position ultimately went to Alfonso Longo, Beccaria's former compatriot in the Academy of Fists. Longo was then teaching public law at the Palatine School, and he had maintained his friendships with both Cesare Beccaria and Pietro Verri. "Although his relationship with Longo was fairly friendly," Marcello Maestro writes of Beccaria, speaking of Beccaria's teaching replacement and Beccaria's reaction to it, "Beccaria was probably a little unhappy about the appointment, not only because he would have liked to help Biumi, but also because Longo was not yet able to replace Beccaria in view of his other duties in the school." Longo had begun teaching public law at the Palatine School in 1769, and because of those ongoing teaching duties, he could not immediately take on a new assignment. "In fact," Maestro writes, "in order to assure the continuity of the course of economics Beccaria had to do one more full year of teaching; and only in 1772 was he finally able to devote all his time to the new career as a public official." After Longo did take over Beccaria's teaching duties, he adopted Pietro Verri's *Meditazioni sull'economia Politica* as recommended reading material for his students and Beccaria's teaching notes went unpublished. Giuseppe Biumi, a student of Beccaria's from January 1769 to April 1771, was thought to be "very promising" by the likes of Pietro Verri, so the person Beccaria had unsuccessfully recommended was certainly a well-qualified applicant for the teaching position.

The eighteenth century witnessed the incorporation of political economy courses into university curricula. "[T]he process of academic institutionalisation of political economy," observes Marco Guidi and Massimo Augello in a book chapter on economic treatises and textbooks in Italy, "started in the 18th century, in Italy as elsewhere." The institutionalization of political economy, they write, "was a phenomenon of a larger circulation of economic ideas throughout Europe that started in the 18th century, and was supported by the circulation of individuals who travelled from a capital to another to attend courses of political economy, gatherings in *salons* and academies, or to meet the masters of the new science." "[T]he introduction of political economy into university curricula was only episodic in Old Regime Italian states," Guidi and Augello explain, giving this brief synopsis of the key dates: "On 5th November 1754, Antonio Genovesi opened his course of 'Commerce and Mechanics' at the University of Naples, which he repeated until his death in 1769. A new course was entrusted to Troiano Odazi in 1782, followed some years later by Domenico Genovese." As Guidi and Augello continue: "As far as Northern Italy is concerned, it was only on 9th January 1769 that Cesare Beccaria started teaching 'political economy' at the *Scuole Palatine* in Milan. He lectured until 1771, when he was followed by Alfonso Longo who taught the same subject until 1782. The only other episode of institutionalisation in the 18th century refers to the University of Modena, where Agostino Paradisi was professor of 'civil economy' from 1772 to 1780."

The institutionalization of political economy instruction was part of a broader reform effort that included monarchs and intellectuals alike. "Political economy," Guidi and Augello emphasize, "was part and parcel of the enlightened reform strategy promoted by some intellectual circles in close connection with local monarchs and political authorities." As those scholars note of two major groups: "The group gathering around Bartolomeo Intieri and Celestino Galiani in Massa Equana, of which Genovesi was a member, or the Accademia dei Pugni created and led by Pietro Verri and Cesare Beccaria in Milan are remarkable examples of this institutional background. Scholars like Verri and Genovesi participated in public non-elected bodies, in which their expertise in political economy was highly recognised." Taking note of the coordination between scholars and the royal figures, Guidi and Augello add: "The enlightened sovereigns of various Italian states promoted the reform of universities and higher education establishments, and made room for subjects like agriculture and political economy in their syllabuses. The teaching of these subjects at the *Scuole Palatine* in Milan was a clear demonstration of the public function that was attributed to them. The 'Plan of direction, discipline and economy' of the University and Palatine Schools issued by the Austrian government of Lombardy in 1771 placed education under the jurisdiction of the State and transformed it into a public service." "The case of the short-lived journal *Il Caffè* (1764–1766), connected to the informal academy gathered by Verri and Beccaria," Guidi and Augello editorialize, "is a vivid example of the way in which the study of political economy was connected to new forms of aristocratic sociability aimed at the modernisation of society and at the creation of a reforming governing class."[16]

While Alfonso Longo taught public economy until 1782, Giuseppe Biumi remained close to Beccaria—his former teacher—and ended up copying various writings and lecture notes of Beccaria that were later published.[17] Those writings on economics included Beccaria's thoughts on value, utility and scarcity, with Beccaria—at one point—emphasizing: "Goods may be considered to have value, first, to the extent to which they contribute to satisfying needs, or adding to the conveniences, or promoting the pleasures of life; and secondly, to the extent that they are scarce and difficult to obtain. Goods which are common, and to be found everywhere, however essential, such as air, and, almost always, water, have no value." "In the same way," Beccaria added, "things which are of no use or convenience, or give no pleasure, however scarce, are of no value." The writings and lectures of Beccaria—the ones he created for use as part of his work at the Palatine School—were ultimately compiled and posthumously published as *Elementi di economia pubblica* as part of a 50-volume series titled *Scrittori Classici Italiani di Economia Politica*. It was Baron Pietro Custodi (1771–1842) who would, in 1804, ten years after Cesare Beccaria's death, finally publish Beccaria's writings and lectures on economics.

At the time of Cesare Beccaria's promotion to the Supreme Economic Council in 1771, Pietro Verri was already serving on it. Though Beccaria was a successful academic, the position on the Supreme Economic Council paid a lot better. And because of his by then dire financial straits because of his familial dependence and his own family, Beccaria—unable at that point to even pay for books he had ordered from his regular book dealer, Chirol in Geneva—was ecstatic to land the better paying position on that body, later called simply the Economic Council. In the new, better-paying role, Beccaria was put in charge of monetary reforms (1771–1773)—a subject he had thought long about—and he supervised matters regarding the food supply (1773), a matter of vital importance for any society. "Already in 1771, while he was still a professor at the Palatine School," Marcello Maestro recounts, "Beccaria was asked to prepare a plan for a new piece of legislation on the bills of exchange and, soon, after, a plan for monetary reform." "Such reform," Maestro emphasizes, "was badly needed because the lack of clear regulations in this field had caused inconveniences and obstacles to the economic development of the region." Another of Beccaria's reports—one on the consumption of grain in Milan that was dated March 26, 1774, just after the death of Beccaria's wife, Teresa, and before his second marriage to Anna—was prepared in collaboration with none other than Pietro Verri, his former friend turned nemesis who became his work colleague. "This study, requested by the government," Maestro writes, "showed that for several reasons a precise calculation of the consumption of grain in Milan was almost impossible, but it gave as accurate figures as possible on the basis of available data."

Their work together on that report on grain—their first cooperative effort since their falling out—seems to have muted or tamped down Pietro's hatred of Cesare. "From then on," Maestro explains, "Pietro Verri's attitude toward Beccaria softened somewhat and, although he continued to talk about him without affection, he now showed more disdain than jealousy or animosity." Their daily interactions with one another was, in part, responsible for the change in perspective. "The two men," Maestro writes, "saw each other every day, worked in the same office, and often had to discuss together the problems submitted to them." "Having, after all, a common goal in their work," Maestro continues of the renewed association between Verri and Beccaria, "they exchanged their points of view and gradually began to feel a little closer to each other." Although Pietro Verri became more introspective about all the barbs and insults he had hurled at Beccaria in his prior correspondence, Pietro could still not bring himself to restore the warm friendship that they had once shared. When Cesare's new wife became pregnant, naturally prompting Pietro to share the news with his brother, Alessandro, Pietro—resorting to old habits—thus could not resist shooting this arrow in his letter: "Beccaria is only a shadow of the sublime man he used to be, you wouldn't recognize in him the philosopher who had in his hand the approving votes of all Europe."[18] By 1778, Pietro—the always diligent letter writer—

was writing to his brother Alessandro yet again. As Pietro wrote, alluding back to their time together in the Academy of Fists: "Beccaria has changed very much from what he used to be fourteen years ago. We are now on fairly friendly terms, and this reciprocal feeling is evident in all the council meetings that we attend. He is very timid, more than any of the women I am acquainted with." "Beccaria is not really a bad man, only weak, and he is not malicious or deceitful," Pietro wrote on yet another occasion, adding that Beccaria has "a good sense of values and knows how to reason on many subjects." In that same letter, Pietro added of Beccaria: "He has put on a lot of weight and seems always sleepy under so much fat; sometimes he is so absent-minded that you have to repeat the same question two or three times." After Beccaria's wife, Anna, and Pietro Verri's wife, Maria or "Marietta," became friends, the two couples also rented a box together for the inaugural season at the La Scala Theater, bringing the two men somewhat closer together again.[19] In 1776, Pietro Verri had married his niece, the much younger Marietta Castiglioni, becoming both the brother-in-law of Milanese botanist Luigi Castiglioni as well as Luigi's uncle.[20]

It was in 1778, after Cesare Beccaria's marriage to Anna, his second wife, that Beccaria—the *cum laude* graduate of the University of Pavia who rose through the ranks of Lombardy's bureaucracy—was named the provincial magistrate of the mint.[21] He had left academia after just a short stint in the classroom, preferring instead to devote his time to the practicalities of economic development in his native Milan. As a member of the Supreme Economic Council, a body whose members submitted proposals that were carefully considered by officials in Vienna, Beccaria focused principally on issues of agriculture, public education, and trade and industry.[22] "The files of the Milan council," Marcello Maestro observes, "show us that Beccaria soon became one of its most active and authoritative members—together with Gian Rinaldo Carli, Pietro Verri, Paolo Frisi, and a few others—and that his suggestions and interventions had a considerable influence on the government's decisions." Economic historian Peter Groenewegen, making reference to the French economist François Quesnay, stresses that one of Beccaria's proposals, a plan for agricultural improvement, followed "physiocratic lines developed by Quesnay in the article 'Grains' as does his division of society into classes."[23]

In those days, news travelled surprisingly fast, especially as regards aristocratic births and deaths and marriages. And the birth of Teresa's only male child, Giovanni Annibale, in 1767, as well as Cesare Beccaria's second marriage, to Anna Barbò, in 1774, were not exceptions (as Pietro Verri's letters make clear). "The news given by Pietro to Alessandro Verri on 27 April," writes Roberto Bizzocchi in *A Lady's Man* of Beccaria's unusually quick remarriage in June 1774 following Teresa's death, "passes over the financial difficulties—which made the help for the Beccaria family from the marriage more than opportune, if not so urgent—and dwells on the more obvious causes of astounded disapproval." Anna Barbò was, herself, related to Pietro and Alessandro Verri, and she was from a wealthy, respectable family. As Pietro Verri's April 27, 1774 letter, noting the new marriage but being highly critical of Beccaria, read:

On 14 March 1774 the Marquis Cesare Beccaria became a widower and on 25 April he had already entered into a marriage contract with Lady Anna

Barbò our cousin. He seemed to be in love with that first wife beyond all measure. If he was away from her, during the autumn while she was a few miles away in a country villa and he had to pass a day in the city, in the evening two or three men on horseback would be sent to have news of her every hour; it seemed as if he would succumb to this loss. Two days later he enters the house, opens the box, examines the dead woman's personal effects, talks freely of the need to have a son, and forty days after she has been buried, he is already tied to a new contract. Calderari, who still loves the dead woman, is indignant; the public hasn't changed its mind about Beccaria, who is full of utter weakness to the core.[24]

In an era of substantial dowries and when property rights were the almost exclusive domain of men, Cesare Beccaria was no doubt anxious to produce a male heir and his second marriage, to Lady Barbò, did at last produce a surviving son, Giulio Bonesana di Beccaria (1775–1858). The couple's only child, Giulio, would not only later marry another respectable woman, Antonio Olimpia Curioni De' Civati, but he would inherit Cesare Beccaria's worldly possessions and his title, too. A collector of coins and the keeper of Cesare Beccaria's papers, Giulio—in the nineteenth century—later renovated the house, now at 6 Via Brera, where his father lived, and inhabited the Villa Beccaria, an eighteenth-century villa on the site of an ancient fort opposite Comacina Island of Italy's famed Lake Como. It was a villa that would later become known as Villa Rachele. Along with Cesare Beccaria and his son Giulio, Alessandro Manzoni—Cesare Beccaria's grandson—would often stay there, admiring all of the beauty of Italy's lake country. Near the entrance to the door at 6 Via Brera where Cesare Beccaria and his family once lived, one now can find a simple inscription reading: "In this house Cesare Beccaria was born in 1738 and died on November 28, 1794." Later in life, it would fall to Cesare Beccaria's son, Giulio, to assemble his father's autographed manuscript for *Dei delitti e delle pene*, consisting of a small leather volume. That manuscript now safely resides in Milan's Biblioteca Ambrosiana along with the text of Beccaria's "Elementi di Economia Pubblica" dated 1769.[25]

As for Cesare Beccaria's first daughter, Giulia Beccaria (July 21, 1762–July 7, 1841), she was raised in a convent before falling in love with Giovanni Verri, a Knight of the Cross of Malta. According to writer Dianne Hales, the author of *La Bella Lingua*, Giovanni "held a quasi-military, quasi-religious rank that forbade marriage at pain of loss of both prestige and income." Despite their love affair, Giovanni Verri, constrained in his own actions and not being considered suitable in any event, was not allowed to marry Giulia and, in 1782, Giulia—then aged twenty—was forced into an unhappy, arranged marriage with Pietro Manzoni, a wealthy 46-year-old nobleman from Lecco. As scholar Roberto Bizzocchi writes in *A Lady's Man*: "Giulia when young had been lively enough to have taken some liberties with her habitual companion Giovanni, one of Pietro Verri's younger brothers. It has already been said that she became pregnant during this period of companionship, and now we can add finally that it is by now commonly accepted that Alessandro's real father was not Pietro Manzoni but Giovanni Verri."[26]

Aristocratic traditions being what they then were, Alessandro Manzoni did not have the kind of childhood that most children have today. Breastfed by a peasant woman who worked as a wet nurse, Alessandro Manzoni instead spent his childhood in a series of boarding schools, attending institutions in Merate, Lugano and Milan operated by Somaschi friars and Barnabite fathers. His schooling ended at age sixteen, and it was in his sixteenth year that Alessandro wrote his first surviving poetry, including his "*Il trionfo della Libertà*" ("The Triumph of Liberty"). He went on to become one of Italy's greatest writers, one still honored today in Milan. According to a summary of Alessandro Manzoni's impressive literary contributions: "Manzoni wrote poetry, fiction, plays, and treatises on language, literature, and religion. Already famous in Europe as a poet (for 'March 1821' and 'The Fifth of May'), he began to write his only novel, *I Promessi Sposi* (*The Betrothed*), in 1821. The first version appeared in 1827 and was an instant success, going through nine editions in four years. Dissatisfied with the novel's language, which Manzoni thought was too reliant on Milanese dialect and French influences, he spent most of the next decade rewriting in the Tuscan vernacular, and the definitive version appeared in 1840." "It enjoyed such widespread popularity," that source reports, "that the novel helped establish the Tuscan dialect as the national language that Italy so desperately needed to become a unified culture and country." As the Penguin Classics edition of the book notes of its plot: "Set in Lombardy during the Spanish occupation of the late 1620s, *The Betrothed* tells the story of two young lovers, Renzo and Lucia, prevented from marrying by the petty tyrant Don Rodrigo, who desires Lucia for himself. Forced to flee, they are then cruelly separated, and must face many dangers including plague, famine and imprisonment, and confront a variety of strange characters—the mysterious Nun of Monza, the fiery Father Cristoforo and the sinister 'Unnamed'—in their struggle to be reunited."[27]

Among eighteenth-century Italian aristocrats, there was—as noted earlier—a now little-remembered practice known as cicisbeism. The role of the *cicisbeo*, according to a prominent Italian dictionary, was defined as follows: "'*Cicisbèo*. A lady's escort who, in accordance with a custom which developed in the eighteenth century, was expected, with the husband's consent, to be in attendance on the lady, accompany her and assist her in all her activities.'" As historian Robert Bizzocchi, of the University of Pisa, describes it: "[A] cicisbeo—or a married woman's escort (*cavalier servente*)— had the public and declared task of living side by side with another man's wife, as part of an arranged and desirable triangle." The cicisbeo would converse and flirt with the husband's wife even in the husband's presence; eat meals seated next to her; bring her coffee and refreshments; take care of all her personal needs; walk with her on prominent streets and walkways of Milan; attend social events and palace receptions with her; and even give orders to servants while at her husband's house. "In Rome, a lady does not appear in society without an escort, who offers her his arm," the French astronomer Joseph-Jérôme de La Lande recorded after a stay in Italy in 1765 and 1766, noting that the escort was "obliged to go and entertain his lady" from morning until dinner time. Simonde de Sismondi, an historian and economist, made this broader observation in *Histoire des Républiques italiennes du moyen âge* (1807–1818): "the rights and duties of cicisbei and ladies' escorts were invented; these rights and duties were based entirely on two laws created by high society, and were: that no woman could decently appear in public alone: and that likewise no husband could, without appearing ridiculous, accompany his wife." "[N]o father," Sismondi observed of this age of gallantry, sociability, conversation and, inevitably, illicit sexual affairs, "could dare to assume that the children of his marriage were really his." One prominent Italian, Giuseppe Baretti, wrote in *An Account of the Manners and Customs of Italy* (1768) that the "custom of almost every man attending on a lady with a lover's attention and respect" was associated with a "spirit of gallantry" as "refined by the revival of the Platonic philosophy in Italy about the thirteenth century." But there is little doubt that initially flirtatious, Platonic relationships sometimes evolved into sexual ones.[28]

Giuseppe Baretti (1719–1789)—the Italian who became so well known in England for his Italian-English dictionaries, his Italian language instruction, and his take on Italian customs and traditions—was once put on trial for murder at the Old Bailey in London. He was "tried for his life"—he faced hanging if convicted—for, as *The London Magazine* put it in 1769, stabbing to death "Evan Morgan, who with others, in company with two street walkers, had grossly insulted and ill used him in the streets." A friend of the English lexicographer Samuel Johnson and other men of letters like Jean-Baptiste le Rond d'Alembert and Edmund Burke, Baretti had many character witnesses at his trial and had three lawyers representing him. Ultimately acquitted of the well-publicized murder charge at his well-attended trial, Baretti described what had happened on the streets of London to his three brothers in Turin, framing his actions as ones justified by self-defense. "That evening, going along one of the largest and most frequented streets of this city," Baretti wrote from London eleven days after the incident that led to his arrest on a cold, wet night, "one of those many poor whores, that go around there every night causing commotion and fornicating and stealing, gave me a big punch in the parts that one doesn't mention." After Baretti relayed that he "returned the compliment with an open hand" to the woman's hand or face, he explained what happened next in his October 17, 1769 letter to his three brothers in Turin: "The slut began to scream like a demon and to give me some nice names. All of the sudden some of her bullies were on top of me with punches. I tried to flee, but the kicks and punches on every side would not permit me."

At trial, Baretti—a lover of books who would've been quite familiar with Beccaria's writings—described the use of his knife to fend off the men. The knife was, he said, a table utensil normally used "to carve fruit and sweetmeats, and not to kill my fellow creatures." "The day of Baretti's trial," an historian of the case reports, giving a sense of the harsh punishments of the era, "three men had been found guilty and sentenced to death—one for highway robbery, another for forgery, and another for 'stealing money and linen.'" Baretti—in a show of confidence—chose to be judged by a jury of Englishmen instead of foreigners, as was his right, and he gave a statement of his innocence. Baretti himself once noted that while English convicted murderers were hanged, those tried and convicted in Italy were confined in a galley, often for life.[29] Baretti had published first in Milan, but he had left for London in 1751, viewing that English city—per one description—as "the city of intellectuals, of Enlightenment, of empiricism; it was anti-academic and anti-pedantic, innovative, receptive to new and open-minded enterprises, such as those offered by the continuing developments in the field of journalism." As that source observes: "Baretti immersed himself as fully as possible in this exciting environment, where he was mentored by writer, critic, and lexicographer Samuel Johnson (1709–1784)." Baretti soon began publishing in English and published a favorable review of Giuseppe Parini's *Il mattino*.[30]

Starting at the end of 1766, a period of time in which Cesare Beccaria's treatise was being read by leading Italian and French *philosophes*, Pietro Verri—Beccaria's mentor—himself served as a *cavalier servente* to Maddalena Beccaria, Cesare's younger sister. Then almost forty years old and still a bachelor, Pietro was twice as old as 20-year-old Maddalena, who, in 1766, had married Giulio Cesare Isimbardi, a man five years older. Her first child was born in 1767, the same year *Dei delitti e delle pene* was first translated into English, and in long letters that Pietro wrote to his brother Alessandro in Rome, Pietro described the intense *cavalier servente* relationship—and the infatuation and personal bond—that he had with Maddalena. Part of the role that Pietro saw for himself was "to release" the husband "from watching over his wife," and the resulting love triangle was full of petulance, jealousy and quarrels. Italian nobles often married later in life, and there was frequently an age gap between spouses, though Maddalena's husband was closer in age to her than most Milanese husbands of that time. In Milan in the first half of the eighteenth century, the average age for men to marry was 33.5 compared to 21 for women. And the *cicisbei* played routine, public roles in the lives of eighteenth-century Italian nobles. As Robert Bizzocchi observes of the family of Beccaria's intellectual mentor: "Pietro Verri writes from Milan in 1777 that one of his younger brothers, Carlo, 'has started his regular service' and, having gone to the lady's country house, stayed there 'for a month as her official escort'...." Pietro Verri's own name appears on the 1766 marriage contract between Maddalena Beccaria and her husband Giulio Cesare Isimbardi—not at that time as a *cavalier servente* but as a *mediatore* (mediator) by which legal matters pertaining to assets and property were worked out.

Pietro Verri's relationship with Cesare Beccaria's sister, Maddalena, which evolved into something far more intimate than a go-between, was described by Pietro Verri in lengthy letters to his brother Alessandro, who settled in Rome after his 1766–1767 trip to Paris and London. Between 1761 and 1766, Alessandro Verri—his brother Pietro's frequent confidante—had diligently worked on his *Saggio sulla storia d'Italia* (*Essay on the History of Italy*), a work "for which he held great expectations" to use the words of one literary encyclopedia. Alessandro was a huge proponent of free speech and after working as a lawyer in his position as "protector of prisoners," he wrote a series of articles about the need for legislative reform. Not only did he share the same perspectives on law reform set forth in Beccaria's *Dei delitti e delle pene*, but he—as the *Encyclopedia of Italian Literary Studies* points out—"pursued a radical change of attitude in literature and in language and engaged in a strong polemic against what he and the *Caffè* group saw as the crystalized academic institutions whose aim was the defense of pedantry and their symbol, the prestigious *Accademia della Crusca*, which, with its influential *Vocabolario*, first published in 1612 and reissued for the fourth time in 1738, set the vernacular of Tuscany as the model of literary

Italian." "Refusing any imposition of language standards," that source emphasizes of Alessandro and his beliefs, "he asserted the right to a free expression in what was to become the most famous article published in *Il Caffè*, 'Rinunzia avanti nodaro degli autori del presente foglio periodico al Vocabolario della Crusca' (Renunciation of the Crusca Vocabulary Made in Front of the Notary by the Authors of This Broadsheet, 1764). Under the motto 'Preferire le idee alle parole' (prefer ideas to words), Verri rejected any restriction imposed 'all'onesta libertà de' loro pensieri, e della ragion loro' (to the honest freedom of their thoughts, and their reason)." "The polemical vigor of this article," that encyclopedia stresses, "brought about a lively debate, to which also contributed, in defence of Alessandro's thesis, both Beccaria and Pietro Verri."

In all, Alessandro Verri wrote 32 articles for the *Il Caffè* gazette, and they reflected the issues and ideas that fascinated intellectuals of that time. After settling in Rome, Alessandro continued his writing career, though he had to be careful about what he published and, over time, he took a much different path than Beccaria's career as a public councilor. "[A]fter his move from Milan to Rome in 1767," the *Encyclopedia of Italian Literary Studies* records of the fate of his *Saggio sulla storia d'Italia*, "aware of the risks connected to the publication of this work and fearing the intervention of the Inquisition, he decided to ask the publisher to stop the printing." "After working on translations of Shakespeare and Homer and on the plays *Pantea* and *I fatti di Milano* (The Events in Milan), published together as *Tentativi drammatici* (Attempts to Drama, 1779)," the encyclopedia summarizes his continued productivity through the years, "he wrote a series of novels that would give him great notoriety: *Le avventure di Saffo poetessa di Mitilene* (The Adventures of Sappho, Poet of Mitilene, 1782); *Le notti romane al sepolcro de' Scipioni* (The Roman Nights; or Dialogues at the Tombs of the Scipios), the first part of which was published in 1792, the second in 1804, while the third remained unpublished until 1967); and *La vita di Erostrato* (The Life of Erostratus, 1815)." Alessandro had studied law with the Barnabite fathers in Milan, but in Rome, after his trip to Paris and London, he had fallen in love with the Marquise Margherita Boccapadule Gentile and ended up residing there.[31]

The letters between Pietro and Alessandro Verri, both of whom shared an interest in poetry, literature and drama, are extremely revealing—as are the early writings of the Verri brothers. In the 1750s, before his brother, Alessandro, and their one-time, fast friend, Cesare Beccaria, had garnered their fame, Pietro had engaged in his own literary pursuits, publishing a collection of satirical poems, *Lo Borlanda impasticciata* (The Messed Up Borlanda, 1751); writing about comedy and theater; penning an almanac titled *Il gran Zoroastro* (The Great Zoroaster), described as "a wry satire of the Milanese aristocracy and of popular prejudices, written in a mixture of languages, including Milanese dialect and Greek"; and translating, with Vittoria Ottoboni, plays by a French writer. When the 38-year-old Pietro began serving as an escort for Maddalena at the end of 1766, she was already pregnant. But Pietro—the new *cavalier servente*—quickly fell in love with Maddalena, writing on June 13, 1767, to his brother Alessandro, referring to himself in the third person: "Would you believe that Pietro is devoted to a single object, scrupulously faithful and very much in love after eight months?" By September of that year, Pietro—who often referred to Maddalena's husband as the "imbecile"—was overflowing about Maddalena, the younger woman: "I, dear Alessandro, have never loved so much in my whole life." Another of Pietro's letters, also sent in September 1767, shows the closeness—the readily apparent intimacy—between Pietro and Maddalena. "Do you know that simply mentioning one of my previous women friends is enough to give rise to indignation, bad temper and terrible quarrels," Pietro confided to his brother about "the storm of jealousy" that was "unleashed" when Pietro simply greeted a woman, Signora Brioschi, in Maddalena's presence, leading to a "miserable evening." "But the good things that adorable creature gives me makes me forget the very acute pain she causes me," Pietro stressed, adding in his letter: "I am loved, just as my heart needs to be loved, that is with passion; I love forcefully: heart and spirit, virtue, generosity, with the vigour of my soul, everything is in that consolation of mine; her feelings are not superficial, she has no vanity, she is a rare being."

In another letter to his brother Alessandro, one dated December 31, 1768, Pietro described some of the emotional difficulties that went along with being a cicisbeo—the purpose of which one Scottish novelist, Tobias Smollett, described in *Travels through France and Italy* (1765). "[T]he custom of choosing cicisbei," Smollett wrote, "was calculated to prevent the extinction of families, which would otherwise often happen in consequence of marriages founded upon interest, without any mutual affection in the contracting parties."[32] In Pietro's letter, which disparaged Maddalena's moody husband, Giulio Cesare Isimbardi, the marital match chosen for her for financial reasons, Pietro wrote:

> I brought the gentleman, Isimbardi, with me to Lodi; I fed him well, and I gave him some good Burgundy to drink; I made sure that he had a good journey by coach; he was in a good mood. When I took him home, Maddalena wraps her arms around his neck, she caresses him; he accepts everything as his due because of his rare beauty, he becomes bad-tempered, he thinks he's important, and he made me spend an unpleasant evening, very boring, in his house.

After Pietro's erstwhile romantic (and at times annoying) rival, Isimbardi, died unexpectedly in June 1778, Pietro bluntly reported to Alessandro that "Cavaliere Isimbardi is dead." Pietro—emotionally invested in Maddalena—later described the circumstances of Isimbardi's death and speculated about Maddalena's own feelings towards her late husband. As Pietro wrote of Isimbardi and then Maddalena, to whom he had once been so close: "He had been at Stradella for the last two years, living in a strange manner; for some days his knees had been very painful; after that he had a terrible fever, and it is said that yesterday night he must have succumbed. If this is so, we'll see whether her conduct was due to love, fear, or a similarity in their characters."[33]

The relationship between Pietro Verri and Maddalena had soured shortly before Isimbardi's untimely death in mid-1778. Several months earlier, in 1776, Pietro—then 47 years of age—had in fact decided to take a wife of his own. Pietro was, by then, an extremely respected and prominent figure in Milanese life. He had become the vice-president of the Chamber of Counts in 1772, with Pietro ultimately becoming that body's president in 1780. Pietro, writing of Cesare Beccaria's sister, Maddalena, once spoke of her "good, amiable" yet "savage" temperament in what was clearly part of a love-hate relationship. In May 1769, less than three years after Cesare Beccaria's 1766 trip to Paris, Pietro was—at that time—still very much torn about Maddalena—and, likely, still deeply in love. In one of his many letters, Pietro had this to report to his brother Alessandro: "The most frivolous illusions give rise to tumults of bad temper and distress; and there is almost always a witness: either the imbecile, or her father or mother; and I, flayed in my deepest sensitivity, can only stifle my feelings, in fact invent pretexts, to make others' outbursts appear natural. To have very bitter disputes and be unable to speak freely is an intolerable situation!" After returning from a trip to Vienna a couple years later, Pietro told Alessandro in October 1771 that he felt "very consoled to be near Maddalena," and in the spring of 1773 he went out of his way to praise Maddalena's devotion to her dying mother. But on December 25, 1773, as Christians around the globe celebrated Christmas, Pietro reported that his feelings for Maddalena had diminished, a decline in affection that no doubt led to his decision to marry another woman. In that letter, he said that he felt "quite lukewarm towards" Maddalena, noting in exasperation: "After seven years we are back at square one. She has never adopted a placid and reserved approach, going to extremes with her husband either tomfoolery or bitterness, and she doesn't control her outbursts of inappropriate jealousy even in front of her husband: this perpetuates a miserable and precarious life." By January 1774, Pietro was resolved to take his life in a new, less volatile direction. As he emphasized at that time to his brother, Alessandro, he no longer felt any passion for Maddalena. Pietro's news of his impending marriage nonetheless led to a six-page letter from Maddalena—the woman who had grown so accustomed to Pietro's attentions—which, Pietro reported of her letter, "breaks my heart."[34]

Pietro Verri's chosen bride, Maria Castiglioni, was 25 years younger than Verri and was actually the daughter of one of his own sisters, Teresa. The sole sister of Pietro, Alessandro, Carlo and Giovanni Verri, Teresa Francesca Castiglioni (Verri), born in 1733, was the daughter of Gabriele Verri (1696–1782) and his wife. But Teresa had died in 1761 before reaching the age of thirty, something not that uncommon in the eighteenth century when knowledge and understanding of illnesses—and the practice of medicine—was still in its infancy. The aristocratic Castiglioni family included Count Luigi Castiglioni (1757–1832) and his brother, Count Alfonso Castiglioni (1756–1834), both talented botanists and, through marriage, related to Pietro and Alessandro Verri. Alfonso and Luigi graduated from the *Collegio dei nobili* between 1775 and 1776, and they wrote extensively about plants and their uses. In the mid-1780s, Luigi Castiglioni—the more adventurous of the brothers—traveled through Genova, Montpellier, Paris and London, then boarded a ship bound for North America, a place that another adventurous Italian noble, Count Paolo Andreani (1763–1823), known for the first hot air balloon flight over Italian soil in 1784, also explored on a trip that began in 1790. In France, Condorcet "graciously received" Luigi Castiglioni and introduced him to Malesherbes, and he dined with Joseph II's ambassador and was "received" by Benjamin Franklin at Passy "with every possible cordiality." It is known that Benjamin Franklin owned a copy of Beccaria's book as the American Philosophical Society, through its treasurer, John Vaughan, authorized its purchase from Franklin's library in September 1801.

Enduring long stretches of travel, Luigi Castiglioni visited all of the original thirteen American states—as well as what is modern-day Canada—in the wake of America's Revolutionary War (1775–1783), later chronicling his trip in a lengthy travelogue, originally published in Italian as *Viaggio negli Stati Uniti dell'America settentrionale fatto negli anni 1785, 1786 e 1787*. It was published in Milan in 1790 by Giuseppe Marelli, and not translated into English until the late twentieth century. On his trip, Castiglioni met a number of leading founders, including Benjamin Franklin, John and Samuel Adams, Robert Morris and John Hancock. Among many other well-known places he visited were George Washington's Mount Vernon and Thomas Jefferson's Monticello. On his own trip in the summer of 1790, Count Andreani—the other adventurer from Milan—traveled along the Hudson and Mohawk Rivers, taking meticulous notes on his voyage. In New York, then the nation's capital, Count Andreani lodged in the same boardinghouse as Thomas Jefferson and James Madison, a guest at Vandine Ellsworth's boardinghouse on Maiden Lane. With Congress in session, Andreani was able—in the words of one account of his journey—"to circulate among the nation's political elite." One of Count Andreani's descendants, Count Antonio Sormani Verri of Milan, later authorized the publication of Count Andreani's journal. Before his departure for North America, Count Andreani—such were his impressive connections—received a letter addressed to George Washington from Oxford University's John Paradise. Andreani and Paradise shared a passion for linguistics, and Paradise asked Andreani to give President George Washington "an ode" written by Count Vittorio Alfieri. In a letter to Thomas Jefferson, John Paradise's wife, Lucy Ludwell Paradise, characterized Count Andreani as "a learned amiable Nobleman ... worthy of every attention" and asked that Jefferson, her fellow American, "take the trouble to introduce Count Andreani by letter to our Friends in Virginia &c. &c. &c."[35]

Prior to tying the knot, Pietro Verri and his late sister's daughter took considerable time to get to know one another. Maria Castiglioni had lived in the Verri home as a guest for four years before their marriage, and Pietro Verri had come to see her good qualities—as well as the benefits of an English-style marriage. As Pietro wrote to his brother Alessandro on December 6, 1775:

> I have at this time made these decisions; I can tell you that although I do not feel passion for our niece, I feel friendship towards her, and I feel able to see to her happiness; her modesty, the nobility of her manners and feelings, her virtual shyness, the ease with which she blushes, her common sense, everything promises me a sweet companion. It is my firm intention to be my wife's friend and lover. I don't like dissipation, on the contrary family life. After lunch going for a walk, in the evening together at the theatre in our permanent box; I no longer want to be involved with gallantries: in London marriages are happy because they live like that, I will not blush at loving my wife and taking care of her.

In a letter written directly to Maria, his bride-to-be, Pietro wrote: "In short, I would like to be worthy of being seen by you as your lover and your best friend, as I will be solely concerned with you and being as good to you as I can." Of course, not all eighteenth-century Italian marriages were arranged or tempestuous, with Giuseppe Baretti's 1769 book, *An Account of the Manners and Customs of Italy*, a defense of *cicisbeism*, arguing that love and jealousy—two common human emotions—are fairly equally distributed between the English and Italians.[36]

In the 1770s, the decade that Cesare Beccaria joined the Supreme Economic Council, Pietro Verri himself was as busy as ever writing even as he courted and chose a wife. He published *Meditazioni sull'economia politica* (*Meditations on Political Economy*, 1771), where he wrote of supply and demand; *Dell'indole del piacere e del dolore* (*Discourse on Pleasure and Pain*, 1773); and in 1777 he wrote *Osservazioni sulla tortura* (*Observations on Torture*, 1804), a work that was only published after his death by Pietro Custodi (1771–1842). The latter manuscript became the main source for Alessandro Manzoni's *Storia della colonna infame* (*The Column of Infamy*, 1840), but Pietro Verri had written about torture—and other issues of law reform—contemporaneously with Beccaria. In *Il mal di milza* (*The Milt of Pain*, 1764), Pietro had parodied the subject of torture, and he was not only, like his brother, a productive writer, but he was not afraid to take on the establishment when it suited him. During the short life of *Il Caffè*, Pietro contributed 37 articles; his "*Sui parolai e sullo spirito della letteratura italiana*" (On Chatterboxes and on the Spirit of Italian Literature, 1765), one of those contributions, sharply "criticized the empty formalistic and purist approach to language of the *Accademia della Crusca* and advocated a new literary language, open to gallicisms and neologisms and based on the social and scientific achievements of his age." In his writings, Verri—like Voltaire—often resorted to the use of satire or parody to get across his points. As his entry in the *Encyclopedia of Italian Literary Studies* explains, referencing Pietro Verri's "Gli studi utili" (The Useful Studies, 1765) and another one of his works published in *Il Caffè*: "The use of a parodic prose to introduce reformist positions also characterizes the *Orazione panegirica sulla giurisprudenza milanese* (*Panegyric Oration on Milanese Jurisprudence*, 1763), an ironic description of the Milanese government."

Pietro Verri, like Cesare Beccaria, had been in a familial dispute with his own father. Pietro came from a tradition-bound aristocratic family, and he had a very traditional education, studying literature and philosophy in Monza, Milan and Rome, before completing his studies in Parma. "When Pietro Verri was born in 1728," one journal article on European history recounts, "his father, Gabriele Verri, with close ties to the court at Vienna and as Vicar of Provision for Milan was the most powerful official in Lombardy." In his mid-twenties, Pietro had travelled to Vienna with his father—a patrician described as "a conservative" and "a magistrate in the *stato Milanese*"—in 1753. But while Gabriele Verri "remained a staunch supporter of the old way," his son, Pietro, "became a moderate liberal reformer." Disgusted with "the old order," Pietro served in the Austrian army from 1759 to 1760 before returning to Milan in 1761 to try to reform the law and the Milanese society that his father so voraciously defended. Pietro Verri—as one source puts it—"repudiated the conservative, judicial, precedent-saturated outlook of his father, Senator Gabriele Verri." As still another history records of Pietro Verri's break with his father, a conflict that was part of a broader societal dispute that pitted one generation of nobles against another: "Pietro Verri's clash with his father was particularly emblematic of this generational conflict. Gabriele Verri had played an important part in the counter-attack of the Milanese establishment against the incursions of the Austrian government, defending in a series of works the local legal and administration traditions of the Lombard region. Pietro, however, bitterly criticised the antiquarian and jurisprudential culture that then dominated in Milan and placed all state affairs in the hands of lawyers and scholars." In his work, Pietro Verri was—time and again—guided by Enlightenment thought as he did his work as a public servant. "I shall always," he observed, "look upon d'Alembert, Voltaire, Helvétius, Rousseau, and David Hume as men of a superior order destined to live for centuries to come."[37]

In his *Discourse on Pleasure and Pain*, published just two years before America's Revolutionary War, Pietro Verri explained that every nation is shaped by its physical locale, climate and landscape as well as by its governing laws. It is only need and pain, defined by a lack of natural resources, Verri asserted, that will arouse a man or nation from *indolenza* (indolence). "His *Ricordi a mia figlia* (Advice to My Daughter), written in 1777," historian Marta Cavazza writes in a book chapter on women and science in eighteenth-century Italy, "seem to reinvent the traditional model of femininity for a secular readership." Verri, Cavazza stresses, was convinced that "a certain level of education was necessary for women in the higher social classes; this was not only so that they might better govern their houses but also so that they might participate in social life and particularly in conversations." For his own daughter, Teresa, Pietro Verri insisted on a liberal arts education that included the study of music, drawing, novels, works by Locke and Rousseau, tragedies and comedies, and history. To allow her "to witness God," Pietro also wanted her to study astronomy and learn from looking into microscopes. Still, Verri's views toward women were, in other ways, rather paternalistic and very much reflective of the time. In *Ricordi*, he wrote that "the singular merit of woman is sweetness and modesty," advising his daughter "you can never be too modest" and that women should avoid "the rash desire for public esteem" that compelled women "to show off what they know." He specifically warned his own daughter, Teresa, against becoming "truly learned and scholarly" as it would inhibit her ability to find a mate. But when Pietro's wife, Maria, died prematurely at age 27 in 1781, it was *he* who resorted to a display of tenderness. As he wrote in a plaintive recollection: "Many times I used to tell Maria that the moment when I had loved her least had been that of our wedding and that now I loved her more than last year, and last year more than the year before."[38]

Just as Pietro Verri had once been a *cicisbeo*, Cesare Beccaria's own marriage to his first wife Teresa—said to be a "very attractive and extremely bubbly" woman—involved, per the custom of the time, a wealthy, aristocratic *cicisbeo*, too. A few years after Cesare married Teresa de Blasco in 1761, "the young couple"—as historian Roberto Bizzocchi notes—"were involved in a well-consolidated *ménage à trois* with an even younger Milanese nobleman, Bartolomeo Calderara (or Calderari), born in 1747." As Bizzocchi writes: "The fact that Calderara frequently kept Teresa company was not only known to Beccaria, it was also a recurring theme in his correspondence with his wife, who, among other things, acted as an intermediary for the affectionate greetings and mutual reminiscences between the two men, as well as for the other members of their *conversazione*." Though Calderara was "the main and permanent escort," the young couple were also often joined by other intellectuals and friends. They included a Milanese nobleman, Count Giuseppe Visconti di Saliceto (1731–1807), and "a man of letters" from Abruzzo—one Troiano Odazzi (1741–1794), often spelled Odazi. Odazi was—it has been written—"a settled guest of Calderara." Count Visconti, an active member of the Academy of Fists, wrote on matters of hygiene and meteorology, while Odazi was, like Pietro Verri and Cesare Beccaria, an economist. Odazi had come to Milan from Naples on the recommendation of his teacher, the prominent Neapolitan philosopher and political economist Antonio Genovesi, and he became close to Beccaria, most likely because of their shared interests and passions. In Naples, Odazi himself had worked as an editor in the printing house of Giovanni Gravier, who had, in 1770, bravely published a collection of Cesare Beccaria's banned writings, including *Dei delitti e delle pene*. "Everything was conducted openly with the greatest nonchalance," Roberto Bizzocchi observes of Teresa's various male escorts.[39]

The historian Marzio Barbagli—an expert on the history of Italian family life— has written that "[t]he cicisbeo was chosen jointly by wife and husband and was sometimes provided for in the nuptial contracts." Formal marriage contracts were then standard, with another commentator, historian Cesare Cantù, also emphasizing that "in nuptial contracts it was stipulated that a *cavalier servente* be given to the lady, and a specific individual was sometimes even named." Cesare Beccaria, his wife Teresa, and her chosen *cicisbeo*, Bartolomeo Calderara (1747–1806), seem to have gotten along swimmingly, and the threesome, whatever their precise interactions and living and sleeping arrangements, lived a luxurious and highly cultured life. In addition to their daily lives in the metropolis of Milan, they spent time in the Lake Como area in a villa near *Isola Comacina* (Comacina Island) built in the first half of the eighteenth century. The villa's locale was originally known as "la Puncia," a dialect term that indicated the estate's position, reaching out into the gorgeous, internationally renowned lake. As a modern-day luxury villa rental website describes Sala Comacina, the village where the villa is located, and its historical connection to Cesare Beccaria:

> If tiny villages with less than 600 residents are your passion, Sala Comacina should be in your visiting list, and certainly not only for its size. Sala Comacina is located in one of the most beautiful areas of Lake Como, in the incredible scenery of the Isola Comacina, close to an inlet called "the oil hollow" for the view of the olive trees on the surrounding hills and the calmness of the water. Apparently, up until a few decades ago, Sala Comacina was one part of a single municipal district with Ossuccio and Colonno. Still today, the old part of the village lies between the church of San Bartolomeo and the lake: the steep little streets that connects the buildings with their characteristic stone gates lead down to the promontory called "La Puncia". It is worth the effort, and the prize is the view of Villa Beccaria, the 18th century

abode of the Beccaria Bonesana marquis, that over the years has hosted many personalities of the Italian culture such as Cesare Beccaria, the author of the famous treatise "On Crimes and Punishments" (1764).[40]

As an aristocrat, Cesare Beccaria hobnobbed with many important and wealthy figures, and he himself had the luxury to ponder the concepts of wealth, luxury and leisure. In *Opera and Sovereignty: Transforming Myths in Eighteenth-century Italy*, Martha Feldman writes that "[l]uxury was a flashpoint in Italian enlightenment discourses of the time." As she explains: "[T]he great Italian writers who engaged the problem of luxury (*lusso*)—Pietro Verri (1728–97) and Cesar[e] Beccaria (1738–94) in Lombardy, economists Antonio Genovesi (1712–69) and Ferdinando Galiani (1728–87) in Naples— fretted along with many others over its relationship to public good and happiness. They deemed luxury a wondrous if sometimes corrupting influence in the arts, and puzzled over its moral ambiguities." Feldman describes *Dei delitti e delle pene* as "the most celebrated work of the Italian enlightenment," with another source noting that Beccaria's book actually "intersects with the world of opera, since it was first published in Livorno by the opera librettist Marco Coltellini, father of the soprano Celeste, and author of reform libretti inspired by Francesco Algarotti's operatic theories and predating Calzabigi's and Gluck's reformed operas."[41] "By the middle of the seventeenth century, the early opera performances held at the courts of the Italian nobility had gained popularity throughout Italy," Alan Sikes writes in *Studies in Eighteenth-century Culture*. "Castrati," Sikes explains of young boys castrated to preserve their vocal characteristics, "played a pivotal role in the spread of opera; many talented castrati, while remaining active within the Church, were also increasingly retained by opera companies."

Italians were serious about their opera, even if it meant castrating pre-teens to produce the voices that gave it some of its life. *Castrati*—as Martha Feldman writes in an essay on the subject—"were first cultivated in the sixteenth century to supply north Italian and papal chapels with powerful high voices." "Pauline doctrine," Feldman writes, "prohibited female speech in church, and falsettists' voices were not as rich and piercing as those of castrati." Eventually, she explains, Italian chapels "came to be staffed with castrati on high parts—not least the pope's chapel, the Cappella Sistina, which employed castrati from the later sixteenth century to 1913; and that castrati could be found in opera houses throughout almost all of Europe from 1607 until 1830." Castrated men were prohibited from marrying, with "the typical castrato"—as Feldman explains—"born into a home of poor or middle-class parents" and castrated "as boy singer sometime between the ages of about seven and thirteen." As Alan Sikes explains of the role that castrati played as Italian operatic themes developed from one century to the next: "While opera of the seventeenth century abounded in sexual adventures pursued across all traditional gender boundaries, the opera of the early eighteenth century witnessed a general turn from salacious stories of illicit passion to honorable tales of virtuous love." Only over time, as the Enlightenment took hold and castrati came to be seen for what they were—as mutilated young men deprived of normal childhoods and the ability to have families of their own—did their popularity decline.[42]

Italy has long been known for its paintings and architecture, its beautiful museums and opera houses, and its pasta and coffeehouses and marble sculptures. A popular eighteenth-century destination for European Grand Tours, Cesare Beccaria got to live—and to soak up the culture—in the place that has inspired so many artists, novelists and other writers, if only for a few months or years at a time. For instance, the English historian Edward Gibbon's three-month, 1764 visit to Rome inspired his well-known, six-volume history, *The Decline and Fall of the Roman Empire* (1776–1783). Because of his aristocratic status, Beccaria himself interacted with many of the leading figures in Italy's arts, music and entertainment scenes. It is known, for example, that after serving as the director of ballet at the Imperial Theatre in Vienna, Gasparo Angiolini—a well-known choreographer and dancer—came back to his native country in 1778 and took up the position of choreographer at the La Scala theatre in Milan. "His villa, Malgacciata, outside the city," writes historian Christopher Duggan, "was frequented by such luminaries as the poet Giuseppe Parini and the jurist Cesare Beccaria." Bartolomeo Calderara, Cesare Beccaria's trusted confidante and the *cavalier servente* of Beccaria's first wife, Teresa, later married Vittoria Peluso, a ballerina nicknamed "Pelusina" who danced on the La Scala stage. "In 1784," one source notes of the "Milanese playboy Marquis Calderara" and his acquisition of an opulent villa in Cernobbio on Lake Como: "the Villa had a new proprietor in the person of Marquis Bartolomeo Calderara," said to be "a dissolute and affluent" aristocrat "who squandered a fortune on wine, women and song."[43] That villa—once a Jesuit spiritual retreat before it passed through the hands of a series of Italian counts and, eventually, a Napoleonic general after Marquis Calderara's death—later became the famous Villa d'Este, now a luxury resort.[44]

In this world of high culture—of endless conversations and contradictions, of light and darkness, of classical music, ballet and opera, of romance and drink, and pronounced class distinctions—Cesare Beccaria's book stood out from other titles of his day. From its initial publication to its serial translations, *Dei delitti e delle pene* was considered either a dangerous text or a *tour de force* by leading intellectuals. It was, in any event, a book not to be ignored, and despite having borrowed many of its ideas from others, it quickly became a bestseller. After it became clear that Beccaria would not be punished for writing *Dei delitti e delle pene* and his authorship became known, no less a figure than the German-born Russian empress, Catherine II, invited him to come to St. Petersburg to assist in legal reforms she was undertaking in Russia. As historian Marcello Maestro recounts: "On November 18, 1766, while Beccaria was still in Paris, a friend of his, Gaspare Angiolini, whose talents as a choreographer were appreciated highly by Catherine, wrote him a letter from Russia in which he referred to the treatise *On Crimes and Punishments*." Gasparo Angiolini (1731–1803), as his name is also spelled, was a famous dancer, composer and choreographer who shaped eighteenth-century ballet, working in Russia from 1766 to 1772 and, later, from 1776 to 1779 and from 1782 to 1786. "I am pleased to tell you," Angiolini wrote in his November 18, 1766 letter, "that our empress has already read your book and that she was touched by the strength with which you have served and sustained the cause of humanity."

The actual offer for Beccaria to come to Russia came from Antonio Greppi (1722–1799), an Italian banker, diplomat, merchant and politician. As Maestro writes: "Antonio Greppi was an indirect representative of Catherine II of Russia; she had given instructions for the offer to Beccaria to a commercial agent of Venice in St. Petersburgh, named Pano Maruzzi, who asked Greppi to get in touch with Beccaria." Greppi inquired as to Beccaria's interest in the position and asked on what terms he would be willing to travel to Russia. For a twentysomething, recent law graduate who aspired to literary fame, it must have been heady stuff indeed, even for a person in Cesare Beccaria's rarified social stratosphere. After being solicited by Catherine the Great for his advice and assistance, Beccaria conferred with his new friends from Paris, the French *philosophes*. Beccaria's translator, André Morellet, vehemently opposed the change, writing: "I don't understand how you can seriously ask if you should go to Russia. If you had no family and no friends, if you were in a country with a bad climate, I would say: go. But in your situation it would be insane, especially with your character and your anxieties: you would certainly be very unhappy if you were far from your friends, from your country, far from the new books and without contacts with writers and men of letters." "You need these things more than anyone else," Morellet emphasized, knowing Beccaria's personality and eccentricities. "Please think well before taking a decision," the French mathematician Jean le Rond d'Alembert further counseled, adding bluntly: "Remember that if you go to Russia you would give up a very beautiful climate for an ugly country, you would give up freedom for slavery, and you would leave your friends for a princess who is full of merits, it is true, but it is better to have her as a mistress than as a wife."

While the French *philosophes* thought that Cesare Beccaria should stay in Italy, Beccaria had the smarts and presence of mind to communicate his offer from Catherine II to Milan's governor, Count Firmian, who in turn reported the Russian empress's enticing offer to his superior, Count Kaunitz, in Vienna. Even if Beccaria decided early on that he was not interested in going to Russia, Catherine II's offer gave him leverage to get the government position in Milan that he had previously sought. Count Karl Joseph Firmian (1716–1782)—the Governor-General of Lombardy, and described as "a sort of King of Milan"—was a highly influential official and patron of the arts, and after getting word of the offer of the Russian empress, he did everything within his power to keep Cesare Beccaria in that highly cultivated city.[45] And the State Chancellor of the Habsburg monarchy from 1753 to 1792, the even more powerful Wenzel Anton Kauntiz—the diplomat said to be virtually "the third head of state" under Empress Maria Theresa and her son, Joseph II—was equally receptive to Firmian's entreaties. "Beccaria was in no hurry to reject the Russian offer," one historian explains, taking note of how Beccaria was exploring the possibility of employment in Milan with Count Firmian and how Catherine II's offer of employment was "an ace in Beccaria's hand and he had decided to use it." Beccaria understood games of chance and the laws of supply and demand, and he played his cards just right, leveraging Catherine II's offer to make a play for a job in his native Milan.

Because Counts Firmian and Kaunitz did not want to lose someone of Beccaria's keen intellect, a chair in political economy was founded for Beccaria in 1768 in Milan's Palatine School under the rubric of *Scienze Camerali*. "The Vienna Imperial Court, opposing Beccaria's emigration," the *History of Universities* recounts of how Beccaria ended up with the chair, "conveniently recalled his earlier interest in an official position in state administration." Beccaria's older friend and fellow *Il Caffè* contributor, the economist, historian and archeologist Gian Rinaldo Carli (1720–1795), had pushed in 1765—via a letter to Count Firmian—for Beccaria to become a member of Lombardy's Supreme Economic Council. Born in Capo d'Istria in the Republic of Venice, Carli had been a professor of astronomy and navigation at the University of Padua and, in 1754, had published *Delle Monete e della Instituzione delle Zecche d'Italia* (*On the History of the Coins and Currency, and on the Institution of the Mints in Italy*), a work that is illustrated with representations of coins throughout the ages and that assessed their value. Carli wrote about antiquities and against sorcery and his writings caught the attention of the Habsburg family, with Carli reportedly received in Vienna "with great distinction" before Joseph II appointed him as his privy councillor. In May 1766, Beccaria himself had appealed to Count Firmian, seeking to be appointed to the vacant position created by the death of Vincenzo Villavecchia. Both efforts—that of Carli and Beccaria—had been unsuccessful, but when Beccaria's book suddenly soared in popularity and Firmian learned of Catherine II's invitation, he became receptive to finding a way to keep Beccaria in Milan—and, ultimately, to employ him in Lombardy in the Austrian government's service. As the *History of Universities* reports: "To dissuade Beccaria from accepting the invitation, Firmian considered offering him the *Scuole Palatine*'s new chair of public law. Kaunitz approved, but Senator Niccolò Pecci, designer of the legal studies programme, seems to have wanted Alessandro Verri for the position, even though Verri had no interest in teaching." "Beccaria, though a lawyer renowned in penal law for his *Delitti*," that source continues, "showed no perceptible interest in this professorship either, coveting instead the planned cameralist chair."

Count Gian Rinaldo Carli—then the president of the Supreme Economic Council—willingly played along with efforts to keep Beccaria in Milan, producing a study plan at Firmian's request that he presented on April 14, 1768. Its title refers to the new chair using the language *scienze camerali* and *economia civile*, and that plan itself used Beccaria's own "Piano d'istruzioni," which, one historian argues, largely plagiarized Cantillon's work and economics—a fact not too surprising since Beccaria had been focused for so long on the reform of the penal law. The notion of "cameralist sciences" was defined as being devoted to increasing public and private wealth and to the just and useful administration of public property. "The course of studies," as the description in the *History of Universities* points out, was "divided into five parts: general principles, sources of wealth (land and soil, work), basic economic terms (labour, value, property etc.), followed by agriculture, trade, manufacture and finances." After Cesare and his wife, Teresa, returned to Milan from a summer 1768 trip to a resort, Bagni di Pisa, a trip that included stops at Bologna, Ferrara and Venice, Count Firmian wrote to Beccaria on November 1, 1768, to tell him that the court in Vienna had approved the proposed chair for *scienze camerali*. The new course of study would be introduced at the *Scuole Palatine* at the beginning of the new academic year. "With space at the Scuole Palatine still limited," it has been noted, "Beccaria was allowed to invite interested students to his own home after the first public lecture at the *Scuole*." Beccaria got the letter from Firmian at Domaso on Lake Como, and quickly thanked him and accepted the position on November 7, 1768, asking only to begin his lectures after Christmas.[46]

Even though he never went to Russia, Cesare Beccaria nonetheless, because of his criminal-law writings, had a major influence on Russian law. The *Nakaz* of Catherine the Great—formally published on July 30, 1767, as *Instruction of Her Imperial Majesty Catherine the Second for the Commission Charged with Preparing a Project of a New Code of Laws*—ended up containing 526 articles, many of which were heavily influenced by Beccaria's book. Of the 526 articles in Catherine II's *Nakaz*, notes Robert K. Massie, Catherine the Great's biographer, 294 articles were adapted from Montesquieu's *The Spirit of the Laws* and 108 articles were drawn from Beccaria's book.[47] Catherine II was a progressive ruler, seeking—in addition to the abolition of torture and capital punishment—the end of serf auctions and the splitting up of serf families in such sales.[48] Among other things, Catherine II said "every punishment which is not inflicted through necessity is tyrannical"; that "[a]ll punishments, by which the human body might be maimed, ought to be abolished"; and that "the use of Torture is contrary to all Dictates of Nature or Reason; even mankind itself cries out against it, and demands loudly the total Abolition of it."[49] Catherine II wrote her instructions for a Grand Commission composed of 652 members—from officials and nobles to burghers and peasants—who met in Moscow to consider the future of the Russian empire. Catherine admitted that her instructions were the result of "pillaging the philosophers of the West," including Beccaria and Montesquieu, and the commission met more than 200 times before being dissolved. Though Beccaria had carefully considered Catherine II's invitation, he ultimately declined it, preferring the beauty and climate of Italy and his native Milan—and the position he accepted teaching economics at the Palatine School—to an uncertain future in Russia.[50]

Voltaire—the renowned French writer and advocate for the wrongfully condemned—himself heavily promoted Beccaria's book, writing a lengthy, though initially anonymously published pamphlet commenting on it. That commentary, *Commentaire sur le livre des délits et des peines*, said to be written by a "provincial lawyer," was likely co-written by Voltaire and a collaborator, Charles Frédéric Gabriel Christin (1741–1799), a young lawyer who worked with Voltaire in a campaign against serfdom. The commentary became a popular adjunct to Beccaria's book, frequently getting reprinted with it. As law professor Bernard Harcourt notes, Voltaire's commentary "was printed regularly as a preface" to André Morellet's French translation in subsequent translations, thus "propelling Beccaria's tract to fame." Voltaire, one source notes, "was unrivaled in stature as an author," so much so that scholars such as Ariel and Will Durant—the husband and wife team who wrote *The Story of Civilization*—have called the eighteenth century the "Age of Voltaire." "I am ashamed to write about these matters after what has been said by the author of *On Crimes and Punishments*," Voltaire offered, adding: "I should limit myself to hope that we all and often reread this great work by this lover of humanity." Voltaire said Beccaria had toiled "on behalf of reason and humanity, both of which have been quashed for so long." In a letter dated May 30, 1768, Voltaire thanked Beccaria "with all my heart," adding that his sentiments were those of all of Europe. "You revive those two sisters, beaten for over sixteen hundred years," Voltaire wrote of reason and humanity, adding of them: "They are finally beginning to walk and talk; but as soon as they do, fanaticism again rears its ugly head."[51]

That ugly fanaticism and brutality, which Beccaria so opposed, was reflected in the French executions that Voltaire himself found so horrifying. As Victor Hugo, the famed French author and poet, described the state-sanctioned killing in 1762 that had so drawn Voltaire's ire—and that had inspired Beccaria's own book—in a tribute to Voltaire on the 100th anniversary of Voltaire's death: "In the month of March, 1762, a man with white hair, Jean Calas, was conducted to a public place, stripped naked, stretched upon a wheel, the members bound upon it, the head hanging.... The executioner lifts the bar of iron, and breaks one of his arms. The victim groans and swoons. The magistrate comes forward; they make the condemned inhale salts; he returns to life. Then another stroke of the bar; another groan." As Hugo's description of Calas's horrific execution—a truly brutal affair—continued: "Calas loses consciousness; they revive him and the executioner begins again; and, as each limb before being broken in two places receives two blows, that makes eight punishments. After the eighth swooning the priest offers him the crucifix to kiss; Calas turns away his head, and the executioner gives him the coup de grâce; that is to say, crushes in his chest with the thick end of the bar of iron." "So died Jean Calas," Hugo stressed matter of factly, with Hugo—a writer as famous as Voltaire himself—also describing the June 5, 1766 torture and execution of a French teenager, the Chevalier François-Jean de la Barre: "La Barre was drawn to the great square of Abbeville, where flamed a penitential fire; the sentence was read to La Barre; then they cut off one of his hands, then they tore out his tongue with iron pincers; then, in mercy, his head was cut off and thrown into the fire. So died the Chavalier de la Barre. He was nineteen years of age."[52]

In one of his own books, *A Philosophical Dictionary*, Voltaire took note of just how influential Beccaria's *Dei delitti e delle pene* became. In a section on "Justice," Voltaire began: "That 'justice' is often extremely unjust, is not an observation merely of the present day; 'summum jus, summa injuria,' is one of the most ancient proverbs in existence. There are many dreadful ways of being unjust; as for example that of racking the innocent Calas upon equivocal evidence, and thus incurring the guilt of shedding innocent blood, by a too strong reliance on vain presumptions." "Another method of being unjust," Voltaire continued, "is, condemning to execution a man who at most deserves only three months imprisonment; this species of injustice is that of tyrants, and particularly of fanatics, who always become tyrants whenever they obtain the power of doing mischief." "We cannot more completely demonstrate this truth," Voltaire wrote, "than by the letter of a celebrated barrister, written in 1766, to the marquis of Beccaria." That letter was printed in Voltaire's book along with—in a subsequent edition—a 1772 letter from Voltaire to Beccaria himself on the subject of M. de Morangiès.[53] A nobleman and spendthrift, Jean-François de Molette, count of Morangiès, was the field marshal in the royal army but in 1771 had borrowed a large sum of money. A scandal arose after the count asserted that only a small sum of the money had been delivered to him, and the cause célèbre—which pitted "the party of the Nobility and that of the Commoners"—lasted two years and involved no less than eight lawyers and fourteen witnesses. Only in September 1773 was the count, who had Voltaire on his side despite Voltaire's regular skewering of aristocratic pretensions in his own writing, cleared of charges of bribery and swindling. A young intermediary in the affair, François Liégard-Dujonquay, ended up being banished from Paris for three years.[54]

In that subsequent edition of his book, Voltaire called Beccaria—then wrapping up his work as a teacher in Milan, having been appointed in 1768, at age thirty, to the Chair in Public Economy and Commerce at the Palatine School[55]—"one of the most celebrated professors of jurisprudence at this time in Europe." Having declined the offer of Catherine II to come to St. Petersburg to assist in the reform of Russia's penal code, Beccaria had taken the professorship at Milan's Palatine School—one of the first chairs in public economy established in Europe. In making the appointment, Empress Maria Theresa noted that in establishing the chair of political economy, Beccaria—to whom the chair was entrusted—had "acquired with his works a good name among learned men." After an opening salutation, "Sir," the elder Voltaire's flattering letter to the much younger Beccaria read: "You are a teacher of laws in Italy, a country from which we derive all laws except those which have been transmitted to us by our own absurd and contradictory customs, the remains of that ancient barbarism, the rust of which subsists to this day in one of the most flourishing kingdoms of the earth." "Your book upon crimes and punishments," Voltaire stressed in his letter, "opened the eyes of many of the lawyers of Europe who had been brought up in absurd and inhuman usages; and men began everywhere to blush at finding themselves still wearing their ancient dress of savages." Voltaire's letter observed that Beccaria's opinion had been requested "on the dreadful execution to which two young gentlemen just out of their childhood had been sentenced," one of whom—Voltaire noted—had "escaped the tortures he was destined to" but the other of whom "died like a sage, by a horrible death, without ostentation and without pusillanimity, surrounded by no less than five executioners." "You replied, that their judges were assassins, and that all Europe was of your opinion," Voltaire added of Beccaria's response.[56]

Cesare Beccaria's teaching stint at the Palatine School in Milan was short-lived, with Beccaria teaching public economy from 1769 to 1771. Beccaria defined public economy—in Italian "*economia pubblica*"—as "the art of preserving and increasing the wealth of nations and putting it to its best possible use." In his preliminary definition, Beccaria wrote: "*Essendo definita la pubblica economia l'arte di conservare e accrescere le ricchezze di una nazione.*" Beccaria went on to discuss the importance of labor to preserving and increasing wealth, a fact noted by later economic historians. For example, in Henry Dunning Macleod's *A Dictionary of Political Economy* (1863), which describes Beccaria "opening discourse, or *Prolusione*," published in 1769, it is emphasized: "Beccaria, in his very excellent discourse, defines Political Economy and Commerce to be the sciences which point out the means of preserving and increasing the wealth of a State, and making the best use of it." "Every Economical action," that entry continues of its summary of Beccaria's beliefs, "resolves itself into procuring the greatest amount of labor, and services, from the members of a nation, *and in this alone consists the true and original riches, much more than in the quantity of the precious metals,* signs only which run to the calls of industry and labor...."[57] Likewise, in *Dictionary of Political Economy* (1894), edited by Sir Robert Harry Inglis Palgrave, the entry for Cesare Beccaria notes that Beccaria's lectures "certainly are very remarkable considering they were written before A. Smith's *Wealth of Nations*." As that source observes: "Beccaria treats political economy as an art to maximise the value of the produce of work, regarding labourers as engines whose *duty* has to be maximised. From this principle he deduces the necessity of a division of labour, a determination of the value of a labourer, and the nature and function of capital."[58]

As another economic historian, a contemporary one, notes: "Beccaria's definitional comments on political economy closely resemble those of Adam Smith in the introduction to Book IV of the *Wealth of Nations*." As that historian, Peter Groenewegen, observes: "Smith may have been aware of Beccaria's definition, since he owned a three-volume edition of his works published in Naples in 1770–1"—an edition that "included Beccaria's 1769 inaugural lecture which contains these views." Beccaria's 1769 inaugural lecture was given after he took up the new chair in political economy at Milan, with Beccaria's two-year course proposal divided into five segments of great importance to students of economics: (1) general principles and theories of economics, (2) agriculture, (3) commerce, (4) industry, and (5) finance. The official appointment of Beccaria came from Vienna. The decree of December 29, 1768, written in Latin, described the name of Beccaria's chair as "*Oeconomia politica*." Foreseeing a future involving greater trade between nations, Beccaria's two-year course plan had concluded: "If there is some time left at the end of the course I propose to further give a general view of European trade as a whole. This will help to enlarge the young people's ideas, because a man can never be great if he confines himself to what he sees within the borders of his own country."[59]

It was as a lecturer at Milan's Palatine School, built by Carlo Buzzi between 1644 and 1645, that Beccaria discussed topics such as the division of labor—a subject that Adam Smith later took up in *The Wealth of Nations* (1776). "Seven years before Smith," Riccardo Faucci writes in *A History of Italian Economic Thought*, "Beccaria gave a precise definition of the division (specialization) of labour." In *History of Political Economy of Europe*, Jérôme-Adolphe Blanqui—taking note of the work of Francesco Algarotti (1712–1764), and referring to Algarotti as a successor to Antonio Genovesi (1713–1769) though Algarotti actually died before Genovesi—similarly writes: "Algarotti, one of his most celebrated successors, has given us the first analysis of the phenomena of the division of labor, of which the Marquis of Beccaria was to complete the theory almost at the very time when it received, in England, the fine demonstrations of Adam Smith." As Beccaria himself put it in 1769: "Through experience everyone draws the realisation that as a person applies his hand and his mind always to the same kinds of works and products, he more easily obtains the results than if he were to make all things by himself, alone and in an isolated context." Count Francesco Algarotti wrote about many subjects—from poetry, philosophy and philology to economics, history, physics, and the visual arts—and he had a friendship with Voltaire. In 1769, one of Algarotti's many works, *Letters from Count Algarotti to Lord Hervey and the Marquis Scipio Maffei containing the State of the Trade, Marine, Revenues and Forces of the Russian Empire*, was published in English, a translation from the Italian version.[60]

Just a few years before Cesare Beccaria's inaugural lecture, the members of the Academy of Fists had themselves grappled with economic policies in their innovative journal, *Il Caffè* (1764–1766). "*Il Caffè,*" Faucci writes, "was the first Italian periodical that aimed at treating, in brilliant literary style, such challenging topics as the role of commerce, the definition of luxury and the meaning of happiness." "*Il Caffè,*" Faucci explains, "exerted a ceaseless pedagogical impulse against leisure in favour of industry and workmanship." Beccaria's first significant contribution as a mathematical economist, in fact, had come with Beccaria's publication in *Il Caffè* of "*Tentativo analitico sui contrabbandi,*" a two-page piece analyzing the issue of smuggling, in 1764. That article contains sophisticated algebraic calculations, an attempt to apply science and reason to a stubborn and perplexing problem for the local economy.[61] This work was novel in its use of algebra to solve an economic issue, but it was but one of many pieces written by Italians on the subject of economics. As one nineteenth-century source, *History of Political Economy in Europe*, stresses: "Italy, which had the honor of lighting the torch of all the sciences, was the first to devote herself to the study of political economy. While most of the great states of Europe were a prey to financial expedients and to poverty, banks were established at Venice, Milan and Genoa; the first budgets of public expenses and receipts were being prepared at Florence; a silk and wool nobility were being substituted for the nobility of the sword."

As that source continues of Italy's early contributions: "Excellent writings on money revealed the secrets of credit and created the science of finance. There was nothing, even in the misfortunes of the Peninsula, which did not favor the progress of political economy, by making the Italians experience, under Charles V, the disastrous influence of monopolies, high taxes and prohibitions." In taking note of individual Italian economists who made contributions even before Antonio Genovesi and Cesare Beccaria, the author of *History of Political Economy in Europe* observes: "In 1582, Gaspard Scaruffi published his work *On Moneys and the True Proportion between Gold and Silver*. He proposed the creation of a *universal medium* of circulation and the mark of all goldsmiths' work. The Neapolitan Serra, who wrote in 1613 his *Treatise on the Causes which make Gold and Silver abound in Kingdoms*, comprehended the productive power of manufactures. Bandini, the precursor of Quesnay and of the Physiocrates, pointed out the advantages of one single tax, as more easy and more economical; Broggia published the first methodical writing on the theory of taxation."[62]

Beccaria's inaugural lecture was delivered on January 9, 1769 in the great hall of the Palatine School. The physiocrat Pierre-Samuel Du Pont de Nemours (1739–1817), the editor-in-chief of *Ephémérides du citoyen ou Bibliothèque raisonnée des sciences morales et politiques*, the physiocrats' journal, had proudly announced Beccaria's appointment to the chair in political economy, though Du Pont vehemently disagreed with some of Beccaria's ideas. Dupont—as his name is also commonly spelled—lauded Beccaria as one of the first recognized economists, published a French translation of Beccaria's inaugural lecture in his journal, but used his 1769 article about the Italian economist to highlight significant differences in outlook between Beccaria and the physiocrats. When Dupont published the translation of Beccaria's inaugural lecture, he in fact annotated the text and heavily criticized Beccaria's method, at times in a vitriolic fashion. As one modern academic writes: "In his lecture, Beccaria had advocated placing tariffs and charges on the importation of value-added products and on the exportation of primary resources. Dupont took issue: 'it is distressing to hear again these alleged maxims that have caused so much harm, especially from a Philosopher, from an illustrious Professor, charged by the state to refute political errors and to substitute them with the knowledge of useful truths.'" Dupont spent eight pages attacking Beccaria's methodology and policy prescriptions before concluding, "we have already said enough perhaps to show a Philosopher as shrewd as *M. le Marquis de* Beccaria that trying to make a *People* more industrial than liberty and instruction would lead them, amounts to a completely wrongheaded understanding of politics."

Beccaria paid attention to the travails of the poor, and he wanted to curtail the harshness of punishments. In *On Crimes and Punishments*, Beccaria had written: "Thefts without violence should be punished with fines." "Since this is generally the crime of poverty and desperation," Beccaria emphasized of theft, "the crime of that unhappy section of men to whom the perhaps 'terrible' and 'unnecessary' right to property has allowed nothing but a bare existence ... the most fitting punishment shall be the only sort of slavery which can be called just, namely the temporary enslavement of the labour and person of the criminal to society....'" Beccaria had also written, however, that the crime of smuggling—one often perpetrated by wealthy citizens—"deserves a fairly heavy punishment, even up to imprisonment or penal servitude." Dupont's critique focused on the question of the right to property, suggesting that Beccaria had not sufficiently recognized the importance of that right. Dupont wrote that "the *right to property* is not *a terrible right*" and that "*contraband* is not *a theft on the Treasury*." "To Dupont," academic Bernard Harcourt explains, "the *real* criminals are not those who smuggle contraband, but those *who regulate* commerce."

Dupont attacked Beccaria for advocating sending merchants engaged in smuggling to the galleys (*aux galères*) and even conjured up a hypothetical merchant—one "Galérien"—and then protested his conjured fate, calling for liberty of commerce and the pursuit of self-interest. As Dupont stressed: "If there is, then, a true *offense that deserves prison and penal servitude*, it's not that of the smugglers, but that of the *Regulators* who have proposed and still propose, who have compelled and still compel the adoption of royal edicts that hamper trade, of fiscal inquisitions, and of monopolistic threats to the natural rights of citizens, to their property, to their civil liberty, deterring useful work, and as fearsome for public as for private wealth." The divergence of opinion between Dupont and Beccaria—and the ideas of Beccaria about crime control and regulation—would in fact intrigue and inspire writings centuries later, as Bernard Harcourt explains of the writings of the twentieth-century French philosopher Michel Foucault in this passage: "It is the regulatory dimension of Beccaria's thought—highlighted by the Physiocrats—that makes sense, perhaps, of why Beccaria's writings would become such a pivotal aspect of Foucault's work on the birth of the prison and the emergence of the disciplinary form in *Discipline and Punish*, in *The Punitive Society*, and in his later lectures." As Harcourt emphasizes: "Foucault's fascination for the emergence of disciplinary techniques drew his interest both to the police regulations of the Parisian markets in the eighteenth century, especially of the Parisian grain markets, and to Beccaria's treatise *On Crimes and Punishments*."

In *On Crimes and Punishments*, Cesare Beccaria had warned against allowing laws favoring the privileged class while Dupont—a member of that class—found Beccaria's economics to be threatening. "A major theme running through the book," Bernard Harcourt explains, "is that the nobility, the rich and the powerful should be subject to the same forms of punishment and should not be able to buy their way out of justice." As Harcourt explains: "It is a constant refrain—barring which, as Beccaria writes, 'wealth feeds tyranny.'" In his 1764 article in *Il Caffè*, "Tentativo analitico su i contraband," Beccaria had in fact earnestly endeavored—as Harcourt puts it—"to figure out the amount of potential contraband that a merchant had to smuggle in order for the merchant to come out even—to retain the same amount of capital as he originally had in his merchandise—given different rates of tariff imposed by the sovereign authorities and given that he would likely lose some of his contraband." Beccaria, Harcourt writes, "was essentially trying to figure out, for the sovereign, how to fix the tariff at the most advantageous level to maximize the return to the treasury." As Beccaria stressed in his *Il Caffè* article: "We are trying to determine how much a merchant ought to defraud the king's right, in terms of the value of any given commodity, such that, even if he loses the rest, he ends up with the same amount of capital as before thanks to the profit from smuggling." "The advantage of this research, for the drafter of tariffs," Beccaria concluded, "will be to know how much smuggling to expect from the merchants even after a certain number of seizures." For tobacco smugglers, Beccaria had proposed a prison regime that included "toil and exertion in the excise service" which the smugglers had "wished to defraud."

In his inaugural lecture, Beccaria praised "*l'immortel* Montesquieu" and spoke of other leading economists, including Hume, Colbert, Vauban, and "*l'abbé* Genovesi," the latter of whom Beccaria called the "*créateur de cette science en Italie*." In *History of Political Economy of Europe*, Jérôme-Adolphe Blanqui—the successor to Jean-Baptiste Say in the Chair of Political Economy in the Conservatory of Arts and Trades (College de France)—himself wrote in the nineteenth century that "the most celebrated of the Italian economists is unquestionably the professor Genovesi, who may be justly considered the rival of Adam Smith, if not in correctness of doctrine, at least in the impulse he gave to the teaching of the science in all Italy." Genovesi, Blanqui emphasized, "contended for free trade in grain, for the abolition of laws on the interest of money and for the reduction of the number of religious communities." As Blanqui also wrote of Genovesi: "He proclaimed the superiority of labor over the productiveness of mines, to enrich nations. He clearly foresaw, in 1764, the independence of the United States of America and the ruin of the colonial system. His high morality, his eloquence, and his vast erudition constantly attracted to him a multitude of disciples, and although his doctrines favored the mercantile system, he may be considered the founder of political economy in Italy."

But Beccaria, who sought to promote yet regulate commerce by injecting criminal sanctions into the economic sphere, did not pay attention to the work of the French physiocrats in his inaugural lecture. Instead, he spent some of his time lauding his sovereign—something that, of course, would have been expected by his fellow Italian aristocrats in such polite society. As Beccaria opened his lecture: "I am appointed by our august sovereign to teach the principles of public oeconomy and commerce, or those sciences which furnish the means or increasing the riches of a state, and applying them to the most useful purposes." The powerful and politically connected Count Firmian was in the audience, and he—for one—was pleased with Beccaria's lecture, taking the time to send a printed copy of it to Vienna as soon as it was available. For his part, Beccaria—from a personal standpoint—wanted to make clear that he would be a different kind of professor. As Marcello Maestro explained of Beccaria and his inaugural lecture: "The new professor had asked and obtained permission to wear a regular suit instead of the academic gown which was customary on such special occasions. Beccaria spoke simply and clearly, without pomposity, and the audience was impressed by his thoughtfulness and serious approach."

In his lecture, Beccaria identified "four principal means of promoting trade"—"concurrence in the price of things, oeconomy in the price of labour, cheapness of carriage, and low interest of money"—and said that "industry is enlivened, by easing the duties on the importation of the first materials, and on the exportation of them when manufactured; and by loading those which are imposed on imported manufactures, and exported materials." Beccaria thus advocated placing higher tariffs on imported goods and higher charges on exports of raw materials, drawing the ire of French physiocrats such as Dupont. The son of a watchmaker and a protégé of François Quesnay, Dupont's 1768 book, *Physiocratie: ou Constitution Naturelle du Gouvernement le Plus Avantageux au Genre Humain*, contained an exposition of this "new science" and advocated low tariffs and free trade among nations. In his critical assessment of Beccaria's inaugural lecture, Dupont declared that Beccaria, the "illustrious Professor" and "Philosopher," had been led "astray," though he hoped that Beccaria "would change considerably his opinions on very many points." While Beccaria's inaugural lecture praised Jean-Baptiste Colbert (1619–1683), Louis XV's finance minister who was skeptical of free trade and who sought to protect French manufacturing from foreign competition, the *physiocrats*—a term derived from the Greek *phýsis*, meaning "nature," and *kràtos*, meaning "power"—believed an economy's power came principally from its agricultural sector and wanted Louis XV's government to deregulate and reduce taxes on French farmers.

François Quesnay (1694–1774), a leading French physiocrat, helped to popularize the term "laissez-faire," the now famous phrase first used by a merchant, Thomas Le Gendre (1638–1706), who, when asked by Colbert what the government could do for trade, reportedly said "*laissez-nous faire*" (leave us alone). Whereas physiocrats sought to decriminalize smuggling while simultaneously urging severe treatment of vagabonds, beggars and thieves, Beccaria sought to punish smugglers—albeit in a proportionate manner, one not designed to dishonor or disgrace such violators—to stop, or at least stem, the flow of contraband. Beccaria specifically sought to keep customs taxes low and retail prices at moderate, reasonable levels, which, he believed, would disincentivize and sharply reduce acts of smuggling.[63] Dupont later initiated direct contact with Beccaria, writing to him on April 8, 1770 with these words: "*Il y a longtemps que j'ambitionne l'honneur d'enter en correspondance avec vous*" ("I have aspired, for a long time, to correspond with you"). "I would be honored," Dupont graciously wrote to Beccaria in that letter, softening his earlier tone, "to learn from your counsel, observations, and even criticisms of the way that the French *philosophers* who are called *economists* envisage the very science that you have had the precious honor of being appointed to the first chaired professorship established by a king."[64]

In his inaugural address, Beccaria—speaking of political economy—said that "one of the great advantages of this science is, that it is not confined to the solitary philosopher in his closet, nor occupied about objects remote from the common business of life." As Beccaria, wanting to spread his ideas beyond the classroom, observed: "Its objects are such as make the most frequent topic of discussion in every company and society of men, and every public occurrence affords an opportunity of applying it." "Yet this science, so useful, and even necessary," Beccaria continued, "has been one of the latest of unfolding itself in the human mind, nor is it yet arrived at that ultimate degree of perfection of which it seems susceptible." If Antonio Genovesi, the Neapolitan, had helped to pioneer the science of public economy along with other early European economists, Cesare Beccaria—his Milanese disciple—wanted to take it even further. "All that remains for me at present," he offered in his inaugural lecture, "is to promise solemnly, that, in laying open the sure principles of agriculture, commerce, manufactures, internal policy, and finances, I am determined never to belye that sacred duty, which ought to bind all those who are intrusted with public instruction, of speaking uniformly the language of truth with clearness, simplicity, and energy." Beccaria expressly noted that his "native country" had "long suffered from the thunderbolt of war which had so often broke upon it," and he complained of "the no less pernicious effects of unequal taxation, and a complicated and confused system of administration."

Naturally, Cesare Beccaria took pains to praise Empress Maria Theresa, the source of his own newly found good fortune. "But, since the accession of the present sovereign," Beccaria graciously praised the monarch who had given him his chair, "we have seen it raised to a happy and flourishing condition, by laws equally simple and comprehensive; laws which have removed the destructive influence of arbitrary power, and yet left in the hands of the prince every salutary means of promoting industry and public felicity." As Beccaria concluded his public lecture:

> The importance of a science which has for its objects the concerns and interest of nations, makes me tremble; but I look for encouragement and assistance from the illustrious youth of Milan. The eager curiosity, the docility, fervor, and indefatigable force of mind, peculiar to the earlier period of life, will all co-operate to prevent the approaches of error, however supple and importunate, and to overthrow the force of barbarous prejudices, or pre-conceived opinions, which might otherwise rise up in this place in opposition to the timid efforts of truth, and attempt to baffle the glorious intentions of government. My wishes will be thoroughly accomplished, if I can, by the most

anxious endeavours, increase the number of enlightened subjects to our sovereign, of true citizens to my country, and of virtuous men, fraught with solid knowledge, to human society.

Beccaria's lecture was quickly published in Italian and also immediately translated into French and then—as noted—distributed, appearing in 1769 in *Éphémérides du citoyen*, the journal of the French physiocrats edited by Pierre-Samuel Dupont de Nemours. Three Frenchmen, Louis-Claude Bigot de Sainte Croix, Jean-Antoine Comparet and Pierre-Samuel Dupont de Nemours actually took the time to produce French translations, with editions published in Paris and Lausanne. For example, as Bernard Harcourt explains in his book, *The Illusion of Free Markets*: "In a letter dated March 17, 1769, the Chevalier de Sainte Croix (secretary at the French embassy in Turin and one of the people behind the *Éphémérides du citoyen*, the journal of the Physiocrats) introduced himself to Beccaria and discussed having read his inaugural lecture. He then proposed translating it into French. Beccaria's first lecture—the subject of much discussion—was also translated into English that same year.[65] The English translator, in a short preface to the translation, pointed out that "the following discourse" was by "the celebrated author of the 'Treatise on Crimes and Punishments' at the opening of a new professorship instituted last winter at Milan, for teaching this science." As the translator, Sylvester Douglas (1743–1823), a recent graduate of the University of Aberdeen in Scotland who had visited Milan in 1767, further emphasized, fully aware of Cesare Beccaria's growing international reputation: "The genius of the author almost insures the merit of his lectures. Though his modesty had long been a bar to that encouragement which his talents deserve, yet it is known that he was invited to Petersburg by the most flattering offers, to assist in digesting the code of laws lately published by the Czarina." "Domestick ties, joined to the desire of devoting his abilities to the service of his own country," the translator stressed of what drove Beccaria's decision, "made him decline those offers, and not many months ago this new chair was instituted for him, and I believe is always to be filled by a person of noble birth."[66]

Sylvester Douglas—who studied law and medicine at the University of Leyden and later became the Chief Secretary for Ireland from 1793 to 1794 under George III—had gotten to know Cesare Beccaria on his second trip to Milan. "The second time of my being at Milan," he recorded, "besides Father Frisi, I made an acquaintance with the Marchese Beccaria, author of the celebrated work, *Dei Delitti e [delle] Pene*, whom I met at Count Firmian's at dinner." Count Firmian hosted lavish dinner parties, such as the farewell dinner he arranged for Leopold and Wolfgang Amadeus Mozart in March 1770 before providing the young prodigy and his father letters of introduction for Parma, Florence, Rome and Naples. "I cannot tell you how gracious he has been to us during the whole period of our stay," Leopold Mozart wrote to his wife from Milan on March 13, 1770. As Marcello Maestro records of how the English translation of Beccaria's inaugural lecture, done by Sylvester Douglas and published by Dodsley of London, came about: "Douglas, who was soon to enter public life and would later have a successful political career, wrote to Beccaria that he had decided to translate the prolusione in order to induce some young men from England to go to Milan and enroll in Beccaria's classes." Sylvester Douglas later quoted Adam Smith, a man in favor of the commercial and political union of Ireland and Britain, to make the case that Scotland and England had benefitted from their relationship with one another. "In the course of an exceedingly long speech," one source observes, "Sylvester Douglas (later Lord Glenbervie), the former chief secretary in the Irish administration of Lord Westmorland, cited Smith at great length."[67]

In studying political economy and its principles, Cesare Beccaria chose the same vocation that had been selected by his erstwhile mentor and one-time best friend, Pietro Verri. Verri—who was not particularly impressed by Beccaria's inaugural lecture on economics, believing it not very original and lacking in clarity (a conclusion no doubt colored by their falling out)—had taken up the topics of commerce and political economy early in his own career. After a year's stay in Vienna, the seat of the Habsburg Empire, Verri had made clear in December 1760 that he was focused on the study of political economy, noting almost a full decade before Beccaria's first lecture that he had "dared, months ago, to draft the elements of commerce." "Through definitions, propositions, consequences and the like I have drawn what seem reasonable conclusions to me from my own thoughts," he explained, emphasizing that he had then "walked to the Imperial Library and started reading on the subject." "I have read Forbannais, Melon, Du Tot, Hume and now I find that my own elements stand up, nor do I feel ashamed of them," he added in 1760, writing in advance of Beccaria's own writings on the subject of economics and referencing the writings of François Véron-Duverger de Forbannais (1722–1800), Jean-François Melon (1675–1738), Nicolas Dutot (1684–1741), and David Hume (1711–1776).

But Pietro Verri harbored more than a modicum of professional jealousy over the almost instant success of *Dei delitti e delle pene*. And his attitude towards Beccaria's genius and successes has strong echoes of the fictionalized jealousies that Antonio Salieri harbored against Wolfgang Amadeus Mozart as depicted in the Academy Award-winning film, *Amadeus* (1994) and or in Alexander Pushkin's drama, *Mozart and Salieri* (1830). Although Pietro Verri had studied political economy before Beccaria, Verri's book, *Meditazioni sulla economia politica* (1771), was only written and published after he had read Beccaria's lecture notes. And Verri's own motive in writing his own book seems to have been jealousy, to try to best Beccaria. As Pietro Verri wrote to his brother in October 1771: "The lesson I will give to the professor of economics (Beccaria) is to teach it to him." Though Verri's *Meditations on Political Economy* is said to have been written in a "concise and energetic style" and to have "contributed not less to the success of the Italian school," one nineteenth-century source, *History of Political Economy in Europe*, also reported that it had "important deficiencies" in it. Moreover, the first English edition of Pietro Verri's *Meditazioni sulla economia politica* (*Meditations on Political Economy*)—prepared by Peter Groenewegen, a scholar of the history of economics—was not published until 1986, giving it far less exposure to a worldwide audience than Beccaria's inaugural lecture, especially in English-speaking countries.[68]

In his critical assessment of Beccaria's inaugural lecture, Pietro Verri—in a letter to his brother, Alessandro, dated January 21, 1769—wrote in a competitive fit of jealousy: "Now that he is on his own Beccaria reveals himself as very mediocre; in his long talk I couldn't find one single bright or new idea.... There were many labored and declamatory sentences, but no real eloquence." In another 1769 letter to his brother, Alessandro, Pietro Verri continued in the same vein, expressing his astonishment and disbelief: "*La prolusione di Beccaria è stata stampata in francese; poi ultimamente in inglese: sono fenomeni strani*." The translation: "The introductory lecture of Beccaria has been printed in French; and then more recently in English: they are strange phenomena." The more senior Verri was bewildered that Beccaria's inaugural lecture was translated so quickly into French and English, and even more miffed that it was admired by Voltaire and sent so quickly by Count Firmian to Vienna to Kaunitz and Joseph von Sperges (1725–1791), the jurist and Austrian diplomat admired by Kaunitz who became the head of Vienna's Italian Department after 1766.[69]

Despite his faults and personal failings and the flaws in some of his assessments, Pietro Verri has long been honored as an important Italian economist. As Luigi Cossa, a professor in the Royal University of Pavia, wrote in *An Introduction to the Study of Political Economy* (1893), in a somewhat mixed review: "In genius as well as in literary culture and scientific attainments Verri was no match for Beccaria, but he outdid him in economics, for his writings are both more numerous and more solid. Verri was not deluded for a moment by the glamour of the physiocratic dictum that all forms of manufacturing industry were barren. Mercantilism, however, had a certain power over his judgment; its prejudices lurk in various writings of his, particularly in his *Elementi del commercio* (1765)." "In his *Meditations on Political Economy* (1771)," Cossa continues, "Verri not only produced something far fuller and far clearer than Beccaria's *Elementi*, but the book is the best compendium published in Italy during the eighteenth century; in fact, but for Turgot's *Reflections*, which came after it, there would be nothing from any quarter to dispute its pre-eminence." According to Cossa's assessment of Verri's book: "His *Meditations* deserve to be called a systematic treatise on economics, inasmuch as they are an investigation into the various causes at work for and against the accumulation of wealth in a given country, the causes allowing or hindering a surplus of production, which he says approaches the maximum only by a continuous increase in population." Verri's *Meditazioni sulla economia politica*, first published in Livorno in 1771, was reprinted several times with additions by its author, and it was first translated into French in 1773 and into German in 1774.[70]

It was only after working as a teacher and appealing directly to Empress Maria Theresa that Beccaria, in 1771, became a member of Lombardy's prestigious Supreme Economic Council. As one historian, Pier Luigi Porta, reports: "A professorship of *scienze camerali*, meaning political economy, was created for him at the Scuole Palatine in Milan in 1769. Beccaria, much like Verri, was also a consultant administrator and a member of the *Supremo Consiglio di Economia* from 1771." Beccaria was a successful teacher, but he had long coveted a position on the reform-minded Supreme Economic Council. As a teacher, Beccaria gave lectures at his house, and he soon had more than 50 students, a number that rose to more than seventy students by February 1769. Per a letter dated February 22, 1769: "*Beccaria ha più di settanta uditori … Alcuni in buona fede, altri per malignità e per riportare le lezioni agli esami dei vari cerchi*" ("Beccaria has more than seventy attending … Some are in good faith, others viciously to report the lectures' content for examination in various circles."). According to other sources, Beccaria had more than one hundred students—an impressive number given that jurisprudence courses at the University of Pavia were normally attended by less than ten students. Beccaria's salary was quickly increased from 2,000 to 3,000 *lire*, though even that salary increase was far from enough to make Beccaria financially independent from his father. It was the lure of an even higher salary—and the prospect of actually *making*, not just *lecturing* on, economic policy—that proved too hard for Beccaria to resist.

Beccaria had unsuccessfully applied to join Lombardy's Supreme Economic Council in 1765 at its creation—and again in 1766. "In May 1766," one source reports, "Beccaria applied directly to Firmian, in a now lost memorandum, for the position in the Council left vacant by the death of Vincenzo Villavecchia." "The only response," that source points out, "seems to have been Firmian's immediate confirmation of receipt of this memorandum, and transmission to Chancellor Kaunitz." But when a vacancy opened up after the death of Francesco Damiani on December 28, 1770, Beccaria applied again—and this time he realized his long-time ambition, getting appointed on April 29, 1771 at a salary of 6,000 *lire*. As members of that body, both Cesare Beccaria and Pietro Verri contributed reports, or *consulte*, within the *Consiglio*. And both men, "probably following Helvétius," Porta emphasizes, "effectively contributed to launch the famous dictum that laws are to be considered—as Beccaria writes in the introduction to his 1764 pamphlet by making use of the formula of Scottish origin (formulated by Francis Hutcheson in 1725)—from the standpoint of 'the greatest happiness of the greatest number.'"[71]

But it was primarily Cesare Beccaria's work on penal reform—not Beccaria's work as an economist, though that was his daily profession after his appointment to the Supreme Economic Council—that garnered so much attention in the 1760s and 1770s. Because it was translated into so many languages, far more than his inaugural lecture on political economy, *Dei delitti e delle pene*—the celebrated book that launched Beccaria's professional career—impacted societies around the globe. For example, the first Spanish translation of Beccaria's book was done by D. Juan Antonio de las Casas and printed by D. Joachin Ibarra.[72] In "Penal Enlightenment in Spain," Alejandro Agüero and Marta Lorente write that "if we look at the legal historiography we find that all the references to the basic patterns of the enlightened reforms in the field of penal thinking lead to the little book written by the Marquis of Beccaria in 1764." Noting that Beccaria's book became "a *tipping point*" in the history of law reform, Agüero and Lorente emphasize that Spanish scholars have "classified the penal thinking" of the second half of the eighteenth century into the "pre Beccaria" and "post Beccaria Spanish Enlightenment."[73] "During the second half of the eighteenth century," one book emphasizes, "the Enlightenment began to influence several Spanish jurists and philosophers." As that book notes: "Francisco Tomás y Valiente demonstrated that Spaniards like Sempere, Jovellanos, Campomanes, and Foronda knew the works of Montesquieu, Rousseau, Beccaria, and others. He concludes that, at least from the 1770s onward, this group of Spanish intellectuals identified themselves with the new ideas."[74]

In *The Formation and Transmission of Western Legal Culture: 150 Books that Made the Law in the Age of Printing*, the editors highlight an array of books that shaped

Western legal systems, including *On Crimes and Punishments*. In taking note of Beccaria's influence on Spanish speakers, one of the contributors notes that "Beccaria and the debate on torture had an enormous impact on Lardizábal's *Discurso*." As that contributor, Alexandro Agüero, observes: "Beccaria's book was known in Spain before its first Castilian translation was published in 1774. At that time, an academic debate on judicial torture in Spain was expressed in two celebrated books: Alfonso Maria Acevedo's *De reorum absolutione* (Madrid 1770) and the response by Pedro de Castro: *Defensa de la tortura y leyes patrias que la establecieron* (Madrid 1778)." Manuel de Lardizábal y Uribe's *Discourse on Punishments* included a 50-page section criticizing torture and Castro's *Defensa*, and though Lardizábal disagreed with Beccaria in some respects, Lardizábal's reform-minded ideas earned him the title of "Spanish Beccaria" among early twentieth-century criminologists.[75] Manuel Miguel de Lardizábal y Uribe (1744–1820) was an academic of the *Real Academia Española de la Lengua* from 1775 until his death, and he became well known as a penal reformer for his *Discurso sobre las penas contrahido a las leyes criminales de España para facilitar su reforma* (1782).[76]

After Beccaria's *Dei delitti e delle pene* was translated into English in 1767 as *On Crimes and Punishments*, it was, in fact, widely read by a vast number of Anglo-American readers. In England, Jeremy Bentham—the British philosopher—read Beccaria's book in 1769 around the time that he was admitted to the bar. He was so taken with *On Crimes and Punishments* that he wrote of Beccaria: "Oh, my master, first evangelist of Reason ... you who have made so many useful excursions into the path of utility, what is there left for us to do?" "When Beccaria came," Bentham wrote in *A Fragment on Government* (1776), "he was received by the intelligent as an Angel from heaven would be by the faithful." "He may be styled the father of *Censorial Jurisprudence*," Bentham wrote, emphasizing the Italian philosopher's highly critical view of then-existing laws—laws full of arbitrary, inhuman and draconian punishments.[77] Bentham went on to write a number of penal codes as well as influential books on penal reform, including *The Rationale of Punishment* and *Panopticon: or The Inspection House*, a proposal for an innovative prison design.[78] Bentham frequently cited Beccaria's work, with the British philosopher H. L. A. Hart observing: "Bentham's debt to Beccaria was great and is well known. Indeed, Bentham himself took the greatest pains to secure that all his readers should realize how greatly Beccaria had contributed to his own thought." "It was from Beccaria's little treatise on crimes and punishments," Bentham acknowledged, "that I drew as I well remember the first hint of the principle by which the precision and clearness and incontestableness of mathematical calculations are introduced for the first time into the field of morals." As Bentham—a writer who corresponded with the likes of James Madison and Aaron Burr—praised Beccaria's pioneering advocacy against capital punishment: "[T]he more attention one gives to the punishment of death the more he will be inclined to adopt the opinion of Beccaria—that it ought to be disused. This subject is so ably discussed in his book that to treat it after him is a work that may well be dispensed with."[79]

In 1769, just two years after Beccaria's treatise was translated into English and the same year that Bentham first read Beccaria's book, the fourth volume of William Blackstone's *Commentaries on the Laws of England* hit the presses. A popular title in

England and colonial America, Blackstone's treatise cited Beccaria and, in it, Blackstone wrote that it is "absurd and impolitic to apply the same punishment to crimes of different magnitude."[80] Although Blackstone still favored executions, he did so for only limited crimes and for limited circumstances, recounting the "melancholy" truth that English law then made approximately 160 different crimes punishable by death.[81] He also favored the use of penitentiaries—the institutions made necessary by the elimination or reduction in the use of executions and by the resort to incarceration. "It is a kind of quackery in government, and argues a want of solid skill," the Beccaria-inspired Blackstone asserted, "to apply the same universal remedy, the *ultimum supplicium*, to every case of difficulty." "It is, it must be owned," Blackstone noted, "much *easier* to extirpate than to amend mankind: yet that magistrate must be esteemed both a weak and a cruel surgeon, who cuts off every limb, which through ignorance or indolence he will not attempt to cure."[82] The legendary Oxford jurist—mimicking Beccarian language—announced in his *Commentaries* that a punishment "ought always to be proportioned to the particular purpose it is meant to serve, and by no means exceed it." "A multitude of sanguinary laws (besides the doubt that may be entertained concerning the right of making them)," Blackstone wrote, "do likewise prove a manifest defect either in the wisdom of the legislature, or the strength of executive power."[83] By 1779, a London journal, *The Literary Fly*, had named Blackstone, Montesquieu, Beccaria and Voltaire as an "enlightened" quartet who had "echoed to each other."[84]

Other intellectuals, including English penologist John Howard, his fellow penal reformer William Eden (1745–1814), and American Quaker and philanthropist Thomas Eddy (1758–1827), were themselves also moved or inspired by Beccaria's ideas on criminal justice to ameliorate the harsh conditions of prisons.[85] But both Blackstone and Bentham, early readers of Beccaria's book, were especially important in promoting Beccaria's ideas. "Another school of prison reformers, greatly influenced by Beccaria's *Dei Delitti e delle Pene*," one history reports, "was led by Beccaria's English disciple, Jeremy Bentham." Bentham's repeated invocations of Beccaria—as well as Blackstone's and Bentham's effusive praise of Beccaria's work—demonstrate just what an impact *Dei delitti e delle pene* had on English thinkers. Blackstone and Bentham, of course, were hardly the only two English penal reformers, but they propagated Beccaria's ideas and drew many disciples of their own. "Bentham," one source notes, for example, "added a detailed criterion of the efficacy of punishment, according to its certainty, immediacy, propinquity, severity, duration, etc, basing it on his psychology of motivation by pleasure and pain."[86] Like classic works by Blackstone, Bentham and figures such as Howard, Eden and Eddy, *On Crimes and Punishments* quickly became a cherished possession of intellectuals throughout the world, and it was frequently cited with approval or reverence. Beccaria's book thus became a must-read text for any serious intellectual or *bona fide* revolutionary.[87] References to *On Crimes and Punishments* can be found in countless books, magazines, newspapers and orations from the late 1760s onward—not only in England, but in continental Europe and in distant America, with Beccaria's ideas inspiring and informing America's Revolutionary War and, later, the French Revolution.[88]

Chapter 5

The Revolutionaries

English subjects and American colonists, as well as those throughout continental Europe, were fascinated by Italian culture long before Cesare Beccaria's book hit the shelves. They studied Italy's history, its ancient and modern rulers, its painters, writers and works of art, and—in many cases—they took pains to learn the Italian language. In late January 1769, for example, Benjamin Franklin, writing from London, sent a letter to fellow Pennsylvanians Charles Thomson and Thomas Mifflin about books ordered for the Library Company of Philadelphia. Among the new books Philadelphians would have had access to at that time, and which are mentioned in the Franklin Papers pertaining to that exchange: Giuseppe M. A. Baretti's *An Account of the Manners and Customs of Italy: with Observations on the Mistakes of Some Travellers* (London, 1768); Cesare Beccaria's *An Essay on Crimes and Punishments, Translated from the Italian; with a Commentary attributed to Mons. de Voltaire, Translated from the French* (London, 1767); Samuel Sharp's *Letters from Italy; Describing the Customs, Manners, Drama, etc. of Italy ... as They Are Described ... by Mr. Baretti* (London, 1768); Laurence Sterne's *A Sentimental Journey through France and Italy, by Mr. Yorick* (new ed., 2 vols., London, 1768) and James Boswell's *An Account of Corsica; the Journal of a Tour to that Island; and Memoirs of Pascal Paoli* (2d ed., London, 1768).[1] On July 13, 1762, Franklin had also written to Father Giambatista Beccaria in Turin to tell his fellow scientist about the musical instrument he had created out of a series of graduated glasses. "In honour of your musical language," Franklin wrote, "I have borrowed from it the name of this instrument, calling it the Armonica." "The advantages of this instrument," Franklin explained, "are that its tones are incomparably sweet beyond those of any other; that they may be swelled and softened at pleasure by stronger or weaker pressures of the finger, and continued to any length; and that the instrument, being once well tuned, never again wants tuning."[2]

The civil law system on the European continent was of special interest to those from a common-law tradition—the centuries-old system of law in Great Britain that vested judges with vast discretion. In a letter written from Paris in 1785, Thomas Jefferson explained to Philip Mazzei—his Italian friend—that "[t]he system of law in most of the United states, in imitation of that of England, is divided into two departments, the Common law and the Chancery." "The Common law," Jefferson explained, "is a *written law* the text of which is preserved from the beginning of the 13th. century downwards, but what preceded that is lost." Jefferson observed that the "substance" of the common law "has been retained in the memory of the people and committed to writing from time to time in the decisions of the judges and treatises of the jurists, insomuch that it is still considered as a lex scripta, the letter of which is sufficiently known to guide the decisions of the courts." The courts of law that applied the common law, Jefferson stressed, "restrain themselves to the letter of the law." The "court of Chancery," Jefferson explained, by contrast, administered "the equity of the law," and the judges overseeing equitable proceedings had even "greater latitude, extending the provisions of every law not only to the cases within it's letter, but to those also which came within the spirit and reason of it." "But it is now very long since certainty in the law has become so highly valued by the nation," Jefferson wrote of America in 1785, in the post-*On Crimes and Punishments* world, "that the judges have ceased to extend the operation of laws beyond those cases which are clearly within the intention of the legislators." "This intention," Jefferson observed, "is to be collected principally from the words of the law: only where these are ambiguous they are permitted to gather further evidence from the history of the times when the law was made and the circumstances which produced it." In the list of books that James Madison prepared in 1783 for the use of Congress, he not only listed Beccaria's works along with ancient titles such as Plato's *Republic* and Aristotle's *Politics*, but he specifically included John Taylor's *Elements of the Civil Law* and Jean Daumat's *The Civil Law in Its Natural Order*.[3]

And the notion of publicizing written laws in the language of ordinary citizens— an idea taken from Beccaria's treatise and the civil-law tradition more broadly—was embraced by many Anglo-American republican thinkers in that era.[4] "In Beccaria's time," one criminology textbook notes, "the laws were often unknown to the populace." As that book, *Introduction to Criminology*, observes: "This was somewhat due to widespread illiteracy but perhaps more due to current laws not being publicly declared. Even when laws were posted, they were often printed in languages (e.g., Latin) that the citizens did not read or speak." In *Dei delitti e delle pene*, Beccaria—wanting everyone to know the law's requirements—stressed: "When the number of those who can understand the sacred code of laws and hold it in their hands increases, the frequency of crimes will be found to decrease." "From the time of the American Revolution," barrister and legal historian Simon Chapple has written, "the reform and codification of the common law of crime was a perennial issue"—a movement "inspired by the work of reformers such as Beccaria and Bentham." "The most important reformer" in the field of criminology notes yet another source, *The Civil Law Tradition*, "was Cesare Beccaria, whose book *Of Crimes and Punishments* exploded on the European scene in 1764 and became the most influential work on criminal law and procedure in Western history."[5]

Enlightenment thinkers, following Beccarian logic, were focused on having laws written in a clear and precise manner. In that way, there would be no ambiguities as regards what the laws asked of citizens and there would be less of a need to have judges interpret those laws, thus giving the people—through their elected representatives— a greater say in their own governance. Thomas Jefferson, who copied numerous passages from Beccaria's treatise, in fact chose excerpts from the fourth chapter of Beccaria's treatise—the one on interpretation—as the first portion of *Dei delitti e delle pene* he began copying into his commonplace book as he read the book.[6] In that chapter, Beccaria began: "Judges, in criminal cases, have no right to interpret the penal laws, because they are not legislators." As Beccaria wrote of his logic and his major and minor premises: "In every criminal cause the judge should reason syllogistically. The *major* should be the general law; the *minor*, the conformity of the action, or its opposition to the laws; the *conclusion*, liberty, or punishment. If the judge be obliged by the imperfection of the laws, or chooses to make any other or more syllogisms than this, it will be an introduction to uncertainty." In other words, the wording of statutes was critical, and a judge simply needed to read the law and analyze the facts of the case before assessing whether a criminal defendant was guilty or innocent. "There is nothing more dangerous that the common axiom, *the spirit of the laws is to be considered*," Beccaria emphasized in a passage that sparked much debate about the *ad hoc* way in which many English chancery or common-law judges—some incredibly corrupt—frequently went about their business, using malleable notions of custom or nebulous community standards or mores to make decisions.[7]

At that time, corruption was rampant and, like it had in prior centuries, posed a clear and present danger to an independent and impartial judiciary. In *Constitution de L'Angleterre* (*The Constitution of England*, 1771), the Swiss and English political theorist Jean Louis de Lolme specifically wrote about the history of "corrupt Judges" in Rome. And England itself had a long history of judges who had not only meted out incredibly harsh sentences, but who had accepted bribes and compromised their integrity for cash payments.[8] That corruption and those draconian sentencing practices even extended to cases involving life and death, with English judges willing to accept money in exchange for particular judicial outcomes. One of the most notorious English judges, Lord Chief Justice George Jeffreys, was still remembered in the late eighteenth century for his ruthlessness. Judge Jeffreys had imposed multiple death sentences, ordering that rebels be drawn and quartered or gibbeted, and, in 1685, he had decided that one man, Titus Oates, be imprisoned, whipped, and pilloried four times a year for the rest of his life. "[I]n the late eighteenth century," a Yale Law School professor, Akhil Amar, recounts, "every schoolboy in America knew that the English Bill of Rights' 1689 ban on excessive bail, excessive fines, and cruel and unusual punishments ... arose as a response to the gross misbehavior of the infamous Judge Jeffreys." De Lolme himself was very familiar with Beccaria's treatise, once writing: "Without repeating here what has been said of the subject by the admirable author of the treatise on *Crimes and Punishments*, I shall observe, that the torture, in itself so horrible an expedient, would, more especially in a free state, be attended with the most fatal consequences."[9]

In the eighteenth century, *On Crimes and Punishments* thus caused European political theorists and Anglo-American lawmakers to rethink their criminal justice systems and the way they approached legislation and the dissemination and interpretation of the laws. According to Ilene Nagel, a former member of the United States Sentencing Commission who previously taught law at Indiana University School of Law in Bloomington, "the Enlightenment and Age of Reason gave rise to the promulgation of new theories regarding man and society." Beccaria's "pioneering work," she wrote in 1990, "laid the foundation for some of the more modern concepts of today's system of criminal justice." As Nagel emphasized of Beccaria's approach: "criminal laws should be codified and defined by theories of social contract, not by vague moral standards." Though Nagel pointed out that the Roman Catholic Church had denounced Beccaria's book, she stressed that Beccaria's ideas "eventually took root, being explored and refined by the likes of John Howard and Jeremy Bentham." As Nagel observed in her article: "The very distinguished Samuel Romilly, in particular, later embraced Beccaria's concerns for the dangers of allowing judges too much discretion in interpreting and applying laws. For Sir Romilly, it was the arbitrary decisions made possible by unfettered discretion that gave rise to the pejorative yet oft-heard characterization of justice as no more than a lottery."[10]

Sir Samuel Romilly (1757–1818)—a fan of both Beccaria's and Bentham's work— was a prominent penal reformer and opponent of the slave trade. In 1808, in discussing manuscripts of Bentham that Pierre Étienne Louis Dumont (1759–1829)—Romilly's friend—was translating into French, Romilly made the following notation in his diary: "One of them, a treatise on punishments, appears to me to have very extraordinary merit, and to be likely to be more popular than most of Bentham's writings, and to produce very good effects. I strongly exhorted Dumont to finish it without delay, and to publish it, if possible, in the ensuring winter; and he has promised to do so." The result: the publication of a translated version of Bentham's work, published as *Théorie des Peines et des Récompenses* in July 1811. In that same August 20, 1808 diary entry, Romilly emphasized immediately after his references to Bentham's then-unpublished manuscripts: "Since the work of Beccaria, nothing has appeared on the subject of the Criminal Law which has made any impression on the public." In March 1810, Romilly published a speech he gave on February 9th of that year as a pamphlet titled *Observations on the Criminal Law as it relates to Capital Punishments, and on the Mode in which it is administered.* In a letter dated February 21, 1810, another one of his friends, Samuel Parr, took note of Romilly's speech and bemoaned to Romilly that "the Legislature has been strangely employed in multiplying capital punishments." In that letter to Romilly, Parr added: "I was very glad to see that you agree with me in lamenting that discretionary power which is so capriciously exercised by Judges." "I observe that your brethren," Parr continued, "seldom or never touch on those great and leading principles of jurisprudence, which Beccaria and Bentham have so well illustrated."[11] Samuel Parr himself regularly cited Beccaria's work, and he expressed the belief that Beccaria had breathed "a spirit of pure and enlightened humanity."[12]

As a highly-educated man, Romilly had of course long been acquainted with Beccaria's treatise, though like many of his day he did not agree with every single idea it in. For example, in a letter he sent from London in 1783, Romilly wrote to the Rev. John Roget: "I am much obliged to you for giving me your sentiments on the question of whether any crime ought to be punished with death. The objection you make to the punishment of death, founded on the errors of human tribunals and the impossibility of having absolute demonstration of the guilt of a criminal, strikes me more forcibly than any argument I have ever before heard on the same side of the question." The opinion that had been expressed to him—one pre-dating by more than two centuries the founding of the Innocence Project in 1992 by Peter Neufeld and Barry Scheck—had made reference to an argument that he had "formerly read in Beccaria." "I confess, however," Romilly continued in his letter, "that to myself it seems absolutely impossible, even if it were to be wished (of which I am not quite sure), to omit death in the catalogue of human punishments; for if the criminal will not submit to the punishment inflicted on him, if he escapes from his prison, refuses to perform the labour prescribed to him, or commits new crimes, he must, at last, be punished with death." As Romilly added: "One reason why I cannot think that death ought so carefully to be avoided among human punishments is, that I do not think death the greatest of evils. Beccaria and his disciples confess that it is not, and recommend other punishments as being more severe and effectual, forgetting, undoubtedly, that, if human tribunals have a right to inflict a severer punishment than death, they must have a right to inflict death itself." "You will not, I hope," Romilly wrote in the paragraph that followed, "conclude from all this that I am perfectly satisfied with the penal codes that now subsist in Europe, and particularly with that in my own country, where theft (pilfering it should rather be called), forgery, and every description of the *Crimen falsi*, are punished with death." "The laws of our country may indeed be said to be written in blood," Romilly observed.[13]

The well-established legal doctrine of *nulla poena sine lege*—the idea that no person shall be punished except in pursuance of a statute that fixes a penalty for criminal behavior before the act of criminality—can itself be seen as an outgrowth, or at least an embrace, of Beccarian principles.[14] That ancient Latin maxim, which has been described as a "fundamental principle" of U.S. law, is now almost taken for granted by legal systems around the world, with both *ex post facto* laws and bills of attainder specifically forbidden by the U.S. Constitution. "In effect," it has been held of what has been called the principle of *legality*, "this means that no one shall be held criminally responsible for conduct which is not specifically forbidden by a statute."[15] With that principle described as "a requisite of due process,"[16] one Massachusetts court—taking notice of the importance of citizens having advance notice of the law—put it this way: "The sense of fairness is that persons subject to the law should have the opportunity, generally or specifically, to know the rules, to understand the consequences of deviation from them, and to behave accordingly. In criminal law the maxim is *nulla poena sine lege*." "The constitutional prohibition against retroactive or ex post facto criminal litigation," that court stressed, "serves this policy of fairness."[17] As another court emphasized: "The maxim *nullum crimen sine lege, nulla poena sine lege* reminds us that the courts may not punish conduct as criminal unless that conduct has transgressed the clear, plain, or fair meaning of the defined offense. In the federal courts, this means a congressionally defined offense, because there is no federal common law of crimes."[18]

Italian thought and the civil-law tradition—as well as specific Italians such as Cesare Beccaria—thus shaped Anglo-American law in fundamental ways, or, in the case of the roving Milanese botanist Luigi Castiglioni, made noteworthy observations on its early history and penal laws through his eighteenth-century *Viaggio*, or travelogue. "Until the middle of the eighteenth century," legal historian Michael Hoeflich writes, "the American legal profession closely resembled that of Great Britain, as befitted a colonial Bar, except that education was less sophisticated and the level of practice in all but the largest eastern cities was well below that in London." "But the generation of lawyers that came of age at the middle of the century," Hoeflich explains, "was also to be the generation who made up the core of the Founding Fathers." As he emphasizes in *Roman and Civil Law and the Development of Anglo-American Jurisprudence in the Nineteenth Century*: "These men were not only trained in the common law but were steeped in the legal and political philosophy of the Continent and much taken with the Roman model of a republic and with the legal system and lawyers that made that republic great." "Many American law libraries (and some general libraries) in the first half of the nineteenth century," Hoeflich writes, "had substantial holdings in civil law and Roman law." Among the books at the library of South Carolina College and many other private and public libraries: Beccaria's treatise on the criminal law.[19] "Among those who best represent the move for both political and criminal law reform at the time," it has been written of the late eighteenth century, "were Cesare Beccaria (1738–1794), Gaetano Filangieri (1752–1788), Gian Domenico Romagnosi (1761–1834) and Paul J.A. Feuerbach (1775–1833)."[20]

Because of their substantial influence on America's founders and eighteenth- and nineteenth-century Americans, continental European writers and thinkers should not be forgotten by modern-day jurists and historians as they trace the origins of law and society. In fact, the Italian-American patriot Philip Mazzei—a close friend of Thomas Jefferson, James Madison and other U.S. founders and framers—was not only a trusted friend to the American cause who, during the Revolutionary War, was sent on an sensitive mission by Virginians to try to secure funds from the Grand Duke of Tuscany, but he materially shaped American political thought.[21] Like so many intellectuals of his era, Mazzei—entrusted by American revolutionaries with a delicate and important assignment—was a big fan of Beccaria's writings, with Mazzei himself writing of liberty and later suggesting that Beccaria be made an honorary member of the Constitutional Society of Virginia. That society, founded in 1784 shortly after the Revolutionary War's end and just a few years before the U.S. Constitution's adoption and ratification, was established to further "those pure and sacred principles of Liberty, which have been derived to us, from the happy event of the late glorious revolution."[22]

The Constitutional Society—an outgrowth of the American Revolution and established after the Treaty of Paris (1783) finally brought the war to a close—counted among its members luminaries such as James Madison, John Marshall, Richard Henry Lee, Patrick Henry, Edmund Randolph and James Monroe.[23] Mazzei and Madison were among the society's founding members, and Mazzei appropriately wanted to honor the French and Italian thinkers who—in one author's words—"represented the spirit of enlightenment and reform." Mazzei had helped to inspire Jefferson's wording in the Declaration of Independence that "All men are created equal," and Mazzei himself observed that the Declaration of Independence is "a true affirmation of the principles necessary to preserve American liberty" and that "the surest mode to secure Republican systems of Government from lapsing into Tyranny, is by giving free and frequent information to the mass of people." "Appropriately," one book on famous Italians records, "Mazzei was later a part of a constitutional society organized by James Madison and James Monroe that had as its goal a free dissemination of information about the new government." In a letter written in Italian, Mazzei proposed to John Blair that "at the first meeting" of the Constitutional Society certain "honored" foreigners be admitted to it, including Duc de la Rochefoucauld, Signor Fontana, Signor Spallanzani, and "Marchese Beccaria in Milano."[24]

Cesare Beccaria and Philip Mazzei both contributed to the American cause, Beccaria indirectly through *Dei delitti e delle pene* and Mazzei more tangibly through his time, intellect and active participation in the American Revolution. Mazzei—the Italian immigrant who had extensive interactions and correspondence with Jefferson and Madison and many other American revolutionaries—has been almost as forgotten by twenty-first century Americans as Cesare Beccaria and his republican associate, Count Giuseppe Gorani (1740–1819). As one source notes of the latter nobleman, Count Gorani—a writer and diplomat from Milan—"frequented the company of Enlightenment philosophers, the Verri brothers and Cesare Beccaria." The author of *Il vero dispotismo* (*True Despotism*), a two-volume work published in Geneva, Gorani's book was—as one source puts it—"an incisive work of political thought composed in Milan, in 1769, and banned by the Inquisition with the full agreement of the forces of *moderazione* in August 1773." "It was," that source, Jonathan Israel's *Democratic Enlightenment*, explains, "a work distinguishing between 'tyranny' as something always malign and 'despotism' that can be bad or good depending on whether or not it is infused by *l'esprit philosophique* and true 'virtue'." Because it was written in Milan in the late 1760s, Gorani's book was naturally shaped by Beccarian impulses.

Giuseppe Gorani was actually a friend of Cesare Beccaria and the Verri brothers, and in *Il vero dispotismo*, he defined despotism as "that will which acts on its own without consulting others, which includes in itself the entire legislative and executive power, which by virtue of the strongest attraction joins and attracts to itself all the vigour and wide-ranging powers of the sovereign, the prince, the government and the whole state, so that the movement of the entire political machine depends on his movement." "Though above the laws, which he can create and destroy at his pleasure," Gorani wrote of a typical despot, "he can through his absolute will arrive at laws as good or better than those existing, which generally and in most countries may be thoroughly bad." Gorani saw rulers such as Catherine II and Leopold of Tuscany as—in one scholar's words—"undertaking a beneficent 'total reform'." As that scholar, Derek Beales, emphasized in his book, *Enlightenment and Reform in Eighteenth-century Europe*, Gorani called upon "'philosophy, the support of thrones, the preserver of liberty, the joy of nations' to come to the aid of his imagined ruler."[25] Though Gorani, part of the Italian aristocracy, wrote that monarchs could work for good or ill, he ended up being put under surveillance by State Inquisitors, and he later found himself in exile in Geneva, where he did his best to keep track of activities back in Milan, including those of Cesare Beccaria's daughter, Giulia. In his *Lettres aux souverains sur la Révolution française* (1792), Gorani—as Jonathan Israel notes of Gorani's later support of the French Revolution—"held that all enlightened men should embrace the Revolution and help overthrow the princely courts and destroy their power."[26]

The physician Philip Mazzei—Gorani's fellow Italian and also known by his given Italian name, Filippo Mazzei—was himself a revolutionary with a penchant for shaking up the status quo. Born in 1730 in a small town near Florence, in Tuscany, Mazzei studied medicine at a hospital in Florence before moving to Pisa. After spending three years in Constantinople, he went to London in 1756 and spent nearly 18 years there, teaching Italian and establishing the firm of Martini & Co. to import wine, champagne, and olive oil into England. An energetic entrepreneur, he later added candies, cheese and pasta to his thriving import business. A successful businessman, Mazzei—an avid reader and writer and a charming networker—traveled frequently, paying one visit to his native country in 1765, just a year after the release of *Dei delitti e delle pene*. At that time, however, he ran into trouble with the Inquisition and faced the charge of importing "forbidden books" into Tuscany. A Roman priest had accused Mazzei of printing works by Voltaire and Rousseau, two writers who had influenced Beccaria himself, and Mazzei got an ominous letter from his friend, Raimondo Cocchi, that advised: "A charge against you has been received here in which it is stated that you put an immense quantity of forbidden books on board a ship bound for Genoa, Leghorn, Civita Vecchia, Naples, and Messina in order to infect all of Italy." Only through some influential friends was the charge ultimately lifted. Mazzei—who simply sought to inform and educate his fellow citizens, the same thing that he and other Virginians would later try to do with the Constitutional Society of Virginia—was, as a result, allowed to travel freely and return to Tuscany, the place he had such close ties to from all the time he lived there. Though Mazzei decided to return to London in 1767 to continue his import business, he was, naturally, as a lover of liberty, determined to "hasten the abolition of the Inquisition in Tuscany."

At that time, Leopold II (1747–1792) was the Grand Duke of Tuscany, a title he held from 1765 to 1790. Leopold II knew Philip Mazzei, and Mazzei, familiar with prominent men in London, facilitated the purchase of two Franklin stoves—one of Benjamin Franklin's many inventions—for the Grand Duke. As one book notes: "In 1767 the Tuscan physician Filippo Mazzei became acquainted with Benjamin Franklin in London. From him he bought two stoves destined to his employer, Leopold of Habsburg, Grand Duke of Tuscany, who later would become Emperor Leopold II." As the capital of the British Empire, American colonists—and later, following independence, full-fledged American citizens—often had reason to travel to London, whether for business, to be trained or educated, or simply to visit family or friends. It was in fact in the British Isles that Mazzei first came to know of *Dei delitti e delle pene*. "[W]hile I was in England," Mazzei wrote in his memoirs, *My Life and Wanderings*, "Beccaria's humane and judicious treatise on crime and punishment came out, and I heartily hailed it." Although Mazzei had originally settled in the British capital with a plan to travel to South America, his contacts with American colonists convinced him to give North America a try instead of sailing further south. "My new American friends," Mazzei would later write, advised him "for some time to go and live among them."

Eventually, Mazzei was convinced to form a company for the promotion in Virginia of silk worms, grapes and olives, commodities he already knew a lot about from his import business. Thomas Adams, a Virginia merchant residing in London, had suggested to Mazzei that Virginia would be an ideal location to grow vines, olive trees, and mulberry trees for silkworms, thus allowing for the creation of a silk industry. Franklin and Adams had also touted America's egalitarian culture, with the receptive Mazzei—a man all too familiar with oppression—later writing that Dr. Franklin and Jefferson's friend Thomas Adams "demonstrated to me that there was no aristocracy, that the people had not their eyes dazzled by the splendour of a throne." "I suspected that their government was but a poor copy of the British Government, and that the foundations of freedom there were consequently even less sound," Mazzei had originally thought. But both Adams and Franklin convinced him "that the head of every family voted in elections and could be elected"; "that they had their city bylaws"; and "that they had adopted only the British laws that suited them." After obtaining the written permission of the Duke of Tuscany for his endeavor, Mazzei set sail and was greeted on American soil by the likes of George Washington and took up quarters in Jefferson's house until his own home was built nearby. Jefferson himself translated articles Mazzei wrote in Italian, they had many long conversations, and Mazzei served in a Virginia militia unit with Patrick Henry as its captain. Among many others, Mazzei—the enlightened thinker—later had contact with D'Alembert in Paris.[27]

The Age of the Enlightenment is well preserved because so many memoirs and letters were written and are still available to read. Mazzei wrote his own memoir in 1811 as a personal letter to his friend, Giovanni Carmignani (1768–1847), at a distance of several decades after his first foray into the literary arts—and after the American and French revolutions, which he had lived through, had played out. Carmignani, who taught criminal law and legal philosophy at the University of Pisa, later gave a speech in Pisa in 1836 in favor of the death penalty's abolition, a subject that interested Mazzei and many other thinkers in the eighteenth and nineteenth centuries. "Carmignani," Carlo Calisse explains in *A History of Italian Law* of Mazzei's friend, "became the founder of an important school of penalists which performed great service for Tuscan criminal legislation and which survives in the illustrious name and work of Francesco Carrara." An Italian politician and jurist, Francesco Carrara (1805–1888)—from a succeeding generation—practiced law in Florence and Lucca and emerged as a leading opponent of capital punishment. His ten-volume *Programma dal corso di diritto criminale* (*Program of Criminal Law*) became a famous and influential text, and Carrara was an important member of the commission that prepared an Italian criminal code, the "Codice Zanardelli" (1889). That code, named for Giuseppe Zanardelli (1826–1903), the prime minister of Italy from 1901 to 1903, banned the death penalty. In 1768, Mazzei himself had written *A Letter on the Behaviour of the Populace on a Late Occasion, in the Procedure against a Noble Lord from a Gentleman to His Countryman Abroad*. In discussing the law and its administration in that political pamphlet, Mazzei utilized Cesare Beccaria's theories of just punishment. Like John Adams and Thomas Jefferson, Mazzei was thus familiar with—and greatly admired—Beccaria's ideas soon after their first appearance.[28]

Social movements are driven by the collective actions of individuals, and Philip Mazzei—like Jefferson and other republicans—had strong feelings about the right of the people to choose their own representatives. After a high-profile, extremely volatile dispute in which the British Parliament refused to seat John Wilkes, a duly elected member of Parliament, following his election by Middlesex voters, Mazzei saw the Parliament's actions as "a death blow to the solid and sacrosanct fundamental law of a free country, which is perfect freedom in the election of the representatives of the people." Wilkes had been expelled from Parliament in 1764 for his reputedly seditious writings, which had impugned the integrity of King George III and his ministers and advisors. After fleeing to France in 1764, he had returned to Britain in 1768 and managed to win a seat in Parliament, though Parliament refused to honor the election results, causing an uproar in England and among American colonists. It was in the 1770s, dispirited by what he'd seen and looking for a new life, that Mazzei had sold his London business, settled his accounts, then returned to Italy to prepare for a move to the New World. In his native land, the Inquisition had forbidden the publication of *Dei delitti e delle pene*—a work that Mazzei had first discovered in London but which had been stigmatized by the Inquisition as having "sprung from the deepest abyss of darkness, horrible, monstrous, full of poison." After recruiting men, gathering supplies, and leaving the port of Leghorn on September 2, 1773, Mazzei and his men— along with Mazzei's mistress, Madame Martin, and her daughter—made their way to Virginia after a three-month voyage. "The Italian émigré Philip Mazzei (1730– 1816)," Chiara Cillerai writes in a book on cultural transformations in the U.S., "is best known for his friendship with Thomas Jefferson, who was his neighbor in Virginia between 1773 and 1785."[29] Because the friendship between Jefferson and Mazzei predates the seminal events of the American Revolution—the signing of the Declaration of Independence and the U.S. Constitution—it is especially noteworthy. To honor Mazzei's contribution, the U.S. Government, in 1980, actually issued an international airmail stamp on the 250th anniversary of Philip Mazzei's birth. A 1790 miniature portrait of Mazzei became the basis for Mazzei's depiction on that postage stamp.[30]

Upon arriving in Virginia, then still a British colony, Philip Mazzei met his friend, Thomas Adams, in Williamsburg. He also quickly befriended George Washington, Thomas Jefferson and Jefferson's friend and mentor, the lawyer and jurist George Wythe. At Monticello, Jefferson and Mazzei walked the grounds and immediately hit it off, so much so that Thomas Adams remarked to Jefferson, "I see by your expression that you've taken him from me; why, I expected as much." With the slave trade then still active, the dwelling at *Colle* (Italian for "hill"), Mazzei's estate next to Monticello, was built by slaves supplied by Jefferson, with the estate itself acquired through funds raised by a company of which Jefferson, Washington, George Mason, and Virginia's then-governor, Lord Dunmore, were members. Jefferson let Mazzei stay at Monticello as Mazzei's acreage was cleared and his new home was built, and the two men had time to discuss books and political philosophy. Shortly after Mazzei's arrival in what would soon become the United States of America, Stefano Bettoia—a good friend of Mazzei who resided in Lucca and who frequently assisted Mazzei in his business affairs—sent two horses and six young men from Italy to aid Mazzei in his Virginia agricultural pursuits. As events unfolded and the American Revolution broke into an armed conflict, Mazzei—already primed for revolution through his own experiences—eagerly joined in the opposition to British rule, speaking in churches on behalf of the American cause. During the Revolutionary War itself, Mazzei sought funds from the Tuscan sovereign to aid the American cause, and Bettoia assisted Mazzei in that endeavor by passing a letter to the Grand Duke of Tuscany from a

"Citizen of the World," a pseudonym that Mazzei used along with "Furioso." Mazzei and Jefferson, who spent a lot of time together at Monticello, were destined to be life-long friends.[31]

Mazzei, like Beccaria, had formative personal experiences with oppression by Italian religious authorities, and Jefferson and Mazzei—political soulmates of sorts—both became zealous advocates of liberty and religious freedom. In the 1774–1775 time period, Mazzei contributed articles to John Pinkney's *Virginia Gazette*, writing under the pseudonym "Furioso" and saying "British liberty" was illusory. Just a year before Jefferson drafted the Declaration of Independence, Mazzei wrote a piece for the *Virginia Gazette*, which Jefferson translated. It read:

> In order to achieve our end, my dear fellow citizens, we must discuss man's natural right and the grounds of a free government. Such a discussion will clearly show us that the British Government has never been free at the peak of its perfection and that our own was nothing more than a bad copy of it.... But the time has come to change ways.... *All men are by nature equally free and independent. Their equality is necessary in order to set up a free government. Every man must be equal of any others in natural rights.* Class distinction has always been and will always be an effective obstacle and the reason for it is very clear. When in a nation you have several classes of men, each class must have its share in the government, otherwise one class will tyrannize the others.

The similarities between Mazzei's ideas and Jefferson's writings, including in the Declaration of Independence that Jefferson drafted with assistance from a committee of four other men, including John Adams and Benjamin Franklin, is—to borrow a familiar expression—self-evident.[32]

The quest to end religious intolerance was a long one, and that task would infuse the work of the American Revolution. In *Tracing the Path of Tolerance: History and Critique from the Early Modern Period to the Present Day*, one writer, Enrico Zucchi, specifically takes note of Voltaire's influence in shaping the debate—and how Beccaria's book may itself have been affected by that advocacy. As that writer explains: "In his *Commentaires sur le livre Des délits et des peines* (1766), Voltaire expressed his great appreciation to the work of Beccaria. The approval by the French philosopher was probably one of the causes of Catholic condemnation of the book."[33] "Beccaria," another source emphasizes, also taking note of Voltaire's direct and substantial influence on him, "set out to free the legal system from religious domination and regain some sense of classical ideals from ancient Greece, which based the state's power to punish in the collective welfare."[34] "The seeds of religious tolerance were planted by Enlightenment scholars," observes still another text. That book stresses that Beccaria had pointed out that the purpose of punishment should be to prevent future wrongdoing and that new Enlightenment ideals—ones forged in part by Voltaire and Beccaria—"came together in the writings of the U.S. Founding Fathers." "The American Revolution," that source emphasizes of its impact across the globe, taking particular note of the newly forged United States of America, served as "a profound lesson to Europe because that was a new government that embodied the philosophies of the Enlightenment."[35]

America's Founding Fathers favored religious toleration and sought to avoid the entanglements of church and state that they had observed or read about in European kingdoms. In the First Amendment, ratified in 1791, the American people issued this foundational directive for their representative democracy: "Congress shall make no law respecting an establishment of religion, or prohibiting the free exercise thereof; or abridging the freedom of speech, or of the press; or the right of the people peaceably to assemble, and to petition the Government for a redress of grievances." In his January 1, 1802 letter to Connecticut's Danbury Baptist Association, Thomas Jefferson wrote "that religion is a matter which lies solely between Man & his God, that he owes account to none other for his faith or his worship, that the legitimate powers of government reach actions only, & not opinion." As Jefferson's letter continued: "I contemplate with sovereign reverence that act of the whole American people which declared that their legislature should 'make no law respecting an establishment of religion, or prohibiting the free exercise thereof,' thus building a wall of separation between Church & State." "Adhering to this expression of the supreme will of the nation in behalf of the rights of conscience," Jefferson emphasized in the letter, "I shall see with sincere satisfaction the progress of those sentiments which tend to restore to man all his natural rights, convinced he has no natural right in opposition to his social duties." One of Jefferson's proudest accomplishments: writing the Virginia Statute for Religious Freedom, a piece of legislation that passed the Virginia General Assembly in 1786 and that served as a forerunner of the First Amendment protections ensuring religious liberty.[36]

James Madison (1751–1836) — Jefferson's frequent collaborator on legislation and a politician who came of age at the apex of Cesare Beccaria's popularity — also favored a separation of religious and secular functions. Later in life, in a July 10, 1822 letter to the American lawyer and penal reformer Edward Livingston, Madison — like Beccaria and Jefferson, deeply interested in penal reform — responded to the receipt of a legislative report Livingston had sent to him pertaining to a newly proposed Louisiana criminal code. After acknowledging receipt of the report, one which referenced Beccaria multiple times and which called for the death penalty's abolition, Madison emphasized: "I should commit a tacit injustice if I did not say that the Report does great honor to the talents & sentiments of the Author. It abounds with Ideas of conspicuous value, and presents them in a manner equally elegant & persuasive." As Madison's letter continued: "The reduction of an entire code of Criminal Jurisprudence into Statutory provisions, excluding a recurrence to foreign or traditional codes, & substituting for technical terms, more familiar ones with or without explanatory notes, can not but be viewed as a very arduous task. I sincerely wish your execution of it may fulfil every expectation." In that letter, Madison went on to say that "there is ample room for improvements in the criminal jurisprudence of Louisiana, as elsewhere," adding: "I observe with particular pleasure the view you have taken of the immunity of Religion from Civil Jurisdiction, in every case where it does not trespass on private rights or the public peace." "This has always," Madison wrote of the separation of church and state, "been a favorite point with me: and it was not with my approbation, that the deviation from it took place in Congress when they appointed Chaplains to be paid from the national Treasury."

In his 1822 letter to Edward Livingston, James Madison staked out his position on the matter of the separation of church and state from his own preferred, yet pragmatic constitutional law perspective: "It would have been a much better proof to their Constituents of their pious feelings, if the members had contributed for the purpose, a pittance from their own pockets. As the precedent is not likely to be rescinded, the best that can now be done may be, to apply to the Constitution, the maxim of the law, de minimis non curat." *De minimis non curat lex*, as translated by *Black's Law Dictionary*: "the law does not concern itself with trifles." "There has been another deviation from the strict principle," Madison added, "in the Executive Proclamations of fasts and festivals; so far at least as they have spoken the language of *injunction*, or have lost sight of the equality of *all* Religious Sects in the eye of the Constitution." As Madison emphasized in his letter: "Every new & successful example therefore of a perfect separation between ecclesiastical & Civil matters is of importance. And I have no doubt that every new example will succeed, as every past one has done, in shewing that Religion & Govt. will both exist in greater purity, the less they are mixed together." "It was the belief of all Sects at one time," Madison noted, "that the establishment of Religion by law was right & necessary; that the true Religion ought to be established in exclusion of all others; and that the only question to be decided was, which was the true Religion." "The example of Holland," Madison continued, "proved that a toleration of Sects dissenting from the established Sect, was safe and even useful." "The example of the Colonies now States, which rejected Religious establishments altogether," he stressed following America's Declaration of Independence, "proved that all Sects might be safely & advantageously put on a footing of equal & entire freedom."[37] "At the time of the Inquisition," John Hostettler, one of Beccaria's biographers writes, "Voltaire opposed the death penalty for heresy and sacrilege and argued for the utmost toleration for all religious sects."[38]

The American Revolution, peppered with deadly skirmishes and major battles from the start of the Revolutionary War at Lexington and Concord onward, took the world in a new direction—one leading to greater liberty and religious toleration. The revolution in political thought and philosophy culminated in America—in Philadelphia—with the issuance of the Declaration of Independence in the summer of 1776. On June 11, 1776, the Continental Congress had appointed a committee of five men—John Adams of Massachusetts, Benjamin Franklin of Pennsylvania, Thomas Jefferson of Virginia, Robert R. Livingston of New York, and Roger Sherman of Connecticut—to draft a declaration of independence. Except for Dr. Franklin, all of the members of the committee were lawyers, and all five—as highly educated men—were familiar with Enlightenment texts, including Beccaria's book, a standard holding in early American law libraries. "Blackstone's *Commentaries*, extensively used by Colonial lawyers on the eve of the Revolution," one 1992 publication points out, "drew heavily on the philosophy of the Italian Beccaria, who attributed crime largely to environmental factors." Robert R. Livingston (1746–1813)—the politician who became the first U.S. Secretary of Foreign Affairs (1781–1783) and the first Chancellor of New York (1777–1801)—had graduated from King's College (later renamed Columbia University) and was the man who administered the presidential oath of office to George Washington in 1789 at Federal Hall in New York City. "In 1768," one source notes, Livingston "wrote about a woman convicted of petty theft who was under sentence of death." "Her execution was delayed," that source, *History of Criminal Justice*, reports, "because of her pregnancy, but would be carried out shortly after her child was born." "Livingston," that history observes, "stressed the harshness and inhumanity of a legal system that left the infant motherless." *A Syllabus of Modern History* (1913)— a selection of the most important events and texts—was curated at Columbia University, Livingston's alma mater, by historian Carlton Hayes. In that book, Montesquieu, Rousseau and Beccaria were specifically listed under the headings "spirit of progress and reform" and "criticism of political institutions."[39]

The Revolutionary War sought to vindicate principles of liberty and equality—if not for all than at least for some. After the war broke out, Mazzei—along with men like Madison and Jefferson—took up the cause of freedom just as he had taken up his pen to write of natural rights. Prior to being tasked with employing his diplomatic skills in Europe, he joined the Independent Company of Albemarle to repel enemy forces, putting his rhetoric and words into action. Writing to John Page on January 11, 1777, Mazzei said he was "preparing to march to the Continental Camp with as many volunteers as I shall be able to persuade." Having written and distributed *Instructions to the Freeholders of Albemarle County to Their Delegates in Convention* (1776), wherein Mazzei sought to restructure relations between the ruled and their ruler, Mazzei also sent the Grand Duke of Tuscany an Italian translation of the Declaration of Independence, a translation published in Tuscan newspapers. In a sign of the trust reposed in him, Mazzei was, as noted, later sent as an envoy to Europe to seek financial assistance from the Grand Duke, with Mazzei also seeking needed provisions and supplies for Virginians during the war effort. In an October 1778 letter to Massachusetts' John Hancock, Thomas Jefferson had sought a solution to the lackluster resources of the Continental force, recommending Mazzei at length in these words:

> An acquaintance with two Italian gentlemen who have settled in my neighborhood has been the means of my becoming acquainted with some facts which may perhaps be of some use to the general cause. The Grand Duke of Tuscany by great œconomy & a particular attention to the affairs of his treasury has I understand a very large sum in ready money which it is thought he would readily put out to interest, more especially if it was proposed not to carry it out of his state, but to invest it in necessaries there. Having also established at his own expence public manufactures for the employment of his poor, it is said he has immense magazines of these which he would without doubt gladly furnish on credit.—The Genoese are among the richest people in Europe.... One of the gentlemen of whom I spoke above (Mr Mazzei) is I think more likely to negotiate this matter to our advantage than perhaps a native alone. He possesses first rate abilities, is pretty well acquainted with the European courts, & particularly those abovementioned, is a native of Tuscany with good connections and I have seen certain proofs of the Grand Duke's personal regard for him. He has been a zealous whig from the begin-

ning and I think may be relied on perfectly in point of integrity. He is very sanguine in his expeditions of the services he could render us on this occasion & would undertake it on a very moderate appointment. This, if Congress were to adopt the plan at all, they would order as they please: He thinks £600 sterl. would enable him to continue there a twelvemonth within which time it might be effected. I think the sum which would be hazarded of little consideration when compared with the benefits hoped for. I have taken the liberty of troubling you with this information, finding there are few others now remaining at Congress of my former acquaintance, & none for whom I have greater esteem. A love for the general cause makes me hazard it for the general service.

Ultimately, the highly respected Mazzei, trusted by Virginians as a loyal supporter of the cause of American independence, travelled by ship to Europe as an agent for Virginia to try to assist the cause of his newly adopted home. As one source describes his appointment and his objective: "Because of his admirable qualifications for this mission—being a Tuscan by birth, a merchant of considerable experience, a judge of men and their motives, a writer—Mazzei received his appointment from Governor Patrick Henry and the Virginia Council, in January, 1779. He was authorized to obtain a loan of gold and silver, not exceeding £900,000, and to purchase goods in Italy for the use of the state troops." Mazzei took an oath of allegiance to the Commonwealth of Virginia on April 21, 1779, and he then set sail from Hob's Hole two months later with his wife, his step-daughter, and a friend, Francesco del Maglio. Unfortunately, from the start, Mazzei's mission ran into hardships and difficulties. For starters, the ship Mazzei boarded for Europe was captured by a British privateer, with Mazzei and his family taken to New York for interrogation and confinement, though not before Mazzei threw overboard a bag containing his official instructions and commission loaded down with a four-pound shot. To avoid a lengthy ordeal and imprisonment, Mazzei—a man accustomed to selling things—insisted he was on a private trip to Tuscany, though he was held in New York anyway for three months. With the Revolutionary War having broken out, it was hard to separate American revolutionaries from British loyalists and neutral parties. And the British navy wasn't taking any chances.

But just as Cesare Beccaria had once encountered seemingly insurmountable obstacles in marrying the woman of his choice, Philip Mazzei would not be deterred. After an English general on Long Island took notice of Mazzei, who was known as a reputable businessman, Mazzei was placed on a cargo ship bound for Cork, Ireland. Although Mazzei fell ill on board that ship, a condition that remained with him for three weeks after his arrival in Ireland, he did not let that stop him either. After befriending a Mr. Cotter, who lodged Mazzei during his illness and provided him with money for a voyage to Paris, Mazzei slipped away in the night to avoid detection and any possibility of the fate—imprisonment in the Tower of London—that had befallen South Carolina's Henry Laurens, a plantation owner-turned-president of the Continental Congress who had been captured by the British at sea. In Paris, Mazzei then called upon Benjamin Franklin, who knew and had corresponded with many Italians, including the University of Turin physics professor, Giambatista Beccaria, an Italian priest and famous electrician (often referred to as Father Beccaria) who shared Franklin's passion for scientific pursuits. Ironically, Mazzei's mission was not stopped by British forces but by his fellow American, Dr. Franklin. Franklin—the seasoned diplomat—felt that foreign affairs should be conducted by Congress, not Virginia, and so Mazzei was left adrift in the diplomatic sea. Lacking his official papers because they had been thrown overboard, all Mazzei was able to do was send back dispatches— from Nantes, Paris, Genoa, Florence, Leghorn and Amsterdam—to then-Governor Thomas Jefferson in Virginia and to his successor, Benjamin Harrison.

Mazzei's diplomatic mission did not achieve its objectives, though Mazzei, in Europe, did write newspaper articles like "The Justice of the American Cause" and "Why the American States Cannot Be Accused of Having Rebelled." Lacking the proper credentials, Mazzei—though not for want of trying—was unable to convince the Grand Duke of Tuscany to extend any credit, with the Grand Duke convinced that Great Britain would never relinquish what it saw as its American colonies. Upon his return to America in November 1783 following the signing of the Treaty of Paris on September 3, 1783, Mazzei was nonetheless greeted warmly—and with great enthusiasm—by his large cadre of Virginia friends. The following resolution, passed by the Board of Trade of Virginia, reflected Virginians' shared sentiments: "And the Board reflecting on the patriotic exertions of Mr. Mazzei in favor of this country in the aforesaid appointment are of the opinion that he has conducted himself therein with activity, assiduity and zeal, and that the ill sweep that has attended his business is by no means imputable to him but to certain coincident circumstances, and that his conduct merits the appreciation of the Board of which this is to be considered as a testimonial." After once more returning to Europe, sailing from New York to France in June 1785, Mazzei reconnected with Thomas Jefferson in Paris and wrote *Recherches historiques et politiques sur les États-Unis de l'Amérique septentrionale*, a work about America and its independence that was published in four volumes in 1788.[40] That book—the title of which, in English, translates as *Historical and Political Researches on the United States of North America*—was hastily written by Mazzei in Italian, mostly from memory, but translated into French by a Norman deputy in Parliament. The text of the very first volume of that work, advertised as written "By a Citizen of Virginia," references the Italian philosopher, Cesare Beccaria, with approval. The first, second and third volumes also discuss *la peine de mort*—the punishment of death.[41]

An examination of Philip Mazzei's history makes clear that he considered himself one of Beccaria's many disciples. In book one, Mazzei notes that "[t]he legislative branch always has the power to absolve delinquents" and that state executives could "pardon any condemned criminal" or "suspend execution in certain cases and grant pardon in others." As translated into English, Mazzei then wrote this: "As long as we retain any vestige of our barbaric laws, the power to abrogate a sentence will be useful, but I hope that in the near future the legislator will be indulgent and humane, following Beccaria's advice, and that the executive power will be inexorable." A footnote to that quoted text—written by the Italian-American with whom Jefferson spent so much time—reads as follows:

All punishments should be proportionate to the offense. When no distinction is made between crimes, men are inclined to commit murder as quickly as to steal. For this reason cruel laws are contrary to justice, as the purpose of punishment is to correct men, not to exterminate them (Article 18 of the Declaration of Rights of New Hampshire, 31 October 1783). The Revolution is responsible for these just and humane reforms.[42]

The Constitution of New Hampshire, adopted on October 31, 1783, became effective the next year, on June 2, 1784. Article 18 of that early American state constitution, titled "Penalties to be Proportioned to Offenses; True Design of Punishment," made the Beccarian call for "penalties" to be "proportioned to the nature of the offense," called "a multitude of sanguinary laws" both "impolitic and unjust," and proclaimed that "[t]he true design of all punishments" is "to reform, not to exterminate mankind."[43]

In fact, Philip Mazzei's recommendation that Cesare Beccaria be added as an international member of Virginia's Constitutional Society along with other Enlightenment figures, including Florentine anatomist, chemist, physicist and philosopher Felice Fontana (1730–1805), shows just how important Beccaria's writings were to him and American revolutionaries more broadly. While Beccaria had penned *Dei delitti e delle pene*, Fontana—the co-founder, with Italian naturalist Giovanni Fabbroni (1752–1822), of a natural history museum—taught logic and physics in Pisa and published scientific works. In 1766, the same year that Cesare Beccaria and Alessandro Verri went to Paris, Fontana was appointed to be the court physicist by Grand Duke Peter Leopold, with Fontana said to be the "driving force" beyond the establishment, in 1775, of the Royal Museum of Physics and Natural History. As Mazzei, in a letter to John Blair, described the purpose of the Constitutional Society, yet another organization and one that sought to further the Beccarian idea of publicizing the laws so all the people would know what they were: "It seems to me that in a truly free country, where national prosperity and happiness stand on the same foundation for everyone, the uneducated portion of the inhabitants has a right to be enlightened and advised by the educated citizens, just as a child is by his father." In another letter to John Adams, dated September 27, 1785, the Constitutional Society's purpose was described this way: "I have always been of the opinion that Freedom cannot subsist for long in any country unless the generality of the people are aware of its blessing, and tolerably well acquainted with the principles on which alone it can be supported."[44] In *On Crimes and Punishments*, Beccaria himself had written of the importance of free speech and education, with Mazzei—like so many Americans—embracing the principles of the "celebrated" Italian philosopher.[45]

Even in the very midst of the Revolutionary War, which ended with the Treaty of Paris in 1783, Beccaria's guidance can be felt. In 1776, the same year the Second Continental Congress issued its Declaration of Independence, Edmund Pendleton—a prominent Virginia lawyer and politician—wrote to Thomas Jefferson: "Our Criminal System of Law has hitherto been too Sanguinary, punishing too many crimes with death, I confess."[46] Indeed, as America's first commander-in-chief, then-General George Washington—having endured the bitter winter of 1777–1778 with his troops at Pennsylvania's Valley Forge—wrote in 1778 to the Continental Congress, at least partially echoing the sentiments of writers such as Voltaire and Beccaria: "Capital crimes in the army are frequent, particularly in the instance of desertion; actually to inflict capital punishment upon every deserter or other heinous offender, would incur the imputation of cruelty, and by the familiarity of the example, destroy its efficacy; on the other hand to give only a hundred lashes to such criminals is a burlesque on their crimes rather than a serious correction, and affords encouragement to obstinacy and imitation."[47] Despite having once served as a British officer and been trained to use harsh corporal punishments and executions to maintain strict military discipline, Washington came to view executions—even in wartime—as too common. Washington thus sought the option, at least for some crimes, of an intermediate punishment, something less than death though more than 100 lashes.[48] In 1769, George Washington—acting as a diligent stepfather—had actually purchased Beccaria's book, *On Crimes and Punishments*, to help educate his own teenage step-son and ward, John Parke Custis.[49]

General Charles Lee, one of Washington's subordinates in the Revolutionary War, once proposed going even further in the way of reform, writing: "With respect to criminal matters, I would adopt Beccaria's scheme; its excellencies have been demonstrated in the Tuscan dominions." Lee—who, in 1776, led forces to repulse a British effort to capture Charleston, South Carolina—specifically noted that the Grand Duke of Tuscany "had read and admired the Marquis of Beccaria,"[50] and that the Grand Duke had "put a stop to all capital punishments, even for the greatest crimes; and the consequences have convinced the world of its wholesomeness." "The galleys, slavery for a certain term of years, or for life, in proportion to the crime," Lee wrote, alluding to Tuscany's abolition of the death penalty in 1786, "have accomplished what an army of hangmen, with their hooks, wheels and gibbets, could not." Praising Beccaria's book as an "incomparable treatise," General Lee emphasized: "In short, Tuscany, from being a theatre of the greatest crimes and villanies of every species, is become the safest and best ordered State of Europe." "I am therefore," Lee concluded, "absolutely and totally against capital punishments, at least in our military community." With non-lethal corporal punishments, such as branding and whipping, then still in use, Lee offered this alternative and his own suggestion: "As to those who have been guilty of crimes of a very deep dye, such as wanton murder, perjury, and the like, let them be mutilated, their ears cut off, their faces stamped with the marks of infamy, and whipped out of State." "Let the loss of liberty, and ignominy," Lee explained elsewhere, "be inculcated as the extreme of all punishments: common culprits therefore are, in proportion to the degree of their delinquency, to be condemned to slavery, for a longer or shorter term of years; to public works, such as repairing high ways, and public buildings, with some ignominious distinction of habit, denoting their condition."[51]

With so many disciples, the momentous impact of Beccaria's *On Crimes and Punishments* can thus be keenly felt in early American law, even though Beccaria's name nowhere appears in early American state constitutions. By the time American states began writing their own constitutions in 1776, Beccaria's treatise had clearly already shaped the framers' thoughts and views. And it dramatically changed the way they talked about tyranny and the concepts of crime and punishment. As Pulitzer Prize-winning historian Gordon Wood emphasizes: "Many of the Revolutionary state constitutions of 1776 evoked the enlightened thinking of the Italian reformer Cesare Beccaria and promised to end punishments that were 'cruel and unusual' and to make them 'less sanguinary and in general more proportionate to the crimes.'"[52] In a series of lectures delivered in the 1890s by Yale University professor John Dillon, one finds similar sentiments. In one of those lectures, later compiled and published in Boston as *The Laws and Jurisprudence of England and America*, Dillon reported: "In this country we never adopted the extreme severities of the English statutes. We were early influenced by the views of Beccaria. Instead of hanging we condemned the criminal to labor for a term of years in what we named a penitentiary." "Pennsylvania," Dillon said, "led the way to this great change by a provision in her Constitution in 1776."[53]

Even after the Revolutionary War came to a close, Beccaria's treatise remained an oft-quoted source for American lawyers and legal commentators. The ideas of Beccaria—and those of other Enlightenment writers—inspired numerous written codes of law, more progressive penal legislation, and the systematic codification of U.S. laws, now reflected in the United States Code and bound volumes containing compilations of state statutes. That the U.S. Constitution and the Bill of Rights—in contrast to the unwritten "English constitution"—are *written* documents reflects this Enlightenment approach and constitutes a very Beccarian impulse favoring codification.[54] While the United States of America is still regularly classed as a *common law* country because part of its legal traditions come from Great Britain, it is—in reality—a mix of common law and civil law traditions. The Rule of Law—dependent on the people's knowledge of the law—was furthered by the systematic codification of important legal principles, whether in constitutions or statutes and whether at the federal, state or local level. Just as codified laws gave the public notice of their rights and responsibilities, the increased use of written judicial opinions—a byproduct of Enlightenment thinkers, such as Beccaria, seeking to curtail runaway judicial discretion—would allow for greater public scrutiny of them. William Cranch, an early American reporter of U.S. Supreme Court decisions, himself whole-heartedly welcomed the practice of the justices of the nation's highest court "of reducing their opinions to writing in all cases of difficulty or importance." It was a practice that would allow for greater transparency and public accountability in regard to such decisions.[55]

Adherence to the Rule of Law, the fabric of which would be strengthened by the people's acceptance of the laws as put in place by their elected representatives, would help eliminate a good portion of the arbitrariness in the law's application.[56] The notion of "due process of law" codified in the text of the U.S. Constitution's Fifth Amendment[57]—and later, repeated in the Constitution's post-Civil War Fourteenth Amendment, which added "equal protection of the laws" as an explicit constitutional guarantee[58]—is rooted in the notion that the law should be applied in an even-handed, non-arbitrary fashion. The very idea of "due process of law," writes one commentator, Giacinto della Cananea, "is often associated with concepts such as non-arbitrariness, legality, and (the prohibition of) denial of justice." The words "due process of law," yet another source notes of those four words that have served to protect so many American citizens, "were intended to secure the individual from the arbitrary exercise of the powers of government."[59] The U.S. Constitution—that out-growth of the American Revolution—thus aims at having like offenders treated alike and at having the law treat everyone, as much as humanly possible, evenhandedly and uniformly, regardless of race, class or gender.[60] The Fourteenth Amendment, ratified in 1868, itself constitutionalized the idea of "like punishment"—part of the wording of the Civil Rights Act of 1866, a landmark piece of legislation passed by Congress after the Civil War. That federal statute sought to ensure that African Americans would have equal access to the courts—and to equal justice before them.[61]

Cesare Beccaria's ideas, when written, were largely theoretical—and it took some time before legislators were willing to experiment with them. By the 1780s and 1790s, however, Anglo-American lawmakers were making strenuous efforts to put Beccaria's theoretical ideas into practice. In 1785, following the end of the Revolutionary War, Thomas Jefferson's bill (drafted in the 1770s) to make punishments more proportionate to crimes finally came to a vote in the Virginia legislature.[62] After it failed to pass by a single vote, James Madison—who pushed for the bill's adoption in Jefferson's absence due to his friend's diplomatic responsibilities abroad—woefully lamented to Jefferson that "our old bloody code is by this event fully restored."[63] That language—perhaps obscure to a modern reader—meant something quite specific to both men. According to Frank McLynn's *Crime and Punishment in Eighteenth Century England*: "The Bloody Code is the name traditionally given to the English system of criminal law during the period 1688–1815." In those years, McLynn notes, "a huge number of felonies punishable by death" were added to the English law. As he further emphasizes: "In 1688 no more than fifty offences carried the death penalty: the crimes so punishable were treason, murder, rape, and arson. By 1765 this figure had risen to about 160; an average of one new capital offence a year was added during the thirty-three-year reign of George II." "A further sixty-five capital felonies added to the Code from 1765 to 1815," McLynn stresses, reflecting the rejection of Beccaria's anti-gallows advocacy among the majority of Britain's tradition-bound elite, "brought the number of crimes that bore the death penalty to about 225 by the end of the Napoleonic wars."[64] In *Criminal Justice in Ireland*, one modern commentator, Paul O'Mahony, emphasizes of what the author of *Dei delitti e delle pene* was up against when he wrote his book: "Beccaria was a man of the Enlightenment concerned to reform the barbaric 'bloody code', then prevailing throughout Europe and meting out extremely brutal and often arbitrary and disproportionate punishment for wrongdoing."[65]

As avid readers and writers, America's Founding Fathers had considerable knowledge of English law as well as considerable contacts with Italian thinkers—among them, scientists and naturalists and Tuscan philosophers who sought to make punishments milder. For example, on April 24, 1796, Thomas Jefferson—writing from Monticello, and having already served as George Washington's Secretary of State from 1790 to 1793—sent a letter to his long-time friend Philip Mazzei, then in Tuscany. "In place of that noble love of liberty, & republican government which carried us triumphantly thro' the war," the politically ambitious Jefferson complained to Mazzei, "an Anglican monarchical, & aristocratical party has sprung up, whose avowed object is to draw over us the substance, as they have already done the forms, of the British government." "The main body of our citizens, however," Jefferson advised, "remain true to their republican principles; the whole landed interest is republican, and so is a great mass of talents." "Against us," Jefferson wrote, "are the Executive, the Judiciary, two out of three branches…, all the officers of the government, all who want to be officers, all timid men who prefer the calm of despotism to the boisterous sea of liberty, British merchants and Americans trading on British capitals, speculators, and holders in the banks of public funds, a continuance invented for the purpose of corruption, and for assimilating us in all things to the rotten as well as the sound parts of the British model." Madison and Jefferson had both disliked some of President Washington's policies and rhetoric, and southerners had strongly opposed the ratification and signing of the Jay Treaty (1794), designed to establish a commission to formalize the border between the U.S. and Canada and to ease tensions with Great Britain. In the fierce political battle that took place in America, John Jay—the first Chief Justice of the United States and Washington's special envoy who was appointed to negotiate the treaty—was hanged in effigy in Philadelphia, with Federalists supporting the treaty and disgruntled Democratic-Republicans portraying the Federalists as monarchists and the heirs of the Tories.

Jefferson's 1796 missive to Mazzei thus contained highly inflammatory language meant to be read and consumed in private. Jefferson's letter to the physician-trained Mazzei, then in Florence, notoriously pulled no punches, and later became the subject of considerable public controversy after its publication, especially since George Washington was an extremely popular figure. As Jefferson's letter continued: "It would give you a fever were I to name to you the apostates who have gone over to these heresies, men who were Samsons in the field and Solomons in the council, but who have had their heads shorn by the harlot England." "In short," Jefferson concluded, worrying about the commitment of some to the principles of the American Revolution, "we are likely to preserve the liberty we have obtained only by unremitting labors and perils." "But," Jefferson pledged, reciting his own unwavering commitment, "we shall preserve it; and our mass of weight and wealth on the good side is so great, as to leave no danger that force will ever be attempted against us." "We have only to awake and snap the Lilliputian cords with which they have been entangling us during the first sleep which succeeded our labors," Jefferson told Mazzei, confiding in him in his private letter never meant for public consumption.[66] George Washington was still the President of the United States when Jefferson sent his letter to Mazzei, and in less than a year's time, Jefferson himself would be the second Vice President of the United States, serving under President John Adams.[67]

A fellow republican, an overzealous Mazzei—anxious to let Jefferson's sentiments be known—translated this letter into Italian and, without Jefferson's permission, had it published in Florence on January 1, 1797. In a world in which periodicals and printing presses were ubiquitous, it was then picked up by the French newspapers, and it was spotted by an American who translated the French version into English and sent it on to the United States. By May 1797, not long after Jefferson's inauguration as Vice President, versions of Jefferson's letter to Mazzei—calling into question George Washington's administration—were appearing in American newspapers. The letter brought down on Jefferson, once a part of that administration, the collective wrath of the Federalist press, which even raised the specter of impeachment.[68] With newspapers often staking out highly partisan turf, Jefferson's letter to Mazzei would be fiercely debated in the press for decades to come and was widely reprinted, albeit with slight variations.[69] As Randall Adkins wrote in *The Evolution of Political Parties, Campaigns, and Elections*: "The controversy surrounding the letter's publication turned out to be highly partisan, and Jefferson was attacked intensely by the Federalists. Jefferson was, of course, an easy target for Federalist propaganda: by the time the letter had been published in the United States, Jefferson was both vice president and leader of the Republican opposition."[70] In the election of 1800, Jefferson squared off against John Adams, with Jefferson believing Federalists were dishonoring the "spirit of 1776." Although Jefferson narrowly beat Adams in the Electoral College vote, 73 to 65, Jefferson only assumed the presidency after beating back a 36-ballot challenge from Aaron Burr. A member of Jefferson's own Democratic-Republican party, Burr had gotten an equal number of electoral votes, tossing the election into the hands of the House of Representatives. The protracted dispute, which finally ended (thanks in part to Alexander Hamilton's dislike of Burr) in Jefferson's favor, led to the Twelfth Amendment, ratified in 1804, requiring electors to cast distinct votes for president and vice-president.[71]

Mazzei, after writing his lengthy history of the American Revolution and an autobiography, *Memorie*, fell ill and died in March 1816, his body buried in his native Pisa — home to the now-famed Leaning Tower of Pisa. After Mazzei's death, in a July 18, 1816 letter to Mazzei's friend, the Italian jurist Giovanni Carmignani (1768–1847), Jefferson — writing from Monticello, and by then an ex-President — paid this tribute to his own long-time friend, the Italian-American Philip Mazzei: "An intimacy of 40 years have proved to me his great worth, and a friendship which had begun in personal acquaintance, was maintained after separation, without abatement by a constant interchange of letters. His esteem too in this country was very general; his early & zealous cooperation in the establishment of our independence having acquired for him here a great degree of favor." Carmignani, who taught criminal law and legal philosophy at the University of Pisa, based his own opposition to capital punishment in Enlightenment principles, grounding the right to punish in juridical necessity just as Montesquieu and Beccaria had previously done. To his friend Thomas Appleton, Jefferson offered these additional personal reflections on Mazzei: "He had some peculiarities, & who of us has not? But he was of solid worth; honest, able, zealous in sound principles Moral & political, constant in friendship, and punctual in all his undertakings. He was greatly esteemed in this country, and some one has inserted in our papers an account of his death, with a handsome and just eulogy of him, and a proposition to publish his life in one 8 vo. volume." "I have no doubt but that what he has written of himself during the portion of the revolutionary period he has passed with us," Jefferson told Appleton, "would furnish some good material for our history of which there is already a wonderful scarcity."[72]

Like Philip Mazzei personally, Cesare Beccaria's book exerted enormous influence on America's founders. As with Jeremy Bentham's exposure to Beccaria's book in England, George Washington, John Adams and Thomas Jefferson — the first three U.S.

presidents, to name just three early American political leaders—bought copies of *On Crimes and Punishments* while places such as Virginia and Massachusetts were still English colonies.[73] And among American colonists, those three men were hardly alone in looking to Beccaria for inspiration and guidance. The book was advertised for sale in colonial America, and many colonists had purchased and eagerly read and used it. In 1770, for example, John Adams had passionately quoted Beccaria's treatise in defending British soldiers at the Boston Massacre trial, demonstrating its familiarity to a broader audience. "I am for the prisoners at the bar," Adams said in open court, "and shall apologize for it only in the words of the Marquis Beccaria: 'If by supporting the rights of mankind, and of invincible truth, I shall contribute to save from the agonies of death one unfortunate victim of tyranny, or ignorance, equally fatal, his blessings and tears of transport shall be sufficient consolation to me for the contempt of all mankind.' "[74] Elsewhere, Adams cited Montesquieu—Beccaria's idol and one of America's founders' go-to French political theorists—for the proposition that "every man invested with power is apt to abuse it." Adams then wrote: "To prevent the abuse of power, it is necessary, that, by the very disposition of things, power should be a check to power."

In the latter source, Adams also quoted Cesare Beccaria in the original Italian: "*Ogni uomo si fa centro di tutte le combinazioni del globo.*"[75] A rough translation: "Every man makes himself the center of his whole world."[76] In *On Crimes and Punishments*, Beccaria had put it this way, employing Rousseau's notion of a social compact: "If it were possible, every one of us would prefer that the compacts binding others did not bind us; every man tends to make himself the center of his whole world."[77] Referring to Montesquieu, Beccaria and other writers as philosophers, John Adams queried: "Shall we say that all these philosophers were ignorant of human nature?" Adams' answer: "With all my soul, I wish it were in my power to quote any passages in history or philosophy, which might demonstrate all these satires on our species to be false. But the phenomena are all in their favour; and the only question to be raised with them is, whether the cause is wickedness, weakness, or insanity?"[78] In *The Wealth of Nations*, Adam Smith had this to say on the subject of self-interest: "It is not from the benevolence of the butcher, the brewer or the baker that we expect our dinner, but from their regard to their own interest." When political theorists like John Adams and economists such as Adam Smith were writing about self-interest, it is clear that they were not writing in a vacuum.[79]

Early American political leaders read a lot of history and political philosophy and they were conversant in economics, literature and the literary arts. John Adams read many English writers—from John Locke (1632–1704) to Algernon Sidney (1623–1683) and from James Harrington (1611–1677) to Thomas Hobbes (1588–1679).[80] But Montesquieu and Beccaria—both from *civil law* countries—shaped Adams' views in important ways, too, with Beccaria's book right there on American bookshelves alongside Montesquieu's *The Spirit of the Laws* and the English and Scottish classics.[81] The writings of John Adams on republicanism and the rule of law are, in fact, put in much better context when Beccaria's writings and those of other Enlightenment thinkers are considered and taken into account. In his 1776 pamphlet, *Thoughts on Government*, Adams wrote that "there is no good government but what is republican" and that "the very definition of a republic is 'an empire of laws and not of men.'" In November 1775, John Adams had been asked by a Virginia politician and revolutionary, Richard Henry Lee, for his thoughts on the proper structure of government should an irreversible break with the British Empire occur, and in March 1776, two North Carolina delegates to Congress, John Penn and William Hooper, had also approached Adams—the talented colonial lawyer—for advice.[82] John Adams ultimately became a member of the Committee of Five charged with drafting the Declaration of Independence, and though Jefferson gets the lion's share of the credit for that document, the suggestions of Adams on governance were in line with Beccaria's views and those of the Enlightenment generally. As Adams wrote: "No man will contend that a nation can be free that is not governed by fixed laws. All other government than that of permanent known laws, is the government of mere will and pleasure, whether it be exercised by one, a few, or many." In his 1811 essay on "A Government of Laws and Not of Men," Adams—the lawyer and revolutionary obsessed by political philosophy—further explained that "it is very true there can be no good government, without laws: but those laws must be good, must be equal, must be wisely made."[83]

John Adams, the drafter of the Massachusetts Constitution of 1780, the oldest continuously operating constitution in the world,[84] thus believed, like Cesare Beccaria and Thomas Jefferson, in a system of fixed and non-arbitrary laws.[85] An avid reader of Beccaria's treatise, Adams had read *On Crimes and Punishments* a full decade before drafting the Massachusetts Constitution of 1780 as he prepared to defend British soldiers accused of murder following the Boston Massacre.[86] Though John Adams would support American independence, he saw fit to ably defend Englishmen being put on trial for their lives regardless of the role they had played in Great Britain's oppression—a position consistent with the notion that *any* person, regardless of nationality or political affiliation, had certain natural rights and was entitled to a fair and vigorous defense with the assistance of counsel, a right now enshrined in the U.S. Constitution's Sixth Amendment. Indeed, in *A Defence of the Constitutions of Government of the United States*, Adams not only later praised American constitutions for their use of separation-of-powers principles—"the legislative, executive, and judicial powers are carefully separated," Adams reflected—but for how "nicely balanced" legislative powers had been calibrated as regards "the powers of the one, the few, and the many" such that "the laws alone can govern." "In all free states," Adams stressed, echoing a theme that both Montesquieu and Beccaria had earlier advanced, "the evil to be avoided is tyranny; that is to say, the *summa imperii*, or unlimited power, solely in the hands of the one, the few, or the many." In railing against tyranny, John Adams was simply voicing the same theme that the Continental Congress, as a whole and invoking Montesquieu and Beccaria, had in 1774 in that body's open letter to the inhabitants of Quebec.

In truth, opposition to tyranny was the driving force behind the American Revolution, and Beccaria's book—as the Continental Congress's 1774 letter makes clear—plainly helped to lay the intellectual foundation for it. In the Declaration of Independence, the document for which John Adams served on the drafting committee, America's founders indicted the King of England in a long series of grievances, published for all to read and justifying the need for independence. "The history of the present King of Great Britain is a history of repeated injuries and usurpations, all having in direct object the establishment of an absolute Tyranny over these States," the Declaration of Independence read. Among the grievances directed at George III: "He has refused his Assent to Laws, the most wholesome and necessary for the public good." "For depriving us in many cases, of the benefit of Trial by Jury." "He has plundered our seas, ravaged our coasts, burnt our towns, and destroyed the lives of our people." "He is at this time transporting large Armies of foreign Mercenaries to compleat the works of death, desolation, and tyranny, already begun with circumstances of Cruelty & Perfidy scarcely paralleled in the most barbarous ages, and totally unworthy the Head of a civilized nation." "He has constrained our fellow Citizens taken Captive on the high Seas to bear Arms against their Country, to become the executioners of their friends and Brethren, or to fall themselves by their Hands." "In every stage of these Oppressions," the Declaration of Independence continued, "We have Petitioned for Redress in the most humble terms: Our repeated Petitions have been answered only by repeated injury. A Prince, whose character is thus marked by every act which may define a Tyrant, is unfit to be the ruler of a free people."[87] America's founders, in laying out the causes for severing the political ties with George III, thus sought to inspire their fellow Americans to join the cause—the fight for liberty and freedom.

Tyranny in all of its forms was seen as the enemy, with George III and the occupying Redcoats becoming symbols of tyranny. John Adams himself wrote about "encroachments of the few upon the rights of the many, and of the many upon the privileges of the few; which ever did, and ever will, conclude in a tyranny; first either of the few or the many, but at least, infallibly, of a *single person*." Consequently, Adams' defense of the British soldiers was fully consistent with Enlightenment and Beccarian principles. "The desires of men, are not only exorbitant, but endless: they grasp at all; and can form no scheme of perfect happiness with less," Adams warned in his own writings, expressing concerns about ambitious men and about the "spirit of cruelty and revenge" and "injustice, sophistry, and fraud." "[A] balance can never be established between two orders in society, without a third to aid the weakest," Adams offered, returning to another Beccarian theme. Explicitly referencing "an inequality of wealth" in Massachusetts as well as another "species of inequality," the happenstance of one's birth and one's ancestors, Adams worried about "severe laws" and "tyrannical laws" executed "in a tyrannical manner." Saying that obedience to "unjust and unequal laws" would be "incompatible with liberty," Adams emphasized with the force of a powerful intellect: "yet no man will contend, that a nation can be free, that is not governed by fixed laws."[88] In the Declaration of Independence itself, America's founders made reference to their "unalienable Rights"—among them, "Life, Liberty and the pursuit of Happiness"—and specifically emphasized: "That to secure these rights, Governments are instituted among Men, deriving their just powers from the consent of the governed." "[W]henever any Form of Government becomes destructive of the ends," the Declaration of Independence stressed, "it is the Right of the People to alter or to abolish it, and to institute new Government, laying its foundation on such principles and organizing its powers in such form, as to them shall seem most likely to effect their Safety and Happiness."[89]

John Adams' views dovetailed with Beccaria's in more ways than one, with the respected legal historian H. Jefferson Powell—a Duke University law professor—once explaining Beccaria's pervasive influence on both American and European thinkers.[90] "In his enormously influential essay on criminal law," Powell observed, "the Italian jurist Cesare Beccaria wrote that judges in criminal cases must not be allowed the authority to interpret the laws because that would make them de facto legislators. Beccaria contrasted 'the constant fixed voice of the law' with 'the erring instability of interpretation,' and his firm conclusion—'the interpretation of laws is an evil'—expressed a view widely shared by educated and 'progressive' individuals in the late eighteenth century."[91] The Beccarian notion of equality of treatment would also show up in Jefferson's Declaration of Independence and in late 1780s debates over the proposed U.S. Constitution itself, with Melancton Smith—at New York's ratifying convention in June 1788—expressly invoking Beccaria's name. In arguing for participation in government by "[t]he middling class," Smith—a delegate worried about the rich assuming disproportionate control over governmental powers for their own benefit—pulled out the exact same quote from *On Crimes and Punishments* that the Continental Congress as a whole had cited to the people of Quebec right before the start of the Revolutionary War.[92] While John Adams' son, John Quincy Adams, later expressed support for America's anti-gallows movement, Beccaria's own proposed alternative for the death penalty—"perpetual slavery"—would itself find expression in the Thirteenth Amendment, which, in 1865, outlawed slavery and involuntary servitude "except as a punishment for crime whereof the party shall have been duly convicted."[93] With the Fourteenth Amendment, ratified in 1868, guaranteeing the "equal protection of the laws," Cesare Beccaria's ideas were still actively shaping American law many decades into the nineteenth century, even in Abraham Lincoln's time.

Most consequentially, Cesare Beccaria's ideas shaped world history at an especially critical time, in the last quarter of the eighteenth century as social and political revolutions took place. In *A Defence of the Constitutions of Government of the United States* (1787–1788), a three-volume work, John Adams specifically wrote of "[t]he checks and balances of republican government," of "Greeks and Romans," and "of governments of laws and not of men." He meticulously studied—and broke out into separate categories—"Democratical Republics," "Aristocratical Republics," "Monarchical Republics," "Ancient Republics, and Opinions of Philosophers," and "Mixed Governments." Before moving on to "Locke, Milton, and Hume," Adams discussed, among the governments of many other locales, "[t]he republic of St. Marino, in Italy"; Genoa and Corsica; "[t]he republic of Venice"; and those of Carthage and Rome.[94] The Italian-speaking Pasquale Paoli (1725–1807), a Corsican leader and revolutionary, inspired many revolutionaries of his day, just as Cesare Beccaria's ideas—and those of other Enlightenment figures—had after they filtered into the public consciousness.[95] James Madison—a lawmaker quite familiar with Beccaria's ideas—would himself stay apprised of events in Italy before—and even long after—he had helped craft the U.S. Constitution and its Bill of Rights. For example, an 1805 letter from Thomas Appleton, sent from Leghorn aboard a vessel departing for the U.S., informed Madison of the goings on of "the Genoese." It described a mode of government "adopted to obtain the votes of the people," and it contained lots of details about what was happening in Italy as regards governance issues.[96] As one modern source emphasizes of the European Enlightenment's vast influence across the Atlantic: "America's most basic documents reflect this history. The Declaration of Independence embraced Locke's version of the social contract, and the Constitution, following Voltaire, rejected aristocratic government; it made use of Montesquieu's checks and balances, and with Beccaria endorsed the rule of law."[97]

The influence of Beccaria's treatise on America's founders is actually readily apparent from a whole host of 1770s newspapers and periodicals, as well as numerous speeches and documents drafted before and after the Declaration of Independence. Early American state constitutions certainly show Beccaria's fingerprints, with early American lawyers and merchants of all political persuasions looking to Beccaria's ideas for guidance. For instance, in 1774, just a year before the onset of the Revolutionary War, John Dickinson—a lawyer and politician from Philadelphia, and one of Pennsylvania's delegates to the First Continental Congress—openly referred to "[t]he genius of a Beccaria" and "the masterly hand of a Beccaria."[98] Likewise, John Hancock—now most remembered for his flamboyant signature on the Declaration of Independence—owned "Beccaria on Crimes," and the Continental Congress, of which Hancock once served as president, was itself familiar with, and evidently impressed by, Enlightenment texts and Beccaria's treatise in particular.[99] In October 1774, the First Continental Congress, meeting in Philadelphia, approved a Declaration of Rights based on "the immutable laws of nature, the principles of the English constitution, and the several charters or compacts" of the colonies.[100] It was in that same month that the Continental Congress—as part of a propaganda campaign aimed at gaining the support of the colonists' northern, French-speaking neighbors for the American cause—issued its now little-remembered letter to the inhabitants of Quebec, quoting both Montesquieu and Beccaria.[101] In 1759, the British had captured Quebec in a pivotal battle as part of the Seven Years' War (known as the French and Indian War in the United States), and the British—anxious to consolidate power—had been quick to employ the death penalty, hanging a former French soldier in November 1759 in Quebec City for inciting resistance to the British occupation.[102]

Addressed to "Friends and Fellow-Subjects," the Continental Congress's October 26, 1774 letter—which put Montesquieu and Beccaria front and center—complained of the audacious and cruel abuse of English subjects and of the withholding of "irrevocable rights" by royal ministers. "The *legislative, executive* and *judging* powers are all moved by the nods of a Minister," the letter lamented, calling the Governor of Quebec "*dependant* on the servant of the Crown in Great-Britain." "Privileges and immunities," the letter asserted acerbically, "last no longer than his smiles." As the Continental Congress's letter, reprinted in the *Pennsylvania Gazette* and elsewhere, read: " 'In every human society,' says the celebrated Marquis *Beccaria*, 'there is an *effort continually tending* to confer on one part the height of power and happiness, and to reduce the other to the extreme of weakness and misery. The intent of good laws is to *oppose this effort*, and to diffuse their influence *universally* and *equally*.' " A major contributor to "Revolutionary ideology," one source observes, writing of colleges in revolutionary America, "was Enlightenment rationalism." As that source, *Educating Republicans: The College in the Era of the American Revolution*, emphasizes: "Colonists read John Locke on natural rights and on the social and governmental compacts. They read Montesquieu on British liberty and the forms of government best designed to preserve it. Voltaire taught them the evils of clerical oppression, Beccaria the necessity for reforming criminal laws."[103]

Eighteenth-century ink thus shows that Beccaria's words—part of a chorus of Enlightenment thought—played a crucial role in the impassioned arguments of the Continental Congress, especially in terms of how British oppression was characterized for a contemporary audience. As the October 1774 letter of Congress continued, returning to Beccaria's themes: "Rulers, stimulated by their pernicious 'effort,' and subjects, animated by the just 'intent of opposing good laws against it,' have occasioned that vast variety of events, that fill the histories of so many nations. All these histories demonstrate the truth of this simple position, that to live by the will of one man, or sett of men, is the production of misery to all men." "On the solid foundation of this principle, Englishmen reared up the fabric of their constitution with such a strength, as for ages to defy time, tyranny, treachery, internal and foreign wars," Congress's letter read, employing the fiery rhetoric of that time and highlighting how far astray the British monarch had gone from the core impulse—liberty—behind that nation's unwritten constitution. "And, as an illustrious author of your nation, hereafter mentioned, observes," the Continental Congress's letter added, then quoting the Frenchman Montesquieu, whose book, *The Spirit of the Laws* (1748), had so impressed the founders, "'They gave the people of their Colonies the form of their own government, and this government carrying prosperity along with it, they have grown great nations in the forests they were sent to inhabit.'"[104] "The American founders," one history, *Montesquieu and His Legacy*, points out, "clearly lifted their view of separation of powers directed from … Montesquieu's *The Spirit of Laws*.…"[105]

The writings of Beccaria and Montesquieu were, in reality, among the most quoted of the 1770s. After quoting Beccaria and Montesquieu, the open letter of the Continental Congress "To the Inhabitants of Quebec"—approved by the strong-willed American colonists then assembled at "a General Congress at Philadelphia"—recited what Americans saw as their fundamental rights. The "first grand right," its letter insisted, is "that of the people having a share in their own government, by the representatives, chosen by themselves, and in consequence of being ruled by *laws* which they themselves approve, not by *edicts* of *men* over whom they have no controul." "This," the letter said, "is a bulwark surrounding and defending their property, which by their honest cares and labours they have acquired, so that no portions of it can legally be taken from them, but with their own full and free consent, when they in their judgment deem it just and necessary to give them for public services, and precisely direct the easiest, cheapest, and most equal methods, in which they shall be collected." Though suspicious of tax collectors, America's founders were wealthy men, some with vast riches. The Jesuit-educated Charles Carroll of Carrollton, the only Catholic signer of the Declaration of Independence, inherited what has been called a "princely" sum of money. But American revolutionaries were intent on not parting with their money—whether hard earned, inherited or accumulated through the exploitation of slaves—unless they had a say in how it would be taxed and spent. "If money is wanted by Rulers who have in any manner oppressed the people, they may retain it, until their grievances are redressed," the letter stressed, drawing a line in the dirt and airing the colonists' full-throated discontent and concerns about taxation without representation.

Although the slave trade remained lawful in the Untied States until 1808, and although slavery itself persisted far longer, America's founders were intent on protecting what they saw as their natural and political rights. The 1774 letter of the Continental Congress also described "[t]he next great right" as "that of trial by jury"—a right supported by Beccaria—so that "neither life, liberty nor property can be taken from the possessor, until twelve of his unexceptionable countrymen and peers, of his vicinage, who from that neighbourhood may reasonably be supposed to be acquainted with his character, and the characters of the witnesses, upon a fair trial, and full enquiry face to face, in open Court, before as many of the people as choose to attend, shall pass their sentence upon oath against him." The letter, which covered a lot of ground, further recited the rights "to the liberty of the person"; to obtain a writ of habeas corpus from a judge if someone was illegally "seized and imprisoned"; and "the freedom of the press" to facilitate "the advancement of truth, science, morality, and arts" and the "ready communication of thoughts between subjects ... whereby oppressive officers are shamed or intimidated into more honourable and just modes of conducting affairs." "These are the invaluable rights, that form a considerable part of our mild system of government," the 1774 letter of the Continental Congress concluded, foreshadowing rights later incorporated into America's founding documents. "The Privilege of the Writ of Habeas Corpus," subject only to suspension "when in Cases of Rebellion or Invasion the public Safety may require it," would be included in Article 1 of the U.S. Constitution, and the rights to freedom of speech and to freedom of the press would make their way into the Bill of Rights, in particular, the First Amendment.[106]

In *Dei delitti e delle pene*, Cesare Beccaria had written of the right to express one's opinion, and that book infused the American founders' discourses and debates. Tracking the then-famous quote from Beccaria's treatise, the 1774 letter to the inhabitants of Quebec spoke of those "invaluable rights" and that "mild system of government" as "sending its equitable energy through all ranks and classes of men," thus defending "the poor from the rich, the weak from the powerful, the industrious from the rapacious, the peaceable from the violent, the tenants from the lords, and all from their superiors." This egalitarian rhetoric closely tracks Beccaria's, showing the power of his enlightened and persuasive appeal to the men who would soon break away from England and forge their own country. "These are the rights," the Continental Congress contended, "without which a people cannot be free and happy, and under the protecting and encouraging influence of which, these Colonies have hitherto so amazingly flourished and increased." "These are rights," the letter proclaimed, attacking George III's administration, "a profligate Ministry are now striving, by force of arms, to ravish from us, and which we are, with one mind, resolved never to resign but with our lives." "These are the rights *you* are entitled to, and ought at this moment in perfection to exercise," the happiness-seeking and tyranny-loathing Americans communicated to their French-speaking counterparts, the people of Quebec.[107]

After taking note of "the late Act of Parliament" and hardships and issues facing the people of Quebec, the 1774 letter of the Continental Congress queried, "What would your countryman, the immortal *Montesquieu*, have said to such a plan of domination, as has been framed for you?" The Quebec Act of 1774, enacted as "An Act for making more effectual Provision for the Government of the Province of Quebec in North America," was passed by the British Parliament to regulate the governance of that province. The Continental Congress' advice to its northern neighbors, returning to Montesquieu, their fellow French speaker and the one who had so inspired Beccaria himself: "Hear his words, with an intenseness of thought suited to the importance of the subject." As Montesquieu — that Madisonian oracle of separation of powers who so shaped the Enlightenment — was quoted by the Continental Congress: "'In a free state, every man, who is supposed a free agent, *ought to be concerned in his own government*: Therefore the *legislative* should reside in the whole body of the *people*, or their *representatives*.'" "'The political liberty of the subject is *a tranquility of mind*, arising from the opinion each person has of his *safety*. In order to have this liberty, it is requisite the government be so constituted, as that one man need not be *afraid* of another.'" "'When the power of *making* laws, and the power of *executing* them, are *united* in the same person, or in the same body of Magistrates, *there can be no liberty*; because apprehensions may arise, lest the same *Monarch* or *Senate* should *enact* tyrannical laws, to *execute* them in a tyrannical manner.'" In short, American colonists were asking their northern neighbors to no longer tolerate the power-thirsty, revenue-hungry, unresponsive British monarchy.[108]

Asking the people of Quebec to consider what advice the "truly great" Montesquieu would give, and citing "[t]he injuries of Boston have roused"[109] along the East Coast, from "Nova-Scotia to Georgia," the Continental Congress invited the ancestors of modern-day Canadians[110] "to meet together in your several towns and districts, and elect Deputies, who afterwards meeting in a provincial Congress, may chuse Delegates, to represent your province in the continental Congress to be held at Philadelphia on the tenth day of May, 1775." "In the present Congress," the October 1774 letter of the Continental Congress read, it had been resolved: "That we should consider the violation of your rights, by the act for altering the government of your province, as a violation of our own, and that you should be invited to accede to our confederation, which has no other objects than the perfect security of the natural and civil rights of all the constituent members, according to their respective circumstances, and the preservation of a happy and lasting connection with Great-Britain, on the salutary and constitutional principles herein before mentioned."[111] Although the people of Quebec were asked to join the American cause, they chose a different path than American colonists, with Canadians not taking the initial step toward declaring their independence from Great Britain until 1867. The Quebec Act of 1774 had given Francophone Quebecers some cultural and religious concessions, and that enactment left the French civil law in place. While America's colonists prepared for war, the Quebec Act of 1774 was enough for the British to placate the 70,000 French-speaking inhabitants in Quebec.[112]

As Americans, angry over British maltreatment and unfair designs on American resources, came to despise the English "Bloody Code," they took up arms and adopted constitutions and declarations of rights that sought to curtail "sanguinary" laws and punishments. Thomas Paine—the American revolutionary and author of *Common Sense* whose writings inspired the Revolutionary War—specifically argued that it is "sanguinary punishments which corrupt mankind."[113] "Sanguinary"—a word little used in common parlance today but ubiquitous in early America—is, as it was understood centuries ago, a synonym for "cruel" and "bloody."[114] In 1776, Maryland delegates approved a declaration expressly providing, "That sanguinary laws ought to be avoided, as far as is consistent with the safety of the State: and no law, to inflict cruel and unusual pains and penalties, ought to be made in any case, or at any time hereafter."[115] American states also routinely included provisions in their constitutions prohibiting "cruel and unusual," "cruel or unusual," or simply "cruel" punishments, with Pennsylvania's 1776 constitution taking specific aim—as in Maryland—at "sanguinary" laws. "The penal laws as heretofore used," read one provision of Pennsylvania's constitution, "shall be reformed by the legislature of this State, as soon as may be, and punishments made in some cases less sanguinary, and in general more proportionate to the crimes." "To deter more effectually from the commission of crimes, by continued visible punishments of long duration," another section declared, "houses ought to be provided for punishing by hard labour, those who shall be convicted of crimes not capital."[116]

In early America and under the English common law, death sentences were the *mandatory* punishment for certain crimes—and a large number of crimes were punishable by death.[117] The English "Bloody Code" made scores of offenses punishable by death, and America's colonial legal system was modeled on that of its mother country, Great Britain.[118] But during the American Revolution, the tide began to turn against capital punishment and that antiquated penal system, in large part because of the influence of Beccaria's treatise. In 1776, Virginians—many under the guiding hand of Beccaria's little treatise—adopted a Declaration of Rights that prohibited "cruel and unusual punishments." It was a clause borrowed from the English Bill of Rights of 1689, but given new content by the Enlightenment, and which prominent Virginians such as Patrick Henry and George Mason viewed as prohibiting torture.[119] Between 1776 and 1779, Thomas Jefferson himself drafted a bill in Virginia to make punishments more proportionate to crimes, a bill that Madison then advocated for in Virginia the following decade but which fell short of passage by just a single vote.[120] In the draft legislation, Jefferson cited Beccaria's treatise multiple times, with Jefferson's bill seeking to eliminate the death penalty for all crimes except murder and treason. "The rage against Horse stealers"—to use Madison's words—doomed the bill's chances of passage that year, but reforms would not be stymied for long and would gradually make their way through American legislatures.[121] As University of Texas law professor Jordan Steiker writes: "Many of our founders—including James Madison, Thomas Jefferson, Benjamin Franklin, and Benjamin Rush—were familiar with Cesare Beccaria's path-breaking critique of the death penalty and accordingly advocated restriction or abolition of capital punishment."[122] The very title of Jefferson's legislation,

"Bill for Proportioning Crimes and Punishments in Cases Heretofore Capital," suggests that Beccaria's influence was hard at work as Jefferson crafted his legislation.[123]

Beccaria pioneered the concept of proportionality, so while Beccaria's *name* was not mentioned in early American state constitutions, his *ideas* can certainly be found there. In addition to Pennsylvania's 1776 constitution speaking of making punishments "more proportionate" to crimes, the requirement of "proportioned" punishments later appeared in the state constitutions of places as diverse as Indiana, Maine, Georgia, Rhode Island and West Virginia.[124] Indeed, by the 1780s and 1790s, American law-makers had made sustained and strenuous efforts to put Beccaria's abstract ideas into practice in the real world.[125] Although Jefferson's and Madison's efforts in Virginia in the 1780s to move beyond the English Bloody Code had narrowly failed, disappointing both men,[126] efforts in Pennsylvania, where the anti-gallows movement had strong Quaker roots dating back to the days of Pennsylvania's founder, William Penn, were more successful.[127] In 1786, the same year the death penalty was totally abolished in Tuscany, Pennsylvania abolished the death penalty for robbery, burglary and sodomy.[128] And eventually, Virginia—along with other American states, joined the reform effort, if not as quickly as dominos falling one by one with great rapidity, then at least with deliberation and purpose. In 1796, ten years after Pennsylvania had taken action, New York and New Jersey specifically voted to reduce the number of capital crimes. In an effort led by George Keith Taylor, John Marshall's brother-in-law and yet another Beccaria disciple, Virginians did the same thing in 1796.[129]

Because of the influence of writers like Montesquieu, Beccaria and William Black-stone, generations of Americans vigorously debated substituting harsh punishments for milder ones. "Even Congress, in one of the first attempts to create a national penal law," writes historian Louis Masur in *Rites of Execution*, "appointed a committee to investigate alterations in the penal laws of the United States that would provide 'milder punishments for certain crimes for which infamous and capital punishments are now inflicted.'"[130] The creation of that committee was urged by Edward Livingston, a 1781 graduate of Princeton and the youngest of eleven children of Robert Livingston, a judge of New York's Supreme Court. Edward's oldest brother, Robert R. Livingston, had been—as noted—a member of the Committee of Five tasked with framing the Declaration of Independence, and Edward himself favorably cited Beccaria's writings in his own writings. Edward Livingston called Beccaria and Montesquieu "names dear to humanity!" In writing of efforts to abolish capital punishment, Edward con-cluded: "If the argument were to be carried by the authority of names, that of Beccaria, were there no other, would ensure the victory." Among the signers of the Declaration of Independence were Dr. Benjamin Rush—early America's premier anti-death penalty crusader—and Philip Livingston, a cousin of Edward Livingston's father. In 1801, Thomas Jefferson—in a show of confidence in the former mayor's intellect and abilities—would appoint Edward Livingston as U.S. attorney for the district of New York. Years later, Edward Livingston wrote a draft penal code for the State of Louisiana advocating the total abolition of capital punishment.[131]

Although Pennsylvanians pushed forward some penal reforms in the 1780s, the Commonwealth of Pennsylvania witnessed even more anti-gallows activity in the

1790s. In 1793, William Bradford—Madison's close friend from their time together at the College of New Jersey, now Princeton—wrote *An Enquiry How Far the Punishment of Death Is Necessary in Pennsylvania*. In that legislative report, Bradford—again invoking Beccaria—argued for the death penalty's abolition for all crimes except pre-meditated murder. Noting that evidence might later show the death penalty to be unnecessary even for pre-meditated murderers, Bradford wrote that, in America, "as soon as the principles of Beccaria were disseminated, they found a soil that was prepared to receive them."[132] In 1794, Pennsylvania ultimately became the first state to divide murder into degrees, with only first-degree murder and felony murders—not murders committed in the heat of passion—punishable by death.[133] Beccaria's writings, one criminologist notes, influenced "reformers such as John Howard and Thomas Jefferson, as well as Quaker reformers in Pennsylvania, and became a driving force behind penal reform in the United States."[134] The very title of William Bradford's widely distributed essay, *An Enquiry How Far the Punishment of Death Is Necessary in Pennsylvania*, confirms that the question early Americans wrestled with so intensely was whether executions were truly necessary.[135] That idea—that punishments had to be justified *by necessity*—came directly from Montesquieu and Beccaria, one of Montesquieu's many admirers.[136]

In the late eighteenth century, a number of Americans invoked Beccaria's name and publicly expressed reservations about executions or their morality, efficacy or frequency.[137] In 1791, James Wilson—then an Associate Justice of the U.S. Supreme Court—instructed a Virginia grand jury as follows: "Let the punishment be proportioned—let it be analogous—to the crime." Wilson—a well-known lawyer who played a significant role at the Constitutional Convention in Philadelphia in 1787—also recited Beccaria's words in another grand jury charge, one delivered in 1793 in Boston, Massachusetts. As Wilson told one set of grand jurors, a body empaneled to check abusive governmental power: "'How happy would mankind be,' says the eloquent and benevolent Beccaria, 'if laws were now to be first formed!' The United States enjoy this singular happiness. Their laws are now first formed." Emphasizing that England's Bloody Code, as Blackstone put it, made "no fewer than one hundred and sixty actions" punishable by death, Wilson added that "sanguinary laws" are "a political distemper of the most inveterate and the most dangerous kind." Wilson—one of only six men to sign both the Declaration of Independence and the U.S. Constitution—would advise that "the people are corrupted" by sanguinary laws and that "[i]t is on the excellence of the criminal laws, says the celebrated Montesquieu, that the liberty of the citizens principally depends." As Wilson, whose mind was described by Dr. Benjamin Rush as "one blaze of light," proudly proclaimed in instructing grand jurors: "How few are the crimes—how few are the capital crimes, known to the laws of the United States, compared with those known to the laws of England!"[138]

For some Americans, the abolition of capital punishment—one of the most talked about focuses of *On Crimes and Punishments*—became a moral imperative, with Beccaria's treatise providing the intellectual rationale for abolition. "The marquis of Beccaria," Dr. Benjamin Rush wrote in *The American Museum* in 1789, "has established a connexion between the abolition of capital punishments and the order and happiness of society."[139] In March of 1787, just a few months before delegates assembled in Philadelphia for the Constitutional Convention that would produce the U.S. Constitution, Dr. Rush specifically invoked Beccaria's name at the house of America's elder statesman, Benjamin Franklin. In his talk, Dr. Rush called death "an improper punishment for any crime."[140] As their writings emphasized, Beccaria and Montesquieu believed that any punishment that goes beyond what is "absolutely necessary" is "tyrannical,"[141] with early Americans—as part of the American Revolution—wholeheartedly embracing that general principle.[142] The rub came with actually deciding *what* punishments were then still necessary. In the pre-penitentiary era when prisoners and those awaiting trial might be held in less-than-secure log jails or crude stone structures, that topic generated heated debate, with the question of the necessity for punishment being the pivotal one. As one North Carolina newspaper wrote in 1846, describing the field on which the debate was waged for many decades in early America: "Every drop of blood which is shed as a penalty for crime when *no necessity* existed for it, is *wrongfully shed*: every life which is taken under such circumstances, amounts to nothing less than murder—cold blooded and tyrannical murder in the Government itself!"[143] Again, the lack of necessity for executions was highlighted by the writer.

On Crimes and Punishments consequently became one of the most popular sources for Americans to cite as they debated whether to abolish executions altogether or to at least curtail their use. At Yale's 1788 commencement exercises, Jeremiah Mason— one of the graduates—squared off in a debate with a classmate later identified as "the Rev. Dr. Chapin." The debate topic: "Whether capital punishment was in any case lawful." As Mason contemporaneously recorded in his diary: "I held the negative. I stole most of my arguments from the treatise of the Marquis Beccaria, then little known in this country. It was new, and consequently well received by the audience; indeed, its novelty excited considerable notice. I was flattered and much gratified by being told that my performance was the best of the day."[144] By then, Beccaria's ideas had actually already been reprinted in American magazines and newspapers, including in the local *New Haven Gazette and Connecticut Magazine*, a fact apparently lost on young Jeremiah Mason. "Had the student realized that just two years earlier a local newspaper had serialized Beccaria's essay," historian Louis Masur notes in *Rites of Execution*, "he might have been less zealous in his plagiarism."[145] The scanning and digitizing of early American sources—now searchable on electronic databases—makes crystal clear just how many times, and in how many ways and places, Beccaria's ideas were cited, discussed and debated in the eighteenth and nineteenth centuries.[146]

Early American lawyers—trained as they were in the English common law—felt somewhat beholden to traditional practices even as they sought to curtail what they viewed as the English legal system's arbitrariness, cruelty and excesses.[147] When Thomas Jefferson drafted his Virginia bill for proportioning crimes and punishments he consequently cited Beccaria as well as a host of more traditional, and far less progressive, sources, some dating back to medieval times.[148] *On Crimes and Punishments* was in fact a book that Jefferson frequently came back to, recommending it to others on multiple occasions. For example, in advising his younger cousin, John Garland Jefferson, Jefferson suggested that he read works by Montesquieu and Beccaria, among others. Likewise, in an 1807 letter to John Norvell, later a U.S. Senator from Michigan, Jefferson—the ardent republican with a fascination for the French and Italian cultures—recommended "Beccaria on crimes & punishments, because of the demonstrative manner in which he has treated that branch of the subject."[149] As American law schools opened up around the country and prominent Americans began teaching law—George Wythe at the College of William and Mary in 1779 and James Wilson at the University of Pennsylvania in 1790, to name two early law professors—Beccaria's ideas were being bandied about by eager and impressionable law students. The first American law school opened up in Litchfield, Connecticut, in 1784, under the direction of Tapping Reeve, and others—from Harvard Law School in 1817 to the University of Maryland in 1824—gradually followed, giving further exposure to Cesare Beccaria's writings. One of Reeve's earliest students, even before he opened his one-room school building next to his house, where he had been instructing students in his parlor, was his brother-in-law, Aaron Burr. Burr, a lawyer and politician who read Beccaria's writings, notoriously, and in disregard of Beccaria's written advocacy against dueling, ended up taking Alexander Hamilton's life in a duel in 1804. In Virginia, Thomas Jefferson, who himself had long recommended Beccaria's book, was instrumental in shaping the future of legal education by recruiting the University of Virginia's first law professor, John Tayloe Lomax, in the mid-1820s.[150]

For his time, Thomas Jefferson might be described as a revolutionary's revolutionary, though his ownership of slaves will forever mar his many biographies. He was the primary drafter of the landscape-changing Declaration of Independence, and he was a lawmaker who, though he failed to free his own slaves, was living in rapidly changing times. He was determined to shift power from monarchs to the people, and he sought to revise the penal laws of his state, spending a good deal of time on that endeavor. Jefferson's draft legislation in Virginia plainly showed Beccaria's influence as it sought to dramatically curtail the use of executions by limiting the number of offenses that would be punishable by death. Still, the concept of proportionality that Jefferson used in his bill—one that he himself later rejected—was largely based on the views of medieval legal commentators and his understanding of the *lex talionis* principle of an eye for an eye and a tooth for a tooth. Jefferson's draft legislation, for example, harkened back to Old Testament-style punishments, calling for poisoning those who poisoned and maiming those who maimed.[151] As he drafted his bill in the 1770s, Thomas Jefferson—who copied twenty-six different passages from *Dei delitti e delle pene* into his commonplace book—nonetheless had major reservations about retaliatory punishments, concerns he forthrightly expressed to Virginia lawyer and jurist George Wythe, his trusted mentor and friend and soon-to-be America's first law professor.[152] "The 'Lex talionis,'" Jefferson told Wythe, another Beccaria reader,[153] "will be revolting to the humanized feelings of modern times." "An eye for an eye, and a hand for a hand," Jefferson wrote in 1778 in the midst of the Revolutionary War, "will exhibit spectacles in execution, whose moral effect would be questionable."[154]

Some of Jefferson's thinking and language closely tracked what appeared in *On Crimes and Punishments*, though Jefferson was a voracious reader and bibliophile who was influenced by scores of books and writers.[155] Jefferson—like other early

American lawyers—was a product of his time and had difficulty completely breaking away from antiquated common law punishments, some of which involved bodily mutilation. For example, Jefferson's draft legislation called for, as a punishment, "boring through the cartilage" of a woman's nose "a hole of one half inch in diameter at the least."[156] Only later did Jefferson reject such grotesque punishments and did his notion of proportionality more closely resemble Beccaria's more progressive approach. While Jefferson's 1770s bill contained notations to Beccaria's treatise, it took a couple more decades before a majority of Virginians embraced penal change, with Jefferson later prominently singling out Beccaria with having changed American views on capital punishment.[157] After Virginia penal reform finally became a reality in 1796 thanks to the determined legislative efforts of George Keith Taylor, John Marshall's brother-in-law, Jefferson—not surprisingly—spoke positively of the change, as he made clear in an 1809 letter to Skelton Jones, a client of Jefferson's and a man later killed in a duel in 1812.[158] Toward the end of his life, in the 1820s, Jefferson expressly went out of his way to expressly laud Beccaria, making this statement in the autobiographical reflection he wrote out by hand: "Beccaria and other writers on crimes and punishments had satisfied the reasonable world of the unrightfulness and inefficacy of the punishment of crimes by death."[159] It was an homage to the Italian *philosophe* who had so shaped Jefferson's thinking on crimes and punishments and the proper functioning of government.

Aside from Jefferson, many other thinkers and revolutionaries piggybacked off of Beccaria's ideas, leading to *Dei delitti e delle pene*'s popularity and other books building upon the ideas in it. Whereas Beccaria focused principally on how to disincentivize and prevent crime, other Italian thinkers—writing in the wake of *On Crimes and Punishments*—focused on the flipside of that coin: how to incentivize virtue. Most notably, the Italian writer Giacinto Dragonetti (1738–1818)—a Neapolitan—was one such thinker who attracted attention among American revolutionaries, English radicals and others. The English-American political activist Thomas Paine—the author of *Common Sense*—went out of his way to quote Giacinto Dragonetti's *Treatise on Virtues and Rewards* (1766) for this proposition: "The science of the politician consists in fixing the true point of happiness and freedom. Those men would deserve the gratitude of ages, who should discover a mode of government that contained the greatest sum of individual happiness, with the least national expense."[160] Dragonetti's ideas—originally published in Italian as *Trattato delle virtu e dei premi*—were in line with Beccaria's, with Beccaria laying the groundwork for them. As Beccaria had previously written in *Dei delitti e delle pene*: "Another means of preventing crimes is to reward virtue. I notice that the laws of all nations today are totally silent on this matter." According to Palgrave's *Dictionary of Political Economy*, Dragonetti showed "considerable knowledge of the most recent economic literature of his time" and regarded agriculture "as the pivot of the economic welfare of the state."[161]

While Cesare Beccaria and Giacinto Dragonetti both inspired American and French revolutionaries, Thomas Paine became an actual revolutionary across the ocean. Dragonetti, a young lawyer from Aquila, Italy, whose Italian treatise, originally published as *Delle virtue de' Premi* in Naples in 1766 before being translated into English, would see his book appear in a bilingual Italian-English edition in 1769. With an historian calling him "Beccaria's disciple," the pro-republican Dragonetti—who asserted "[w]e have made numberless laws to punish crimes, and not one is established to reward virtue"—had learned about Beccaria's book by 1765, the same year that Ferdinando Facchinei penned his accusatory and highly critical book review, the 191-page *Note ed osservazioni sul libro intitolato Dei delitti e delle pene*. In *Common Sense*, Thomas Paine—called the "Father of the American Revolution" for his passionate call in January 1776 for American independence—described Dragonetti, also a disciple of Antonio Genovesi (one of Beccaria's influences), as "that wise observer on governments."[162] A close friend of Dr. Benjamin Rush, Paine had spoken extensively with Dr. Rush before the publication of *Common Sense*; Dr. Rush in fact reviewed Paine's draft manuscript and even suggested the title for Paine's book. Originally, Paine had thought he might call his book "Plain Truth."[163]

In modern times, Giacinto Dragonetti has been aptly described as "an obscure Italian," and the scarcity of copies of *Treatise on Virtues and Rewards*—making it an extremely rare book, indeed—is likely due to a 1770 fire that destroyed the stock of the radical printer Joseph Johnson.[164] As the scholar David Wootton has explained, there are many misconceptions about Dragonetti and his writings, some caused by variant French and English translations of the Italian text. As Wootton writes of misconceptions about Dragonetti: "He was a conservative author, we are told: a strange claim to make about an enemy of feudalism. He was an opponent of Beccaria, we are told: he was in fact a disciple." On the issue of translations, often a subject of controversy, especially in the eighteenth century when many unauthorized editions were produced, Wootton notes:

> We can summarize the differences between the texts straightforwardly: the French editor thinks Dragonetti too radical, revises him in a monarchist direction, and adds conservative remarks in the notes; the English editor thinks the resulting text too conservative, refuses to translate at least one monarchist sentiment, and quarrels in his notes with the monarchism of his French counterpart. Dragonetti admires Rousseau; his French translator criticizes Rousseau; his English translator defends him. Paine, reading Dragonetti in English, was reading a distinctly republican text, one whose editor wanted to assimilate all kings to tyrants.

In the Enlightenment, the exchange of ideas could be fierce, and writers were known to expropriate ideas from other sources—and from wherever they could find them—for their own purposes. "Then, as now," Wootton adds, "the only way to find out about Dragonetti is to read him," with Wootton speculating that the reason Thomas Paine would have had a quotation from Dragonetti at his fingertips in Pennsylvania in 1776 is that he had likely "brought a copy of *Virtues and Rewards* with him in his luggage as he traveled (first class) across the Atlantic." In any case, what seems crystal clear is that Dragonetti's book came about only after the runaway success of Beccaria's treatise. As Wootton writes: "Both in England and in France, Dragonetti was published to capitalize on the publishing success recently enjoyed by Beccaria. Beccaria had discussed the criminal law, the philosophy of punishment, in utilitarian terms, and had attacked capital punishment in particular." "Dragonetti's purpose," Wootton explains, "was to balance Beccaria by looking at the positive functions of government: How could government reward virtue, and foster happiness?" "The Age of Paine," Wootton concludes, "was an age of iron bridges, as well as paper constitutions; an age of public benefits as well as private profits; an age of new learning as well as classical traditions; of Beccaria as well as of Machiavelli and Locke."[165]

The American founders' intense interest in Italian history and culture, especially in the lead up to the 1787 Constitutional Convention in Philadelphia, is thus written all over the record. For example, in a May 1787 letter to Richard Cranch, her Harvard College-trained relative, Abigail Adams noted that her husband, John, was then "considering the I[t]alian Republicks through the middle age," what she called "a work of no small labour" and an "expensive" project in terms of all the books involved in the endeavor.[166] John Adams developed such a close familiarity with Italian rulers and forms of government that Thomas Jefferson, in an 1819 letter to Adams, felt comfortable writing this: "Your intimacy with their history, antient, middle and modern, your familiarity with the improvements in the science of government at this time, will enable you, if any body, to go back with our principles and opinions to the times of Cicero, Cato, and Brutus, and tell us by what process these great and virtuous men could have led so unenlightened and vitiated a people into freedom and good government...."[167] America's founders, looking for the best way to structure government and foster liberty and reduce crime, familiarized themselves with books of all kinds from all over the world, including ones written by French and Italian writers. And the French and Italians, in turn, came to greatly admire American revolutionaries a world away. "By the 1830s," one source notes of those living on the Italian peninsula, "it became commonplace for Italian writers of democratic persuasion to praise the American war of independence and the Founding Fathers."[168]

Beccaria's writings, in connection with a whole series of events and other Enlightenment-era writings, stirred reformers and American, French, Spanish and Italian revolutionaries to action. "Cesare Beccaria," a source on the Enlightenment points out, "was the leading intellectual of the Italian Enlightenment in Milan, which focused on *la questione de la lingua* (the Question of Language, the controversy surrounding the proper form of Italian) as part of the even larger debate regarding politics." "The calls by Italian Enlightenment thinkers for legal and political reform," that source notes, "led to a more popular desire to throw off foreign oppression—in nineteenth-century Milan, now by the Austrians—and to a more general move toward Italian nationalism. The French Revolution was a symbol for nineteenth-century Italian intellectuals of what could be accomplished against tyranny, and the rise of Napoleon did not weaken this sentiment." As that book continues, noting later developments: "The Revolutions of 1848 in Italian cities, especially in Milan and Naples, were motivated by nationalism and led to the triumph of Italian unification a couple of decades later."[169] Of course, it was the American Revolution that preceded both the French Revolution and Italy's unification as well as revolutions in Central and South America.

Not only did several of the Founding Fathers, including Benjamin Franklin, Thomas Jefferson, James Madison, John Adams and John Quincy Adams, study and speak and read Italian to one degree or another,[170] but those men were enamored of—in some cases, obsessed by—the history of Greece and Italy and the early Greek, Italian and Roman writers and republics.[171] "Caesar, by destroying the Roman Republic, made himself perpetual Dictator," John Adams wrote in June 1771; in May 1777—to give another representative example—Adams wrote to Continental Army Major-General Nathanael Greene from Philadelphia to describe "the civil Wars in Rome, in the Time of Sylla." In the latter instance, Adams paraphrased language from Abbé René Aubert de Vertot's *The History of the Revolutions that Happened in the Government of the Roman Republic*. James Madison recommended that very book for the Library of Congress along with books on the history of the Venetian republic and the Republic of Geneva as well as Edward Wortley Montagu's *Reflections on the Rise and Fall of the Antient Republicks*. Madison's recommendations also included texts on law and political philosophy, including "Beccaria's works," as well as an assortment of books on both the civil law and the common law.[172] Cesare Beccaria's ideas materially shaped the views of America's founders and framers, with Nathanael Greene—one of the general's in George Washington's army—himself owning a beautifully bound copy of Beccaria's book.[173]

A couple of additional examples show the mutual admiration between American revolutionaries and Italian *philosophes*. The Italian playwright Vittorio Alfieri, in 1788, published a play, *Bruto Primo*, dedicated to George Washington, the political icon—and much-revered figure—described as "the deliverer of America." And numerous American revolutionaries were receiving, reading and studying Italian writers. For example, in a 1793 letter to Alexander Hamilton, Samuel Paterson—an Edinburgh bookseller—wrote this: "I have Sent you the Speech of Mr. Erskine at London on the Liberty of the Press—also a Translation on Legislation from the Italian of Filangieri."[174] Benjamin Franklin had become enamored of Filangieri's writings, and he was not the only one. "The problem of education, considered by Beccaria the most effective means to prevent crime," a source on the Enlightenment reports, "is at the center of the Neapolitan Gaetano Filangieri's *Scienza della legislazione* (The Science of Legislation, 1780–1785), in which legal problems expand into a vast consideration of civil and social relations, confronting questions of property, divisions between social classes, civil and penal legislation, religion, and public education and including a plan of national education to close the gap between the people and the elite."[175]

The introduction to the translation of Filangieri's work that Samuel Paterson sent Hamilton stated forcefully: "The present common object of thinking men is legislation. The errors of jurisprudence surround us: every writer seeks to expose them; and from each extremity of Europe to the other, one voice alone is heard, which tells us, the laws of Latium are no longer calculated for Europe." "This union of voices, this universal clamour, this cry of reason and philosophy," the introduction continued, "has at length reached the Throne. The scene has changed, and Princes have begun to discover, that the lives, and the tranquility of men, demand greater regard; that there are means, independent of force and arms, to arrive at greatness; that good laws are the only support of national happiness; that the goodness of laws is inseparable from their uniformity; and that this uniformity is not to be found in a legislation framed at intervals during twenty-two centuries … with all the cruelty of the Lombards."[176] A central theme of Beccaria's own work, of course, had been the pursuit of good laws—ones that could be read and easily understood by the common person in his or her native language, and ones that would further the public good, equality, and the public's happiness.

Though America's Founding Fathers were themselves pioneers in political philosophy, they sought out the best thinkers of the past—along with contemporary texts like *On Crimes and Punishments*—as they crafted America's founding documents. "The American Constitution," NYU law professor David Richards writes, "is a historically remarkable attempt to use the best political theory and political science of the age, combined with a diverse practical experience of democratic self-rule, to give a written text of substantive and procedural constraints on and definitions of state power that would achieve in America what has never been achieved elsewhere: enduring republican government in a large territory." As Richards explains: "The Constitution, followed shortly by the Bill of Rights, is a self-conscious product of reflection on past republican experiments (Greece, Rome, the Florentine and Venetian republics, the Cromwellian commonwealth) and the republican political theory and science of their emergence, stability, and decline (Polybius, Machiavelli, Guicciardini, Giannotti, Harrington, Locke, Sidney)."[177] Indeed, the central question posed in Adams' *A Defence of the Constitutions of Government of the United States of America* echoes themes found in *On Crimes and Punishments*. As Adams framed what he called "[t]he great question": "What combination of powers in society, or what form of government, will compel the formation of good and equal laws, an impartial execution, and faithful interpretation of them, so that the citizens may constantly enjoy the benefit of them, and be sure of their continuance."[178]

American society was then divided by the issue of slavery, but the American Revolution—taking place in the context of Beccaria's focus on an egalitarian administrative state—prompted much debate over the slave trade and human bondage. As one source puts it: "The revolutionary war, and the questions which then arose, turned the thoughts of men, as never before, to the injustice and impolicy of slavery." In 1774, Thomas Jefferson—who was born into a world of plantations and slavery—wrote that "[t]he abolition of domestic slavery is the great object of desire" of the American colonists, adding that, in England's colonies, slavery "was unhappily introduced in their infant state." The first anti-slavery society—"The Society for the Relief of Free Negroes unlawfully held in Bondage"—was formed by Quakers in Philadelphia on April 14, 1775, at the Sun Tavern on Second Street. It met four times in 1775, though because of the onset of the Revolutionary War, which began on April 19, 1775 with the Battles of Lexington and Concord, it did not meet again until February of 1784. That society held regular meetings until April 1787, when its constitution was revised to include the "Abolition of Slavery" as well as the "Relief of Free Negroes," with two signers of the Declaration of Independence—Benjamin Franklin and Benjamin Rush—chosen as its president and secretary, respectively. In 1791, Jefferson—a slave owner still struggling with the issue of human bondage—wrote this to Benjamin Banneker, an African-American surveyor, mathematician and astronomer in Maryland who had written to him urging that he (Jefferson) apply the principles of the Declaration of Independence for the benefit of *all* people regardless of color: "Nobody wishes more than I do to see such proofs as you exhibit, that nature has given to our black brethren, talents equal to those of the other colors of men, and that the appearance of a want of them is owing merely to the degraded condition of their existence." By 1837, just eleven years after John Adams and Thomas Jefferson's deaths on July 4, 1826, there were more than one thousand anti-slavery societies in the United States, seventy-seven of which were made up solely of women.[179]

As early American lawmakers did their work, Beccaria, Dragonetti and Filangieri were not the only Italian writers who were studied—or who came to the attention of revolutionaries and the public. Milan, like Naples and other parts of Italy, produced many writers and intellectuals who opposed tyrannical practices. One of those was Giuseppe Gorani, the author of *Il vero dispotismo* (*True Despotism*, 1770) who has been described as "an adventurous, well-travelled nobleman" and who had personal experience with censorship and the Inquisition. Gorani spent time abroad as an officer in the Habsburg Austrian army, as a prisoner in Prussia, and in Parisian high society where he interacted with leading French *philosophes*. He first garnered attention in the period from 1767 to 1769 among the Milanese men who produced *Il Caffé*. "His principal mentor in 'philosophy,'" Jonathan Israel notes, "was Beccaria whom he venerated and who read his drafts, encouraging his ambitions as a political thinker." "His original goal," Israel notes of Gorani's project, making a reference to Joseph II's policies and reforms, "was to combine Austrian enlightened despotism, or Josephism, with more individual and collective freedom." "On appearing, in two volumes at Geneva in January 1770," Israel writes of Gorani's *Il vero dispotismo*, "his book met with critical reactions ranging from qualified approval, as with Verri who noted its kinship with Beccaria's masterpiece, to outrage at what commentators considered undisguised sedition and irreligion." *Il vero dispotismo*, Israel notes, "brims with references to Machiavelli, Sarpi, Giannone, and Beccaria, besides Helvétius and Diderot, both of whom he warmly praises besides Rousseau."[180]

In August 1792, in the midst of the French Revolution, France's National Assembly granted honorary French citizenship to a select number of persons who had promoted the cause of liberty. Giuseppe Gorani—who, by 1787, the year of America's Constitutional Convention in Philadelphia, had rejected "enlightened despotism" in favor of representative democratic republicanism—was one of the chosen honorees. Among the others: American and English luminaries such as George Washington, Alexander Hamilton, James Madison, Thomas Paine, Jeremy Bentham, William Wilberforce and Joseph Priestley. Writing from Paris to Alexander Hamilton, Jean-Marie Roland (1734–1793)—a leader of the French Revolution, an economist, and the minister of interior in King Louis XVI's government in 1792—enclosed the printed act of August 26, 1792, "which confers the title of Citizen François" upon "several foreigners," with the French Minister of the Interior adding that the French Republic had placed the honorees "among the friends of humanity & society." The "whereas" clauses in the act made clear its purpose: "whereas men who, through their writings and by their courage, have served the cause of freedom, and prepared the emancipation of the people, can not be regarded as foreign"; "if five years of residence in France, are sufficient for a foreign citizen François title, this title is more justly due to those who, regardless of the soil they inhabit, have devoted their arms & their watches to defend the cause of the people against the tyranny of kings, to banish the stigma of the earth, and to push the limits of human knowledge."[181] Jeremy Bentham—the hard-core Beccaria disciple—also had conferred upon him an honorary citizenship of the French republic. In his *Fragment on Government* (1776), Bentham—tracking Beccaria—had publicly declared that "it is the greatest happiness of the greatest number that is the measure of right and wrong."[182]

The French Revolution (1789–1799), like the American Revolution before it, took place in the wake of the publication of Beccaria's book—and in the aftermath of Beccaria's ideas, both big and small, seeping into societies. During the French Revolution, Louis-Marie Prudhomme (1752–1830)—a Frenchman who founded *The Révolutions of Paris*, a prominent radical newspaper—was just one of many French revolutionaries who cited Beccaria in opposing the death penalty.[183] And along with the writings of Montesquieu, Cesare Beccaria's book shaped key documents of the French Revolution. The Declaration of the Rights of Man and of the Citizen of 1789—introduced in France's National Constituent Assembly by the Marquis de Lafayette (1757–1834), the French aristocrat and military officer who fought in America's Revolutionary War—emphasized the value of equality and articulated principles of criminal law reform. A close friend of Thomas Jefferson, George Washington and Alexander Hamilton, Lafayette fought in Revolutionary War battles and served on Washington's staff. And French revolutionary assemblies passed two acts in 1791 that—in Catherine Elliott's words—"amounted to a criminal code."

Lafayette had come to America at age nineteen, was commissioned as a major general, and later wrote the Declaration of the Rights of Man and of the Citizen with the assistance of Thomas Jefferson, America's envoy to France. That French declaration set out core principles. "Men are born free and remain equal in rights," Article 1 declared. "All that is not forbidden by the law cannot be prevented and no one can be forced to do what it does not order," Article 5 of the Declaration of the Rights of Man of 1789 proclaimed, articulating the principle now called *legality*. "Law is the expression of the general will," Article 6 proclaimed, emphasizing that "[i]t must be the same for all, whether it protects or punishes." Article 8 of that Declaration—now part of the French constitution—then added: "[T]he law can only lay down punishments that are strictly and obviously necessary and a person can only be punished by virtue of a law established and promulgated prior to the wrongful conduct and legally applicable." As Elliott describes the effect of the two French acts of 1791 that followed the issuance of the Declaration: "The sentences were greatly reduced, corporal punishments were abolished, and capital punishment was preserved for only a few offenses." "The legislation," she notes, held up "the principle of equality and took this to an extreme by imposing fixed sentences and abolishing pardons."[184]

The Napoleonic Code of 1810 also shows signs of Montesquieu's and Beccaria's reformist philosophies, though the times were turbulent ones. Influenced by their writings, the French revolutionary assemblies had made considerable reforms to the criminal law (*e.g.*, abolishing corporal punishments and reducing the number of offenses punishable by death) and the Napoleonic Code incorporated various notable features, too. As Catherine Elliott writes: "[T]he ideas of Beccaria and Montesquieu, which had directly inspired the revolutionary Criminal Code of 1791, left their traces on the imperial code. Thus the principle of legality was included in the Criminal Code of 1810, and it imposed an egalitarian system founded on the mental responsibility of the offender." In *The Handbook of Comparative Criminal Law*, Elliot notes, however, that "social unrest at the time had given rise to lawless behavior and led to the imposition of a fairly harsh criminal system, which reflect the severity of the prerevolutionary law."[185] As another source notes: "In revised form, Beccaria's influence was most undeniably felt in the early years of the nineteenth century when the Napoleonic Code was promulgated. That Code, reflecting the influence of Beccaria but with modifications which allowed for some mitigation and flexibility, became the basis for the criminal code in most continental European and Latin American countries."[186]

The Enlightenment thus produced real change, part of it driven by Beccarian impulses. The Declaration of Independence—though influenced by many sources—itself carries echoes of Beccaria's philosophy, famously reading: "We hold these truths to be self-evident, that all men are created equal, that they are endowed by their Creator with certain unalienable Rights, that among these are Life, Liberty and the pursuit of Happiness."[187] Though most early Americans were not familiar with the writings of Cesare Beccaria's Italian mentor, Pietro Verri,[188] Verri's 1763 book, *Meditazioni sulla felicitá* (*Meditations on Happiness*), was—in the words of one source—"immediately considered a manifesto of the Milanese Enlightenment." Pietro Verri's treatise, that source reports, "follows the lines of Locke, Helvétius, and especially Rousseau."[189] Verri's book—as another source stresses—argued that "it was man's inbuilt dissatisfaction with things as they are that led to progress, a fundamental idea, grounded in empiricist thinking, which he elaborated on later in his *Discorso sull'indole del piacere e del dolore* (*Discourse on the Nature of Pleasure and Pain*, 1773)."[190] Because Pietro Verri personally influenced Beccaria, his own ideas cannot—and should not—be dismissed, neglected or ignored by modern historians. Indeed, Verri's ideas—albeit indirectly—influenced Americans and others throughout the world to the extent that they shaped the views expressed by Beccaria in *On Crimes and Punishments*, the book that took Europe and the Americas by storm.[191]

George Washington, Thomas Jefferson and James Madison—three of the most prominent Virginia politicians of the age—were all influenced by Enlightenment impulses and, more specifically, by Beccaria's writings. Washington bought a copy of Beccaria's treatise in 1769, as did Jefferson, the principal drafter of the Declaration of Independence (1776). Before drafting the Declaration of Independence, Jefferson had read Beccaria and a host of other Enlightenment writers, including John Locke, Francis Hutcheson, David Hume, William Blackstone, Thomas Hobbes and Jean-Jacques Burlamaqui.[192] John Locke had used the exact phrase "pursuit of happiness" in *An Essay Concerning Human Understanding* (1689), and had written, in particular, "Of Modes of Pleasure and Pain."[193] Jefferson, Madison and other penal reformers were fascinated by these ideas, and Beccaria's treatise—whether read in Italian,

French, English or some other language—was part of the mix.[194] "The art of life is the art of avoiding pain, and he is the best pilot who steers clearest of the rocks and shoals with which it is beset," Jefferson once wrote.[195] Madison—the father of the U.S. Constitution—in fact led the effort, at Jefferson's urging, to ratify the U.S. Bill of Rights, a document that—along with the Declaration of Independence and the U.S. Constitution—is now on display at the National Archives in Washington, D.C.[196] Madison—who pushed for penal reform as the fourth U.S. President—once wrote that, in early America, Cesare Beccaria was "in the zenith of his fame as a philosophical legislator."[197] As President, Madison himself personally called for reform of the nation's criminal law, though he did not agree with everything Beccaria had written. While serving as the nation's commander-in-chief, Madison specifically asked Congress to mitigate penalties "adopted into it antecedent to experiment" and recommended "a more lenient policy."[198]

On Crimes and Punishments—as other sources make clear, taking note of Europe's eighteenth-century "enlightened despots"—became a "turning point" and "led to reforms in the criminal-justice systems of many European countries." In the 1770s, Beccaria's book stimulated the abolition of torture in Denmark (1771) and Austria (1776) and a Spanish prohibition on torturing those not yet convicted of crimes (1775).[199] In Prussia, the powerful and long-reigning king, Frederick II (1712–1786), also known as Frederick the Great, drew particular inspiration from Beccaria's book and began work on a new criminal code for his realm in the late 1770s. It was—as one source puts it—"consciously modeled on Beccaria's writings." As Frederick II observed: "Beccaria has left nothing to glean after him; we need only to follow what he has so wisely indicated."[200] Frederick II ruled Prussia from 1740 until his death in 1786, but the law code later promulgated—in 1794—was partly the product of his efforts. That code did not abolish the death penalty for all cases, but it did restrict its application. In 1794, in the same year that Pennsylvania divided murder into degrees, Prussia became the first German state to abolish capital punishment for sodomy, death sentences being replaced with the lesser penalties of flogging and imprisonment.[201]

The writings of Beccaria and his many disciples—as just one example—led to a seismic shift in Scandinavian law. "[B]y the 1760s," one source notes, "enlightened reforms had come on thick and fast in Denmark-Norway, affecting matters administrative, judicial, economic, and penal. As in the rest of Europe, Beccaria's famous treatise on crimes and punishment set off a lively debate about reforming the penal codes." As that source, a history of the eighteenth century, explains: "A new general law on murder introduced by Danish crown in 1767 was plainly based on Beccaria. This statute was part of a flurry of other crown initiatives, which in hindsight appeared to be the first of three short but vigorous bouts of legal, institutional, and cultural reform." "While Copenhagen University's theologians," that source continues, "considered the death penalty both proper and mandatory in all cases of murder (since this penalty was biblically prescribed), key reformers urged the need to adapt penalties to both the nature and social circumstances of crimes." "The Danish law of 1767," it observes, "marked the point in Scandinavian legal history when automatically imposing the death penalty in murder cases, as stipulated under earlier customary law and then the *Code Danoise* of 1683, formally ended."[202]

The Danish decree of 1767 was limited in scope, applying only to "melancholy and other dismal persons" who murdered "for the exclusive purpose of losing their lives."[203] Under that decree, suicidal murderers who killed (but who did not die during the commission of their crimes) would be branded, publicly whipped annually, and be imprisoned for life to perform "the most strenuous and demeaning work." "The decree of 1767," historian Tyge Krogh notes of its significance, "was epochal in a Lutheran context, with its public break with the mandatory and divinely ordained death penalty for murder, and indeed it represented a landmark throughout Europe in prescribing a penalty other than the death sentence for premeditated murder."[204] Indeed, the Danish law of 1767 was—as historian Ditlev Tamm writes in *La peine*—"the first example of the non-use of the death penalty in cases of murder."[205] In the seventeenth and eighteenth centuries, the idea of the "divine right" of kings was still a popular one, and kings were seen to possess the power to take lives or to grant pardons or reprieves. "The theory of the Divine Right of Kings in its completest form," one late nineteenth-century source emphasized, "involves the following propositions": (1) "*Monarchy is a divinely ordained institution*"; (2) "*Hereditary right is indefeasible*"; (3) "*Kings are accountable to God alone*"; and (4) "*Non-resistance and passive obedience are enjoined by God.*"[206]

The Danish decree was drafted by Henrik Stampe (1713–1789), a Danish legal advisor, in 1757. Drafted well before the publication of Beccaria's *Dei delitti e delle pene*, it was driven by a spate of suicidal murderers. The records for the city of Copenhagen for 1750 to 1759 document—as Tyge Krogh writes in *A Lutheran Plague: Murdering to Die in the Eighteenth Century*—"the execution of ten suicide murderers and only two executions for other crimes." "In early 1757," Krogh notes, "no fewer than three suicide murders were committed in the course of three weeks." With a permanent scaffold then erected in the middle of Copenhagen, the executions took place in full view of the city's leading citizens. Anxious to prevent these types of murders, the Danish king had asked his legal advisors to consider how such crimes might be deterred—a task they dutifully took up. But Henrik Stampe's then revolutionary proposal languished until 1767, after the publication of Beccaria's book, with *On Crimes and Punishments* prompting and provoking extensive public debate over capital punishment. Before Beccaria's *Dei delitti e delle pene* appeared, arguments over the proper interpretation of the Mosaic law took place largely behind closed doors or in obscure Latin texts, with judges and civil servants only privately questioning the use of mandatory death sentences for criminals. After its release, all that changed, with Beccaria's book kick-starting more debate in Denmark. As one source writes: "It is quite possible that Beccaria's ideas had sown the seed for the revival of Stampe's proposal in 1767, but the proposal was actually written in 1757, eight years before the publication of *Dei delitti e delle pene.*"

After the Danish king, in 1761, had the permanent scaffold taken down, executions were moved out of town. But six years later, Henrik Stampe's proposal—initially resisted by theologians who saw the death penalty as part of God's natural law—was finally implemented in that society in the post-*Dei delitti e delle pene* time frame. It happened after Christian VII—a more enlightened ruler—ascended to the throne in 1766 and there were nine more suicide murders in Copenhagen in 1766 and 1767. "According to Stampe," writes Tyge Krogh, "suicide murderers were melancholy, depressed people who considered life not as something precious but as a heavy and unbearable burden." Instead of executing these offenders and fulfilling their wishes to die, Stampe sought a different yet still severe punishment, one designed to deter their homicidal acts. As Krogh summarized Stampe's view on the best alternative punishment: "[T]he most effective punishment for these people was not the death sentence but the continuation of the life of which they were so tired, and making this life as unbearable as possible." Under the Danish decree, after suicidal murderers were branded, whipped every year for life, and then died after toiling away at hard labor in prison, their bodies were to be taken to the customary place of execution and, at night, unceremoniously buried there.[207]

In the rough-and-tumble world of the seventeenth century, full of intrigue, power struggles, and quests for influence and control, many executions and acts of torture took place. In Denmark itself, Count Johann Friedrich Struensee and Count Enevold Brandt, ex-ministers to the mentally ill King Christian VII, were publicly put to death on the morning of April 28, 1772, for crimes against the crown. The king's physician, Count Struensee, had issued over one thousand edicts in the king's name as he sought to reform Danish society, but Struensee had an affair with 21-year-old Queen Caroline Matilde. It took three blows of the executioner's axe to sever Struensee's head before the two men's bodies were quartered and their heads and hands impaled on poles and publicly displayed. Struensee had effectively seized power until he was removed by conservative forces, put on trial, and executed.[208] Ironically, one of the many reforms put in place during Struensee's brief stint in power was to abolish judicial torture and the death penalty for burglary and for stealing cattle or horses. Instead of being executed, convicted burglars and thieves would be branded, publicly whipped, and forced to labor for life. "After Struensee's fall in 1772," it has been emphasized, "the new conservative government overturned several of his reforms," though "the abolition of the death penalty for offences against property remained in force, and so did the decree of 1767."[209]

Scandinavian countries proved to be particularly receptive to experimentation with Beccarian principles. In 1777, for example, Sweden's monarch, King Gustav III, sent a letter to all appeals courts in the country decreeing that no death sentence was to be carried out before being signed by him.[210] That same year, he also submitted a bill to the Swedish parliament to curtail the death penalty. "It is well documented," one source notes, "that the young Crown Prince later King Gustav III (1746–92) read Beccaria, probably in a French translation, and that Beccaria's ideas strongly influenced him in his decision to abolish torture, and at his coronation, to issue a decree on pardon (1772)." As that text observes: "The King declared all types of torment unlawful. He tried in vain to abolish the death penalty but succeeded in restricting the number of capital offences and the amount of executions."[211] In writing about Scandinavia's history, sociologist Finn Hornum stresses: "Imprisonment became the predominant form of punishment and capital punishment was the exception." After Beccaria's book appeared, torture was abolished and barbaric Scandinavian executions gradually gave way to the Italian philosopher's suggested alternative, "penal servitude for life," a punishment set forth in the Norwegian Penal Code of 1842. That code allowed capital punishment for treason and murder, though, in time, executions ended up giving way to the viable alternative of imprisonment even for the worst of the worst crimes. Ultimately, the last execution in Norway took place in 1876, with abolition coming in 1905; Sweden abolished capital punishment in 1921; and Denmark did the same in 1930.[212]

The publication of Beccaria's book — as one writer put it — "produced an electrifying effect across Europe."[213] And the world, history shows, would never be the same. "No sooner had Beccaria arrived at Paris," Carlo Calisse writes in *A History of Italian Law*, "than Baron d'Holbach invited him to his suppers, where Helvetius, Rousseau and all who called themselves followers of the philosophy of humanity met and by their discussions prepared the social revolution."[214] In line with philosophers like Thomas Hobbes and John Locke, Rousseau believed that a society had a right to take a murderer's life, though Rousseau, like Montesquieu and Beccaria, only believed in *necessary* punishments.[215] But Beccaria reconceived Montesquieu's proportionality principle and Rousseau's social compact and envisioned a world without the penalty of death — a world in which no citizen would ever authorize the state to take the lives of convicted criminals and in which no state would ever do so. Over the many decades to come, Beccaria's arguments for proportionality and against the death penalty and torture would get cited again and again, and around the globe individual abolitionists would turn to Beccaria's book for guidance on crafting criminal codes. Although the anti-gallows movement suffered almost as many setbacks as steps forward as nations sometimes brought back executions after periods of abolition, *On Crimes and Punishments* was always right there to be consulted in the movement's darkest days.

Chapter 6

The Celebrated Marquis

Though Cesare Beccaria's contributions to Western thought may have been forgotten over time, they were significant. In Quaker-filled Pennsylvania, Beccaria's ideas found a particularly receptive audience. For example, Dr. Benjamin Rush—the Philadelphia physician and a signer of America's Declaration of Independence—was an undying and fervent Beccaria disciple, often invoking Beccaria's name in public settings. One of the first Americans to call for the total abolition of capital punishment, Dr. Rush announced in March 1787, at his friend Benjamin Franklin's house, that the death penalty was an inappropriate punishment for *any* crime. "The Duke of Tuscany, soon after the publication of the Marquis of Beccaria's excellent treatise upon this subject," Rush emphasized shortly before the Constitutional Convention, "abolished death as a punishment for murder."[1] "I suspect the attachment to death as a punishment for murder, in minds otherwise enlightened," Dr. Rush wrote in one essay, "arises from a false interpretation of a passage contained in the old testament, and that is, 'he that sheds the blood of man, by man shall his blood be shed.'"[2] James Wilson—a Pennsylvania lawyer perhaps second only in importance to Madison in terms of his role at Philadelphia's Constitutional Convention, held between May and September 1787—also repeatedly brought up Beccaria's ideas in his own writings and law lectures.[3] Throughout America's founding era, Beccaria was, in fact, regularly hailed as "benevolent," "celebrated," "learned," "immortal," of "great genius," and as a "sublime philosopher,"[4] the kind of monikers reserved for the most revered Enlightenment figures, such as Newton, Locke and Montesquieu.[5]

In America's founding period, as well as in the generations that came after those who lived through the hard-fought Revolutionary War, scores of Americans—along with many reform-minded Europeans—devoted their energies to replacing "sanguinary" laws and punishments with a new "penitentiary" system.[6] Though continental Europe had penal institutions—bridewells and workhouses, for example—as far back as the 1500s and 1600s, Americans and Englishmen, in the late eighteenth century, became fascinated by the potential for penitentiaries, places where criminals could be reformed and housed for long periods of time. Those incarcerated were sometimes called *penitents*, with the root word of *penitentiaries* being *penitent*, meaning to show sorrow and regret for having done something wrong. Inspired by Quakers and other like-minded civic leaders, Philadelphia's Walnut Street Prison—considered to be America's first modern penitentiary, and which facilitated a switch from executions to periods of incarceration—opened its doors in 1790.[7] Prior to that time, U.S. jails and prisons were often make-shift or decrepit facilities, full of vice and disease. They resembled—or actually were—horrid dungeons, as was the case of a Connecticut prison that made use of a former copper mine to house offenders in the 1770s. In the caverns of Connecticut's Simsbury prison, inmates labored underground and were chained in overcrowded cages.[8]

Over time, the American political system and its lawmakers—intent on rejecting England's "Bloody Code"—gradually moved away from reliance on capital offenses to deter crime and sought to further the rehabilitation of offenders. As one writer, penning an article for *The Christian Examiner and Theological Review*, later editorialized of the "Sanguinary" system: "As a system, it has completely failed." "The Penitentiary System," by contrast, that writer emphasized, "had its origin in the United States, and trial has been made of it by the principal members of the Union."[9] Virginia governor James Monroe—later the fifth U.S. President—would describe Virginia's penitentiary, on which construction began in 1797, as a "benevolent system." The penitentiary system, Monroe observed, was based on the idea that "in punishing crime, the society or rather the government ought not to indulge in the passion of revenge."[10] A similar movement in England—to "put a stop to sanguinary punishments," considered by some English intellectuals and radicals to be "a disgrace"—had also gotten underway across the Atlantic, with English lawmakers approving the Penitentiary Act of 1779, though the first English penitentiaries were not built right away because of concerns over cost.[11] To be sure, a number of Enlightenment authors provided the impetus for the creation of the Anglo-American penitentiary system, from—in the words of one source—"Mr. Howard's Work on Prisons" and "Mr. Buxton's Essay on Prisons" to "the Essay on Crimes and Punishments, by the celebrated Marquis Beccaria." As that source, Anthony Highmore's *Philanthropia Metropolitana: A View of the Charitable Institutions*, stressed in 1822, taking note of the religious impulses beyond part of the shift in societal attitudes: "In all of these much knowledge and solid judgment are imparted on this subject, now happily made peculiarly interesting by these benevolent visitors of mercy, to whom I trust it will be said at the last day, 'I was sick and in prison, and ye visited me; for inasmuch as ye did it to one of the least of these, my brethren, ye did it unto me!'"[12]

The development of America's penitentiary system—built out on a state-by-state basis, and intended to reign in "sanguinary" punishments and to give prisoners a chance to repent for their sins—would take considerable time to mature. That system started to be built out shortly before Cesare Beccaria's death in Milan in 1794, but it quickly accelerated thereafter.[13] After Pennsylvania's Walnut Street Prison opened in 1790, shortly before the ratification of the U.S. Bill of Rights in 1791, other states quickly followed suit. New York passed legislation in 1796 providing for the construction of the Newgate state prison in Greenwich Village; New Jersey completed its state penitentiary in 1797; and penitentiaries in Virginia and Kentucky opened in 1800, the same year Massachusetts appropriated money for one.[14] A new penitentiary also opened in Maryland in 1811, and it wasn't long before other penitentiaries got built.[15] New York's Auburn Prison, like Maryland's state prison, was built in the 1810s; New York's Sing Sing Prison began operating in 1825; Connecticut started building its Wethersfield penitentiary in 1827; Pennsylvania's Eastern State Penitentiary opened in 1829; and other state prisons around the U.S. were built from the 1820s to the

1850s. A federal penitentiary, at Fort Leavenworth, Kansas, opened in the 1890s, a few decades after America's Civil War, so the movement extended over multiple generations and shaped both federal and state laws.[16] In 1839, in *A History of Philadelphia*, author Daniel Bowen, commenting on Dr. Benjamin Rush's eighteenth-century, anti-death penalty advocacy, made this telling observation: "From these early endeavors have arisen the great improvements made in our Penitentiary systems, and the certainty of regulated punishments seems, so far to promise, much more in the correction of crime, than the sanguinary code, of former times."[17]

Around the time of her father's death, Giulia Manzoni—Cesare Beccaria's eldest daughter—had relocated to France and spent time in Paris in the aftermath of an ill-fated arranged marriage to a much older Italian count, Don Pietro Manzoni, a wealthy widower. By 1791, Giulia's marriage to Pietro Manzoni had become unsustainable, and Giulia had asked Pietro Verri to intervene with her father, Cesare, to help arrange a separation, which he did, making favorable financial arrangements for his daughter, Giulia. Although Giulia—like Cesare Beccaria's brothers and Cesare's sister, Maddalena—got involved in litigation over assets in the Beccaria family's estate (in Giulia's case, after the death of Cesare's second daughter, Maria, when Giulia claimed that her father had forced her to marry a man who repulsed her and she sought a larger share of Maria's inheritance), she was well taken care of financially, became a well-known personality in Paris, and materially furthered Cesare Beccaria's legacy as she made her own way through the world. As reported in *France in Eighteen Hundred and Two: Described in a Series of Contemporary Letters by Henry Redhead Yorke*: "Madame de Beccaria ... is the daughter of the celebrated Marquis de Beccaria, author of the book on Crimes and Punishments. Elegant in her manners, she is possessed of a pleasing person, and is modest, affable, and good-natured. Though a rigid Catholic, she does not pose as a saint, nor does she keep a coterie, or wish to take advantage of her father's celebrity to collect around her the fops of philosophy." As that source further relayed, noting her concern with her father's literary legacy: "Madame de Beccaria will go to England very shortly for the purpose of having her father's writings translated there. She made me a present of her father's portrait, assuring me that he never wrote an Italian work entitled *Saggio sopra la Politica e la Legislatione Romana*."[18] That 1772 work, critical of Roman law, was written by Count Ugo Vincenzo Botton di Castellamonte (1754–1828) and has been said to echo the "celebrated and influential *Difetti dell Gurisprudenza* (1742)" of the Italian cleric, Ludovico Antonio Muratori. After separating from her husband, Giulia would travel to Paris—and then to England and Switzerland—with Carlo Imbonati, a rich merchant banker.[19]

Giulia's older husband Pietro Manzoni—the man her father had arranged for her to marry, no doubt with her long-term financial security in mind—treated Alessandro Manzoni as his son, though scholars mostly believe that the boy's biological father was actually the charismatic playboy Giovanni Verri. A musician and liberal Milanese intellectual with whom Giulia fell in love, Giovanni—the brother of Pietro and Alessandro Verri—was Giulia's lover in the mid-1780s.[20] As the daughter of an international celebrity, Giulia led a cosmopolitan lifestyle, especially after her separation in 1792 from Don Pietro Manzoni and her move to Paris. In *A Tour of Switzerland*, one writer, Helen Maria Williams, spoke of Giulia's house near Lugano—the place just across the Swiss border where many wealthy and noble families of Milan owned properties and retreated. As Williams put it in 1798, just four years after Cesare Beccaria's death: "One of the mansions, in the neighborhood of Lugano, is inhabited by Madame Beccaria, the daughter of the illustrious Beccaria, who inherits from her father an understanding of the first class, and unites with the graces of person, and the most charming simplicity of manners, that independence of soul, and love of rational liberty, which is the characteristic of superior minds."[21] It was in Lugano, in 1766, that the Verri brothers had anonymously published their reply, *Risposta ad uno scritto che s'intitola Note ed osservazioni sul libro Dei delitti e delle pene*, to Ferdinando Facchinei, written in the first person, as if it had been written by Beccaria himself. And it was in Lugano—as well as in Merate and Milan—that Giulia's son, Alessandro, had been educated.[22]

Giulia had married Pietro Manzoni (1736–1807) in Milan in 1782 when Milan was still under the control of Joseph II. "Arranged as a marriage of convenience (since Giulia was not wealthy) by Giulia's father, Marquis Cesare Beccaria, and by Count Pietro Verri," one source emphasizes, "the union soon proved unhappy, more on account of incompatibility of character than the wide age gap." As that source notes: "Don Pietro was of aristocratic descent, a widower without heirs who lived in a modest home on the Navigli with his seven unmarried sisters, one of whom was a former nun. He had a brother who was Canon at Milan Cathedral, and owned a villa in the Lecco countryside that he called Villa Caleotto." "Solitary and melancholy by nature," that source continues of Pietro Manzoni, "he shunned the kind of social life enjoyed by Giulia, who was young, beautiful, intelligent, lively, strong-minded and accustomed to expressing her ideas freely." After a stifling marriage and the birth of her son Alessandro in 1785, Giulia separated from her husband in 1792 and developed a relationship with Count Carlo Imbonati. In 1796, a few months after the French, under Napoleon, entered Milan, she went to Paris, later to be joined by her son Alessandro Manzoni—the novelist and poet who adored his mother and who, in France, is said to have "imbibed Voltairean principles." Alessandro Manzoni later became famous for his own works.[23] Donna Giulia Beccaria—as Manzoni's mother was known—became a celebrity in Paris, with her son Alessandro joining her in 1805 and coming into his own as a writer shortly thereafter. Alessandro Manzoni—basking in the association with Cesare Beccaria, his famous grandfather—got married in 1808, had nine children, and reportedly "liked being called Manzoni-Beccaria, or even Signor Beccaria."[24]

As penitentiaries got built before and after Cesare Beccaria's death, anti-death penalty activism grew and the anti-gallows movement matured and became more organized. In Western countries, that sentiment was reflected in the formation of England's Quaker-dominated Society for Diffusing Information on the Subject of the Punishment by Death (1808), the British Anti-Capital Punishment Society (1828), and the American Society for the Abolition of Capital Punishment (1845).[25] Though those societies were not organized until the nineteenth century, the intellectual foundation for them was laid in Beccaria's lifetime, as was reflected in a number of constitutions, laws and edicts. For example, New Hampshire's 1784 constitution—

echoing the language of Montesquieu, Beccaria and Blackstone—provided in part: "All penalties ought to be proportioned to the nature of the offence. No wise legislature will affix the same punishment to the crimes of theft, forgery and the like, which they do to those of murder and treason; where the same undistinguished severity is exerted against all offences, the people are led to forget the real distinction in the crimes themselves, and to commit the most flagrant with as little compunction as they do those of the lightest dye." As that provision of New Hampshire's 1784 constitution continued: "For the same reason a multitude of sanguinary laws is both impolitic and unjust. The true design of all punishments being to reform, not to exterminate mankind."[26] After the adoption of New Hampshire's constitution, the death penalty's abolition in Tuscany and Austria came soon thereafter in the decade before Beccaria's death. The Edict of the Grand Duke of Tuscany, issued "by the Grace of God," proclaimed then-existing criminal laws "too severe, in consequence of their having been founded on maxims established either at the unhappy crisis of the Roman empire, or during the troubles of anarchy." That edict abolished "the pains of death, together with the different tortures and punishments, which were immoderate, and disproportioned to the transgressions." As regards "those who are guilty of the crimes formerly deemed capital," the edict continued, they "should continue to live, to atone by some good actions for the bad ones they have committed." In lieu of being put to death, such offenders were ordered to perform "public labour" during "the term of their natural life"—the punishment designated "as the greatest punishment for the men," the punishment of death being abolished.[27]

With penitentiaries being authorized and built in America and Great Britain and elsewhere, jurisdictions gradually began to curtail the death penalty for certain offenses, though legislative reform came to different places at different times. In England, Sir Samuel Romilly (1757–1818)—a man who thoroughly embraced penal reform—called for the death penalty's repeal for shoplifting in the early nineteenth century. His bill passed the House of Commons in 1813, but it failed in the House of Lords. It was only after Romilly's death that, in 1820, England abolished the death penalty for that crime. In the 1820s and 1830s, Sir James Mackintosh and Sir Robert Peel also introduced legislation in Parliament to do away with capital punishment for forgery, an effort that eventually bore fruit in the British Isles.[28] It was in 1820s America that penal reformer Edward Livingston—the former New York City mayor and future U.S. Secretary of State—drafted his code for Louisiana that sought to abolish the death penalty for all crimes. His effort wasn't successful in that locale, but he became a much-celebrated figure in his day.[29] In France, which had embraced *Dei delitti e delle pene* so early on after its first appearance, Victor Hugo's *Le Dernier Jour d'un Condamné* (*The Last Day of a Condemned Man*), published in 1829, also reinvigorated the death penalty debate. In that book's preface, added in 1832, Hugo spoke of abolishing the death penalty as "the highest, holiest, most noble aim" and specifically gave a nod to Montesquieu and Beccaria, both, by then, long deceased. As Hugo wrote: "*On Crimes and Punishments* is an offshoot of *On the Spirit of the Laws*. Montesquieu fathered Beccaria." In particular, Hugo sought with his book, *The Last Day of a Condemned Man*, "to do his best to deepen the incision that, sixty-six years ago, Beccaria made into the old gibbet that has loomed over Christianity for centuries."[30]

It is perhaps no coincidence that, in many states, penitentiaries were authorized in close proximity to the curtailment of death eligibility for certain classes of offenders. For example, the Philadelphia Society for Alleviating the Miseries of Public Prisons was formed in 1787, with Dr. Benjamin Rush attending that organization's first meeting. As one source explains of that society, whose members included Dr. Rush, Benjamin Franklin and William Bradford: "In 1789, the society, with Rush as its primary spokesperson, attempted to improve the lot of inmates incarcerated at Philadelphia's Walnut Street Jail. The General Assembly agreed and designated the facility a peniten- tiary." By the act of the Pennsylvania assembly of April 5, 1790, the old Walnut Street Jail—built in 1776—was, in the words of one historical source, "transformed into the first American penitentiary."[31] Penitentiaries—whether in Europe or the Americas— developed in the wake of writings inspired by *Dei delitti e delle pene* and these new prisons were seen as a more humane alternative to frequent executions, just as English authorities, over time, often imposed sentences of "transportation," or exile, in lieu of death sentences and the gallows.[32] An English sheriff, John Howard (1726–1790), had brought the maltreatment of prisoners into focus, with Howard—himself inspired by Beccaria—lobbying the House of Commons in 1774 to reform horrendous prison con- ditions. After Howard published a 1777 account of the state of prisons in England and Wales, he himself earned many disciples and the British Parliament eventually took ac- tion, passing the Penitentiary Act of 1779. Howard, Sir William Blackstone and William Eden—all of whom were influenced by Beccaria's treatise—drafted that legislation.[33]

In America, as in Europe, the building of penitentiaries thus came to be seen as a progressive, forward-looking measure. Virginia—Jefferson and Madison's home state—provides a good example and shows Cesare Beccaria's impact. As a member of Virginia's House of Delegates, George Keith Taylor—a leading lawyer from Peters- burg, Virginia—is considered "the father of penal reform in Virginia" for leading the effort to amend that state's antiquated penal code.[34] It was once written of George Keith Taylor that he "embodied the principles of Beccaria in the criminal code of a state"—the Commonwealth of Virginia—"and founded a penitentiary, the comple- ment of that enlightened measure."[35] Much of that humanitarian sentiment can be traced back in one way or another to Milan, to Pietro Verri and his protégé Cesare Beccaria, both of whom shared a disdain for cruelty and barbaric practices. In Milan, a Column of Infamy actually stood in that city until the year 1778. It had been erected in 1631 to commemorate the wrongful execution of two men falsely accused of spread- ing a poison that, in 1630, was erroneously thought to have caused a deadly plague. As one source puts it: "This miscarriage of justice haunted future generations of Mi- lanese. At the end of the 18th century, several Enlightenment thinkers—above all Pietro Verri and Cesare Beccaria—began to see the infamy attached not to the men who were executed, for it had become increasingly clear that they were innocent, but to the legal system that had led to this great miscarriage of justice." Pietro Verri—that source reports—"dealt explicitly with the matter in his *Osservazioni sulla tortura*, writ- ten in 1766 but not published until 1804, while Beccaria's engagement with this trial was more abstract but nonetheless evident in his *Dei delitti e delle pene* (*On Crimes and Punishments*) published in 1764."[36] Using those sources, Beccaria's own grandson, Alessandro Manzoni (1785–1873),[37] later wrote a famous historical novel, *I Promessi Sposi* (*The Betrothed*), to which was later appended his *La Storia della Colonna infame* (*The Story of the Column of Infamy*) about that infamous miscarriage of justice.[38]

Beccaria himself had direct contacts with figures who played a role in shaping the Enlightenment itself. In the mid-1760s, for example, Beccaria met the French nobleman Étienne Bonnot, better known as the abbé de Condillac (1714–1780), during the latter's visit to Milan, and the two later stayed in contact as reflected in letters sent in late 1765. Condillac studied human psychology, served as a court-appointed tutor to an orphaned duke in the Duchy of Parma, and corresponded directly with Beccaria on smallpox, then a major threat, especially in large European cities. Jean-Jacques Rousseau had tutored Condillac's nephews, and Rousseau and Condillac—along with Denis Diderot, a co-contributor to the *Encyclopédie*—developed a lasting friendship. "In his preparatory *Essai sur l'origin des connaissances humaines* (1746), in *Traité des systèms* (1749), and then in *Traité des sensations* (1754)," one criminology text notes, "Condillac developed Locke's doctrine of sensationalism, positing that the human mind is at birth a *tabula rasa*, which operates through sensations." "Like Locke," that source notes, "Condillac championed the rigidly materialistic conclusion that 'man' is simply what he has acquired through his sensations." As Condillac wrote a decade before the first appearance of *Dei delitti e delle pene*: "It is pleasures and pains compared, that is to say, our needs which exercise our faculties. As a result, it is to them that we owe the happiness that is ours to enjoy." As his 1754 essay concluded: "We have as many needs as different kinds of enjoyment; as many degrees of need as degrees of enjoyment. And there you have the germ of everything that we are, the source of our unhappiness or of our happiness. To observe the influence of this principle is thus the sole means to study ourselves."

After returning from Italy in 1768, Condillac published works like *Le Commerce et le Gouvernement* (1776) on the subject of economics. In his theory of "*vrai prix*" (true price), he called progress the rational use of resources and characterized decline as upper classes behaving poorly and encouraging excess and luxury. As a remedy for "false prices," Condillac proposed his "*vrai prix*," a true price to be created by deregulation and the forces of supply and demand. Beccaria's *Dei delitti e delle pene* itself emphasizes that "sentiment is always proportional to the result of the impressions made on the senses" and that punishments have "a direct impact on the senses and appear continually to the mind to counterbalance the strong impressions of individual passions opposed to the general good." Other influential Frenchmen, including Condorcet, also corresponded with Beccaria, who, in 1765, reported to Archduke Ferdinand—the Austrian governor of Lombardy—that he hadn't enjoyed the study of law and wanted to serve his country not in a judicial robe but by engaging in sciences more pertinent to economics. Like Cesare Beccaria, Pietro Verri also favored a career in economics instead of one focused on the legal profession. In *Modern Italian Literature*, historian Lacy Collison-Morley writes of Pietro Verri's career path: "To escape his father's profession of the law, which he detested, he entered the army and saw some active service with the Austrians. But he soon found he was not made for a soldier, resigned his commission in 1760, and returned to Milan." After leaving the army, Collison-Morley observes, Verri "threw himself heart and soul into the study of finance and political economy."[39]

Cesare Beccaria, who followed Pietro Verri into the field of economics, developed a global reputation, one that far exceeded Verri's celebrity. As one academic paper emphasizes of the kind of reformist sentiment Beccaria inspired: "In letters to Beccaria of 1771, Condorcet condemned the injustices of existing criminal jurisprudence and he expressed his desire to follow Beccaria's lead in using mathematics to search for rationality in judicial decision making." In that particular paper, "Inventing Criminology," Professor Piers Beirne argues that *Dei delitti e delle pene*—what he calls "an instant and dazzling success"—was influenced and inspired by the precepts of French humanism, English philosophy, and the Scottish notion of the "science of man." The cross-cultural dialogue led to innovations on both sides of the intellectual exchange. Along with readily acknowledging his indebtedness to the French *philosophes*, Beccaria and his fellow Milanese *Accademia* members read and no doubt passionately discussed works by Bacon, Locke and Shakespeare as well as leading Scottish philosophers such as Hume and Francis Hutcheson. Beccaria's 1762 essay addressing the problems associated with currency in Milan drew inspiration from both Hume and Locke, and *Dei delitti e delle pene* includes this revealing sentence: "Mankind owes a debt of gratitude to the philosopher who, from the despised obscurity of his study, had the courage to cast the first and long fruitless seeds of useful truths among the multitude!" Beccaria, Piers Beirne writes of that sentence, "was undoubtedly referring to Hutcheson, who had explicitly termed himself 'an obscure Philosopher.'" "It is almost certain that Beccaria had read Hutcheson's *Inquiry into the Original of Our Ideas of Beauty and Virtue*, probably in a French translation of 1749," Beirne explains, emphasizing Francis Hutcheson's book was popular in Italy and that "[n]early every page" of Beccaria's book was shaped "by Hutcheson's towering influence." "Careful comparison," Beirne writes, "reveals that whole sections of *Dei delitti* either restate or develop the proposals for law and criminal justice in Hutcheson's *System*"—a reference to Hutcheson's *System of Moral Philosophy* (1755).[40]

Though the U.S. penitentiary system was not completed in their lifetimes, America's Enlightenment-inspired Founding Fathers expressed great hopes for that system, one that—if properly built out—would eliminate the need for barbarous punishments. In the 1820s, James Madison wrote one Quaker reformer, Roberts Vaux, that "the Penitentiary System" was "an experiment so deeply interesting to the cause of Humanity."[41] In 1823, James Madison even wrote to a veteran from Kentucky, a physician, who had written to ask the former President about his views on capital punishment. That veteran and honorary member of the Lexington Medical Society, G. F. H. Crockett, had sent Madison a copy of Crockett's extended essay, *An Address to the Legislature of Kentucky on the Abolition of Capital Punishments, in the United States, and the Substitution of Exile for Life*, an essay that specifically invoked Beccaria's name as it evangelized against the punishment of death.[42] Madison's response: "I should not regret a fair and full trial of the entire abolition of capital punishments by any State willing to make it: tho' I do not see the injustice of such punishments in one case at least."[43] In 1827, Madison also wrote a letter to another correspondent who had sent the ex-

President a report on Pennsylvania's penal system. In that letter, Madison said he was "attracted to what related to the penitentiary discipline as a substitute for the cruel inflictions so disgraceful to penal codes."[44] In other words, unduly harsh punishments such as executions and the pillory were on their way out, with legislative bodies actively exploring more humane alternatives.

It was in the nineteenth and early twentieth centuries that, in English-speaking countries, the anti-gallows movement had its first major successes in eliminating the death penalty for murder. Before America's Civil War (1861–1865), three U.S. states — Michigan (1846), Rhode Island (1852), and Wisconsin (1853) — abolished the death penalty for that crime. Michigan thus became the first English-speaking jurisdiction to abolish the death penalty for murder, and abolition in Rhode Island came after a 43-page legislative report concluded that "the spirit of the age in which we live, the sublime principles of Christianity, as well as the ends of justice, demand the abolition of death as a penalty for crime." In Wisconsin, it was a state legislator — Marvin Bovee — who led the fight in the Wisconsin State Senate to put an end to the practice, calling capital punishment "a dark spot resting on us Christians."[45] Christopher Latham Sholes, a Wisconsin assemblyman and the publisher of the *Kenosha Telegraph*, partnered with Bovee in leading the legislative effort. Sholes had witnessed the 1851 execution of John McCaffary in Kenosha, Wisconsin, and he was appalled by it. "The crowd has been indulged in its insane passion for the sight of a judicially-murdered man," Sholes' newspaper reported, adding: "We do not complain that the law has been enforced. We complain that the law exists."[46] Sholes — the passionate social reformer — later invented the typewriter as a way to allow people to communicate more effectively and efficiently.[47]

Unfortunately, the Civil War halted the momentum of America's anti-death penalty movement. Bovee's anti-gallows manifesto, *Christ and the Gallows*, was ready for release in 1861, but Bovee put its publication on hold in light of the war. To have presented such a work during the Civil War, Bovee wrote in 1869 when his book finally came out, "would have been 'ill-timed,' to say the least."[48] But after the Civil War, anti-death penalty activism resumed across the country. Early in 1869, a state senator in Maine, John L. Stevens, sought the death penalty's abolition in his home state.[49] The movement was fueled there by the March 12th, 1869 hanging in the state prison of Clifton Harris, a black nineteen-year-old who moved to Maine after serving in the Civil War. Though it took some time, the Maine legislature abolished capital punishment in 1876, more than 80 years after Cesare Beccaria's death.[50] In addition to *Christ and the Gallows*, Marvin Bovee later published *Reasons for Abolishing Capital Punishment* (1878), a book dedicated to his 84-year-old mother, who — as Bovee's inscription read — taught him "to hate nothing but Injustice and Cruelty." In his book, Bovee highlighted prominent abolitionist voices, including Beccaria's, with Bovee emphasizing: "The Marquis Beccaria, in 1764, published a work entitled, *Dei Delitti e delle Pene*, which produced a marked effect upon the public sentiment of that day."[51]

The pervasive influence of Beccaria's book on American law can be gleaned from a 1786 letter that William Bradford, Jr., then Pennsylvania's attorney general, sent to Luigi Castiglioni, the botanist from Milan who toured the United States in the mid-

1780s, leaving America shortly before the country's 1787 Constitutional Convention in Philadelphia.[52] Castiglioni—the nephew of Pietro and Alessandro Verri, the brothers from Milan who had encouraged Beccaria to write *On Crimes and Punishments* in the first place[53]—came to America to study its trees and plants but also met a who's who of America's civic and political leaders.[54] George Washington, the citizen-soldier who became the first President of the United States, hosted Castiglioni for four days at Mount Vernon, and even though Thomas Jefferson was away in France as a diplomat, Castiglioni got a tour of his impressive, beautifully designed Virginia home, Monticello. Like Count Paolo Andreani, a later Italian traveler, Castiglioni met with a whole host of American founders. Castiglioni developed a strong enough bond with American leaders like Benjamin Franklin that Dr. Franklin—at the instigation of his friend, Luigi Castiglioni—was, in 1786, named a corresponding member of the Patriotic Society of Milan. In turn, Dr. Franklin later sent Castiglioni—after the Italian botanist had returned home to Milan—a copy of the proposed U.S. Constitution, the one later ratified by the American people.[55] It was a legal document that would forever change the course of world history as one of its core elements—the separation of powers—was emulated in other places.

In the dynamic, cross-cultural exchange that took place in the eighteenth century, Luigi Castiglioni had initially been made known to Dr. Franklin through a letter of introduction from Paolo Frisi, a mathematician from Milan who knew Cesare Beccaria and those in his social circle.[56] In a letter to Castiglioni dated October 14, 1787, Franklin had written from Philadelphia in the wake of the Constitutional Convention: "Supposing that a Gentleman who had so much Curiosity respecting the *natural* Productions of our Country, may have some respecting its *political* Productions, I send you enclos'd a Copy of the new federal Constitution propos'd by the Convention of all the States lately held in this City. It is a singular Thing in the History of Mankind, that a great People have had the Opportunity of forming a Government for themselves. This Plan is now to be submitted to the Consideration of separate State Conventions, and probably will be adopted by most if not all of them."[57] Writing in Italian in November 1784 from his residence in France, in Passy, Benjamin Franklin—in another letter referencing Castiglioni—had previously sent to another Italian, Lorenzo Manini, translated copies of the early constitutions of the American states. A letter to Franklin from an Italian language teacher, Alphonse Pellegrini, also spelled Pelligrini, referenced Castiglioni, too, with that 1785 letter written in French and specifically taking note of the botanist's trip to America.[58]

In his 1786 letter, William Bradford—James Madison's close friend—effusively lauded *On Crimes and Punishments*, with Bradford going so far as to give Castiglioni a newly printed American edition of Beccaria's book. The son of a printer, Bradford volunteered as a private during the Revolutionary War, became a general's aide, served at Valley Forge and was promoted through the ranks to a lieutenant colonel, and later became the second Attorney General of the United States during George Washington's presidency. Washington named him to that post in 1794, the year of Cesare Beccaria's death and just shortly after Bradford had published his influential, Beccaria-inspired legislative report and essay, *An Enquiry How Far the Punishment of Death Is Necessary in Pennsylvania* (1793).[59] In 1786, in presenting the new edition of Beccaria's treatise as a gesture of good will, William Bradford—who believed Castiglioni to be *Beccaria's* nephew and who was then serving as Pennsylvania's attorney general—wrote: "It is a new proof of the veneration my countrymen harbor for the opinions of your famous relative. I should like it to be known by the author of this book, so well received in the Old World, that his efforts to extend the domain of humanity have been crowned in the New World with the happiest success." "Long before the recent Revolution," Bradford explained in his letter, "this book was common among lettered persons of Pennsylvania, who admired its principles without daring to hope that they could be adopted in legislation, since we copied the laws of England, to whose laws we were subject." "However," Bradford continued, "as soon as we were free of political bonds, this humanitarian system, long admired in secret, was publicly adopted and incorporated by the Constitution of the State, which, spurred by the influence of this benign spirit, ordered the legislative bodies to render penalties less bloody and, in general, more proportionate to the crimes."[60]

The impact of *On Crimes and Punishments* on the American psyche—and on American law—is clear. Just as the Italian botanist Luigi Castiglioni traveled throughout the United States, Beccaria's fame extended throughout the former British colonies, shaping everything from legislation to newspaper editorials. In the April 14, 1780 edition of *The Maryland Gazette*, published in Annapolis, "A Republican" wrote a letter addressed "To the PEOPLE of MARYLAND." "The power of punishing offences, which are merely so, because they are prohibited by the laws of society, in the state of Maryland," that letter began, "is founded on the contract contained in the declaration of rights and the form of government." "To this government," the letter continued, "is also transferred the right of punishing offences against the law of nature, which every individual, in a state of nature, would possess, and which is clearly derived from the principle of self-preservation." "It is this alone," the letter writer asserted, "which can justify capital punishment."[61] In *On Crimes and Punishments*, Beccaria had proposed a version of the social compact in which individuals only transferred to the state the smallest portion of their liberty necessary to secure law and order. As one scholar, David Luban, has explained: "Beccaria condemns punishments that are more cruel than is absolutely necessary to deter crime, arguing that on classical-liberal grounds that people in the state of nature will surrender only the smallest quantum of liberty necessary to secure society: 'The aggregate of these smallest possible portions of individual liberty constitutes the right to punish; everything beyond that is an abuse and not justice, a fact but scarcely a right.'"[62]

The views of the Marylander, "A Republican," were clearly shaped by Beccaria's writings. "Wherever the necessity of enforcing a law by the death of the transgressor, is not dictated by this ruling principle," the letter writer continued, referencing Beccaria's theory of the social compact, "I make no scruple of denying the right of a legislature to take away the life of a human creature." Asserting that "[a]n excessive severity is moreover so repugnant to common sense," the writer further contended that "the grand cause of the imperfection in the penal laws is this, they are framed by the rich and powerful, and contrived principally for their own security."[63] Citing the author of *On Crimes and Punishments*, "A Republican" also made this observation: "If my *memory* does not deceive me, the marquis Beccaria denies the right of capital punishment, because it is not fairly derived from the original compact. He also contends, that the execution of a criminal does not operate so powerfully by way of example as some other punishments, which might in another view contribute to the benefit of the public."[64]

Less than three years before the all-important Constitutional Convention in Philadelphia, *The Pennsylvania Gazette*—in October 1784—published an extensive excerpt from Beccaria's treatise on "THE OBSCURITY OF LAWS." These words, the newspaper reported, were "Written by the Marquis BECCARIA, of Milan":

If the power of interpreting laws be an evil, obscurity in them must be another, as the former is the consequence of the latter. This evil will be still greater, if the laws be written in a language unknown to the people; who, being ignorant of the consequences of their own actions, become necessarily dependent on a few, who are interpreters of the laws, which, instead of being public and general, are thus rendered private and particular. What must we think of mankind, when we reflect, that such is the established custom of the greatest part of our polished and enlightened Europe? Crimes will be less frequent, in proportion as the code of laws is more universally read and understood; for there is no doubt, but that the eloquence of the passions is greatly assisted by the ignorance, and uncertainty of punishments.

Hence it follows, that without written laws, no society will ever acquire a fixed form of government, in which the power is vested in the whole, and not in any part of the society; and in which the laws are not to be altered, but by the will of the whole, nor corrupted by the force of private interest. Experience and reason shew us, that the probability of human traditions diminishes in proportion as they are distant from their sources. How then can laws resist the inevitable force of time, if there be not a lasting monument of the social compact?

Hence we see the use of PRINTING, which alone makes the public, and not a few individuals, the guardians and defenders of the laws. It is this ART, which, by diffusing literature, has gradually dissipated the gloomy spirit of cabal and intrigue. To this ART it is owing, that the attrocious crimes of our ancestors, who were alternatively slaves and tyrants, are become less frequent. Those who are acquainted with the history of the two or three last centuries, may observe, how from the lap of luxury and effeminacy have sprung the most tender virtues, humanity, benevolence, and toleration of human errors. They may contemplate the effects of what was so improperly called, ancient simplicity, and good faith; humanity groaning under implacable superstition; the avarice and ambition of a few, staining, with human blood, the thrones and palaces of Kings; secret treasons, and public massacres; every noble a tyrant over the people; and the Ministers of the Gospel of Christ bathing their hands in blood, in the name of the God of all Mercy. We may talk as we please of the corruption and degeneracy of the present age, but happily we see no such horrid examples of cruelty and oppression.[65]

In William Bradford's 1786 letter to Luigi Castiglioni, Bradford specifically emphasized: "The name of Beccaria has become familiar in Pennsylvania, his authority has become great, and his principles have spread among all classes of persons and impressed themselves deeply in the hearts of our citizens." "You yourself must have noticed the influence of these precepts in other American states," Bradford wrote to the Italian botanist, aware that Castiglioni had been traveling throughout the American states on his extended overseas trip.[66] Castiglioni, in fact, would spend more than two years in North America, visiting what is modern-day Canada and all thirteen of the original U.S. states.[67] Castiglioni had originally been introduced to America's senior statesman, Benjamin Franklin, by Paolo Frisi, the mathematician and astronomer, and that introduction bore delicious fruit as Castiglioni traveled throughout America and gained entrée to America's most important civic and political leaders. Frisi was a member of Milan's Society of Fists, the self-described "Coffeepot Society" of mostly young men that included the Verri brothers, Cesare Beccaria, and other influential thinkers.[68] "Coffee," Pietro Verri wrote, celebrating the popular stimulant, "cheers the spirit, awakens the mind, is diuretic for some, keeps away sleep for many, and it is particularly useful to people who do not move around much, and who cultivate the sciences."[69]

Coffee became a symbol of refinement and sophistication in the seventeenth and eighteenth centuries. In London, cafés and coffeehouses sprung up around the Royal Exchange, and Lloyd's—a famous shipping and insurance society—got its name from a coffeehouse of the same name on Lombard Street. Parisian cafés and coffeehouses likewise became gathering spots, whether for checkers, chess or card games, and they found their way into literature and plays such as Carlo Goldoni's *La bottega del caffè* (*The Coffee House*, 1736) and Voltaire's comedy, *Le café ou L'ecossaise* (*The Café; or, the Scottish Woman*, 1760). Milan's Academy of Fists—as one historian reiterates, recounting the short-lived but highly influential salon—"derived specifically from gossip circulated around Milan in the summer of 1763, according to which Verri and Beccaria had resolved an intellectual dispute by resorting to 'powerful punches,' giving life to the idea of an *Academy of Punches*."[70] And the products of their meetings produced much discussion around Milan, just as gatherings at Europe's cafés and coffeehouses did over the years in places throughout that continent. For example, after *Dei delitti e delle pene* first appeared, Gian Rinaldo Carli—for many years the president of Milan's Supreme Economic Council, the body that Beccaria joined after a concerted lobbying effort—had embraced Beccaria's treatise as "an example of independent thought in favor of humanity." Carli did so even though he had written to Paolo Frisi that he (Carli) still saw the death penalty as a necessary criminal sanction to be used against "enemies of society, guilty of deliberate murder."[71]

Writing of Beccaria's ideological influence in the newly forged United States of America, just a small portion of Beccaria's geographic reach brought about by the many translations of *Dei delitti e delle pene*, Bradford explained in his 1786 letter: "The tyranny of prejudice and injustice has fallen, the voice of a philosopher has stilled the outcries of the masses, and although a bloody system may still survive in the laws of many of our states, nevertheless the beneficent spirit sown by Beccaria works secretly in behalf of the accused, moderating the rigor of the laws and tempering justice with compassion."[72] The "bloody system" to which Bradford referred—the English legal system that was then littered with capital crimes—had been inherited from England, America's mother country, and Bradford was keen to get rid of it as Pennsylvanians would begin to do in the 1780s and 1790s.[73] In his little-known Italian travelogue, published in Milan in 1790 but only translated into English in 1983 as *Viaggio: Travels in the United States of North America, 1785–1787*,[74] Luigi Castiglioni specifically referenced sections 38 and 39 of the Pennsylvania Constitution. Those sections of Pennsylvania's constitution dealt with the type of penal reform—"hard labour" and "less sanguinary" punishments—inspired in part by Pennsylvania's founder, William Penn, as well as by Enlightenment texts such as Cesare Beccaria's *On Crimes and Punishments*.[75]

In fact, an array of eighteenth- and nineteenth-century newspapers and other sources make reference to Beccaria and other thinkers inspired by him.[76] In the October 18, 1787 edition of the *New York Journal*, "Brutus," in making a point, wrote: "I shall content myself with quoting" only two "illustrious authorities," namely, Montesquieu and Beccaria. In a June 21, 1788 speech at New York's ratifying convention, Melancton Smith likewise quoted Beccaria from the Continental Congress's 1774 address to the inhabitants of Quebec.[77] And those are but two prominent examples. Numerous American colonists and early Americans owned Beccaria's treatise or read it in libraries, with one scholar stressing: "In America, Beccaria's radical book soon became highly influential among the Founders, especially Adams and Jefferson."[78] American judges—tasked with administering justice—themselves routinely looked to Beccaria's book, or were guided by it, as part of their work in giving jury instructions or carrying out their other duties. In a grand jury charge before the ratification of the U.S. Bill of Rights, the Hon. James Duane—a New York district court judge—paraphrased more than one passage from Beccaria's treatise. "Severe laws may be necessary to support despotic power," Judge Duane instructed jurors, "and it is the interest of tyrants to inspire their vassals with fear and servility; but a free republic calls for moderation." Having echoed Beccaria's themes against tyranny and in favor of milder penalties, Judge Duane continued: "The celebrated Beccaria observes, that the countries and times most notorious for severity of punishment were always those in which the most inhuman and atrocious crimes were committed."[79] In other words, tyrannical monarchs, like the British monarchy, used draconian edicts to enforce their will, but republics, including the newly formed United States of America, should—by their very nature—employ milder laws.

Ultimately, Beccaria's writings shaped penal codes throughout the world.[80] And those writings continue—from a distance of more than 250 years—to educate criminologists and to shape and inform the world's death penalty debate amidst a growing chorus of voices calling for an end to executions.[81] Initially, *Dei delitti e delle pene* helped to catalyze milder, written penal codes and to persuade members of the Habsburg Dynasty to abolish the death penalty. In 1786, Grand Duke Leopold of Tuscany adopted a Tuscan penal code (known as the *Codice Leopoldino*) that totally eliminated the death penalty. And in 1787, Holy Roman Emperor Joseph II, Leopold's brother, went almost as far, abolishing Austria's death penalty save for crimes of revolt against the state.[82] Emperor Joseph II, through secret decrees issued in 1781 and 1783, had previously ordered that every case involving the death penalty be submitted to him personally, and only one execution—in 1786—took place before his 1787 decision to reject the death penalty. That execution, of nobleman Franz Zahlheim, a convicted murderer, was publicly carried out on March 10, 1786 by way of hot pincers and breaking on the wheel.[83] Indeed, Holy Roman Empress Maria Theresa (1717–1780), of Austria, eventually abolished torture at the urging of Austrian law professor Joseph von Sonnenfels, a Beccaria admirer and a key advisor of the powerful sovereign. A law professor at the University of Vienna, Sonnenfels wrote Empress Maria Theresa a letter in opposition to the use of torture, with Sonnenfels later penning a German language book, *Über die Abschaffung der Tortur* (*On the Abolition of Torture*, 1775) that was soon translated into Italian.[84]

Central themes of Beccaria's book also got repeated in the 1789 French Declaration of the Rights of Man and the Citizen after the success of the American Revolution inspired the French Revolution.[85] Montesquieu's writings had influenced Beccaria, and the works of both men—the French jurist and the Italian economist, philosopher and criminal-law theorist—were often cited side by side, shaping laws far and wide. As *The Handbook of Comparative Criminal Law* emphasizes of the impact of the Montesquieu/Beccaria dynamic duo before and during the tumultuous French Revolution: "Translated into French in 1766, the book of Beccaria was received with enthusiasm in France. Influenced by his and Montesquieu's ideas, the Revolutionary Assemblies made considerable reforms to the criminal law." For instance, in June 1791, during the midst of the French Revolution, there was much anti-death penalty advocacy even though the Reign of Terror is what most people remember now. Maximilien Robespierre—the architect of that Reign of Terror—actually himself opposed the death penalty's use in a 1791 speech to the Constituent Assembly. Though he later changed his mind as the Reign of Terror, with its many executions, unfolded, Robespierre was guillotined on July 28, 1794—perhaps concentrating and changing his mind a final time as the blade fell before a throng of Parisians. A new French penal code was crafted from 1790 to 1791, and capital punishment—at least at the beginning of the French Revolution—was very much on the agenda.[86] The French Penal Code of 1791 reduced the number of capital crimes, though the 1789 Declaration of the Rights of Man—the penal code's predecessor—took a more aggressive stance, providing in Article 8 in no uncertain terms: "[T]he law can only lay down punishments that are strictly and obviously necessary and a person can only be punished by virtue of a law established and promulgated prior to the wrongful conduct and legally applicable."[87]

There were many skeptics of capital punishment in eighteenth- and nineteenth-century Europe and the Americas. For example, Etienne Michel Le Pelletier de Saint-Fargeau (1760–1793) presented to the French Assembly a penal code that has been characterized as a "synthesis of Enlightenment thought." The proposed system, developed in the wake of the American Revolution, was based on "humane," "proportionate" and "fixed" punishments. While Le Pelletier and others, following Beccaria, sought the death penalty's abolition, the reformers did not achieve all that they sought—societies not being ready for the scale of legal reform that Beccaria sought.[88] Along with works by Montesquieu and Voltaire, Beccaria's work "at the end of the eighteenth century," the author of *The Civil Law in Spain and Spanish-America* emphasizes, nevertheless "produced a revolution in European penal legislation."[89] Thus, *On Crimes and Punishments* was nothing short of a landscape-changing text, even if it didn't immediately achieve all that it set out to do—most significantly, the elimination of executions. "For thinkers such as Montesquieu, Voltaire, and Beccaria," David Garland explains in *Peculiar Institution*, his award-winning book on America's death penalty, "the death penalty was emblematic of the absolutist *ancien regime* with its arbitrary use of power and crushing disregard for individual life and liberty."[90]

Cesare Beccaria's advocacy against the death penalty, though it achieved only limited, tangible successes in his lifetime, certainly shaped attitudes throughout Europe and the Americas.[91] In Colombia, President José Hilario Lopez (1798–1869)—elected in 1849—signed into law the abolition of the death penalty for political crimes.[92] The country of Venezuela, following the Revolutions of 1848, also abolished the death penalty for political crimes in 1849 before doing away with the death penalty entirely in the 1860s under the leadership of Juan Crisóstomo Falcón (1820–1870).[93] "In 1863," one source notes, "Venezuela became the first country in the world to abolish the death penalty for all crimes, and by the mid-twentieth century Brazil, Colombia, Costa Rica, Ecuador, Uruguay, and Argentina had removed the punishment in peacetime."[94] Brazil, which declared its independence in the 1820s, had—history reveals—long flirted with the death penalty's abolition. When that country's Constituent Assembly deliberated over the substance of its 1824 constitution, a committee chosen by the emperor, Dom Pedro I, did the drafting. As law professor Robert Cottrol describes the outcome: "The constitutional text specifically included *libertos* in this group. All citizens were equal before the law and equally entitled to the law's protection. Citizens were guaranteed freedom from religious persecution provided that their actions did not offend public morals. Harsh physical punishment was prohibited." "In the Constituent Assembly," Cottrol adds, "a minority went even further in their advocacy of human rights, urging the abolition of the death penalty." "Their efforts failed," Cottrol explains, "but the attempt showed the influence of the modern Enlightenment on at least some of the members."[95]

In Central and South America, the death penalty—as in the United States of America—came to be viewed with increasing skepticism, in some cases eventually leading to its outright abolition. "'In 1887,'" one late nineteenth-century source reported, quoting Frederick Gerhard of New York, "'the Central-American States Honduras, Costa Rica, Nicaragua, and Guatemala entered into negotiations for forming a Union, similar to the United States, with the express condition, that the death-penalty in those states should be abolished.'"[96] Leaders in these countries had ties to liberal thinkers who were steeped in the Italian Enlightenment. As Maurizio Isabella observes in *Connections After Colonialism: Europe and Latin America in the 1820s*: "José Cecilio del Valle, widely known as the father of Guatemalan independence, numbered among his most faithful correspondents an Italian exile in England, Giuseppe Pecchio. Formerly the leader of the anti-Austrian plot in Milan in 1820, Pecchio had been a civil servant working for the Napoleonic kingdom of Italy and, after the Restoration, a leading figure in Milan's romantic and liberal circles." "During his exile," that source notes of Giuseppe Pecchio (1785–1835), who left Milan in March 1821 and lived in Switzerland, Spain and Portugal before arriving in England in July 1823, "he had a hand in all revolutionary events in Europe, from Spain to Greece, and was at the center of a vast network of liberals across Europe, including other exiles and some of the most prominent intellectuals of the time."

Del Valle, historian Maurizio Isabella notes, "never left Guatemala, but he had a wide range of international correspondents, including Álvaro Flórez Estrada, the famous exiled Spanish economist, Jeremy Bentham, Alexander von Humboldt, Dominique de Pradt, and several Latin American diplomats stationed in Europe, as well as Pecchio." According to Isabella: "Del Valle sought the guidance of his European peers in order to realize a vision that he felt was his own, but which was also indebted to their intellectual tradition. Since he perceived his nation to be at the periphery of civilization, and Europe as the center of progress and culture, he sought a formal recognition of his intellectual credibility by corresponding with European elites." As Isabella continues of del Valle in the essay, "Entangled Patriotisms: Italian Liberals and Spanish America in the 1820s": "Pecchio sent him his own publications, along with the collection of the Italian eighteenth-century economists and the writings of Cesare Beccaria, which del Valle prided himself upon having quoted in his speeches in the congress."[97] "In London," another source notes, also taking note of del Valle's admiration for Beccaria's ideas, "Giuseppe Pecchio and Fortunato Prandi were directly involved in the exchanges between Bentham's circle and the Guatemalan patriots." As that source adds: "In England Jeremy Bentham, one of the staunchest supporters of the Spanish American cause, furnished the many Spanish American patriots of his acquaintance with intellectual tools to make their case. He justified independence on the basis of the greatest happiness of the greatest number, a principle he used to attack any and every form of colonial power and imperial government."[98]

Count Giuseppe Pecchio, in his *Storia dell' Economica Pubblica in Italia* (*History of Public Economy in Italy*, 1829) penned a chapter titled "Comparison between Italian and English Writers." There, Pecchio observed: "One of the most distinctive features among economists of these two nations is the definition they give of public economy and how they deal with it. For the English it is an isolated science; it is the science of how to make nations wealthy, and that is the exclusive subject of their research. On the other hand, Italians regard it as a complex science, as the administrator's science, and they treat it in all its relationships with ethics and public happiness." In one of his books, *Semi-Serious Observations of an Italian Exile, During His Residence in England* (1833), Count Pecchio specifically took note of Cesare Beccaria's influences, both big and small. Pecchio referred to "the fruit we have gathered from the immortal works of Beccaria" and further emphasized: "Beccaria, in his 'Lessons on Political Economy,' demonstrated, by comparing the strength and longevity of horses with those of oxen, that in many provinces it would be an improvement to substitute horses for oxen in rural labour." One English barrister who knew Pecchio recorded this in his diary on July 22, 1830: "I was instructed by reading Pecchio's 'History of the Science of Political Economy.' He taught me that the Italian writers had the merit of showing the effect of commerce, agriculture, &c., on the *moral state* and happiness of a country; while English writers confined their inquiry to the *mere wealth* of nations." "Beccaria and Filangieri," that barrister, Henry Crabb Robinson, wrote, "are their prime writers, economists as well as philanthropists."[99]

Centuries after Cesare Beccaria lived, his intellectual legacy continued to thrive — and that legacy still lives on. Not only was state legislator George MacKenzie — the prime mover behind the State of Minnesota's decision to abolish capital punishment in 1911 — a reader of Cesare Beccaria's words,[100] but entire countries, adopting Beccaria's preferred policy, decided to abandon the death penalty. For example, the Constitution of the Republic of Honduras — a legal instrument adopted in 1982 and in force since 1985 — succinctly states in Article 66: "The death penalty is abolished." Likewise, Article 23 of the Constitution of Nicaragua (1987) expressly states: "The right to life is inviolable and inherent to the human person. In Nicaragua there is no death penalty."[101] In Nicaragua, opposition to the death penalty actually has roots that are more than a century old, with the foundation for abolition laid even earlier. As one source puts it, the "liberal-leaning" nationalist general José Santos Zelaya "took power in 1893" and "did much to improve the rule of law in Nicaragua," introducing "a new constitution in 1893 that abolished the death penalty, separated church and state, recognized private property, and introduced universal education."[102] As one textbook focused on U.S.-Latin American relations observes of his background: "The son of a wealthy Managua planter, José Santos Zelaya López (1853–1915) was educated at the *Instituto de Oriente* in Granada and then, at age 16, sent to France for further studies. Zelaya returned home in 1872 at age 19 and immediately became involved in politics. He became Nicaragua's president in 1893 following a series of liberal-instigated revolts."[103] In *Latin America: Its Rise and Progress*, it is noted that Beccaria, Filangieri and Adam Smith "were among the prophets."[104]

Cesare Beccaria's treatise thus brought monumental changes to the Americas as political leaders rethought their approach to crime and punishment and the role of government. "South and Central America have been in the vanguard of the abolitionist movement," Roger Hood and Carolyn Hoyle emphasize in *The Death Penalty: A World-wide Perspective*. As they write in the fifth edition of their book: "Venezuela, Costa Rica, and Brazil, which had already abolished capital punishment by the end of the nineteenth century, were followed soon afterwards by Ecuador, Uruguay, Colombia, Argentina, Panama, and most of the Mexican states." Although there have been notable setbacks — both Argentina and Brazil reintroduced capital punishment before abolishing it yet again — the trend in the Americas is plainly toward abolition.[105] Six American states — New Jersey, New York, New Mexico, Illinois, Connecticut and Maryland — have abolished capital punishment since 2007, and even U.S. jurisdictions that retain the death penalty have witnessed a decline in the number of death sentences and executions.[106] And in 2011, the Inter-American Commission on Human Rights issued a lengthy report, the title of which — *The Death Penalty in the Inter-American Human Rights System: From Restrictions to Abolition* — itself speaks volumes. Among the recommendations of that report to member States pertaining to the death penalty:

"Impose a moratorium on executions as a step toward the gradual disappearance of this penalty"; "Ratify the Protocol to the American Convention on Human Rights to Abolish the Death Penalty"; and "Refrain from any measure that would expand the application of the death penalty or reintroduce it."[107]

Indeed, many countries south of the U.S. border now outlaw capital punishment altogether in their constitutions. Article 11 of the 1991 Constitution of Colombia reads: "The right to life is inviolable. There will be no death penalty." Article 8 of the Constitution of the Dominican Republic, promulgated in 1966, also refers to "the inviolability of life" and states: "neither the death penalty, torture, nor any other punishment or oppressive procedure or penalty that implies loss or diminution of the physical integrity or health of the individual may be established." Article 19 of the 1979 Constitution of the Republic of Ecuador likewise contains a provision on "[t]he inviolability of life" and further provides: "There is no death penalty." Article 30 of the Constitution of the Republic of Panama, in a title on "Individual and Social Rights and Duties," also reads: "There is no death penalty."[108] "The more than one-hundred-year tradition of abolition in South and Central America now holds sway," Roger Hood and Carolyn Hoyle point out in their book. "Most countries," they note of those regions, "appear to support abolition because in this respect they see themselves as heirs of the European Enlightenment and share many of the human rights values of Western Europe."[109] Giuseppe Garibaldi—the hero of Italian unification who had risen to military fame in South America and who had spent some time in New York—was himself a self-professed disciple of Cesare Beccaria and an opponent of capital punishment. "As a follower of Beccaria, I am opposed to capital punishment," Garibaldi wrote in his memoirs. Along with declaring himself a follower of Beccaria, Garibaldi considered Voltaire and Rousseau "veritable granite pillars on which universal intelligence was built."[110]

Many early leaders in the Americas were directly influenced by the Enlightenment and—in some cases—had direct contact with Cesare Beccaria himself. A 1943 issue of *Political Science Quarterly* puts it this way: "[T]he eighteenth-century philosopher who had the greatest influence on Latin American penal codes was Cesare Beccaria, whose original treatise *On Crimes and Punishments*, first published in 1764, soon became widely known through a later French edition with a commentary ascribed to Voltaire."[111] Francisco de Miranda—a Venezuelan general—spent extended periods of time in the United States and Europe, meeting with U.S. presidents, participating in the French Revolution, and trying to liberate Spanish America from colonial rule. In August 1788, while in Milan, Miranda specifically sought out Cesare Beccaria and—according to Miranda's biographer—"the two had a lengthy conversation about America."[112] Francisco de Miranda was also personally acquainted with Jeremy Bentham, one of Beccaria's biggest disciples. According to one source: "Miranda, the Spanish revolutionist in South America, had known Bentham in London, and Bentham would have been glad to follow him to Venezuela, for he was convinced that his laws would be received there with glad acclaim, but Miranda died in a Spanish prison." As that source further notes: "It is computed that in 1830 forty thousand volumes of Bentham's works in French were sold in Spanish America alone."[113] Of the Beccaria-citing Jeremy Bentham, that source, *Great Jurists of the World*, emphasizes:

"In the department of the penal law his influence has been of great and constantly increasing value. The amelioration of punishments and the adaptation of penalties to offences, through the work of Bentham re-enforcing Beccaria, can be traced in the legislation of every civilized country."[114]

In truth, footprints reflecting Cesare Beccaria's global impact can be found in region after region and country after country. In Argentina, Cesare Beccaria's writings were well known in Buenos Aires, the country's capital and Argentina's largest city. The University of Buenos Aires was created in 1821, and the city's *academia de jurisprudencia*—proposed in 1814—became a forum for the discussion of republican ideas and penal reform. Beccaria's ideas shaped those debates, and the writings of Beccaria and Bentham were well known in that locale. As noted in one book: "Florencio Varela wrote the first thesis on criminal law at the University of Buenos Aires in 1827. In his 'Disertación sobre los delitos y las penas,' Varela elaborated on Beccaria's concept of proportionality between crime and punishment and Bentham's principle of utilitarianism as the keystones for the new penal system in the Río de la Plata." As that source, *Crime and the Administration of Justice in Buenos Aires, 1785–1853*, explains: "Although Varela vindicated the principles stated by Beccaria and Bentham, he and many others ... were reluctant to apply them in the Río de la Plata right away. In other words, the ideas were fine but the timing was not."[115] "The European legal experts whose works were most often quoted by Argentine legal professionals," stresses another commentator, included Cesare Beccaria and Jeremy Bentham, two of the Enlightenment's leading lights.[116] Only later did Argentina—along with many other countries in the Americas—follow Beccaria's advice and abolish the death penalty.[117]

Naturally, Beccaria's ideas—being so energetically discussed and debated in Europe—also made their way to Mexican soil and influenced the law there.[118] After Mexican independence, "[c]onservatives"—as one historian puts it—"looked back on the stability once provided by the Spanish crown, while liberals sought to eradicate the colonial heritage, doing away with the legal privileges of the Church, the army, and large landholders."[119] Under Charles III, the ruler of Spain from 1759–1788,[120] Don Manuel de Roda was appointed Spain's minister of mercy and justice. And King Charles III—also known as Carlos III—"exhibited," in the one scholar's words, "some concern about several points such as the principle of proportionality between crime and punishment, the wisdom of maintaining, suppressing, or reducing the application of the death penalty, and the rationality of permitting torture as a means of obtaining evidence."[121] The impact of Beccaria's treatise was summed up this way by one source: "[T]he best-known representative of *Illuminismo* was the Milanese Cesare Beccaria (1738–94). His treatise *Dei delitti e delle pene* (*Of Crimes and Punishments*), published in 1764, became one of the textbooks of the campaign to abolish the death penalty and mitigate the severity of the criminal law all over Europe."[122] "Early on," another source observes, citing Beccaria's writings, "Enlightenment-inspired works on crime and punishment had found a sympathetic ear in Mexico."[123]

Just as French, English and Germans had, Spanish and Portuguese speakers gravitated over time—as if in a magnetic field—to Beccaria's ideas. The powerful *Sala de Alcaldes*—a court in Madrid—had Gaspar Melchor de Jovellanos as a judge in the 1770s, with Juan Meléndez Valdés and Manuel de Lardizábal serving as prosecuting attorneys (*fiscales*) for that tribunal in the 1780s and 1790s.[124] The Spanish jurist and dramatist Gaspar Melchor de Jovellanos was reportedly "affected by Beccaria's impassioned, sentimental style" and "greatly influenced by Beccaria in his advocation of humanitarian treatment for the criminal, in his censure of torture and in his condemnation of the anti-dueling laws."[125] Indeed, in the twentieth century, Beccaria's book was still being read with great interest in countries such as Brazil. As one Brazilian playwright who attended law school at the University of São Paulo wrote about one of her plays from the 1970s: "Torture at that time had reached its most intense level because of the dictatorship. I spoke about a person whom we had studied in law school in the criminal-law course, Cesare Beccaria." "During the 18th century," Renata Pallottini wrote of Beccaria, "he had written a book entitled *Dos delitos e das penas* [*On Crimes and Punishments*] where he had expressed ideas in opposition to torture as a way of determining the truth."[126] In *Torture*, historian Edward Peters — an expert on the subject — describes Beccaria's importance this way: "The most famous indictment of torture came from the pen of Cesare Beccaria, the eighteenth-century Italian publicist whose essay *On Crimes and Punishments* became the foremost treatise on penal reform produced by the Enlightenment. The work circulated widely in both the original Italian and in many translations."[127]

Though conceived on Italian soil, Beccaria's ideas had quickly made their way to Spain, and they would also quickly become known in Spanish colonies in the Americas. In 1776, jurist Manuel de Lardizábal y Uribe (1744–1820) — an academician and devout Catholic who taught at the *Real Academia Española de la Lengua* from 1775 to 1820 — had been tasked with reviewing Spanish criminal jurisprudence. Influenced by Beccaria, he produced his *Discurso sobre las penas contrahido á las leyes criminales de España, para facilitar su reforma* (1782), first published in Madrid. That book, *Discurso sobre las penas*, became extremely well known among Spanish jurists and intellectuals, and Beccaria — identified in that text as "Marques de Becaría" — is in fact repeatedly cited in it. That Spanish language work on penology later ended up in Thomas Jefferson's library, with Lardizábal — though departing from Beccaria in particular ways — concluding that "after learning the value of life and the liberty of man," humanity "could no longer avoid the indispensable necessity of reforming criminal laws."[128] Lardizábal — in a manner similar to Beccaria — favored prompt, public and proportionate punishments, arguing for well-ordered prisons and punishments that would be certain and swiftly imposed.[129] In some sources, Cesare Beccaria is referred to as "César Bonesana, Marqués de Beccaria" or "marqués de Becaria."[130]

Leading criminologists and contemporary writers on comparative criminal law continue to document how Cesare Beccaria's writings shaped today's world — and their findings are notable. "Modern Spanish criminal law," Kevin Heller and Markus Dubber observe in *The Handbook of Comparative Criminal Law*, "was influenced by the humanist and utilitarian ideals of the Enlightenment and, more specifically, by Cesare Beccaria's *Dei delitti e delle pene* (1764)." As that source details: "The Spanish constitution of 1812 required the enactment of a penal code reflecting the principles of the nineteenth-century European liberal tradition of codification. Because the drafters of the first code (1822) were greatly influenced by the ideas of Jeremy Bentham and Beccaria, they attempted to limit judicial discretion in sentencing and to curb the imposition of disproportionate punishments." "The rapidly changing social environment that followed," Heller and Dubber emphasize, "led to a series of reforms that culminated in the enactment of the Penal Code in 1870, which was supposed to be in force only for a short time. Although it was dubbed the 'Summer Code' in light of its transitory nature, it was ironically still in force in 1928."[131] As another source puts it of what led up to that code and how it endured for so long despite the temporal label it originally had: "The Penal Code (*Código Penal*) was first voted into law in 1821 and revised in 1848 and 1870. The 1870 Code was in force in Puerto Rico as of 1879…."[132]

The humanity expressed in *On Crimes and Punishments* spoke to a wide array of individuals. In Gabriel Haslip-Viera's *Crime and Punishment in Late Colonial Mexico City, 1692–1810*, the author notes: "Manuel de Roda, another royal advisor, suggested that a complete reform of the penal codes be instituted and called for the elimination of torture, mutilation, and other inhumane practices. He noted that these punishments were ineffective and called for the expansion of convict labor and other rational or 'rehabilitative' forms of correction." Haslip-Viera adds: "In addition to Roda, Juan Meléndez Valdés, Gaspar Melchor de Jovellanos, Manuel de Lardizábal, and other influential persons were inspired by the ideas of the noted Italian criminologist Cesare Beccaria, whose work, *On Crimes and Punishments*, was first translated into Spanish in 1774."[133] "The purest exponent of Enlightenment ideals in classic Mexican criminology was influential liberal theorist José María Luis Mora," Robert Buffington emphasized in *Criminal and Citizen in Modern Mexico*, relaying that Mora was influenced by both Beccaria and Bentham (as so many others had been).[134] In the 1830s and 1840s, the Mexican publisher Ignacio Cumplido also devoted substantial ink and copy to prison reform in the popular periodical *El Mosáico Mexicano*, with Cumplido even visiting the Cherry Hill Penitentiary in Philadelphia and Sing-Sing Prison in New York. Many other Mexican nationals also pressed for the building of a penitentiary system.[135]

Like other nations around the world, Mexico — a country with rich cultural and religious traditions — thus followed the United States in moving from the sanguinary system to the penitentiary system. In the 1850s, the Mexican journalist Ignacio Ramírez spoke out against capital punishment, arguing that no good could come from vengeance and piling "corpse upon corpse." Mariano Navarro — alluding to Beccaria — also took up the cause of the death penalty's abolition at a patriotic celebration in mid-September 1850.[136] Navarro — from the town of Jilotepec, Mexico — reflected on how "modern civilization" had brought reforms as he argued for the death penalty's abolition while standing outside a new penitentiary. "The philosophers of the last century have fought the law that forces society to impose the death penalty, and since then its reputation has fallen into discredit, as much in practice as in opinion," Navarro said, in an obvious allusion to Beccaria and his disciples. "The penitentiary system," he said, "has established a new era that will become famous in the philosophical history of punishment, and it makes death [as punishment] unnecessary."[137] Almost a century after its initial publication, *Dei delitti e delle pene* was continuing to shape the law and public policy debates.

Beccaria's book thus impacted countless thinkers south of the U.S. border—from Argentina to Mexico. The case of Mexico, where legal reforms came before the U.S. Civil War, provides a representative example, though many others could be referenced. After an unsuccessful war with the United States, Mexico's President, Antonio López de Santa Anna, eventually fled the country, leaving on August 9, 1855, for Cuba. With liberals taking control of the national government in Mexico City, delegates gathered there to reform the country's laws. Article 22 of the Mexican Constitution of 1857 prohibited the corporal punishment of convicts with branding, flogging, mutilation, torture, excessive fines, and beating with clubs, while Article 23—unanimously adopted—barred the death penalty's use for political crimes. Article 23, as one scholar notes, "reserved the death penalty for bandits and pirates and anyone convicted of treason, arson, parricide, murder, or military crimes." The delegates made the full abolition of the death penalty contingent on the construction of a national penitentiary system, the viable alternative to executions then being debated. "When the deputies finally moved to vote on whether the death penalty should be abolished once the government constructed a penitentiary regime," historian Patrick Timmons notes, "sixty-three deputies voted in favor and sixteen against." "By making the abolition of the death penalty contingent upon the construction of a penitentiary regime," he adds, "liberals affirmed their belief in the general direction of progressive change."[138] After a subsequent, decades-long struggle, one that spanned the nineteenth and twentieth centuries, as well as the early twenty-first century, Mexico formally abolished the death penalty for all crimes in 2005.[139]

Beccaria's ideas on penal reform got play in the Caribbean, too, with a Puerto Rican historian noting that Caribbean thought was influenced by "leading thinkers and reformers of the period like Voltaire and Rousseau, Adam Smith and Bentham, Locke and Beccaria, Turgot and Jovellanos." "[T]he general ideas of those authors had become part of the mental climate of the age, and were, so to speak, in the air," Gordon Lewis explains in *Main Currents in Caribbean Thought*.[140] In *A Political Account of the Island of Trinidad*, the author—in a section of the book on the use of torture—repeated "some of the remarks of Beccaria, from his Essay on Crimes and Punishments."[141] A history of Cuba, written in 1898, further noted on the cusp of a new millennium: "During the great Revolutionary and Napoleonic periods there was considerable chaos in the island, and the vigilance of the censorship became so relaxed, that the large towns were flooded with French and Italian literature of an advanced kind, and the ex-pupils of the Jesuits devoured the translated works of Voltaire, Rousseau, and Beccaria with an avidity which must have sorely scandalized their orthodox instructors."[142] While some Caribbean countries continue to authorize the death penalty's infliction,[143] that is not true everywhere. For example, Article 19 of the Constitution of the Republic of Haiti (1987) provides: "The death penalty is abolished in all cases."[144]

Debates and laws around the globe were thus molded in fundamental ways by *On Crimes and Punishments*. As one source on the European Enlightenment's influence in far away Australia—a much larger island nation—emphasizes: "Though Beccaria's influence was often subsumed within that of his disciple, Bentham, he was a name which conferred authority and hence was invoked by would-be penal reformers in colonial Australia." John Dunmore Lang quoted Beccaria on the need for punishments to be "public, immediate and necessary; the least possible in the case given, proportionate to the crime, and determined by the laws." Alexander Maconochie—an active reformer of Australian penal policies—also cited Beccaria,[145] arguing in 1839 that existing practices contravened the Beccarian notion that "Nothing can produce a worse moral effect than a striking and obvious disproportion between the quality of an offence committed, and the degree of punishment awarded for it." Nathaniel Kentish of Hobart, seeking the death penalty's abolition, himself appealed to the Italian philosopher in arguing that capital punishment was "in contravention of the paramount and indefeasible rights of man." Kentish called Beccaria "[o]ne of the most efficient auxiliaries in this cause ... who, by his powerful publication on crimes and punishments ... had the high honour of introducing humanity into the criminal codes of Europe."[146]

Though Cesare Beccaria had borrowed liberally from other Enlightenment thinkers as he wrote *On Crimes and Punishments*, it had been written in an accessible style—one highly readable by lawyers and non-lawyers alike. Its style, no doubt, is partly what made it so successful. It was short and concise, and its arguments could be understood by anyone—from farmers and mechanics to kings and barristers. After noting that *On Crimes and Punishments* "turned out to be very influential," one worldwide study of the death penalty put it this way in explaining its effects on the anti-gallows movement: "The first countries to abolish the death penalty were generally situated on the American continent, more specifically in South America." After taking note of Venezuela's abolition in 1863, that comparative study explains: "Costa Rica abolished the death penalty for all crimes in 1877 and, by the year 1910, Ecuador, Uruguay, and Colombia had followed the example."[147] Within the United States of America, a republic forged in 1776, it was individual state legislatures that, one by one, acted to curtail the use of executions after independence, which showed the sweep of Beccaria's reach as well as the impact of Beccaria's views on Beccaria's disciples. As Robert Cottrol, a law professor at George Washington University, explains: "State criminal codes were being amended to make punishments less severe. The new nation was a leader in limiting capital punishment."[148] Indeed, Beccaria's influence is apparent *throughout* the Americas, though the scope and extent of Beccaria's influence naturally varies by locale, dependent upon how individual readers of *On Crimes and Punishments* responded to it.

From north to south and east to west, Beccaria's writings certainly made a lasting impression and a profound impact on a variety of thinkers in the Americas. In a history of Ontario, historian Peter Oliver notes that Beccaria's influence "penetrated deeply into the psyche of Upper Canadian law reformers." Chief Justice John Robinson had absorbed Beccarian messages, as Oliver explains in this way: "Like the English reformers, the Upper Canadian chief justice had accepted Cesare Beccaria's condemnation of old-regime legal codes, and especially discretionary justice." "It is an admitted truth," Robinson reported to Home District jurors in October 1831, "that it is the *certainty* more than the *severity* of punishment which deters offenders." That language was taken directly from Beccaria's treatise.[149] The criminal law in Upper Canada would be reformed in 1833, the same year the legislature passed an "Act to Defray Expenses of Erecting a Penitentiary." An 1834 statute authorized the creation of a penitentiary, and—as historian Peter Oliver puts it—"the principal effect of the Tory law reform would be to end capital punishment for over a hundred offences." "For several years before the criminal law reform of 1833," Oliver writes, "Robinson and his fellow judges had been forced to work within the sentencing procedures of the old criminal code." "In applying these antiquated rules they had participated in the farce of sentencing criminals to death knowing they would be pardoned, and had resorted to fines, whippings, and brief gaol sentences, none of which Robinson regarded as satisfactory punishments for serious felonies." The statute of 1833 reportedly "marked a turning point in the administration of criminal justice in Upper Canada," reducing the number of capital offenses from about one hundred and fifty to twelve. "This firmly Beccarian statute," Oliver emphasized, "pronounced in favour of certain and proportionate punishment, uniformly applied." "It does not seem to be indispensable for the security and well being of society," the statute's preamble proclaimed, "that punishment of death should be inflicted in any other cases than those hereinafter mentioned."[150]

And the Upper Canadian experience was no aberration. "In view of their metropolitan prominence, and the derivative character of much of North America's early penal law," another historian notes, "it is unsurprising that monographs by Beccaria and Bentham found their way into Lower Canada, where their presence in original, translated, and edited versions can be readily documented." In *Essays in the History of Canadian Law*, that historian, Blaine Baker, puts it this way: "Although neither Bentham nor Beccaria drafted criminal-law codes for legislative enactment, their outlines for codification and their utilitarian justifications for liberalizing penal law supplied the cornerstones for several generations of transatlantic debate on criminal-law reform." The writings of American statesman and penal reformer Edward Livingston—"widely acknowledged as the early-nineteenth-century's leading publicist of Beccarian and Benthamite ideas about criminal-law reform on the North American continent," Baker stresses—were also circulated in Lower Canada, sometimes translated into French.[151]

Throughout Europe and the Americas, Cesare Beccaria's work thus found innumerable dedicated admirers, so many that its followers had a whole school of thought named after them. "The followers of Beccaria's theories," one book observes, "became known as the *classical school* of criminology, its first and founding school."[152] In that respect, Mexico, which gained its independence in 1821, and which adopted its liberal constitution in 1824,[153] provides a good—but again, but one—illustrative example. "Mexican liberals," historian Patrick Timmons explains, echoing the sentiments of other historians, "saw themselves as the Enlightenment's heirs." "In this regard, literate nineteenth-century Mexicans of the political class were aware of philosopher Cesare Beccaria's assessment of the futility of capital punishment," Timmons notes.[154] As St. John's University historian Robert Buffington stresses: "As 'enlightened' Bourbon reformers and post-Independence Mexican policy makers struggled with the perceived increase in crime that accompanied political and economic modernization, the legal theories of European social reformers like Beccaria and Bentham played an important role in informing the educated public imagination." Even before Mexico's break with Spain, the Mexican-born jurist Manuel de Lardizábal offered that "nothing is more important to a nation than having good criminal laws because they ensure civil liberty and, in large part, the well-being and security of the State."[155] "It is Beccaria," one criminology textbook emphasizes, identifying him as the leader of the classical school, "who pulled together many of the most powerful 18th-century ideas of democratic liberalism and connected them to issues of criminal justice."[156]

The Americas had indigenous populations, but lands there—in time—became European colonies. Consequently, in those European-centric days of colonialism, those colonies were subjected to Europe's then extremely harsh laws. What was being read and well received in Europe, and influencing laws (or at least the debate) there, thus became equally important, if not more so, to those colonized by the great European powers, especially those being subjected to tyrannical practices. Although the Inquisition and state censors had attempted to regulate the publication of books, anyone in power could not ignore Enlightenment thought and revolutionary impulses as they were to be found everywhere in that era, often in spite of the censors. For example, the writings of Montesquieu and Beccaria arrived in Spain in the 1760s and 1770s and were—in the words of one criminal justice annual—"espoused with great enthusiasm by a group of Spanish enlightenment thinkers."[157] As Alejandro Agüero and Marta Lorente explain in "Penal Enlightenment in Spain," the first translation of Beccaria's book was published in Spain, in Castilian, in 1774, but "Beccaria was known by the members of the Spanish enlightened elite even before 1774." "For their posts at the Royal Court," Agüero and Lorente write of those elites, "they had been sponsoring a wide range of economic and social reforms, in a context ideologically dominated by 'Enlightened Despotism' and known as the time of 'Bourbon reformism.'" "One of the prominent men of the Royal Court, Minister Campomanes," Agüero and Lorente note, "was personally involved, from both the Royal Council and the Royal Academy of History, in getting the required license for the translation of 'On crime and punishment' to be printed and published."[158] Even where it was banned, black-market copies might be obtained by enterprising intellectuals.

Centuries later, Beccaria's writings laid the foundation for the University of Chicago's now famed "Law and Economics" movement.[159] As Professor Bernard Harcourt writes of the work of Judge Richard Posner and American economist Gary Becker, both closely associated with the Chicago School of Economics: "Beccaria developed theories of marginal deterrence that later became a cornerstone of Becker and Posner's economic model of crime. 'If an equal punishment is laid down for two crimes which damage society equally, men will not have a stronger deterrent against committing the greater crime if they find it more advantageous to do so,' Beccaria wrote, prefacing later economic analysis of crime."[160] While Cesare Beccaria's work in the field of economics never became as well-known as or accessible internationally as his thoughts on penal reform as set forth in *On Crimes and Punishments*, Beccaria—along with his Milanese mentor, Pietro Verri—made important contributions to that field, too. "In 1769," *The Edinburgh Review* once reported, "the Empress Maria Theresa founded a similar chair in the University of Milan, and appointed the justly celebrated Marquis Beccaria its first professor."[161] Beccaria himself took on a number of tasks pertaining to economic development for the Habsburg dynasty in Austrian Lombardy. For example, in 1769, one publication, *Critical Memoirs of the Times*, gave this telling report for "*Jan. 14*" for Milan, Italy: "A society for the encouragement of agriculture and commerce, has lately been established here, under the auspices of her imperial majesty: the celebrated marquis de Beccaria, author of the Essay on Crimes and Punishments, is appointed president."[162]

In his role as a civil servant, Beccaria studied and tried to find solutions to numerous problems. He proposed the creation of academies to conduct agricultural research, with Beccaria looking for ways to increase the fertility of soil and boost crop yields. He organized competitions and prizes for the best crops, and through printing and distributing instructions, he helped peasants learn how best to sow and cultivate crops. He took up the subject of forestry and tree conservation, warning against the indiscriminate cutting of trees for commercial uses because of the long period of time it would take to regrow them. He advised that only as much timber should be cut in a given year as would regrow in that year—the sage words of an early conservationist. He recognized the importance of botany, chemistry and mineralogy, believing research in those areas would lead to innovation and new discoveries. He also studied trade between Lombardy and Switzerland and the state of pastures in Lombardy, and he wrote reports on the need for medical services for the rural poor, proposing that subsidies be provided so that doctors could afford to treat people of modest means. Anticipating subsidized modern-day health care for the needy, Beccaria stressed the need for free hospitalization for impoverished peasants as well as access to a free supply of drugs and medicines. And to improve the output and efficiency of mining operations in Lombardy, Beccaria suggested bringing in experts from Hungary.

In the 1770s, the Patriotic Society of Milan (*Società Patriotica di Milano*)—modeled after other societies formed in other cities in the Habsburg Empire—was formed to promote the "useful arts," especially agriculture, and Beccaria would become one of its presidents. Members of the Patriotic Society, Pietro Verri asserted, were expected to be "mediators between the educated physicist and the artisan machinist." In a book on the spread of Italy's scientific revolution, it is noted of the Patriotic Society that "[e]ven a rapid review of its activities provides many illustrations of the close interrelationships that existed between various sectors of society—public and private, professional and dilettante, middle class and aristocratic, secular and religious." The "very respectable" Patriotic Society, as *The Monthly Review* put it in the 1790s, published volumes of information on the arts and agriculture, and those volumes were described in English language publications. For example, *The Monthly Review* extracted a passage from one of the papers of the Patriotic Society on the culture of vines written by Don Giulio Bramieri, a patrician of Placentia.[163] It was noted in another publication—one published later—that an "ingenious" kneading machine, to mix things, was "first described in the Transactions of the Patriotic Society at Milan."[164]

The Patriotic Society of Milan was founded during the reign of Empress Maria Theresa, who died in 1780. As Denis Mack Smith writes in *The Making of Italy* of the parochial interests associated with the Lombard region: "A 'Patriotic Society' was formed at Milan in 1776, but its concern was Lombard and not Italian patriotism; and when it permitted itself some 'foreign' members, these included Venetians and Piedmontese as well as English and Germans." In its very first year, Milan's Patriotic Society for the Improvement of Agriculture, the Arts and Manufacturing offered a prize for anyone who could help identify a treatment for *pellagra*, a disease associated with four "D's": diarrhea, dermatitis, dementia and death. It was suggested as early as 1762 that the horrific disease—a vitamin deficiency now known to be caused by a chronic lack of niacin—could be caused by one's diet, and cases of pellagra were documented by Francesco Frapolli, a physician who, in 1771, published his work, "Animadversiones in Morbum Vulgo Pelagram," spelling *pellagra* with a single *l*. The prize ended up going to a Dr. Viemar, a physician who believed poverty and malnutrition to be the cause. Among the founders of the Milanese Patriotic Society was Marsilio Landriani, a man who was also a contributor to *Il Caffè*. In *The Medical Enlightenment of the Eighteenth Century*, it is noted that Beccaria's 1769–1770 lectures on "political agriculture" argued that "priestcraft and peasant prejudice were principal obstacles to the use of medical science in rural improvement."

Beccaria saw the world as interconnected, and he believed in shared prosperity, writing, for example, of agriculture: "We come now to a useful thought, that a nation can prosper at the expense of another only to a certain point; beyond that point our prosperity, in order to be a real one, must bring about the prosperity of others, because it is impossible to be happy or to be miserable in isolation: a sign, this, of a community of things, of a tacit brotherhood that nature has decreed for the whole human species." "This thought of a universal brotherhood," Beccaria declared, anticipating the Universal Declaration of Human Rights (1948) by many decades, "should lead us to a virtuous path—away from the narrow and petty views of selfish gain, toward the serene areas of justice and goodwill." The work of the Patriotic Society of Milan was, itself, specifically directed to the advancement of agriculture, the local economy and human happiness, with members grappling with such issues as olive production, "the cultivation of vines," "the best method of making and preserving the wines of Austrian Lombardy" and "the best method of preparing leather and skins." Other topics or technologies that the society took up: "a moveable tablet for the use of engravers," "microscopic lenses" and "a new machine for making them," and the best means for reaping corn. According to one source, *The New Annual Register*, published in 1790, the second volume of *The Transactions of the Patriotic Society of Milan* "contains a great variety of valuable dissertations, memoirs, answers to questions, and descriptions of new machines, which are intended to facilitate improvements in agriculture, manufactures, and commerce, that are too numerous to be specified by us." As *The New Annual Register* reported of the writings of Milan's Patriotic Society and their importance: "Many of them are of a more local nature, and calculated chiefly for the benefit of the country where they are published. Others of them, however, relate to objects of universal importance, and which have a considerable influence on the happiness of mankind in general."[165]

Perhaps most significantly, Cesare Beccaria was speaking and writing about economics before the appearance of *The Wealth of Nations* by Adam Smith, making Beccaria's academic notes—as well as his inaugural lecture at the Palatine School— of particular interest to historians. In 1769, Beccaria published *Piano d'Istruzione e Piano di Lezioni di Economia Pubblica*, also referred to as *Discourse on Public Economy and Commerce*. And in 1771, the same year Pietro Verri published his *Meditazione sulla Economia Politica* (1771), Beccaria began writing *Elementi di Economia Pubblica*, though that work—comprised of his lecture notes written from 1771 to 1772—was not published until 1804 after Beccaria's death. In the early 1770s, Pietro Verri clearly saw himself as an intellectual competitor to Cesare Beccaria, with both men making contributions to their society—and to posterity—in their own ways. Shortly before his own book was published in 1771, Pietro Verri—on January 23, 1771—wrote a letter to his brother Alessandro, with the rivalry between Pietro and Cesare as evident as ever, though one can sense at least a little softening—but much haughtiness—in Pietro's harsh rhetoric. As Pietro's letter to his brother reads: "Beccaria is not so haughty anymore; a few days ago I saw him and talked to him. He was so nice, just as he used to be. We talked about economics, and without boasting I can say that of the two it was not he who seemed to be a teacher. I talked freely because by now he is not in time to steal my ideas." Pietro Verri's book—a popular one—would get reprinted six times in two years and was translated into Dutch, French and German.[166] Meanwhile, Beccaria's project faltered as his administrative duties took up so much of his time.

In *Elementi di Economia Pubblica*, Beccaria defined "economia pubblica" as the art of preserving and increasing the wealth of nations while putting those resources to the best possible use.[167] "In his *Elementi di economia pubblica*, written in 1769 and posthumously published by Baron Custodi in 1804," writes Riccardo Faucci in *A History of Italian Economic Thought*, "Beccaria presented a model of the circular flow of an economy, illustrating the ways in which the different social classes spend their incomes and transform them into demand for the goods and services which the same classes cooperate in producing." In his *Of the Disorder and Remedies of Currencies in the State of Milan* (1762), Beccaria had written that "in most men there is a lack of vigour to work back to great and universal principles"—and throughout his life Beccaria was intent on trying to understand those principles. "Beccaria," Faucci explains, "assumed that non-agricultural workers need their wages in advance—while agricultural workers may directly draw from what they produce—under the classical assumption that wages exactly cover subsistence." As Faucci writes of Beccaria and his thinking on economics: "After sketching his general model, he examined the main features of growth, which consists of the increase of *prodotto contrattabile* [marketable product]. This result is achieved by maximizing the *travaglio utile* [useful labour], which in turn influences the population level." Productive, profitable work—and competition and productive capital—were thus priorities for Beccaria, who opposed monopolies. "The relationship between population and subsistence," Faucci summarizes Beccaria's line of thought, "is taken in the sense that the capacity of the latter to grow is seen as a limiting factor affecting the increase of the former."[168]

In a reflection of the analytical nature of the Enlightenment, Beccaria's *Elementi di Economia Pubblica* is broken into several distinct parts. Part I — "Principles and general view" — has three chapters. Chapter 1 discusses "capital, reproduction, division of labour, exchange, value, sectors in production of wealth"; Chapter 2 explores "[t]he nature of labour and consumption, value, wages and profits"; and Chapter 3 covers "population, its increase, decrease and measurement." Part II then covers "agriculture," including obstacles to its improvement, "small-scale and large-scale cultivation of the soil," "different methods of cultivation," and such diverse topics as "regulations in staple commodities," "pastoral activity," and "mining, fishing and hunting." The rest of *Elementi di Economia Pubblica* systematically covers other issues of interest to his contemporaries and to modern-day economists. While Part III covered "arts and manufacturing," Part IV takes on the broad issue of "commerce," with nine separate chapters in the latter part titled: (1) "Of value and price," (2) "Of money," (3) "Of circulation and competition," (4) "Of commerce," (5) "Of luxury," (6) "Of the interest of money," (7) "Of exchange rates," (8) "Of banking and credit," and (9) "Of public credit." An intended final part of Beccaria's *Elementi* was to have dealt with public finance, including the need for taxation, public administration and public goods, statistical information, and different types of government.[169]

It was not just some of Adam Smith's ideas in *The Wealth of Nations* that Cesare Beccaria presaged. In Beccaria's *Elements of Public Economy*, he also anticipated arguments made by Thomas Robert Malthus (1766–1834) as regards the relationship between population growth and the food supply. In his *Elements of Public Economy*, Beccaria emphasized: "Excessive population becomes a liability to a nation when there is not enough work for all the people; this is due to the fact that the idle inhabitants must be fed at the expense of the useful population." "Man is able to live and propagate as long as there are products that can feed him," he wrote, noting that "the population can increase as long as the means of subsistence increase." "These means," he continued, "may be augmented in a certain area thanks to a more perfected system of agriculture, or to the importation of products from other areas in exchange for services or work done in behalf of the foreign exporters — whose number, however, cannot increase beyond their own means of subsistence." In *An Essay on the Principle of Population* (1798), Malthus wrote about population size, procreation, and the scarcity of food, though — one source notes — "Cesare Beccaria had already declared the problem of population to be intimately connected with that of the means of subsistence." "The eclectic Beccaria," another text emphasizes, "is also credited with anticipating the economic notions of Thomas Malthus and Adam Smith and creating one of the world's first veterinary schools; he was also an early proponent of a decimal system of weights and measures." Beccaria in fact played in instrumental role in organizing and selecting the location for Lombardy's first veterinary school — one formed in the late 1780s after a couple of similar schools opened up in France in 1761 and 1765.

Cesare Beccaria saw the need for societal reform everywhere, and given that food shortages could occur, he was greatly concerned about population levels, productivity and the needs of the populace. "[T]he problems of population seem to have fascinated Beccaria," historian Marcello Maestro observes, noting that Beccaria discouraged bachelorhood as it would increase licentiousness. "Neither has he great sympathy for religious celibacy, which in his opinion should be limited to those who are clearly inspired by a spiritual vocation and voluntarily prefer that status to any other," Maestro explains of Beccaria, summarizing his views—and his personal experiences—as follows: "He condemns without reservation the habit of confining men and women to a life of seclusion because of financial considerations, such as the interest of certain families to keep their properties intact for reasons of power and prestige. This was an accepted custom at that time, and Beccaria had seen it adopted in his own family, as his father's brothers and sisters had had to enter religious orders. Beccaria considers this habit not only cruel, but potentially harmful if too many young people are thus taken away from productive life." Ever the mathematician, Beccaria—the aristocrat who tried to help his own brothers find suitable employment—produced mortality tables and collected data on life expectancies in various countries.[170] "Beccaria," historian Garry Wills explains in *Inventing America: Jefferson's Declaration of Independence*, taking particular note of Beccaria's frequent use of probabilities and statistics, "also uses '*il calculo delle probabilità*,' part of his '*aritmetica politica*,' to establish the unlikelihood of procuring truthful evidence from torture ... and the greater likelihood of false testimony in the more atrocious crimes."[171]

As a civil servant in Milan, Beccaria served in a variety of roles and took on many different projects and tasks. For instance, he wrote a report on a system of measures that led France to start using the metric system. As Lynn McDonald writes in *The Early Origins of the Social Sciences*: "Beccaria's economic reforms included a new, metric system of weights and measures, which the French National Assembly adopted in 1790."[172] Measurements in old European systems—a *foot* to mark the distance between planted potatoes and an *ell*, an abbreviation for *elbow*, to measure cloth—were inexact, something that Beccaria recognized impeded trade. "In the 1770s," a history of the metric system notes of the role that Beccaria played, "he was asked by the Austrian rulers of Milan to reform weights and measures in their Italian possessions, and so at the same time his friend Condorcet was trying and failing to give France a uniform, scientifically based system of measurement, Beccaria was succeeding in doing just that for Lombardy."[173] Although Beccaria had proposed a decimal system to the government of Milan in 1780, that scheme had not been adopted at that time, largely because of financial concerns.

Beccaria's report, "On the reduction of the measures of length to uniformity in the state of Milan," was presented on January 25, 1780. It acknowledged Paolo Frisi for his precise mathematical calculations, with Beccaria building a model of the new standard and creating tables showing the ratio between the new measures and the old measures. While Beccaria, with Frisi's assistance, had proposed an innovative decimal system (with all measures to be divided in decimal fractions "in view of the great simplicity that this type of arithmetic brings to all sorts of operations"), the scheme he and Frisi devised did not come to fruition—at least not in full—in Beccaria's lifetime. Frisi and Beccaria has proposed using geodetic measurements, with the proposal calling for a new unit of length that would be divisible into 1/10ths, 1/100ths, and 1/1000ths (and that could be multiplied by 10, 100, and 1,000) to form other measures. "In the end," Witold Kula writes in *Measures and Men*, "on 30 January 1781, Joseph II and Ferdinand signed in Vienna a decree that laid down a 'minimalist' reform program: measures of length alone were to be standardized for the time being, the ell of Milan providing the standard, and the reform was restricted to the state of Milan."[174]

Between 1771 and 1782, the Austrian Habsburgs launched a reform program in Milan to standardize local measurements, and Cesare Beccaria—under Chancellor Kaunitz's supervision—had been instructed to examine the length of the Milanese *ell*. A decree signed in Vienna in 1781 called for standard measurement of lengths in Milan, and the Milanese *ell* was to be used as the standard. The stated rationale for reform: "The dimensions and diversity of the measures in use in different regions of our state, although it has one law and obeys one ruler, and the absence or inexactitude of the standards employed by the agencies of control—these are matters that have always been considered as sources of errors ... and a hindrance to the flow of secure internal and foreign trade."[175] This decree came about as a result of a report that Beccaria prepared. As one London publication, *The Foreign Review*, later observed in 1829, lauding that report and Beccaria himself: "Nor is the idea of applying the decimal system, taken from the system of the earth, to weights and measures, an exotic in Italy. *Beccaria*, whose book '*Dei delitti e delle pene*,' has eclipsed so many other titles which that great man had to the esteem of the world, as far back as 1780, suggested this very system in a report which he made to the government of Lombardy on the subject."[176] Lombardy, one journal, *Studies in Eighteenth-Century Culture*, points out, had "a bewildering variety of standards of measurement," with Beccaria proposing "a simple, universal, decimal system, a suggestion that anticipated the metric system in many respects."[177]

Although Cesare Beccaria's dream of a truly universal system of measurement did not come to pass during his life, it wasn't long before such a system became compulsory in France. "[I]n 1790, in the climate of reform that was brought about by the French Revolution," historian Marcello Maestro writes in a chapter of his biography about Beccaria's work for Milan's Supreme Economic Council, "Charles de Talleyrand presented to the French National Assembly a report in which a universal system of measures was advocated." A member of the French National Assembly, Charles Maurice de Talleyrand-Périgord (1754–1838) presented the work of a committee that had been appointed by France's National Assembly to consider the suitability of adopting a fraction of the meridian as the new length of measure. Ultimately, that committee had chosen to use as the new unit of measure the *meter* (*i.e.*, 1/40,000,000 of the earth's circumference); "[t]hus," Maestro explains, "a decimal system was developed in which the square meter, the liter, and the kilogram became the units in their categories, all being based on the meter as the unit of length." Between 1796 and 1797, sixteen prototype meters were carved in marble and placed around Paris, two of which—marked "METRE"—still remain today. As Maestro records of the significance of what ultimately transpired in France just a few years after Beccaria's death: "In 1799 a law established the new standards officially; the new system became compulsory in France in 1801, and soon after in many other countries. Beccaria was dead by then, but his dream of a universal system of weights and measures had come true: a system almost identical in principle to the one he had first outlined, with all the standards interrelated and based on a unit of length derived from the terrestrial circumference, the whole system made simple by the adoption of the decimal scale."[178]

During his lifetime, Cesare Beccaria became a valued and respected member of the Austrian Habsburg administration. In 1778, Beccaria was appointed Officer of the Mint and he became a member of an inquiry into monetary reform—something he had long considered. In Milan, his native city, Beccaria was also tapped in 1786—at a pivotal moment in Italian history—to lead the Department of Agriculture, Industry and Commerce. "At the time of the grave silk crisis of 1787," one history of Italy notes, "Cesare Beccaria stressed how the 'disorder' created by unemployment was not 'particular to the city of Como, but general to the whole State'." Shortly thereafter, in 1790, Emperor Joseph II died, to be replaced by his brother, Leopold II, who had been a liberal ruler as the Grand Duke of Tuscany. Around that time, Beccaria had been tasked by the Habsburg dynasty with making recommendations about fixing labor relations in the textile industry. As one historian observes: "The development of the silk industry in the Como area had been accompanied by growing tensions between the factory owners and the workers. Since there were no labor contracts, wages were lowered when work was scarce and men were dismissed without compensation. The ups and downs of silk production meant a precarious existence for the workers and a constant fear of remaining without a job." Beccaria felt that the city of Como owed a duty to its workers because the local economy had benefitted greatly from their labors. After the city council rejected Beccaria's advice to grant a subsidy to the unemployed and to diversify local industries, labor demonstrations and violence broke out in Como and Beccaria was asked to go to Como to help restore peace and tranquility.

Like many of his friends and fellow Italian economists, Cesare Beccaria emerged as a voice for the downtrodden and as an opponent of primogeniture—the legal custom whereby the first-born son would inherit his father's estate in preference to any daughters. "Italian primogeniture," author Maurizio Isabella explains, "had been attacked by economists like Antonio Genovesi, Pietro Verri, Alfonso Longo, and Cesare Beccaria on the grounds that it served to perpetuate the power of a parasitic aristocracy, constituted a symbol of privilege and a major obstacle to a more entrepreneurial exploitation of the land, and hence was a hindrance to the development of commerce, agriculture, and population growth." Beccaria favored productivity over privilege, and idle hands meant less productive lands. "Primogeniture," historian R. B. Bernstein writes in his biography of Thomas Jefferson, the politician who successfully advocated for the abolition of the practice, "required that, if a landowner had not made a will directing who should get his property, the oldest son would get the whole estate." In a report he issued on September 17, 1790, on the situation in Como, Beccaria specifically rejected a policy of repression and a policy, suggested by the industrialists, of rounding up disgruntled laborers and putting them in the army. Instead, Beccaria—a proponent of social justice and equality—expressed concern about "the odious and irritating contrast between the poverty of the pleading workers and the wealth of the citizens armed in defense against them."

But though economic development activities—and fighting poverty—took up most of his time as an administrator, Cesare Beccaria never lost his interest in penal reform. In 1789, in fact, Cesare Beccaria became the head of the Department of Justice, with the preparation of reports—as in any bureaucracy—becoming a big part of his job. In 1791, he was specifically appointed as a member of a commission that took up the subject of the reformation of criminal legislation in Lombardy. Chancellor Kaunitz told Beccaria that the new emperor had specifically requested Beccaria's participation on the commission, which was to study the possibility of applying the Austrian code to Lombardy. In that role, the question of the death penalty's efficacy came up again. And just as he had opposed the use of executions in 1764, Beccaria opposed their use more than 25 years later. Thus, in 1792, in articulating the minority position of the commission charged with drafting a new penal code for Austrian Lombardy, Beccaria—joined by two other men, Francesco Gallarati Scotti and Paolo Risi—articulated once more the long-standing rationales for his anti-death penalty views and added yet another: the irrevocability of capital punishment. Written in the midst of the French Revolution, that minority report favored "forced labour" and "perpetual enslavement" for criminals committing the most serious crimes. "[W]e believe," the three dissenters wrote, "that the death penalty is not suitable" because "it is not just"; "it is not necessary," "because it cannot be undone"; and "because it is less efficacious than perpetual punishment equipped with a good deal of continuous publicity."[179]

In addition to economic and criminal justice matters, Cesare Beccaria thought a lot about issues of style, the thing that made *Dei delitti e delle pene* such a phenomenal success. After his trip to Paris in 1766, Beccaria needed a new subject to write about— and he ended up returning to a topic, the skillful use of language, he had written about before. As a member of the Academy of Fists, Cesare Beccaria had written for the *Il Caffè* a "Fragment on Style," a subject that continued to hold his attention and imagination even after the publication of his popular treatise on crime and punishment. After his trip to Paris, Beccaria had considered two separate projects—a book on style or one on the development of civilization, from a barbaric state to one focused on the importance of law to the development of an organized society. Ultimately, Beccaria chose to write on the first topic, writing an essay titled *Ricerche intorno alla natura dello stile* (*Research on the Nature of Style*) that was published in the early 1770s. "The best styles," Beccaria concluded, "are those which vary continually the ways of presenting the largest possible number of feelings and thus maintain for a longer period an air of novelty and keep our attention always engaged." "[I]n 1770, when he was teaching economics at the Palatine School," Marcello Maestro recounts, "the book was printed in Milan by the publisher Galeazzi. It was, to be exact, only the first part of his projected book, and Beccaria promised in the introduction that a second part would follow in a short time." The increasingly busy Beccaria, however, never completed the second part, and he only ended up writing one additional chapter that went unpublished in his lifetime. Giuseppe Galeazzi was the royal printer and a bookseller in Milan, and he published a wide array of titles, from works on opera to, in 1784, a proposed design for a "flying boat" to be powered by rowing and sails.[180]

Unlike *Dei delitti e delle pene*, Beccaria's essay on style met with little success, though it was translated from Italian into French in 1771 as *Recherches sur le style* by André Morellet. Its reception in France, historian Marcello Maestro reports, "was far from enthusiastic." "Apart from this French version of Morellet," Maestro notes, "no other translation was made, but there have been reprints of the Italian text in several editions of Beccaria's writings." The ideas on language and usage, Maestro emphasizes, "were not developed, and the book remained somewhat uneven and incomplete." The work, Maestro concluded, was "badly organized and lacking the systematic order and discipline of the treatise *On Crimes and Punishments*." Containing disjointed little essays, Beccaria's treatment of style discussed the use of language and had chapters on adjectives and human passions in which he discussed, among other things, the causes of laughter. But despite its noted deficiencies, the book was dedicated to Count Karl Joseph von Firmian, Beccaria's "old friend and protector." It was with these words of appreciation that Beccaria dedicated his new book to Count Firmian: "With the most sincere feelings of gratitude I offer you this work which perhaps will have the sole, although glorious, merit of having your name in the front and of giving the author the hope that he will still have in the future your highly appreciated patronage." In the preface to his exploration of the nature of style, Beccaria wrote that "beauty, goodness, and usefulness are closely related to one another and have all one thing in common: the love of happiness." "[M]orality, politics, and the fine arts," Beccaria added, are "the sciences of goodness, usefulness, and beauty" and "all have their origin in one first science, the science of man."[181]

After Beccaria died at age 56 in 1794, possibly of a stroke (then called *apoplexy*), his *Elements of Public Economy* was published posthumously in 1804, a full decade later. It was to be his last book-length treatment of a subject. During his lifetime, Beccaria had worked to improve the Italian economy and people's lives and living conditions, and he wrote on the nature of human happiness and the elements of style, trying his best to express how one should live and best express oneself. "Beccaria, apart from opposing capital punishment and torture," Lynn McDonald writes in *The Early Origins of the Social Sciences*, "promoted monetary and trade reform, fairer taxes, a health care system, job creation, and the metric system."[182] Whereas *Elements of Political Economy* was cobbled together after Beccaria's death, *On Crimes and Punishments*—written in a clear manner, making it highly accessible—is reflective of his overall approach to rhetoric and communication, at least when he was writing at his best and had some editorial assistance.[183] In the end, Pietro Verri—the prime motivator behind Cesare Beccaria's writing of *Dei delitti e delle pene*, and the man who contributed so much to its style, its ideas, and its success—made peace with Cesare Beccaria, his younger friend and one-time rival, if not fully in life, than at least after Beccaria's death. Three years after Beccaria died, as one book, *Criminal Justice Masterworks*, points out, Pietro Verri—"to demonstrate Milan's esteem for Beccaria"—passionately "urged the city to erect a statue of Beccaria."[184]

The foundational role that Cesare Beccaria's book played in the American Revolution—the revolution that, more than any other, shaped the modern world—is now crystal clear from the historical record. In *An Oration Pronounced on the 4th July, 1805, at Pembroke; at the Request of a Convention of Republicans, from Various Parts of the County of Plymouth*, a Massachusetts native, John Danforth Dunbar, specifically invoked Beccaria's name in a Fourth of July celebration. "This is the birth day of our nation, and it again finds us celebrating the joyous event," Dunbar said near the outset, invoking the names of prominent American founders who had carefully read Beccaria's little treatise before the issuance of the Declaration of Independence. "Nine and twenty times has the earth performed its annual revolution since the Charter of our Independence, penned by Jefferson and subscribed by Hancock, announced freedom and sovereignty to this western world," Dunbar said on the anniversary of America's independence. "It was then a new era commenced in the history of the world," Dunbar said, emphasizing that "a nation was born in a day" and that "thirteen colonies scattered over an immense extent of territory ... united as a band of brothers" to "form a sovereignty by the appellation of the United States of America." "Fellow Citizens," he added, "we yet enjoy all the privileges and immunities of freemen, that were acquired by our soldiers and statesmen." Among the figures who shaped American views of what those privileges and immunities are, one must list Cesare Beccaria.

Beccaria's words, as history shows, were not only invoked by the Continental Congress in 1774, just before the Revolutionary War broke out; they were also still being quoted—often with great fanfare—during the ratification period for America's U.S. Constitution and its Bill of Rights, as well as in the decades that followed.[185] In his speech, John Danforth Dunbar, for example, laid out the principles—freedom and equality—for which the American Revolution was fought. "It is proper on this occasion," Dunbar said in his own Fourth of July oration, "not only to rejoice and be thankful for what we possess; but to call to mind the principles on which those rights were established; and the means by which they may be preserved; the dangers (if any) which threaten their existence; and to contemplate that political character, which influenced us as a nation to the acquisition, and without which they cannot be continued." "The principles for which we contended," he stressed, "were our natural freedom and equality." Dunbar then detailed a whole smorgasbord of rights for which Americans had fought and, in many cases, died: "[t]he right to worship God as conscience dictates"; "the right of self government residing in the People"; "the accountability of all vested with authority to the People"; "the right of the People to reform, alter, or change their government when their happiness requires it"; "the right to free and frequent elections"; "the right to a trial by jury"; "security from unreasonable searches and seizures"; "the liberty of the Press"; "the right to keep and bear arms"; and "the right of assembling and consulting for the public good." "These," Dunbar emphasized, "are all of them rights of which Britain sought to deprive us: they are the rights which this country fought to defend, and which were maintained at the point of the bayonet." "These principles," he observed, "are totally inconsistent with monarchical, and aristocratical power, of course they are objects of hatred to those who are ambitious of those powers."

It was at that point that, returning to the quotation from Beccaria that the Continental Congress itself used in 1774 on the eve of the Revolutionary War, John Danforth Dunbar chose to invoke Cesare Beccaria's name in his Fourth of July oration. As Dunbar told his fellow Massachusetts republicans: "We must not be surprised to find in this happy country a junto of men adverse to these principles. There is, says the celebrated Marquis Beccaria, 'in every human society an effort constantly tending to confer on one part the heighth of power and happiness; and to reduce the other to the extreme of weakness and misery.'" Dunbar's oration then continued, returning to themes and subjects that Beccaria had taken up in *Dei delitti e delle pene* four decades earlier: "The adventitious influence of wealth, when increased to excess, has as invariably produced that pride and hauteur, that disdain of equality, and that itch of arbitrary power which constitutes the first principle of aristocracy; as an excessive richness of soil produces rank, noisome and destructive weeds."[186] The role played by the Italian Enlightenment and by Cesare Beccaria's writings had now come full circle: not only had Beccaria's words inspired the American Revolution, they were then being used—on the anniversary of the Declaration of Independence—to celebrate the success of that revolution.

At that time, John Danforth Dunbar was concerned about Federalist ambitions that he felt contradicted republican principles—the principles that imbued the American Revolution itself. As Dunbar's oration, seeking to stamp out monarchical and aristocratic impulses, reads: "As it is the business of a wise cultivator to eradicate those destructive weeds, and destroy the very nests of those insects and reptiles which feed upon them; and to compel this excessive luxuriance to contribute to the support and comfort of life: so it is the object of every free government to counteract the effect of excessive wealth, and compel its too rich possessor to contribute to the public weal; to discountenance those pimps and parasites who for ever attend the levees of wealth and grandeur, and to prevent that corruption which none but the wealthy can practice." Pitting "virtue and republicanism" against "wealth and corruption," Dunbar passionately asserted and warned that—as regards the "propensity so natural to human ambition," the one identified by Beccaria—"[a]ll the Republics, ever established, except our own, have fallen victims to this corrupt principle." "It extinguishes," Dunbar said of the corrupting principle of ambition, "the principles of piety, virtue, temperance, moderation, industry and frugality, without which, freedom cannot be maintained."[187]

In the eighteenth century, America's economy was predominantly predicated on agriculture and the U.S. Constitution itself had rejected aristocratic governance—one fueled, more often than not, by greed and the quest for more power. According to Article I, section 9 of the Constitution: "No title of nobility shall be granted by the United States: and no person holding any office of profit or trust under them, shall, without the consent of Congress, accept of any present, emolument, office, or title, of any kind whatever, from any king, prince, or foreign state."[188] Dunbar himself found distinct advantages in that broad-based agricultural economy, comparing it with republics of old. As Dunbar spoke of the republics of the past: "Ancient Republics were chiefly confined to cities; few of the electors were the owners and cultivators of land. When the Roman arms extended their limits, they reduced the conquered countries to provinces. The plunder of those countries accumulated in the hands of a few individuals: corruption prevailed, and to such a degree, that Pompey, Cæsar and Crassus, and their rich connections, were able to purchase a majority of the votes in Rome." "Even Cato himself descended to this practice, and publicly purchased the votes of the people," Dunbar said. In its heyday and in hindsight, the Roman Republic had frequently been held up and glorified as a model of government. "At about the same time that popular government was introduced in Greece, it also appeared on the Italian Peninsula in the city of Rome," one source emphasizes. As that book, *Forms of Government and the Rise of Democracy*, reports: "[T]he Romans called their system a *rēspūblica*, or republic, from the Latin *rēs*, meaning thing or affair, and *pūblicus* or *pūblica*, meaning public—thus, a republic was the thing that belonged to the Roman people, the *populus romanus*." "[T]hroughout the republican era (until roughly the end of the 1st century BCE)," that book emphasizes, "Roman assemblies were held in the very small Forum at the centre of the city."[189]

Rome had been founded way back in 753 B.C.,[190] but Dunbar and others in the eighteenth and nineteenth centuries still carefully studied the Roman republic. As Dunbar emphasized: "Rome then afforded an example, never to be forgotten by a free people. Luxury and debauchery were prevalent among all classes of citizens: every favor was to be purchased with money: and the priests of Rome prostituted the rights of religion to the purposes of faction." "Amidst this universal corruption of morals," Dunbar recounted, noting that Julius Cæsar became "sole master" of the Roman republic, "monarchy arose as a necessary appendage of wickedness." "Thank Heaven the great body of the people of our Republic are farmers," Dunbar said of the United States, emphasizing: "not only farmers but enlightened and independent farmers" who were "in full possession of the free elective franchise established by our constitutions, with sufficient knowledge to understand those instruments, and appreciate their value." Dunbar then quoted "Col. Humphries"—said to be "[o]ne of our best writers"—as follows: "[T]here is something elevating to the soul in the consciousness of being lord of the soil. It converts the farmer into a species of rural philosopher, by inspiring an honest pride in his rank as a freeman, flattering the natural propensity for personal independence, and nourishing an unlimited hospitality and philanthropy in his social character." "Our almost unlimited extent of territory promises an inexhaustive supply of farms to our encreasing population," Dunbar said, anticipating western expansion without taking account of the involuntary removals of Native Americans—what came to be known as the Trail of Tears, one marked by death, disease and starvation—that would ensue as tribal nations were forced off their ancestral lands. As Dunbar, living at a time of the egregious exploitation of Native peoples, indentured servants and slaves, declared without flushing out such exploitation: "The ease with which land is acquired, and the profits of their cultivation has raised the price of labor to such a degree, as almost to invert the obligations of master and servants. A hired servant, in a short time, is able to purchase a farm and live independently. This will prevent those born without a patrimony from becoming the tools of some rich employer."[191]

In ancient Rome, Emperor Justinian had, in the sixth century A.D., codified Roman law, a subject Cesare Beccaria would have studied carefully at the University of Pavia.

"For hundreds of years," a book on Justinian I observes, "Roman laws were written in books and tablets." As another source notes of that ancient history and an erstwhile code that authorized death for a variety of crimes: "The Twelve Tables of Rome, developed in 450 B.C., were the first written laws of the Roman Republic. These laws were an attempt by the plebeians to ensure that Roman judges did not favor one class over another." Dissatisfied with the way in which the law had developed, Justinian, the Byzantine emperor who reigned from 527 to 565 A.D., asked a group of men with special knowledge of the laws to gather together all of the Roman laws and to systematically compile them in an order that made logical sense. This new system of laws, a multi-year revision effort that came to be known as the Justinian Code, was then written down in one place and called the *Corpus Juris Civilis* (*The Body of Civil Law*). Though Greek was the Byzantine language of administration, the *Corpus Juris Civilis* was written in Latin, the language of Roman law and the elite. The project itself actually had four distinct components: the *Code*, containing imperial enactments; the *Digest*, containing the writings of jurists; the *Institutes*, a kind of textbook for students to learn the law; and the *Novels*, or Justinian's own new enactments. Many of the ideas in Justinian's Code, such as the concept that a person is "innocent until proven guilty," remain part of modern law today. It was in the latter half of the eleventh century, in Italy, that a manuscript containing the *Corpus Juris Civilis* was rediscovered in a library in Pisa and that scholars in Bologna's university began to intensely study Roman law, sparking renewed interest in it.[192]

Harkening back to a Beccarian theme, John Danforth Dunbar—yet another admirer of *On Crimes and Punishments*, one in a long line—worried about situations "where the extreme inequality of wealth renders one portion of men subservient to the other." In his oration, he specifically emphasized the following advantages of America's still relatively new republic: "The yeomanry of this country are generally well instructed. Our town schools equally open to the rich and poor, diffuse knowledge so generally to a certain degree, as keeps the people from being their own enemies through ignorance; and so long as knowledge is generally diffused, tyranny will show his head only to lose it." Praising religious freedom and the separation of church and state, the ideals Jefferson and Madison fought so hard for, Dunbar then observed: "The universal freedom of religious sentiments, established by the several state constitutions, and by the constitution of the United States, will always remain an insurmountable barrier to the introduction of arbitrary governments." "The priests of an established religion, where the dictates of conscience are silenced by the terrors of human laws and punishments," he said, "have never failed, in any country, to assume the attributes of Deity." "The power of forgiving sins is claimed by the English clergy," he noted, well aware of the tradition of *benefit of clergy*, a legal doctrine allowing death sentences to be set aside.[193] Touting "the most republican features in our constitution," Dunbar contrasted republican principles with those of ambitious Federalists, it being crystal clear which side Dunbar put himself on:

> The constitution establishes a liberal suffrage to protect the rights of the people.

They wish to confine suffrage to a few, the better to control the many.

The constitution establishes a militia.

They want a standing army.

The constitution directs economy that the people may be happy. They wish for excises lest the people should be too happy.

The constitution declares the people sole guardians of their own rights.

They declare the people their own worst enemies.

Near the end of his speech, sounding a very Beccarian tone, Dunbar spoke of "pursuing our own happiness, and enjoying all the good things that Providence may bestow" and of "laws of kindness administered by the wisdom and mildness of an angel."[194]

While Cesare Beccaria's ideas had a global reach, *On Crimes and Punishments* indisputably had an almost immediate impact on American soil—a fact that Dunbar himself acknowledged through his carefully chosen words. Beccaria argued against the arbitrary power of judges, favoring a fixed code of laws instead of the whim of a multitude of judges making capricious decisions. America's Founding Fathers, favoring equality (at least for men of their own race), themselves railed against monarchical power and arbitrary government. And the development of *written* codes and *written* constitutions—found at both the state and federal levels in the United States—helped to further the Rule of Law in a Beccarian fashion. As George Washington—in his valedictory statement as he prepared to step off the public stage and return to his life as a farmer and plantation owner—said of the new American government in his famous 1796 Farewell Address:

> Respect for its authority, compliance with its laws, acquiescence in its measures, are duties enjoined by the fundamental maxims of true liberty. The basis of our political systems is the right of the people to make and to alter their constitutions of government. But the Constitution which at any time exists, till changed by an explicit and authentic act of the whole people, is sacredly obligatory upon all. The very idea of the power and the right of the people to establish government presupposes the duty of every individual to obey the established government.

The Rule of Law—as enforced by the world's courts—is now a bedrock feature of America's representative democracy as well as that of other Western democracies.[195]

Cesare Beccaria's impact, both immediate and long lasting, was explicitly acknowledged even decades after America's founding in the country's breadbasket, its heartland. For example, an Indiana legislative report from 1842, inquiring into whether life imprisonment should be substituted for capital punishment, called that question—one inspired by Beccaria—"of deep and abiding interest." Indiana state senator Robert C. Gregory made this statement in his report: "We live in an age when *mere* regard for old and long established customs is not permitted to outweigh the dictates of sound reason and enlightened policy; if capital punishment is right it can be proven to be so by sound logical reasoning; if it is wrong, no sophistry can long shield it from the scrutinizing gaze of the public eye." "It is the remark of the celebrated Marquis Beccaria whose philosophic eye penetrated as deep into the hidden springs of human action as any other writing on this subject," Gregory's report continued, "'that crimes are more effectually prevented by the *certainty* than the *severity* of punishment,' and the history of the human race abundantly proves this to be true; if there were no other instances, the twenty years reign of Elizabeth empress of Russia, would be sufficient to convince every unprejudiced mind."[196] Of course, Cesare Beccaria's writings on capital punishment were just one aspect of Beccaria's broader influence on eighteenth- and nineteenth-century legal systems. Beccaria's insistence that laws further human happiness and the public good was likewise instrumental in convincing people to abandon archaic practices in favor of a new, much more progressive approach to law and governance.

Sadly, in twenty-first century America, Beccaria's influence on American law—and the impact of the Italian Enlightenment more broadly—has largely been forgotten. This is true even though the French Enlightenment's impact on early American law remains well known by most U.S. lawyers and judges. A lot of that probably has to do with the fact that Beccaria's name does not appear in any of *The Federalist Papers*, while Montesquieu's name appears in four—*No. 9, No. 43, No. 47* and *No. 78*. Alexander Hamilton referred to Montesquieu four separate times in *Federalist No. 9* in discussing republicanism and confederate republics,[197] with James Madison—in *Federalist No. 43*—bringing up Montesquieu's name two additional times, also in the context of discussing confederate republics.[198] In *Federalist No. 47*, Madison refers to Montesquieu by name five more times, giving Montesquieu particular prominence. As regards the idea that "the three great departments of power should be separate and distinct," Madison wrote, speaking of legislative, executive and judicial powers, "[t]he oracle who is always consulted and cited on this subject is the celebrated Montesquieu."[199] And in the now much-invoked *Federalist No. 78*, Hamilton—in discussing the judiciary—also cites "[t]he celebrated Montesquieu."[200] Beccaria, though once on the tip of every founder's tongue, is left out in the cold in spite of the fact that Beccaria's writings were hugely influential in both Europe and America when *The Federalist Papers* were written. Victor Hugo himself once wrote that "Montesquieu engendered Beccaria" and that the writings of Beccaria and Montesquieu are, in fact, "closely connected."[201]

In the haste of their preparation, or, more likely, simply because the proposed U.S. Constitution was an instrument to govern the structure of America's *federal* government, *The Federalist Papers* never made explicit mention of Cesare Beccaria. At that time, there were only a few federal crimes, with *state* governments—not the *federal* government—playing the predominant role in administering the criminal law and in bringing criminal prosecutions.[202] The crime of treason came up in Madison's *Federalist No. 43*, with Madison writing of one of only a handful of federal crimes: "As treason may be committed against the United States, the authority of the United States ought to be enabled to punish it." "But as new-fangled and artificial treasons, have been the great engines, by which violent factions, the natural offspring of free Governments, have usually wrecked their alternative malignity on each other," Madison warned of the risks. "[T]he Convention," he stressed, assuring New Yorkers, the original audience for *The Federalist Papers*, "have with great judgment opposed a barrier to this peculiar danger, by inserting a constitutional definition of the crime, fixing the proof necessary for conviction of it, and restraining the Congress, even in punishing it, from extending the consequences of guilt beyond the person of its author." "In a confederacy founded on republican principles, and composed of republican members," Madison concluded, "the superintending government ought clearly to possess authority to defend the system against aristocratical or monarchical innovations."[203]

In *Federalist No. 74*, Alexander Hamilton—in another reference to "crime" found in *The Federalist Papers*—wrote about the President's role as commander-in-chief. Though Hamilton, like Madison, did not explicitly reference Beccaria's treatise either, it is clear from the text of *Federalist No. 74* that Hamilton was living in the Age of Beccaria. In addressing the proposed power in the U.S. Constitution for the President "to grant reprieves and pardons for offences against the United States," Hamilton wrote: "Humanity and good policy conspire to dictate, that the benign prerogative of pardoning should be as little as possible fettered or embarrassed. The criminal code of every country partakes so much of necessary severity, that without an easy access to exceptions in favor of unfortunate guilt, justice would wear a countenance too sanguinary and cruel."[204] While Beccaria opposed the use of pardons, believing that punishments should be mild and certain rather than harsh and subject to later remediation, he also rejected punishments that were not absolutely necessary. Until criminal codes became less sanguinary, there would be a need to retain the power of executive clemency to mitigate the effects of such draconian codes. Beccaria's influence, in truth, is all over the historical record, though not explicitly acknowledged in the *Federalist Papers* or by name in American constitutions. "Many of the revolutionary state constitutions," writes historian Gordon Wood in *The Radicalism of the American Revolution*, "had promised in Beccarian fashion to end punishments that were 'cruel and unusual' and to make them 'less sanguinary, and in general more proportionate to the crimes.'"[205] Prohibitions on "sanguinary" punishments—and in favor of "proportionate" punishments—were frequently included in various early American state constitutions, reflecting the sentiment of the day.[206]

Indeed, in *Federalist No. 84*, Alexander Hamilton—in discussing the protections provided in the proposed Constitution for trial by jury and habeas corpus, and against *ex post facto* laws and bills of attainder—struck a very Beccarian chord. As Hamilton wrote: "The creation of crimes after the commission of the fact, or in other words, the subjecting of men to punishment for things which, when they were done, were breaches of no law, and the practice of arbitrary imprisonments have been in all ages the favourite and most formidable instruments of tyranny." "The observations of the judicious Blackstone," Hamilton continued, referencing the English jurist who had, in his own *Commentaries on the Laws of England*, praised Beccaria by name, "are well worthy of recital." Hamilton then quoted Blackstone: "'To bereave a man of life (says he) or by violence to confiscate his estate, without accusation or trial, would be so gross and notorious an act of despotism, as must at once convey the alarm of tyranny throughout the whole nation; but confinement of the person by secretly hurrying him to gaol, where his sufferings are unknown or forgotten, is a less public, a less striking, and therefore a *more dangerous engine* of arbitrary government.'"[207] Beccaria had also advocated public punishments, an idea largely embraced in America's founding period, though Dr. Benjamin Rush ended up opposing them after a period of experimentation and experience in Pennsylvania. A Pennsylvania law had required offenders to work on the streets of Philadelphia dressed in prison garb, with the hair on their heads shaved off as a form of humiliation.

In post-Revolutionary War Pennsylvania, the state, in Beccarian fashion, had quickly begun experimenting with new kinds of punishments. In lieu of executing certain offenders, those convicted of non-homicidal crimes were ordered to do hard, public labor on canals, roads and other public works. They infamously came to be known as "wheelbarrow men," so named because the state legislature, in 1786, enacted a penal code that provided that all convicts other than those sentenced to be hanged be put to "servitude" as "wheelbarrowmen" on the state's highways, forts, roads and mines. "In echoes of Beccaria and the English parliament's failed Dock Yards bill," Rebecca McLennan writes in *The Crisis of Imprisonment*, "Pennsylvania lawmakers reasoned that the sight of convicts, shorn of their hair and beards, working silently and obediently, in distinctive garb whose markings identified the convict's particular crime, would both impress upon free passers-by the idea that ignominious punishment awaited anyone who committed a crime and allow the elimination of bodily chastisements from the state's penal system."

The wheelbarrow men went to work during the summer of 1786. Soon thereafter, however, problems arose. During the Constitutional Convention, for example, one group of wheelbarrow men who had escaped attempted to rob Alexander Hamilton and his wife as they rode in their carriage. Not only did almost three dozen wheelbarrow men escape at the same time in 1788, but Dr. Rush and others came to believe that the practice would not help to reform the offenders but would instead mark and stigmatize them for life. As a result, Pennsylvanians moved to having convicted offenders labor in a "house of repentance" or a "penitentiary-house." "Under this penitential mode of punishment," McLennan explains of the way the system was initially designed, "the majority of inmates ate, slept, and worked together in one large household and, theoretically, submitted to the hard, Christian labor of repenting their sins and repairing their souls." As McLennan summarizes of the shift in thought that took place: "As criticism of the wheelbarrow scheme intensified, Rush's ideas began to find traction in the Pennsylvania legislature. Following intensive lobbying by Rush and the Philadelphia Society for Alleviating the Miseries of Public Prisons, the legislature directed, in 1790, that all people convicted of crimes (other than murder and a handful of similarly grave offenses) or misdemeanors be committed to the Walnut Street Jail for a term of hard labor; shortly thereafter, renovations began on the old Walnut Street Jail: Several workshops were built, as well as a series of large rooms in which the prisoners were to sleep."[208]

Though American public executions were then still in use, new sensibilities arose in the Victorian Era—the period of Queen Victoria's reign from 1837 to 1901. Driven by reforms that started with Dr. Rush in Philadelphia, the American system of punishment gradually transformed from one based on the English "Bloody Code" to one based on the use of penitentiaries. As Rebecca McLennan writes of the initial influence of Pennsylvania's reforms, in particular, the Walnut Street Jail's renovation into a penitentiary: "Quite quickly, similar houses of repentance sprang up in other states:

In 1796, the New York legislature abolished corporal punishment, reduced capital crimes to just three in number (treason, murder, and theft from a church), and directed the construction in lower Manhattan of what was to become Newgate penitentiary. Thomas Eddy, its architect and first 'agent,' modeled the institution on Walnut Street." From the 1830s to the 1930s, on a state-by-state basis, and only after the Founding Fathers had passed from the scene, the American people abandoned public executions altogether and embraced non-public executions behind thick prison walls.[209]

The all-important Constitutional Convention in Philadelphia, as well as the national debate over the U.S. Bill of Rights, took place in close proximity to early American penal reform efforts. But despite the lack of any explicit mention of *On Crimes and Punishments* in *The Federalist Papers*, Beccaria's book—then around for more than 20 years—had not somehow fallen out of favor by the time of America's Constitutional Convention in 1787 (or by the nineteenth century), not by a long shot; on the contrary, it was a cherished possession in many American households and libraries, including on the bookshelves of the founders.[210] In fact, James Madison reported that, in the eighteenth century, Beccaria was "in the zenith of his fame as a philosophical legislator."[211] And Beccaria's ideas—which, by the time the U.S. Constitution was drafted, had already fundamentally shaped the Founding Fathers' beliefs as well as many *state* constitutions—were still being regularly bandied about in eighteenth-century America.[212] "[I]n every society," one writer in a Philadelphia newspaper wrote in mid-January 1788, referencing Beccaria's by then familiar words during the ratification debate, "there is an effort constantly tending to confer on one part the height and to reduce the other to the extreme of weakness." "[T]his is of itself," that writer explained in *The Freeman's Journal* in a discussion of standing armies, "sufficient to employ the people's attention."[213] The U.S. Constitution's explicit prohibitions on *ex post facto* laws and bills of attainder—legislative acts that, in the past, operated retroactively or that, before being outlawed, condemned men to death without jury trials—itself reflects a Beccarian approach to the law.[214]

Although once celebrated by America's founders,[215] in early American verse,[216] and by eighteenth- and nineteenth-century lawmakers and death penalty foes,[217] Cesare Beccaria's name is now mostly missing from the pages and indexes of leading books on the American Revolution and U.S. constitutional law.[218] The best-informed legal historians may know Beccaria's name and recognize his contributions, but the general public's level of awareness of Beccaria and his ideas is nil or almost nil. Other important figures of the Italian Enlightenment—Pietro and Alessandro Verri, Gaetano Filangieri and Giacinto Dragonetti, to name but four—are even more obscure, though they once inspired—or were inspired by—Beccaria's game-changing treatise. And this is to say nothing of other Italian writers, such as Ferdinando Galiani, a man who wrote on the topic of trade and whom at least some of America's founders were familiar.[219] Despite the neglect of many U.S. historians, the Italian Enlightenment— or *Illuminismo*, as the Italians call it[220]—played a crucial role in the development of American law, with Beccaria's treatise, *On Crimes and Punishments*, and Gaetano Filangieri's *The Science of Legislation*, leading the way.[221] In fact, early American sources—among them, books, magazines, newspapers and early state legislative and congressional debates—frequently sang the praises of *both* Montesquieu and Beccaria, the two European philosophers (the baron and the marquis) who so materially shaped America's founding period.[222]

In truth, the contributions of Beccaria and his disciples to American law have long been underappreciated and underreported—more often than not, not mentioned at all—by twenty-first century historians and legal scholars. Everyday Americans may know the name of Montesquieu or that of Voltaire, the French writer, philosopher and playwright who penned famed works such as *Candide* (1759) and *Traité sur la tolerance* (1763), who opposed religious intolerance, and who advocated for freedom of religion and a separation of church and state. But because Beccaria has gotten such short shrift in the history books, few Americans likely know that Voltaire—known for his signature wit and a figure who still commands at least some attention in pop culture—wrote a lengthy and influential commentary on Beccaria's treatise almost a decade before the Revolutionary War broke out and that Voltaire dedicated his 1766 account of the death of the Chevalier de La Barre to Beccaria.[223] Beccaria's name does appear in four U.S. Supreme Court opinions,[224] but through the passage of time, the American people—living in an age of mass incarceration and lethal injection—have largely lost sight of a major focus of the American Revolution: the elimination of sanguinary and unnecessary punishments. Only by studying Beccaria's writings and the founding generation's reaction to them can one fully appreciate the full extent of Beccaria's enormous contributions to the origins of American law—and, perhaps, gain insights into where Americans should go from here in terms of future penal reform.[225]

Increasingly, the death penalty itself is being described as a cruel and inhuman—indeed, as a torturous—punishment.[226] In 1972, in *People v. Anderson*, the California Supreme Court—in striking down the death penalty as unconstitutional—described "the process of carrying out a verdict of death" as "so degrading and brutalizing to the human spirit as to constitute psychological torture." And later that same year, in *Furman v. Georgia*, the U.S. Supreme Court struck down death penalty laws as imposing "cruel and unusual punishments" in violation of the U.S. Constitution's Eighth Amendment. The California Supreme Court's decision was later abrogated by a state constitutional amendment, and the U.S. Supreme Court, in its 1976 decision in *Gregg v. Georgia*, ultimately reversed course—and once more upheld the death penalty's constitutionality. The nation's highest court took that step after thirty-five American states reenacted death penalty statutes. But other countries have moved away from the punishment of death, and the death penalty—it must be said—has *immutable* characteristics, with *mock*—or simulated—executions already considered to be a classic example of psychological torture. The U.S. Supreme Court has yet to take up the issue of the psychological torment associated with death sentences and executions and the prolonged—often decades' long—stays on death row that inmates now endure. Way back in 1890, though, the U.S. Supreme Court, in a case called *In re Medley*, recognized in a candid moment that "when a prisoner sentenced by a court to death is confined in the penitentiary awaiting the execution of the sentence, one of the most horrible feelings to which he can be subjected during that time is the uncertainty during the whole of it."[227]

While the U.S. Supreme Court continues to allow the death penalty's use, the Connecticut Supreme Court recently declared that state's death penalty unconstitutional in *State v. Santiago*—and many other foreign jurisdictions have expressly outlawed the use of capital punishment. In *State v. Santiago*, the Connecticut Supreme Court, in reciting the long history of death penalty opposition, actually referenced Cesare Beccaria's early American influence. In particular, the Connecticut Supreme Court pointed out in 2015 that, centuries earlier, during "the first half of 1786," the *New Haven Gazette* "had reprinted Cesare Beccaria's entire 1764 treatise 'On Crimes and Punishments,' a seminal Enlightenment era work that condemned torture and the death penalty, and that led to widespread questioning of the latter throughout Europe and the United States."[228] In 1995, the Constitutional Court of South Africa—acting in a post-apartheid world at the inception of that court's creation (and at a distance of more than 200 years after Beccaria's burial in Milan)—explicitly declared that country's death penalty unconstitutional, putting an end to the barbaric practice in the landmark ruling of *S v. Makwanyane*.[229] Finding capital punishment a "cruel, inhuman or degrading treatment or punishment," the South African court—relying, among other things, on principles of human dignity—noted in its judgment that "[a]n account of the history of the death sentence, the growth of the abolitionist movement, and the application of the death sentence by South African courts is given by Prof. B. van Niekerk in *Hanged by the Neck Until You Are Dead....*" In his own work, Professor Barend van Niekerk had credited Beccaria's influence on the anti-death penalty movement—yet another example of Beccaria's extensive influence and geographic reach.[230]

While colonial legal systems were heavily reliant on executions to instill terror and fear in the populace, Beccaria's writings broke through barriers of all kind, whether colonial or otherwise. In Africa and Asia, colonial rule brought European oppression to those continents but also, in time, Beccaria's ideas about crime and punishment. As one source notes: "European prison systems were instituted in Asia and Africa as an important component of colonial rule. In India, for example, the English prison system was introduced during the second half of the 18th century, when jails were established in the regions of Calcutta and Madras."[231] In the latter country, Cesare Beccaria is in fact still remembered as "the father of modern criminology" and as a thinker who criticized torture and the death penalty.[232] In a 2013 judgment of the Supreme Court of India, that court considered the history of capital punishment and quoted an earlier judicial opinion that had referenced Beccaria's name and the Beccarian principle that "crimes are only to be measured by the injury done to society."[233] "In his *Essay on Crimes and Punishments*," Somya Deshwal stressed in a paper written for the Indian National Bar Association on contemporary issues pertaining to the death penalty, "Beccaria asserted that the certainty of punishment, rather than its severity, was a more effective deterrent."[234]

While the *death penalty* and *torture* have, themselves, traditionally been viewed in separate legal silos, that is starting to change in light of pressure from U.N. officials, due to the fact that a host of *non-lethal* acts and punishments are considered torturous under international law, and in light of the abandonment of capital punishment by so many countries. The U.N. Convention Against Torture has long strictly prohibited physical and psychological torture when it comes to punishment, and in many places death sentences and executions are no longer being authorized or used, not even for the worst of the worst offenders. For example, the Rome Statute, which created the International Criminal Court, does not permit the punishment of death. Instead, the maximum punishment for genocide, crimes against humanity, and war crimes is life imprisonment. Though the United States and an increasingly small number of nations continue to put people to death under the auspices of "lawful sanctions" (to use the words of the Convention Against Torture), death sentences and state-sanctioned executions bear the unmistakable *indicia* of torture. And in many nations, including throughout Europe, such sentences and executions are simply no longer lawful as they are expressly prohibited by law. The United Nations now seeks the death penalty's complete abolition, with repeated calls by the U.N. General Assembly to put a worldwide moratorium on executions. And with U.N. officials, academics, and abolitionist leaders such as Sister Helen Prejean calling executions acts of torture, calls have been made for the recognition of a peremptory, international law norm against the death penalty's use.[235] An April 2017 report of the Human Rights Clinic at the University of Texas School of Law concluded that "the current conditions of confinement on Texas' death row, including mandatory indefinite isolation, amounts to a severe and relentless act of torture."[236]

The anti-death penalty movement has, certainly, come a long way since the publication of Cesare Beccaria's *Dei delitti e delle pene* in 1764. Through the transmission of information online, Beccaria's once handwritten thoughts—and those of his many intellectual successors—have transformed the global conversation about crime and punishment and the death penalty in particular. Indeed, since its publication, central tenets of Beccaria's *On Crimes and Punishments* have penetrated many non-Western societies—ones with very different legal customs and traditions—far beyond Europe and the Americas.[237] China remains the world's top user of executions, with thousands executed every year. But in recent decades, its own legal scholars have developed their own proportionality principle (*zuixing xiang shiying yuanze*). As a book on Chinese law reports of China's 1979 criminal law: "The Chinese principle of proportionality is fundamentally based on the theory developed by the 18th century Italian scholar Cesare Beccaria in his seminal work *On Crimes and Punishments*."[238] "The People's Republic of China (PRC) did not have a codified criminal law approved and passed by the legislative body until 1979," another book emphasizes,[239] pointing out how late China has been to the codification of the law compared to its Western counterparts. Abolition in China, where the death penalty remains popular, is not likely to come soon. But the future is hard to predict, and there are, already, glimmers of hope throughout the developing world. In general, Amnesty International's annual reports on the death penalty—digitized and widely distributed online and throughout much of the international community—continue to reflect an abolitionist trend despite China's countless executions.[240]

Recently, one Chinese law professor has in fact struck a different, more progressive tone than past Chinese officials and academics, encouraging his fellow citizens "to learn from the fathers of Western legal philosophy in order to turn around China's flawed legal system." "Prof. He," Tom Rousseau writes in *Chinese Heroes*, has "mustered the courage of addressing very controversial topics like the death penalty." In 2007, Professor He wrote an entire essay, "*Eight reasons why the death penalty should be abolished*," that reflects the changing attitudes, at least in some quarters in Chinese society. Professor He's arguments, Rousseau writes, "followed partly the lines delineated in the famous '*Of Crimes and Punishment*' by Italian philosopher Cesare Beccaria, while at the same time not losing sight of the specific Chinese cultural context: the death penalty does not produce desired results in terms of crime control; it does not play a preventive role, and may actually cause more crimes; it encourages vengeful feelings within society; it is a violation of human dignity." In 1979, Rousseau points out, China's Criminal Code and Criminal Procedure Law moved "the country away from the arbitrary lawlessness applied in the administration of justice in the previous 20 years." In 2011 and 2013, China reduced the number of death-eligible crimes, though the list remains a long one and executions are still extremely common.[241]

Still, the Chinese death penalty has come under relentless attack in the international community, leading one scholar to conclude in 2013: "the debate between China and the global community against the death penalty has come to centre on *how*, not *whether*, to restrict the death penalty with the final goal of abolition."[242] The Dui Hau Foundation has promoted death penalty reform in China since 2007, when its executive director, John Kamm, chaired a plenary session on China at the World Congress Against the Death Penalty in Paris. According to estimates it publishes, the use of executions in China has been declining, though they still number in the thousands annually and the actual number remains an official state secret. As part of the debate in China surrounding the death penalty's use, Beccaria's treatise, *Dei delitti e delle pene*, is now helpfully available in a new Chinese translation, with Beccaria's name also showing up in Chinese law reviews. "As early as 200 years ago," an article in the *Renmin Chinese Law Review* points out, "Beccaria pointed out that 'confession by torture can only free strong criminals, and convict the weak and innocent'" and thus put the innocent "'in a much worse plight than the criminal.'" Translated by Professor Huang Feng, of the Beijing Normal University Law School, *On Crimes and Punishments* can now more readily shape China's death penalty debate, with Chinese editions of it printed in 2002 and 2005 in Beijing, the latest by China Legal Publishing House.[243]

Of course, Cesare Beccaria's *On Crimes and Punishments*—widely available before these recent developments—has long impressed its countless global readers, including in at least some quarters in Asia. In Petra Schmidt's book, *Capital Punishment in Japan*, one gets a sense of how the transmission of Beccaria's ideas occurred in Eastern cultures. In that book, it is noted that due to "the influx of Western thought since the *Meiji* Period, gradually the arguments of the Western discussion on capital punishment became known." As Schmidt explains:

> As early as 1868, Kanda Kôhei, a Holland-Scholar, introduced the debate in his article "Criminal Procedure in the West" (*Seiyô shokoku kôji saiban no*

koto). Tsuda Mamichi, who at the end of the *Tokugawa* Period had studied in the Netherlands and brought his knowledge on Western legal science back to Japan, was the first Japanese who, based on Beccaria's ideas, openly demanded that the death penalty be replaced with penal servitude.[244]

During the Meiji period—the time period between 1868 and the early twentieth century—the Itsukaichi "Learning and Debating Society" took up the subject of capital punishment. After debating "Should there be capital punishment?", the society concluded: "Persons convicted of crimes against the state shall not be subject to capital punishment. Moreover, guilt or innocence in such trials shall be determined by trial by jury."[245]

In societies without a Western tradition, there was—perhaps not surprisingly— greater resistance to the ideas in Cesare Beccaria's writings because they were seen to be coming from an unfamiliar source. In her book, Petra Schmidt explains the results of the Japanese exposure to Beccaria's ideas as follows: "Although Tsuda found a weighty supporter in Nishi Amane (1829–1897), the *Meiji* Period's representative philosopher and enlightener, the thought of an abolition did not even cross the minds of early *Meiji* legislators. It was only from the second decade of that period that a substantial debate on capital punishment materialised among practitioners and scholars in the magazine *Kangoku Kyôkai Zasshi* of the 'Japanese Prison Association.'" An August 1875 issue of another publication, *Meiroku zasshi*, actually called for the entire abolition of the death penalty. As one source puts it of one writer: "Citing passages from the Chinese classics in tandem with the example of Beccaria in Europe, he argued that the aim of punishment should be to reform and correct criminals, not to match one act of violence with another."[246] "This slowly developing discussion," Schmidt writes in *Capital Punishment in Japan*, "culminated, when Ogawa Shigejirô, then editor of the magazine, in 1907 published a special issue as well as a number of articles in regular issues on 'prison', in which forty prison officials presented their—overwhelmingly negative—views on capital punishment."[247] In 1880, Japan put in place a penal code based on a French model, with another penal code—with mostly German influences—promulgated in 1908.[248]

These kind of historical nuggets—an entry for Cesare Beccaria appears in a Chinese-English dictionary published in Shanghai in 1908 (replete with Chinese characters for his name)—shows that Beccaria's ideas, even if viewed skeptically, filtered into Asian and other non-Western societies long ago.[249] According to a 2013 presentation by Angelo Paratico at an Asia Society meeting in Hong Kong, it was Eugenio Zanoni Volpicelli, a Neapolitan consular official, who actually translated Beccaria's *Dei delitti e delle pene* into Chinese almost a full century ago. The consul general of Italy in Hong Kong, Macau and Canton from 1899 to 1919, Volpicelli retired to Canton in 1919 before moving to Japan, where he died in 1936.[250] Beccaria's name has appeared in judges' opinions in Indian courts, including the Supreme Court of India,[251] and in such varied sources as the *Philippine Law Journal* and *The Chinese Human Rights Reader*.[252] Yasoji Kazahaya did a Japanese translation of Beccaria's book in 1929, and another Japanese translation of the book's French version, by Haruo Satô, appeared in 1976.[253] "In short," criminologist Marvin E. Wolfgang once observed, alluding to all the translations of Beccaria's work, "the influence" of Beccaria's *Dei delitti e delle pene* "was enormous in Europe, in Asia, and in the United States."[254]

Whereas the latest Japanese translation of Beccaria's book, by Masao Kontani, was published by the University of Tokyo Press in 2011, the first ever Arabic translation of Beccaria's book—printed in Lebanon—only appeared in 2008, giving only a few readers in the Middle East (*i.e.*, those familiar with languages in which Beccaria's treatise had previously appeared) exposure to his ideas.[255] Consequently, in the Arab world, a place where Beccaria's ideas have yet to fully penetrate, scores of executions are still carried out in a handful of countries every year. Still, Beccaria's ideas have been discussed—at least in passing—in several texts about Islamic law or pertaining to historical events in the Arab world. For example, in *The Application of Islamic Criminal Law in Pakistan*, Tahir Wasti has written about Beccaria's theory of punishment. "According to Beccaria," Wasti emphasized, "averting the recurrence of the offence is not only the prime objective but the sole permissible purpose of inflicting a criminal punishment."[256] During a December 18, 1913 debate in the Italian parliament, Filippo Turati—in discussing events unfolding in Libya—offered these words:

> I heard the words of the King, just a few days ago, to the effect that the acquisition of Libya gives Italy a great civilizing mission, and that our foremost objective is to make those peoples our friends, by respecting their religion, property, families, and by imparting to them the advantages of civilization. Instead, what I see is an all-encompassing shadow of the gallows extending over your endeavor! ... Every solider who performs the noble task of executioner receives, through the office of the Carabinieri, a special bonus of five francs.... I ask myself, is this really Italy, is the government aware that someone named Cesare Beccaria was born in Italy?[257]

And while Beccaria's ideas have yet to be implemented in some nations, they have resulted in big changes in others. As one 1999 book about Islamic law in modern Arab legal systems reported: "In the criminal law field, Saudi Arabia and other Gulf States continue to adhere to traditional Islamic law in whole or in part, even where modern penal codes have been adopted, as is the case in the United Arab Emirates. All the other Arab states, on the other hand, have basically discarded the penal principles of classical Islamic law and adopted instead the European notions of criminality and punishment, which were first developed by the Italian jurist Beccaria in the 18th century."[258]

The slow, insufficient penetration of Beccaria's ideas into the Islamic world has meant that many executions—as well as other brutal corporal punishments—continue to be carried out in those parts of the world. Consider the case of Saudi Arabia, profiled in a 2013 news story from the United Kingdom titled "Execution Central: Saudi Arabia's Bloody Chop-Chop Square." That article took note of that country's strict interpretation of Islamic law, with Saudi Arabian courts imposing a slew of corporal punishments ranging from flogging to hand amputation to "cross amputation"—right hand and left foot, the prescribed punishment for highway robbery. In a rare interview, one of the country's executioners, Muhammad Saad al-Beshi, described his technique: "I use a special sharp knife, not a sword. When I cut off a hand I cut it from the joint. If it is a leg the authorities specify where it is to be taken off, so I follow that." Other Saudi Arabian punishments have included eye-gouging and tooth extraction, with the 2013 news article highlighting a court decision ordering the severance of a man's spine in an "eye-for-an-eye" punishment after Ali al-Khawahir allegedly paralyzed one of his friends from the waist down when he was fourteen. "After 10 years in jail," the article reported, "a court in the town of Al-Ahsa ruled that al-Khawahir, now 24, is to receive the same treatment unless he pays 1 million Saudi riyals (£176,000) in compensation to the victim." "Paralysing someone as punishment for a crime would be torture," Ann Harrison, Amnesty International's Middle East and North Africa Deputy Director, aptly asserts, with the 2013 article also pointing out that Saudi executions are carried out by beheading. As was reported of the country's frequent use of public executions: "In the capital Riyadh, public executions take place in the central Deera square, usually at 9 a.m." "The wide ochre square has been grimly dubbed 'chop chop square'," the article observes, noting that it had seen "dozens of condemned men and women put to death in recent years." After reading the execution order to the condemned person in the square, al-Beshi indicated in his interview, "at a signal I cut the prisoner's head off." "Beheadings," the article stressed of the region of the world where punishments are still sometimes tied to religious texts, "are imposed mainly for murder or drug offences, but cases of apostasy (renunciation of one's faith), sorcery and witchcraft can also end up in Chop Chop square."[259]

Despite these outlier practices in theocratic, totalitarian or authoritarian regimes, the impact of Montesquieu and Beccaria on the modern world — and on penal codes in particular — is evident. In general, harsh punishments have given way to milder ones since the Enlightenment, and arbitrary punishments are more closely scrutinized by legal systems around the world, with constitutions and codified legal codes seeking the administration of equal justice. As Marc Ancel wrote in 1958 in the *University of Pennsylvania Law Review* in recognition of that fact: "The twentieth-century codes flow largely from those of the nineteenth century, which in turn arise directly from the penal reform which swept irresistibly through Europe at the end of the eighteenth century. So Montesquieu and Beccaria are at the heart of the European movement for codification, and it is important to grasp this." As Ancel adds: "A rupture occurred at the end of the 'century of enlightenment' between the repressive system of the Old Law and the system which arose from the claims of the philosophers and the movement for penal reform."[260] The connection between Beccaria's ideas and the development of new, more egalitarian penal codes — and, ultimately, the penitentiary system — is thus incontestable. "The humanitarian movement for penal reform at the end of the eighteenth century was followed," Marc Ancel emphasized, "by a strictly liberal movement aiming at the lessening of sentences and the abolition of certain punishments incompatible with the idea … of the dignity of man."

The origins of the law's progression — from grotesque brutality to systems predicated on human dignity — cannot even be traced properly by historians without considering Cesare Beccaria's work. "At the beginning of the nineteenth century," Ancel continued, "the object of the national legislatures of new Europe had been above all to provide penal codes suited to their political, social and ideological state." "The firm aim," he notes, "had been to meet the basic demands of Beccaria, then to incorporate the teachings of Bentham." It was Beccaria's philosophical approach—one aimed at eliminating unnecessary bodily punishments, including executions—that inexorably led to the building of penitentiaries around the world. As Ancel explained the consequences of this seismic shift in thinking wrought by Beccaria and the proponents of prisons: "The substitution of imprisonment for corporal punishment, or, in many cases, for capital punishment, brought about a considerable increase in the number of persons detained in penitentiaries." As Ancel emphasized in his article: "As the number of persons so held and the length of detention increased, the fate of these condemned persons became a subject for concern. Thus, it was practical necessity, arising from the new legislation, that gave rise to penitentiary science."[261] From public executions to penitentiaries, it was Cesare Beccaria's writings which helped to usher in the changes. Of course, Beccaria also cautioned that punishments should only be inflicted when absolutely necessary.

In *Law Miscellanies: An Introduction to the Study of the Law*, Hugh Henry Brackenridge—an early American jurist who served on the Supreme Court of Pennsylvania—specifically wrote of Beccaria's impact on the American polity in 1814. As Brackenridge observed: "Elementary writers, at the head of whom is the marquis de Beccaria, have with great plausibility, questioned the right of society to punish, by taking life at all."[262] Brackenridge was a Princeton classmate of James Madison, and the two men were good friends. For example, in a 1774 letter to William Bradford, Jr., another friend of James Madison from their college days together, Madison wrote: "When you have an opportunity and write to Mr. Brackenridge, pray tell him I often think of him, and long to see him, and resolved to do so in the spring." Along with Philip Freneau, sometimes called the "Poet of the American Revolution," Madison and Brackenridge wrote a poetical dialogue called "The Rising Glory of America" that was read at Princeton's graduating exercises and printed in 1772, shortly before the onset of the Revolutionary War.[263]

Some early bibliophiles owned multiple editions of *Dei delitti e delle pene* as well as Beccaria's book on style. Others read Beccaria's book in the original Italian to better grasp its intended meaning, or, as in Basil Montagu's case, cited Beccaria's book dozens of times in his own, anti-gallows text, *The Opinions of Different Authors upon the Punishment of Death* (1809). And wherever his words were read, Cesare Beccaria made an indelible impression. For example, in his early nineteenth-century travelogue, Englishman John Bramsen—in a book dedicated in April 1818 to "The Most Noble The Marquis of Sligo, Earl of Altamont, Viscount Westport, &c. &c. &c."—discussed the cruelty of European punishments. After describing gruesome bodily punishments, Bramsen—who took notice of the presence of a "good English society" in Rome—specifically credited Beccaria with affecting a change in attitude toward the laws. As Bramsen wrote: "The laws, as understood in our age of superior light and civilization, and as explained by the celebrated Marquis Beccaria, in his book of Crimes and Punishments, disclaims all idea of being influenced by a vindictive spirit; their only object being to deter others from the commission of crimes."[264]

Conclusion

In *A History of Italian Law*, Carlo Calisse writes that "[n]o book" upon penal law "created a greater stir in Europe, was more read, or brought greater fame" than Cesare Beccaria's *Dei delitti e delle pene*.[1] It came at an opportune time in world history, in the wake of influential works by Montesquieu and Voltaire on the division of power and religious tolerance, and it shaped—indeed, helped to frame—the American Revolution. "In founding a democratic republic upon law and establishing a system of checks and balances," writes Timothy Snyder, a professor of history at Yale University, "the Founding Fathers sought to avoid the evil that they, like the ancient philosophers, called tyranny." "They had in mind," Snyder emphasizes, "the usurpation of power by a single individual or group, or the circumvention of law by rulers for their own benefit." In *On Crimes and Punishments*, Cesare Beccaria—like Montesquieu had in *The Spirit of the Laws* before him—had railed against tyranny, and Beccaria's book was front and center in the founders' minds as, in state after state, they drafted their revolutionary constitutions and fought for their freedom. As Snyder, writing of later events, observes: "Much of the succeeding political debate in the United States has concerned the problem of tyranny within American society: over slaves and women, for example."[2] The section of Beccaria's treatise on egalitarian treatment brought the problem of inequality of treatment into sharp focus.

After Cesare Beccaria's death, the Italian philosopher's ideas—on the death penalty and other subjects—continued to be passionately debated even as people's memories of Beccaria, the man, faded. In a 1798 edition of *The Monthly Magazine, and British Register*, published in London, printed at St. Paul's Church Yard, and finally taking notice of Cesare Beccaria's death, a "Philo-Italicus" wrote a letter to the editor about the Italian thinker. As that letter to the editor began: "I am not certainly informed whether the Italians have written the eulogium of the late Marquis Beccaria. Any particulars relating to the life of that illustrious character, whose name is already synonymous to those of philosophy and humanity, deserve to be transmitted to the remotest posterity, with all the instructive singularities that accompany the exertions of great minds." Though the letter writer, who wrote that Beccaria "was born about the year 1720," got the year of Beccaria's birth all wrong, Philo-Italicus correctly emphasized that *On Crimes and Punishments* "raised its author to the pinnacle of fame, and also exposed him to some dangers." "This work," Philo-Italicus stressed, "was justly celebrated all over Europe; and the author's ideas were so well understood, that we need not scruple to assert, that few books ever produced so memorable a revolution in the human mind, in government, and in courts of justice, as this; so that Voltaire, who almost immediately after published some commentaries upon it, could affirm with justice, that this little book was in *morals*, what in *medicine* the discovery of a small drug would be, competent to effect [a] universal cure for the distempers of mankind." "The Marquis Beccaria," the letter writer continued, heaping praise upon him, "was a great lover of learned men, cordial in friendship, and a general Mæcenas to all Tiro's in the career of literature."[3]

As time passed, memories of Beccaria were replaced by simple memorials. "In the strada di Brera is a handsome hotel which was inhabited by Beccaria, whose medallion and those of eight other celebrated Milanese of both sexes are seen on the front," a Parisian writer, Antoine Claude Pasquin (1789–1847), better known as Valéry, wrote in a travel guide in the 1830s about Italy. "Beccaria, a genius full of paradox in his passionate love of virtue and humanity, a philosopher whose opinions were daring and rash, while his life was prudent, virtuous, and peaceable," Valéry stressed, "has recently acquired partizans in the old and new worlds; his principles on the punishment of death have regained favour with the friends of enlightenment." The librarian of the Royal Libraries of Versailles and Trianon, Valéry acknowledged "the superior merit" of some of Beccaria's "discourses and essays," but nonetheless favored the *lex talionis* doctrine, taking the position that the death penalty's abolition—"an innovation"—could not "be compared to civil liberty, religious toleration, the abolition of slavery, and other just and natural improvements."[4] Even while acknowledging Beccaria's greatness, Valéry thus took issue with one of Beccaria's premier ideas—that the death penalty is not necessary.

Described as "the celebrated jurist" in a book published in distant Philadelphia in 1832, Cesare Beccaria—at least before the Civil War—once ranked as one the world's best-known authors.[5] "[T]he modern world opened a glorious page in the progress of criminal science with the modest little book of Cesare Beccaria," one lecturer, Enrico Ferri, stressed in 1901 at the University of Naples in Italy, with another commentator offering this assessment of what happened after the initial publication of *Dei delitti e delle pene*: "The name of Beccaria soon became synonymous with indignation and demands for reform. His ideas, which influenced Jeremy Bentham and the Utilitarians, stressed the interdependence of individual liberties."[6] On the 150th anniversary of Italy's unification, one twenty-first century book summarized Beccaria's substantial contributions this way: "Cesare Beccaria advocated an equitable legal system that rendered all men equal before the law; greater humanity in criminal proceedings; the banning of torture; setting punishment at the lowest possible level; abolition of the death penalty and, first and foremost, measures setting out to avert criminal behavior through education. He argued that the real curb on criminal behavior was not the cruelty of the punishment, but the certainty that the culprit would be punished, albeit with a more lenient, but certain and inevitable sentence."[7]

Such glowing tributes, many to the "celebrated Marquis Beccaria," had certainly been made many times before—and will no doubt be made again in the future. In a preface to the second edition of *The Theory of Political Economy* by William Stanley Jevons (1835–1882), its author wrote in 1879: "If we overlook Hutcheson, who did not expressly write on Economics, the earliest mathematico-economic author seems to be the Italian Ceva, whose works have just been brought to notice in the *Giornale degli Economisti*." "The next author in the list," Jevons observed, taking note of Beccaria's *Tentativo analitico sui contrabbandi*, "is the celebrated Beccaria, who printed a very small, but distinctly mathematical, tract on Taxation as early as 1765." *Tentativo analitico sui contrabbandi* first appeared in *Il Caffè* in 1764, and it has been described as "a remarkable piece of mathematical economics."[8] As Jevons emphasized, comparing the timing of relevant works of economics: "Italians were thus first in the field. The earliest English work of the kind yet discovered is an anonymous *Essay on the Theory of Money*, published in London in 1771, five years before the era of the *Wealth of Nations*." Jevons noted that he had found *An Essay on the Theory of Money*—the book later attributed to Henry Lloyd and first published by the English printer John Almon—"by accidentally finding a copy on a bookseller's stall" and that it was only owing "to Professor Luigi Cossa, of the University of Pavia," that Jevons learned that the book had been "written by Major-General Henry Lloyd," the soldier who formed a friendship with both Pietro Verri and Cesare Beccaria.[9]

Cesare Beccaria's *Dei delitti e delle pene*—found in libraries across the world, from the London Library to the Library of Congress, after its publication[10]—thus marks a pivotal demarcation point between the *Ancien régime* and modernity. "Some of the most important reforms of the last years of the *ancien régime* and many more to follow into the revolutionary decade," Geoffrey Treasure emphasized in the early twenty-first century in *The Making of Modern Europe, 1684–1780*, "constitute a memorial to Beccaria and those like him who dared to articulate their faith in human reason into words."[11] In fact, in the 1880s, thousands of miles from Beccaria's birthplace and nearly a full century after the Italian philosopher's death, a whole group—the now-defunct Beccaria Club—was organized in New York City to pay homage to the great Italian philosopher and "to promote the study and practice of scientific penology."[12] Though his legacy lives on, Cesare Beccaria died in Milan in 1794 after—as one source puts it—"a life richly rewarded with honorary titles and recognitions." He had been toasted in 1766 in Paris by the French *philosophes*, and he had received adulation and lavish praise in letters for his little masterpiece, *Dei delitti e delle pene*. But the shy young man who preferred his native Milan to the salons of Paris had aged and his time had come. "One day," one of Beccaria's biographers notes of his death on November 28, 1794, after a period of ill health, "he was alone in the house and later was found dead of apoplexy."[13]

Cesare Beccaria loved to eat and drink, and his lifestyle eventually caught up with him. Over time, he became overweight, which no doubt contributed to his death at age 56. In 1792, his ill health and awareness of his own mortality had actually prompted him to take proactive measures and to guarantee, in the event of his death, 12,000 *lire* for his wife, Anna; a demise or bequest that prompted a lawsuit against him from his two brothers—an unsuccessful lawsuit (but one that he faced from family members in his lifetime) seeking to annul the provision in his wife's favor. "The last two years of Beccaria's life," biographer Marcello Maestro explains, "were not happy ones and his only comfort was his little family: his wife and young Giulio." "His last paper, dated April 3, 1794," Maestro notes of the often mundane, everyday work as part of Beccaria's administrative duties, "was a study of the sanitary situation in Lombardy, with suggestions on how to better organize that department."[14] It was a life spent in the economic development trenches, trying to improve the lives of Italians bit by bit and one by one. But it was a worthy one—and one that, in time, found recognition in the pages of the world's histories. "Among the Italian economists who were most under the influence of the modern spirit, and in closest harmony with the general movement which was impelling the Western nations towards a new social order," the *Encyclopædia Britannica* reported in 1885, "Cesare Beccaria (1738–1794) holds a foremost place."[15]

Cesare Beccaria's body was interred in Milan's Mojazza Cemetery—a burial place outside Porta Comasina where the famous poet Giuseppe Parini, Beccaria's compatriot in the *Accademia dei Trasformati*, also was laid to rest.[16] He was buried—in the words of his biographer, Marcello Maestro, "[w]ith a very simple funeral and without any special ceremony." As Maestro emphasized after taking note of the intra-familial squabbles that marred Beccaria's final years: "No one except his wife and son seemed to care about Beccaria's passing. In the turmoil of a rapidly changing world his death went almost unnoticed even in his native city. There was no word of it in the newspapers, nor were speeches made to honor or praise him." Per Maestro's concluding observations: "This silence may well appear as a last tribute to his modesty and to his feeling of uneasiness at being in the limelight. Some time later, at the grave in which he was buried, his son, Giulio, laid a simple stone with a Latin inscription saying that there lay Cesare Beccaria, 'councillor in the public administration, expert in criminal jurisprudence, writer of clear intellect.'"[17] Even that simple gesture was more than Giuseppe Parini, Cesare Beccaria's one-time associate, would have wanted. As the official tourism website for Milan notes: "Parini was buried in Milan, in a mass grave in the Cemetery of Mojazza, just out of Porta Comasina. His funeral was made very humble, according to his testament: 'I want, demand and order that my funeral service is made humble and bare, as in the habits of the lowest classes.'"

In fact, Cesare Beccaria's own bodily remains are now lost to history, in part because of a governmental act that Beccaria himself was involved with as a public servant. Because of the population growth in Milan and legitimate concerns over illnesses and hygiene, the burial of bodies in churches or the chapels of family palaces had been forbidden, and individual or family graves in public cemeteries were not yet in use. As a result, Beccaria's body had been buried in a common grave—the same way in which Giuseppe Parini's body had been laid to rest, and in a manner reminiscent of how Wolfgang Amadeus Mozart's body was buried in Vienna in 1791, just three years before Beccaria passed away. As a biography of Mozart notes of the practice of the time in Habsburg-controlled lands: "individual graves were the exception, not the rule, in Josephine Vienna and while the nobility and some wealthy merchants may have erected family vaults, gravestones were otherwise permitted only along cemetery walls; Joseph's 'court decree on religious and police matters' of 23 August 1784 makes it clear that bodies were to be sewn into linen sacks and that if several bodies arrived at the cemetery at the same time, they could be placed in a single grave." After Joseph II's reforms, another source notes, "mass burials were the rule; only the very wealthy could afford to have a family vault, and the tending of individual graves was virtually unknown." As that modern guide to Vienna observes: "Funeral services took place in churches (Mozart's in the Stephansdom), and it was not customary for mourners to accompany the funeral cortège to cemeteries. In fact, bodies were only allowed to be taken to the cemetery after nightfall, where they were left in the mortuary overnight for burial the next day."

Given Cesare Beccaria's sundry achievements, there was later regret that his remains had not been interred in a different, more befitting manner. Pietro Verri—who, along with his brother Alessandro, had once despised and privately ridiculed Beccaria—wanted people to be able to pay homage to the immortal Beccaria, regretting that a monument to Beccaria had never been built in the city where the Academy of Fists once met. A fellow Italian also later griped about Giuseppe Parini's burial in 1799, lamenting that "he was lying without a grave, with his bones lost in the desolate countryside, maybe mixed up to those of a thief who expiated his crimes on the gallows."[18] In 1838, Milan's city council announced a competition to build a new burial ground to replace the six graveyards, including San Gregorio at Porta Venezia and La Mojazza at Porta Comasina, located outside the municipality's Spanish walls. Though all the submitted proposals proved too unwieldly and expensive, another competition was held by the city council in 1863 that led to the creation of the Monumental Cemetery, designed by architect Carlo Maciachini (1818–1899). After that new cemetery was constructed, there was a desire to convey to it the bodies of Parini and Beccaria, but by then, it was no longer possible to distinguish their bones from the others that had been laid to rest in the Mojazza Cemetery.[19] Those wanting to pay homage to Beccaria today thus have no specific gravesite to go to in Milan; instead, they must content themselves with reading and mulling over Beccaria's ideas, perhaps while sipping an espresso at a lively Milanese coffeehouse.

Cesare Beccaria's older, erstwhile mentor, Pietro Verri, would outlive Beccaria by more than two years, and in his remaining time, Verri would dedicate himself to keeping Beccaria's memory alive. After French forces entered Milan in May 1796, the French decreed that all titles of nobility were abolished, a development welcomed by the aging Pietro Verri, who, as an elder statesman, agreed to serve on the municipal council at the request of French authorities. As Pietro wrote to his brother Alessandro: "From now on please address your letters simply: Citizen Pietro Verri. I never liked titles anyway and if I used mine it was only because others did." "I don't now feel deprived of anything, only an empty illusion has disappeared," Pietro assured his brother. In his last public speech before he died, Pietro Verri urged his fellow citizens to remember his late friend, Cesare Beccaria. In his speech to the city council, Verri asked: "Where is the monument to Beccaria, the monument that you Milanese have erected to that immortal genius who first proclaimed that the goal of social science must be the greatest happiness shared by the greatest number? How have you shown your gratitude to the man who gave luster to your city, whose book on justice has been translated into all languages and is now placed among the most sublime works in all the world libraries?" "It would be unforgivable," Verri said, "not to honor now the great man who dared, not without danger, to defend the cause of the oppressed and who opened the way to the triumph of justice and humanity."[20]

It took a few more decades before the monument to Cesare Beccaria in Milan was actually built and dedicated. But to this day, thanks to Pietro Verri, Beccaria's surviving children, and the impact that Beccaria made during his own lifetime, Cesare Beccaria continues to be studied and admired by jurists, criminologists and legal historians—and, at least occasionally, by ordinary citizens hungry for knowledge of the world's history. While he remains best known for his novel approach to the law and for his passionate anti-death penalty advocacy, leading scholars in the "law and economics" movement also regularly point to *On Crimes and Punishments* and his *Il Caffè* article on smuggling as foundational texts. As one biographical sketch of Beccaria emphasizes: "the leading theorists of the 'Law and Economics' movement—Gary Becker and Richard Posner—have legitimately credited Beccaria as a pioneer of the utilitarian project of a 'mathematical approach' to the study of crime and punishments, and a strong supporter of a rational evaluation of the deterrent effect of punishment."[21] The debate over how best to deter crime—a debate begun in earnest in Beccaria's book, where the contours of deterrence theory were systematically explored—thus continues, with modern-day economists, criminologists and other social scientists still using Beccarian terminology. "The origins of law and economics may be traced to eighteenth century writings on crime by Beccaria (1767) and Bentham (1789)," the preface to the *Handbook of Law and Economics* stresses.[22] Among the vast majority of the world's people, though, Beccaria's pivotal influence—an impact that was especially pronounced in the eighteenth and nineteenth centuries—is now badly in need of rehabilitation, if not resurrection.

There are many reasons, perhaps, why Cesare Beccaria is no longer a household name. Part of it has to do with his reserved personality, and part of it has to do with the fact that he mostly worked behind the scenes as an administrator within the Habsburg Empire. But Beccaria was once—and perhaps will be again—recognized for his innovative economic ideas and his genius. In *A Dictionary of Political Economy* (1863), Henry Dunning Macleod of Trinity College in Cambridge called Cesare Beccaria the "very celebrated philosopher, one of the great founders of the science of Political Economy in Italy." Noting that Beccaria delivered his 1769 inaugural lecture seven years before the publication of Adam Smith's *The Wealth of Nations*, Macleod freely acknowledged the significance of Beccaria's ideas. "Beccaria," Macleod wrote, "saw that the fundamental conception of Political Economy was *exchange*." Beccaria's view: "In every age there has been an exchange of products for products, reciprocally superfluous and necessary, of services for products, and of services for services." After recounting the key points of Beccaria's economic ideas, Macleod emphasized: "Thus it will be seen that Beccaria entirely anticipated the doctrine of Adam Smith, and Ricardo, when the one said that the value of things was measured by *labor*, and the other by the *cost of production*. But he skillfully avoided the errors to which the doctrines of these eminent writers lead; for he shews that though this is the tendency of prices under equal circumstances of production, yet if any could produce cheaper than the rest, these would gain the benefit of the reduced cost of production, until increased competition reduced the price."

"It is by no means uncommon to see it stated that Adam Smith was the founder of Political Economy and the father of Free Trade," Macleod stressed before adding of his Italian predecessors: "But such opinions only proceed from inaccurate historical knowledge. The fact is, that, as in the early stages of every other science, England was far in arrear of France and Italy." "[T]here was," Macleod pointed out, "a much greater number of earnest advocates for free trade, both in France and Italy, before the *Wealth of Nations* was published, than in England." "To suppose, therefore, that Adam Smith was either the father of Free Trade or of Political Economy is a most profound error," Macleod concluded, further observing: "We see that Italy is entitled to a very high rank indeed in the science of Political Economy. But Beccaria's name has been comparatively little known in connection with it, and this arose from his constitutional failing. Beccaria was endowed with a great, a piercing, and a generous mind, but it was vastly overshadowed by a most pusillanimous soul." As Macleod judgmentally wrote of what—whether true or not—he felt had led to the Italian thinker's lost opportunity: "Finding the sentiments expressed in his lectures likely to create opposition, he stopped, and left them unfinished, and he never published them. They first saw the light in 1804, in Custodi's collection of the Italian Economists. And thus he has deservedly missed the fame which would otherwise have been his legitimate due."[23]

Though Cesare Beccaria became a worldwide celebrity for writing *Dei delitti e delle pene*, his failure to achieve the fame as an economist that Adam Smith did was a near miss, a fact of history due, in large part, to Beccaria's failure to publish and to develop his ideas in greater detail. As William Spalding writes in *Italy and the Italian Islands: From the Earliest Ages to the Present Time* (1841): "[O]ne of the most celebrated of all names was that of Beccaria, whose essay 'On Crimes and Punishments,' speedily translated into every language of Europe, had an influence on public opinion not easily conceivable by those who, living in a later age, think the truths demonstrated in the little book unquestionable and trite. The concisely sententious, yet imaginative style of this early composition, was tran[s]fused with tenfold vigour into the author's Lectures on Political Economy, which, delivered in the years after 1768 from a chair then instituted for him at Milan, were never printed till they adorned Custodi's collection in 1804." Of those lectures on economics, Spalding concluded: "In plan and form, the lectures deserve to rank among the best of all philosophical works;—systematic in their arrangement even to excess; pointed and energetic in diction, though not unfrequently obscure through brevity; and studded with original expressions and images, which fix ideas in the memory by a single stroke." "The most successful disquisitions," Spalding added, "are those on the division of labour, on the circumstances that determine its price, and on the nature of productive capitals; in all of which Beccaria came very near, in the abstract, to the theories of Smith."[24]

Adam Smith's *The Wealth of Nations* was not produced in isolation; it was written in the context of a profusion of thinking, writings, and European lectures on economics—on money, agriculture and manufacturing, trade, finance, and economic development—that came before it.[25] Many of those lectures were delivered on the Italian peninsula, and in Beccaria's case, they were open to the public and—at least for two years—were attended by more than one hundred pupils.[26] In *The Encyclopædia Britannica*, it is specifically emphasized that Cesare Beccaria's lectures at Milan's Palatine School in the late 1760s and early 1770s "attracted much notice" in spite of the fact that they were not published in his lifetime. In comparing Beccaria's posthumously published *Elementi di Economia Pubblica* (the collection of Beccaria's teaching notes transcribed by his students) and Smith's *Wealth of Nations*, a mid-nineteenth-century edition of that encyclopedia relays: "In perspicuity of language, and distinct and patient illustration, the style of these discourses bears a considerable resemblance to that of the *Wealth of Nations*; but the coincidence between the two works, in some general and fundamental doctrines, is still more remarkable and interesting. Beccaria does not appear to have adopted the particular theory of the French economists, which was developed about that time; although his practical doctrines on some of the most important points were conformable to the conclusions deduced from that system."[27] The Verri brothers and Beccaria himself quoted liberally from English, French and Scottish works, and the translation of Enlightenment texts—whether in Paris, on the Italian peninsula, or in the British Isles—clearly fertilized cross-cultural communication.[28]

Not only were the French physiocrats and Italian thinkers such as Antonio Genovesi, Pietro Verri and Cesare Beccaria writing about economic matters,[29] but English, German, Scottish and Irish intellectuals—and other Europeans more broadly, if not as vocally—became obsessed with the study of political economy before Adam Smith's famous book first appeared in 1776.[30] General Henry Lloyd—Pietro Verri's close friend since 1759 and a frequent presence in Milan after their service together in the Austrian army—was just one such person, with Lloyd writing extensively about issues pertaining to political economy. Like Beccaria's lectures, Lloyd's anonymously published book, *An Essay on the Theory of Money* (1771), a work said to stand "as an early form of liberal economics," pre-dates Smith's famous book, with Lloyd reportedly becoming "a favorite of Catherine the Great."[31] The economic historian Sophus Reinert, a Harvard Business School professor, specifically takes note of this fascinating history. In exploring Lloyd's life and writings, Reinert emphasizes that Lloyd spent "[t]he years between 1766 and 1771" traveling across Europe and "fraternizing with Milanese intellectuals" who embodied "the coffee culture." The Milanese journal *Il Caffè*, Reinert stresses, had become "both the incubator (as coffee shop) and medium (as journal)" of the *Accademia dei pugni*'s "message of reform."[32] The members of the Academy of Fists were, themselves, fixated on social and economic development—along with art, theater, music, food and wine, and love—as they went about their daily lives.[33]

Because of *The Wealth of Nations* (1776), Adam Smith—the Scottish economist and moral philosopher—has been described as "the intellectual founder of capitalism." In his best-selling book, Smith described the way in which division of labor works and how self-interested individuals, through their labor and industry, serve the public good, whether intentionally or unintentionally. "By pursuing his own interest," Smith wrote of a typical eighteenth-century participant in commerce, "he frequently promotes that of society more effectually than when he really intends to promote it." As Smith observed: "As every individual, therefore, endeavours as much as he can both to employ his capital in the support of domestic industry, and so to direct that industry that its produce may be of the greatest value; every individual necessarily labors to render the annual revenue of the society as great as he can." "[B]y directing that industry in such a manner as its produce may be of the greatest value," he stressed of the commercial participant, "he intends only his own gain, and he is in this, as in many other cases, led by an invisible hand to promote an end which was no part of his intention." Italian economic writers, such as Pietro Verri and Cesare Beccaria, were similarly interested in furthering private gain as well as the public good, with Verri writing in 1771 that "the private interest of each individual, when it coincides with the public interests, is always the safest guarantor of public happiness."

But Smith, like Beccaria, believed that government was necessary—indeed, indispensable—to protect members of society from violence, oppression, and invasion; to build infrastructure and regulate commerce; and to foster the public interest. He also recognized the potential moral hazards of the economic system he so convincingly promoted (*e.g.*, the problem of cartels and monopolies and the rich being inordinately admired by society's members at the expense, and to the detriment, of the poor). When a regulation "is in favor of the workmen," Smith wrote, "it is always just and equitable." "Monopoly," Smith stressed, "is a great enemy to good management," with Smith observing: "A monopoly granted either to an individual or to a trading company has the same effect as a secret in trade or manufactures. The monopolists, by keeping the market constantly understocked, by never fully supplying the effectual demand, sell their commodities much above the natural price, and raise their emoluments, whether they consist in wages or profit, greatly above their natural rate." Just as Beccaria and Verri worried about seasonal unemployment and monopolies for commodities such as salt and tobacco, Smith cared a lot about "the general welfare of the society," stressing that "the interest of the laborer is strictly connected with that of the society." To characterize Adam Smith's work as promoting runaway greed—or a total hands-off approach by government in all economic matters—would thus be a complete distortion of Smith's life's work. As one commentator notes of Adam Smith's economics: "One important role of the government, according to Smith, was to provide the institutional framework required for competitive markets to function."

Adam Smith, in truth, cared deeply about morality and the outcomes of human activity, and he believed that a good and efficient government should tax fairly and spend frugally—and only when necessary to provide services and infrastructure that are required for a healthy society. He recognized that unregulated markets would result in a disparity of wealth in free societies, with Smith—favoring free enterprise as the best means to further the collective public good—writing as follows of the resulting need for government to protect private property: "The acquisition of valuable and extensive property, therefore, necessarily requires the establishment of civil government. Where there is no property, or at least none that exceeds the value of two or three days labour, civil government is not so necessary." In fact, Smith was very concerned, like Verri and Beccaria, about the wages of "the laboring poor," and he specifically declared it a matter of "equity" that those "who feed, clothe, and lodge the whole body of people, should have such a share of the produce of their own labor as to be themselves tolerable well fed, clothed, and lodged." "No society," Smith wrote, "can surely be flourishing and happy, of which the far greater part of the members are poor and miserable." Above all else, Smith felt that all "political disquisitions" should—as he wrote in *The Theory of Moral Sentiments* (1759), in which he frequently referred to his much-admired mentor, Dr. Hutcheson—"animate the public passions of men, and rouse them to seek out the means of promoting the happiness of the society." "It is a remarkable fact that Smith's systematic course of instruction on economic subjects," the editors of his work recite, "closely follows the order used by his old teacher, Francis Hutchinson, in his *System of Moral Philosophy* (published posthumously in 1755)."[34]

In their landscape-changing books, Adam Smith and Cesare Beccaria were heavily influenced by Francis Hutcheson (1694-1746), Smith's moral philosophy professor at the University of Glasgow—Smith in person and Beccaria from afar. In 1725, Dr. Hutcheson—in an idea echoed and promoted by both Smith and Beccaria—had written in *An Inquiry into the Original of Our Ideas of Beauty and Virtue*: "*that Action is* best, which accomplishes the *greatest Happiness* for the *greatest Numbers*; and that, worst, which in *like manner*, occasions *Misery*."[35] While Smith's *Wealth of Nations* applied that basic principle in the economic arena, Beccaria's *Dei delitti e delle pene* applied it in the sphere of both economics and the criminal law. "As an economic order," James Q. Wilson perceptively writes in a thoughtful essay, "capitalism in Smith's judgment was more just than the mercantilist alternative because it would produce greater prosperity for a greater number of people, albeit at the cost of greater inequality of wealth." As Sophus Reinert editorializes of Smith's Italian counterpart in an anthology titled *Economic Growth and the Origins of Modern Political Economy*: "The greatest legal theorist of political economy in Enlightenment Europe was undoubtedly the Milanese reformer and later professor of Cameralism Cesare Beccaria, who, though certainly building on Genovesi's work on the topic of sociability and commercial society in the tradition of '*economia civile*', resolutely went beyond it, with his epochal 1764 *On Crimes and Punishments* forcing him to engage with the practice of banditry in a fashion that was both more nuanced and more immediate."[36]

Neither Adam Smith nor Beccaria ever used the word "capitalism."[37] Smith's goal, like Beccaria's, however, was to maximize societal prosperity and the greatest happiness for the greatest number of people.[38] In the mid-1760s, Beccaria was pejoratively labeled a "socialista" by a defender of the Inquisition and the Old Order. But that was when the concept of *socialism* meant something very different than what it means today. In the eighteenth century, the idea of the *social contract* was associated with people having a say in their own governance—and, ultimately, with republicanism.[39] In fact, Beccaria favored increased productivity and private and free enterprise, though he also saw an important role for government to help foster broad-based societal prosperity. "In the ideal world, Beccaria was clear, 'absolute liberty' should be the aim of the political economy," Sophus Reinert explains in *Commerce and Peace in the Enlightenment*.[40] While Cesare Beccaria's role as a civil servant in the Habsburg Empire meant his work was often done behind the scenes and thus went unnoticed and unrecognized,[41] Beccaria's 1780 proposal to Habsburg administrators for the adoption of the metric system—as just one example—was itself designed to better facilitate *private* commerce.[42] Beccaria's efforts to standardize weights and measures, as well as his lectures and work in the field of economics more broadly, represented Beccaria's best efforts—in his own time, and in his own way—to advance the science of public economy and to improve the local economy.[43] As Reinert, the author of histories of capitalism, points out: "[I]f one accepts the vague if commonplace equation of the eighteenth-century idiom 'commercial society' with the modern concept of 'capitalism'… then an inescapable proposition emerges: the first 'socialists' were at the time Europe's greatest proponents of 'capitalism.'"[44]

"The Milanese school," economic historian Pier Luigi Porta further explains of this intriguing period of economic history, "provides a characteristic example of the construction of what we choose to call here the 'economic theory of civil society.'" In a section of Porta's book chapter titled "*Economia civile*: a tradition based on competition, institutions and creativity," he explicitly glories in "[t]he outstanding contributions" of "Cesare Beccaria, Pietro Verri, Gianrinaldo Carli in the late eighteenth century."[45] In his *Lectures on Political Economy* (1877), Dugald Stewart—a professor of moral philosophy at the University of Edinburgh—described decades earlier how "[t]he maintenance of the poor is intimately connected" with "[t]he means of encouraging among the body of the people habits of industry, and of a regularity of morals; and of effecting, where it is possible, a reformation in the manners of those who have rendered themselves obnoxious to the laws of their country." After taking note of "the projects of penitentiary houses," institutions Beccaria's *Dei delitti e delle pene* had helped to inspire, Stewart emphasized: "With a review of these establishments, the general principles which ought to regulate the *punishment of crimes* have a very close connexion, and accordingly, they have attracted, in the course of the last century, the attention of some very distinguished writers, and more particularly of the Marquis *Beccaria*, whose humane and eloquent *Treatise on Crimes and Punishments* forms one of the most valuable illustrations that has yet appeared, of the connexion between the principles of Ethical Philosophy and the Science of Legislation."[46]

Both Cesare Beccaria and Adam Smith, the record shows, premised their intellectual inquiries on mostly shared values and ideas, including the idea that the accumulation or increase of wealth for the betterment of the populace was a primary objective for societies. In fact, Beccaria—in defining "*economia pubblica*"—used the phrase "*ricchezze di una nazione*" ("the wealth of nations" or "the riches of nations"). His mentor, Pietro Verri, by contrast, had referred to "*ripulimento delle nazioni*" (refinement of nations) in his mid-1760s "Elementi del commercio" in *Il Caffè*. While Smith wrote in *The Wealth of Nations* about the self-interested conduct of butchers, brewers and bakers, Beccaria—in *On Crimes and Punishments*—recognized years earlier that humans acted in their own self-interest and could be incredibly selfish or self-centered, with Beccaria concluding in his native language: "*Ogni uomo si fa centro di tutte le combinazioni del globo.*" The American revolutionary John Adams, a pivotal figure in America's quest for independence who recognized the value of separation of powers to temper or restrain that human impulse, himself transcribed that exact Italian phrase from Beccaria, words that translate into English as follows: "[e]very man makes himself the center of his whole world" or "every man sees himself as the center of all the world's affairs." While self-interest and the profit motive lay at the foundation of Adam Smith's conception of the economic system that came, in time, to be known as capitalism, Beccaria, too, recognized that people rationally act in their own self-interest—and for their own private gain—in accordance with their needs, wants and desires. "No man ever freely surrendered a portion of his own liberty for the sake of the public good," Beccaria once observed in a reflection of that core belief in human nature. Beccaria himself saw punishment as necessary to combat "the despotic spirit of every individual" and the instinct of individuals to "withdraw not only their share but also to usurp that belonging to others."[47]

More broadly, Beccaria—in grappling with crime and punishment and issues of economic development—believed in the concept of free will, and he recognized the rationality of individual actions driven by the pursuit of pleasure or happiness and the desire to avoid pain. He also believed in the ability of lawmakers to structure government—and governmental policies—to incentivize virtue and disincentive vice. As one source notes: Beccaria believed that individuals freely make choices, look out for their own personal satisfaction, and that rational self-interest makes human actions—at least to a degree—predictable, capable of manipulation, or controllable.[48] "Of all the writings on punishment produced during the eighteenth century, a century so prominently marked by the profusion of ideas on the subject," historian Anthony Draper of the University College London writes, "Beccaria's small book *On Crimes and Punishments* was, and remains, of distinct and considerable importance." In effect, Beccaria, while drawing upon the writings of many others, from Montesquieu and Rousseau to Dr. Hutcheson, innovatively combined rationale-choice and social contract theory and, with his directed focus on human happiness, thus managed to influence laws and societies around the world in a unique way. "[T]he work was eagerly adopted, most obviously by lawyers and the rising middle classes," Draper explains of *Dei delitti e delle pene*'s reception, "as a declaration of the fundamental principles that ought to underpin the application of the penal sanction in an 'improved' civilisation." Not only did Beccaria provide "a contractarian vision of civil organisation," as Draper emphasizes, but he (Beccaria) asserted that all members of the social contract should be equal before the law.[49]

Cesare Beccaria's writings, including *Dei delitti e delle pene* and his inaugural 1769 lecture on economics, were translated into other languages. Described as "a masterpiece of the Italian Enlightenment,"[50] *Dei delitti e delle pene* was translated into far more languages than any of his other writings—and, by far, it drew the most attention of any of them.[51] The book had what one writer calls "extraordinary success," with that writer noting that Beccaria's name will forever be linked with the anti-death penalty movement. "Well may it be said of the Marquis di Beccaria," that historian, Thomas Rawling Bridgwater, stresses after alluding to the laws and legislative proposals that Beccaria's compact treatise shaped and produced, that Beccaria's book "is indeed one of the most important Works that has ever been written, and that he, by writing, has contributed towards the enduring happiness of nations." "The age in which Beccaria wrote," another commentator, M. Lerminier, notes, "was one in which the rights of humanity (before ignored and violated) were suddenly and quickly sought to be established."[52] Beccaria's book even inspired one Asian reformer, Tsuda Mamichi

(1829–1908), in distant Japan during that nation's reform-minded Meiji period, to call for the complete elimination of the death penalty in the nineteenth century.[53] Italian economists had long focused on human happiness, and Beccaria—in an especially prominent way given the success of his book—was, in reality, simply a part of that storied and humanistic tradition.[54]

Revolutionaries and intellectuals were drawn to Beccaria's ideas like moths to brightly lit lampposts, with leading Enlightenment figures debating—and often genuinely revering—Beccaria's cogent insights. To be sure, some thought Beccaria's ideas impractical or even naïve.[55] As Philipp Blom writes of one thinker's reaction to *Dei delitti e delle pene* in *A Wicked Company: The Forgotten Radicalism of the European Enlightenment*: "Friedrich Melchoir Grimm, the official voice of the radical Enlightenment in Europe, dismissed both the book and its author as facile and immature. The social contract, on which Beccaria's ideas were based, was a mere illusion born out of a life of wealth, Grimm wrote in his *Correspondance littéraire*, a pious dream by a young man who had no idea how harsh the world could be and how quickly a social contract could cede to total, murderous anarchy." But others, whether immediately or in the decades to come, recognized Beccaria's intellectual gifts and raw intelligence and saw the enormous potential for Beccaria's ideas to transform the world, be it in the social and political or the penal or economic spheres. For example, in 1802, in the wake of the American and French Revolutions, a prominent figure of the Greek Enlightenment, Adamantios Coray (or Koraes or Korais as his name is also often spelled), chose to translate Beccaria's *Dei delitti e delle pene*, dedicating it to the young Republic of the Ionian Islands.[56] An 1823 edition of that Greek translation of Beccaria's book would end up in Thomas Jefferson's library.[57]

Though it was Beccaria's *On Crimes and Punishments*, along with other Enlightenment texts, that helped inspire America's all-important Declaration of Independence (1776),[58] the fact that Beccaria's inaugural lecture at Milan's Palatine School so quickly made its way into French and English translations is also revealing. Indeed, one of the many students who attended the Marquis Beccaria's lectures at the *Scuole* Palatine recorded that, on the subject of division of labor, Beccaria had made this statement years before the appearance of Smith's *The Wealth of Nations*: "everyone can prove by experience, that by constantly applying his hand and his understanding to the same kind of works and products, he will attain easier, more abundant and better results, than in the case in which everybody would produce in isolation all the things he needs."[59] Neither Smith nor Beccaria, in fact, actually originated the concept of division of labor, though they both elaborated on it and thus publicized it.[60] In *The Fundamental Institutions of Capitalism*, it is written: "The role of the division of labour in arousing increasing returns to scale had already been recognized at the time of Cesare Beccaria and Adam Smith."[61] In *Civilization and Capitalism*, the French historian Fernand Braudel (1902–1985) offers this recitation of the applicable history: "Adam Smith did not invent the idea of the division of labour. He merely conferred the status of a general theory on an ancient idea already adumbrated by Plato, Aristotle and Xenophon, and mentioned long before his own time by William Petty (1623–87), Ernest Ludwig Carl (1687–1743), Adam Ferguson (1723–1816) and Cesare Beccaria."

"But from the time of Adam Smith," Braudel emphasized, referencing the Scottish economist who has garnered the lion's share of the credit for the concept and the pioneering scientist, Isaac Newton (1643–1727), who, through his own celebrity, had unwittingly given Beccaria his childhood nickname, "economists regarded the idea as something akin to Newton's law of gravity."[62]

In the Enlightenment, scientists and other thinkers frequently built on the ideas of other scientists and thinkers—and sometimes people even plagiarized them or were accused of misappropriating them, an accusation made by the Verri brothers in private that, in truth, was at least partially behind the rift that developed in 1766 between Cesare Beccaria and the Verri brothers. As one scholar writes, for example, of what transpired after *Dei delitti e delle pene* first appeared: "Rumour began spreading that Beccaria might have taken credit for the Verri brothers' *Reply* to Facchinei while on a visit to Paris, and soon Alessandro Verri sought to convince the *philosophes* in Paris that Beccaria had merely supplied 'the style and organization' to their own 'material' in his *On Crimes and Punishments.*" Behind the scenes, at least in the initial years after the publication of *Dei delitti e delle pene*, the Verri brothers certainly called into question Beccaria's literary achievement, leading one political economist, "Il marchese" Giovan Battista Freganeschi (1710-1793), Pietro Verri's close friend, to judgmentally remark of Beccaria's *On Crimes and Punishments* in 1783: "what is good in it is not his" and "what is his is not good."[63] But as history makes clear, it was *Beccaria*, not Verri or Freganeschi, who became the eighteenth- and nineteenth-century global celebrity. Because of *Dei delitti e delle pene*, as a recent criminology text stresses, "most experts consider Beccaria not only the Father of Criminal Justice and the Father of the Classical School of Criminology but, perhaps most important, the Father of Deterrence Theory."[64]

Dei delitti e delle pene, because of the sharp-edged framing of its ideas, set the stage for the coming battle against slavery—and for equality of treatment by the law. While Cesare Beccaria saw hard labor and imprisonment of convicts as "the only type of slavery that can be called just,"[65] and while he saw *la schiavitú perpetua* (perpetual slavery) as a reasonable alternative to torture and executions, the language he employed in *On Crimes and Punishments* represented a powerful call to action against the *Ancien Régime*'s focus on absolute power and privilege. "The rich and the powerful," Beccaria wrote in 1764, "should not be able to make amends for assaults against the weak and the poor by naming a price; otherwise, wealth, which is the reward of industry under the tutelage of the laws, becomes fodder for tyranny." "There is no liberty," Beccaria emphasized, "whenever the laws permit a man in some cases to cease to be a *person* and to become a *thing*: then you will see the efforts of the powerful dedicated entirely to eliciting from the mass of civil relations those in which the law is to his advantage." As Beccaria presciently warned: "This discovery is the magic secret that transforms citizens into beasts of burden and that, in the hands of the strong, is the chain that fetters the actions of the incautious and the weak. This is why in some governments that have every appearance of liberty, tyranny lies hidden or insinuates itself unseen into some corner neglected by the legislator, where imperceptibly it gathers strength and grows." "Generally," Beccaria concluded, "men set up the most solid embankments against open tyranny, but they do not see the tiny insect that gnaws away at them and opens a path for the river's flood, a path that is all the more certain to develop the more hidden it is."[66]

Beccaria's advocacy of a system of federalism, of which the United States of America is now but one prominent example, was itself part of a broader project of curtailing tyranny. In his 1764 work, historian Alex Körner writes, "Beccaria pronounced himself in favor of a federal organization of smaller states." As Körner explains of Beccaria's *Dei delitti e delle pene* in *America in Italy: The United States in the Political Thought and Imagination of the Risorgimento, 1763–1865*: "Although this is by no means his main argument, he might have been thinking about Rousseau's small-community-based democracy. Small states help to foster republican sentiment against the dangers of despotism; and a confederation protects them from foreign intervention." As Beccaria himself put it: "as a society grows larger, the significance of each member becomes less and the republican sentiment is diminished if the citizen is not protected by the laws." "A republic that is too large," Beccaria added, "cannot save citizens from despotism unless it subdivides itself and then reunifies as numerous federal republics." "Writing before the outbreak of conflict in the American colonies," Körner observes, "Beccaria made his argument independent of America's constitutional experiences, at a time when federalism (with the exception of the Holy Roman Empire, the United Provinces, and Switzerland) was largely posed as a theoretical problem."[67]

Although the title of Beccaria's most famous book, *On Crimes and Punishments*, thus suggests that it is only about the criminal law, it actually covers much more ground than that and is really about how to properly structure government itself to maximize human happiness and the public's welfare. Employing the same proportionality principle that he suggested for use as regards readjusting punishments in relation to crimes, Beccaria made this mathematics-like argument in *On Crimes and Punishments* about the consequences of states becoming too large and, therefore, too unaccountable: "In proportion to the increase of society, each member becomes a smaller part of the whole; and the republican spirit diminishes in the same proportion, if neglected by the laws. Political societies, like the human body, have their limits circumscribed, which they cannot exceed without disturbing their œconomy. It seems as if the greatness of a state ought to be inversely as the sensibility and activity of the individuals; if on the contrary, population, and activity increase in the same proportion, the laws will with difficulty prevent the crimes arising from the good they have produced." "An overgrown republic," Beccaria, as his words were translated into English, sagely advised, "can only be saved from despotism, by subdividing it into a number of confederate republics."[68] It was this insight that inspired a Pennsylvania lawyer, John Dickinson, to write of "the masterly hand of a *Beccaria*" and "[t]he genius of a *Beccaria*" — the Italian who, in Dickinson's words in *An Essay on the Constitutional Power of Great-Britain Over the Colonies in America* (1774), had warned with such great foresight of "the condition of a large empire verging into servitude." "What was argument in *Italy*, is reality to *Great-Britain*," Dickinson opined in his 1774 essay, written on the cusp of the Revolutionary War in a last-ditch effort to get Great Britain to rethink its mistreatment of the American colonies.[69]

The plethora of historical evidence about Cesare Beccaria's enormous impact could not be clearer. Beccaria's treatise, *On Crimes and Punishments*, was said in 1846 to have acquired a "general reputation" and to have "exercised much influence."[70] The book was purchased and read by countless individuals, both famous and not, and it was acquired by assorted public and private libraries in the eighteenth and nineteenth centuries.[71] For instance, the inventory of the library of William Chambers—a young Pennsylvania lawyer who died at age 27—was recently rediscovered. The holdings in his carefully selected personal library—one of which he must have been enormously proud—reveal the importance of Beccaria's book to well-educated citizens such as that young attorney. The son of a Revolutionary War veteran, William Chambers (1796–1823) was, himself, the brother of George Chambers, a justice of the Pennsylvania Supreme Court in a state that had scores of Beccaria admirers. The executors of William Chamber's estate cataloged 266 books, one of which, perhaps not surprisingly, was Cesare Beccaria's *On Crimes and Punishments*. Among the other titles in the library of William Chambers: Adam Smith's *The Wealth of Nations* (1776); Adam Ferguson's *The History of the Progress and Termination of the Roman Republic*; *The Percy Anecdotes*, which contains an entry on Beccaria wherein he is described as a "philosopher of humanity"; and *Reports of Cases Argued and Determined in the Court of King's Bench in the Nineteenth, Twentieth, and Twenty-First Years of the Reign of George III* by Sylvester Douglas of Lincoln's Inn. While Beccaria's *Dei delitti e delle pene* was readily available in English translations, including in Scotland, after 1767,[72] it was none other than Sylvester Douglas who translated Cesare Beccaria's 1769 inaugural lecture at the Palatine School into English.[73]

Scores of attorneys, barristers and advocates—at the Inns of Court in London, at the Faculty of Advocates in Scotland, and elsewhere throughout the world—were thus highly conversant with Beccaria's *On Crimes and Punishments*. They carefully read it, mining its perceptive wisdom, and the treatise can be found in countless early Anglo-American estate-sale catalogues along with being discussed in innumerable books, periodicals, and other sources.[74] Multiple editions of Beccaria's treatise were, in multiple languages, in circulation from the mid-1760s onward. And it is crystal clear that scores of prominent figures, including Sir William Blackstone and penal reformers Jeremy Bentham and Samuel Romilly, were intrigued—even deeply moved—by Beccaria's ideas.[75] Beccaria's book became one of those texts that entered—indeed, deeply penetrated—the public's collective consciousness. Indeed, once it was published—and especially once highly respected writers like Voltaire and Blackstone offered lavish praise for it—the world could not stay the same.[76] In *Reflections on Hanging* (1957), the Budapest-born, British author Arthur Koestler—looking back at Beccaria's massive intellectual impact in Europe many decades later after discussing what he called Beccaria's "principle of the 'minimum effective punishment'"—put it this way: "I have already mentioned the influence which Beccaria's teaching gained all over Europe, from Russia to France, from Sweden to Italy. There was perhaps no single humanist since Erasmus of Rotterdam, who, without being attached to a definite political or religious movement, had such a deep effect on European thought."[77]

In England, though Cesare Beccaria's anti-death penalty views initially found few initial adherents within the British government or its complacent, Old Line aristocracy, Beccaria's writings were well received by others in English society on a variety of matters.[78] Progressive British thinkers certainly eagerly read its contents, with Edward Augustus (1739–1767), the Duke of York and a man very close to the throne, reportedly "one of the very few English admirers of Beccaria" from the uppermost, royal echelon of English high society. The younger brother of King George III, the Duke of York was reportedly "the first member of the English Royal Family to visit Italy as a tourist." He travelled to Italy from 1763 to 1764, where he met Pope Clement XIII, who held a reception in his honor and presented him with gifts. While in Milan, the Duke of York—according to a letter between the Alessandro and Pietro Verri—actually met Cesare Beccaria's wife, Teresa, and was given a copy of *Dei delitti e delle pene*, which had only recently been clandestinely published in Leghorn. As historian Jeremy Black describes the Duke of York's trip in *George III: America's Last King*: "After Rome, where he also sat for his portrait by Pompeo Batoni, York pressed on to Bologna, Parma, Venice, Padua and Milan, where he was interested in the copy he was given of Beccaria's *Dei delitti e delle pene*, a call for the end of capital punishment, not a cause close to George's heart." The "marchesnia Beccaria" also reportedly "corresponded with the Duke after his return home," with the duke apparently planning to have the book translated into English.[79] Peter Molini—the Italian publisher and bookseller associated with the first English translation of *Dei delitti e delle pene*—was himself a well-known figure in London who had hosted Alessandro Verri in that city after Alessandro Verri's own unsatisfying 1766 trip to Paris ended with Beccaria's premature departure.[80]

Cesare Beccaria's worldview, the one that catapulted him to fame, was forged by the patriarchal society in which he lived—and by the tyranny he had experienced in his own life. Beccaria's formative experience with his own father when he unsuccessfully attempted to gain his father's blessing to marry Teresa de Blasco must have remained etched in his mind throughout his adult life. While the Beccaria family had an estate in Gessate, the Blasco family—headed by Domenico, a Lieutenant Colonel of the Engineers of the Brigade of Italy who had nine brothers—had a nearby house in Gorgonzola, a locality northeast of Milan now best known for its cheese, but not the vast wealth or social standing that Cesare's father originally sought for his son. After Cesare had courted and pledged to marry Teresa, expressing his undying love, Beccaria's father and uncle had stridently opposed the marriage, with both men finding Teresa unsuitable. In a then fully legal maneuver, Cesare—experiencing a total loss of control, as well as a loss of his freedom and liberty in that highly patriarchal society—had been placed under house arrest. Though Cesare and Teresa persevered and ultimately went forward with their marriage in spite of the Beccaria family's opposition to it, Cesare and Teresa—for a time—were forced to live modestly on a 1,000 *lire* annual stipend (and in a rented house).

While his new wife, Teresa, was pregnant, Cesare had to rely on pity and his friend, Pietro Verri, for support and to help him reunite with his family. Cesare felt that he had been reduced to the condition of a beggar, prompting him to write two letters to Count Firmian, the Austrian minister of plenipotentiary to Milan. Cesare felt miserable and in a state of despair, and it took the staging of a pregnant Teresa fainting in front of the Beccaria family home to reset the trajectory of Cesare and Teresa's young lives. While Cesare was later staying in Gessate with his new wife, Teresa, "the rakish Count Pietro Verri" (as he was once described), in an October 1764 letter to Livorno publisher Giuseppe Aubert, called Teresa a "*bella moglie*" (beautiful wife). It was jealousies, whether literary or of a much more personal nature, or perhaps both, that later drove a wedge between the older Pietro Verri and the younger Cesare Beccaria. Verri, a man known to have had affairs with married women, actually had his own relationship with Beccaria's wife, Teresa, between 1763 and 1764, though it was Bartolomeo Calderara—Teresa's subsequent lover—who is thought to be (and almost certainly was) the biological father of Teresa's short-lived, first-born male child, Giovanni Annibale. Born on August 20, 1767, Giovanni Annibale was the baby who was delivered—and who, tragically, died shortly following childbirth—a few months after Cesare Beccaria's hasty return from his 1766 trip to Paris.[81]

Because of his humanitarian vision, it has been written that Cesare Beccaria was not a "typical" eighteenth-century aristocrat. In his work, the Italian economist and philosopher often referred to as "the humane Beccaria" expressed great concern and empathy for the poor and the downtrodden—a concern and empathic impulse that, perhaps unsurprisingly, found a sympathetic audience in many quarters around the globe. The Italian peninsula, the place of Beccaria's own birth, had large numbers of poor and poorly educated agricultural and industrial workers, and many were illiterate. The reform-minded Beccaria sought to better educate the populace, something that captivated others, too. For example, Robert Coram—a Revolutionary War veteran and a self-educated librarian and schoolteacher from Wilmington, Delaware—advocated for a system of universal public education. He recognized, as had Beccaria, that education was the key to bettering societies and to preventing crime. As historian Seth Cotlar tellingly writes in *Tom Paine's America*: "Coram drew on Beccaria—a major influence on the Painite radicals of the 1790s—in making the argument that the poor have no choice but to break the laws regarding property in order to survive." "For Coram," Cotlar explains, "Beccaria's work had conclusively demonstrated that poverty, not the inherent vice of the poor, was the cause of most crime: 'It is a melancholy reflection that in almost all ages and countries men have been cruelly butchered for crimes occasioned by the laws and which they never would have committed, had they not been deprived of their natural means of subsistence.'"

A fellow American, the Connecticut poet and Yale College graduate Joel Barlow, known today for writing his poem, *The Hasty-Pudding* (1796), himself noted in *Advice to the Privileged Orders in the Several States of Europe*: "the compassionate little treatise of Beccaria, *[D]ei delitti e delle pene*, is getting to be a manual in all languages." In his essay, Barlow specifically wrote of then-existing governments: "As far as any rule can be discovered in their gradation of punishments, it appears to be this, That the severity of the penalty is in proportion to the injustice of the law." That little treatise, Barlow observed, taking note of Beccaria's ideas on reforming barbaric penal codes, "has already served as an introduction to many luminous essays on the policy and right of punishment, in which the spirit of inquiry is pursued much farther than that benevolent philosopher, surrounded as he is by the united sabres of feudal and ecclesiastical tyranny, has dared to pursue it."[82] As one source on Joel Barlow (1754-1812), a bookseller, lawyer and legal philosopher who supported the French Revolution and who served as an American diplomat in France, notes: "Barlow was greatly influenced by Beccaria in his views on capital punishment and debtor imprisonment. The firm of Barlow and Babcock had sold Beccaria's Essays on Crime and Punishment, which was widely read in the colonies."[83] In *The Expanding Blaze: How the American Revolution Ignited the World, 1775-1848*, Enlightenment expert and historian Jonathan Israel emphasizes that, in truth, a large number of Americans and Europeans alike cited and invoked Beccaria's treatise during this pivotal period of world history.[84]

Sophus Reinert, who teaches a course on globalization and emerging markets at Harvard Business School, has called *Dei delitti e delle pene* "the most lionized work to emerge from the Italian Enlightenment," though he points out that fragments from Beccaria's unpublished writings, including *Ripulimento della nazioni* (*Refinement of Nations*), demonstrate that Beccaria sought to pacify people—to end endless wars—through benevolent commerce and trade. *Ripulimento della nazioni*, planned "between 1764 and 1770," Reinert writes, "was ostensibly meant to redraw the history and, perhaps, future of civilization through the lens of political economy." Primitive societies had become more sophisticated and cultured, with Antonio Genovesi, Italy's first professor of political economy, once emphasizing that people in his time were seeing the world through "the eyes of a merchant." In his planned *Refinement of Nations*, to be an ambitious study of the history of human progress, Beccaria wanted to produce a book that—as the Verri brothers put—would be a "second, equal book" to *Dei delitti e delle pene*. Though that goal was never achieved, it was a noteworthy project. "In one of the few surviving fragments of the *Refinement of Nations*, entitled *Thoughts on the Barbarism and Culture of Nations and the Savage State of Man*," Sophus Reinert points out, "Beccaria had suggested a conceptual matrix for analyzing nations at all stages of their historical development." As Reinert describes Beccaria's matrix: "On one axis he proposed a spectrum stretching from barbarism to culture, a measure of a nation's 'ignorance of things that are useful to it' and the best 'means' of achieving 'individual happiness'. The other axis stretched from savagery to sociability, gauging the degree of a nation's distance 'from the greatest union that can exist between men, and from the greatest absolute happiness possible divided among the greatest possible number'."[85]

In nation after nation, Cesare Beccaria had an impressive, lasting impact. In a 1793 Irish grand jury charge, Beccaria was described as a "humane Philosopher."[86] But it was Beccaria's *ideas*—in many ways ahead of their time—that made the biggest impression or that show his impressive intellect. "*The political boundaries of a state*," Beccaria once wrote, centuries before the creation of the United Nations, the European Union, and the World Trade Organization, "*are almost never the same as its economic boundaries*"; countries, "*however divided by sovereignty and reciprocally independent with respect to their political laws*," he observed, were "*really a single nation tightly united by physical laws and dependent one on the other through their economic relations*." Beccaria earnestly worried about imperialism and exploitation of the poor, but he also saw the potential that trade could contribute to peace and prosperity. As Reinert summarizes the Italian economist's ideas: "Beccaria embraced the possibility that a fair international exchange of manufactures might pave the way to a pacification of the world system." Beccaria, believing that the "introduction" of certain goods might be "opportune to open an exit for our things, and a communication with other nations," expressed the view that "up to a certain point a nation can prosper at the expense of another." Beccaria, however, also aptly observed that "beyond a certain point our true prosperity produces the prosperity of others, given man was not given an exclusive happiness or misery." This, he felt, provided "a clear indication" that "nature wished" for a "brotherhood of the human species."[87]

After Adam Smith's death, in the introduction to Smith's posthumously published *Essays on Philosophical Subjects* (1799), its compiler, Dugald Stewart, specifically mentioned Beccaria's influence on eighteenth-century societies. "It is evident," Stewart wrote in that book, "that the most important branch of political science is that which has for its object to ascertain the philosophical principles of jurisprudence; or (as MR. SMITH expresses it) to ascertain 'the general principles which ought to run through and be the foundation of the laws of all nations.'" "I cannot help adding," Stewart continued, "that the capacity of a people to exercise political rights with utility to themselves and to their country, presupposes a diffusion of knowledge and of good morals, which can only result from the previous operation of laws favorable to industry, to order, and to freedom." "Of the truth of these remarks," Stewart stressed, "enlightened politicians seem now to be in general convinced; for the most celebrated works which have been produced in the different countries of Europe, during the last thirty years, by SMITH, QUESNAI, TURGOT, CAMPOMANES, BECCARIA, and others, have aimed at the improvement of society,— not by delineating plans of new constitutions, but by enlightening the policy of actual legislators."[88] *Dei delitti e delle pene* was not only read, whether in the original Italian or in translation, by many such lawmakers, but it was regularly referred to as a "celebrated work," even though it was still being censored in some European locales into the nineteenth century.[89]

Cesare Beccaria's earliest critics have been judged harshly in the history books. For example, Ferdinando Facchinei expressed the view that author of *Dei delitti e delle pene* was a "false Christian" and that Beccaria's book was a "true daughter" of Rousseau's *Social Contract*. Although Facchinei himself had made clear in January 1763 that he was about to finish a "letter regarding the sum of pleasures and pains" and that he aimed to show "it is only schmucks [*minchioni*] who don't find more pleasures than pains in this world," the appearance of Pietro Verri's anonymously published *Meditations on Happiness* and Beccaria's anonymously published *Dei delitti e delle pene* somehow set him off. Then mistakenly believing both books had been written by the same person, Facchinei derided them as "monstrous twins." "The Social Contract is an impossible Chimera," Facchinei declared, derisively concluding that the author of *Dei delitti e delle pene* wished to be viewed as "the *Rousseau* of the Italians." Viewing harsh punishments, what he called "the Wolf's bite," favorably, Facchinei expressed the view that "fear conserves realms" and that without such draconian measures humans would still be living "in the forests, and the deserts, the way Bears and Lions live." As Sophus Reinert, the modern economic historian, writes of Facchinei and his blistering, eighteenth-century attack on *Dei delitti e delle pene* that appeared just a year after Beccaria's book was published: "History has not been kind to Facchinei, who complained late in life of having been 'hated and defamed', not to mention forced into 'silence, slandered and oppressed' for his *Notes and Observations*." As Reinert speaks of Facchinei and the public wrath that was soon visited upon him (and not Beccaria): "One of his more inventive critics even described him as having 'a truly amphibious and hermaphroditic head', and it has been argued that Facchinei became 'almost proverbial as a symbol of obtuse fanaticism.'"[90]

Not only did Beccaria's ideas on law and economics, however obscure or in the background in modern times, shape the Enlightenment, but they continue to be felt—and to be relevant—to this day. What history reveals is that Beccaria's lucid ideas on a broad range of subjects—from happiness to tyranny and from cruelty to infamy and torture—were an integral part of eighteenth- and nineteenth-century debates in Europe, the Americas, and elsewhere. Those ideas, which the Roman Catholic Church attempted to censor, led to *Dei delitti e delle pene* being put on the Index of Forbidden Books. But despite the efforts of the Inquisition and state censors, Beccaria's ideas could not be suppressed. Instead, they had a profound civilizing effect on Western cultures, an effect that rippled across the globe and that can still be identified today worldwide. Most significantly, Beccaria's ideas about equality, proper governance, and the orderly regulation of crime and punishment—pillars of modernity—shaped and molded societal attitudes and the world's constitutions and statutes, leading to clearer and less barbaric penal codes.[91] As Beccaria's biographer, John Hostettler, writes in *Champions of the Rule of Law*: "As part of the fabric of the rule of law, Beccaria held that the law must be clear and precise, not arbitrary. Trial by a person's peers was essential, secret accusations should be outlawed, proof of a crime should be perfect and laws should be passed by legislation and should not be created by judges."[92]

In the seventeenth century, Europe's monarchs regularly resorted to torture and executions to induce fear and dread among the populace. "Capital punishment is underpinning the whole system, really, until the 19th Century," criminal justice historian Matthew White, of the University of Hertfordshire, recently emphasized. For example, in a story about Execution Dock, the London gallows on the River Thames where pirates were hanged, White underscored the intent of the "bloody" or sanguinary system that once pervaded European societies: "It's legal terror, effectively; it is preventing crime by means of terror. The original goal of the judicial system is to terrorise everybody by, as they call it, the might of the law." London scaffolds—whether at Execution Dock or Tyburn, another conspicuous site for hanging—were specifically designed to showcase the state's limitless power. "Between 1735 and 1830 alone," the BBC's story reported, "Execution Dock"—the site of execution for those condemned to death by the High Court of Admiralty for crimes ranging from mutiny to murder to piracy—"saw at least 78 hangings." By tradition, the riverfront executions at Execution Dock occurred at low tide, with authorities letting the tide wash over the dead body. For notorious convicts, the bodies would be tarred and then hung in cages so that anyone sailing up the Thames would see the bodies hanging there. At Tyburn, a far more popular execution site, it is estimated that between 1196 and 1783 more than

50,000 people were put to death for crimes against the King or the state.[93] The revolution in penal reform that Beccaria sparked did not change or abolish the world's
sanguinary laws overnight, but his ideas set in motion an ongoing, multi-generational
reform movement that continues to this day. It was a movement that led to the dismantling of many scaffolds, including those in England.

Though he lived exclusively in the eighteenth century, scattered physical traces of
Cesare Beccaria's legacy still remain. Today, if one strolls through the shrub- and bust-
lined paths on the hilltop park adjoining Rome's Villa Borghese gardens, one can still
encounter the sculpted head of the Enlightenment philosopher and economist.[94] There,
one can also find busts of Beccaria's mentor, fellow economist and philosopher Pietro
Verri; the Neapolitan Gaetano Filangieri (1752–1788), the Italian legal reformer who,
in life, corresponded with both Benjamin Franklin and Beccaria himself; and the Piedmont poet and playwright Vittorio Alfieri (1749–1803), who wrote of America's independence, even dedicating a play to George Washington, the first U.S. President.[95]
Count Vittorio Alfieri—a rich nobleman who, like Beccaria, read Montesquieu,
Voltaire, Helvétius, Rousseau and other Enlightenment writers—was one of many
Italians who admired the American Revolution, writing his own ode to American independence in 1788 (*L'America libera*) as well as a treatise on tyranny (*Della tirannide*).[96]
Count Alfieri became the first Italian to call for national unity, using the term *risorgimento* (resurgence) before Italy's unification in the nineteenth century. With a street
in Rome, Via Cesare Beccaria, not far from the Villa Borghese, the adjoining park also
contains a bust of General Pasquale Paoli (1725–1807), the Italian speaker who also
inspired American revolutionaries with his own quest for Corsican independence.[97]

Among the sculpted busts to be admired along the Roman park's walking paths
in the Villa Borghese gardens are also ones of Alessandro Manzoni (1785–1873),
Cesare Beccaria's grandson and a famous Italian writer and poet in his own right,[98]
and of the historian Carlo Botta (1766–1837), who decided to write a multi-volume
history of the American Revolution after attending a Parisian party at the home of
Cesare Beccaria's daughter, Giulia. A still much-celebrated literary figure, Manzoni
wrote books that were translated from Italian into English and sold in America,
though his fame in Italy, at its height, was unsurpassed.[99] A street in Milan, Via
Alessandro Manzoni, is now named after Cesare Beccaria's grandson, and in the city
there is also an impressive bronze statue of Alessandro Manzoni—a monument to
the great writer—near the church on the Piazza San Fedele, the place where Manzoni
worshipped during his life.[100] As one guidebook describes the piazza and the church
overlooking the square: "Piazza San Fedele is an elegantly aristocratic corner of Milan
that was particularly dear to one of the city's most illustrious sons, Alessandro Manzoni, who lived a stone's throw away for almost 60 years." "Overlooking the square
is the church of the same name, which boasts a long and noble history." "In San
Fedele, in 1771," that source notes, "Mozart directed his *Passion Cantata*, and later
on Alessandro Manzoni regularly attended Mass here."[101]

Alessandro Manzoni's mother, Giulia, whose portrait was painted by Maria Cosway
(1760–1838) in the first decade of the 1800s, was reportedly "a woman of rare intelligence and refinement."[102] Giulia was said to be a "poetess" of "literary ability" who

"was crucial to her son's intellectual and religious development," and she gave her son many opportunities after he came to Paris to live with her.[103] As one source reports of the literary success of Giulia's son: "Alessandro Manzoni must be considered … as the most brilliant Italian novelist of the nineteenth century. As a poet his achievement was also far from negligible." Alessandro's first poem, written in 1801, was *Il Trionfo della Libertà*, "an exaltation of the French Revolution and its triumph over tyranny and superstition." The national motto of France—*Liberté, égalité, fraternité*—originated in the French Revolution, though the original version that appeared on eighteenth-century placards read *Liberté, égalité, fraternité ou la mort* (Liberty, equality, fraternity or death). Because of its association with the Reign of Terror— the horrific brutality wrought by thousands of executions that made Cesare Beccaria, while alive, cringe—the *death* part of the slogan was later dropped from the country's now famed motto.[104]

Born in 1785 in Milan, Alessandro Manzoni lived in Paris from 1805 to 1810. He married Henriette Blondel, the sixteen-year-old daughter of a Swiss banker, in 1808, and they started what would become a large family. The marriage of Alessandro's parents had ended in 1792, with Alessandro's mother, wanting a change in scenery and a new life after her separation, settling in Paris with the Italian aristocrat Carlo Imbonati—a "handsome, rich, and well-connected nobleman." Carlo Imbonati, the son of the founder of the Academy of the Transformed, was close friends with Sophie de Condorcet, the widow of the Girondin leader, the Marquis de Condorcet, who—to escape the guillotine's indignities—is said to have poisoned himself in 1794 after being arrested during the Reign of Terror.[105] The last embroidery made by Marie Antoinette during her imprisonment—a portrait of a young girl that now resides at Alessandro Manzoni's house in Milan—was actually latter presented by Sophie de Condorcet to her friend, Giulia Beccaria.[106] As one source describes Giulia and Alessandro's time in Paris: "The daughter of progressive jurist Cesare Beccaria, Giulia was heir to the cultural tradition of the Enlightenment, which profoundly affected young Alessandro's intellectual development. After separating from her husband in 1792, Giulia moved to Paris, where her son Alessandro joined her in 1805. Manzoni spent five years in Paris, where he met the most prestigious intellectuals of the day." As that source notes: "With Donna Giulia and historian Claude Fauriel, Manzoni frequented the salon of Mme de Condorcet and sympathized with the idéologues, a group of philosophers who shared his progressive political views and skepticism in religious matters. From the idéologues Manzoni derived methodological rigor and analytical precision."[107]

Before his death, the Marquis de Condorcet (1743–1794) actively took part in Voltaire's campaign to reform French criminal procedure in the aftermath of the 1766 trial in Abbeville of the chevalier de La Barre. As Enlightenment expert David Williams writes in *Condorcet and Modernity*: "Condorcet became closely involved in the ongoing controversy, stoked by Voltaire, arising from the case of La Barre, a sixteen-year-old youth tortured and burnt by the Abbeville magistrates for vandalism of a crucifix." "Condorcet worked hard with Voltaire to rehabilitate the young blasphemer's memory," Williams observes, emphasizing that "[t]he affair turned Condorcet into Voltaire's apostle and *trompette* in Paris." Condorcet, the French intellectual, also had contact with Beccaria, knew Thomas Paine, corresponded with leading American founders such as John Adams, Benjamin Franklin and Thomas Jefferson, and had a close friendship with Turgot, the French Controller-General. As Williams stresses of Beccaria's own influence on the Marquis de Condorcet, the two having corresponded decades before their deaths in the same year, 1794: "Impressed by Beccaria's argument about proportionality in the matter of judicial punishments, Condorcet's opposition to French medieval court practices, the judicial use of torture, the infamous rules of evidence, and in particular to the profligate use of the death penalty, hardened. Condorcet knew Beccaria personally, having met him in Sophie de Grouchy's circle. His own *Réflexions sur la jurisprudence criminelle* appeared in 1775."[108]

The project of the Enlightenment took a chorus of intellects and courageous voices to take shape, and Condorcet and his wife played their own part in the Republic of Letters that flowered in the eighteenth century. Born Marie-Louise-Sophie de Grouchy, the daughter of the 1st Marquis de Grouchy but better known after her marriage as Madame de Condorcet, Madame de Condorcet was a popular hostess and a gifted writer who, fluent in both English and Italian, produced translations of works by Thomas Paine and Adam Smith. Her translation of Adam Smith's *Theory of Moral Sentiments* included an appendix of her own *Letters on Sympathy*. The Marquis de Condorcet—a Jesuit-educated son of a noble cavalry captain—was a mathematician, and he had married the much younger Sophie de Grouchy in 1786, with Madame de Condorcet reportedly presiding "in their apartment at the Mint over the last salon favored by liberal Paris in the old regime." As one historian observes of that salon: "It was noted for serious conversation, not for wit." Its guests included both local politicians as well as foreign leaders and dignitaries, including Cesare Beccaria, Olympe de Gouges, Thomas Jefferson, André Morellet, Thomas Paine and Adam Smith. A lover of liberty and a fierce opponent of religious intolerance, the Marquis de Condorcet visited Voltaire at Ferney and wrote biographies of both Turgot and Voltaire. Those biographies, *Vie de M. Turgot* (1786) and *Vie de Voltaire* (1789), reveal—as one source reports—"his sympathy with Anne-Robert-Jacques Turgot's economic theories about mitigating the suffering of the French populace before the French Revolution and with Voltaire's opposition to the church."[109]

Cesare Beccaria's contemporaries—many versed in political philosophy and mathematics and economics—were major Enlightenment figures. Anne-Robert-Jacques Turgot—one of Condorcet's mentors, along with d'Alembert—was said to be "the very model of the enlightened administrator, appointed Minister of Finance by Louis XVI in 1774." As the editors of that source, *Condorcet: Political Writings*, explain of Turgot: "For Turgot, humanity's progress was inevitable, but in the here and now fiscal reforms were urgently needed: free trade across the French provinces, the end of compulsory unpaid labour by the peasants on the roads, a single land tax for all property-holders, including the clergy, a system of elected local assemblies, the dismantling of feudal privileges and the promotion of commerce." "Inevitably," those editors continue, "all this threatened too many vested interests and Turgot was dismissed within two years, to Condorcet's despair." Both Turgot and Beccaria—the two economists—felt compelled to speak out and air their views, even if all their ideas were not immediately embraced. "Turgot's major economic work, 'Reflections on the Production and Distribution of Wealth,'" Peter Groenewegen emphasizes in *Eighteenth-century Economics*, "was hurriedly composed and completed in November 1766; it is a short work of 101 paragraphs or sections, and was not intended as a major work at all."

The Marquis de Condorcet, the *Encyclopædia Britannica* recounts of Turgot's mentee, "was the friend of almost all the distinguished persons of his time and a zealous propagator of the progressive views then current among French literati." "He was," that source notes, "a protégé of the French philosopher and mathematician Jean Le Rond d'Alembert and took an active part in the preparation of the *Encyclopédie*." As the *Encyclopædia Britannica* sums up Condorcet's pivotal role in the French Revolution: "Condorcet was one of the first to declare for a republic, and in August 1792 drew up the declaration justifying the suspension of the king and the summoning of the National Convention. In the convention he represented the *département* of Aisne and was a member of the committee on the constitution." As that encyclopedia then recounts of the series of events that ultimately led Condorcet to take his own life—or so the common story goes—after being arrested and labeled a traitor: "His draft of a new constitution, representative of the Girondins, the more moderate political group during the Revolution, was rejected, however, in favour of that of the Jacobins, a more radical political group whose dominating figure was Robespierre. In the trial of Louis XVI he voted against the death penalty. But his independent attitude became dangerous in the wake of the Revolution when Robespierre's radical measures triumphed, and his opposition to arrest of the Girondins lead to his being outlawed." Before his death, the Marquis de Condorcet published *De l'admission des femmes au droit de cité* (*For the Admission to the Rights of Citizenship for Women*) in 1790 and penned a final essay, *Esquisse d'un tableau historique des progrès de l'esprit humain* (*Sketch for a Historical Picture of the Progress of the Human Mind*) that was posthumously published in 1794 shortly after his death. The latter essay posited the continuous progress of the human race and predicted the end of inequality between nations and classes and the perfectibility of human nature. "The equality to which he represents nations and individuals as tending," the *Encyclopædia Britannica* emphasizes, "is not absolute equality but equality of freedom and of rights."[110]

Cesare Beccaria and the Marquis de Condorcet had much in common besides their titles, and each influenced the other. Just as Cesare Beccaria had taken charge of the mint in his native land, Condorcet oversaw the operations of his country's mint. Condorcet—as Steven Luke and Nadia Urbinati, the editors of his writings, recount—had been appointed by Turgot to be Inspector General of the Mint, a position he retained until 1791. "In this capacity," they note, "he made a series of technical contributions to practical problems, such as the building of canals and the measurement of tonnage in ships, and he worked out the first coherent account of insurance." As Luke and Urbinati further emphasize: "Condorcet not only shared Turgot's vision of progress, his belief in free trade and freedom of contract, and his idea of the need to institute locally elected assemblies, but he was also at one with Turgot's rejection of the utilitarians' narrow view of self-interested motivation, with his concern to protect the poor from market failures and, above all, with his commitment to practical political engagement." The co-founder of an anti-slavery society, Condorcet was "in contact with the leading Enlightenment figures of the time, both at home and abroad, including Adam Smith, Cesare Beccaria and David Hume, and later Tom Paine, as well as Thomas Jefferson and Benjamin Franklin." An admirer of the American Declaration of Independence, which Condorcet once described as "a restoration of humanity's long-lost title-deeds," Condorcet and his wife, along with Thomas Paine and two others, co-founded the first Republican club in 1791, published a new journal, *Le Républicain*, associated with it, and hosted in their home a pioneering women's rights group known as *Le Cercle social*.[111] "It would be difficult to overstate Beccaria's influence on the movement for French legal reform," one history of the French Revolution observes. "*On Crimes and Punishments*," that source notes of its ubiquitous impact, "deepened the thinking of a long line of liberal magistrates, lawyers, and philosophers, from Voltaire and Michel Antoine Servan to Jacques Pierre Brissot and Marquis de Condorcet."[112]

Like the Marquis de Condorcet's wife, Madame de Condorcet, Giulia Beccaria—Cesare Beccaria's daughter—became a prominent member of Parisian high society. "About the year 1806," *The Romanic Review* notes of one of Cesare's surviving children, "there was in Paris Madame Beccaria, daughter of the celebrated Marquis Beccaria, author of the famous book *Dei Delitti e delle Pene*, and mother of Signore Alessandro Manzoni, whose name has become very famous...."[113] Giulia—whose portrait was painted in Paris between 1802 and 1803 by the Italian-English painter Maria Cosway—lived for years in the City of Light after her famous father's death.[114] Cosway, whose paintings and engravings are now on display at the British Museum and art galleries around the world, was born in Florence, was an accomplished artist, composer and musician, and—perhaps, most famously—became the object of Thomas Jefferson's affections when Jefferson, a widower, represented America in France as an envoy.[115] Jefferson and Maria Cosway spent several weeks together seeing the sights in Paris until Maria's husband, English portrait painter Richard Cosway, insisted the Cosways depart for London. As historian Cynthia Kiemer writes of Jefferson's "famous flirtation with Maria Cosway" before Jefferson himself departed for Italy: "Jefferson and Maria Cosway enjoyed opera, theater, art, and each other's company during the early autumn of 1786, when she returned to London. In late February 1787, Jefferson left Paris for a tour of France and northern Italy that lasted three and a half months."[116]

Thomas Jefferson's famous missive, a long love letter sent to the younger Maria in 1786 after Jefferson saw Maria off in her carriage at the Pavillon de St. Denis, was a dialogue between "Head" and "Heart" in which Jefferson wrote of being "[o]verwhelmed with grief" and said he felt "more fit for death than life." In that letter, Jefferson also wrote of Americans as "a people occupied as we are in opening rivers, digging navigable canals, making roads, building public schools, establishing academies, erecting busts & statues to our great men, protecting religious freedom, abolishing sanguinary punishments, reforming & improving our laws in general."[117] Many of those beautiful busts and statues, including ones of George Washington, the first U.S. President, and John Jay, the first Chief Justice of the U.S. Supreme Court, were sculpted by Italian artists, with much of the artistic ornamentation in the U.S. Capitol also executed by Italian artisans. George Washington's bust—sculpted by Antonio

Capellano—now resides in the Capitol, and John Jay's bust—sculpted by Giuseppe Ceracchi—is on display in the U.S. Supreme Court building. Ceracchi actually executed twenty-seven busts of America's most prominent leaders, including ones of Washington, Jefferson and Alexander Hamilton. James Madison, another client, called Ceracchi "an artist celebrated by his genius."[118]

Both Alessandro Manzoni and Carlo Botta—two of the Italian writers represented in the Villa Borghese gardens—became famous literary figures in their own right.[119] After leaving college, a young Alessandro Manzoni had joined his mother in Paris, where he penned an elegiac poem, *In Morte di Carlo Imbonati* (*On the death of Carlo Imbonati*, 1806), before becoming a world-renowned author. Born at San Giorgio in the Piedmont region in 1766, Carlo Botta—one of Giulia Beccaria's many guests at her Parisian salon—was a poet and a prolific writer. He had studied medicine at the University of Turin, was part of the medical staff of the French army, and went on to become—as one text puts it—"one of the leading historians of his age." Botta had emigrated to France after being confined for two years in the citadel of Turin for his involvement in the French Revolution, and he was a fierce proponent of liberty and of the power of history and literature. After the turn of the century, he was elected to the French legislature and prepared his *Storia della Guerra dell' Indipendenza d'America* (*History of the War of Independence of the United States of America*), published in Turin in 1809 and in Paris in 1810. That book, translated into English by a prominent American, George Alexander Otis, appeared in ten editions in the United States from the 1820s to the 1850s.[120] That an Italian should write a history of the American Revolution was not at all surprising; the pursuit of human rights was of *universal* concern and the affinity between Italian writers and American revolutionaries was, by then, decades-old, starting—most prominently—with *Dei delitti e delle pene*.

The story of Botta's history of America's Revolutionary War (1775–1783) is recorded in George Washington Greene's *Italian Literature in the Nineteenth Century*. George Washington Greene (1811–1883), the grandson of Continental Army Major General Nathanael Greene (1742–1786), a Revolutionary War hero, wrote of Botta's inspiration this way: "The first idea of his history of the American Revolution was suggested by a conversation that took place in the house of Madame Manzoni, or as the Italians, out of reverence to the memory of her father, called her, Madama Beccaria. The choicest society in Paris met in the rooms of this lady, and it may readily be supposed that Botta was of the number." "One evening," George Washington Greene reported, "the conversation chanced to fall upon the great events of modern history, and their adaption to epic poetry. The discussion was long and animated, and scarce an event but found its advocate; but it was at last unanimously decided in favor of our Revolution, as furnishing, of all others, the characters and the incidents most worthy of the sublimity of the epic." As Botta walked home through a square near the Tuileries, the place "so closely associated with the most horrid excesses of the French Revolution," Botta said to himself, "Why, if it be a fit subject for a poem, should it not be fitter still for a history?" "It is, and I will write it," Botta resolved.[121] Because Cesare Beccaria's writings played such a sizable role in inspiring the American Revolution, it is only fitting, perhaps, that Botta's history of it should have been inspired in the salon of

Beccaria's own daughter. As with *Dei delitti e delle pene*, Thomas Jefferson thought especially highly of Botta's history, with Botta himself corresponding with the man from Monticello.[122]

The Enlightenment—what the Germans call *Aufklärung*, the Italians call the *Illuminismo*, and the French call *le Siècle des Lumières* (literally, "the Century of Lights")—was a period of intense scientific and social inquiry. It was the Age of Reason, of Thomas Paine's *Rights of Man* (1791), of Milanese *illuminista* Pier Domenico Soresi's *Essay on the Necessity and the Facility of Educating Girls* (1774), and of Mary Wollstonecraft's *A Vindication of the Rights of Woman* (1792), a pioneering, much-publicized work that set women on their own long path towards equality of treatment in the eyes of the law. Although the women's suffrage movement took many more decades to mature and bear fruit, it found its origins in the Enlightenment. Cesare Beccaria himself believed that women should be allowed to testify as witnesses just as men regularly appeared in court as part of judicial proceedings. As Beccaria, writing in the eighteenth century, emphasized: "it seems ridiculous to exclude the testimony of women on account of their weakness." At the time that he wrote that in *Dei delitti e delle pene*, women were generally excluded from the witness stand in Italy, and women throughout the world, in fact, had few legal rights and were notorious labeled "the weaker sex."[123] The novelist Mary Shelley, the author of *Frankenstein* (1818) and Mary Wollstonecraft's own daughter, married the Romantic poet Percy Bysshe Shelley, a known reader of an Italian edition of Beccaria's work—a work that promoted equal justice under the law. In *Rambles in Germany and Italy in 1840, 1842, and 1843*, Mary Shelley herself, in discussing Italian literature, emphasized that Cesare Beccaria's daughter, Giulia—the mother of the "devout Catholic" Alessandro Manzoni—"was an accomplished and active-minded woman." In that travelogue, she further described *Dei delitti e delle pene*—Cesare Beccaria's classic treatise—as "the well-known work."[124]

The Age of Beccaria was a time of Grand Tours, both through cosmopolitan Europe and the cities and vast stretches of wild places in the Americas. It was also a time of great political upheaval, and of leisurely—and sometimes heated—coffee-shop debates over everything from pleasure and pain, to tyranny and slavery, to equality and ending cruelty and arbitrariness. In Britain, William Wilberforce (1759–1833) and Thomas Clarkson (1760–1846) campaigned against the slave trade, while Beccaria "most profoundly"—as one modern source puts it—"advocated equality of punishment for aristocrats and commoners alike" in these words: "I assert that the punishment of a noble should in no wise differ from that of the lowest member of society."[125] In *Dei delitti e delle pene*, Beccaria himself did not reject the use of perpetual slavery as an alternative for state-sanctioned executions. For convicted criminals, Beccaria saw long-term imprisonment as a better deterrent than either torture or executions, and he believed that those condemned to a life of slavery in prisons would serve as a powerful deterrent to others. With essays, pamphlets and books, as well as volumes of verse, being produced in abundance, the transatlantic Republic of Letters flourished as brand new, even radical ideas—as well as strong literary and social friendships—were forged through intellectual exchange.[126]

Anti-slavery campaigners sometimes shared an affinity with anti-gallows campaigns, as was the case among some early English reformers. For example, Thomas Clarkson was among the early subscribers to the Capital Punishment Society—also known as The Society for Diffusing Information on the Subject of the Punishment of Death—that was organized in England in the early nineteenth century, with the legendary William Wilberforce also taking an interest in its activities. The small group's first meeting took place in Basil Montagu's chambers in Lincoln's Inn on April 12, 1808, with the express purpose of forming "a little society … to endeavor to diminish the number of capital punishments." Aside from Montagu, among its members and supporters were the Quaker philanthropist William Allen, the Scottish jurist and politician Sir James Mackintosh, the Rev. Francis Wrangham, and Sir Thomas Fowell Buxton, a member of Parliament and a brewer and committed anti-slavery abolitionist. Other members included Peter Bedford, Stephen Lushington, Luke Howard, Joseph Gurney Bevan and Richard Phillips. One historian, Richard Follett, takes note of Beccaria's influence among late eighteenth- and early nineteenth-century English intellectuals, but stresses that, in 1819, the English "Bloody Code" still had 223 capital crimes on the books. As Follett emphasizes of the society's inaugural work and its debt to Beccaria and others influenced by him: "The first 'diffusion' resulting from this ambitious society was Montagu's collection of opinions on capital punishment in 1809. He included quotations from Samuel Johnson, William Blackstone, the Marquis Beccaria, William Paley, Erasmus and even a translation from French of one of Bentham's works published by Dumont."[127]

On Crimes and Punishments was avidly read by many intellectuals, from soon after it was published to long after its first appearance. Though editions produced in Europe made their way around the world, the first American translations of the book appeared in Charleston in 1777 and in Philadelphia in 1778.[128] That American printers chose to print them during the middle of the Revolutionary War speaks volumes as regards Beccaria's importance to America's founders. And intellectuals did not stop reading Beccaria even after independence had been achieved, with Beccaria's influence extending far beyond his own lifetime as new generations of readers discovered *On Crimes and Punishments*. Notably, George Washington Greene—who once served as the American consul to Rome—befriended the American poet Henry Wadsworth Longfellow in France after Beccaria's ideas had already permeated Western culture. In 1828, for example, Greene spent time with Longfellow in Rome and Naples.[129] Henry Wadsworth Longfellow, that American literary light, himself visited Alessandro Manzoni, his equivalent Italian counterpart and Cesare Beccaria's grandson. Indeed, in 1849, Longfellow—then living in the Victorian Era—would ask his own brother, Alexander Wadsworth Longfellow, to purchase a number of Enlightenment era books for his use. Among the titles he sought: John Locke's *An Essay Concerning Human Understanding*, William Blackstone's *Commentaries on the Laws of England*, Emmerich de Vattel's *The Law of Nations*, and Cesare Beccaria's *An Essay on Crimes and Punishments*.[130] Clearly, Beccaria's book had not lost its currency, even by the mid-nineteenth century.

In *The Philosophy of Religion* (1847), one writer, Thomas Dick, cited and quoted "the Marquis Beccaria" for taking a stand against torture before writing of his own disdain for "the *Slave Trade*—the eternal disgrace of individuals and of nations calling themselves *civilized*." After referring to Beccaria's *On Crimes and Punishments*, Dick went on to list "the principal punishments that have been adopted by men, in different countries, for tormenting and destroying each other." Under the rubric of "*Capital* punishments," he listed this assortment of barbarous methods of execution: "Beheading, strangling, crucifixion, drowning, burning, roasting, hanging by the neck, the arm, or the leg; starving, sawing, exposing to wild beasts, rendering asunder by horses drawing opposite ways; shooting, burying alive, blowing from the mouth of a cannon, compulsory deprivation of sleep, rolling in a barrel stuck with nails, cutting to pieces, hanging by the ribs, poisoning, pressing slowly to death, by a weight laid on the breast; casting headlong from a rock, tearing out the bowels, pulling to pieces with red hot pincers, stretching on the rack, breaking on the wheel, impaling, flaying alive, cutting out the heart, &c. &c. &c." "Nothing shows the malevolent dispositions of a great portion of the human race, in so striking a light, as the punishments they have inflicted on one another," Dick wrote in his essay on Christianity and what he called the moral laws of the universe.[131]

In modern-day Milan, a city rich with art and fashion and music, history and architecture, the presence of Pietro Verri and Cesare Beccaria still looms large. In their native city, the Pinacoteca di Brera—one of the city's premier art museums—contains life size, if not larger-than-life size, statues of both men. A standing Pietro Verri is found in the inner courtyard of the museum on Via Brera, and just a short stroll away, up a flight of stairs, sits the statue of Beccaria, reclining in a chair holding a copy of *Dei delitti e delle pene* (1764), his most important book.[132] In an homage to his other works, Beccaria's *Ricerche intorno alla natura dello stile* (*Research on the Nature of Style*, 1770) and *Elementi di economia pubblica* (*Elements of Public Economy*, 1804) are at his feet.[133] The statue of Beccaria was created in 1838 by Pompeo Marchesi (1783–1858), a talented Roman-trained sculptor and a professor at the Milan Academy.[134] His three-dimensional stone masterpiece brings Cesare Beccaria to life in a way much different than two-dimensional French and Italian representations, such as the 1766 engraving—a side profile of Beccaria—by Carlo Faucci (1729–1784), an artist from Florence.[135] The available artistic renderings of Beccaria show his progression from a handsome, determined young man to a distinguished, if somewhat portly, middle-aged nobleman.

The statue depicting the Italian criminal-law theorist at the Pinacoteca di Brera is, of course, not the only image of—or homage to—the great man to be found in his native city. Across town, near Milan's impressive Duomo, the Italian Gothic cathedral dedicated to St. Mary of the Nativity, one also finds a street named after Cesare Beccaria and the stately Piazza Cesare Beccaria, a monument to the memory of the author of *Dei delitti e delle pene*. The monument's impressive bronze statue by Alberti Achille, a reproduction of a marble sculpture by Italian artist Giuseppe Grandi, sits on the spot formerly occupied by the executioner's home.[136] One source describes Milan's public executioner as having "dressed in red" and as being "armed with a long and shining sword" ready to be used on "a new victim to the offended laws of the state."[137] Other descriptions of Milanese executions refer to a noble "torn to pieces by the public executioner" for stabbing to death the Duke of Milan in 1476 and to "[a] brazier of live charcoal" containing "the pincers with which the flesh was to be torn" as well as "a large platform" on which two victims had "their limbs broken by an iron bar, preparatory to their exposure on the wheel for six hours."[138] The piazza named for Beccaria is a place not far from where he and his friends used to gather and drink cups of coffee and debate the pressing issues of the day, earnestly looking for solutions to their society's most vexing problems.[139] Having studied in Milan and Turin, Grandi had obtained the commission for the monument near the Palace of Justice in a competition.[140] The massive stone pedestal on which the large bronze statue of Beccaria now rests showcases a short excerpt from *Dei delitti e delle pene*. Its translation from the Italian: "If I can demonstrate that the death penalty is neither useful nor necessary, I shall have won the cause of humanity."[141] "It is comments such as these," writes Paul Friedland in a book on the history of public executions in France, "that have allowed Beccaria to go down in history as one of the first to support the abolition of the death penalty."[142]

At the time the monument in Piazza Cesare Beccaria was erected, Professor Pasquale Stanislao Mancini—a civic-minded scholar looking to the world's future—optimistically offered a 500 *lire* prize for the best essay promoting the death penalty's abolition. "When it was decided to dedicate a statue to Cesare Beccaria," an architectural guide of Milan notes of the site of the former executioner's home, "the City had the statue put in front of it."[143] According to a sketch of Cesare Beccaria in a nineteenth-century biographical dictionary: "When, in 1865, the Lower House in the Italian Parliament passed the bill against capital punishment, the memory of the Milanese publicist was honoured by popular demonstrations, and a national subscription was opened for the erection of a monument to him in his native town."[144] On the stone pedestal on which the figure of Cesare Beccaria stands is also a bronze cast of Lady Justice, a fitting homage, perhaps, to the famous frontispiece that appeared in early editions of *Dei delitti e delle pene* that depict *Justice*—the allegorical figure—rejecting a group of three severed heads from an executioner.[145] Decades earlier, in 1846, a book on the literature of southern Europe had itself praised "the celebrated Marquis Beccaria,"[146] with other sources regularly referring to the Italian nobleman—the jurist justly honored in Milan—as "[t]he celebrated Marquis."[147]

Another Piazza Cesare Beccaria, a public square in Florence, is also dedicated to the memory of the legendary Italian economist and penal reformer.[148] A large open space, laid out by Giuseppe Poggi (1811–1901) and Giacomo Roster (1837–1905) between 1865 and 1877, that piazza—as an architectural guide for that city points out—was "named after the marchese della Beccaria," "a notable Enlightenment figure who tried to reform the judicial system; his views of 'equality for all before the law' were highly influential."[149] "Curiously," *The Companion Guide to Florence* observes, "when it came to commemorating Beccaria, the man responsible for ending capital punishment in Italy, the piazza chosen to honor him was not the site of the old public gallows but the next piazza up the Viale." As another sources notes of how Florence's condemned criminals—not unlike Italian offenders elsewhere—had been dealt with in the past: "Although public executions were common in late-fifteenth-century Florence, occurring at a rate of more than one a week, they were usually performed in a designated field on the outskirts of the city, rather than in a central square, a venue reserved for high-profile criminals. Most of the offenders, as many as fifteen at a time, were led out through the eastern part of the city, past the church of Santa Croce, to the gallows by way of the via de' Malcontenti (the Street of the Malcontents)—so named because many individuals were sentenced to death for allegedly conspiring against aristocratic families."[150]

It is actually impossible to conceive of the modern world without the publication of *On Crimes and Punishments*. Cesare Beccaria's face, whether as it appears on a painter's canvas or as it has been chiseled into stone, has, in fact, been admired for more than two centuries, though scores of people today have entirely forgotten Beccaria's contributions, not to mention his aristocratic garb. Back in 1816, while in Milan, the English poet and politician Lord Byron—who spent several years in Italy and who owned a copy of Beccaria's little treatise—once gazed upon a marble bust of Cesare Beccaria. That *Herma of Cesare Beccaria* was sculpted by the Italian artist Giuseppe Franchi (1731–1806), a neoclassical sculptor who taught at the Brera Academy in Milan. It had been installed in the city's famed Biblioteca Ambrosiana for all to see.[151] The façade of the Palazzo Brentani, the historic mansion built in 1829 and located in the center of Milan on Via Manzoni, also has long featured large, neoclassical medallions of important Italian historical figures, including Leonardo da Vinci, Pietro Verri, Giuseppe Parini, and Cesare Beccaria.[152] The creation of those works of art was in keeping with Beccaria's long-standing reputation as a figure of international renown and importance. Decades before the façade of the Palazzo Brentani was erected, a book published in London in 1781 had itself referred to "the celebrated Marquis Beccaria," "the justly-celebrated Marquis Beccaria," and "the celebrated Marquis Beccaria," referencing or citing his name fifteen times.[153]

After the publication of *Dei delitti e delle pene*, Cesare Beccaria—the Italian thinker who was sculpted, drawn, and even painted in miniature in a portrait, *Ritratto di Cesare Beccaria*—was celebrated throughout the civilized world as a transformational thinker. "Beccaria is a philosopher who deals with his subject from the most useful point of view for humanity," his French translator, André Morellet, once observed. Indeed, a series of portraits—among them, Cesare Beccaria's—were executed in the early nineteenth century by artists Jean-François Bosio and Antoine-François Sergent-Marceau. These portraits were done for an ambitious Milanese work, *Serie di vite e ritratti de'famosi personaggi degli ultimi tempi* (1815–1818), a collection of biographical sketches highlighting famous personalities of then-recent times. Among those selected for the high honor of being represented in the copper-plate etchings, later acquired by The Metropolitan Museum of Art in New York City: Cesare Beccaria, Benjamin Franklin, George Washington, Marquis de Condorcet, Count Vittorio Alfieri, Gaetano Filangieri, the Corsican revolutionary Pasquale Paoli, the Milanese mathematician and philosopher Maria Gaetana Agnesi, Russian czar Alexander I, the King of Naples Joseph Bonaparte, and the Tuscan poet and republican Giovanni Fantoni (1755–1807) whose own writings celebrated Beccaria's celebrity and contributions.[154] The National Gallery of Art in Washington, D.C., itself owns an engraving of Beccaria by Giovanni Antonio Sasso, one modeled after Bosio's rendering. An

Italian artist, Sasso also did an engraving of Wolfgang Amadeus Mozart—the child prodigy who delighted audiences throughout Europe, including in Vienna and Milan—based off of Bosio's now-lost painting of the great composer.[155]

Eighteenth- and nineteenth-century homages to Cesare Beccaria—whether in books, speeches, or sculpture—were commonplace, be they in Milan or far afield from the Italian peninsula. As John Hostettler observes in *Champions of the Rule of Law*: "Law reformers Jefferson, Bentham, Romilly and the Criminal Law Commissioners all paid fulsome tributes to Beccaria and all used his arguments in their own efforts to give meaning and life to the concept of the rule of law. In truth, Beccaria was perhaps the greatest exponent of the rule of law in history." The membership of the Criminal Law Commission that Hostettler references—a royal commission authorized by King William IV in 1833—included David Jardine, a graduate of Glasgow University. In *A Reading on the Use of Torture in the Criminal Law of England prior to the Commonwealth* (1836), Jardine himself exposed the use of torture by royal prerogative during the reigns of the Tudors and the Stuarts, the very kind of brutality Beccaria had railed against in *Dei delitti e delle pene*.[156] In *Law Miscellanies: An Introduction to the Study of the Law*, Hugh Henry Brackenridge—a member of the Supreme Court of Pennsylvania—also wrote of Beccaria's impact on the American polity. As Brackenridge observed in 1814: "Elementary writers, at the head of whom is the marquis de Beccaria, have with great plausibility, questioned the right of society to punish, by taking life at all."[157]

In *Great Jurists of the World*, a book published in Boston in 1914 under the auspices of the Association of American Law Schools, Cesare Beccaria is featured along with other major figures in the history of law, including Francis Bacon, Hugo Grotius, Samuel von Pufendorf, Montesquieu and Emerich de Vattel. As that source reported of Beccaria's *Dei delitti e delle pene*: "Perhaps no book of the kind was ever received with more avidity, more generally read, or more universally applauded." "*The Essay on Crimes and Punishments*," that book observed, "is one of the books of the eighteenth century from which one can even at this day draw some lessons." As another writer emphasized of Beccaria's book in that source: "All the world now recognizes that Beccaria took up the reform of penal legislation, which he pleaded with a luminous reason, an eloquent passion, and won almost immediately an honour no one could share with him. One must not forget that Beccaria was the first publicist to question the law as to the punishments of death. His name will ever be associated with the idea of the suppression of the scaffold." "When the *Essay* appeared," yet another writer concluded in *Great Jurists of the World*, "Beccaria was stamped with that immortality which belongs only to geniuses, born to be benefactors of their times." After recounting how executions had, by then, already been abolished or significantly curtailed in various countries and states around the globe, the 1914 compilation of great jurists made this final observation: "Well may it be said of the Marquis di Beccaria, looking at these results of his *Essay*, that it is indeed one of the most important Works that has ever been written, and that he has contributed towards the enduring happiness of nations."[158]

Across the globe, Cesare Beccaria is still honored by those involved in—and by those who study—the criminal justice system. In Philadelphia, a bust of Beccaria—the brainchild of a local lawyer, the late Michael Rainone—was installed in 2006 in the Jury Assembly Room of the city's Criminal Justice Center at 13th and Filbert Streets. That bust was unveiled at the aptly named Beccaria Award ceremony co-sponsored by the Philadelphia Bar Association's Criminal Justice Section and The Justinian Society, an organization named for Justinian, the emperor associated with the origins of the civil law system. The Beccaria Award "represents the highest honor that the Justinian Society," in cooperation with the Criminal Justice Section, "can give to any member of the Bar ... who exemplifies the ideals of the career of Cesare Beccaria, the 18th century Italian scholar whose writings presaged the dawn of the modern penal system." The Louisiana Chapter of the National Italian American Bar Association also presents a Cesare Beccaria Award, as does the International Society of Social Defence and Humane Criminal Policy ("ISSD"). A non-profit, the ISSD focuses on crime studies and research on crime prevention and combatting recidivism, and it regularly gives out its Cesare Beccaria Award for Young Researchers. In addition, the ISSD's annual Cesare Beccaria medal is awarded "to the scholar who has most contributed," through research or teaching, "to the diffusion worldwide of the underlying principles inspiring the Society's existence."

Thus far, the ISSD medal has been awarded to scholars in Argentina, Chile, Egypt, France, Germany, Italy, Mexico, and the United Kingdom, reflecting its international character. Those honored include Robert Badinter and Roger Hood, both leading advocates for the death penalty's abolition. As a young French lawyer, Badinter represented Roger Bontems, a man convicted of participating in a 1971 prison riot and executed by the guillotine the next year. He also served as the Minister of Justice under President François Mitterrand, leading to the death penalty's abolition in France in 1981, and he wrote the preface to a 1991 translation of Beccaria's famous treatise. Roger Hood—another dedicated abolitionist and a frequenter lecturer on death penalty issues—is now Professor Emeritus of Criminology at the University of Oxford's Centre for Criminology.[159] In 2009, the ISSD also awarded a Cesare Beccaria medal to an American lawyer, Sandra Babcock, for her commitment to the defense of individuals facing the death penalty. A talented, Harvard Law School graduate who now teaches at Cornell Law School, Babcock has represented many death row inmates and has created an online database, Death Penalty Worldwide, that tracks the use of the death penalty by every retentionist country.[160]

For criminologists and capital punishment foes alike, Cesare Beccaria is still a greatly admired figure. On the 250th anniversary of the publication of *Dei delitti e delle pene*, Professor Dirk Verhofstadt at Belgium's University of Ghent called Beccaria "one of the most influential representatives of the Enlightenment." In cataloging his contributions, Professor Verhofstadt emphasized that Beccaria "substantially contributed to the humanization of criminal law by ridding it of arbitrariness, abuse of power, and religious dogmas." In calling for clear and precise laws to be published in advance for all people to read and comprehend, Beccaria thus embraced transparency and the principle of *legality*, also simultaneously rejecting the notion that laws should only be published in inaccessible Latin (as was sometimes then the case). As Beccaria wrote: "The use of such a foreign language makes the people dependent on a small minority, reduces respect for the legal code—which is intended for openness and for the benefit of everyone—and turns it into an obscure manual, exclusively for the convenience of a few adepts." "The larger the number of citizens that understand the wording of the law and have the legal code in their hands," Beccaria observed, "the less criminality there will be." Beccaria's demand that all citizens "be equally subjected to the law" and that criminal sanctions "be the same for the first citizen as well as for the humblest" also appealed to Enlightenment thinkers throughout the globe.[161]

The most prominent advocates of the "Law and Economics" movement have consistently credited Cesare Beccaria's work as being ground-breaking or pioneering in nature. For example, in *The Economics of Justice*, Richard Posner acknowledges the intellectual debt that both Sir William Blackstone and Jeremy Bentham—on issues of criminal justice and marginal deterrence theory in particular—owed to Beccaria.[162] In tracing the history of utilitarianism and economics as well as referencing Adam Smith's work in his book, Posner emphasized that while Beccaria's foundational ideas were largely theoretical, it was Bentham who, building off of Beccaria's core principles, took the field of "applied utilitarianism" to a new level. As Posner—the recently retired federal appellate court judge—has explained: "Although the origins of utilitarianism, like those of economics, are earlier than *The Wealth of Nations*—they are found in the writings of Priestley, Beccaria, Hume, and others—utilitarianism did not reach a state of development comparable to economics until Bentham's work in the generation after Smith."[163] Though Posner has noted that utilitarian ideas date back to Aristotle, he freely acknowledges the historic and important role that Beccaria played in promoting them—and, of course, the material influence that Beccaria had in shaping many, many others and modern conceptions of utilitarianism more broadly.[164] "It was Beccaria," another writer has observed, "who effectively contributed to the launch of the famous *dictum* that laws are to be considered from the standpoint of 'the greatest happiness of the greatest number'—as he writes in the introduction (*A chi legge*) of his 1764 pamphlet, thus making use of a formula of Scottish origin."[165] Because of the foundational role that Beccaria's writings played in shaping thinkers from Blackstone and Bentham to Gary Becker and Richard Posner, Beccaria's ideas have been called "a precursor to the law and economics movement."[166]

In the world of criminologists, there are actually few names more consequential to the history of criminology than that of Cesare Beccaria—or, as he is identified in *Great Jurists of the World*, Cæsar Bonesana, Marquis di Beccaria.[167] A crime prevention conference in Hannover, Germany, is named in Beccaria's honor, and the New German Society of Criminology also honors the work of criminologists with its own Beccaria medal. In addition, the "Beccaria standards for ensuring quality in crime prevention projects" are explicitly named after the Italian *philosophe*, the illustrious economist and philosopher who so shaped the modern world. Those standards, developed by the European Commission of Human Rights and available in sixteen languages, provide recommendations for preventing crime. In *On Crimes and Punishments*, Beccaria himself had emphasized: "It is better to prevent crime than to punish it."[168] In the drawing of Beccaria at The Metropolitan Museum of Art and replicated in the National Gallery of Art's etching, he is seated in an elegant chair, his right arm resting on a book on his desk. "In his limited purpose of showing each celebrity in a typical moment of activity," it is noted in one article, Jean-François Bosio—the Monaco-born French artist who sketched Beccaria and who, in Milan, went by Giovanni Battista Bosio—chose to portray him working at his desk. In that drawing, Beccaria's elegant attire—as well as the decorative sword hanging from Beccaria's left side—reveal his nobility while the books on his desk represent his learning and intellectual pursuits.[169]

In assessing Cesare Beccaria's rightful place in the history of economics, Joseph Schumpeter—the economist who called Beccaria "the Italian" Adam Smith—emphasized that the bulk of Beccaria's economic writings consisted of government reports. Beccaria, he notes, did not publish his own lectures on economics but "left them in his files for nearly a quarter of a century." In comparing Cesare Beccaria's legacy with that of Adam Smith's, Schumpeter highlighted some key differences and similarities in their lives. While Beccaria "was much more of a public servant" than Smith, Schumpeter wrote in *History of Economic Analysis*, "Smith was much more of a professor than Beccaria, who taught for only two years." "Both," Schumpeter stressed, though, "were sovereign lords of a vast intellectual realm that extended far beyond what, even then, was possible for ordinary mortals to embrace." "Both," Schumpeter added, "swam joyfully in the river of their time, but with a difference: whereas Beccaria not only accepted all utilitarianism stands for but also was a leading force in shaping it, A. Smith quite clearly showed some critical coolness towards it; and whereas A. Smith not only accepted (almost) all that free trade and *laissez-faire* stand for but also was a leading force in their victory (so far as economic literature is concerned), Beccaria clearly showed some critical coolness toward them." "[T]he great Beccaria," Schumpeter editorialized, "went to the length of asserting that man is wholly egotistic and egocentric and does not trouble at all about any other man's (or the common) good." Yet, Cesare Beccaria—in his native Milan—continually worked to *promote* the common good, to channel free enterprise, entrepreneurship and regulatory structures to further the public good.[170]

Cesare Beccaria—as another history of economic thought notes—was, like Antonio Genovesi and Pietro Verri, "in favour of economic freedom," but took a "pragmatic attitude towards *laissez-faire*," limiting the application of free trade to within national boundaries. "In regard to foreign trade," Ernesto Screpanti and Stefano Zamagni write of Italian economists of that period in *An Outline of the History of Economic Thought*, "they believed that the State had to guide and regulate the flows of imports and exports in the national interest, which might not coincide with the interests of the individual citizens." In recounting Beccaria's "original contributions," Screpanti and Zamagni emphasize that "Beccaria sketched out a theory of the division of labour and of increasing returns in industry, besides having an insight about the indeterminacy of prices in a duopoly." "Beccaria and Verri," they further observe, "shared a subjectivist and hedonistic conception of economic phenomena." As Screpanti and Zamagni explain: "Starting from a sensist and materialist philosophy, they tried to explain human behaviour in utilitarian terms, by maintaining that individuals are driven, in their economic choices, exclusively by the search for pleasure and the fear of pain. It was not only in this that the two Milanese economists anticipated Bentham, but also in the proposal that the State should aim at creating—in Beccaria's words—the 'maximum happiness divided among the greatest number.'"[171]

Today, the general public's awareness (or lack of knowledge) of Cesare Beccaria's legacy is, in part, a function of education and geography and is dependent on the placement of monuments erected in his honor. "If you are visiting Milan," two Italian scholars note, "you will discover that 'Cesare Beccaria' is a Milanese household name." As their 2014 article on Beccaria emphasizes of the Italian thinker's almost ubiquitous presence in Milan: "Walking through the streets downtown—in an area familiar to shoppers—is Cesare Beccaria Square, and everyone has heard of the high school, or of the juvenile prison, named after this illustrious citizen of the past." "We have not forgotten Beccaria's name," University of Milan professor Mario Ricciardi and Italian scholar Filippo Santoni de Sio emphasize in their biographical sketch, "and indeed we associate it with the struggle for justice and humanity in punishment that was one of the dominant themes of the Enlightenment."[172] A street in the 12th *arondissement* in Paris, Rue Beccaria, is also named after Cesare Beccaria, so christened in 1864—perhaps hopefully, perhaps simply to honor him on the 100th anniversary of *Dei delitti e delle pene*'s publication—in the midst of all of the violence of the U.S. Civil War.[173] Rue Beccaria fittingly intersects with Boulevard Diderot and is just a short stroll away from the Seine, the river that flows by the Eiffel Tower and around a much smaller replica of New York Harbor's iconic Statue of Liberty. That a street in Paris is named after Beccaria is a particularly fitting honor because of Cesare Beccaria's 1766 trip to the City of Light—a trip taken when the success of *Dei delitti e delle pene* was still in its infancy.

In the late eighteenth and early nineteenth centuries, Cesare Beccaria certainly held a special place in the hearts and minds of European intellectuals and America's founders. And nowhere did Beccaria's star shine more brightly in America than in Pennsylvania, the site of the signing of the Declaration of Independence, the birthplace of the U.S. Constitution, and the home of the Liberty Bell and what is now known as Independence Hall, the historic site now managed by the National Park Service. In 1807, after the ratification of the U.S. Constitution and the Bill of Rights and just a few years before the start of the War of 1812, Beccaria Township in Clearfield County, Pennsylvania was itself named in Cesare Beccaria's honor.[174] Long inhabited by Native Americans, that part of Pennsylvania was settled by Captain Edward Ricketts, a Revolutionary War veteran and one of the first settlers in Clearfield County. A pioneer, Ricketts filed his claim in 1783—the year the Revolutionary War came to an end—and he cleared some trees and built a log cabin. In 1807, the year Beccaria Township got its name, *On Crimes and Punishments* was of course still being offered for sale in America; the *Raleigh Register, and North-Carolina State Gazette*, whose motto was "Libertas," reprinted a report of the Pennsylvania legislature that referred to "the learned and benevolent Beccaria"; and *The Centinel*—a newspaper in Gettysburg, Pennsylvania whose tagline was "TRUTH, OUR GUIDE—THE PUBLIC GOOD, OUR AIM"—published a news item that quoted "the enlightened and humane Beccaria."[175]

In fact, Cesare Beccaria—the law-trained economist and philosopher—was once known and respected worldwide for his humane vision. "The Italian writers of the eighteenth century, who have been celebrated by their prose writings, are rather Philosophers than Poets," *The Gentleman's Magazine* reported in 1824, adding of Cesare Beccaria: "About the same period flourished the celebrated Marquis Beccaria, who has defended with such animation the cause of humanity."[176] Although a member of the Italian aristocracy, a small, privileged class of eighteenth-century nobles, Cesare Beccaria is remembered today not for his family's crest or coat of arms or his familial assets or estate but for his humane call for all people to receive equal justice under the law.[177] That philosophy—"EQUAL JUSTICE UNDER LAW"—is now carved in stone on the front of the Cass Gilbert-designed U.S. Supreme Court building in Washington, D.C.[178] In *The Progress*, a newspaper published in Clearfield, Pennsylvania, it was noted as late as 1969 in a discussion of place names that Beccaria Township was named for "the celebrated Italian publicist and philosopher."[179] The *History of Clearfield County, Pennsylvania* noted in 1887 that "no reliable information is obtainable" as to why Beccaria Township was "so named in his honor."[180] But if one knows the massive impact that *On Crimes and Punishments* had in eighteenth- and nineteenth-century America, it is actually easy to understand why Cesare Beccaria would be honored in that fashion.

Even after Cesare Beccaria's death in 1794, Beccaria's legacy lived on through his descendants—and through the laborious work and human rights advocacy of scores of reformers that followed in the wake of the publication of *On Crimes and Punishments*. While Cesare Beccaria's ideas, in the pre-Internet era, continued to filter through the world's societies and multi-varied cultures, Giulio Beccaria—Cesare's son—assembled and preserved his father's autographed manuscript of *Dei delitti e delle pene* and that of "Elementi di Economia Pubblica," now in the possession of Milan's Biblioteca Ambrosiana. A facsimile of the original edition of *Dei delitti e delle pene*, published anonymously in Livorno in 1764, was later published in 1965 with handwritten notations in the margins long after the Marquis Giulio Beccaria organized his father's papers. Cesare Beccaria had, two centuries earlier, given the original manuscript of *Dei delitti e delle pene* to Pietro Verri in February 1764 for a final review and to transmit it to the publisher in Livorno. But Pietro Verri had made a copy and had kept the original, though Verri eventually, at Cesare Beccaria's request, had returned the manuscript to Beccaria as reflected in a January 21, 1769 letter from Pietro Verri to his brother, Alessandro. It fell to Cesare Beccaria's heirs to safeguard Cesare Beccaria's writings before their transmission to the Biblioteca Ambrosiana.[181]

Guilio Beccaria—an avid coin collector, reflecting his father's own interest in the monetary system—maintained the Beccaria family's residence at 6 Via Brera in Milan and also frequented the family villa on Lake Como. As a modern website describes the villa on Lake Como where Guilio is now buried in a family tomb: "The first portion of the building was built in the mid-eighteenth century, but the villa as it appears today was completed in the early nineteenth century." "The extraordinary gardens of this luxurious villa," that website observes, "can only be glimpsed from the lake," with the description of the villa noting that on the side of the residence "a shady driveway of cypresses leads to the clearing where the tomb of Antonietta Curioni and Giulio Beccaria was built in 1858." "The three-floor Villa Beccaria," it is emphasized, "was built on a semicircular terrace overlooking the lake." "After Giulio's death," the rental website notes of the fate of Alessandro Manzoni's uncle and the estate itself, "the villa was passed on to Cesare Cantù, a scholar and patriot, and the daughter

Rachele, wife of Angelo Villa Pernice, deputy to the first Italian parliament in Florence, who used it as his main residence, where a literary salon known by the name 'Academy of pedantics' once gathered."[182]

In *The Genius of Italy: Being Sketches of Italian Life, Literature and Religion*, Alessandro Manzoni—Cesare Beccaria's grandson—was described in 1849 as "a man of fine character and resplendent genius, who has attained equal celebrity in prose and verse." As that sketch described Manzoni, the much-revered Italian writer whose own statue now appears in Milan's San Fedele square: "He was born at Milan in 1784, of a noble family, and early distinguished himself by his poetical talent. His mother was a daughter of the celebrated Marquis Beccaria, one of the noblest men, and one of the best writers on political subjects that Italy has produced." In *The Poets and Poetry of Europe*, written by Henry Wadsworth Longfellow, Manzoni is also said to be "distinguished as a lyrist, tragic poet, and novelist" whose "excellent novel, 'I Promessi Sposi,' appeared at Milan in 1827." As that source emphasizes, *I Promessi Sposi*—Manzoni's only novel—got "translated into most of the languages of Europe" and it "holds the highest rank among the Italian romances."[183] That novel, the title of which translates as *The Betrothed*, was an enormously popular book written in the Italian language.[184] An historical romance, the book was set in seventeenth-century Lombardy, then under Spanish rule (the Spanish said to represent the Austrians of Manzoni's day). Its plot: about a priest and a nobleman who interfere with a couple's wedding plans.[185] The novel was immediately hailed as a masterpiece and is still considered an Italian classic. Pope Francis—the head of the Catholic Church—himself encourages newly engaged couples to read it as it tells the story of two people who are called to trust each other as they encounter obstacles in their journey toward marriage.[186]

Beyond Italy, the names of Italian writers such as Cesare Beccaria, Pietro Verri, Gaetano Filangieri and Alessandro Manzoni are largely unfamiliar to the general public. But the writings of those men shaped the modern world, with Manzoni supporting Italian unification and Giuseppe Verdi (1813–1901)—the great Italian composer—dedicating his *Requiem* (1874) to Manzoni's memory.[187] Beccaria's writings—calling for proportion between crimes and punishments and opposing both torture and capital punishment[188]—are still as relevant today as they were when they first appeared in print in the 1700s. Indeed, the contributions of the Italian Enlightenment—of which Beccaria's writings were a part—were profound. Pietro Verri and his equally literary-minded brother, Alessandro, inspired Beccaria to write *Dei delitti e delle pene*, a book that George Washington purchased, that American revolutionaries Thomas Jefferson and John Adams read in the original Italian and made notes on, and that countless intellectuals in the Americas and Europe effusively praised. Beccaria's and then Filangieri's writings inspired Americans and others to make laws less severe, with Philip Mazzei's history of the American Revolution, as well as Carlo Botta's book, *History of the War of Independence of the United States of America* (1809), documenting the transformation of American life.[189] "The work of Cesar Becaria, at the end of the eighteenth century, produced a revolution in European penal legislation," the author of *The Civil Law in Spain and Spanish-America* emphasizes of his profound impact there.[190]

Beccaria's treatise and Montesquieu's *Spirit of the Laws*, along with a host of other Enlightenment books authored by writers such as Rousseau and de Lolme, were actually must-read texts for any republican or any progressive, reform-minded judge or legislator. As Nathaniel Chipman (1752–1843)—a U.S. Senator from Vermont and, at one time, the Chief Justice of the Vermont Supreme Court—wrote, singling out Beccaria's book for praise: "The world is more indebted to the Marquis Beccaria, for his little treatise on Crimes and Punishments, than to all other writers on the subject."[191] The result of that influence, as Alexis de Tocqueville recorded in *Democracy in America* in 1840: "In no other country is criminal justice administered with more mildness than in the United States. Whilst the English seem disposed carefully to retain the bloody traces of the Middle Ages in their penal legislation, the Americans have almost expunged capital punishment from their codes." The fact that Tocqueville and his companion, Gustave Beaumont, made their trip to America to study the country's penal system is itself revealing.[192] After all, a society's treatment of its lowliest citizens—its criminals and its homeless, poor and disabled—says a lot about how far that society has advanced. In that regard, Cesare Beccaria—the Italian economist and philosopher—was far ahead of his time, expressing concern for impoverished and unemployed workers at a time when slavery and serfdom were still in use.

Cesare Beccaria's egalitarian and anti-tyrannical rhetoric became a fixture of American legal thought, reflecting the sentiments shared by many revolutionaries about the needless severity of traditional, centuries-old English common-law punishments. By the time Uriah M. Rose—the founder and first president of the Arkansas State Bar Association[193]—delivered an address to his colleagues in the legal profession in 1900, he had this to say: "If we except Montesquieu, whose work was rather critical and suggestive than constructive, Beccaria was the first of the modern law reformers in point of time; and, if we judge solely by benefits conferred, he was by far the greatest of all." "It may be," Rose wrote, "that Beccaria was not profound; but he was a thoroughly sane man, with that rare kind of common sense, possessed by men like Washington, which easily adjusts itself to great subjects." Noting that Beccaria's book "made a great stir everywhere" after its publication, especially in Paris where Beccaria's achievement had been toasted in 1766, Rose concluded: "The victory of Beccaria has become complete. The principles that he announced are now embodied in every criminal code in Christendom: and they have even penetrated the distant Orient."[194]

Cesare Beccaria's advocacy of clear written laws to minimize judicial discretion, as well as his advocacy of proportionate punishments to make the law itself more humane, ultimately led to the adoption of many international treaties, constitutions and laws reflective of those core principles. After the publication of *Dei delitti e delle pene*, Beccaria's name was, in fact, invoked side by side with Montesquieu's and Filangieri's as illustrated in this reference, words of advice given to an English knight: "As a lawyer, my Lord, you ought to have those celebrated foreign authors, 'Beccaria, on Crimes and Punishments,' 'Filangeri, on Legislation,' and 'Montesquieu's Spirit of Laws.' These eminent writers would have taught you the reflection which is necessary in endeavouring to proportion the punishment to the crime, and the circumstances of the individual; and to temper justice with mercy."[195] Freely giving credit where credit was due, Beccaria himself acknowledged Montesquieu's greatness as well as the greatness of other thinkers on whose shoulders Beccaria stood. According to the *Encyclopedia of Law and Society*, Beccaria followed in Montesquieu's footsteps in pointing out the cruelty of then-existing laws. As scholar Mario Cattaneo writes in that source: "Beccaria recognized his debt toward Charles-Louis de Montesquieu (1689–1755), who had already written — mainly, in *Esprit des lois* (*Spirit of the Laws*) and *Lettres Persanes* (*Persian Letters*) — against injustice and cruelty in criminal law." "Montesquieu and Beccaria," another writer, Francesco Pagano (1748–1799), stressed, "were the two thinkers who most importantly contributed to the reform of criminal law."[196]

Cesare Beccaria's *Dei delitti e delle pene* "was a sensation of the Enlightenment when it was published in 1764," yet another source observes, albeit editorializing that, in Eastern Europe, one eighteenth-century writer — taking note of the harsh conditions there — wrote that "[i]f M. de Beccaria had seen all the cutthroats of this land, he would be less disposed to be tender (*s'attendrir*)."[197] Though Cesare Beccaria died in the late eighteenth century, his humane ideas were then transmitted from generation to generation — and from country to country — and remain an essential part of twenty-first century public discourse. In *The Illusion of Free Markets*, a modern-day scholar, Professor Bernard Harcourt of Columbia Law School, confirms Beccaria's foundational importance to the field of law and economics: "[C]ontemporary scholars of law and economics have embraced Beccaria as one of their own. Richard Posner traces his intellectual genealogy, in the area of penal law, specifically to Beccaria. In introducing his economic model of criminal law in 1985, Posner explicitly wrote: 'The economic analysis of criminal law began on a very high plane in the eighteenth and early nineteenth centuries with the work of Beccaria and Bentham, but its revival in modern times dates only from 1968, when Gary Becker's article on the economics of crime and punishment appeared.'" *On Crimes and Punishments*, Harcourt further explains of the importance of that book, extended "economic rationality to the penal sphere, so as to achieve there what had been achieved in the field of commercial exchange."[198] Not only did Pietro Verri end up reconciling with Beccaria and promoting his legacy, but both of Cesare Beccaria's two surviving children, Giulia and Giulio, played a central role in promoting their father's work, too. It is thus fitting that portraits of Giulia Beccaria (1762–1841) and Giulio Beccaria (1774–1856) would be made, thus immortalizing both of Beccaria's surviving children in paintings.[199]

While global capitalists still revere Adam Smith's *The Wealth of Nations*, it was Cesare Beccaria's book that, more than a decade earlier, set the stage for society's jump to modernity. By railing against tyranny and the most cruel of punishments, Beccaria's ideas shed light on the world's dark past and promised a better future. The death penalty and the scaffold had been used for centuries, but Beccaria had the foresight to see a better, less violent way. Beccaria's call for equality of treatment also represented a major break with past practice in a world in which the rich had been consistently treated much differently (and much more favorably) by judges than the poor. It was also Beccaria's little treatise that laid a solid foundation for the rule of law—an idea that is central not only to human rights but to creating a legal climate that fosters stability and in which contracts and commercial transactions are held to be enforceable. With its call for clearly worded written laws and less barbarous punishments, *Dei delitti e delle pene* changed Western civilization and must be seen, above all else, as a progressive and *civilizing* influence. It began a worldwide conversation on capital punishment that continues to this day, and it helped to consolidate an emerging consensus against torture and for laws that would bind all equally.

Today, a number of international treaties and declarations adopted at the U.N.— as well as various constitutions and laws in individual countries—address the very subjects that Beccaria took up in *On Crimes and Punishments*. The Universal Declaration of Human Rights, for example, provides: "No one shall be subjected to torture or to cruel, inhuman or degrading treatment or punishment."[200] And that prohibition is repeated verbatim in the U.N.'s International Covenant on Civil and Political Rights,[201] which also has an optional protocol providing that "[e]ach State Party shall take all necessary measures to abolish the death penalty within its jurisdiction."[202] The Convention Against Torture and Other Cruel, Inhuman or Degrading Treatment or Punishment, which entered into force in 1987, likewise has roots in Beccaria's advocacy more than two centuries earlier.[203] Such declarations, conventions and treaties are part of Beccaria's enduring legacy, though these legal instruments were, of course, shaped by many individuals and a variety of events and intervening influences. As for the principle of *legality*, or the rule of law requiring advance notice of the law itself, one source points out that "Beccaria's masterpiece remains the milestone on this topic."[204]

Ironically, while America still retains capital punishment in the twenty-first century, the very country from which America's founders inherited executions and the prohibition on "cruel and unusual punishments," no longer allows executions. Great Britain abolished capital punishment altogether in 1998, with the last executions in England taking place in 1964, a full two hundred years after *Dei delitti e delle pene* first appeared.[205] Europe itself is now a death penalty-free zone, with specific protocols—Protocol No. 6 and Protocol No. 13 to the European Convention on Human Rights—prohibiting the death penalty's use in both peacetime and wartime.[206] Indeed, a number of African countries—among them Rwanda and South Africa, with their respective histories of genocide and apartheid—no longer allow state-sanctioned killing either.[207] This puts America, with its use of death sentences and executions, in the odd and uncomfortable company of totalitarian or authoritarian regimes like China, Iran, North Korea, Saudi Arabia, Sudan and Yemen.[208] Beccaria's writings caused many eighteenth- and nineteenth-century lawmakers to question the use of executions; in many cases, they voted to abolish or restrict capital punishment in their time. But Beccaria's vision—of a world without the death penalty, and one in which only *necessary* punishments are imposed—has not yet been realized, not by a long shot.[209] Still, Beccaria's prescient words in *Dei delitti e delle pene*—his admonitions against arbitrariness, tyranny and cruelty, and his cry for the death penalty's abolition and equality of treatment under the law—endure, forever inviting change into the future.

Cesare Beccaria, it has been observed, "revolutionized the world of thought" on punishment. His book, "which passed through more editions in more languages than any other book on the subject for one hundred and fifty years thereafter," led—as that source emphasizes—to "the break of ideas" that put an end to the *Ancien Régime*.[210] In 1826, more than thirty years after Beccaria's death, a Swiss philanthropist, Count Jean-Jacques de Sellon, held an international essay competition for those seeking the death penalty's abolition—a quest began by Beccaria himself. "Only a century and half before," one source notes, "his country had been burning witches." Before his death in 1839, Count Sellon erected a monument to commemorate the foundation of the *Société de la Paix de Genève* (Peace Society of Geneva) in 1830. The obelisk—a solid block of marble—bears the names of those who had sought or advanced peace or who, as with Count Sellon himself, campaigned to end slavery or state-sanctioned killing. Among those memorialized on the obelisk: Henry IV, the King of France who proposed a congress of nations—a predecessor to the League of Nations and the United Nations—to arbitrate international disputes; William Wilberforce, whose efforts resulted in the abolition of the British slave trade; Leopold, the Grand Duke of Tuscany, who abolished capital punishment in his dominions; Edward Livingston, the American and Beccaria disciple who proposed the death penalty's abolition in the criminal code he drafted for the State of Louisiana; and Cesare Beccaria himself. It is a fitting tribute to the historic figures, and to the eighteenth-century Italian economist and philosopher—the Milanese nobleman—who so shaped the modern world in which we live.[211]

Notes

Introduction

1. Lars Magnusson, *Mercantilism: The Shaping of an Economic Language* (London: Routledge, 2002), p. 199. I summarized some of Cesare Beccaria's intellectual contributions to Western civilization and the American Revolution in two recent journal articles. *See* John D. Bessler, *The Economist and the Enlightenment: How Cesare Beccaria Changed Western Civilization*, 42 Eur. J. Law & Econ. 1 (2016); John D. Bessler, *The Italian Enlightenment and the American Revolution: Cesare Beccaria's Forgotten Influence on American Law*, 37 Mitchell Hamline L.J. of Pub. Pol'y & Practice, Iss. 1, Article 1 (2016). This book and my prior book, *The Birth of American Law: An Italian Philosopher and the American Revolution*, represent my attempt to fully rehabilitate Cesare Beccaria's contributions to, and influence on, the civilized world.

2. Bernard E. Harcourt, *The Illusion of Free Markets: Punishment and the Myth of Natural Order* (Cambridge, MA: Harvard University Press, 2011), p. 57.

3. Esben Sloth Andersen, *Joseph A. Schumpeter: A Theory of Social and Economic Evolution* (New York: Palgrave Macmillan, 2011), pp. 1, 119–31.

4. Peter Groenewegen, *Eighteenth-century Economics: Turgot, Beccaria and Smith and Their Contemporaries* (London: Routledge, 2002), pp. 20 & 40 n.6 ("Beccaria's *Elementi* was written during 1771–2 as his lecture notes; this is a much larger work than that of Turgot but is clearly unfinished....").

5. Yuichi Shionoya, "Reflections on Schumpeter's History of Economic Analysis in Light of His Universal Social Science," *in* James P. Henderson, ed., *The State of the History of Economics: Proceedings of the History of Economics Society* (London: Routledge, 1997), p. 96 ("In comparing Smith and Beccaria too, Schumpeter remarked, Beccaria's *Elementi di economia pubblica*, though only lecture notes, was superior to Smith's lectures at the University of Glasgow. Schumpeter reflected that if Beccaria had spent his time expanding the notes instead of working for the Milanese administration, for as many years as Smith had, the outcome would have been comparable to the *Wealth of Nations*.").

6. Adolph Caso, *We, the People ... : Formative Documents of America's Democracy* (Wellesley, MA: Branden Publishing Co., 2011).

7. Preserved Smith, *A History of Modern Culture* (London: George Routledge & Sons, 1934), Vol. 2, p. 224.

8. Groenewegen, *Eighteenth-century Economics*, pp. 4, 7–14; P. D. Groenewegen, *The Economics of A. R. J. Turgot* (The Hague: Martinus Nijhoff, 1977), p. xvi; Anita Wolff, ed., *Britannica Concise Encyclopedia* (Chicago, IL: Encyclopedia Britannica, 2008), p. 1950; Björn Bjerke, *About Entrepreneurship* (Cheltenham, UK: Edward Elgar, 2013), p. 23; F. C. Schlosser, *History of the Eighteenth Century and of the Nineteenth Till the Overthrow of the French Empire* (London: Chapman and Hall: D. Davison, trans. 1845), p. 163; Joseph T. Salerno, "Two Traditions in Modern Monetary Theory: John Law and A. R. J. Turgot," *Journal des Économistes et des Études Humaines*, ISSN (Online) 2153-1552, ISSN (Print) 2194-5799 (1991); Richard van den Berg, ed., *Richard Cantillon's Essay on the Nature of Trade in General: A Variorum Edition* (New York: Routledge, 2015), p. 1; "Richard Cantillon: The Founding Father of Modern Economics," Mises Institute, https://mises.org/library/richard-cantillon-founding-father-modern-economics; Peter Groenewegen, "Sir James Steuart and Richard Cantillon," *in* Ramón Tortajada, ed., *The Economics of James Steuart* (London: Routledge, 1999), p. 34 ("Quesnay, Turgot, Beccaria, Verri and Adam Smith all drew directly on Richard Cantillon's *Essai*, which they specifically cited and more than likely had studied *in toto*.").

9. David Williams, ed., *The Enlightenment* (Cambridge: Cambridge University Press, 1999), p. 61; *see also* Caso, *We, the People.*

10. Richard Alan Ryerson, *John Adams's Republic: The One, the Few, and the Many* (Baltimore, MD: Johns Hopkins University Press, 2016), pp. 74, 77; Eric Burns, *Infamous Scribbler: The Founding Fathers and the Rowdy Beginnings of American Journalism* (New York: Public Affairs, 2006), p. 151; Boston Massacre Historical Society, http://www.bostonmassacre.net.

11. John M. Murrin, Paul E. Johnson, James M. McPherson, Gary Gerstle, Emily S. Rosenberg & Norman L. Rosenberg, *Liberty, Equality, Power: A History of the American People* (Belmont, CA: Thomson Higher Education, 2009), p. 148; S. E. Forman, *Advanced American History* (New York: The Century Co., 1921), p. 169.

12. J. Johnston, *Popular Handbook of the British Constitution: Giving the History of Its Origin and Growth* (London: Thomas Burleigh, 1899), p. 62; Pat Blakeley, "Stamp Act Rebellion to Hit Streets—249 Years Later," http://www.newportthisweek.com/news/2014-08-14/Front_Page/Stamp_Act_Rebellion_to_Hit_Streets__249_Years_Late.html.

13. Rebecca Stefoff, *Furman v. Georgia: Debating the Death Penalty* (New York: Marshall Cavendish, 2008), p. 29; Travis C. Pratt, Jacinta M. Gau & Travis W. Franklin, *Key Ideas in Criminology and Criminal Justice* (Thousand Oaks, CA: Sage Publications, 2011).

14. Groenewegen, *Eighteenth-century Economics*, pp. 16, 172, 343.

15. In that book, Ortes observed: "All men by nature are led to the pleasure of the senses." "[F]or this reason," he continued, "all external objects become at the same time the particular object of desire of each man." Italo Calvino, *Why Read the Classics?* (Boston: Mariner Books, Martin McLaughlin, trans. 1991), pp. 114–18. Ortes studied math and metaphysics as a young man, then turned to political economy in his later years, penning works on economics and population such as *Economia Nazionale* (1774) and *Riflessioni sulla popolazione delle nazioni per rapporto all' economia nazionale* (1790). His "main title to fame," economist Joseph Schumpeter explains, "is in his contribution to the 'Malthusian' theory of people," with his *Economia Nazionale* contributing to the idea that consumption is a limiting factor in total output. Luigi Cossa, *An Introduction to the Study of Political Economy* (London: Macmillan and Co., Louis Dyer, trans. 1893), p. 167; *Journal of the Royal Statistical Society* (London: The Royal Statistical Society, 1901), p. 686; Joseph A. Schumpeter, *History of Economic Analysis* (New York: Routledge, 1997), p. 178.

16. Jean Le Rond d'Alembert, *Preliminary Discourse to the Encyclopedia of Diderot* (Chicago: The University of Chicago Press, Richard N. Schwab, trans. 1995) (1751), pp. ix–x; Edward Grant, *God and Reason in the Middle Ages* (Cambridge: Cambridge University Press, 2001), p. 325; Elizabeth S. Radcliffe, ed., *A Companion to Hume* (West Sussex, UK: Wiley-Blackwell, 2011), p. 24.

17. Shannon M. Barton-Bellessa, eds., *Encyclopedia of Community Corrections* (Thousand Oaks, CA: Sage Publications, 2012), p. 22; Luigino Bruni & Pier Luigi Porta, eds., *Handbook of Research Methods and Applications in Happiness and Quality of Life* (Cheltenham, UK: Edward Elgar Publishing, 2016), p. 505.

18. Merry E. Wiesner-Hanks, *Early Modern Europe, 1450–1789* (Cambridge: Cambridge University Press, 2013), p. 385; Groenewegen, *Eighteenth-century Economics*, pp. 29, 37, 43 n.21; Bernard E. Harcourt, "Beccaria's *On Crimes and Punishments*: A Mirror on the History of the Foundations of Modern Criminal Law," *in* Marcus D. Dubber, ed., *Foundational Texts in Modern Criminal Law* (Oxford: Oxford University Press, 2014), ch. 2; "Cesare Bonesana, marquis de Beccaria," Larousse, http://www.larousse.fr/encyclopedie/personnage/Cesare_Bonesana_marquis_de_Beccaria/108100; The ARTFL Encyclopédie, http://encyclopedie.uchicago.edu.

19. J. R. McCulloch, *The Literature of Political Economy: A Classified Catalogue of Select Publications in the Different Departments of that Science, with Historical, Critical, and Biographical Notices* (London: Longman, Brown, Green, and Longmans, 1845), pp. 26–28.

20. Solveig C. Robinson, *The Book in Society: An Introduction to Print Culture* (Buffalo, NY: Broadview Press, 2014), p. 101; Carol Strickland, *The Illustrated Timeline of Western Literature: A Crash Course in Words and Pictures* (New York: Sterling, 2007), p. 42; Dayna Mergenthaler, The Enlightenment, PowerPoint® Presentations in World History (Culver City, CA: Social Studies School Service, 2005), S15; William Smyth, *Lectures on the French Revolution* (London: William Pickering, 1842), Vol. 1, p. 86; Stuart Brown, ed., *British Philosophy and the Age of Enlightenment* (London: Routledge,

2003), p. 188; Lawrence S. Cunningham, John J. Reich & Lois Fichner-Rathus, *Culture and Values: A Survey of the Western Humanities* (Stamford, CT: Cengage Learning, 8th ed. 2015), Vol. II, p. 555; Ian Davidson, *Voltaire: A Life* (New York: Pegasus Books, 2012); Eckart Förster, ed., Immanuel Kant, *Opus Postumum* (Cambridge: Cambridge University Press, Eckart Förster & Michael Rosen, trans. 1998), p. 266 n.49; *see also* Michael C. Carhart, *The Science of Culture in Enlightenment Germany* (Cambridge, MA: Harvard University Press, 2007), p. 52 ("More than ten years before Beccaria published *On Crimes and Punishments* (1764), Samuel Johnson wrote that 'to equate robbery with murder is to reduce murder to robbery,' commenting that 'the frequency of capital punishments rarely hinders the commission of a crime.'").

21. Daniela Rogobete, Jonathan P. A. Sell & Alan Munton, eds., *The Silent Life of Things: Reading and Representing Commodified Objecthood* (Newcastle upon Tyne, UK: Cambridge Scholars Publishing, 2015), p. 76; Margaret Bald, *Banned Books: Literature Suppressed on Religious Grounds* (New York: Facts on File, rev. ed. 2006), p. 93.

22. Groenewegen, *Eighteenth-century Economics*, p. 27; Harcourt, "Beccaria's *On Crimes and Punishments*," in Dubber, *Foundational Texts in Modern Criminal Law*, p. 42; Philipp Blom, *Enlightening the World* Encyclopédie: *The Book that Changed the Course of History* (New York: St. Martin's Press, 2005), p. 141; Inna Gorbatov, *Catherine the Great and French Philosophers of the Enlightenment: Montesquieu, Voltaire, Rousseau, Diderot and Grimm* (Bethesda, MD: Academica Press, 2006), p. 65; Piers Beirne, *Inventing Criminology: Essays on the Rise of 'Homo Criminalis'* (Albany: State University of New York Press, 1993), p. 13.

23. "This Day Is Published," *The Public Advertiser* (London, England), May 1, 1767, p. 1 (noting that *The Critical Review* for April 1767 contains "Beccaria's Essay on Crimes and Punishments"); "This Day Is Published," *The Public Advertiser* (London, England), June 2, 1770, p. 3 (noting the publication of various pamphlets, including "A Discourse upon Oeconomy and Commerce, from the Italian of the celebrated Marquis Cæsar Beccaria, Author of the Treatise on Crimes and Punishments"); "This Day Is Published," *The Public Advertiser* (London, England), June 2, 1772, p. 4 (noting the publication of "A Discourse on Oeconomy and Commerce, by the celebrated Marquis Cæsar Beccaria, Author of the Treatise on Crimes and Punishments"); "This Day Is Published," *The Public Advertiser* (London, England), June 13, 1777, p. 1 (noting the publication of "[t]he Fourth Edition of, An Essay on Crimes and Punishments: Translated from the Italian of the Marquis Beccaria; with a Commentary, attributed to Voltaire, translated from the French"); "To the Printer of the Public Advertiser," *The Public Advertiser* (London, England), Aug. 31, 1778, p. 1 (quoting Beccaria's *Dei delitti e delle pene* in the original Italian).

24. "Ought Transportation to Be Abolished?" *The British Controversialist and Impartial Inquirer* (London: Houlston and Stoneman, 1852), Vol. 3, p. 464.

25. Lyon N. Richardson, *A History of Early American Magazines 1741–1789* (New York: Octagon Books, 1966), pp. 252–58; Thomas Keymer, ed., *Laurence Sterne's* Tristram Shandy: *A Casebook* (Oxford: Oxford University Press, 2006), pp. 80–81; Lynn Hunt, *Inventing Human Rights: A History* (New York: W. W. Norton & Co., 2007).

26. John D. Bessler, *Cruel and Unusual: The American Death Penalty and the Founders' Eighth Amendment* (Boston: Northeastern University Press, 2012), pp. 51–53.

27. Ibid., p. 90; Brian McCartin, *Thomas Paine: Common Sense and Revolutionary Pamphleteering* (New York: PowerPlus Books, 2002), p. 55.

28. *The Pennsylvania Packet* (Philadelphia, PA), Sept. 15, 1778, p. 4. The same advertisement later ran in a subsequent edition of that newspaper. *The Pennsylvania Packet* (Philadelphia, PA), Sept. 26, 1778, p. 4; *see also The Pennsylvania Packet* (Philadelphia, PA), Dec. 19, 1778, p. 3 (noting "Beccaria on Crimes, may be had at Bell's Book-Store, next door to St. Paul's Church, in Third-street, Philadelphia").

29. Laura I. Appleman, *Defending the Jury: Crime, Community, and the Constitution* (Cambridge: Cambridge University Press, 2015), pp. 25–26 & n.69.

30. "Founding Father's Library," Online Library of Liberty, http://oll.libertyfund.org/pages/founding-father-s-library?q=Beccaria#.

31. Luigino Bruni & Pier Luigi Porta, eds., *Handbook on the Economics of Happiness* (Cheltenham, UK: Edward Elgar Publishing, 2007), p. 97.

32. John Kells Ingram, *A History of Political Economy* (1888), ch. 5, *available at* Online Library of Liberty, http://oll.libertyfund.org/titles/ingram-a-history-of-political-economy?q=Beccaria#Ingram_ 1286_116; *see also* Katrin Van Bragt, *Bibliographie des Traductions Françaises* (Presses Universitaires de Louvain, 1995), pp. 280–81.

33. John D. Bessler, *The Birth of American Law: An Italian Philosopher and the American Revolution* (Durham, NC: Carolina Academic Press, 2014), pp. 13, 17, 93–94, 124–25, 136–39, 141, 144, 204, 234, 261, 315, 362–63.

34. Bruni & Porta, *Handbook on the Economics of Happiness*, p. 98; John P. McKay, Bennett D. Hill, John Buckler, Clare Haru Crowston, Merry E. Wiesner-Hanks & Joe Perry, *Understanding Western Society: A Brief History* (Boston: Bedford/St. Martin's, 2012), p. 541; Lisa Shapiro, "Pleasure, Pain and Sense Perception," *in* Aaron Garrett, ed., *The Routledge Companion to Eighteenth Century Philosophy* (New York: Routledge, 2014), pp. 400–17; http://enlightenment_revolution.org/index.php/Beccaria,_ Cesare_Bonesana,_Marchese_di.

35. Bessler, *The Birth of American Law*, pp. 41, 95–100; "A Biography of Edmund Randolph 1753– 1813," American History: From Revolution to Reconstruction, http://www.let.rug.nl/usa/biographies/ edmund-randolph/; F. C. Montague, ed., Jeremy Bentham, *A Fragment on Government* (Union, NJ: The Lawbook Exchange, 2001), p. 27; Bessler, *Cruel and Unusual*, p. 57; Philip Whitehead, *Modernising Probation and Criminal Justice: Getting the Measure of Cultural Change* (Kent, UK: Shaw & Sons, 2007), p. 64; Gunnar Skirbekk & Nils Gilje, *A History of Western Thought: From Ancient Greece to the Twentieth Century* (New York: Routledge, 2001), pp. 229, 247; *The Philosophical Works of David Hume* (Edinburgh: Adam Black and William Tait, 1826), Vol. 2, p. 132; John D. Greenwood, *A Conceptual History of Psychology: Exploring the Tangled Web* (Cambridge: Cambridge University Press, 2d ed. 2015), p. 126; Sally Mitchell, ed., *Victorian Britain: An Encyclopedia* (New York: Routledge, 2011), p. 828; *see also The Courier-Journal* (Louisville, KY), p. 14 ("*Greatest Happiness of the Greatest Number.*—This expression is used by Beccaria in the introduction to his 'Essay on Crimes and Punishment' (1764)."); ibid. ("'That action is best which procures the greatest happiness for the greatest numbers.'—[*Hutcheson's Inquiry Concerning Moral Good and Evil.* (1720)"; ibid. ("'Priestly was the first (unless it was Beccaria) who taught my lips to pronounce this sacred truth—that the greatest happiness of the greatest number is the foundation of morals and legislation.'—*Bentham's Works.*"); William Robert Scott, *Francis Hutcheson: His Life, Teaching and Position in the History of Philosophy* (Cambridge: Cambridge University Press, 1900), p. 273 (discussing Beccaria's and Bentham's influences, tracing back, in part, to Francis Hutcheson).

36. Daniel R. Coquillette & Neil Longley York, eds., *Portrait of a Patriot: The Major Political and Legal Papers of Josiah Quincy Junior* (Boston: The Colonial Society of Massachusetts, 2007), Vol. 2, pp. 62–66, 68, 179–82, 185, 227–29, 325, 340–41, 344–45 (quoting Josiah Quincy, Jr.'s law commonplace book); *compare* ibid. at 66 ("Some of Quincy's excerpts seem directly contradictory, such as the section from *Hobart's Reports* (1641), 'Judges have liberty + authority over statutes to mould them to the truest + best use, according to reason + best use, according to reason + best convenience.'"). Quincy's commonplace book also included material from Montesquieu's *L'Esprit des Lois* (1748) and on the subject of natural law, copying, for example, the ideas of Jean Jacques Burlamaqui (1694– 1748) and Emmerich de Vattel (1714–1767). Elsewhere, Quincy carefully recorded in Latin "Maxims of the Civil Law."

37. Terry M. Mays, *Historical Dictionary of Revolutionary America* (Lanham, MD: The Scarecrow Press, 2005), p. 33; Coquillette & York, *Portrait of a Patriot*, Vol. 6, pp. 185–86, 202, 235 nn. 39– 40. Dated May 14, 1774, Josiah Quincy's *Observations*—commenting on George III's statute "*to discontinue, in such Manner, and for such Time as are therein mentioned, the landing and discharging, the lading or shipping of Goods, Wares, Merchandize, at the Town, and within the Harbour of Boston*"— were said by Quincy himself to reflect the appearance of being "*thrown together in haste*" as "*the Writer was out of Town on business, almost every day, the Sheets were printing off.*"

38. Coquillette & York, *Portrait of a Patriot*, Vol. 1, pp. 122–23, 127, 202–3. In the first entry, on the topic "Of Society," Josiah Quincy, Jr. recorded the ever-popular passage from Beccaria's treatise: "In *every* human society, there is an effort *continually* tending to confer on one part the height of power and happiness, and to reduce the other to the extreme of weakness and misery. The intent of good laws is to oppose this effort, and diffuse their influence universally and *equally.*" Quincy also

transcribed this passage from Beccaria: "The sum of all the portions of the liberty of each Individual constitute the sovereignty of a State." In his political commonplace book, Josiah Quincy, Jr. also recorded passages from Scottish author James Boswell's book on Corsica, noting, among other things: "Liberty is so natural, and so dear to mankind, whether as Individuals, or as members of society, that is indispensably necessary to our happiness. Everything great and worthy ariseth from it." "Particular punishments are the cure for accidental distempers in the State; they inflame rather than allay those heats which arise from settled mismanagement of government, or from a natural indisposition in the people. It is of the utmost moment not to make mistakes in the use of strong measures...." Ibid., pp. 165–66.

39. C. H. Timperley, *A Dictionary of Printers and Printing, with the Progress of Literature, Ancient and Modern* (London: H. Johnson, 1839), p. 822.

40. Rosamaria Loretelli, "The First English Translation of Cesare Beccaria's *On Crimes and Punishments*: Uncovering the Editorial and Political Contexts," *Diciottesimo Secolo*, anno II, 2017, p. 9.

41. John S. C. Abbott, *The French Revolution of 1789, as Viewed in the Light of Republican Institutions* (New York: Harper & Brothers, 1859), p. 379; Robert A. Silverman, Terence P. Thornberry, Bernard Cohen & Barry Krisberg, eds., *Crime and Justice at the Millennium: Essays by and in Honor of Marvin E. Wolfgang* (New York: Springer Science + Business Media, 2002), p. 399; David J. Siemers, *Presidents and Political Thought* (Columbia: University of Missouri Press, 2009), p. 43.

42. Bessler, *Cruel and Unusual*, pp. 48–49; Bessler, *The Birth of American Law*, p. 147.

43. Kent S. Miller & Michael L. Radelet, *Executing the Mentally Ill: The Criminal Justice System and the Case of Alvin Ford* (Newbury Park, CA: Sage Publications, 1993), p. 111 n.5; John Ferling, *Adams vs. Jefferson: The Tumultuous Election of 1800* (Oxford: Oxford University Press, 2004), pp. xi–xii.

44. Mitchel P. Roth, *Crime and Punishment: A History of the Criminal Justice System* (Belmont, CA: Wadsworth, 2d ed. 2011), p. 90.

45. Bessler, *The Birth of American Law*, p. 373.

46. Bessler, *Cruel and Unusual*, p. 51.

47. Bessler, *The Birth of American Law*, pp. 3, 5, 34–35, 50, 65, 79–80, 147, 164, 166–67, 172, 192, 206, 270, 312, 331, 366, 369–70, 385, 396.

48. Ibid., pp. 9, 29, 48, 147, 180, 220, 333, 343, 366; Petra T. C. Kampen, *Expert Evidence Compared: Rules and Practices in the Dutch and American Criminal Justice System* (Cambridge, UK: Intersentia, 1998), p. 28.

49. J. Mitchell Miller, *The Encyclopedia of Theoretical Criminology* (West Sussex, UK: Wiley Blackwell, 2014), Vol. 1, p. 260; Stacy L. Mallicoat, *Crime and Criminal Justice: Concepts and Controversies* (Thousand Oaks, CA: Sage Publications, 2017), p. 78.

50. E. Antonello, "Boscovich and the Brera Observatory," Paper presented on May 18, 2011, Istituto Lombardo, Palazzo Brera, Milano, pp. 1, 3.

51. Roberto Curti, *Italian Crime Filmography 1968–1980* (Jefferson, NC: McFarland & Co., 2013), p. 193; G. Colombo, *Who's Who in Italy* (2001), p. 1812; https://en.wikipedia.org/wiki/Beccaria_Township,_Clearfield_County,_Pennsylvania.

52. C. Beccaria liceo classico statale, http://www.liceobeccaria.gov.it/pvw/app/MILG0001/pvw_sito.php?sede_codice=MILG0001&from=-1&page=1814377&from=0.

53. Felice Venosta, *The Traveller's Guide of Milan and Its Environs* (Milan: Ronchi, E. C. Cornaro tran., 1875), pp. 43–44 (describing the monument); John D. Bessler, *The Italian Enlightenment and the American Revolution: Cesare Beccaria's Forgotten Influence on American Law*, 37 Mitchell Hamline L.J. Pub. Pol'y & Practice, Iss. 1, Article 1 (2016), pp. 3–4; September 24, 2014—Beccaria and Religion—250 Years after "Dei delitti e delle pene" (On crimes and punishments, 1764–2014), Fondazione Bruno Kessler, Trento, http://www.fbk.eu/events/september-24-2014-beccaria-and-religion-250-years-after-dei-delitti-e-delle-pene-crimes-and; *see also* William M. Johnston, *Celebrations: The Cult of Anniversaries in Europe and the United States Today* (New Brunswick, NJ: Transaction Publishers, 1991), p. 99 ("In 1988 the city of Milan commemorated the 250th anniversary of the jurist Cesare Beccaria (1738–1794), whose book *On Crimes and Punishments* (1764) advocated reforms of penal law that have benefited all mankind."); Conference on the Legacy of Beccaria 250 Years after the P[u]blication of "Of Crimes and Punishments" (Rome, 29–30 October 2014), http://esclh.blogspot.com/2014/10/

conference-on-legacy-of-beccaria-250.html. A conference marking the 250th anniversary of the publication of the English translation of Cesare Beccaria's book, *An Essay on Crimes and Punishments*, also took place in 2017. http://www.academia.edu/26709677/CESARE_BECCARIAS_ON_CRIMES_AND_PUNISHMENTS_AND_EIGHTEENTH-_CENTURY_BRITAIN_LAW_HISTORY_PHILOSOPHY_LITERATURE._A_TWO-_WAY_PERSPECTIVE (highlighting details of the conference and the call for papers).

54. Bessler, *The Birth of American Law*, p. 431; Cesare Beccaria, *On Crimes and Punishments* (New Brunswick, NJ: Transaction Publishers, Graeme R. Newman & Pietro Marongiu, eds. & trans., 5th ed. 2009), p. lxvii; Aaron Thomas, ed., On Crimes and Punishments *and Other Writings* (Toronto: University of Toronto Press, Aaron Thomas & Jeremy Parzen, trans. 2008), p. xxix; Amato Amati & Antonio Buccellati, *Cesare Beccaria: L'Abolizione Della Pena Di Morte* (Milano: Francesco Vallardi, ed., 1872), pp. 315–17. Professor Amato Amati, of Milan, was a member of the commission that raised funds and supported the memorial to Cesare Beccaria's life that can still be found in Milan. Ibid.; *see also* John Hostettler, *Cesare Beccaria: The Genius of 'On Crimes and Punishments'* (Hampshire, UK: Waterside Press, 2011), p. 33.

55. Bessler, *Cruel and Unusual*, p. 47. Many early Americans read Montesquieu's *Spirit of the Laws. E.g.*, W. Stull Holt, "Charles Carroll, Barrister: The Man," 31 *Maryland Historical Magazine* 112, 123 (1936).

56. Giuseppe Barigazzi, *La Scala racconta: Nouva edizione riveduta e ampliata a cura di Silvia Barigazzi* (Milano: Hoephi, 2014) (reprinting Antonio Perego's painting and noting it is part of a private collection); Fernando Mazzocca, Alessandro Morandotti, Enrico Colle & Eugenia Bianchi, *Milano Neoclassica* (Milano: Longanesi, 2001), Vol. 177, p. 478 (identifying Antonio Perego's *L'Accademia dei Pugni* (1766) as in the "collezione Luisa Sormani Andreani Verri"); Sophus A. Reinert, "Patriotism, Cosmopolitanism and Political Economy in the *Accademia dei pugni* in Austrian Lombardy, 1760–1780," *in* Koen Stapelbroek & Jani Marjanen, eds., *The Rise of Economic Societies in the Eighteenth Century: Patriotic Reform in Europe and North America* (New York: Palgrave Macmillan, 2012), p. 131 (making reference to the "1766 group-portrait" of the Accademia dei Pugni by Antonio Perego); Stephen P. Halbrook, *A Right to Bear Arms: State and Federal Bills of Rights and Constitutional Guarantees* (Westport, CT: Greenwood Press, 1989), pp. 43, 132 n.81; Richard J. Goy, *Florence: A Walking Guide to Its Architecture* (2015); Mario Ricciardi & Filippo Santoni de Sio, "Cesare Beccaria: Utilitarianism, Contractualism and Rights," *philinq II*, 2-2014, pp. 79–86; Richard B. Sher, *The Enlightenment and the Book: Scottish Authors and Their Publishers in Eighteenth-Century Britain, Ireland and America* (Chicago: The University of Chicago Press, 2006), pp. 571–72; *The Pennsylvania Packet* (Philadelphia, PA), June 24, 1786, p. 4 (the bookseller William Prichard "Begs leave to inform the Gentlemen of the Law, that he has just received the following most excellent professional Authors, viz.... Beccaria on crimes and punishments"); "New Books for Sale at Rice's," *The Pennsylvania Packet* (Philadelphia, PA), Mar. 16, 1787, p. 4 (noting that "Beccaria's essay on crimes and punishments" was for sale at "Rice's Book-Store and Music Shop, Market, near Second street"); "Imported in the late vessels from London, and to be sold by Joseph Crukshank," *The Pennsylvania Packet* (Philadelphia, PA), May 18, 1787, p. 4 (advertising "Beccaria on crimes & punishments" for sale); "Imported in the late vessels from London, and to be sold by Joseph Crukshank," *The Pennsylvania Packet* (Philadelphia, PA), May 24, 1787, p. 4 (advertising "Beccaria on crimes & punishments" for sale); "Law," *The Pennsylvania Packet* (Philadelphia, PA), June 30, 1787, p. 4 ("Just Imported from London and Dublin, and to be Sold by William Prichard ... Beccaria on crimes and punishments").

57. Hostettler, *Cesare Beccaria*, p. 22.

58. *Florence: A Complete Guide to the Renaissance City, the Surrounding Countryside, and Chianti Region* (Milano: Touring Club of Italy, 1999), p. 94; Beccaria 2.5: Convegno Internazionale a 250 Anni Dalla Prima Edizione Di *Dei Delitti e Delle Pene* (23 e 24 Octtobre 2014—Milano). In anticipation of the 250th anniversary of the publication of *Dei delitti e delle pene*, the University of Geneva, in Switzerland, also hosted a multi-day conference on Beccaria's book and Cesare Beccaria's legacy. That conference was organized by Michel Porret and Elisabeth Salvi, two scholars of Beccaria's work. Cesare Beccaria: Reception et Heritage, Feb. 21–23, 2013, http://www.unige.ch/lettres/istge/hmo/Colloques/ColloqueBeccaria2013.html. That conference resulted in the publication of a book in French highlighting Beccaria's many varied intellectual contributions. Michel Porret & Élisabeth Salvi, eds., *Cesare*

Beccaria: La controverse pénale XVIIIe–XXIe siècle (Rennes Cedex, France: Presses Universitaires de Rennes, 2015).

59. Cesare Beccaria regularly fails to make the list of great economists. *See, e.g.*, Mark Skousen, *The Big Three in Economics: Adam Smith, Karl Marx and John Maynard Keynes* (New York: Routledge, 2015); David Daiches Raphael, Donald Winch & Robert Jacob Alexander Skidelsky, eds., *Three Great Economists: Smith, Malthus, Keynes* (Oxford: Oxford University Press, 1997); *see also* Phil Thornton, *The Great Economists: Ten Economists Whose Thinking Changed the Way We Live* (Harlow, UK: Pearson Education, 2014) (listing the following ten economists, Beccaria not among them: Daniel Kahneman, Paul Samuelson, Friedrich Hayek, David Ricardo, Adam Smith, John Maynard Keynes, Alfred Marshall, Milton Friedman, Gary Becker and Karl Marx); Steven Pressman, *Fifty Major Economists* (New York: Routledge, 3rd ed. 2014) (failing to list Beccaria among fifty influential economists, though listing Adam Smith and Jeremy Bentham, both readers of Beccaria's work).

60. *E.g.*, James R. Otteson, *Adam Smith* (New York: Bloomsbury Academic, 2013); Nicholas Phillipson, *Adam Smith: An Enlightened Life* (New York: Penguin Books, 2010); Ian Simpson Ross, *The Life of Adam Smith* (Oxford: Oxford University Press, 2d ed. 2010); Knud Haakonssen, ed., *The Cambridge Companion to Adam Smith* (Cambridge: Cambridge University Press, 2006); Samuel Fleischacker, *On Adam Smith's* Wealth of Nations (Princeton: Princeton University Press, 2004); Charles L. Griswold, Jr., *Adam Smith and the Virtues of Enlightenment* (Cambridge: Cambridge University Press, 1999); John Cunningham Wood, ed., *Adam Smith: Critical Assessments* (New York: Routledge, 1996).

61. *See generally* Hostettler, *Cesare Beccaria*; Marcello T. Maestro, *Cesare Beccaria and the Origins of Penal Reform* (Philadelphia, PA: Temple University Press, 1973). Some of the biographies have been published in Italy, while Beccaria is not the sole focus of others. Dominic R. Massaro, *Cesare Beccaria—The Father of Criminal Justice: His Impact on Anglo-American Jurisprudence* (Cecina, Italy: Universitas Internationalis Coluccio Salutati, 1991); Coleman Phillipson, *Three Criminal Law Reformers: Beccaria, Bentham, Romilly* (Glen Ridge, NJ: Patterson Smith, 1970).

62. Samuel Fleischacker, "Adam Smith's Reception among the American Founders, 1776–1790," *William and Mary Quarterly*, 3d Series, Vol. LIX, No. 4, Oct. 2002.

63. Groenewegen, *Eighteenth-century Economics*, p. 4 ("In the history of political economy, three figures of the Enlightenment stand out at the end of the third quarter of the century: Turgot, Beccaria and Smith."); ibid. ("Of these three figures from the Enlightenment who all wrote extensively on political economy, only one, Adam Smith, has been given a prominent place in the history of economic thought. Turgot has generally been given a more minor, but nevertheless relatively important place, while Beccaria has been almost totally ignored in the histories of economics.").

64. Russ Roberts, *How Adam Smith Can Change Your Life: An Unexpected Guide to Human Nature and Happiness* (New York: Penguin, 2014).

65. Federalist No. 78 (Alexander Hamilton).

66. Christopher Berry Gray, ed., *The Philosophy of Law: An Encyclopedia* (New York: Routledge, 2012), pp. 307–8; Bessler, *The Birth of American Law*, pp. 157–58, 163.

67. Antonio Andreoni, "The Political Economy of Industrial Policy: After the Crisis, Back on the Agenda," *in* Ugo Mattei & John D. Haskell, eds., *Research Handbook on Political Economy and Law* (Northampton, MA: Edward Elgar Publishing, 2015), p. 342.

68. Cesare Beccaria, "An Attempt at an Analysis of Smuggling," *in* William J. Baumol & Stephen M. Goldfeld, eds., *Precursors in Mathematical Economics: An Anthology* (London: The London School of Economics and Political Science, 1968), pp. 147–50 (originally printed in Italian as "Tentativo analitico sui contrabbandi," *Il Caffè*, Vol. I, Brescia, 1764, pp. 118–19, and available in the English translation at http://www.lawlib.utoronto.ca/bclc/crimweb/foundation/Beccaria%20smuggling%20small.pdf).

69. Melissa Goodwin & Catherine Sommervold, *Creativity, Critical Thinking, and Communication: Strategies to Increase Students' Skills* (Lanham, MD: Rowman & Littlefield, 2012), pp. 24, 27–28; Horace Mann, ed., *The Common School Journal* (Boston: William B. Fowle & N. Capen, 1845), Vol. VII, p. 157; "The Education to Be," *The Continental Monthly* (New York: J. R. Gilmore, 1862), Vol. 1, p. 592; *see also* Board of Commissioners of Common Schools, *The Connecticut Common School Journal*, Vols. I–IV (1838–1842) (Hartford, CT: Case, Tiffany & Burnham, Henry Barnard, ed., 1842),

p. 190 ("In Ireland education is most neglected; the gibbet takes account of it. Beccaria, in 1767, pre-dicted that the punishment of death would not survive that happy period, 'when knowledge instead of ignorance shall become the portion of the greater number.' "); Benjamin Rush, "A Plan for the Es-tablishment of Public Schools and the Diffusion of Knowledge in Pennsylvania; to Which Are Added, Thoughts upon the Mode of Education, Proper in a Republic," *available at* http://oll.libertyfund.org/ titles/hyneman-american-political-writing-during-the-founding-era-1760-1805-vol-1.

70. John P. Kaminski & Richard Leffler, eds., *Federalists and Antifederalists: The Debate Over the Ratification of the Constitution* (Lanham, MD: Madison House, 2d ed. 1998), Vol. 1, pp. 193–96.

71. Bessler, *The Birth of American Law*, p. 8.

72. John C. Hamilton, ed., *The Works of Alexander Hamilton* (New York: John F. Trow 1850), Vol. 2, pp. 435, 438, 445.

73. Bessler, *The Birth of American Law*, pp. 421–29.

74. Ibid, pp. 88–92; *see also* "Law Books, &c. for Sale by Rice and Co.," *The Pennsylvania Packet* (Philadelphia, PA), Dec. 1, 1787, p. 3 (advertising "Beccaria on crimes and punishments" by Rice and Co., "Booksellers and Stationers, South Side of Market-street, next door but one to Second-street"); "Books Lately imported, and to be Sold by Joseph Crukshank," *The Pennsylvania Packet*, June 14, 1788, p. 3 (advertising "Beccaria on crimes and punishments" for sale). The U.S. Constitution was ratified on June 21, 1788. Robert A. Brady, *The Constitution of the United States* (Washington, DC: Government Printing Office, 2007), p. 1.

75. Bessler, *The Birth of American Law*, pp. 124–26; "Books Lately imported, and to be Sold by Joseph Crukshank," *The Pennsylvania Packet* (Philadelphia, PA), June 27, 1788, p. 4 (advertising "Bec-caria on crimes and punishments"); "Books Lately imported, and to be Sold by Joseph Crukshank," *The Pennsylvania Packet* (Philadelphia, PA), June 30, 1788, p. 4 (same); "This Day is published, and to be sold, by Parry Hall, No. 149, Chesnut-street, near Fourth-street," *The Pennsylvania Gazette* (Philadelphia, PA), Dec. 5, 1792, p. 4 (listing "Beccaria" for sale); "The following Books, may be had at the Printing-Office of H. Wills," *State Gazette of North-Carolina* (New Bern, NC), Dec. 5, 1794, p. 4 (listing "Beccaria on Crimes" for sale in a newspaper printed by Henry Wills, "JOINT PRINTER TO THE STATE WITH A. HODGE"); "For Sale at the Printing-Office, (Newbern) the Following Books," *North-Carolina Gazette* (New Bern, NC), Feb. 14, 1795, p. 4 (listing "Beccaria on Crimes" for sale); "A. Hodge has just received from New-York and offers for sale at Raleigh, during the sitting of the Legislature, the following," *The North-Carolina Journal* (Halifax, NC), Nov. 16, 1795, p. 4 (listing "Beccaria on Crimes" for sale); "New Books," *Weekly Raleigh Register* (Raleigh, NC), May 19, 1801, p. 3 ("J. GALES has just received from Philadelphia, the following Addition to his Stock of Books, viz.... Beccaria on Crimes and Punishments"); "New English Books," *Raleigh Register and North-Car-olina State Gazette* (Raleigh, NC), Mar. 30, 1802, p. 1 (offering for sale Beccaria's *On Crimes and Punishments*); "New Books," *Raleigh Register and North-Carolina State Gazette* (Raleigh, NC), Aug. 20, 1804, p. 1 (same); "Just Received, and for Sale at the Office of the Journal," *The North-Carolina Journal* (Halifax, NC), July 6, 1807, p. 4 (same); *The Evening Post* (New York, NY), Dec. 12, 1810, p. 3 (noting "A VALUABLE COLLECTION of about 1200 volumes of English, French and Italian BOOKS, *London* and *Paris* editions — For sale by JOHN GOURGAS," including "WORKS OF ... Beccaria"); "Gould, Banks & Gould," *The Evening Post* (New York, NY), Mar. 15, 1811, p. 3 ("Have at their Book-stores at New-York and Albany, quantities of the following BOOKS ... Beccaria on Crimes and Punishments, 1 dol."); "Book Store," *Western Carolinian* (Salisbury, NC), Feb. 22, 1825, p. 3 (noting that Beccaria's treatise was for sale at Allemong & Locke after "an extensive assortment of *Books* from Philadelphia" were received); "Book Store," *Western Carolinian* (Salisbury, NC), Mar. 1, 1825, p. 4 (same).

76. Robert Ernst, *Rufus King: American Federalist* (Chapel Hill: University of North Carolina Press, 1968), pp. 14–20.

77. *E.g.*, Bessler, *The Birth of American Law* (noting and detailing Beccaria's substantial influence in the United States).

78. Carlo Scognamiglio Pasini, *L'arte della ricchezza: Cesare Beccaria economista* (Milano: Mondadori Education S.p.A., 2014).

79. Bessler, *The Birth of American Law*, p. 27.

80. Pasini, *L'arte della ricchezza*.

81. Armando Massarenti, "Rome Celebrates Beccaria, 250 Years after the Publication of 'On Crimes

and Punishments,'" *Il Sole 24 Ore* Digital Edition, Nov. 26, 2014, http://www.italy24.ilsole24ore.com/art/arts-and-leisure/2014-11-25/beccaria-161810.php?uuid=AB1AaxHC.

82. Gianmarco Gaspari, ed., *Scritti economici* (Milano: Mediobanca, 2014), Vols. 1–3.

83. Rother, "The Beginning of Higher Education in Political Economy in Milan and Modena," *in History of Universities*, p. 120 ("The great success of *Dei delitti e delle pene* overshadowed Beccaria's economic work, but never entirely eclipsed it. After Schumpeter resurrected the 'underrated economist', Angelo Bignami produced a first evaluation, followed by Oscar Nuccio's more extensive analysis of Beccaria's theories. His role has since been studied mainly by Italian economic historians.").

84. Rebecca Newberger Goldstein, "Don't Overthink It," *The Atlantic*, May 2015, http://www.theatlantic.com/magazine/archive/2015/05/dont-overthink-it/389519/.

85. Rae Paoletta, "Can Candidates Please Stop Misquoting the Founding Fathers? It's Embarrassing," MTV.com, Oct. 19, 2015, http://www.mtv.com/news/2353756/candidates-founding-fathers-quote-john-oliver/.

86. The full title of Adam Smith's famous book—as published—is *An Inquiry into the Nature and Causes of the Wealth of Nations* (1776). Smith wrote of the "invisible hand" in chapter 2 of book four. *See* Bert Tieben, *The Concept of Equilibrium in Different Economic Traditions: An Historical Investigation* (Cheltenham, UK: Edward Elgar Publishing, 2012), p. 171; *see also* Heinz Lubasz, "Adam Smith and the 'Free Market,'" *in* Stephen Copley & Kathryn Sutherland, eds., *Adam Smith's* Wealth of Nations*: New Interdisciplinary Essays* (Manchester, UK: Manchester University Press, 1995), p. 46 ("What chiefly attracts Adam Smith's latter-day champions to the *Wealth of Nations* is undoubtedly the concept they call 'the invisible hand of the market', what Smith called simply the 'invisible hand', and which turns out on closer examination of the full text of the book to be the hand not of the market but of nature."). Adam Smith used the term "invisible hand" three times in his published writings. Warren J. Samuels, *Erasing the Invisible Hand: Essays on an Elusive and Misused Concept in Economics* (Cambridge: Cambridge University Press, 2011), p. 30.

87. Jonathan A. Knee, "In 'Misbehaving,' an Economics Professor Isn't Afraid to Attack His Own," *New York Times*, May 5, 2015; N. Gregory Mankiw, "Economists Actually Agree on This: The Wisdom of Free Trade," *New York Times*, Apr. 24, 2015.

88. James C. Miller III, "What Would Adam Smith Say?" *Wall Street Journal*, June 29, 2004 ("As an economist, I'm painfully aware that Adam Smith is one of the most over-quoted and least-understood figures in the history of Western civilization.").

89. *E.g.*, Adam Davidson, "In Code We Trust," *New York Times Magazine*, Apr. 30, 2015; Sendhil Mullainathan, "Why a Harvard Professor Has Mixed Feelings When Students Take Jobs in Finance," *New York Times*, Apr. 10, 2015. There were also mentions of Beccaria in the *New York Times* in 2011 and 2010. *See* Kathryn Harrison, "Empress of All the Russias," *New York Times Book Review*, Nov. 16, 2011; Jeffrey Rosen, "Prisoners of Parole," *New York Times*, Jan. 8, 2010.

90. David Siegal, "How Efficiency Is Wiping Out the Middle Class," *New York Times*, Jan. 25, 2017.

91. "Adam Smith T-Shirts & Tees," http://www.cafepress.com/+adam-smith+t-shirts.

92. Richard Posner, *An Economic Theory of the Criminal Law*, 85 Colum. L. Rev. 1193 (1985) ("The economic analysis of criminal law began on a very high plane in the eighteenth and early nineteenth centuries with the work of Beccaria and Bentham, but its revival in modern times dates only from 1968, when Gary Becker's article on the economics of crime and punishment appeared."); Gary Becker, *Crime and Punishment: An Economic Approach*, 76 J. Pol. Econ. 169 (1968) ("Lest the reader be repelled by the apparent novelty of an 'economic' framework for illegal behavior, let him recall that two important contributors to criminology during the eighteenth and nineteenth centuries, Beccaria and Bentham, explicitly applied an economic calculus.").

93. Harcourt, *The Illusion of Free Markets*, p. 60. "Beccaria's economic writings," Harcourt notes elsewhere, "have been forgotten by history and never translated into English." As Harcourt notes of Beccaria: "Beccaria was primarily an economist. Joseph Schumpeter referred to him as the 'Italian Adam Smith'—but in importance only. His economics, as you will see, were radically different than Smith's." Prof. Bernard Harcourt, author of *The Illusion of Free Markets*, speaking to *Harper's Magazine* blog on September 8, 2011.

94. Bessler, *The Birth of American Law*, pp. 3–9.

95. Ibid., pp. 431–36.

96. Osvaldo Barreneche, *Crime and the Administration of Justice in Buenos Aires, 1785–1853* (Lincoln: University of Nebraska Press, 2006), pp. 21–22; J. H. R. Pelt, *Gaspare Melchor de Jovellanos* (New York: Twayne Publishers, 1971), p. 70; Owen Chadwick, *The Popes and European Revolution* (New York: Oxford University Press, 1981), p. 333; Gabriel Haslip-Viera, *Crime and Punishment in Late Colonial Mexico City, 1692–1810* (Albuquerque: University of New Mexico Press, 1999), p. 43; Michel Delon, *Encyclopedia of the Enlightenment* (New York: Routledge, 2013), p. 759; Robert Buffington, "Looking Forward, Looking Back: Judicial Discretion and the Mexican Revolutionary State," 2 *Crime, History & Societies: International Association for the History of Crime and Criminal Justice* (Droz, 1998), pp. 15, 18, 32; *see also* Roger Hood & Carolyn Hoyle, *The Death Penalty: A Worldwide Perspective* (Oxford: Oxford University Press, 5th ed. 2015), p. 71 ("Argentina first abolished the death penalty for political offences in 1853 and for all crimes in 1921, five years after the last execution had been carried out in 1916."); Timothy J. Coates, *Convict Labor in the Portuguese Empire 1740–1932* (Leiden, The Netherlands: Koninklijke Brill, 2014), p. 26 (noting Beccaria's influence in Portugal); Guilherme Braga da Cruz, *O movimiento abolicionista e a abolição da pena de morte em Portugal: resenha histórica* (Ministerio da Justiça, 1967), p. 34 (referencing Beccaria).

Chapter 1

1. Frederick Converse Beach & George Edwin Rines, ed., *The Americana: A Universal Reference Library* (New York: Scientific American Compiling Department, 1912), Vol. II (entry for "Beccaria, Cesare Bonesana, Marchese di"); John Hostettler, *Cesare Beccaria: The Genius of "On Crimes and Punishments"* (Hampshire, UK: Waterside Press, 2010), pp. xii, 23; *Opere di Cesare Beccaria* (Milano: Dalla Societa Tipogr. Dei Classici Italiano, 1821), p. vii; Henry Dunning Macleod, *A Dictionary of Political Economy: Biographical, Bibliographical, Historical, and Practical* (London: Longman, Brown, Longmans, and Roberts, 1862), Vol. 1, p. 252; *Il Politico* (Università degli studi di Pavia, 1983), Vol. 48, p. 704; Rev. Joel Foote Bingham, *The Sacred Hymns [Gl' Inni Sacri] and The Napoleonic Ode [Il Cinque Maggio] of Alexander Manzoni* (London: Henry Frowde, 1904), p. 6; David Young, trans., Cesare Beccaria, *On Crimes and Punishments* (Hackett Publishing Co., 1986), pp. 95–96. Cesare Beccaria's mother is also known as Maria Visconti di Saliceto.

2. Massimo Leone, *Saints and Signs: A Semiotic Reading of Conversion in Early Modern Catholicism* (Berlin: Walter de Gruyter, 2010), p. 327 & n.4.

3. *Life of S. Francis Xavier: Apostle of the Indies* (London: Burns and Lambert, 1858), p. 174; Frederick Converse Beach, ed., *The Encyclopedia Americana: A Universal Reference Library* (New York: Scientific American Compiling Dep't, 1905) (entry for Francis Xavier).

4. Bernard E. Harcourt, "Beccaria's *On Crimes and Punishments*: A Mirror on the History of the Foundations of Modern Criminal Law," *in* Markus D. Dubber, ed., *Foundational Texts in Modern Criminal Law* (Oxford: Oxford University Press, 2014), p. 40 n.6.

5. Renzo Zorzi, *Cesare Beccaria: Il dramma della giustizia* (Milano: Mondadori, 1996), p. 53; *see also* Giovanni Treccani degli Alfieri, *Storia di Milano* (Fondazione Treccani degli Alfieri per la storia di Milano, 1959), p. ii.

6. Cesare Beccaria, *Des délits et des peines/Dei delitti e delle pene* (Lyon: Ens Éditions: Philippe Audegean & Gianni Francioni, trans. & comp., 2009, p. 9; Gionatan Iosa, *Il buongiorno si legge dal mattino* (2014) (entry for Beccaria); *see also* Maria G. Vitali-Volant, *Cesare Beccaria (1738–1794): Cours et discours d'économie politique* (Paris: L'Harmattan, 2005), Note Bio-Bibliographique ("Cesare Beccaria Bonesana, troisième marquis de Gualdrasco et Villareggio, naît à Milan le 15 mars 1738 du marquis Giovanni Saverio et de Maria Visconti di Saliceto.").

7. http://italy.places-in-the-world.com/8959604-place-villareggio.html; http://italy.places-in-the-world.com/8949544-place-gualdrasco.html.

8. Federica Cengarle & Maria Nadia Covini, eds., *Il ducato de Filippo Maria Visconti, 1412–1447: Economia, politica, cultura* (Firenze, Italy: Firenze University Press, 2015); Domenico Sella, *Crisis and Continuity: The Economy of Spanish Lombardy in the Seventeenth Century* (Cambridge: Harvard University Press, 1979), pp. 18, 114, 182–83. A book published in Milan in 1839 is about an armory of C. A. Uboldo, a noble of Villareggio. *See* Domenico Biorci, *L'armeria del Signore C. Ambrogio Uboldo,*

nobile de Villareggio socio onorardio di Varie accademie e banchiere in Milano (Milano: Giuseppe Crespi, 1839).

9. John Wilkes, comp., *Encyclopædia Londinensis, or, Universal Dictionary of Arts, Sciences, and Literature* (London: J. Adlard, 1812), p. 456; Michael Bush, *Noble Privilege* (Manchester, UK: Manchester University Press, 1983), Vol. 1, pp. 133–34; Roland Sarti, *Italy: A Reference Guide from the Renaissance to the Present* (New York: Facts on File, 2004), p. 122.

10. Giovanni Bosco, *A Compendium of Italian History: From the Fall of the Roman Empire* (London: Longman, Green, and Co., J. D. Morell, trans. 1881), p. 66.

11. John Millard, *The New Pocket Cyclopædia: Or, Elements of Useful Knowledge, Methodically Arranged* (London: Sherwood, Neely, and Jones, 1813), p. 260; *see also* Edward Hutton, *The Cities of Romagna and the Marches* (New York: The Macmillan Co., 1913), p. 156 ("Ancona in the Lombard invasion appears as the second city of the maritime Pentapolis and, as might be expected, was plundered by those barbarians. They governed it by an officer with the title of Marquis.").

12. *Political Dictionary; Forming a Work of Universal Reference, Both Constitutional and Legal; and Embracing the Terms of Civil Administration, of Political Economy and Social Relations, and of All the More Important Statistical Departments of Finance and Commerce* (London: Charles Knight & Co., 1846), Vol, 2, p. 318; *see also* John Wilkes, comp., *Encyclopædia Londinensis; Or, Universal Dictionary of Arts, Sciences, and Literature* (London: J. Adlard, 1816), Vol. XIV, p. 404 ("Marquis, as a title of honour among us, dates as far back as the year 1385...."); *Elegant Arts for Ladies* (London: Ward and Lock, 1856), p. 223 ("A Marquis ... is the next degree of nobility. His office, formerly, was to guard the frontiers and limits of the kingdom, which was called the marches, from the Teutonic word *marche*, a limit; as in particular were the marches of Wales and Scotland, before those countries were annexed to Britain."); Charles R. Dodd, *A Manual of Dignities, Privilege, and Precedence: Including Lists of the Great Public Functionaries, from the Revolution to the Present Time* (London: Whittaker & Co., 1842), p. 176 ("A marquis is personally styled 'My Lord,' and the superscription of his letters is, 'The Most Honourable the Marquis of ___,'....").

13. George Ripley & Charles A. Dana, eds., *The New American Cyclopædia: A Popular Dictionary of General Knowledge* (New York: D. Appleton & Co., 1863), Vol. XI, p. 208.

14. Gregory Hanlon, *Italy 1636: Cemetery of Armies* (Oxford: Oxford University Press, 2016), p. 64; George Procter, *The History of Italy, from the Fall of the Western Empire to the Commencement of the Wars of the French Revolution* (London: Whittaker and Co., 2d ed. 1844), pp. 99, 133, 142–43; Gregory Lubkin, *A Renaissance Court: Milan under Galeazzo Maria Sforza* (Berkeley, CA: University of California Press, 1994), p. 8; Martin John Cable, *"Cum essem in Constantie ...": Raffaele Fulgosio and the Council of Constance 1414–1415* (Lieden: Brill, 2015), pp. 71–72, 74–76, 82–86, 265, 290–91, 293, 295–300, 329–38; Hugh James Rose, *A New General Biographical Dictionary* (London: B. Fellowes, 1841), Vol. 3, p. 467.

15. Hugh James Rose, *A New General Biographical Dictionary* (London: B. Fellowes, 1853), Vol. 3, p. 467; Corinne Saunders, ed., *A Companion to Medieval Poetry* (West Sussex, UK: Wiley-Blackwell, 2010), p. 517.

16. Cable, *"Cum essem in Constantie ..."*, pp. 82–83.

17. Massimo Mazzotti, *The World of Maria Gaetana Agnesi, Mathematician of God* (Baltimore, MD: The Johns Hopkins University Press, 2007), ch. 1; Angelo Heilprin & Louis Heilprin, *Geographical Dictionary of the World* (New Delhi: Logos Press, 1990), p. 1217; https://en.wikipedia.org/wiki/Montù_Beccaria.

18. Paula Findlen, "Calculations of Faith: Mathematics, Philosophy, and Sanctity in 18th-Century Italy (New Work on Maria Gaetana Agnesi)," *Historia Mathematica*, Vol. 38(2), pp. 248–91 (May 2011); Snezana Lawrence & Mark McCartney, *Mathematicians and Their Gods: Interactions Between Mathematics and Religious Beliefs* (Oxford: Oxford University Press, 2015), pp. 151–52.

19. "Marquis de Sade," http://www.poet.me.uk/english-language-poets/Marquis-de-Sade.htm.

20. William Bates, "Queries: Beccaria," *in Notes and Queries: Medium of Inter-Communication for Literary Men, General Readers, Etc.* (London: Bell & Daldy, 1863), pp. 228–29; *Mozart-Jahrbuch 1978/79* (Bärenreiter, 1978), p. 154; Robert Dessaix, ed., *Speaking Their Minds: Intellectuals and the Public Culture in Australia* (ABC Books, 1998), p. 25; Da Agostino Olivieri, *Rivista della Numismatica antica e moderna* (Asti: Tipografia raspi e compagnia, 1864), p. 350 n.4; *The Italian Scene* (Centro per gior-

nalisti esteri, 1964), p. 108.

21. Bush, *Noble Privilege*, Vol. 1, p. 134.

22. Christopher F. Black, *Early Modern Italy: A Social History* (London: Routledge, 2001), p. 135.

23. Robert Panzarella & Daniel Vona, *Criminal Justice Masterworks: A History of Ideas about Crime, Law, Police, and Corrections* (Durham, NC: Carolina Academic Press, 2006), p. xxv; Sarti, *Italy*, p. 167.

24. Stefano D'Amico, *Spanish Milan: A City Within the Empire, 1535–1706* (New York: Palgrave Macmillan, 2012), pp. 1, 148; Charles A. Truxillo, *By the Sword and the Cross: The Historical Evolution of the Catholic World Monarchy in Spain and the New World, 1492–1825* (Westport, CT: Greenwood Press, 2001), p. 51; Karen Owens, *Franz Joseph and Elisabeth: The Last Great Monarchs of Austria-Hungary* (Jefferson, NC: McFarland & Co., 2014), pp. 171, 177; Benjamin Wiker, *Worshipping the State: How Liberalism Became Our State Religion* (Washington, DC: Regency Publishing, 2013), p. 322; George Holmes, ed., *The Oxford Illustrated History of Italy* (Oxford: Oxford University Press, 1997), p. 364; Ole Peter Grell, Andrew Cunningham & Jon Arrizabalaga, eds., *Health Care and Poor Relief in Counter-Reformation Europe* (London: Routledge, 1999), p. 45.

25. Panzarella & Vona, *Criminal Justice Masterworks*, p. 7.

26. William Young, *International Politics and Warfare in the Age of Louis XIV and Peter the Great* (Lincoln, NE: iUniverse, 2004), p. 330; Michael A. Sommers, *France: A Primary Source Cultural Guide* (New York: PowerPlus Books, 2005), p. 29; Sylvia Neely, *A Concise History of the French Revolution* (Lanham, MD: Rowman & Littlefield Publishers, 2008), p. 35; M. S. Anderson, *The War of Austrian Succession 1740–1748* (New York: Routledge, 2013), p. 73.

27. J. N. Hays, *Epidemics and Pandemics: Their Impacts on Human History* (Santa Barbara, CA: ABC-CLIO, 2005), p. 151; Matthew White, "Health, Hygiene and the Rise of 'Mother Gin' in the 18th Century," British Library, https://www.bl.uk/georgian-britain/articles/health-hygiene-and-the-rise-of-mother-gin-in-the-18th-century.

28. "Condillac (1714–1780)," Online Library of Liberty, http://oll.libertyfund.org/pages/condillac-1714-1780 (citing Shelagh Eltis & Walter Eltis, *Commerce and Government Considered in Their Mutual Relationship* (Indianapolis, IN: Liberty Fund, 2008)); *see also* ibid. ("In the autumn [of 1765] he [Condillac] was at Genoa and then Milan, where he met the Marchese Beccaria whose *Dei Delitti e delle pene* gained much attention in France. Beccaria was himself honoured to meet Condillac as he wrote to Morellet.").

29. Victoria S. Harrison, *Religion and Modern Thought* (London: SCM Press, 2007), p. 61; Wiker, *Worshipping the State*, p. 322.

30. Chris Cook & Philip Broadhead, *The Routledge Companion to Early Modern Europe 1453–1763* (New York: Routledge, 2006), p. 85; Ian Barnes, *The Historical Atlas of the American Revolution* (New York: Routledge, 2000), p. 48.

31. Francis Coghlan, *Handbook for Travellers in Italy* (London: Tallant and Allen, 1857), p. 150; Charles Ingrao, Nikola Samardžić & Jovan Pešalj, eds., *The Peace of Passarowitz, 1718* (West Lafayette, IN: Purdue University Press, 2011), p. 10; William R. Nester, *The French and Indian War and the Conquest of New France* (Norman: University of Oklahoma Press, 2014), p. 72; U. C. Mandal, *Dictionary of Public Administration* (New Delhi: Sarup & Sons, 2007), pp. 389–90.

32. Julia P. Gelardi, *In Triumph's Wake: Royal Mothers, Tragic Daughters, and the Price They Paid for Glory* (New York: St. Martin's Press, 2008), p. 166; *The Hutchinson Illustrated Encyclopedia of British History* (Chicago, IL: Fitzroy Dearborn Publishers, 1998), p. 27; Rex D. Matthews, *Timetables of History of Students of Methodism* (Nashville, TN: Abingdon Press, 2007), p. 20; R. J. W. Evans, *Austria, Hungary, and the Habsburgs: Central Europe c. 1683–1867* (Oxford: Oxford University Press, 2006), p. xiv; M. S. Anderson, *The War of Austrian Succession 1740–1748* (New York: Routledge, 2013), pp. 202, 210, 215.

33. Dana Facaros & Michael Pauls, *Lombardy and the Italian Lakes* (Guilford, CT: The Globe Pequot Press, 2006), p. 26; Harry Hearder, *Italy in the Age of the Risorgimento 1790–1870* (New York: Routledge, 2013), ch. 1; Julia P. Gelardi, *In Triumph's Wake: Royal Mothers, Tragic Daughters, and the Price They Paid for Glory* (New York: St. Martin's Press, 2008), p. 167; Mark Jarrett, *The Congress of Vienna and Its Legacy: War and Great Power Diplomacy after Napoleon* (London: I.B. Tauris, 2014), p. 13.

34. Jerzy Lukowski, *The European Nobility in the Eighteenth Century* (New York: Palgrave Macmillan, 2003), pp. 20, 37.

35. Luca Mocarelli, "The Attitude of Milanese Society to Work and Commercial Activities. The Case of the Porters and the Case of the Elites," *in* Josef Ehmer & Catharina Lis, eds., *The Idea of Work in Europe from Antiquity to Modern Times* (Surrey, England: Ashgate, 2009), pp. 117–18.

36. Hugh James Rose, *A New General Biographical Dictionary* (London: B. Fellows, et al. 1848), Vol. 3, p. 141; John McClintock & James Strong, *Cyclopaedia of Biblical, Theological, and Ecclesiastical Literature* (New York: Harper & Brothers, 1894), Vol. XI, p. 207; Jane Black, *Absolutism in Renaissance Milan: Plenitude of Power under the Visconti and the Sforza 1329–1535* (Oxford: Oxford University Press, 2009), p. 59; Massimo Zaggia, "Culture in Lombardy, 1535–1706," *in* Andrea Gamberini, ed., *A Companion to Late Medieval and Early Modern Milan: The Distinctive Features of an Italian State* (Leiden: Brill, 2015).

37. André Vieusseux, *Italy and the Italians in the Nineteenth Century: A View of the Civil, Political, and Moral State of that Country* (London: Charles Knight, 1824), Vol. 1, p. 243; Franz A. J. Szabo, *Kaunitz and Enlightened Absolutism 1753–1780* (Cambridge: Cambridge University Press, 1994), p. 216; Charles Osborne, *The Complete Operas of Mozart: A Critical Guide* (New York: Da Capo Press, 1978), p. 54; Otto Erich Deutsch, *Mozart: A Documentary Biography* (Stanford, CA: Stanford University Press, Eric Blom, Peter Branscombe & Jeremy Noble, trans. 1965), pp. 110–11; Ulrich L. Lehner & Michael Printy, *A Companion to the Catholic Enlightenment in Europe* (Leiden: Brill, 2010), p. 137; Piers Beirne, *Inventing Criminology: Essays on the Rise of 'Homo Criminalis'* (Albany: State University of New York Press, 1993), p. 18; Walter W. Davis, *Joseph II: An Imperial Reformer for the Austrian Netherlands* (The Hague: Martinus Nijhoff, 1974), pp. 77–78; Heinz Gärtner, *John Christian Bach: Mozart's Friend and Mentor* (Portland, OR: Amadeus Press, Reinhard G. Pauly, trans. 1989), p. 149.

38. Roland Sarti, *Italy: A Reference Guide from the Renaissance to the Present* (New York: Facts on File, 2004); Gaetana Marrone, ed., *Encyclopedia of Italian Literary Studies* (New York: Routledge, 2007), pp. 1350–51.

39. Cara Camcastle, *The More Moderate Side of Joseph de Maistre: Views on Political Liberty and Political Economy* (Montreal: McGill-Queen's University Press, 2005), p. 61; Palazzo delle Scuole Palatine, https://en.wikipedia.org/wiki/Palazzo_delle_Scuole_Palatine; Wolfgang Rother, "The Beginning of Higher Education in Political Economy in Milan and Modena: Cesare Beccaria, Alfonso Longo, Agostino Paradisi," *in* Mordechai Feingold, ed., *History of Universities* (Oxford: Oxford University Press, 2004), Vol. XIX/1, p. 120. Three of the chairs at the *Scuole Palatine* ended up being "occupied by former members of the *Accademia dei Pugni*: Beccaria, Longo, and Frisi, who between the winter of 1761/2 and 1765 had collaborated on the *Caffè*, the mouthpiece of the Italian Enlightenment." Ibid.

40. Edward Eldefonso, Alan Coffey & Richard C. Grace, *Principles of Law Enforcement: An Overview of the Justice System* (New York: John Wiley & Sons, 1982) p. 329; Jacob Burckhardt, *The Civilisation of the Period of the Renaissance in Italy* (London: Swan Sonnenschein & Co., 1892), Vol. 1, p. 472 n.3; Christopher Kleinhenz, ed., *Medieval Italy: An Encyclopedia* (New York: Routledge, 2004), p. 866; Maestro, *Cesare Beccaria and the Origins of Penal Reform*, p. 105 & n.8; Henry Dunning Macleod, *A Dictionary of Political Economy: Biographical, Bibliographical, Historical, and Practical* (London: Longman, Brown, Longmans, and Roberts, 1863), p. 252; Angelo de Gubernatis, "The Social Classes in Italy," *The Atlantic Monthly* (1904), Vol. 94, pp. 322, 324; F. Bottarelli, *The New French, Italian, and English Pocket-Dictionary* (London: 4th ed. 1805), Vol. III, p. 408; Maria Teresa Borgato, "I matematici italiani e l'avvio in Italia del sistema metrico," Società Italiana di Storia delle Matematiche: La matematica nel Mediterrraneo Storia della matematica e insegnamento, 16-17-18 Nov. 2006, Napoli, p. 14, *available at* http://www.sism.unito.it/node/congressi/VIcongresso/sunti.pdf; *see also* Maria Teresa Borgato, "The first applications of the metric system in Italy," The Global and the Local: The History of Science and the Cultural Integration of Europe, Proceedings of the 2nd ICESHS (Cracow, Poland, Sept. 6–9, 2006, M. Kokowski, ed.), p. 431 ("A new attempt at standardisation of weights and measures in Lombardy was initiated in 1772: in 1781 the Milanese *braccio* replaced all the other *bracci* used up to then in Lombardy and its exact length was fixed by Annibale Beccaria who devised a sample into *once*, *punti* and *atomi*; however, after various consultations that dragged on until 1783, they were unable to reduce the various *bracci* to the single Milanese *braccio da legname*.").

41. Karl Smári Hreinsson & Adam Nichols, eds. & trans., *The Travels of Reverend Ólafur Egilsson:*

The Story of the Barbary Corsair Raid on Iceland in 1627 (Washington, DC: The Catholic University of America Press, 2016), p. 47 n.3.

42. *The Encyclopædia Britannica: A Dictionary of Arts, Sciences, Literature and General Information* (Cambridge: Cambridge University Press, 11th ed. 1911), Vol. XVIII, pp. 438–39.

43. Mazzotti, *The World of Maria Gaetana Agnesi, Mathematician of God*, ch. 4; R. W. McColl, ed., *Encyclopedia of World Geography* (New York: Facts on File, 2005), p. 956 ("The history of Vatican City can be traced to Roman times where, originally, summer villas were constructed on Vatican Hill. Caligula built his private circus in the area, and in 65 C.E., the Romans reportedly sacrificed Christians in the Circo Vaticano. Saint Peter, the Roman Catholic Church's first pope, was killed on this spot by the Romans. Around 100 years after his death, a monument was built for Saint Peter, and between 324 and 326, Emperor Constantine ordered a basilica to be built above Saint Peter's tomb.").

44. Stefano D'Amico, *Spanish Milan: A City Within the Empire, 1535–1706* (New York: Palgrave Macmillan, 2012), p. 102; Sarti, *Italy*, p. 615.

45. *The Penny Cyclopædia of the Society for the Diffusion of Useful Knowledge* (London: Charles Knight and Co., 1840), Vol. XVII, p. 282; Cesare Beccaria, *On Crimes and Punishments* (Indianapolis, IN: Hackett Publishing Co., David Young, trans. 1986), p. 100 n.6.

46. H. de Ridder-Symoens, ed., *A History of the University in Europe* (Cambridge: Cambridge University Press, 1996), Vol. 2, p. 319; *Encyclopædia Americana* (Philadelphia: Carey and Lea, 1831), p. 52; *see also* Alberto Cadoppi, *Lo Studio di Ranuccio: La Rifondazione dell'Università di Parma nel 1600* (Parma: Grafiche Step editrice, 2013), p. 40.

47. M. Valery, *Historical, Literary, and Artistical Travels in Italy: A Complete and Methodical Guide for Travellers and Artists* (Paris: Baudry's European Library, C. E. Clifton, trans. 1839), p. 285.

48. Aaron Thomas, On Crimes and Punishments *and Other Writings* (Toronto: University of Toronto Press, 2008), p. xvi; *The Encyclopædia Britannica* (New York: The Werner Co. 1903), Vol. 3, p. 477; Knud Haakonssen, ed., *The Cambridge History of Eighteenth-Century Philosophy* (Cambridge: Cambridge University Press, 2006), Vol. II, p. 1147; *Collier's Encyclopedia* (New York: P. F. Collier & Son Corp., 1958), Vol. 15, p. 450; Ellen Frankel Paul, Fred D. Miller, Jr. & Jeffrey Paul, eds., *Natural Rights: Liberalism from Locke to Nozick* (Cambridge: Cambridge University Press, 2005), p. 11; Graeme R. Newman & Pietro Marongiu, trans., Cesare Beccaria, *On Crimes and Punishments* (New Brunswick, NJ: Transaction Publishers, 5th ed. 2009), p. lxvii; Paul F. Grendler, *The Universities of the Italian Renaissance* (Baltimore, MD: The Johns Hopkins University Press, 2002); K. Baedeker, *Italy: Handbook for Travellers* (Leipsic: Karl Baedeker, 1892), Vol. 1, p. 269; Cristiano Catalina, "Building a Duchy to the Greater Glory of God: The Jesuits and the Farnesian Educational Policy in Parma (1539–1605)," *EDUCAZIONE: Giornale di pedagogia critica*, IV, pp. 37–38, 44; "A Brief History of the National College Maria Luigia," http://tutorsofmluigia.altervista.org/home/convitto-mluigia-qcenni-storiciq/83?showall=1. The Jesuits were banished from Parma in 1768. B.N., *The Jesuits: Their Foundation and History* (New York: Benziger Brothers, 1879), pp. 221–222; Germano Maifreda (University of Milan), "Flowing" Rather Than "Digging": Scientific Knowledge and Political Economy in the Lombard Enlightenment, Paper Delivered at David Nichol Smith Seminar in Eighteenth-Century Studies XV (10–12 December 2014), The University of Sydney, Sydney, Australia, p. 6, *available at* http://www.academia.edu/9715214/_Flowing_rather_than_Digging_Scientific_Knowledge_and_Political_Economy_in_the_Lombard_Enlightenment_-_Paper_delivered_at_David_Nichol_Smith_Seminar_in_Eighteenth-Century_Studies_XV._IDEAS_AND_ENLIGHTENMENT_THE_LONG_EIGHTEENTH_CENTURY._10-12_December_2014_The_University_of_Sydney_Australia. After the Pope dissolved the Jesuit order, Maria Theresa supported the suppression of the Jesuits in her domains in 1773. Julia P. Gelardi, *In Triumph's Wake: Royal Mothers, Tragic Daughters, and the Price They Paid for Glory* (New York: St. Martin's Press, 2008), p. 184.

49. Peter R. Anstey, *The Oxford Handbook of British Philosophy in the Seventeenth Century* (Oxford: Oxford University Press, 2013), pp. 311, 511; David A. Dieterle, ed., *Economic Thinkers: A Biographical Encyclopedia* (Santa Barbara, CA: Greenwood, 2013), pp. 213–15; John D. Bessler, *Cruel and Unusual: The American Death Penalty and the Founders' Eighth Amendment* (Boston: Northeastern University Press, 2012), p. 33; George Thomas Kurian, ed., *The Encyclopedia of Christian Literature* (Lanham, MD: The Scarecrow Press, 2010), Vol. 1, p. 195; Alexis Clairaut, "Du systeme du monde, dans les principes de la gravitation universelle," *in* "Histoires (& Memoires) de l'Academie Royale des Sciences"

for 1745 (published 1749), p. 329 (noting Clairaut's paper was read in November 1747).

50. Frans De Bruyn & Shaun Regan, ed., *The Culture of the Seven Years' War: Empire, Identity, and the Arts in the Eighteenth-Century Atlantic World* (Toronto: University of Toronto Press, 2014), p. 3; Herbert J. Redman, *Frederick the Great and the Seven Years' War, 1756–1763* (Jefferson, NC: McFarland & Co., 2015), pp. 3–5; Elizabeth Raum, *A Revolutionary War Timeline* (North Mankato, MN: Capstone Press, 2014), p. 5; Wiker, *Worshipping the State*, p. 322.

51. Christina Antenhofer, Günter Bischof, Robert L. Dupont & Ulrich Leitner, eds., *Cities as Multiple Landscapes: Investigating the Sister Cities of Innsbruck and New Orleans* (Frankfurt: Campus Verlag, 2016), p. 63; Paolo de Vecchi, *Modern Italian Surgery and Old Universities of Italy* (New York: Paul B. Hoeber, 1921), pp. 145–46; *The Scrap Book* (New York: The Frank A. Munsey Co., 1908), Vol. VI, p. 1017; Bessler, *Cruel and Unusual*, p. 34; University of Pavia (brochure documenting the University of Pavia's history), *available at* 26609UNIPV_en_2016.pdf.

52. Mario Ricciardi and Filippo Santoni de Sio, "Cesare Beccaria: Utilitarianism, Contractualism and Rights," *philinq II*, 2-2014, p. 80; Gennaro Barbarisi, ed., *Scritti di argomento familiare e autobiografico* (Roma: Edizioni di Storia e Letteratura, 2003), Vol. 5, p. 118 & n.176. Don Nicola Beccaria served as a judge in Milan for two periods, from 1746 to 1747 and from 1758 to 1759. Ibid.

53. Marcello Maestro, *Cesare Beccaria and the Origins of Penal Reform* (Philadelphia: Temple University Press, 1973), p. 6; Margaret Ruth Butler, *Operatic Reform at Turin's Teatro Regio* (Libreria Musicale Italiana, 2001), pp. 34–35; Anthony Trollope, ed., *Saint Pauls [afterw.] The Saint Pauls Magazine*, Vol. 3 (Oct. 1868–Mar. 1869), pp. 226–27; Vernon Lee, *Studies of the Eighteenth Century in Italy* (London: T. Fisher Unwin, 2d ed. 1907), p. 14.

54. Anna Cattoretti, *Giovanni Battista Sammartini and His Musical Environment* (Turnhout: Brepols, 2004), p. 3; Robert M. Place, *The Tarot: History, Symbolism, and Divination* (New York: Jeremy P. Tarcher/Penguin, 2005), pp. 17–20, 96, 113, 115, 132, 138, 146–47, 156; https://it.wikipedia.org/wiki/Palazzo_Imbonati; https://en.wikipedia.org/wiki/Visconti-Sforza_tarot_deck; Emily E. Auger, *Tarot and Other Meditation Decks: History, Theory, Aesthetics, Typology* (Jefferson, NC: McFarland & Co., 2004), p. 2; Michael A. E. Dummett, *The Visconti-Sforza Tarot Cards* (New York: G. Braziller, 1986), p. 11, 30; Karen Hamaker-Zondag, *Tarot as a Way of Life: A Jungian Approach to the Tarot* (York Beach, ME: Samuel Weiser, 1997), p. 17; Nevill Drury, *Stealing Fire from Heaven: The Rise of Modern Western Magic* (Oxford: Oxford University Press, 2011), p. 17.

55. Thomas, Cesare Beccaria, *On Crimes and Punishments and Other Writings*, p. xvii; Vernon Lee, *Studies of the Eighteenth Century in Italy* (London: T. Fisher Unwin, 1978), p. 7; Massimo Mazzotti, *The World of Maria Gaetana Agnesi, Mathematician of God* (Baltimore, MD: The Johns Hopkins University Press, 2007), p. 83; Lacy Collison-Morley, *Giuseppe Baretti and His Friends* (London: John Murray, 1909), pp. 27, 34, 131–32; Butler, *Operatic Reform at Turin's Teatro Regio*, p. 34; *Miscellanea di studi* (Torino: Centro studi piemontesi, 2003), Vol. 5, p. 148; *Componimenti in morte del Conte Giuseppe Maria Imbonati* (Milano: Appresso Giuseppe Galeazzi Regio Stampatore, 1769); Antonella Cupillari, *A Biography of Maria Gaetana Agnesi, an Eighteenth-century Woman Mathematician: With Translations of Some of Her Work from Italian into English* (Lewiston, NY: Edwin Mellen Press, 2007), p. 219; https://it.wikipedia.org/wiki/Giuseppe_Maria_Imbonati.

56. Collison-Morley, *Giuseppe Baretti and His Friends*, pp. 27, 131; *Prose*, Issue 215 (Edizioni Universitarie di Lettere Economia Diritto, 2005), p. 659; Catherine M. Sama, ed. & trans., *Elisabetta Caminer Turra: Selected Writings of an Eighteenth-Century Venetian Woman of Letters* (Chicago: The University of Chicago Press, 2003), p. 211 n.152; *Il Settecento: L'Arcadia e l'età riforme*, Vol. 6 (1973), p. 464; Daniel Heartz, *Music in European Capitals: The Galant Style, 1720–1780* (New York: W.W. Norton & Co., 2003), p. 232; Anna Cattoretti, *Giovanni Battista Sammartini and His Musical Environment* (Turnhout: Brepols, 2004), p. x; *The American Universal Cyclopædia: A Complete Library of Knowledge* (New York: S. W. Green's Son, 1882), p. 715; *Pinacoteca Ambrosiana: Tomo terzo—Dipinti dalla metà del Seicento alla fine del Settecento—Ritratti* (Milano: Mondadori Electra S.p.A., 2007), pp. 107, 239–40, 246; *Philological Quarterly* (University of Iowa, 1948), Vol. 27, p. 104; Francesco Galeazzi, *The Theoretical-Practical Elements of Music, Parts III and IV* (Urbana: University of Illinois Press, Deborah Burton & Gregory W. Harwood, trans. 2012), p. 195 n.175; Cupillari, *A Biography of Maria Gaetana Agnesi, an Eighteenth-century Woman Mathematician*, p. 219.

57. Mazzotti, *The World of Maria Gaetana Agnesi, Mathematician of God*, pp. 81–83, 86, 130–

31, 134.

58. *Miscellanea di studi* (Centro studi piemontesi, 2003), Vol. 5, pp. 146–49; Julian Rushton, *The New Grove Guide to Mozart and His Operas* (Oxford: Oxford University Press, 2007), pp. 34, 126; Thomas, Cesare Beccaria, On Crimes and Punishments *and Other Writings*, p. xvii; *The Athenæum*, Mar. 12, 1859, pp. 347–49; *The Penguin Companion to Literature* (Middlesex, England: Penguin Books, 1969), Vol. 2, pp. 82, 596; Peter Brand & Lino Pertile, eds., *The Cambridge History of Italian Literature* (Cambridge: Cambridge University Press, rev. ed. 1996), pp. 380, 393; Peter Bondanella, Julia Conaway Bondanella & Jody Robin Shiffman, eds., *Cassell Dictionary of Italian Literature* (London: Cassell, 1996), p. 464; Hermann W. Haller, *The Other Italy: The Literary Canon in Dialect* (Toronto: University of Toronto Press, 1999), p. 108; Paola Govoni & Zelda Alice Franceschi, eds., *Writing About Lives in Science: (Auto)Biography, Gender, and Genre* (Göttingen: V&R unipress GmbH, 2014), p. 107; Gaetana Marrone, ed., *Encyclopedia of Italian Literary Studies* (New York: Routledge, 2007), Vol. 1, pp. 129, 1349–50, 1979; Ann Hallamore Caesar & Michael Caesar, *Modern Italian Literature* (Cambridge: Polity Press, 2007), pp. 40–41; Lacy Collison-Morley, *Modern Italian Literature* (Boston: Little, Brown, and Co., 1912), pp. 100–2; http://www.gettyimages.com/detail/news-photo/portrait-of-giovan-mauro-mazzucchelli-italian-writer-member-news-photo/122320433?#portrait-of-giovan-mauro-mazzucchelli-italian-writer-member-of-the-picture-id122320433.

59. Daniel Heartz, *Music in European Capitals: The Galant Style, 1720–1780* (New York: W. W. Norton & Co., 2003), pp. 231–32; Jennifer Homans, *Apollo's Angels: A History of Ballet* (New York: Random House, 2010), ch. 2.1.

60. H. M. Scott, *The Emergence of the Eastern Powers, 1756–1775* (Cambridge: Cambridge University Press, 2001), p. 49; Daniel Coetzee & Lee W. Eysturlid, eds., *Philosophers of War: The Evolution of History's Greatest Military Thinkers* (Santa Barbara, CA: Praeger, 2013), pp. 96–97.

61. Gilbert Faccarello, *Studies in the History of French Political Economy: From Boudin to Walras* (London: Routledge, 1998), p. 99; Paola Zanardi, "Italian Responses to David Hume," *in* Peter Jones, ed., *The Reception of David Hume in Europe* (London: Thoemmes Continuum, 2005), pp. 163–64 & n.11; https://www.britannica.com/biography/Paolo-Frisi; http://www.groups.dcs.st-and.ac.uk/history/Biographies/Frisi.html.

62. Koen Stapelbroek & Jani Marjanen, eds., *The Rise of Economic Societies in the Eighteenth Century* (New York: Palgrave Macmillan), p. 137; Mark H. Danley & Patrick J. Speelman, eds., *The Seven Years' War: Global Views* (Lieden: Brill, 2012), pp. 42–43; Cesare Beccaria, *On Crimes and Punishments* (Indianapolis, IN: Hackett Publishing Co., David Young, trans. 1986), p. 96 (translator's notes); Michel Delon, ed., *Encyclopedia of the Enlightenment* (London: Routledge, 2001), Vol. 1, p. 724; Orlandi Balzari & Vittoria Roberta Rossella, "Gabriel Verri giurista, politico e uomo di cultura," Università Cattolica del Sacro Cuore, XX ciclo, a.a. 2007/08, Milano; Azar Gat, *A History of Military Thought: From the Enlightenment to the Cold War* (Oxford: Oxford University Press, 2001), p. 70; Riccardo Faucci, *A History of Italian Economic Thought* (New York: Routledge, 2014), pp. 47–48; Gaetana Marrone, ed., *Encyclopedia of Italian Literary Studies* (New York: Routledge, 2007), p. 1979; Bernard E. Harcourt, *The Illusion of Free Markets: Punishment and the Myth of Natural Order* (Cambridge, MA: Harvard University Press, 2011), p. 59; *An Essay on the Theory of Money*, pp. 53–54, 67, 69–70, 144 (London: J. Almon, 1771) (attributed to Henry Lloyd). In another chapter, titled "Luxury, corruption of manners and national poverty are in proportion to the inequality of circulation," Henry Lloyd said something that seems to mirror the popular quotation from Cesare Beccaria's treatise that was invoked in 1774 by the Continental Congress. In that chapter, Lloyd wrote: "A great inequality of fortunes necessarily implies a national and general poverty. Some few, will have infinitely more than they want, while the remainder can have only what they procure by their industry, and as this is precarious, the least accident, the least interruption in trade, will reduce them to misery." Ibid., p. 75.

63. Sophus A. Reinert, "The Italian Tradition of Political Economy: Theories and Policies of Development in the Semi-Periphery of the Enlightenment," *in* Jomo K.S. & Erik S. Reinert, eds., *The Origins of Development Economics: How Schools of Economic Thought Have Addressed Development* (London: Zed Books, 2005), pp. 37–38; *see also* ibid., p. 47 (noting Pietro Verri's early writings on commerce and economics). Pietro Verri's views are discussed in detail elsewhere. *See* Pier Luigi Porta & Roberto Scazzieri, "Pietro Verri's Political Economy: Commercial Society, Civil Society, and the

Science of the Legislator," 34 *History of Political Economy* 83 (2002).

64. Stephen E. Brown, Finn-Aage Esbensen & Gilbert Geis, *Criminology: Explaining Crime and Its Context* (New York: Routledge, 8th ed., 2015), p. 159; Emily Anderson, ed., *The Letters of Mozart and His Family* (London: Macmillan, 3d ed. 1997), p. 365; Marita P. McClymonds, *Niccolò Jommelli: The Last Years, 1769–1774* (Ann Arbor, MI: UMI Research Press, 1980), p. 373 n.57; Charles J. Hall, *An Eighteenth-Century Musical Chronicle: Events 1750–1799* (New York: Greenwood Press, 1990), p. 56; Carlo Monza, allmusic.com/artist/carlo-monza-mn0001208006/biography.

65. Madalina Valeria Veres, "Unravelling a Trans-Imperial Career: Michel Angelo de Blasco's Map-making Abilities in the Service of Vienna and Lisbon," *Itinerario*, Vol. XXXVIII (2004), pp. 75, 79.

66. Ibid., pp. 75, 78–79; *The Complete Militia-Man, or a Compendium of Military Knowledge* (London: R. Griffiths, 1760), p. 141; Sawyer F. Sylvester, *The Heritage of Modern Criminology* (Cambridge, MA: Schenkman Publishing Co., 1972), p. 9.

67. Stephen E. Brown, Finn-Aage Esbensen & Gilbert Geis, *Criminology: Explaining Crime and Its Context* (New York: Routledge, 8th ed., 2015), p. 159; Barry Nicholas, *An Introduction to Roman Law* (Oxford: Oxford University Press, 2008), p. 66; Hostettler, *Cesare Beccaria*, p. 23; William Dwight Whitney, comp., *The Century Dictionary: An Encyclopedic Lexicon of the English Language* (New York: The Century Co., 1906), p. 4329 (entry for "patria potestas").

68. Maestro, *Cesare Beccaria and the Origins of Penal Reform*, p. 8.

69. *A General Biographical Dictionary* (London: Henry G. Bohn, 1851), Vol. 1 (entry for "Beccaria").

70. Randolph Paul Runyon, *The Art of the Persian Letters: Unlocking Montesquieu's "Secret Chain"* (Newark: University of Delaware Press, 2005), pp. 13–14.

71. Mario Ricciardi and Filippo Santoni de Sio, "Cesare Beccaria: Utilitarianism, Contractualism and Rights," *philinq II*, 2-2014, p. 82.

72. Lynn Hunt, *Inventing Human Rights: A History* (New York: W.W. Norton & Co., 2007), pp. 38–39 & 237 n.24.

73. Jean-Jacques Rousseau, *Julie, or the New Heloise: Letters of Two Lovers Who Live in a Small Town at the Foot of the Alps* (Lebanon, NH: Dartmouth College Press, 1997), p. x.

74. Brian Hamnett, *The Historical Novel in Nineteenth-Century Europe: Representations of Reality in History and Fiction* (Oxford: Oxford University Press, 2011), p. 150.

75. Peter Brand & Lino Pertile, *The Cambridge History of Italian Literature* (Cambridge: Cambridge University Press, rev. ed. 1999), p. 427; Pietro Manzoni (1736–1807), La Famiglia Manzoni, www.casadelmanzoni.it/content/la-famiglia-manzoni#n0; Brian Hamnett, *The Historical Novel in Nineteenth-Century Europe: Representations of Reality in History and Fiction* (Oxford: Oxford University Press, 2011), p. 150; https://it.wikipedia.org/wiki/Pietro_Manzoni.

76. Jean-Jacques Rousseau, *La Nouvelle Héloïse: Julie, or the New Eloise* (University Park, PA: Penn State University Press, Judith H. McDowell, trans. 2004), pp. 1–2; Philip Stewart & Jean Vaché, trans., *Jean-Jacques Rousseau, Julie, or the New Heloise: Letters of Two Lovers Who Live in a Small Town at the Foot of the Alps* (Hanover, NH: Dartmouth College Press, 1997), p. x.

77. Mario Ricciardi and Filippo Santoni de Sio, "Cesare Beccaria: Utilitarianism, Contractualism and Rights," *philinq II*, 2-2014, p. 81; Germaine Mason, *A Concise Survey of French Literature* (Lanham, MD: Rowman & Littlefield, 2014), p. 152; Nicholas Dent, *Rousseau* (New York: Routledge, 2005), pp. 32–33; Margaret Bald, *Banned Books: Literature Suppressed on Religious Grounds* (New York: Facts on File, 2006), p. 89.

78. Luigino Bruni & Pier Luigi Porta, *Handbook of Research Methods and Applications in Happiness and Quality of Life* (Cheltenham, UK: Edward Elgar Publishing, 2016), p. 506; Mario Ricciardi and Filippo Santoni de Sio, "Cesare Beccaria: Utilitarianism, Contractualism and Rights," *philinq II*, 2-2014, p. 81; Benjamin Constant, *Principles of Politics Applicable to All Governments* (Indianapolis, IN: Liberty Fund, Dennis O'Keeffe, trans. 2003) (1815), *available at* Online Library of Liberty, http://oll.libertyfund.org/titles/constant-principles-of-politics-applicable-to-all-governments?q=Beccaria#Constant_0452_85.

79. Jonathan I. Israel, *Democratic Enlightenment: Philosophy, Revolution, and Human Rights 1750–1790* (Oxford: Oxford University Press, 2011), p. 338.

80. Ibid., p. 337; C. A. Helvetius, *De l'esprit; or, Essays on the Mind, and Its Several Faculties* (Lon-

don: M. Jones, 1807), p. 58.

81. Helvetius, *De l'esprit*, pp. 291–92.

82. Rita J. Simon & Dagny A. Blaskovich, *A Comparative Analysis of Capital Punishment: Statutes, Policies, Frequencies, and Public Attitudes the World Over* (Lanham, MD: Lexington Books, 2007), p. xiii; John E. McDonough, *Experience Politics: A Legislator's Stories of Government and Health Care* (Berkeley, CA: University of California Press, 2000), p. 296.

83. Maestro, *Cesare Beccaria and the Origins of Penal Reform*, p. 8; Veres, "Unravelling a Trans-Imperial Career," *Itinerario*, pp. 75, 98–99 n.63. Cesare Beccaria's marriage to Teresa de Blasco is discussed in Giovanni Albertocchi, "Dietro il *Retablo*: 'Addio Teresa Blasco, addio Marchesina Beccaria,'" *Quaderns d'Italià*, Vol. 10 (2005), pp. 95–111.

84. Matthew Bunson, *OSV's Encyclopedia of Catholic History* (Huntington, IN: Our Sunday Vistor Publishing Division, rev. 2004), p. 263; D'Amico, *Spanish Milan*, p. 69; Nicholas Davidson, "Toleration in Enlightenment Italy," *in* Ole Peter Grell & Roy Porter, eds., *Toleration in Enlightenment Europe* (Cambridge: Cambridge University Press, 2000), p. 233.

85. Fredrik Thomasson, *The Life of J. D. Åkerblad: Egyptian Decipherment and Orientalism in Revolutionary Times* (Leiden: Brill, 2013), p. 328; Gaetana Marrone, ed., *Encyclopedia of Italian Literary Studies* (New York: Routledge, 2007), p. 4; Hanns Gross, *Rome in the Age of Enlightenment: The Post-Tridentine Syndrome and the Ancien Regime* (Cambridge: Cambridge University Press, 1990), pp. 293–94; Peter Bondanella & Julia Conaway Bondanella, eds., *Cassell Dictionary of Italian Literature* (London: Cassell, 1996), pp. 14–16.

86. John W. O'Malley, Gauvin Alexander Bailey, Steven J. Harris & T. Frank Kennedy, eds., *The Jesuits II: Cultures, Sciences, and the Arts, 1540–1773* (Toronto: University of Toronto Press, 2006), p. 539; Vernon Lee, *Studies of the Eighteenth Century in Italy* (London: F. Fisher Unwin, 2d ed. 1907), pp. 49–51, 85; Peter Bondanella & Andrea Ciccarelli, eds., *The Cambridge Companion to the Italian Novel* (Cambridge: Cambridge University Press, 2003), p. 39; Hermann J. Real, ed., *The Reception of Jonathan Swift in Europe* (London: Continuum, 2005), p. 27; Peter Bondanella & Julia Conaway Bondanella, eds., *Cassell Dictionary of Italian Literature* (London: Cassell, 1996), p. 30; "Carlo Pertusati," http://www.bibliotecauniversitariapavia.it/bu/index.php?en/186/carlo-pertusati.

87. In a 1769 letter to Charles Thomson and Thomas Mifflin, Benjamin Franklin—speaking about the Library Company of Philadelphia—wrote: "I think we should have, in some one of our public Libraries, all the Transactions of every Philosophical Society in Europe, vizt. The Memoirs of the Academy of Sciences at Paris; those of Petersburgh; of Haerlem in Holland; of Bononia in Italy &c. with the Continuations as they come out Yearly; and also the French Encyclopedia." Benjamin Franklin to Charles Thomson and Thomas Mifflin, July 7, 1769. A "List of Learned Societies" from late 1801—and endorsed by Thomas Jefferson in early 1802—notes "[t]ransactions ordered for" the following societies: Royal Academy of Sciences Turin; Society of Milan; Society of Bologna; Society of Florence; Academy of Mexico; Academy of Lyons; Academy of Rouen; Royal Academy of Bells Lettres at Sevill; Society for Promoting Arts & Manufac[.] & Commerce in London. In the 1780s, the new *Società Patriotica* of Milan began to exchange publications with the American Philosophical Society. Benjamin Franklin and Dr. Benjamin Rush were made corresponding members of that Milan association. In the 1770s, Philip Mazzei took charge of correspondence with the academies of Bologna and Turin. Enclosure: List of Learned Societies, Dec. 29, 1801, *available at* www.founders.archives.gov. Jefferson himself associated and corresponded with Italians such as Philip Mazzei, Carlo Bellini and Adamo Fabbroni, often receiving letters in Italian. *E.g.*, Thomas Jefferson to Adamo Fabbroni, Antoine Gouan, Lacépè, Marc Auguste Pictet, and André Thoüin, Mar. 6, 1815 (noting that "Doctr Barton, my friend," "one of the Vice presidents of the American Philosophical society," would be traveling to Florence "in the course of his travels"); Carlo Bellini to Thomas Jefferson, Mar. 16, 1801.

88. Mario Ricciardi and Filippo Santoni de Sio, "Cesare Beccaria: Utilitarianism, Contractualism and Rights," *philinq II*, 2-2014, pp. 81–82; J. Robert Lilly, Francis T. Cullen & Richard A. Ball, *Criminological Theory: Context and Consequences* (Thousand Oaks, CA: Sage Publications, 6th ed. 2014), p. 19; Brown, Esbensen & Geis, *Criminology*, p. 159; Knud Haakonssen, ed., *The Cambridge History of Eighteenth-Century Philosophy* (Cambridge: Cambridge University Press, 2006), Vol. II, p. 1147.

89. turismo.milan.it.

90. Mario Ricciardi and Filippo Santoni de Sio, "Cesare Beccaria: Utilitarianism, Contractualism

and Rights," *philinq II*, 2-2014, p. 81; Israel, *Democratic Enlightenment*, pp. xiii, 337; Marco Guidi & Nanda Torcellano, *Europe 1700–1992: History of an Identity* (Electa, 1987), pp. 155, 158; Michel Porret, *Beccaria et la Culture Juridique des Lumières* (Genève: Libraire Droz S.A., 1997) (containing engraving of Beccaria at age 28 in 1765).

91. These portraits can be seen on the websites art.com and gettyimages.ie.

92. Maestro, *Cesare Beccaria and the Origins of Penal Reform*, p. 9 & n.6; Thomas Kuehn, *Family and Gender in Renaissance Italy, 1300–1600* (Cambridge: Cambridge University Press, 2017), p. 332; Rother, "The Beginning of Higher Education in Political Economy in Milan and Modena," *in* Feingold, *History of Universities*, Vol. XIX/1, pp. 121–22 & 149 n.16; *Atti delle Fondazione Giorgio Ronchi: Fondata da Vasco Ronchi* (Firenze: Lucia Ronchi, 2007), p. 30; Margaretta Jolly, ed., *Encyclopedia of Life Writing: Autobiographical and Biographical Forms* (London: Fitzroy Dearborn Publishers, 2001), Vol. 1, p. 481; Marrone, *Italian Literary Studies*, pp. 663; Richard Bellamy, ed., *Beccaria:* On Crimes and Punishments *and Other Writings* (Cambridge: Cambridge University Press, 1995), pp. xxxiii, xxxvi–xxxvii; *Historical Abstracts: Modern History Abstracts, 1775–1914*, Vol. 46 (Santa Barbara, CA: ABC-CLIO, 1995), p. 760; "Guiseppe Visconti di Saliceto," https://fr.wikipedia.org/wiki/Giuseppe_Visconti_di_Saliceto.

93. Mariam J. Levy, *Governance and Grievance: Habsburg Policy and Italian Tyrol in the Eighteenth Century* (West Lafayette, IN: Purdue University Press, 1988), p. 36.

94. Marrone, *Encyclopedia of Italian Literary*, p. 1980; Helmut C. Jacobs & Gisela Schlüter, *Beiträge zur Begriffsgeschichte der italienischen Aufklärung im europäischen Kontext* (Wien: Peter Lang, 2000), p. 135; Rebecca Messbarger & Paula Findlen, eds. & trans., *The Contest for Knowledge: Debates over Women's Learning in Eighteenth-Century Italy* (Chicago: The University of Chicago Press, 2007), p. 12; "Franci, Sebastiano," Dizionario Biografico degli Italiani, Vol. 50 (1998), http://www.treccani.it/enciclopedia/sebastiano-franci_(Dizionario-Biografico)/.

95. Messbarger & Findlen, *The Contest for Knowledge*, p. 12.

96. Rebecca Messbarger, *The Century of Women: Representations of Women in Eighteenth-Century Italian Public Discourse* (Toronto: University of Toronto Press, 2002), p. 76.

97. Richard Bellamy, ed., *Beccaria:* On Crimes and Punishments *and Other Writings* (Cambridge: Cambridge University Press, Richard Davies, trans. 2003), pp. xxxiii, 126; Franco Venturi, *The End of the Old Regime in Europe, 1776–1789, Part II: Republican Patriotism and the Empires of the East* (Princeton, NJ: Princeton University Press, R. Burr Litchfield trans. 1991), p. 711; Pietro Verri, *Memorie* (Modena: Enrico Mucchi Editore, 2001), p. 255; Marica Forni, *Giuseppe Pollack Architetto di Cas Belgiojoso: Villa e tenimento Belgiojoso giulini della porta a velate* (Roma: Gangemi Editore), p. 137; "Ludovico, Count di Belgiojoso," https://www.revolvy.com/topic/Ludovico,%20Count%20di%20Belgiojoso&item_type=topic; *see also Milan and the Lakes* (New York: DK Publishing, 2011), p. 121 ("Milan's modern art gallery is housed in a splendid Neo-Classical villa built by the Austrian architect Leopold Pollack in 1790 for Count Ludovico Barbiano di Belgioioso. It was lived in by Napoleon in 1802….").

98. Pier Francesco Asso, ed., *From Economists to Economists: The International Spread of Italian Economic Thought, 1750–1950* (David Brown Book Co., 2001), p. 93.

99. Erik S. Reinert, Jayati Ghosh & Rainer Kattel, eds., *Handbook of Alternative Theories of Economic Development* (Cheltenham, UK: Edward Elgar, 2016), pp. 49–50.

100. Sophus A. Reinert, ed., Antonio Serra, *A Short Treatise on the Wealth and Poverty of Nations* (1613) (London: Anthem Press, Jonathan Hunt, trans. 2011), pp. 74–75.

101. Paola Zanardi, "Italian Responses to David Hume" & Emilio Mazza, "Translations of Hume's Works in Italy," *in* Peter Jones, ed., *The Reception of David Hume in Europe* (London: Thoemmes Continuum, 2005), pp. 171, 184.

102. Richard Bellamy, *Croce, Gramsci, Bobbio and the Italian Political Tradition* (ECPR Press, 2013), p. 50; Imogene L. Moyer, *Criminological Theories: Traditional and Nontraditional Voices and Themes* (Thousand Oaks, CA: Sage Publications, 2001), p. 15; Geoffrey K. Ingham, ed., *Concepts of Money: Interdisciplinary Perspectives from Economics, Sociology and Political Science* (Cheltenham, UK: Edward Elgar Pub., 2005), pp. 257–58; Luca Einaudi, Riccardo Faucci & Roberto Marchionatti, eds., *Luigi Einaudi: Selected Economic Essays* (New York: Palgrave Macmillan, 2006), pp. 163–64; Frederic C. Lane, ed., *Enterprise and Secular Change: Readings in Economic History* (Homewood, IL: Richard

D. Irwin, 1953), pp. 241–44; Maestro, *Cesare Beccaria and the Origins of Penal Reform*, pp. 10–11; Cesare Beccaria, *On Crimes and Punishments* (New Brunswick, NJ: Transaction Publishers, Graeme R. Newman & Pietro Marongiu, trans. 5th ed. 2009), p. lxvii.

103. Bellamy, *Beccaria*, p. xxxi; Shaun L. Gabbidon, "Cesare Beccaria (1738–1794)," *in* Imogene L. Moyer, *Criminological Theories: Traditional and Nontraditional Voices and Themes* (Thousand Oaks, CA: Sage Publications, 2001), p. 16; Robert A. Silverman, Terence P. Thornberry, Bernard Cohen & Barry Krisberg, eds., *Crime and Justice at the Millennium: Essays by and in Honor of Marvin E. Wolfgang* (Boston: Kluwer Academic Publishers, 2002), p. 392; Panzarella & Vona, *Criminal Justice Masterworks*, p. 8; Robert J. Mutchnick, W. Timothy Austin & Randy Martin, *Criminological Thought: Pioneers Past and Present* (Upper Saddle River, NJ: Prentice Hall, 2009), p. 2.

104. Bernard E. Harcourt, "Beccaria's 'On Crimes and Punishments': A Mirror on the History of the Foundations of Modern Criminal Law," Coase-Sandor Institute for Law & Economics Working Paper, No. 648 (2013), p. 13, *available at* http://chicagounbound.uchicago.edu/cgi/viewcontent.cgi?article=1633&context=law_and_economics; *see also* ibid., p. 14 ("Joseph Schumpeter, in his magisterial review of the history of economic thought, recognized only three precursors to modern econometrics: Daniel Bernouilli for a 1731 article on probabilities; Achille Nicolas Isnard for a treatise in 1781; and Beccaria for this article [*Tentativo analitico su i contraband*] published in 1764.").

105. William M. Odom, *A History of Italian Furniture: From the Fourteenth to the Early Nineteenth Centuries* (Garden City, NY: Doubleday, Page & Co., 1919), Vol. 2, pp. 293–95.

106. John J. Butt, *The Greenwood Dictionary of World History* (Westport, CT: Greenwood Press, 2006), p. 270.

107. Alberto Capatti & Massimo Montanari, *Italian Cuisine: A Cultural History* (New York: Columbia University Press, Aine O'Healy, trans., 1999), p. 113.

108. John F. Mariani, *How Italian Food Conquered the World* (New York: St. Martin's Press, 2011), p. 19.

109. Rebecca Messbarger, *The Century of Women: Representations of Women in Eighteenth-century Italian Public Discourse* (Toronto: University of Toronto Press, 2002), pp. 88–102; Marrone, *Encyclopedia of Italian Literary Studies*, p. 1980; Messbarger & Findlen, *The Contest for Knowledge*, p. 12; Elisabetta Graziosi, "Women and Academies in Eighteenth-Century Italy," *in* Paula Findlen, Wendy Wassyng Roworth & Catherine M. Sama, eds., *Italy's Eighteenth Century: Gender and Culture in the Age of the Grand Tour* (Stanford, CA: Stanford University Press, 2009), p. 103; Roger Chartier, "The Man of Letters," *in* Michel Vovelle, ed., *Enlightenment Portraits* (Chicago: The University of Chicago Press, Lydia G. Cochrane, trans. 1997), p. 175; Maestro, *Cesare Beccaria and the Origins of Penal Reform*, pp. 47–51.

110. Groenewegen, *Eighteenth-century Economics*, pp. 17, 19 (citing Beccaria to Morellet, 26 January 1766, in Romagnoli, 1958, II, p. 865); Hostettler, *Cesare Beccaria*, p. 25; William Roberts, *Printers' Marks: A Chapter in the History of Typography* (London: George Bell & Sons, 1893), p. 226; Bellamy, *Beccaria*, p. xxxi; https://it.wikipedia.org/wiki/Il_Caffè_(Verri); Christoph Grafe & Franziska Bollerey, *Cafes and Bars: The Architecture of Public Display* (New York: Routledge, 2007), p. 72; *Milan and the Lakes* (New York: DK Publishing, 2000), p. 33; Marjorie Perlman Lorch, "Explorations of the Brain, Mind and Medicine in the Writings of Jonathan Swift," *in* Harry Whitaker & C.U.M. Smith & Stanley Finger, eds., *Brain, Mind and Medicine: Neuroscience in the 18th Century* (New York: Springer, 2007), p. 345.

111. *Cesare Beccaria and the Origins of Penal Reform*, p. 47 n.1; Robert Darnton, *The Business of Enlightenment: A Publishing History of the* Encyclopédie *1775–1800* (Cambridge, MA: The Belknap Press of Harvard University Press, 1979), p. 316; Giambattista Mancini, *Practical Reflections on the Figurative Art of Singing* (Boston, MA: The Gorham Press, Pietro Buzzi, trans. 1912); "Il Caffè," Illuminismo, http://illuminismolombardo.it/autori/il-caffe/. A whole website on the Italian Enlightenment gives information about (and reprints in the original Italian the editions of) *Il Caffè*, and also provides information about both Cesare Beccaria and Pietro Verri. *See, e.g.*, http://illuminismolombardo.it/testo/il-caffe-tomo-i/?tipo=1.

112. John D. Bessler, *The Birth of American Law: An Italian Philosopher and the American Revolution* (Durham, NC: Carolina Academic Press, 2014), p. 30; Geoffrey Treasure, *The Making of Modern Europe, 1648–1780* (London: Routledge, 2003), p. 134.

113. Claudia Baldoli, *A History of Italy* (New York: Palgrave Macmillan, 2009), pp. 157, 167.

114. Maestro, *Cesare Beccaria and the Origins of Penal Reform*, pp. 11–12.

115. Cesare Beccaria, *On Crimes and Punishments* (New Brunswick, NJ: Transaction Publishers, Graeme R. Newman & Pietro Marongiu, trans., 5th ed. 2009), p. lviii; Ezzat A. Fattah, *Criminology, Past, Present and Future: A Critical Overview* (New York: St. Martin's Press, 1997), p. 201; Cesare Cantù, *Beccaria: E Il Diritto Penale* (Firenze: G. Barbèra, 1862); Mario Ricciardi and Filippo Santoni de Sio, "Cesare Beccaria: Utilitarianism, Contractualism and Rights," *philinq II*, 2-2014, p. 82.

116. "Cesare Cantù (1804–1895)," Bartleby.com, http://www.bartleby.com/library/prose/1173.html; "Cesare Cantù," https://en.wikipedia.org/wiki/Cesare_Cantù.

117. Miriam J. Levy, *Governance and Grievance: Habsburg Policy and Italian Tyrol in the Eighteenth Century* (West Lafayette, IN: Purdue University Press, 1988), p. 36; Frederick Converse Beach, ed., *The Americana: A Universal Reference Library* (New York: Scientific American Compiling Department, 1912), Vol. 11 (entry for "Italy-Literature").

118. Sophus A. Reinert, "Patriotism, Cosmopolitanism and Political Economy in the *Accademia dei pugni* in Austrian Lombardy, 1760–1780," *in* Koen Stapelbroek & Jani Marjanen, eds., *The Rise of Economic Societies in the Eighteenth Century: Patriotic Reform in Europe and North America* (New York: Palgrave Macmillan, 2012), p. 131.

119. William H. Ukers, *All About Coffee* (New York: The Tea and Coffee Trade Journal Co., 1922), pp. 25–30, 558; Toby Miller, *Cultural Citizenship: Cosmopolitanism, Consumerism, and Television in a Neoliberal Age* (Philadelphia: Temple University Press, 2007), p. 114.

120. 3 Luigi Alberto Franzoni, "Tax Evasion and Avoidance," *in* Nuno Garoupa, *Criminal Law and Economics* (Cheltenham, UK: Edward Elgar Pub., 2d ed. 2009), p. 290; Cesare Beccaria, "Attempt at an Analysis of Smuggling," http://www.lawlib.utoronto.ca/bclc/crimweb/foundation/Beccaria%20smuggling%20small.pdf.

121. Groenewegen, *Eighteenth-century Economics*, pp. 3–4.

122. Ibid., pp. 4, 6; Murray N. Rothbard, "Introduction," in David Gordon, ed., *The Turgot Collection: Writings, Speeches, and Letters of Anne Robert Jacques Turgot, Baron de Laune* (Auburn, AL: Mises Institute, 2001), pp. ix–xiii.

Chapter 2

1. Joseph A. Melusky & Keith Alan Pesto, *Capital Punishment* (Santa Barbara, CA: Greenwood, 2011), p. 13 ("Through the Middle Ages and into the Renaissance, capital punishment was accompanied by what we would consider torture. Most barons had drowning pits as well as gallows, and they were used for major as well as minor crimes."); ibid., p. 436 ("The dungeons of the Inquisition were like all those constructed in the Middle Ages."); ibid. ("The prisoner was seated upon a kind of raised stool placed opposite the Inquisitor; when, after a long interrogatory, he failed to avow his guilt, he was taken to the *torture-chamber....*").

2. James Hitchcock, *History of the Catholic Church: From the Apostolic Age to the Third Millennium* (San Francisco, CA: Ignatius Press, 2012), p. 278.

3. John Hostettler, *A History of Criminal Justice in England and Wales* (Hampshire, UK: Waterside Press, 2009), p. 196; John D. Bessler, *Cruel and Unusual: The American Death Penalty and the Founders' Eighth Amendment* (Boston, MA: Northeastern University Press, 2012), p. 266; "A Brief History of Abolition," Amnesty International, https://web.archive.org/web/20070930223055/http://www.amnesty.org.uk/content.asp?CategoryID=10403.

4. William Monter, "Witch Trials in Continental Europe 1560–1660," *in* Bengt Ankarloo, Stuart Clark & William Monter, *Witchcraft and Magic in Europe: The Period of the Witch Trials* (London: The Athlone Press, 2002), p. 13 ("Germany's leading expert has established a baseline figure of about 15,000 confirmed witchcraft executions within contemporary Germany").

5. Roger Hood & Carolyn Hoyle, *The Death Penalty: A Worldwide Perspective* (Oxford: Oxford University Press, 5th ed. 2015), p. 11.

6. Bessler, *Cruel and Unusual*, p. 266; John Middleton, ed., *World Monarchies and Dynasties* (London: Routledge, 2005), p. 295 ("In the sixteenth and seventeenth centuries, Germany and England

used the Headman's Axe to execute both royal and nonroyal individuals. In England, the Tower of London was the site of many notable beheadings and was used for only the aristocracy."); Alfred Marks, *Tyburn Tree: Its History and Annals* (London: Brown, Langham & Co., 1908), pp. 274–79 (listing various executions).

7. Stephen G. Tibbetts & Craig Hemmens, *Criminological Theory: A Text/Reader* (Thousand Oaks, CA: Sage Publications, 2010), p. 87 n.11.

8. Klaus Epstein, *The Genesis of German Conservatism* (Princeton, NJ: Princeton University Press, 2015), p. 400; Rosita Rindler Schjerve, ed., *Diglossia and Power: Language Policies and Practice in the 19th Century Habsburg Empire* (Berlin: Mouton de Gruyter, 2003), p. 74; Catherine Toal, *The Entrapments of Form: Cruelty and Modern Literature* (New York: Fordham University Press, 2016), p. 166 n.40; Derek Beales, *Joseph II: In the Shadow of Maria Theresa, 1741–1780* (Cambridge: Cambridge University Press, 1987), p. 236.

9. Alexis M. Durham III, *Crisis and Reform: Current Issues in American Punishment* (Boston, MA: Little, Brown and Co., 1994), p. 303; Bryan F. Le Beau, *The Story of the Salem Witch Trials* (Upper Saddle River, NJ: Prentice Hall, 1998), p. 33.

10. Scott Vollum, Rolando V. Del Carmen, Durant Frantzen, Claudia San Miguel & Kelly Cheeseman, *The Death Penalty: Constitutional Issues, Commentaries, and Case Briefs* (New York: Routledge: 3d ed., 2015), p. 2; John R. Rice, *"In the Beginning ...": A Verse-by-Verse Commentary on the Book of Genesis* (Murfreesboro, TN: Sword of the Lord Publishers, 1975), pp. 232–33.

11. Finn Hornum, "The Executioner: His Role and Status in Scandinavian Society," *in* Charles H. Ainsworth, ed., *Selected Readings for Introductory Sociology* (New York, NY: MSS Information Corp., 1972), p. 70.

12. Barry Latzer & David McCord, *Death Penalty Cases: Leading U.S. Supreme Court Cases on Capital Punishment* (Amsterdam: Elsevier, 3d ed., 2010), p. 15.

13. The Massachusetts Body of Liberties (1641), ¶ 94 ("Capital Laws"); Henry W. Farnam, *Chapters in the History of Social Legislation in the United States to 1860* (Washington, DC: Carnegie Institution of Washington, 1938), p. 15.

14. Edward Lawson, *Encyclopedia of Human Rights* (Washington, DC: Taylor & Francis, 2d ed. 1991), p. 168; William Tallack, *George Fox, the Friends, and the Early Baptists* (London: S.W. Partridge & Co., 1868), p. 171; George Fox, *To the Parliament of the Commonwealth of England* (London: Thomas Simmons, 1659).

15. Robert M. Bohm, *DeathQuest: An Introduction to the Theory and Practice of Capital Punishment in the United States* (Waltham, MA: Anderson Publishing, 4th ed. 2012), p. 1; David Whitten Smith & Elizabeth Geraldine Burr, *Understanding World Religions: A Road Map for Justice and Peace* (Lanham, MD: Rowman & Littlefield, 2d ed., 2015), p. 128.

16. Stuart Banner, *The Death Penalty: An American History* (Cambridge, MA: Harvard University Press, 2002), p. 89.

17. Sydney G. Fisher, *The Quaker Colonies: A Chronicle of the Proprietors of the Delaware* (New Haven, CT: Yale University Press, 1919), pp. 1, 4, 9–10, 14–15; Lawrence M. Friedman & Harry N. Scheiber, eds., *American Law and the Constitutional Order: Historical Perspectives* (Cambridge, MA: Harvard University Press, enlarged ed., 1988), pp. 55–56; Bryan Villa & Cynthia Morris, *Capital Punishment in the United States: A Documentary History* (Westport, CT: Greenwood Press, 1997), p. 10; Jeremy Mercer, *When the Guillotine Fell: The Bloody Beginning and Horrifying End to France's River of Blood, 1791–1977* (New York: St. Martin's Press, 2008), p. 97.

18. Ken I. Kersch, *Freedom of Speech: Rights and Liberties Under the Law* (Santa Barbara, CA: ABC-CLIO, 2003), p. 243.

19. William C. Kashatus, "William Penn's Legacy: Religious and Spiritual Diversity," *Pennsylvania Heritage*, Vol. XXXVII, No. 2 (Spring 2011).

20. "To the Inhabitants of the Province of Quebec," *The Pennsylvania Gazette* (Philadelphia, PA), Nov. 9, 1774, pp. 5–6.

21. Cesare Beccaria, *On Crimes and Punishments* (New Brunswick, NJ: Transaction Publishers, Graeme R. Newman & Pietro Marongiu, eds. & trans. 2009), pp. viii, 9, 11, 42, 77; Richard Bellamy, ed., Cesare Beccaria, On Crimes and Punishments *and Other Writings* (Cambridge: Cambridge University Press, Richard Davies, trans. 1995), p. 35; Cesare Beccaria, *Of Crimes and Punishments*, ch.

23, *available at* http://www.laits.utexas.edu/poltheory/beccaria/delitti/delitti.ch23.html.

22. Christopher N. Phillips, *Epic in American Culture: Settlement to Reconstruction* (Baltimore, MD: The Johns Hopkins University Press, 2012), p. 77.

23. U.S. Const., arts. I, II & III; U.S. Const., amends. I, V & VI.

24. U.S. Const. (signed Sept. 17, 1787; ratified June 21, 1788), preamble.

25. Danny Danziger & John Gillingham, *1215: The Year of Magna Carta* (New York: Touchstone, 2004), p. xxi; English Translation of Magna Carta, https://www.bl.uk/magna-carta/articles/magna-carta-english-translation.

26. Magna Carta Quotations, Magna Carta Trust, http://magnacarta800th.com/schools/downloads-and-resources/magna-carta-quotations/.

27. J. Neil Schulman, *Nasty, Brutish and Short Stories* (Culver City: Pulpless.com, 1999), p. 15.

28. Alison Weir, *The Six Wives of Henry VIII* (New York: Grove Press, 1991), pp. 282, 319.

29. T. B. Howell, comp., *A Complete Collection of State Trials and Proceedings for High Treason and Other Crimes and Misdemeanors from the Earliest Period to the Year 1783, with Notes and Other Illustrations* (London: Longman, Hurst, Rees, Orme & Brown, 1816), Vol. IV, pp. 1071–72.

30. Mitchell Cohen & Nicole Fermon, eds., *Princeton Readings in Political Thought* (Princeton, NJ: Princeton University Press, 1996), p. 243.

31. Claire P. Curtis, *Postapocalyptic Fiction and the Social Contract: We'll Not Go Home Again* (Lanham, MD: Lexington Books, 2010), p. 9; David Williams, ed., *The Enlightenment* (Cambridge: Cambridge University Press, 1999), pp. 85–86; Jacques Véron, Sophie Pennec & Jacques Légaré, *Ages, Generations and the Social Contract: The Demographic Challenges Facing the Welfare State* (Dordrecht, The Netherlands: Springer, 2007), p. xii; Mark G. Spencer, ed., *The Bloomsbury Encyclopedia of the American Enlightenment* (New York: Bloomsbury Academic, 2015), Vol. 1, p. 985; David Lay Williams, *Rousseau's Social Contract: An Introduction* (Cambridge: Cambridge University Press, 2014), p. 39 & n.32.

32. Deborah A. Rosen, *Border Law: The First Seminole War and American Nationhood* (Cambridge, MA: Harvard University Press, 2015), pp. 46, 187; Antonio Trampus, "The Circulation of Vattel's *Droit des gens* in Italy: The Doctrinal and Practical Model of Government," *in* Antonella Alimento, ed., *War, Trade and Neutrality: Europe and the Mediterranean in the Seventeenth and Eighteenth Centuries* (Milano: FrancoAngeli, 2011), pp. 221–22, 224, 228.

33. Joseph Early Jr., *A History of Christianity: An Introductory Survey* (Nashville, TN: B&H Publishing, 2015), pp. 300–1; Sarah M. S. Clarke, *Mayflower Stories* (Edinburgh: William Oliphant and Co., 1876), pp. 53–54; E. D. Hirsch, Jr., Joseph F. Kett & James Trefil, *The New Dictionary of Cultural Literacy: What Every American Needs to Know* (Boston, MA: Houghton Mifflin Co., 2002), p. 267.

34. Jane A. Grant, *The New American Social Compact: Rights and Responsibilities in the Twenty-First Century* (Lanham, MD: Lexington Books, 2008), p. 1.

35. Jean-Jacques Rousseau, *The Basic Political Writings* (Indianapolis: Hackett Publishing Co., Donald A. Cress, trans. & ed., 2d ed. 2011), p. 3 n.1; Jean-Jacques Rousseau, *A Discourse on a Subject Proposed by the Academy of Dijon: What Is the Origin of Inequality Among Men, and Is It Authorised by Natural Law?* (1754), *available at* http://www.constitution.org/jjr/ineq.htm.

36. David Lay Williams, *Rousseau's Platonic Enlightenment* (University Park, PA: The Pennsylvania State University Press, 2007), p. 147.

37. James Miller, *Rousseau: Dreamer of Democracy* (New Haven: Yale University Press, 1984), p. 134.

38. Claire P. Curtis, *Postapocalyptic Fiction and the Social Contract: We'll Not Go Home Again* (Lanham, MD: Lexington Books, 2010), pp. 9–10; John Adams to Abigail Adams, Dec. 2, 1778; Abigail Adams to John Thaxter, Feb. 5, 1781; "Thursday. February 21st. 1765.," *Founders Online*, National Archives, last modified July 12, 2016, http://founders.archives.gov/documents/Adams/01-01-02-0009-0001-0004 [Original source: *The Adams Papers*, Diary and Autobiography of John Adams, vol. 1, *1755–1770*, L. H. Butterfield, ed. Cambridge, MA: Harvard University Press, 1961, pp. 253–255.].

39. "Reply of the House to Hutchinson's Second Message, 2 March 1773," National Archives, Founders Online, https://founders.archives.gov/?q=rousseau&s=1111311111&sa=&r=6&sr=; R. G. F. Candage, "The Gridley House, Brookline, and Jeremy Gridley," *in Publications of the Brookline Historical Society* (Brookline, MA: Brookline Historical Society, 1903), pp. 1, 3, 15.

40. John Julius Norwich, ed., *The Italians: History, Art, and the Genius of a People* (New York: Harry N. Abrams, 1983), p. 98; Archive Bencivenni, folder 13, insert 170; Philippe Audegean, "Le *Discourso della pena di morte* de Giuseppe Pelli (1760–1761)," *Corpus: Revue de Philosophie* (2012), pp. 135–56; Giuseppe Pelli, *Contro la pena di morte* (Padoue: CLEUP, Philippe Audegean, ed. & Gregorio Piaia, préf. 2014); Catherine M. Sama, ed. & trans., *Elisabetta Caminer Turra: Selected Writings of an Eighteenth-Century Venetian Woman of Letters* (Chicago, IL: The University of Chicago Press, 2003), p. 7 n.18.

41. Stefano Castelvecchi, *Sentimental Opera: Questions of Genre in the Age of Bourgeois Drama* (Cambridge: Cambridge University Press, 2013), pp. 103–4; R. Burr Litchfield, *Emergence of a Bureaucracy: The Florentine Patricians, 1530–1790* (Princeton, NJ: Princeton University Press, 1986), p. 309; Sama, *Elisabetta Caminer Turra*, p. 32.

42. William A. Schabas, *The Abolition of the Death Penalty in International Law* (Cambridge: Cambridge University Press, 3d ed. 2002), p. 4.

43. Anne M. Cohler, Basia C. Miller & Harold S. Stone, trans. & eds., *Montesquieu, The Spirit of the Laws* (Cambridge: Cambridge University Press, 1989), p. 75.

44. Ibid., p. 82.

45. *See generally* Rebecca E. Kingston, ed., *Montesquieu and His Legacy* (Albany, NY: State University of New York Press, 2009). Montesquieu's *The Spirit of Laws* was translated into English by Thomas Nugent in 1750, with Montesquieu, in a letter to his English translator, praising him for his work. "Your translation has no blemishes but those of the original, which are to be charged to my account; and I am much obliged to you for your ability in concealing them from the public eye," Montesquieu wrote. M. De Secondat, Baron De Montesquieu, *The Spirit of Laws* (Cincinnati: Robert Clarke & Co., Thomas Nugent, trans. & M. D'Alembert, ed. 1873), Vol. 1.

46. Cohler, Miller & Stone, *Montesquieu, The Spirit of the Laws*, p. 489.

47. Ibid. "In a word," Montesquieu wrote, "history teaches us well enough that the penal laws have never had any effect other than destruction." Ibid.

48. Bessler, *Cruel and Unusual*, pp. 94–95, 173–74; Rod Gragg, *Forged in Faith: How Faith Shaped the Birth of the Nation 1607–1776* (New York: Howard Books, 2010), pp. 57–58.

49. Cohler, Miller & Stone, *Montesquieu, The Spirit of the Laws*, p. 85.

50. Ibid., p. 91.

51. Ibid., p. 189.

52. Piet Strydom, *Discourse and Knowledge: The Making of Enlightenment Sociology* (Liverpool: Liverpool University Press, 2000), p. 206.

53. Cohler, Miller & Stone, *Montesquieu, The Spirit of the Laws*, p. 191; *The Memoirs of Jacques Casanova* (1894), Vol. 5, p. 33; *The Memoirs of Giacomo Casanova di Seingalt* (1922), Vol. 5, p. 22.

54. Jane Kamensky, *Governing the Tongue: The Politics of Speech in Early New England* (New York: Oxford University Press, 1997), p. 251; Frank Chalk & Kurt Jonassohn, *The History and Sociology of Genocide: Analyses and Case Studies* (New Haven, CT: Yale University Press, 1990), p. 6.

55. Maestro, *Cesare Beccaria and the Origins of Penal Reform*, p. 13.

56. 2 James Harvey Robinson & Charles A. Beard, *Outlines of European History* (Boston, MA: Ginn and Co., 1912), p. 34 ("Among all the books advocating urgent reforms which appeared in the eighteenth century none accomplished more than a little volume by the Italian economist and jurist, Beccaria, which exposed with great clearness and vigor the atrocities of the criminal law. The trials (even in England) were scandalously unfair and the punishments incredibly cruel. The accused was not ordinarily allowed any counsel and was required to give evidence against himself. Indeed, it was common enough to use torture to force a confession from him.... After a criminal had been convicted he might be tortured by the rack, thumbscrews, applying fire to different parts of his body, or in other ways, to induce him to reveal the names of his accomplices. The death penalty was established for a great variety of offenses besides murder....").

57. Reg Hamilton, *Colony, Strange Origins of One of the Earliest Modern Democracies* (Kent Town, South Australia: Wakefield Press, 2010), p. 107 ("Punishment was a public spectacle, designed to teach good conduct. The pillory, stocks, a whipping post, and cage, stood in the market place until about 1830. A man might be punished by a whipping, for example, for stealing a rabbit."); J. Lewis Peyton, *History of Augusta County, Virginia* (Staunton, VA: Samuel M. Yost & Son, 1882), p. 55 ("The

ancient laws of Virginia declared that the court in every county shall cause to be set up near the court-house a pillory, pair of stocks, a whipping-post and a ducking-stool, in such place as they shall think convenient...."); P. H. Ditchfield, *Vanishing England* (Folk Customs 2014), p. 218 ("The stocks, pillory, and whipping-post were three different implements of punishment, but, as was the case at Wallingford, Berkshire, they were sometimes allied and combined. The stocks secured the feet, the pillory 'held in durance vile' the head and the hands, while the whipping-post imprisoned the hands only by clamps on the sides of the post.").

58. Tanya Kevorkian, *Baroque Piety: Religion, Society, and Music in Leipzig, 1650–1750* (Hampshire, England: Ashgate, 2007), p. 116 ("Benedict Carpzov's other major work, for which he is best known, was the criminal-law compendium *Practica Nova Imperialis Saxonica Rerum Criminalium*. First published in 1635 and reprinted fourteen times to 1758, the *Practica Nova* became the standard work of criminal law in Saxony and throughout much of the Holy Roman Empire. It resembled the *Jurisprudentia Ecclesiastica* in its organization and empirical focus. Carpzov extensively applied the precepts of Christian natural law. He organized the two main books of the *Practica Nova* thematically around the Ten Commandments and referred extensively to Scripture."); ibid. ("Many of the crimes discussed in the *Practica Nova* themselves had a religious dimension. They included witchcraft, which fell under the category of heresy and was not an abstract issue at the time. Contrary to legend, Carpzov did not sentence 20,000 or even 300 women to death as witches while he was a Juror's Court judge. From 1661 he actually worked against the implementation of death sentences in Saxony. However, the trial and torture of suspects of witchcraft in Leipzig and elsewhere followed the guidelines of the *Practica Nova*. The torture was harsh: in the 1650s at least two women died under it, and another did as late as 1699.").

59. Tyge Krogh, *A Lutheran Plague: Murdering to Die in the Eighteenth Century* (Leiden, The Netherlands: Koninklijke Brill NV, 2012), p. 101.

60. Bessler, *Cruel and Unusual*, pp. 43–44; Brian Davies, *Thomas Aquinas's* Summa Contra Gentiles: *A Guide and Commentary* (Oxford: Oxford University Press, 2016), p. 285; Erica Benner, *Machiavelli's Ethics* (Princeton, NJ: Princeton University Press, 2009), pp. 316–18; Gerald Lee Ratliff, *Niccolò Machiavelli's* The Prince (Hauppauge, NY: Barron's Educational Series, 1986), p. 78; Keith Hopkins, *Death and Renewal: Sociological Studies in Roman History* (Cambridge: Cambridge University Press, 1983), pp. 1–2.

61. Mauro Pomo, *Discovering the Colosseum: Between Myth and Reality* (Narcissus, 2015); Mary-Lou Galician & Debra L. Merskin, eds., *Critical Thinking about Sex, Love, and Romance in the Mass Media: Media Literacy Applications* (Mahwah, NJ: Lawrence Erlbaum Associates, 2007), p. 318; George P. Monger, *Marriage Customs of the World: An Encyclopedia of Dating Customs and Wedding Traditions* (Santa Barbara, CA: ABC-CLIO, 2013), p. 665.

62. Bessler, *Cruel and Unusual*, p. 42; Derek Beales, *Joseph II: In the Shadow of Maria Theresa, 1741–1780* (Cambridge: Cambridge University Press, 1987), p. 236; Ken Armstrong, "Broken on the Wheel," *The Paris Review*, Mar. 13, 2015 (The Daily blog).

63. Albert Henry Smyth, comp., *The Writings of Benjamin Franklin* (New York: The Macmillan Co., 1907), Vol. IV, pp. 267–69; *Traité sur la Tolérance*, John Adams Library (Boston Public Library), https://archive.org/details/traitsurlatol02volt.

64. Aaron Thomas, ed., Cesare Beccaria, On Crimes and Punishments *and Other Writings* (Toronto: University of Toronto Press, Aaron Thomas & Jeremy Parzen, trans. 2008), pp. 117, 119.

65. Simon Harvey, ed., Voltaire, Treatise on Tolerance *and Other Writings* (Cambrige: Cambridge University Press, Brian Masters, trans. 2000), p. 19.

66. Kees Schuyt, "Tolerance and Democracy," *in* Douwe Fokkema & Frans Grijzenhout, eds., *Dutch Culture in a European Perspective: Accounting for the Past, 1650–2000* (New York: Palgrave Macmillan, 2004), Vol. 5, p. 114.

67. Piers Beirne, *Inventing Criminology: Essays on the Rise of 'Homo Criminalis'* (Albany: State University of New York Press, 1993), pp. 13–14; Charles Toth, *Liberté, Egalité, Fraternité: The American Revolution and the European Response* (Troy, NY: Whitston Pub. Co., 1989), pp. 104–5.

68. Voltaire, *Relation de la mort du Chevalier de la Barre* (1766); Online Library of Liberty, http://oll.libertyfund.org/titles/voltaire-the-works-of-voltaire-vol-iv-philosophical-dictionary-part-2?q=Beccaria#Voltaire_0060-04_1740 (citing William F. Fleming, ed., Voltaire, *The Works of Voltaire: A*

Contemporary Version (New York: E. R. DuMont, Tobias Smollett, trans., Vol. IV — *Philosophical Dictionary*, Part 2).

69. https://en.m.wikipedia.org/wiki/Gabriel_Malagrida.

70. Simon Harvey, ed., Voltaire, Treatise on Tolerance *and Other Writings* (Cambridge: Cambridge University Press, Simon Harvey, trans. 2000), p. xiv, xxi; Williams, *The Enlightenment*, p. 176; J. Thomas, *Universal Pronouncing Dictionary of Biography and Mythology* (Philadelphia: J. B. Lippincott and Co., 1870), Vol. 1, p. 274; William Monter, *Judging the French Revolution: Heresy Trials by Sixteenth-Century Parlements* (Cambridge, MA: Harvard University Press, 1999), pp. 15–17; "Voltaire and the La Barre affair," Voltaire Foundation (posted June 30, 2016), https://voltairefoundation.wordpress.com/tag/relation-de-la-mort-du-chevalier-de-la-barre/.

71. John D. Bessler, *The Birth of American Law: An Italian Philosopher and the American Revolution* (Durham, NC: Carolina Academic Press, 2014), pp. 48–57.

72. Ibid., p. 355.

73. Bellamy, Beccaria, On Crimes and Punishments *and Other Writings*, pp. 4–5, 22–23.

74. Ibid., pp. 83–86.

75. Ibid., pp. 39–41, 47; Walter A. Shumaker, George Foster Longsdorf & James C. Cahill, eds., *The Cyclopedic Law Dictionary* (Chicago, IL: Callaghan & Co., 1922), p. 528. According to that law dictionary, an "infamous crime" is "[a] crime which works infamy in one who has committed it." That dictionary pointed out that, in the United States, "[i]t has been held that only those crimes are infamous that were so at common law, but the general rule is that any offense is infamous that may be punished by death, or by imprisonment in the penitentiary, with or without hard labor." At common law, "[t]reason and all felonies, and certain misdemeanors affecting the public interest most closely, were infamous crimes, the nature of the crime being the test." Ibid., p. 527. In English law, an *amende honorable* — sometimes employing a visit to a church in disgraceful garb to atone for a sin — was defined as follows: "A penalty imposed upon a person by way of disgrace or infamy, as a punishment for any offense, or for the purpose of making reparation for any injury done to another, as the walking into church in a white sheet, with a rope about the neck and a torch in the hand, and begging the pardon of God, or the king, or any private individual, for some delinquency." Ibid., p. 52.

76. Bruce Caldwell, ed., *The Collected Words of F. A. Hayek: The Market and Other Orders* (London: Routledge, 2014), Vol. 15, p. 46 n.13.

77. Stephen G. Tibbetts & Craig Hemmens, *Criminological Theory: A Text/Reader* (Thousand Oaks, CA: Sage Publications, 2010), p. 86.

78. Emmanuelle de Champs, *Enlightenment and Utility: Bentham in French, Bentham in France* (Cambridge: Cambridge University Press, 2015), p. 58.

79. Christopher F. Black, *Early Modern Italy: A Social History* (London: Routledge, 2001), p. 213.

80. *See* Michel Delon, ed., *Encyclopedia of the Enlightenment* (London: Routledge, 2001), p. 76 ("The Italian jurist Cesare Bonesana Beccaria had reason to complain about Cevallos, insofar as the latter's *Analisis del libro intitulado 'Delitos y penas'* (Analysis of the Book Entitled 'Crimes and Punishments') contributed to the condemnation [of] Beccaria's book by the Inquisition in 1777.").

81. Bessler, *Cruel and Unusual*, pp. 32, 47–48.

82. Graeme R. Newman & Pietro Marongiu, trans., Cesare Beccaria, *On Crimes and Punishments* (New Brunswick, NJ: 5th ed., 2009), pp. 75–76.

83. David Garland, *Peculiar Institution: America's Death Penalty in an Age of Abolition* (Cambridge: The Belknap Press of Harvard University Press, 2010), p. 136.

84. Maestro, *Cesare Beccaria and the Origins of Penal Reform*, p. 26; Richard Bellamy, ed., *Beccaria: On Crimes and Punishments and Other Writings* (Cambridge: Cambridge University Press, 1995), p. 92; Dirk Verhofstadt, *Cesare Beccaria: 250 Years on Crimes and Punishments* (Lexington, KY: July 24, 2016), pp. 15, 17; William Whiting, *War Powers under the Constitution of the United States* (Union, NJ: The Lawbook Exchange, 10th ed. 2002), pp. 102–3; *A New Law-Dictionary: Containing the Interpretation and Definition of Words and Terms used in the Law* (London: Giles Jacob, 8th ed., 1762) (entry for "Forfeiture").

85. Elena Past, *Methods of Murder: Beccarian Introspection and Lombrosian Vivisection in Italian Crime Fiction* (Toronto: University of Toronto Press, 2012), p. 31.

86. Cesare Bonesana di Beccaria, *An Essay on Crimes and Punishments* [1764], Online Library of

Liberty, http://oll.libertyfund.org/titles/beccaria-an-essay-on-crimes-and-punishments.

87. Jeremy D. Bailey, *Thomas Jefferson and Executive Power* (Cambridge: Cambridge University Press, 2007), p. 42.

88. Voltaire, Philosophical Dictionary (entry on "Inquisition"), *available at* https://ebooks.adelaide.edu.au/v/voltaire/dictionary/chapter279.html.

89. Galileo and the Inquisition, *available at* http://physics.ucr.edu/~wudka/Physics7/Notes_www/node52.html.

90. Toby Green, *Inquisition: The Reign of Fear* (London: Pan Books, 2011) (e-book edition); https://en.wikipedia.org/wiki/List_of_authors_and_works_on_the_Index_Librorum_Prohibitorum.

91. Beccaria, *On Crimes and Punishments* (Graeme R. Newman & Pietro Marongiu, eds. & trans. 2009), pp. lix–lx.

92. *A History of English Criminal Law and Its Administration from 1750* (London: Stevens & Sons Limited, 1948), p. 277; Marcello T. Maestro, *Cesare Beccaria and the Origins of Penal Reform* (Philadelphia, PA: Temple University Press, 1973), p. 20; Frank A. Kafker, *Notable Encyclopedias of the Late Eighteenth Century: Eleven Successors of the Encyclopédie* (Oxford: Voltaire Foundation, 1994), pp. 51, 73; Roy Osborne, *Books on Colour 1495–2015: History and Bibliography* (Lulu.com, 2016); Ian Chilvers, ed., *The Oxford Dictionary of Art* (Oxford: Oxford University Press, 3d ed. 2004), p. 16; Enrico Fubini, *Music and Culture in Eighteenth-Century Europe: A Source Book* (Chicago: The University of Chicago Press, Wolfgang Freis, Lisa Gasbarrone & Michael Louis Leone, trans. 1994), p. 233; Jaynie Anderson, *Tiepolo's Cleopatra* (Melbourne: Macmillan, 2003), pp. 98–109; Philip Steadman, *Vermeer's Camera: Uncovering the Truth Behind the Masterpieces* (Oxford: Oxford University Press, 2001), p. 27; "Vermeer and the Camera Obscura (part one)," Essential Vermeer 2.0, http://www.essentialvermeer.com/camera_obscura/co_one.html#.WOrD7VKZOqA; Alberto Colzani, *Il teatro musicale italiano nel Sacro Romano Impero nei secoli XVII e XVIII: atti del VII Convegno internazionale sulla musica italiana nei secoli XVII–XVIII, Loveno di Menaggio (Como), 15–17 luglio 1997* (Antiquae Musicae Italicae Studiosi, 1999), p. 503; Sir John MacDonell & Edward Manson, eds., *Great Jurists of the World* (Boston: Little, Brown, and Co., 1914), Vol. 2, p. 506; Clorinda Donato & Robert M. Maniquis, eds., *The Encyclopédie and the Age of Revolution* (Boston, MA: G. K. Hall, 1992), p. 53; Marcello T. Maestro, *Gaetano Filangieri and His* Science of Legislation (Philadelphia, PA: American Philosophical Society, 1976), p. 43.

93. Robert M. Bohm & Brenda L. Vogel, *A Primer on Crime and Delinquency Theory* (Belmont, CA: Wadsworth, 3d ed. 2011), p. 16; Alette Smeulers & Fred Grünfeld, *International Crimes and Other Gross Human Rights Violations: A Multi- and Interdisciplinary Textbook* (Lieden: Martinus Nijhoff Publishers, 2011), p. 122; Werner J. Einstadter & Stuart Henry, *Criminological Theory: An Analysis of Its Underlying Assumptions* (Lanham, MD: Rowman & Littlefield, 2d ed. 2006), p. 69.

94. Franklin Mesa, *Opera: An Encyclopedia of World Premieres and Significant Performances, Singers, Composers, Librettists, Arias and Conductors, 1597–2000* (Jefferson, NC: McFarland & Co., 2007), p. 14; Richard Wigmore, *The Faber Pocket Guide to Haydn* (London: Faber and Faber, 2009), p. 309; Daniel Heartz, *Haydn, Mozart and the Viennese School 1740–1780* (New York: W.W. Norton & Co., 1995), p. 210; John A. Rice, *Antonio Salieri and Viennese Opera* (Chicago, IL: The University of Chicago Press, 1998), p. 45; Giacomo Casanova (Chevalier de Seingalt), *History of My Life* (Baltimore, MD: The Johns Hopkins University Press, Willard R. Trask, trans. 1971), Vols. 11–12, p. 360 n.82; Robert Darnton, *The Business of Enlightenment: A Publishing History of the* Encyclopédie *1775–1800* (Cambridge, MA: The Belknap Press of Harvard University Press, 1979), pp. 33–34, 315 n.140; Frank A. Kafker, *Notable Encyclopedias of the Late Eighteenth Century: Eleven Successors of the* Encyclopédie (Oxford: The Voltaire Foundation), p. 73; "Coltellini, Marco (1724–1777), librettist," http://oxfordindex.oup.com/view/10.1093/gmo/9781561592630.article.06159.

95. Darnton, *The Business of Enlightenment*, p. 315; Franco Venturi, *The End of the Old Regime in Europe, 1776–1789: The Great States of the West* (Princeton, NJ: Princeton University Press, R. Burr Litchfield, trans. 1991), pp. 82–86; Roy Domenico, *The Regions of Italy: A Reference Guide to History and Culture* (Westport, CT: Greenwood Press, 2002), p. 313; Alessandro P. d'Entrèves, "The Italian Renaissance of the Eighteenth Century," *in Arts and Ideas in Eighteenth-Century Italy: Lectures Given at the Italian Institute 1957–1958* (Roma: Edizioni di Storia e Letteratura, 1960), p. 16; Francis Steegmuller, *A Woman, a Man, and Two Kingdoms: The Story of Madame D'Epinay and Abbe Galiani* (New

York: Alfred A. Knopf, 1991), p. 46; http://www.philipwine.com/The-Marchesi-Mazzei/A-Wine-Dynasty/; *see also* Philip Mazzei, *My Life and Wanderings* (American Institute of Italian Studies, S. Eugene Scalia, trans. 1980), p. 151 ("I wrote the necessary details to Signor Giuseppe Aubert in Leghorn, asking him to please go to Auditor Franceschini on my behalf, inform him of everything, and tell him that I ought to go by sea."); ibid., p. 167 ("Aubert, who had placed his foot on the first step, stood still till the end of the stanza. Then he leisurely went up, entered the room without having as yet opened his mouth, sat on a sofa, and pretending to wipe his face (as does a preacher on the pulpit to give himself more time to collect his thoughts), he answered with an ottava rima.").

96. Beccaria, *On Crimes and Punishments* (Graeme R. Newman & Pietro Marongiu, eds. & trans. 2009), p. lx; Piers Beirne, *Inventing Criminology: Essays on the Rise of 'Homo Criminalis'* (Albany: State University of New York Press, 1993), p. 61, n.134; Andrea S. Norris & Ingrid Weber, *Medals and Plaquettes from the Molinari Collection at Bowdoin College* (Brunswick, ME: Bowdoin College, 1976), p. 47; http://www.italicon.it/it/museo/I298-009.htm.

97. Bellamy, Beccaria, On Crimes and Punishments *and Other Writings*, p. xliii.

98. Dino Carpanetto & Giuseppe Ricuperati, *Italy in the Age of Reason, 1685–1789* (New York: Longman, 1987), Vol. 5, p. 213.

99. Gaetana Marrone, ed., *Encyclopedia of Italian Literary Studies* (New York: Routledge, 2007), Vol. 1, p. 147.

100. Bellamy, Beccaria, On Crimes and Punishments *and Other Writings*, p. xlvi.

101. Aaron Thomas, ed., Cesare Beccaria, On Crimes and Punishments *and Other Writings* (Toronto: University of Toronto Press, Aaron Thomas & Jeremy Parzen, trans. 2008), p. xxx.

102. Michel Delon, ed., *Encyclopedia of the Enlightenment* (New York: Routledge, 2001), p. 724. American colonists were certainly not oblivious to events in Milan and other parts of Europe. Newspapers, in fact, regularly reported on events in major European cities, including the goings on in places such as Milan. *The Virginia Gazette* (Williamsburg, VA), Aug. 1, 1766, p. 1 ("MILAN, *April 12. It is at length determined that the Court de Firmian, Minister Plenipotentiary from Austrian Lombardy, shall make his publick entry into this city the 25th instant....").

103. Bernard E. Harcourt, *The Illusion of Free Markets: Punishment and the Myth of Natural Order* (Cambridge: Harvard University Press, 2011), p. 59; *compare* Javier Moscoso, *Pain: A Cultural History* (New York: Palgrave Macmillan, 2012), p. 60 ("A year before the publication of *On Crimes and Punishments*—the text that made him truly famous—Beccaria's cousin, Pietro Verri, had published his *Meditations on Happiness* in which this promoter of the Italian Enlightenment circle known as the *Society of the Fist* maintained that the search for well-being depended on a rational fight against the impediments to pleasure."); ibid. ("The second of the Verri brothers ... had also published a brief text denouncing the use of pain....").

104. James V. Bennett, *I Chose Prison* (New York: Alfred E. Knopf, 1970), p. 63.

105. Cesare Beccaria, *An Essay on Crimes and Punishments* (Edinburgh: James Donaldson, 1788), p. 233.

106. Cesare Beccaria, *On Crimes and Punishments* (New Brunswick, NJ: Transaction Publishers, Graeme R. Newman & Pietro Marongiu, trans., 5th ed. 2009), p. lviii.

107. Jonathan I. Israel, *Democratic Enlightenment: Philosophy, Revolution, and Human Rights 1750–1790* (Oxford: Oxford University Press, 2011), p. 339; Madoka Futamura & Nadia Bernaz, eds., *The Politics of the Death Penalty in Countries in Transition* (New York: Routledge, 2014), p. 219.

108. Maestro, *Cesare Beccaria and the Origins of Penal Reform*, pp. 35–37; Owen Chadwick, *The Popes and European Revolution* (Oxford: Clarendon Press, 1981), p. 332; Charles E. Little, *Cyclopedia of Classified Dates with an Exhaustive Index* (New York: Funk & Wagnalls Co., 1900), p. 1085; Mary Seidman Trouille, *Sexual Politics in the Enlightenment: Women Writers Read Rousseau* (Albany: State University of New York Press, 1997), p. 16.

109. James Anson Farrer, *Crimes and Punishments: Including a New Translation of Beccaria's 'Dei delitti e delle pene'* (London: Chatto & Windus, 1880), p. 16; Piers Beirne, "Inventing Criminology: The 'Science of Man' in Cesare Beccaria's *Dei delitti e delle pene* (1764)," *in* Marilyn McShane & Frank P. Williams III, eds., *Criminal Justice: Contemporary Literature in Theory and Practice* (New York: Garland Publishing, 1997), p. 26.

110. Margaret Plant, *Venice: Fragile City, 1797–1997* (New Haven, CT: Yale University Press, 2001),

p. 23; Marianna D'Ezio, "Isabella Teotochi Abrizzi's Venetian Salon: A Transcultural and Transnational Example of Sociability and Cosmopolitanism in Late Eighteenth- and Early Nineteenth-Century Europe," *in* Ileana Baird, ed., *Social Networks in the Long Eighteenth Century: Clubs, Literary Salons, Textual Coteries* (Newcastle upon Tyne, UK: Cambridge Scholars Publishing, 2011), p. 179.

111. Larry Wolff, *Paolina's Innocence: Child Abuse in Casanova's Venice* (Stanford, CA: Stanford University Press, 2012), p. 28.

112. Ann Caesar & Michael Caesar, *Modern Italian Literature* (Cambridge, UK: Polity Press, 2007), p. 39; Thomas, Cesare Beccaria, On Crimes and Punishments *and Other Writings*, p. 175 n.1.

113. Paolo Rambaldi & Dante Pattini, eds., *Index Librorum Prohibitorum: Historical Notes on a Collection* (Studio Bibliografico Rambaldi), *available at* http://www.rambaldirarebooks.com/clientfiles/ upload/241.pdf; Marvin Perry, *Western Civilization: A Brief History* (Boston, MA: Wadsworth, 10th ed. 2013), p. 255.

114. Stuart Henry & Werner Einstadter, *The Criminology Theory Reader* (New York: New York University Press, 1998), p. 21. The Catholic Church has now long opposed the use of capital punishment. Elizabeth Bruenig, "The Catholic Church Opposes the Death Penalty. Why Don't White Catholics?" *New Republic*, Mar. 6, 2015, https://newrepublic.com/article/121231/national-catholic-publications-announce-opposition-death-penalty. Pope Francis has himself spoken out against the death penalty. "Pope: No to Death Penalty and to Inhuman Prison Conditions," Vatican Radio, http:// en.radiovaticana.va/news/2014/10/23/pope_no_to_death_penalty_and_to_inhuman_prison_ conditions/1109301; Letter of His Holiness Pope Francis to the President of the International Commission Against the Death Penalty, Mar. 20, 2015, *available at* https://web.archive.org/web/201605 22173223/http://w2.vatican.va/content/francesco/en/letters/2015/documents/papa-francesco_201503 20_lettera-pena-morte.html.

115. Luis Arroyo Zapatero, "Francisco de Goya: Against the Cruelty of the Penal System and the Death Penalty," *in* L. Arroyo Zapatero, W. Schabas & K. Takayama, eds., *Death Penalty: A Cruel and Inhuman Punishment* (Cuenca: Ediciones de la Universidad de Castilla-La Mancha, 2013), p. 131; Williams, *The Enlightenment*, p. 60; Stuart Henry & Werner Einstadter, eds., *The Criminology Theory Reader* (New York: NYU Press, 1997), p. 21; Piers Beirne, *Inventing Criminology: Essays on the Rise of 'Homo Criminalis'* (Albany: State University of New York Press, 1993), pp. 14–15; James Crimmins, ed., *The Bloomsbury Encyclopedia of Utilitarianism* (London: Bloomsbury Academic, 2017), p. 397; John Rogerson, ed., *Theory and Practice in Old Testament Ethics* (London: T&T Clark International, 2004), p. 15; Stephen G.H. Roberts & Adam Sharman, eds., *1812 Echoes: The Cadiz Constitution in Hispanic History, Culture and Politics* (Newcastle upon Tyne, UK: Cambridge Scholars Publishing, 2013), pp. 40–41.

116. Williams, *The Enlightenment*, pp. 58, 440; Stuart Henry & Werner Einstadter, eds., *The Criminology Theory Reader* (New York: NYU Press, 1997), p. 21.

117. Bessler, *The Birth of American Law*, p. 27; 48 *Il Politico* 707 (Università degli studi di Pavia, 1983) ("After much discussion and various further suggestions and revision this work was edited by Pietro Verri and published in July 1764 in Leghorn, when Beccaria was still only 26 years old, as 'Dei Delitti e delle Pene' or 'On Crimes and Punishments.'").

118. Lynn Hunt, *Inventing Human Rights: A History* (New York: W. W. Norton & Co., 2007), p. 103; Maestro, *Cesare Beccaria and the Origins of Penal Reform*, p. 127; *see also* Kostas Gavroglu, ed., *The Sciences in the European Periphery During the Enlightenment* (Dordrecht, The Netherlands: Kluwer Academic Publishers, 1999), p. 107 ("In February 1766, the Santo Uffizio condemned the major work of Cesare Beccaria (1738–1794), *Dei delitti e delle pene* [On Crimes and Punishments], first published anonymously in Leghorn in the summer of 1764, and immediately famous all over Europe.").

119. Israel, *Democratic Enlightenment*, p. 339.

120. Maestro, *Cesare Beccaria and the Origins of Penal Reform*, p. 128.

121. Maria Rogacka-Rzewnicka, "Unconventional Ways of Adjudication in Criminal Cases within the Solutions in the Polish Trial," *Ius Novum* (Feb. 2016), p. 143.

122. Samuel Fiszman, *Constitution and Reform in Eighteenth-century Poland: The Constitution of 3 May 1791* (Bloomington: Indiana University Press, 1997), pp. 386, 398, 403, 410; Teodor Waga, https://pl.wikipedia.org/wiki/Teodor_Waga.

123. "Description and Character of the King of Poland," *The Virginia Gazette* (Williamsburg, VA),

July 1, 1773, p. 2.

124. Stanisław Waltoś, *Humanitarian Traditions of the Polish Criminal Procedure: On the History of the Torture Abolition and Free Expression in the Polish Criminal Procedure* (Naukowe, 1983), p. 51.

125. Jean Carpentier, ed., *The Emergence of Human Rights in Europe: An Anthology* (Strasbourg: Council of Europe Publishing, 2001), p. 87.

126. 3 David S. Clark, ed., *Encyclopedia of Law and Society: American and Global Perspectives* (Thousand Oaks, CA: Sage Publications, 2007), p. 117.

127. Johan van der Zande & Richard H. Popkin, eds., *The Skeptical Tradition Around 1800: Skepticism in Philosophy, Science, and Society* (Dordrecht, The Netherlands: Springer Science+Business Media, 1998).

128. Maestro, *Cesare Beccaria and the Origins of Penal Reform*, p. 127; Ulrich L. Lehner & Michael Printy, eds., *A Companion to the Catholic Enlightenment in Europe* (Lieden: Brill, 2010), p. 232.

129. Wolfgang Rother, "The Beginning of Higher Education in Political Economy in Milan and Modena: Cesare Beccaria, Alfonso Longo, Agostino Paradisi," *in* Mordechai Feingold, *History of Universities* (Oxford: Oxford University Press, 2004), Vol. XIX/1, p. 123; Lehner & Printy, *A Companion to the Catholic Enlightenment in Europe*, p. 232.

130. Richard J. Evans, *Rituals of Retribution: Capital Punishment in Germany, 1600–1987* (Oxford: Oxford University Press, 1996), p. 133; Terry Pinkard, *Hegel: A Biography* (Cambridge: Cambridge University Press, 2000), p. 72.

131. David Brion Davis, *From Homicide to Slavery: Studies in American Culture* (New York: Oxford University Press, 1986), p. 30 n.43; Isabel V. Hull, *Sexuality, State, and Civil Society in Germany, 1700–1815* (Ithaca: Cornell University Press, 1997), p. 139 n.114.

132. Michael C. Carhart, *The Science of Culture in Enlightenment Germany* (Cambridge, MA: Harvard University Press, 2007), pp. 45–46, 51–52; *see also* ibid., p. 291 ("Michaelis offered reasoned and gentle arguments, perhaps derived from Beccaria, as he worked his way through the Mosaic law.").

133. Kevin Jon Heller & Markus D. Dubber, eds., *The Handbook of Comparative Criminal Law* (Stanford: Stanford University Press, 2011), p. 210; Harcourt, *The Illusion of Free Markets*, p. 54.

134. Bessler, *The Birth of American Law*, p. xi.

135. Owen Chadwick, *The Popes and European Revolution* (New York: Oxford University Press, 1981), p. 333; Gabriel Haslip-Viera, *Crime and Punishment in Late Colonial Mexico City, 1692–1810* (Albuquerque: University of New Mexico Press, 1999), p. 43. The first Spanish translation of Beccaria's book, published in Madrid, appeared as *Tratado de los delitos y de las penas*.

136. Lineide Salvador Mosca (org.), *Discursco, argumentação e produção de sentido* 99 (Sãn Paulo: Associação Editorial Humanitas, 2006).

137. Ibid., p. 8.

138. Cesare Beccaria, *On Crimes and Punishments* (New Brunswick, NJ: Transaction Publishers, Graeme R. Newman and Pietro Marongiu, trans., 5th ed. 2009), p. lxiv.

139. Harvey Chisick, *Historical Dictionary of the Enlightenment* (Lanham, MD: The Scarecrow Press, 2005), p. 99; N. B. Ghodke, *Encyclopaedic Dictionary of Economics* (Delhi, India: Mittal Publications, 1985), Vol. 1, p. 141; Andre Wakefield, "Cameralism: A German Alternative to Mercantilism," *in* Philip J. Stern & Carl Wennerlind, eds., *Mercantilism Reimagined: Political Economy in Early Modern Britain and Its Empire* (Oxford: Oxford University Press, 2014), pp. 134–36; Rother, "The Beginning of Higher Education in Political Economy in Milan and Modena" *in* Feingold, *History of Universities*, Vol. XIX/1, pp. 119–58.

140. As those scholars write:

> Beccaria's lecture notes collected in *Elementi* reveal traces of an old-style approach to political economy, based on the role of government in encouraging agriculture and other economic activities. One of his models seems to be Joseph von Sonnenfels' *Grundsätze der Polizei, Handlung und Finanzwissenschaft*, a work that reveals a narrowly defined and quite old-fashioned role of police regulations. However among Beccaria's sources there are also Cantillon, Hume, and a dash of Physiocracy. Furthermore, the text reveals a methodology that is closer to that adopted in "Tentativo" and based on a "Galilean" scientific approach to the analysis of economic phenomena. Policy recommendations are selected consistently with

the results of economic analysis. The laws that regulate the growth of wealth—which can be discovered through 'political arithmetic' and probability calculus—are natural and providential. The existence of such laws only makes the economic science applicable and useful.
Marco E. L. Guidi & Massimo M. Augello, "Economic Treatises and Textbooks in Italy: A Comparative Analysis of 18th- and 19th-century Political Economy," *in* Jesús Astigarraga & Javier Usoz, eds., *L'économie politique et la sphère publique dans le débat des lumières* (Madrid: Casa de Valázqvez, 2013), p. 120.

141. Jörg Guido Hülsmann, *Mises: The Last Knight of Liberalism* (Auburn, AL: Ludwig von Mises Institute, 2007), p. 62 & n.4; Georg Knepler, *Wolfgang Amadé Mozart* (Cambridge: Cambridge University Press, J. Bradford Robinson, trans. 1997), p. 83; William O. McCagg Jr., *A History of Habsburg Jews, 1670–1918* (Bloomington: Indiana University Press, 1989), p. 24; Jürgen Georg Backhaus, ed., *The Liberation of the Serfs: The Economics of Unfree Labor* (New York: Springer, 2012), p. 23.

142. Patrick J. Charles, *Restoring "Life, Liberty, and the Pursuit of Happiness" in Our Constitutional Jurisprudence: An Exercise in Legal History*, 20 Wm. & Mary Bill Rts. J. 457, 495 (2011) ("The founding generation's incorporation of Hutcheson and Beccaria's language of 'the greatest happiness of the greatest number' was just one way of phrasing the representative political theory embodied by preserving liberty and ensuring the 'pursuit of happiness.' Often the terms 'public good,' 'common good,' or 'good of the whole' were alternative and interchangeable ways of phrasing the same principle.").

143. Comprehensive collections of Pietro Verri's and Cesare Beccaria's extensive writings have been published in Italian. Michelis, "Letters from London," p. 38 (referencing "the National Editions of the *Works* of Cesare Beccaria, edited by Luigi Firpo and Gianni Francioni, and the *Collected Works* of Pietro Verri, edited by Carlo Capra"). Pietro Verri's best-known works include *Discourse on Happiness* (1763), *Reflections on Political Economy* (1771), and *Discourse on Pleasure and Pain* (1773). Peter Groenewegen, "Scritti di Economia, Finanza e Amministrazione," *Contributions to Political Economy*, Vol. 28, pp. 103–113 (reviewing Pietro Verri, *Scritti di Economia, Finanza e Amministrazione*, edited by Giuseppe Bognetti, Angelo Moioli, Pier Luigi Porta & Giovanni Tonelli, *Edizione Nationale delle Opere di Pietro Verri*, two volumes, *Edizioni di Storia e Letteratura*, Roma, 2006, 2007); *see also* Pier Luigi Porta, "Lombard Enlightenment and Classical Political Economy," http://www.eshet.net/public/lecture2.pdf; Harcourt, *The Illusion of Free Markets*, p. 59 ("'The end of the social pact,' Verri wrote in 1763, 'is the well-being of each of the individuals who join together to form society, who do so in order that this well-being becomes absorbed into the public happiness or rather the greatest possible happiness distributed with the greatest equality possible.'"); ibid. ("Beccaria wrote, in the very introductory pages of his short tract, that the litmus test of state intervention should be whether 'they conduce to *the greatest happiness shared among the greater number.*'"). "Beccaria's—and Verri's—conception of welfare," Bernard Harcourt writes, "was somewhat unique in its emphasis on equality." Ibid.

144. Bessler, *The Birth of American Law*, pp. 375–90; Pietro Verri, *Osservazioni sulla tortura* (Milano: BUR, 2006). Both Verri and Beccaria—leading thinkers of the Italian Enlightenment—wanted to reform Lombardy's penal justice system. Claudia Baldoli, *A History of Italy* (New York: Palgrave Macmillan, 2009), ch. 6 ("[B]etween 1770 and 1777, Pietro Verri contributed by writing a pamphlet on torture, *Osservazioni sulla tortura* ('Observations on torture'), which was published posthumously in 1804, when torture was abolished in Lombardy by Joseph II…. Verri had previously written a pamphlet against torture in 1763….").

145. Austin Sarat & Jürgen Martschukat, *Is the Death Penalty Dying? European and American Perspectives* (Cambridge: Cambridge University Press, 2011), p. 178 (discussing the views of Sonnenfels, "who advocated strict restrictions on capital punishment," and noting that, "[l]ike Beccaria, Sonnenfels pointed to the nondeterrability of criminals motivated by fanaticism or revenge"); William A. Schabas, *The Abolition of the Death Penalty in International Law* (Cambridge: Cambridge University Press, 3rd ed. 2002), p. 5 ("The modern abolitionist movement establishes its paternity with the great Italian criminologist, Cesare Beccaria.").

146. Jackson J. Spielvogel, *Western Civilization* (Boston, MA: Wadsworth, 8th ed. 2012), p. 601.

147. Peter Brand & Lino Pertile, eds., *The Cambridge History of Italian Literature* (Cambridge: Cambridge University Press: rev. ed. 1996), pp. 371, 378–80; *The Edinburgh Review, or Critical Journal:*

For November 1825 ... February 1826 (London: Archibald Constable and Co./Longman, Rees, Orme, Brown and Green, 1826), p. 18:

> England is the native country of Political Economy: But she has not treated it with a kind and fostering hand: She cannot boast of being the first to perceive the advantage of rendering it a branch of popular instruction, or to form establishments for that purpose. It is to Italy, or rather to an Italian citizen, Bartholomew Intieri, a Florentine, celebrated by his countrymen for the variety of his useful attainments, and the benevolence of his character, that this honour is due. Having resided long in Naples, in the capacity of manager of the estates of the Corsini and Medici families, Intieri necessarily became familiar with many of the abuses with which every part of the internal administration of that country was infected; and being strongly impressed with a conviction, that the easiest, safest, and most effectual reform of these abuses, would be produced by rendering the public generally acquainted with the genuine sources of national wealth and prosperity, and of poverty and misery, he determined to show his gratitude to the Neapolitans for the kindness he had experienced during his residence amongst them, by instituting a course of lectures on this science. For this purpose, Intieri applied to the Neapolitan government to be permitted to found a professorship of Political Economy in the University of Naples, to which a salary of 300 scudi should be attached, stipulating that the lectures should be given in the Italian language; that his distinguished friend Genovesi should be the first professor; and that, after his death, no individual in holy orders should be appointed to the chair. The government having, greatly to its credit, agreed to these conditions, Genovesi opened his class on the 5th of November 1754. His lectures, which were very successful, were published in 1764, in two volumes 8vo, under the title of *Lezioni di Commercio o sia di Economia Civile*.

148. Barbara Cassin, ed., *Dictionary of Untranslatables: A Philosophical Lexicon* (Princeton, NJ: Princeton University Press, 2014), p. 521; Terry J. Tekippe, *What Is Lonergan Up to INSIGHT?: A Primer* (Collegeville, MN: The Liturgical Press, 1996), p. 5.

149. Maestro, *Cesare Beccaria and the Origins of Penal Reform*, p. 46.

Chapter 3

1. John Hailman, *Thomas Jefferson on Wine* (Jackson: University Press of Mississippi, 2006), p. 75; Marcello Maestro, *Cesare Beccaria and the Origins of Penal Reform* (Philadelphia: Temple University Press, 1973), pp. 39–40 & n.6, 68; Michael L. Coulter, Richard S. Myers & Joseph A. Varacalli, eds., *Encyclopedia of Catholic Social Thought, Social Science, and Social Policy* (Lanham, MD: The Scarecrow Press, 2012), Vol. 3, p. 380; Robert Louis Stevenson, *The Art of Writing* (Cheshire, England: Cool Publications, 2003), p. 61; Roselyne de Ayala, Jean-Pierre Guéno & John Goodman, *Belles Lettres: Manuscripts by the Masters of French Literature* (New York: Harry N. Abrams, 2001), p. 50; "'Arator': On the Price of Corn, and Management of the Poor," Nov. 29, 1766, https://founders.archives.gov/? q=Morellet&s=1111311111&sa=&r=3&sr=; Benjamin Franklin to Matthew Boulton, June 15, 1772, https://founders.archives.gov/?q=Morellet&s=1111311111&sa=&r=4&sr=; "March 7: André Morellet (1727)," http://freethoughtalmanac.com/?p=6890.

2. J. Thomas, *The Universal Dictionary of Biography and Mythology* (New York: Cosimo Classics, 2009), Vol. II, p. 1159; C. A. Helvetius, *De L'Esprit; or, Essays on the Mind, and Its Several Faculties* (Albion Press, new ed. 1810), pp. 18, 135, 291, 343.

3. Derek Jones, ed., *Censorship: A World Encyclopedia* (London: Routledge, 2015), pp. 899–900, 1482; William J. Landon, *Politics, Patriotism and Language: Niccolò Machiavelli's "Secular Patria" and the Creation of an Italian National Identity* (New York: Peter Lang Publishing, 2005), p. 95; https:// en.wikipedia.org/wiki/Pietro_Giannone.

4. Maestro, *Cesare Beccaria and the Origins of Penal Reform*, pp. 40–42.

5. Francesco Flamini, *A History of Italian Literature (1265–1907)* (The National Alumni: Evangeline M. O'Connor, trans., 1909), p. 299; Omid Shahibzadeh, Penal Philosophy in 18th Century Italy: A Historical Enquiry into the Ideas of Francesco Mario Pagano, Master Thesis in the History of Ideas, Department of Philosophy, Classics, History of Art and Ideas, Faculty of Humanities at the University

of Oslo (Spring 2016), p. 16.

6. Franco Venturi, "Church and Reform in Enlightenment Italy: The Sixties of the Eighteenth Century," 48 *The Journal of Modern History* 215 (1976).

7. Ferenc Hörcher, "Beccaria, Voltaire, and the Scots on Capital Punishment: A Comparative View of the Legal Enlightenment," *in* Deidre Dawson & Pierre Morère, eds., *Scotland and France in the Enlightenment* (Lewisburg: Bucknell University Press, 2004), pp. 306, 317; Iain McDaniel, *Adam Ferguson in the Scottish Enlightenment: The Roman Past and Europe's Future* (Cambridge: Harvard University Press, 2013), pp. 47–48; Alex. Fraser Tytler, *Memoirs of the Life and Writings of the Honourable Henry Home of Kames* (Edinburgh: T. Cadell & W. Davies, 2d ed. 1814), Vol. 3, pp. 110–11, 118, 128, 131–35, 143, 346, 396; https://en.wikipedia.org/wiki/Henry_Home,_Lord_Kames; Piers Beirne, "Inventing Criminology: The 'Science of Man' in Cesare Beccaria's *Dei delitti e delle pene* (1764)," *in* Marilyn Mc-Shane & Frank P. Williams III, eds., *Criminal Justice: Contemporary Literature in Theory and Practice* (New York: Garland Publishing, 1997), p. 25; *see also* Franco Venturi, "Scottish echoes in eighteenth-century Italy," *in* Istvan Hont and Michael Ignatieff, eds., *Wealth and Virtue: The Shaping of Political Economy in the Scottish Enlightenment* (Cambridge: Cambridge University Press, 1983), p. 346 ("The similarities between Beccaria's ideas and those of the Scottish Enlightenment impressed other contemporaries. The great debate on the death penalty stimulated by Beccaria during his journey to Paris in 1766 drew interventions not only from Voltaire, Morellet, Marmontel and Grimm, but also from the Scottish painter and writer, Allan Ramsay. In January 1766, Ramsay sent to Diderot 'some reflections on the treatise of Crimes and Punishments which you and Suard mentioned at the Baron d'Holbach's during my stay in Paris'. Ramsay could not accept the Lockean and Rousseauian elements in Beccaria's work. He despised its egalitarian spirit, and dismissed the idea of a social contract as 'the product of all the petty grumbling that the liberty of each individual can engender'."); ibid., p. 349 ("[O]n 15 March 1767, the Baron d'Holbach had written to [Beccaria] from Paris: 'In England, a *History of Civil Society* by M. Ferguson is expected shortly, of which they speak very highly—we shall see if the author has freed himself from the national tendency to Platonism, which makes it very difficult to write good philosophy.'").

8. Thomas Jefferson was so taken with Beccaria's treatise that he copied—in Italian—more than two dozen passages from it into his commonplace book. John D. Bessler, *The Birth of American Law: An Italian Philosopher and the American Revolution* (Durham, NC: Carolina Academic Press, 2014), pp. 182–91. Although Jefferson admired Beccaria's work, it took considerable time for him to shake off the influence of more medieval sources of law in terms of his thinking on the criminal law. Markus D. Dubber, "'An Extraordinarily Beautiful Document': Jefferson's 'Bill for Proportioning Crimes and Punishments' and the Challenge of Republican Punishment," *in* Markus D. Dubber & Lindsay Farmer, eds., *Modern Histories of Crime and Punishment* (Stanford, CA: Stanford University Press, 2007), pp. 134–35 (discussing the influences on Jefferson—from Beccaria and Blackstone, to Montesquieu and Pufendorf, to Coke and Bracton, to Hale's seventeenth-century criminal law treatise—as he drafted a bill to revise Virginia's criminal law in the 1770s).

9. Janet Semple, *Bentham's Prison: A Study of the Panopticon Penitentiary* (Oxford: Clarendon Press, 1993), p. 63.

10. Bessler, *The Birth of American Law*, p. 4; John D. Bessler, *Cruel and Unusual: The American Death Penalty and the Founders' Eighth Amendment* (Boston: Northeastern University Press, 2012), p. 48.

11. Bessler, *The Birth of American Law*, p. 76.

12. *Archæologia Americana: Transactions and Collections of the American Antiquarian Society* (1874), Vol. 6, p. 629.

13. Joseph Priestley, *An Essay on the First Principles of Government, and on the Nature of Political, Civil, and Religious Liberty* (London: J. Johnson, 2d ed. 1771), pp. 73–74.

14. H. A. Washington, ed., *The Writings of Thomas Jefferson* (Cambridge: Cambridge University Press, 2011), Vol. 5, p. 91; Jack McLaughlin, *To His Excellency Thomas Jefferson: Letters to a President* (New York: Avon Books, 1993), p. 89; Nathaniel Chipman, *Sketches of the Principles of Government* (Rutland, VT: J. Lyon, 1793), pp. 70, 74, 190, 193; Jean-Baptiste Say, *A Treatise on Political Economy, or the Production, Distribution, and Consumption of Wealth* (Philadelphia: Claxton, Remsen & Haffelfinger, new Am. ed., C. R. Prinsep, trans., 1880), pp. xxxvi, 91 n.* (introduction by Clement C.

Biddle); *see also* ibid., p. 458 n.* ("The efficacy of the characteristics of punishment has been placed beyond all doubt by Beccaria, in his tract, *Dei delitti e delle pene.*"). Cesare Beccaria's writings on the division of labor have been consulted and cited by a wide range of economists, from ardent capitalists to Karl Marx. Rob Beamish, *Marx, Method, and the Division of Labor* (Urbana: University of Illinois Press, 1992), pp. 81, 98–99 & nn.43 & 48, 159 n.97, 170.

15. "Presents Received by the American Philosophical Society, Since the Publication of Their 2d Vol. of Transactions," *Transactions of the American Philosophical Society* (1793), Vol. 3, pp. 351, 355; *Early Proceedings of the American Philosophical Society for the Promotion of Useful Knowledge, Compiled by One of the Secretaries, from the Manuscript of Minutes of Its Meetings from 1744 to 1838* (Philadelphia: McCalla & Stavely, 1884), pp. 144, 162–63, 211; *Catalogue of the Library of the American Philosophical Society Held at Philadelphia for Promoting Useful Knowledge* (Philadelphia: Joseph R. A. Skerrett, 1824), pp. 4, 141; *Catalogue of the American Philosophical Library* (Philadelphia: M'Calla & Stavely, 1878), Vol. 3, pp. 879; John G. Gazley, *The Life of Arthur Young, 1741–1820* (Philadelphia: American Philosophical Society, 1973), p. 248; Jared Sparks, ed., *The Works of Benjamin Franklin* (Boston: Whittemore, Niles, and Hall, 1856), Vol. 1, p. 319; Murphy D. Smith, *Oak from an Acorn: A History of the American Philosophical Library, 1770–1803* (Scholarly Resources, 1976), p. 75; *The Biographical Dictionary of the Society for the Diffusion of Useful Knowledge* (London: Longman, Brown, Green, and Longmans, 1843), Vol. 2, Part II (entry for "Amoretti, Carlo"); Dino Carpanetto & Giuseppe Ricuperati, *Italy in the Age of Reason, 1685–1789* (New York: Longman, 1987), Vol. 5, pp. 225, 304; *The Foreign Quarterly Review* (London: Treuttel and Würtz, Treuttel, Jr. and Richter, 1828), Vol. 2, p. 631; *Atti della Società Patriotica di Milano* (Milano: Nell' Imperial Monistero di S. Amrrogio Maggiore, 1783), Vol. 1, p. 25.

16. Bessler, *The Birth of American Law*, p. 4.

17. Ibid.

18. William Eden, *Principles of Penal Law* (London: B. White, 1771), pp. 235, 264, 296.

19. Bessler, *The Birth of American Law*, p. 80.

20. Francis Gribble, *Lake Geneva and Its Literary Landmarks* (New York: E. P. Dutton & Co., 1901), pp. 271, 274.

21. Maestro, *Cesare Beccaria and the Origins of Penal Reform*, p. 43.

22. Pier Luigi Porta, "Lombard Enlightenment and Classical Political Economy," p. 34, *available at* http://www.eshet.net/public/lecture2.pdf; Cesare Beccaria Biography, http://www.biography.com/people/cesare-beccaria-39630#economics; *see also* Hiroshi Mizuta, *Adam Smith's Library: A Supplement to Bonar's Catalogue with a Check-list of Whole Library*, pp. 4, 149 (Cambridge: Cambridge University Press, 1967) (noting that Adam Smith's library contained " 'Opere del Marchese Beccaria Bonesana 3 Toms.' [Opere diverse. Napoli 1770–71. 3 vols.]" and listing Pietro Verri's "Meditazioni sulla economia politica. [Anon.]"); John Cunningham Wood, ed., *Adam Smith: Critical Assessments* (New York: Routledge, 1996), p. 102 ("The Italians are represented by Beccaria's *Works* and by Verri's *Meditazione sulla economia politica....*"). The comprehensive scope of Beccaria's *Elementi* is described elsewhere, along with the sources and authorities, including Montesquieu's *l'Esprit des Lois* (1748) and Pietro Verri's *Meditazione Sulla Economia Politica* (1771), known to Beccaria at the time. Ibid., pp. 21–23, 25–27, 277. Adam Smith's own library contained some of Cesare Beccaria's writings and the 1772 Livorno edition of Pietro Verri's book. Mizuta, *Adam Smith's Library*, pp. 4, 149. Smith also owned an Italian dictionary, and Smith's "reading ability in Italian is well documented." Ibid., p. 106; Groenewegen, *Eighteenth-century Economics*, pp. 273, 278; *see also* W.P.D. Wightman, J.C. Bryce & I.S. Ross, eds., *Adam Smith: Essays on Philosophical Subjects* (Oxford: Oxford University Press, 1980), pp. 217–25 (reprinting Smith's essay "Of the Affinity Between Certain English and Italian Verses").

23. James Bonar, ed., *A Catalogue of the Library of Adam Smith: Author of the 'Moral Sentiments' and 'The Wealth of Nations'* (London: Macmillan and Co., 1894), pp. 12, 70–71, 177.

24. Adam Smith, *An Inquiry into the Nature and Causes of the Wealth of Nations* (1776), Vol. 2, *available at* http://oll.libertyfund.org/titles/smith-an-inquiry-into-the-nature-and-causes-of-the-wealth-of-nations-cannan-ed-vol-2?q=Milan#Smith_0206-02_777.

25. Groenewegen, *Eighteenth-century Economics*, pp. 16–17; Keith Tribe & Hiroshi Mizuta, eds., *A Critical Bibliography of Adam Smith* (New York: Routledge, 2016), pp. 73–75; Richard Vann De Berg & Christophe Salvat, "Scottish Subtlety: André Morellet's Comments on *The Wealth of Nations*,

European Journal of the History of Economic Thought, Vol. 8, Iss. 2 (2001).

26. Groenewegen, *Eighteenth-century Economics*, pp. 10–11, 20–21 & Table 1.1; Adam Smith, *The Theory of Moral Sentiments* (London: A. Millar, 2d ed. 1761).

27. Dennis C. Rasmussen, *The Problems and Promise of Commercial Society: Adam Smith's Response to Rousseau* (University Park, PA: The Pennsylvania State University Press, 2008), pp. 52–53; "Victor Riqueti, marquis de Mirabeau," Encyclopædia Britannica, https://www.britannica.com/biography/Victor-Riqueti-marquis-de-Mirabeau; Mark G. Spencer, ed., *David Hume: Historical Thinker, Historical Writer* (University Park, PA: The Pennsylvania State University Press, 2013); Friedrich List, *The Natural System of Political Economy* (New York: Routledge, 2016); Steven N. Durlauf & Lawrence E. Blume, eds., *The New Palgrave Dictionary of Economics* (New York: Palgrave Macmillan 2d ed. 2008), pp. 237, 424; Oscar Gelderblom, *The Political Economy of the Dutch Republic* (Surrey, England: Ashgate, 2009), p. 33; Erik S. Reinert, "Full Circle: Economics from Scholasticism through Innovation and Back into Mathematical Scholasticism — Reflection on a 1769 Price Essay: 'Why is it that economics so far has gained so few advantages from physics and mathematics?'", 27 *Journal of Economic Studies* 364, 369 (2000). For the latter point and the list of economists cited in Cesare Beccaria's lectures on economics, I am grateful to Carlo Scognamiglio Pasini. François Forbonnais (1722–1800), the French economist and contributor to the *Encyclopédie*, published *Elémens du Commerce* in 1754 and *Principes et observations oeconomiques* in 1767. Forbonnais uses mathematical symbols in his *Elémens du Commerce*. Durlauf & Blume, *The New Palgrave Dictionary of Economics*, p. 447.

28. Bernard E. Harcourt, "Beccaria's *On Crimes and Punishments*: A Mirror on the History of the Foundations of Modern Criminal Law," *in* Markus D. Dubber, ed., *Foundational Texts in Modern Criminal Law* (Oxford: Oxford University Press, 2014), p. 41; Dominic R. Massaro, *Cesare Beccaria: The Father of Criminal Justice: His Impact on Anglo-American Jurisprudence* (Cecina: Tecnostampa, 1991), p. 11; Ian Davidson, *Voltaire in Exile: The Last Years, 1753–78* (New York: Grove Press, 2006), p. 154; A. Esmein, *A History of Continental Criminal Procedure: With Special Reference to France* (Boston: Little, Brown, and Co., John Simpson, trans. 1913), pp. 364, 371–72.

29. Michael Sonenscher, ed., *Emmanuel Joseph Sieyès: Political Writings: Including the Debate Between Sieyès and Tom Paine in 1791* (Indianapolis, IN: Hackett Publishing Co., 2003), pp. 123–24.

30. Bessler, *The Birth of American Law*, p. 63; Bessler, *Cruel and Unusual*, p. 39; Margaret Plant, *Venice: Fragile City 1797–1997* (New Haven, CT: Yale University Press, 2002), p. 24; John W. Freeman, *The Metropolitan Opera Stories of the Great Operas* (New York: W. W. Norton & Co., 1984), p. 307; Christopher F. Black, *Early Modern Italy: A Social History* (London: Routledge, 2001), p. 213; Richard Bellamy, ed., *Beccaria: On Crimes and Punishments and Other Writings* (Cambridge: Cambridge University Press, Richard Davies, trans. 2003), p. xxxv; The Doge's Palace, http://www.reidsitaly.com/destinations/veneto/venice/sights/palazzo_ducale.html.

31. Ardis B. Collins, ed., *Hegel on the Modern World* (Albany: State University of New York Press, 1995), p. 222; Francis T. Cullen & Pamela Wilcox, eds., *Encyclopedia of Criminological Theory* (Thousand Oaks, CA: Sage Publications, 2010), p. 76.

32. Serge Dauchy, Georges Martyn, Anthony Musson, Heikki Pihlajamäki & Alain Wijffels, eds., *The Formation and Transmission of Western Legal Culture: 150 Books that Made the Law in the Age of Printing* (Cham, Switzerland, Springer, 2016), p. 292.

33. Piers Beirne, *Inventing Criminology: Essays on the Rise of 'Homo Criminalis'* (Albany: State University of New York Press, 1993), p. 48; Bernard E. Harcourt, "Beccaria's *On Crimes and Punishments*: A Mirror on the History of the Foundations of Modern Criminal Law," *in* Markus D. Dubber, ed., *Foundational Texts in Modern Criminal Law* (Oxford: Oxford University Press, 2014), p. 41.

34. Groenewegen, *Eighteenth-century Economics*, p. 12; Lidia De Michelis, "Letters from London: A 'Bridge' Between Italy and Europe," *in* Frank O'Gorman & Lia Guerra, eds., *The Centre and the Margins in Eighteenth-Century British and Italian Cultures* (Newcastle upon Tyne, UK: Cambridge Scholars Publishing, 2013), p. 54 n.70; Voltaire Foundation, "Never the twain shall meet: the correspondence of Pietro and Alessandro Verri (1766–1797)," May 26, 2016, https://voltairefoundation.wordpress.com/2016/05/26/never-the-twain-shall-meet-the-correspondence-of-pietro-and-alessandro-verri-1766-1797/.

35. Maestro, *Cesare Beccaria and the Origins of Penal Reform*, pp. 51–52.

36. Ibid., pp. 52–55.

37. Groenewegen, *Eighteenth-century Economics*, pp. 12, 16, 20, 41 n.13, 92 n.6, 134, 136, 382–83; Bonar, *A Catalogue of the Library of Adam Smith: Author of the 'Moral Sentiments' and 'The Wealth of Nations'*, pp. 70–71.

38. Maestro, *Cesare Beccaria and the Origins of Penal Reform*, pp. 86–87, 94.

39. Antoine Lilti, *The World of the Salons: Sociability and Worldliness in Eighteenth-Century Paris* (Oxford: Oxford University Press, Lydia G. Cochrane, trans. 2015), pp. 33, 59, 129; *see also* Marta Cavazza, "Between Modesty and Spectacle: Women and Science in Eighteenth-Century Italy," *in* Paula Findlen, Wendy Wassyng Roworth & Catherine M. Sama, eds., *Italy's Eighteenth-Century: Gender and Culture in the Age of the Grand Tour* (Stanford: Stanford University Press, 2009), p. 294 ("Eighteenth-century aristocratic society, both in Bologna and Milan, was different from that of preceding centuries. New forms of sociability had arisen. On the one hand, there were the salons, which were private forms of aggregation and political and cultural influence; on the other hand, there were the public institutions of culture—academies and museums—desired by and financed by a political power which had begun to consider the problem of the education and the consent of its subjects.").

40. Groenewegen, *Eighteenth-century Economics*, p. 273.

41. Mia Pia Donato, "The Temple of Female Glory: Female Self-Affirmation in the Roman Salon of the Grand Tour," *in* Findlen, Roworth & Sama, *Italy's Eighteenth Century*, pp. 66–67.

42. Waltraud Heindl, "People, Class Structure, and Society," *in* Raymond Erickson, ed., *Schubert's Vienna* (New Haven: Yale University Press, 1997), p. 46.

43. Lisa Curtis-Wendlandt, Paul Gibbard & Karen Green, eds., *Political Ideas of Enlightenment Women: Virtue and Citizenship* (New York: Routledge, 2016), p. 10.

44. Marianna D'Ezio, "Italian Women Intellectuals and Their Cultural Networks: The Making of a European 'Life of the Mind,'" *in* Gibbard & Green, *Political Ideas of Enlightenment Women*, p. 113 n.21.

45. Karen Green, *A History of Women's Political Thought in Europe, 1700–1800* (Cambridge: Cambridge University Press, 2014), pp. 93–94. In the eighteenth century, Italian women got involved in journalism, too. For example, Elisabetta Caminer Turra, who went by "Bettina" and who was the daughter of a journalist and publisher, Domenico Caminer, started her journalistic activity in 1768 at age seventeen. "The topics she wrote on," *A History of Women's Writing in Italy* emphasizes, "were wide-ranging: literature, with much attention paid to contemporary European literature, scientific matters, pharmaceutics, medicine, botany, agriculture, history, politics, entomology, religion, geography, economics, education, even philosophy (for example she reviewed Soave's Italian translation of John Locke, in *Giornale enciclopedico*, May 1777)." As that source continues of her writings: "There is much emphasis on Voltaire, and on typical Enlightenment concerns, such as issues of legislation and opposition to torture (she wrote in praise of Beccaria in *Giornale enciclopedico*, May 1782), not neglecting current affairs (in October 1789 she expressed guarded approval of the recent revolutionary events in Paris)." Verina R. Jones, "Journalism, 1750–1850," *in* Letizia Panizza & Sharon Wood, eds., *A History of Women's Writing in Italy* (Cambridge: Cambridge University Press, 2000), pp. 122–23.

46. Nancy W. Collins, The Problem of the Enlightenment Salon: European History or Post-Revolutionary Politics 1755–1850, UCL Department of History (2006), pp. 130–31.

47. "Conqueror of Paris," *The New York Review of Books*, Dec. 17, 1992 (book review).

48. Roger Chartier, "The Man of Letters," *in* Michel Vovelle, ed., *Enlightenment Portraits* (Chicago: The University of Chicago Press, Lydia G. Cochrane, trans. 1997), p. 152; Carlo Capra, "The Functionary," *in* Vovelle, *Enlightenment Portraits*, p. 336; Daniel Roche, *France in the Enlightenment* (Cambridge, MA: Harvard University Press, Arthur Goldhammer, trans. 1998), p. 45.

49. Karen Sullivan, *The Inner Lives of Medieval Inquisitors* (Chicago: The University of Chicago Press, 2011), p. 169.

50. Antoine Lilti, *The World of the Salons: Sociability and Worldliness in Eighteenth-century Paris* (Oxford: Oxford University Press, Lydia G. Cochrane, trans. 2015), pp. 71, 85–86; Maestro, *Cesare Beccaria and the Origins of Penal Reform*, pp. 61–63.

51. Michael Rapport, *Nationality and Citizenship in Revolutionary France: The Treatment of Foreigners 1789–1799* (Oxford: Clarendon Press, 2000), p. 63.

52. Richard Butterwick, *The Polish Revolution and the Catholic Church, 1788–1792* (Oxford: Oxford University Press, 2012), p. 285; Dieter Rössner & Jörg-Martin Jehle, eds., *Beccaria als Wegbereiter der*

Kriminologie: Verleihung der Beccaria-Medaille durch die Neue Kriminologische Gesellschaft (Mönchengladbach: Forum Verlag Godesberg GmbH, 2000), p. 29.

53. Francis Steegmuller, *A Woman, a Man, and Two Kingdoms: The Story of Madame D'Épinay and Abbé Galiani* (New York: Alfred A. Knopf, 1991), pp. 60–61; Roberto Bizzocchi, *A Lady's Man: The Cicisbei, Private Morals and National Identity in Italy* (New York: Palgrave Macmillan, Noor Giovanni Mazhar, trans. 2014), pp. 75–79; Koen Stapelbroek, *Love, Self-Deceit, and Money: Commerce and Morality in the Early Neapolitan Enlightenment* (Toronto: University of Toronto Press, 2008), p. 3; T. Adolphus Trollope, "The Homes and Haunts of the Italian Poets," *Belgravia: An Illustrated London Magazine* (London: Chatto and Windus, 1879), Vol. 39, pp. 159, 168–70; *The Athenæum: Journal of Literature, Science, and the Fine Arts* (London: James Holmes, 1859), p. 349 (March 12, 1859 issue); Philipp Blom, *A Wicked Company: The Forgotten Radicalism of the European Enlightenment* (New York: Basic Books, 2010), p. 171; "Ferdinando Galiani: Italian economist," https://www.britannica.com/biography/Ferdinando-Galiani; *compare* Sylvanus Urban, *The Gentleman's Magazine: and Historical Chronicle* (London: John Nichols, 1789), Vol. 65, p. 39 ("*Tric-trac* is a game more intricate and far superior to that of backgammon. It is still played by the French, and the board or tables are called by them *le tric-trac*, which are made with pegholes in the margin or border, for insertion of pegs to mark the progress of the game.").

54. Lacy Collison-Morley, *Modern Italian Literature* (Boston: Little, Brown, and Co., 1912), p. 46.

55. Cavazza, "Between Modesty and Spectacle," *in* Findlen, Roworth & Sama, *Italy's Eighteenth-Century*, p. 286; Giuliano Pancaldi, *Volta: Science and Culture in the Age of Enlightenment* (Princeton, NJ: Princeton University Press, 2003), p. 33; E. Cobham Brewer, *Dictionary of Phrase and Fable* (London: Cassell & Co., 1885), p. 151; C. A. M. Fennell, *The Stanford Dictionary of Anglicised Words and Phrases* (Cambridge: Cambridge University Press, 1892), p. 221; Arnold J. Cooley, *The Toilet and Cosmetic Arts in Ancient and Modern Times* (London: Robert Hardwicke, 1866), p. 85; Bizzocchi, *A Lady's Man*, pp. 75–79.

56. Robert Casillo, *The Empire of Stereotypes: Germaine de Staël and the Idea of Italy* (New York: Palgrave Macmillan, 2006), pp. 109–10.

57. Randolph Trumbach, *The Rise of the Egalitarian Family: Aristocratic Kinship and Domestic Relations in Eighteenth-century England* (New York: Academic Press, 1978), p. 126.

58. Dena Goodman, *The Republic of Letters: A Cultural History of the French Enlightenment* (Ithaca, NY: Cornell University Press, 1994), pp. 108, 166.

59. Harcourt, "Beccaria's *On Crimes and Punishments*," *in* Dubber, *Foundational Texts in Modern Criminal Law*, pp. 41–42; *Studies on Voltaire and the Eighteenth Century* (Institut et musée Voltaire, 1978), Vol. 174, p. 197; Serge Dauchy, Georges Martyn, Anthony Musson, Heikki Pihlajamäki & Alain Wijffels, eds., *The Formation and Transmission of Western Legal Culture: 150 Books that Made the Law in the Age of Printing* (Cham, Switzerland, Springer, 2016), p. 90; Maestro, *Cesare Beccaria and the Origins of Penal Reform*, pp. 47, 56–58; Lilti, *The World of the Salons*, p. 60; Bizzocchi, *A Lady's Man*, pp. 196–98; Massaro, *Cesare Beccaria*, p. 9; "The Chateau Ferney," http://www.visitvoltaire.com/voltaire's_later_life_chateau_ferney.htm; Maestro, *Cesare Beccaria and the Origins of Penal Reform*, p. 45. The bookseller's full name was Barthélemy Chirol. *The Complete Works of Voltaire* (Institut et Musée Voltaire, 2006), Vol. 63, p. 131; *see also The History of the Book in the West: 1700–1800*, Vol. 3, p. 241 (Burlington, VT: Ashgate, 2010) ("Cesare Beccaria bought most of the classics of *philosophic* during the 1760s and 1770s, mainly through the Swiss bookseller Barthélemy Chirol, but he sold his library to the Turin-based French booksellers Reycends in 1777.... The inventory of Pietro Verri's library enumerates only some 300 works; but he enjoyed free access to all the libraries of the aristocracy in Milan, including the prestigious 40,000-volume collection of the Habsburg Plenipotentiary in Lombardy, count Carlo di Firmian.").

60. Maestro, *Cesare Beccaria and the Origins of Penal Reform*, pp. 44–45; Simon Harvey, ed., Voltaire, *Treatise on Tolerance and Other Writings* (Cambridge: Cambridge University Press, Brian Masters, trans. 2000), p. xxiv; *The Complete Works of Voltaire* (Institut et Musée Voltaire, 2006), Vol. 63, p. 131. On August 1, 1767, Chivol—a bookseller in Geneva—wrote to Cesare Beccaria, inquiring if Beccaria would travel to Ferney and noting that the great Voltaire would be pleased to know him personally. In May 1771, Giuseppe Gorani also wrote to Cesare Beccaria to tell him that Voltaire spoke

highly of him (Beccaria) when he (Gorani) visted Voltaire at Ferney. M. César Cantù, *Beccaria et le droit penal: essai* (Paris: Librairie de Firmin-Didot et Cie, 1885), p. 100; *see also* A. v. Rinaldini, *Beccaria: Biographische Skizze nach Cesare Cantù "Beccaria e il diritto penale"* (Wien: Wilhelm Braumüller, 1865), p. 51.

61. Rosamaria Loretelli, "The First English Translation of Cesare Beccaria's *On Crimes and Punishments*: Uncovering the Editorial and Political Contexts," *Diciottesimo Secolo*, anno II, 2017, pp. 1–22; *see also* ibid., p. 20 ("As to the presence of the *Commentary*, it should be noted that this was the very first translation of Voltaire's text, which had been published anonymously in France in early September 1766 and which, by February 1767, had run through six editions, plus a few pirated ones. An Italian version would appear as a separate volume a few months after the English translation, and only in 1769 would be issued in one volume with Beccaria's *Dei delitti e delle pene*.").

Chapter 4

1. Harcourt, *The Illusion of Free Markets*, p. 55; Peter Brand & Lino Pertile, eds., *The Cambridge History of Italian Literature* (Cambridge: Cambridge University Press, 1996), p. 380.

2. *Encyclopædia; or A Dictionary of Arts, Sciences, and Miscellaneous Literature* (Philadelphia: Thomas Dobson, 1798), Vol. VIII, p. 146.

3. Richard Bellamy, ed., Cesare Beccaria, On Crimes and Punishments *and Other Writings* (Cambridge: Cambridge University Press, Richard Davies, trans. 1995), pp. 79–82; Maestro, *Cesare Beccaria and the Origins of Penal Reform*, pp. 64–67.

4. Wayne R. Dynes, ed., *Encyclopedia of Homosexuality* (New York: Routledge, 1990), Vol. 1, pp. 121–22; *see also* ibid., p. 600 ("Cesare Beccaria, in his treatise *Dei delitti e delle pene* (1764), attacked the concept of infamy in the Roman law of late feudal and early modern Europe, and the favorable reception of his work in the early Republic accounted for the reference to 'a capital, or otherwise infamous crime' in the Fifth Amendment to the American Constitution.").

5. *Italian Americana* (State University of New York at Buffalo, 1976), Vol. 3, pp. 86–87.

6. Bizzocchi, *A Lady's Man*, pp. 209–10.

7. Emiliana Pasca Noether, *The American Constitution as a Symbol and Reality for Italy* (Boston, MA: Pirandello Lyceum Press, 1989), p. 38.

8. Lidia De Michelis, "Letters from London: A 'Bridge' Between Italy and Europe," *in* Frank O'Gorman & Lia Guerra, eds., *The Centre and the Margins in Eighteenth-Century British and Italian Cultures* (Newcastle upon Tyne, UK: Cambridge Scholars Publishing, 2013), pp. 36, 43–47. In one of her novels, *The Valley of Decision*, set in late eighteenth-century Italy, Edith Wharton included passages about both Pietro Verri and Cesare Beccaria, and she took note of "the brilliant gazette" which "Verri and his associates were then publishing in Milan, and in which all the questions of the day, theological, economic and literary, were discussed with a freedom possible only under the lenient Austrian rule." Edith Wharton, *The Valley of Decision* (1902), *available at* https://www.mirrorservice.org/sites/gutenberg.org/4/3/2/4327/4327-h/4327-h.htm. According to another source: "The 'Caffe' was to be thoroughly popular in style and to encourage the average reader to take an interest in the new theories that were springing up abroad, in science, art, trade and, above all, in agriculture, as the chief source of the nation's wealth." Lacy Collison-Morley, *Modern Italian Literature* (Boston: Little, Brown, and Co., 1912), p. 42. "The 'Caffe'," that source notes, "was strongly opposed to the narrow provincialism of the day and one of its best articles is directed against the habit of calling natives of other parts of the peninsula foreigners, for Italy was essentially a single country." Ibid., p. 43. Although the trip to Paris "caused a misunderstanding between Beccaria and the Verris, in which both sides were probably to blame," that source further notes, "many years later the breach was healed and they died friends." Ibid., p. 47.

9. Graeme R. Newman & Pietro Marongiu, eds. & trans., Cesare Beccaria, *On Crimes and Punishments* (New Brunswick, NJ: Transaction Publishers, 5th ed. 2009), p. lxii; Lidia De Michelis, "Letters from London: A 'Bridge' Between Italy and Europe," *in* Frank O'Gorman & Lia Guerra, eds., *The Centre and the Margins in Eighteenth-Century British and Italian Cultures* (Newcastle upon Tyne: Cambridge Scholars Publishing, 2013), p. 47; Kevin J. Hayes, *The Road to Monticello: The Life and*

Mind of Thomas Jefferson (Oxford: Oxford University Press, 2008), p. 282; *An English Ilustrado: The Reverend John Bowle* (Bern: Peter Lang, 1977), p. 56; Giuseppe Marc'Antonio Baretti, https://en. wikipedia.org/wiki/Giuseppe_Marc'Antonio_Baretti; Molini, http://edpopehistory.co.uk/entries/ molini/1802-04-20-000000; *Travellers in Northern Italy: States of Sardinia, Lombardy and Venice, Parma and Piacenza, Modena, Lucca, Mass-Carrara, and Tuscany, as Far as the Val D'Arno* (London: John Murray and Son, 1842), p. 487; Christina Ionescu, ed., *Book Illustration in the Long Eighteenth Century: Reconfiguring the Visual Periphery of the Text* (Newcastle upon Tyne, UK: Cambridge Scholar Publishing, 2011), p. 84; *The European Indicator or Road-Book for Travellers on the Continent* (Florence: Félix le Monnier, 1841) pp. 108–9; Josiah Henry Benton, *John Baskerville: Type-Founder and Printer 1706– 1775* (Boston, 1914), pp. 41–42; *The Bodleian Library Record* (1982), Vol. 10, p. 55; *Mélanges de l'Ecole française de Rome: Italie et Méditerranée*, Vol. 102 (L'Ecole, 1990), pp. 27, 262–63; Herbert Edmund Poole, ed., *Music, Men, and Manners in France and Italy, 1770: Being the Journal Written by Charles Burney during a Tour through Those Countries Undertaken to Collect Material for a General History of Music* (London: Eulenburg Books, 1969), p. 106; Giovanni Claudio Molini (1724–1812), http://data.bnf.fr/atelier/12230833/giovanni_claudio_molini/; "Molini, Giovanni Claudio (1724– 1812)," https://www.idref.fr/031006795; Kristian Jensen, *Revolution and the Antiquarian Book: Reshaping the Past, 1780–1815* (Cambridge: Cambridge University Press, 2011), p. 214 n.105; *The Athenæum: Journal of Literature, Science, and the Fine Arts* (London: Dec. 17, 1859 issue), p. 811. Another guide-book for Florence contains this information: "Sig. Giuseppe Molini has a good Printing-office … and likewise a large Library for sale. He has also kept for several years, in the Via degli Archibusieri, a large Bookseller's Shop; containing, besides books and engravings, English paper, pens, pencils, &c." Mariana Starke, *Information and Directions for Travellers on the Continent* (London: John Murray, 1828), p. 493.

10. Massaro, *Cesare Beccaria*, p. 8; *Italy: A Complete Guide to 1,000 Towns and Cities and Their Landmarks, with 80 Regional Tours* (Milano: Touring Club of Italy, 1999), p. 228.

11. Cesare Beccaria, *On Crimes and Punishments* (New Brunswick, NJ: Transaction Publishers, Graeme R. Newman & Pietro Marongiu, trans. 5th ed. 2009), p. lxvii; Ronald Findlay, Rolf G.H. Henriksson, Håkan Lindgren & Mats Lundahl, eds., *Eli Heckscher, International Trade, and Economic History* (Cambridge, MA: The MIT Press, 2006), p. 294 n.30; Maestro, *Cesare Beccaria and the Origins of Penal Reform*, p. 68; Giovanni Di Leonardo, *L'illuminista abruzzese Don Trojano Odazj: dalle lezioni di Genovesi all'amicizia con Beccaria, dalla cattedra di economia alla cospirazione* (Media Edizioni 2003), p. 46; Maria Bonesana di Beccaria, https://www.geni.com/people/Maria-Bonesana-di-Beccaria/ 6000000028919142914; Giovanni Annibale Bonesana di Beccaria, https://www.geni.com/people/ Giovanni-Annibale-Bonesana-di-Beccaria/6000000028919151155; Margherita Bonesana di Beccaria, https://www.geni.com/people/Margherita-Bonesana-di-Beccaria/6000000028918719107.

12. Constance Jocelyn Ffoulkes & Rodolfo Maiocchi, *Vincenzo Foppa of Brescia, Founder of the Lombard School: His Life and Work* (New York: John Lane Company, 1909), p. 53. Alessandro Manzoni was born in 1783. Bizzocchi, *A Lady's Man*, p. 216.

13. Robert Ignatius Letellier, ed. & trans., *The Diaries of Giacomo Meyerbeer: The Years of Celebrity, 1850–1856* (Cranbury, NJ: Associated University Presses, 2002), Vol. 3, p. 413 n.120; Rebecca Harris-Warrick & Bruce Alan Brown, eds., *The Grotesque Dancer on the Eighteenth-Century Stage: Gennaro Magri and His World* (Madison, WI: The University of Wisconsin Press, 2005), pp. 15–16, 44, 173, 298.

14. Renée Baernstein, *A Convent Tale: A Century of Sisterhood in Spanish Milan* (London: Routledge, 2002), p. 181; *The Conservation of Tapestries and Embroideries: Proceedings of Meetings at the Institut Royal du Patrimoine Artistique, Brussels, Belgium September 21–24, 1987* (The Getty Conservation In-stitute, 1989), p. 31; Maestro, *Cesare Beccaria and the Origins of Penal Reform*, p. 103; San Paolo Converso, https://en.wikipedia.org/wiki/San_Paolo_Converso.

15. *Italian Journal* (Italian Academy Foundation, 2002), Vols. 18–19, p. 46.

16. Marco E. L. Guidi & Massimo M. Augello, "Economic Treatises and Textbooks in Italy: A Comparative Analysis of 18th- and 19th-century Political Economy," in *L'Économie politique et al sphère publique dans le débat des lumières* (Jesús Astigarraga & Javier Usoz, eds.) (Madrid: Case de Valázqvez, 2013), pp. 110–11, 114–16; *see also* Franco Venturi & R. Burr Litchfield, *The End of the Old Regime in Europe, 1776–1789, Part I: The Great States of the West* (Princeton, NJ: Princeton Uni-

versity Press, R. Burr Litchfield, trans. 1991), p. 206 ("In the summer of 1788 Pietro Verri received direct news from Portugal from Michele Blasco, the brother of Teresa, Beccaria's first wife. He had been a 'captain of engineers in Brazil for ten years' and had ruined his career by leaving it without permission. For this he had spent eight months in prison and was finally liberated by the new queen.").

17. Maestro, *Cesare Beccaria and the Origins of Penal Reform*, pp. 96–97, 114; Richard Bellamy, ed., *Beccaria: On Crimes and Punishments and Other Writings* (Cambridge: Cambridge University Press, Richard Davies, trans., 1995), p. xlv; Feingold, *History of Universities*, p. 126; "Biumi, Giuseppe," *Dizionario Biografico degli Italiani*, Vol. 10 (1968), http://www.treccani.it/enciclopedia/giuseppe-biumi_(Dizionario-Biografico)/. A portion of Cesare Beccaria's lecture notes have never been located. As academic Bernard Harcourt explains: "Beccaria understood the science of public economy to include, at its very core, the science of the police. By a curious twist of fate, however, Beccaria's lecture notes on 'police'—as well as those on taxation and public finance—are missing. The *Elementi* that have come down to us today contain parts 1, 2, 3, and 4—but go no further. The lectures on 'police' have never been found, an accident of history that has proven strangely productive and come to distort our reading of Beccaria's writings on punishment." Harcourt, *The Illusion of Free Markets*, p. 66. Beccaria's ideas on economics nonetheless continued to be sought out even many decades after Beccaria delivered his lectures. For example, in the July 1, 1905 edition of *The Publishers' Circular*, it was noted under the heading "BOOKS WANTED" that a J. G. Glover—a bookseller at 8 Terminus Buildings in Eastbourne—was seeking a 1769 edition of "Beccaria's Lecture on Political Economy." *The Publishers' Circular and Booksellers' Record of British and Foreign Literature*, Vol. 83, p. 25 (containing the July 1, 1905 edition of The Publishers' Circular).

18. Christopher John White, Competition and Cooperation in Economic and Christian Thought: Towards a Better Understanding, Ph.D. thesis, The Australian National University (Aug. 2016), p. 260; Jesús Astigarraga & Javier Usoz, eds., *L'Économie politique et la Sphère publique dans le débat des lumières* (Madrid: Casa de Valáquez, 2013), p. 114; Maestro, *Cesare Beccaria and the Origins of Penal Reform*, pp. 95, 101–2.

19. Maestro, *Cesare Beccaria and the Origins of Penal Reform*, pp. 103–4.

20. Antonio Pace, ed. & trans., *Luigi Castiglioni's Viaggio: Travels in the United States of North America 1785–87* (Syracuse, NY: Syracuse University Press, 1983), p. xii.

21. John Hostettler, *Cesare Beccaria: The Genius of 'On Crimes and Punishments'* (Hampshire, UK: Waterside Press, 2011), pp. 32–33; Gaetana Marrone, ed., *Encyclopedia of Italian Literary Studies* (New York: Routledge, 2007), Vol. 1, pp. 147–48; Bizzocchi, *A Lady's Man*, p. 216; Groenewegen, *Eighteenth-century Economics*, p. 10; Maestro, *Cesare Beccaria and the Origins of Penal Reform*, pp. 98–100; Alessandro Manzoni Biography, https://www.enotes.com/topics/alessandro-manzoni; The House, http://www.casadelmanzoni.it/content/house?language=en.

22. David Williams, *The Enlightenment* (Cambridge: Cambridge University Press, 1999), p. 440; Maestro, *Cesare Beccaria and the Origins of Penal Reform*, pp. 60–61, 97–99.

23. Groenewegen, *Eighteenth-century Economics*, pp. 36, 254; Maestro, *Cesare Beccaria and the Origins of Penal Reform*, pp. 100–101.

24. Bizzocchi, *A Lady's Man*, pp. 197–99. Notably, Cesare Beccaria and Bartolomeo Calderara seem to have quickly patched up their relationship after Teresa's death. As Roberto Bizzocchi points out: "Calderara overcame his indignation towards his friend, and perhaps resumed with him and his new wife the habit of a *ménage à trois*, in view of the fact that on 23 August 1775 a foreign correspondent wrote to Beccaria: 'I pray to pay my best regards to Madame the Marquise, and my compliments to the Marquis Calderara.'" Ibid., p. 199.

25. Another copy of "Elementi di Economia Pubblica" dated 1769, probably written by a secretary under dictation of Cesare Beccaria, now resides in the Biblioteca Braidense. It was that text that was probably used by Pietro Custodi in 1804 for the published edition of Beccaria's economic writings. Differences between the manuscripts held in the Biblioteca Ambrosiana and the Biblioteca Braidense are—as Italian economist Carlo Scognamiglio Pasini points out in discussing those manuscripts—small or negligible.

26. Hostettler, *Cesare Beccaria*, p. 33; Bessler, *The Birth of American Law*, p. 71; Bizzocchi, *A Lady's Man*, pp. 194, 216; Marrone, *Encyclopedia of Italian Literary Studies*, p. 147; Art & History: Manzoni House: A Tour of the Museum, http://www.hotelwindsormilan.com/en/manzoni-house-a-

tour-of-the-museum/; Villa Beccaria Lake Como, http://www.villaatlakecomo.com/villadetails/villa-beccaria-lake-como.html; https://translate.google.com/translate?hl=en&sl=it&u=https://it.wikipedia.org/wiki/Giulia_Beccaria&prev=search; Biography of Cesare Beccaria, https://edukalife.blogspot.com/2016/04/biography-of-cesare-beccaria.html.

27. Bessler, *The Birth of American Law*, p. 74; Alessandro Manzoni, *The Betrothed* (London: Penguin Books, 1983); The Betrothed (by Alessandro Manzoni), http://www.encyclopedia.com/arts/culture-magazines/betrothed.

28. Bizzocchi, *A Lady's Man*, pp. 1–5, 11, 18–19, 176–77.

29. Matthew Francis Rusnak, The Trial of Giuseppe Baretti, October 20th 1769: A Literary and Cultural History of the Baretti Case, Ph.D. dissertation, Graduate School-New Brunswick, Rutgers, The State University of New Jersey, Graduate Program in Italian (May 2008), pp. 80–88, 90–93, 109, 125, 191–93, 240, 245, 266–67, 278, 283–85, 302–3, 306–9, 339, 385–86, 403–4. Matthew Francis Rusnak, the author of a Ph.D. thesis on the Baretti murder trial, notes that the October 1769 trial "occurred in a vital moment in a criminal justice system at once barbaric and enlightened, primitive and modern, brutal and humane." Ibid., p. 246. "The Baretti case," he notes, "came on the heels of the publications of two of the seminal works in the history of jurisprudence: Cesare Beccaria's *Crimes and Punishments* ... and Sir William Blackstone's *Commentaries on the Laws of England* (1765–1769)." Ibid. "In the eighteenth century," Rusnak points out, "nearly every aspect of legal procedure and philosophy was examined, discussed and evaluated against new standards of justice and liability." Ibid. The acquittal of Baretti would be a subject of controversy in the decades to come. Ibid., pp. 336–37. "One of the men who assaulted Baretti," Rusnak observes, however, was later "hanged at Tyburn for highway robbery." Ibid., p. 341. Giuseppe Baretti, who went by Joseph Baretti during his time in England, was visited by Pietro (Peter) Molini, an Italian bookseller, shortly after the stabbing. Ibid., p. 383. Molini also served as a character witness for Baretti. Lidia De Michelis, "Letters from London: A 'Bridge' Between Italy and Europe," in Frank O'Gorman & Lia Guerra, eds., *The Centre and the Margins in Eighteenth-century British and Italian Cultures* (Newcastle upon Tyne: Cambridge Scholars Publishing, 2013), p. 47; Kevin J. Hayes, *The Road to Monticello: The Life and Mind of Thomas Jefferson* (Oxford: Oxford University Press, 2008), p. 282; *An English Ilustrado: The Reverend John Bowle* (Bern: Peter Lang, 1977), p. 56; Giuseppe Marc'Antonio Baretti, https://en.wikipedia.org/wiki/Giuseppe_Marc'Antonio_Baretti.

30. Anne Urbancic, *Reviewing Mario Pratesi: The Critical Press and Its Influence* (Toronto: University of Toronto Press, 2014), pp. 11–12.

31. Marrone, *Encyclopedia of Italian Literary Studies*, Vol. 2, pp. 1977–79.

32. Bizzocchi, *A Lady's Man*, p. 213.

33. Ibid., p. 201. Because of concerns over paternity, a cicisbei might not begin escorting a married woman until after the newlyweds had conceived a child—though this custom was not universally observed. For example, a German writer, Christian Joseph Jagemann, reported in *Letters about Italy* (1778) that in the "first months" of married life, aristocratic spouses lived in country houses and new wives were only permitted to see close relatives. "Many people have assured me," Jagemann explained, "that this happens so that the father will not have any doubts about the paternity of the first-born son, who will be responsible for the propagation of the family and for the whole inheritance." "Generally," he noted, "the wives return from the countryside pregnant, and later begin for the first time to pair off with their cicisbei." Ibid., pp. 204–5. "It is certainly possible that the cicisbeo was chosen at the time of the nuptial agreement, but that the service would begin later," Roberto Bizzocchi explains. Ibid., p. 205; *compare* ibid. ("Maddalena Beccaria Isimbardi was already expecting her first and only child when she began her relationship with Pietro Verri. Her sister-in-law Teresa Blasco Beccaria conceived a daughter before and another daughter and a son after the beginning of the triangle with Bartolomeo Calderara. Her niece Giulia Beccaria Manzoni conceived her only child during the period when she was accompanied by Giovanni Verri.").

34. Bizzocchi, *A Lady's Man*, pp. 38–39, 69, 75, 84–85, 182–85; Gaetana Marrone, ed., *Encyclopedia of Italian Literary Studies* (New York: Routledge, 2007), p. 1981.

35. Venturi & Litchfield, *The End of the Old Regime in Europe, 1776–1789*, pp. 74–75; *Dictionary of Literary Biography: American Book Collectors and Bibliographers* (Farmington Hills, MI: Gale Research, 1997), p. 86; Pace, *Luigi Castiglioni's Viaggio*, p. xxxii; Cesare Marino & Karim M. Tiro, eds. & trans.,

Along the Hudson and Mohawk: The 1790 Journey of Count Paolo Andreani (Philadelphia: University of Pennsylvania Press, 2006), pp. ix, 11, 13; Marco Beretta & Alessandro Tosi, *Linnaeus in Italy: The Spread of a Revolution in Science* (Sagamore Beach, MA: Science History Publications/USA, 2007), pp. 165–66; John D. Bessler, "The American Enlightenment: Eliminating Capital Punishment in the United States," *in* Lill Scherdin, ed., *Capital Punishment: A Hazard to a Sustainable Criminal Justice System?* (New York: Routledge, 2014), p. 98; Luigi Castiglioni, *Storia delle piante forastiere: Le più importanti nell'uso medico, od economico* (Milano: Jaca Book, Luigi Saibene, ed. 2008); Pietro Verri, http://gw.geneanet.org/fcicogna?lang=en&pz=francesco+maria&nz=cicogna+mozzoni&ocz=1&p=pietro&n=verri&oc=1; Luigi Castiglioni, 1757–1832, https://www.myheritage.com/names/luigi_castiglioni; Portrait of Count Alfonso Castiglioni by Giovanni Pock, oil on wood, 1830–1832, http://www.gettyimages.com/detail/photo/portrait-of-count-alfonso-castiglioni-by-high-res-stock-photography/109268405.

36. Robert Casillo, *The Empire of Stereotypes: Germaine de Staël and the Idea of Italy* (New York: Palgrave Macmillan, 2006), p. 111.

37. Marrone, *Encyclopedia of Italian Literary Studies*, p. 1981; Shahibzadeh, *Penal Philosophy in 18th Century Italy*, p. 18; Cesare Beccaria, *On Crimes and Punishments* (Indianapolis, IN: Hackett Publishing Co., David Young, trans. 1986), p. 96 n.1; Donald A. Limoli, "Pietro Verri: A Lombard Reformer under Enlightened Absolutism and the French Revolution," *Journal of Central European Affairs*, Vol. XVIII, no. 3, pp. 254, 258–59; Richard Bellamy, *Croce, Gramsci, Bobbio and the Italian Political Tradition* (Colchester, UK: ECPR Press, 2013), p. 48. The ideas of Cesare Beccaria and Pietro and Alessandro Verri have been the subject of much study. As one academic writes: "Beccaria and his closest intellectual allies, the brothers Pietro and Alessandro Verri, positioned themselves politically against the traditional, ecclesiastical power structure of their aristocratic Lombard parents and in favor of reforms, some of which they helped introduce on behalf of the Austrian Habsburg Empire. The Verris and Beccaria endorsed systemic change aimed at a more organized and centralized economic power; greater government intervention as a way to increase state revenues; and more formal legal structures and regulatory mechanisms." "Like Verri," Richard Bellamy has further asserted, Beccaria sought "the substitution of the existing irregular, particularist and custom-bound legal system, based on hereditary rights and the personal rule of the monarch and nobility, by a regular centralized and rational system of justice that was equal for all and grounded in the rule of law." Harcourt, *The Illusion of Free Markets*, p. 66; *see also* Alessandro Roncaglia, *The Wealth of Ideas: A History of Economic Thought* (Cambridge: Cambridge University Press, 2006), p. 110 ("Both Verri and Beccaria adopted a subjective theory of value based on comparison between scarcity and utility; in general, they conceived the market as the point where buyers and sellers met (and this held true also for the rate of interest, determined by demand for and supply of loans). Moreover, both Verri and Beccaria took a wide interest in practical issues, from the fiscal and monetary situation to problems of custom duties, seasonal unemployment, and concession to private agents of monopolies for commodities such as salt and tobacco. On the latter issue, for instance, Verri, in his capacity as a high-ranking functionary in the Austro-Hungarian empire, succeeded in obtaining an important victory with abolition of the concessions in 1770."). "In his *Reflections*, fragments of a projected work on the *Ripulimento delle nazioni*, Beccaria wrote: 'The ruler and governor is required to know what is advantageous to his people and how to secure it for them, and to have a desire to do so.' In Beccaria's view, Professor Bernard Harcourt stresses, "the task of public economy was to mold self-interest so as to make it conform to the larger interests of society." "It is characteristic of human beings to throw themselves blindly into their present and immediate concerns, neglecting the future," Beccaria lamented in his inaugural lecture. Harcourt, *The Illusion of Free Markets*, pp. 66–68.

38. Bizzocchi, *A Lady's Man*, pp. 222–23; Marrone, *Encyclopedia of Italian Literary Studies*, Vol. 2, pp. 1797–80, 1978; Rebecca Messbarger, *The Century of Women: Representations of Women in Eighteenth-Century Italian Public Discourse* (Toronto: University of Toronto Press, 2002), p.76; Cavazza, "Between Modesty and Spectacle," *in* Findlen, Roworth & Sama, *Italy's Eighteenth Century*, p. 289; Marc J. Neveu, Ph.D. thesis, Architectural Lessons of Carlo Lodoli (1690–1761): Indole of Material and of Self, School of Architecture, McGill University, Montrèal (2005), pp. 179–80; Gabriele Verri, https://www.geni.com/people/Gabriele-Verri/6000000028879176133; "Maria Verri (born Castiglioni), 1753–1781," https://www.myheritage.com/names/maria-verri; Teresa Francesca Castiglioni, https://

www.geni.com/people/Teresa-Castiglioni/6000000028879188040. It was in April 1785 that the Milanese botanist Luigi Castiglioni—the nephew of Pietro and Alessandro Verri—embarked on his long voyage to North America. That voyage resulted in the publication of his travelogue, later translated into English as *Travels in the United States of North America in the Years 1785–87. See generally* Pace, *Luigi Castiglioni's Viaggio*. Luigi Castiglioni was interested in studying trees and plants, but he also wanted to see America following the Revolutionary War. As he wrote in his preface:

> The Revolution which had taken place in the last few years in North America is one of the most memorable events of this century and may in time produce important consequences for Europe. No wonder, therefore, if after such an epoch reports on things having to do with the United States are more sought after than before and that various travelers have visited this country hitherto little frequented by them. Among these, I too was moved by curiosity to see the political birth of a Republic composed of diverse nationalities, scattered over vast provinces far removed from one another, and varied in climate and products.

"Castiglioni's journal," one source notes of its significance, "is in all probability the only late eighteenth-century account by an Italian traveler to the United States." Stefania Buccini, *The Americas in Italian Literature and Culture 1700–1825* (University Park, PA: The Pennsylvania State University Press, Rosanna Giammanco, trans. 1997), pp. 149–50. *But see* Cesare Marino & Karim M. Tiro, eds. & trans., *Along the Hudson and Mohawk: The 1790 Journey of Count Paolo Andreani* (Philadelphia, PA: University of Pennsylvania Press, 2006) (describing the journey of Count Paolo Andreani, an Italian nobleman born in 1763 in Milan, who traveled to Halifax, Nova Scotia and New York, and who kept a diary of his travels). The Castiglioni family is depicted in a painting by Francesco Corneliani that commemorates Luigi Castiglioni's trip to America. In the painting, an art historian writes, "Luigi Castiglioni sits at a desk and retraces his travels on the map while the two girls at his side follow the itinerary on the globe." "The young children," the art historian writes of the girls in the artist's painting, "hold rare plant specimens, perhaps flowers from a locust, a plant that Castiglioni brought back from America and introduced in Lombardy." Daniela Tarabra, *European Art of the Eighteenth Century* (Los Angeles, CA: The J. Paul Getty Museum, Rosanna M. Giammanco Frongia, trans. 2006), p. 188. A brief sketch of Luigi Castiglioni and his travels can be found online. *See* Luigi Castiglioni, https://www.thefreelibrary.com/Luigi+Castiglioni.+Lettere+dalla+Francia+(1784).+Viaggio+in...-a0266224592.

39. Bizzocchi, *A Lady's Man*, pp. 191–95; Giuseppe Visconti di Saliceto, https://translate.google.com/translate?hl=en&sl=fr&u=https://fr.wikipedia.org/wiki/Giuseppe_Visconti_di_Saliceto&prev=search; Marco Guidi & Nanda Torcellano, *Europe 1700-1999: History of an Identity* (Electa, 1987), Vol. 1, p. 158; *Memorie Della Società Astronomica Italiana* (1997), p. 544; Istituto Italiano Per Gli Studi Filosofici, http://www.iisf.it/pubblicazioni/studi_economia.pdf, pp. 424, 426; *Opere diverse del marchese Cesare Beccaria Bonesana patrizio Milanese* (Napoli : nella stamperia di Giovanni Gravier, 1770-1771), http://www.catalogobibliotecheliguri.it/opaclib/opac/cbl/scheda_sim.jsp?sim_bid=TO0E045776&pager.offset=24&bid=SBLE015818 (noting as follows: "A cura di Troiano Odazzi: cfr. L. Firpo, Le edizioni italiane del "Dei delitti e delle pene", n. 15—Prima raccolta delle opere di Beccaria, con nome dell'autore e luogo di stampa autentico, nonostante la condanna all'Indice."); Lot 296, Cesare Beccaria, Opere diverse del marchese Cesare Beccaria Bonesana patrizio Milanese (Napoli: Nella Stamperia di Giovanni Gravier, 1770), https://www.the-saleroom.com/en-gb/auction-catalogues/forumauctions/catalogue-id-forum-10010/lot-8d1b6cfe-767d-474b-bb08-a69500caf1ac; Troiano Odazi, http://www.wikiwand.com/it/Troiano_Odazi; Antonio Genovesi, https://en.wikipedia.org/wiki/Antonio_Genovesi.

40. Roberto Bizzocchi, "Cicisbei: Italian Morality and European Values in the Eighteenth Century," *in* Findlen, Roworth & Sama, *Italy's Eighteenth Century*, p. 38; Rosmarie Macri, *Fascinating Lake Como: Travel Guide for Discoverers* (Troubador Publishing, 2015) (entry for "Sala Comacina"); Italian Lakes Holiday Rentals, Villa Beccaria also called Villa Rachele (Sala Comacina), http://www.italianlakes-holidayrentals.com/villa-beccaria-also-called-villa-rachele-sala-comacina/; "Sala Comacina," Property at Lake Como, http://www.propertyatlakecomo.com/eng/pagina/como-and-surroundings/1466834875/1468417098.

41. Martha Feldman, *Opera and Sovereignty: Transforming Myths in Eighteenth-Century Italy* (Chicago: The University of Chicago Press, 2010), pp. 216, 219, 253; Pierpaolo Polzonetti, *Italian*

Opera in the Age of the American Revolution (Cambridge: Cambridge University Press, 2011), p. 49 n.33.

42. Martha Feldman, "Strange Births and Surprising Kin: The Castrato's Tale," *in* Findlen, Roworth & Sama, *Italy's Eighteenth Century*, pp. 175–76; Catherine Ingrassia & Jeffrey S. Ravel, eds., *Studies in Eighteenth-century Culture* (Baltimore: The Johns Hopkins University Press, 2005), Vol. 34, pp. 206, 222. The definiton of *castrato*, per the *Dictionnaire de l'Académe française* (1773): "A man who has been castrated so that his voice may preserve a quality similar to that of women. *There are many castrati in Italy.*" Thomas A. King, *The Gendering of Men, 1600–1750: Queer Articulations*, Vol. 2, p. 521 n.28 (Madison, WI: The University of Wisconsin Press, 2008) (italics in original).

43. Christopher Duggan, *The Force of Destiny: A History of Italy Since 1796* (Boston, MA: Houghton Mifflin Co., 2008), p. 5; Paula Findlen, "Gender and Culture in Eighteenth-Century Italy," *in* Findlen, Roworth & Sama, *Italy's Eighteenth Century*, pp. 1–2, 4; http://www.villadeste.com/fileUpload/downloads/30/Historical_Notes_VilladEste.pdf.

44. Jim Dobson, "The Legendary Villas of Lake Como: Where to Go and What to See," *Forbes*, June 8, 2016, *available at* https://www.forbes.com/sites/jimdobson/2016/06/08/the-legendary-villas-of-lake-como-the-ultimate-guide-of-where-to-go-and-what-to-see/3/#41d8cbe55189 (the entry for "Villa D'Este (Cernobbio)" reads: "Gerardo Landriani, Bishop of Como, founded a female convent here in 1442. A century later Cardinal Tolomeo Gallio demolished the nunnery and commissioned Pellegrino Tibaldi to design a residence for his own use. The Villa del Garovo, together with its luxurious gardens, was constructed during the years 1565–70, and during the cardinal's lifetime, it became a resort of politicians and brilliant minds. On Gallio's death, the villa passed to his family who allowed it to sink into a state of decay. From 1749 to 1769 it was a Jesuit spiritual retreat, before being acquired first by Count Mario Odescalchi, and then in 1778 by Count Marliani. In 1784, it passed to the Milanese Calderari family who undertook a major restoration project and created a new park with an impressive temple displaying a seventeenth-century statue of Hercules hurling Lichas into the sea. After the death of Marquis Calderari, his wife Vittoria Peluso, a former ballerina at La Scala and known as *la Pelusina*, married a Napoleonic general, Count Domenico Pino and a mock fortress was erected in the park in his honor.").

45. Ruth Halliwell, *The Mozart Family: Four Lives in a Social Context* (Oxford: Clarendon Press, 1998), p. 55; Marina Riztarev, *Eighteenth-century Russian Music* (Hampshire, England: Ashgate, 2006), p. 140 n.3; Maestro, *Cesare Beccaria and the Origins of Penal Reform*, pp. 68–69 & n.6.

46. Mordechai Feingold, ed., *History of Universities: Volume XIX/1* (Oxford: Oxford University Press, 2004), pp. 121–22; Maestro, *Cesare Beccaria and the Origins of Penal Reform*, pp. 70–72; *The National Encyclopædia: A Dictionary of Universal Knowledge* (London: William Mackenzie), Vol. 4, pp. 199–200; *The Penny Cyclopedpædia of the Society for the Diffusion of Useful Knowledge* (London: Charles Knight and Co., 1836), Vol. VI, p. 296; *Chambers's Encyclopædia: A Dictionary of Universal Knowledge for the People* (Philadelphia: J. B. Lippincott Co., 1886), Vol. II, p. 617.

47. Bessler, *The Birth of American Law*, p. 20; Franz A. J. Szabo, *Kaunitz and Enlightened Absolutism 1753–1780* (Cambridge: Cambridge University Press, 1994); James H. Billington, *Icon and Axe: An Interpretive History of Russian Culture* (New York: Knopf Doubleday, 2010) (citing T. Cizova, "Beccaria in Russia," *SEER*, June 1962, pp. 384–408); Henry Dunning Macleod, *A Dictionary of Political Economy: Biographical, Bibliographical, Historical, and Practical* (London: Longman, Brown, Longmans, and Roberts, 1863), Vol. I, p. 253.

48. Mark A. Kishlansky, Patrick J. Geary & Patricia O'Brien, *Civilization in the West: Since 1555* (New York: HarperCollins, 1991), p. 559.

49. Robert A. Silverman, Terence P. Thornberry, Bernard Cohen & Barry Krisberg, eds., *Crime and Justice at the Millennium: Essays by and in Honor of Marvin E. Wolfgang* (New York: Springer Science+Business Media, 2002), p. 398.

50. Bessler, *The Birth of American Law*, p. 3; *The Encyclopædia Britannica: A Dictionary of Arts, Sciences, Literature and General Information* (New York: The Encyclopædia Britannica Company, 11th ed. 1911), Vol. 23, pp. 900–1.

51. Harcourt, *The Illusion of Free Markets*, p. 55; Florian Schui, *Early Debates about Industry: Voltaire and His Contemporaries* (New York: Palgrave Macmillan, 2005), p. 152; Bernard E. Harcourt, "Beccaria's *On Crimes and Punishments*," *in* Dubber, *Foundational Texts in Modern Criminal Law*, p.

42; *A Study Guide for Voltaire's "Candide"* (Farmington Hills, MI: Gale Research, 1999), intro.

52. Lewis Copeland, Lawrence W. Lamm & Stephen J. McKenna, eds., *The World's Great Speeches: 292 Speeches from Pericles to Nelson Mandela* (Mineola, NY: Dover Publications, 4th ed. 1999), pp. 91–93; Maestro, *Cesare Beccaria and the Origins of Penal Reform*, p. 44.

53. Voltaire, *A Philosophical Dictionary*, Vol. 4, pp. 260–61.

54. Sarah Maza, *Private Lives and Public Affairs: The Causes Célèbres of Prerevolutionary France* (Berkeley, CA: University of California Press, 1993), pp. 19–23.

55. Hostettler, *Cesare Beccaria*, pp. 31, 57; Hans Göran Franck, *The Barbaric Punishment: Abolishing the Death Penalty* (The Hague: Martinus Nijhoff Publishers, William Schabas, ed., 2003), p. 49; *see also* John Robertson, *Enlightenment: A Very Short Introduction* (Oxford: Oxford University Press, 2015), p. 110 ("In Lombardy, Beccaria followed the publication of his work *On Crimes and Punishments* (1764) by lecturing on political economy, and subsequently served as an official of the Austrian government, as did the economist Pietro Verri.").

56. Marcello Maestro, *Cesare Beccaria and the Origins of Penal Reform* (Philadelphia: Temple University Press, 1973), pp. 70–72.

57. Henry Dunning Macleod, *A Dictionary of Political Economy: Biographical, Bibliographical, Historical, and Practical* (London: Longman, Brown, Longmans, and Roberts, 1863), Vol. 1, p. 254.

58. R. H. Inglis Palgrave, ed., *Dictionary of Political Economy* (London: Macmillan and Co., 1894), Vol. 1, p. 127.

59. Groenewegen, *Eighteenth-century Economics*, pp. 4, 20, 42 n.20, 120 & 123; Maestro, *Cesare Beccaria and the Origins of Penal Reform*, p. 73. The information about the date and circumstances of Beccaria's appointment is courtesy of Carlo Scognamiglio Pasini.

60. Richard R. E. Kania & Richards P. Davis, *Managing Criminal Justice Organizations: An Introduction to Theory and Practice* (New York: 2d ed. 2015), pp. 44–45; Giulia Brasca, *Milan 360°: A Metropolis to Discover, Among Art, Culture, Technology and Fashion* (Chiasso, Switzerland: OlliService Multimedia, Elizabeth Lowrie, trans. 2014), p. 95; Marrone, *Encyclopedia of Italian Literary Studies*, Vol. 1, pp. 26–27; Henry Higgs, *Bibliography of Economics 1751–1775* (Cambridge: Cambridge University Press, 1935), p. 452. Antonio Genovesi's actual successor in his chair was Traiano Odazzi. Jesús Astigarraga & Javier Usoz, "The Enlightenment in Translation: Antonio Genovesi's Political Economy in Spain, 1778–1800," 28 *Mediterranean Historical Review* 24 (2013); https://www.britannica.com/place/Italy/The-Papal-States; Pier Francesco Asso & Luca Fiorito, eds., Economics and Institutions — Contributions from the History of Economic Thought, Selected Papers from the 8th Aispe Conference (Milano: FrancoAngeli, 2007), p. 347.

61. Riccardo Faucci, *A History of Italian Economic Thought* (New York: Routledge, 2014), pp. 46–47, 54; Gilbert Faccarello & Heinz D. Kurz, eds., *Handbook on the History of Economic Analysis: Schools of Thought in Economics* (Cheltenham, UK: Edward Elgar Publishing, 2016), Vol. II, p. 102; Jérôme-Adolphe Blanqui, *History of Political Economy of Europe* (New York: G. P. Putnam's Sons, Emily J. Leonard trans. 1880), p. 523.

62. Blanqui, *History of Political Economy of Europe*, pp. 522–23.

63. Groenewegen, *Eighteenth-century Economics*, p. 211; Murray N. Rothbard, *Economic Thought Before Adam Smith: An Austrian Perspective on the History of Economic Thought* (Auburn, AL: Ludwig von Mises Institute, 2006), Vol. 1, pp. 217–18, 246–49, 261; Luigino Bruni & Pier Luigi Porta, *Handbook of Research Methods and Applications in Happiness and Quality of Life* (Cheltenham, UK: Edward Elgar Publishing, 2016), p. 516; Blanqui, *History of Political Economy of Europe*, p. 523. Marshal Vauban was an early French economist. *The British Quarterly Review* (London: Jackson & Walford, 1854), Vol. 19, p. 470; Harcourt, "Beccaria's *On Crimes and Punishments*," in Dubber, *Foundational Texts in Modern Criminal Law*, pp. 54–56; Bernard E. Harcourt, "Beccaria's 'On Crimes and Punishments': A Mirror on the History of the Foundations of Modern Criminal Law," Coase-Sandor Institute for Law & Economics Working Paper, No. 648 (2013), pp. 8, 10–11, 14, 18, *available at* http://chicagounbound.uchicago.edu/cgi/viewcontent.cgi?article=1633&context=law_and_economics; Michael Kwass, *Contraband: Louis Mandrin and the Making of a Global Underground* (Cambridge, MA: Harvard University Press, 2014), pp. 286, 299, 306; Maestro, *Cesare Beccaria and the Origins of Penal Reform*, pp. 74, 81; Feingold, *History of Universities*, p. 125; François Quesnay (1694–1774), The Concise Encyclopedia of Economics, http://www.econlib.org/library/Enc/bios/Quesnay.html.

64. Harcourt, "Beccaria's *On Crimes and Punishments*," *in* Dubber, *Foundational Texts in Modern Criminal Law*, p. 255 n.46. Not only did Dupont send Beccaria a copy of his journal, *Les Éphémérides du citoyen*, but he also sent him, under separate cover, a copy of *Physiocratie*, his collected edition of physiocratic writings. Dupont, who later immigrated to America, was, during the French Revolution's Reign of Terror, condemned to death and almost guillotined.

65. 2 George Ripley & Charles A. Dana, *The American Cyclopædia: A Popular Dictionary of General Knowledge* (New York: D. Appleton and Co., 1881), p. 437; James J. McLain, *The Economic Writings of Du Pont de Nemours* (Newark: University of Delaware Press, 1977), p. 98; Groenewegen, *Eighteenth-century Economics*, p. 19; Harcourt, *The Illusion of Free Markets*, p. 255 n.45.

66. Caesar Beccaria, *A Discourse on Public Economy and Commerce*, *available at* http://socserv2.socsci.mcmaster.ca/econ/ugcm/3ll3/beccaria/pubecon.

67. Garland Greever, ed., *The Diaries of Sylvester Douglas (Lord Glenbervie)* (Boston, MA: Houghton Mifflin Co., 1928), p. 85; Maestro, *Cesare Beccaria and the Origins of Penal Reform*, pp. 81–82; John Cunningham Wood, ed., *Adam Smith: Critical Assessments* (London: Routledge, 1996), Vol. 1, p. 798 n.45; *Speech of the Right Honourable Sylvester Douglas in the House of Commons, Tuesday, April the 23d, 1799, on Seconding the Motion of the Right Honourable the Chancellor of the Exchequer, for the House to Agree with the Lords in an Address to His Majesty Relative to a Union with Ireland* (London: J. Wright, 1799), pp. 35, 92, 118–22. Because of the large invitation list, it seems highly likely that Cesare Beccaria would have been at Wolfgang Amadeus Mozart's performance in Milan in 1770. As Leopold Mozart's March 13, 1770 letter to his wife, sent from Milan, also read: "It was impossible for me to write last Saturday, because Wolfgang had to compose for the concert held yesterday at Count Firmian's, three arias and a recitative with violins, and I had to copy the violin parts myself and then have them duplicated, so that they should not be stolen. Over one hundred and fifty members of the leading nobility were present, the most important of them being the Duke, the Princess and the Cardinal." Emily Anderson, *The Letters of Mozart and His Family* (London: Macmillan Reference Limited, 1997), pp. 118–19.

68. Pier Luigi Porta, "Happiness: What Kahneman could have learnt from Pietro Verri," *in* Richard Arena, Sheila Dow & Matthias Klaes, eds., *Open Economics: Economics in Relation to Other Disciplines* (New York: Routledge, 2009), pp. 48–49; Jérôme-Adolphe Blanqui, *History of Political Economy in Europe* (New York: G. P. Putnam's Sons, Emily J. Leonard, trans. 1880), pp. 523–24.

69. Maestro, *Cesare Beccaria and the Origins of Penal Reform*, p. 82; Franz A. J. Szabo, *Kaunitz and Enlightened Absolutism 1753–1780* (Cambridge: Cambridge University Press, 1994), p. 51.

70. Luigi Cossa, *An Introduction to the Study of Political Economy* (London: Macmillan and Co., Louis Dyer, trans. 1893), pp. 280–83; *compare* J. R. McCulloch, *The Principles of Political Economy: With Sketch of the Rise and Progress of the Science* (London: Alex. Murray and Son, 1870), p. 35 ("The Count di Verri, whose *Meditations on Political Economy* were published in 1771, demonstrated the fallacy of the opinions of the French Economists respecting the superior productiveness of the labour employed in agriculture; and showed that all the operations of industry really consist of *modifications of matter already in existence*. But Verri did not trace the consequences of this important principle; and, possessing no clear and definite notions of what constituted wealth, did not attempt to discover the means by which labour might be facilitated. He made some valuable additions to particular branches of the science, and had sufficient acuteness to detect errors in the system of others; but the task of constructing a better system in their stead required talents of a far higher order. At length, in 1776, our illustrious countryman Adam Smith published the 'Wealth of Nations,'—a work which has done for Political Economy what the Essay of Locke did for the philosophy of mind."); William Spalding, *Italy and the Italian Islands: From the Earliest Ages to the Present Time* (Edinburgh: Oliver & Boyd, 1841), Vol. 2, p. 391 ("Among the numerous works of Verri, some are local or historical, like his invaluable Memoirs on the Administration of the State of Milan. Another dissertation, 'On the Policy of Restrictive Laws, with especial reference to the Trade in Corn,' is a lucid and temperate argument in favour of free trade in grain as the only system suitable for Austrian Lombardy. But the former of these pieces, through written in 1768, lay in manuscript till 1804; and the latter, composed in 1769, was published only in 1796. The author's fame during his lifetime rested on what is still his most valuable composition,—the Meditations on Political Economy,—the acuteness and originality of which have been acknowledged more cheerfully than usual by the writers of other nations. Perhaps,

indeed, as an overthrower of popular errors, no political economist of the century, except Smith alone, was either so bold or so successful.").

71. Porta, "Happiness," *in Open Economics*, p. 50; Feingold, *History of Universities*, pp. 121–22, 125–26. The figures about the number of students who attended Beccaria's course, as well as various information in this section and the translations from Italian to English, were provided by Carlo Scognamiglio Pasini.

72. *Tratado de los delitos y de las penas* (Madrid, 1774); German E. Berrios, *The History of Mental Symptoms: Descriptive Psychopathology Since the Nineteenth Century* (Cambridge: Cambridge University Press, 1996), p. 460; Jonathan I. Israel, *Democratic Enlightenment: Philosophy, Revolution, and Human Rights 1750–1790* (Oxford: Oxford University Press, 2011), p. 339.

73. Alejandro Agüero and Marta Lorente, "Penal enlightenment in Spain: from Beccaria's reception to the first criminal code" (Nov. 2012), *available at* http://www.forhistiur.de/es/2012-11-aguero-lorente/?l=en. In the preface to the 1821 edition of Jean-Baptiste Say's *Tratado de economía política* (1803), its translator, Juan Sánchez Rivera, attributed "a great number of laws and dispositions of the Spanish legislature of 1820" to "the brilliant ideas" of Beccaria, Filangieri, Say, Smith "and other celebrated writers." Cheng-chung Lai, ed., *Adam Smith Across Nations: Translations and Receptions of The Wealth of Nations* (Oxford: Oxford University Press, 2003), pp. 329, 364.

74. *Crime and the Administration of Justice in Buenos Aires, 1785–1853* (Lincoln: University of Nebraska, Osvaldo Barreneche, trans. 2006), pp. 21–22.

75. Serge Dauchy, Georges Martyn, Anthony Musson, Heikki Pihlajamäki & Alain Wijffels, eds., *The Formation and Transmission of Western Legal Culture: 150 Books that Made the Law in the Age of Printing* (Cham, Switzerland, Springer, 2016), pp. 90, 305.

76. Manuel de Lardizábal y Uribe, https://en.wikipedia.org/wiki/Manuel_de_Lardizábal_y_Uribe.

77. Marilyn McShane & Frank P. Williams III, eds., *Criminal Justice: Contemporary Literature in Theory and Practice* (New York: Garland Publishing, 1997), p. 24 n.7; Bessler, *The Birth of American Law*, p. 48; Jeremy Bentham, *A Fragment on Government; Being an Examination of What Is Delivered, on the Subject of Government in General, in the Introduction to Sir William Blackstone's* Commentaries (1776), *reprinted in* F. C. Montague, ed., Jeremy Bentham, *A Fragment on Government* (Union, NJ: The Lawbook Exchange, 2001), p. 105 n.2.

78. Semple, *Bentham's Prison*, p. 13; Jeremy Bentham, *The Rationale of Punishment* (London: Robert Heward, 1830); *see also* Thomas D. Lynch & Todd J. Dicker, eds., *Handbook of Organizational Theory and Management: The Philosophical Approach* (New York: Marcel Dekker, 1998), p. 115 ("Bentham developed his view on utilitarianism principally from Beccaria, Priestley, Hume, and Helvetius. Bentham read Beccaria's *Trattato Dei Delitti e Delle Pene*, or *Crimes and Punishments*, (1764), and Priestley's *Essay on the First Principles of Government* (1768) both of which contained the utilitarian principle.").

79. H. L. A. Hart, *Essays on Bentham: Jurisprudence and Political Theory* (Oxford: Oxford University Press, 2011), Pt. II; Steven J. Macias, *Legal Science in the Early Republic: The Origins of American Legal Thought and Education* (Lanham, MD: Lexington Books, 2016), p. 60.

80. Bessler, *Cruel and Unusual*, pp. 48–49.

81. Ibid.

82. Ibid.

83. Ibid., p. 49.

84. William Prest, *William Blackstone: Law and Letters in the Eighteenth Century* (Oxford: Oxford University Press, 2008), p. 308; *see also* David S. Clark, ed., *Encyclopedia of Law and Society: American and Global Perspectives* (Thousand Oaks, CA: Sage Publications, 2007), p. 117 ("Francesco Pagano (1748–1799) indicated that Montesquieu and Beccaria were the two thinkers who most importantly contributed to the reform of criminal law.").

85. Edwin G. Burrows & Mike Wallace, *Gotham: A History of New York City to 1898* (Oxford: Oxford University Press, 1999), p. 366; Emma Christopher, *A Merciless Place: The Lost Story of Britain's Convict Disaster in Africa* (Oxford: Oxford University Press, 2011), ch. 4.

86. Ursula R. Q. Henriques, *Before the Welfare State: Social Administration in Early Industrial Britain* (London: Longman, 1979), p. 161; Hart, *Essays on Bentham*, part II (discussing Bentham's admiration of Beccaria's work).

87. Bessler, *The Birth of American Law*, p. 125. Beccaria's book would remain a popular title—and would be discussed and debated in America and abroad for decades to come. Ibid., pp. 421–29; "Books," *Raleigh Register and North-Carolina State Gazette* (Raleigh, NC), Dec. 19, 1803, p. 4 (noting a donation of Beccaria's *On Crimes and Punishments* to the University of North Carolina "by the Citizens of Johnson County"); "Mr. Peel's Improvement of the Criminal Law," *The Times* (London, England), June 15, 1827, p. 8 (referencing Beccaria); *Raleigh Register and North-Carolina Gazette* (Raleigh, NC), Nov. 25, 1830, p. 4 (quoting Beccaria's views on pardons and clemency).

88. *See generally* Bessler, *The Birth of American Law.*

Chapter 5

1. Benjamin Franklin to Charles Thomson and Thomas Mifflin, Jan. 27, 1769, *available at* www.founders.archives.gov.

2. *The Annual Report of the Library Company of Philadelphia for the Year 1959: Presented at the Annual Meeting, May, 1960* (Philadelphia: The Library Company of Philadelphia, 1960), p. 24.

3. A. London Fell, *Origins of Legislative Sovereignty and the Legislative State* (Westport, CT: Praeger, 2004), Vol. 6, p. 183; Thomas Jefferson to Philip Mazzei, Nov. 1785, *available at* www.founders.archives.gov; Report on Books for Congress, [23 Jan.] 1783, *available at* www.founders.archives.gov.

4. "Reverend O'Leary's Address to the Common People of Ireland," *The Freeman's Journal* (Dublin, Ireland), Mar. 7, 1786, p. 2:

> In foreign countries when new laws, affecting the lives of the people, are enacted, they are posted up on the gates of the churches in all the parishes, and their non-promulgation is pleaded in justification of the fact. This before mentioned conduct corresponds with Beccaria's wishes, who says, that every citizen should have the code of laws which affect his life: and that the conduct of Censors and Magistrates, who punish the ignorant, is *a kind of tyranny which surrounds the confines of political liberty*. If the laws are made for the people, the people should know them, and laws which affect the lives of the multitude, should not be confined to the lawyer's library.

5. Pamela J. Schram & Stephen G. Tibbetts, *Introduction to Criminology: Why Do They Do It?* (Thousand Oaks, CA: Sage Publications, 2014), p. 42; Simon Chapple, "Origins of Transnational Governance in the Nineteenth Century," *in* Michael Head, Scott Mann & Simon Kozlina, eds., *Transnational Governance: Emerging Models of Global Legal Regulation* (London: Routledge, 2016), pp. vii, 22; John Henry Merryman & Rogelio Pérez-Perdomo, *The Civil Law Tradition: An Introduction to the Legal Systems of Europe and Latin America* (Stanford, CA: Stanford University Press, 3d ed. 2007), p. 125. In the United States, notices were often posted on church doors. *See, e.g.*, Ron Chernow, *Washington: A Life* (New York: Penguin Books, 2010) ("Like other major planters, Washington owned more slaves than his overseers could effectively monitor, and so the only way to control a captive population was to convince them that runaways would be severely punished. Virginia had perfected a system of terror for capturing fugitive slaves. Under a 1748 law, a master could seek out two justices of the peace and have them issue a proclamation against runaways. To give the slaves fair warning, the proclamation had to be posted on church doors throughout the county. If the slave still didn't surrender, the law said that 'it shall be lawful for any person ... to kill and destroy such slaves by any ways or means, without accusation or impeachment of any crime for the same.'").

6. John D. Bessler, *The Birth of American Law: An Italian Philosopher and the American Revolution* (Durham, NC: Carolina Academic Press, 2014), p. 182; Christopher L. Tomlins & Bruce H. Mann, eds., *The Many Legalities of Early America* (Chapel Hill: University of North Carolina Press, 2001), p. 116 (published for the Omohundro Institute of Early American History and Culture, Williamsburg, Virginia).

7. Cesare Beccaria, "Of the Interpretation of Laws," *Of Crimes and Punishments*, http://www.constitution.org/cb/crim_pun04.htm.

8. J. L. de Lolme, *The Constitution of England; or, An Account of the English Government: In Which It Is Compared, Both with the Republican Form of Government, and the Other Monarchies in Europe* (London: C. G. J. & J. Robinson, new ed. 1789), pp. 350, 352; Jennifer Hole, *Economic Ethics in Late*

Medieval England, 1300–1500 (Cham, Switzerland: Palgrave Macmillan, 2016), p. 80.

9. *The British Prose Writers: De Lolme on the Constitution* (London: John Sharpe, 1819–1821), p. 151; John D. Bessler, ed., Stephen Breyer, *Against the Death Penalty* (Washington, DC: Brookings Institution Press, 2016), pp. 46 & 127–28 n.1.

10. Ilene H. Nagel, *Structuring Sentencing Discretion: The New Federal Sentencing Guidelines*, 80 J. Crim. L. & Criminology 883, 890–91 (1990); Ilene H. Nagel, Russell Reynolds Associates, http://www.russellreynolds.com/consultants/ilene-nagel.

11. *Memoirs of the Life of Sir Samuel Romilly, Written by Himself; with a Selection from His Correspondence* (London: John Murray, 2d ed. 1840), Vol. 2, pp. 258–59, 309–10 (edited by Sir Samuel Romilly's sons).

12. John Johnstone, *The Works of Samuel Parr, LL.D.* (London: Longman, Rees, Orme, Brown, and Green, 1828), Vol. 1, p. 553; ibid., Vol. 4, pp. 139–40, 163, 175–76, 202, 209, 226–27, 238, 240, 253–54, 273, 284, 288, 298–99, 308.

13. *Memoirs of the Life of Sir Samuel Romilly, Written by Himself; with a Selection from His Correspondence* (London: John Murray, 3d ed. 1841), Vol. 1, pp. 206–11; Innocence Project, https://www.innocenceproject.org/about/.

14. Jerome Hall, *Nulla Poena Sine Lege*, 47 Yale L. J. 165, 165 (1937); *see also* ibid. ("Employed as *nullum crimen sine lege*, the prohibition is that no conduct shall be held criminal unless it is specifically described in the behavior-circumstance element of a penal statute. In addition, *nulla poena sine lege* has been understood to include the rule that penal statutes must be strictly construed. A final, important signification of the rule is that penal laws shall not be given retroactive effect."); ibid., p. 177 ("The rule of strict construction of penal statutes played a peculiar and important role in eighteenth century England when a humanitarian ideology propagated by Beccaria, Romilly, Howard, Buxton and others rose against a severe and undiscriminating written law."); ibid., pp. 168–69:

> Long before the French Revolution, the movement for codification had advanced some of the ideas underlying *nulla poena* on its technical side. Indeed, it was in the Code of the Austrian monarch, Joseph II, (1787) that specific prohibition of analogy first entered the modern criminal law. The English tradition of the rule of law, translated by eighteenth century French philosophers into terms expressive of the Revolutionary ideology, joined with the continental movement for codification to provide *nulla poena* with its particular, current meanings.

15. F. & A. Ice Cream Co. v. Arden Farms Co., 98 F. Supp. 180, 184 (S.D. Cal. 1951).

16. United States v. Bodiford, 753 F.2d 380, 382 (5th Cir. 1985).

17. Apostolopoulos v. Massachusetts Registry of Motor Vehicles, 21 Mass. L. Rptr. 616, No. 2006-3623-A *5 (Mass. Sup. Ct. 2006).

18. United States v. Davis, 576 F.2d 1065, 1069 (3d Cir. 1978); *see also* State of Maryland v. Kramer, 318 Md. 576, 582 (Md. Ct. App. 1990) (" 'Basic to our theory of justice is the principle that there can be no punishment for harmful conduct unless it was so provided by some law in existence at the time.' This is expressed in the maxim *nullum crimen sine lege, nulla poena sine lege* (no crime or punishment without law)."); Nunley v. State of Alaska, 26 P.3d 1113, 1116 (Alaska Ct. App. 2001) ("[O]ne of the cardinal principles of our law is *nullum crimen sine lege, nulla poena sine lege*—the principle that no person shall suffer criminal punishment unless the legislature (or an agency with power delegated by the legislature) has enacted a statute or regulation that makes the person's conduct a crime."); Bynum v. State of Texas, 767 S.W.2d 769, 773 n.5 (Tex. Crim. Ct. App. 1989) ("The principle of 'legality,' or *nulla poena sine lege*, condemns judicial crime creation.").

19. Michael H. Hoeflich, *Roman and Civil Law and the Development of Anglo-American Jurisprudence in the Nineteenth Century* (Athens: The University of Georgia Press, 1997), pp. 5, 56.

20. Aniceto Masferrer, "The Liberal State and Criminal Law Reform in Spain," *in* Mortimer Sellers & Tadeusz Tomaszewski, eds., *The Rule of Law in Comparative Perspective* (Dordrecht: Springer Science + Business Media, 2010), p. 27.

21. Hoeflich, *Roman and Civil Law and the Development of Anglo-American Jurisprudence in the Nineteenth Century*, pp. 107–8, 112, 114–15, 118–19, 195–98, 407–9; Luciano J. Iorizzo & Ernest E. Rossi, eds., *Italian Americans: Bridges to Italy, Bonds to America* (Youngstown, NY: Teneo Press, 2010), p. 211; Reneé Critcher Lyons, *Foreign-Born American Patriots: Sixteen Volunteer Leaders in the*

Revolutionary War (Jefferson, NC: McFarland & Co., 2014), p. 14; "From the Gazette of the United States," *The North-Carolina Journal* (Halifax, NC), May 29, 1797, p. 4; "Jefferson's Life and Times," *The New York Times*, Aug. 10, 1874, p. 3 ("Virginia sent Mazzei, an Italian of strong Republican sympathies, on a financial mission to the Duke of Tuscany. This was after the Declaration of Independence—in 1778…."); *see also* "Mr. Pickering's Address to the People of the United States," *The Pennsylvania Gazette* (Philadelphia, PA), May 29, 1811, p. 1 ("Mr. Jefferson, in his memorable letter to his friend Mazzei, dared to represent 'the executive power,' meaning Washington, in whom, as President, the executive power was then vested, 'the judiciary,' and 'all the officers of government,' as engaged in a conspiracy against republicanism!").

22. Bessler, *The Birth of American Law*, p. 196.

23. Ibid.

24. Franco Venturi & R. Burr Litchfield, *The End of the Old Regime in Europe, 1776–1789: The Great States of the West* (Princeton, NJ: Princeton University Press, R. Burr Litchfield, trans., 1991), Part I, pp. 93–94; Stephen J. Spignesi, *The Italian 100: A Ranking of the Most Influential Cultural, Scientific, and Political Figures, Past and Present* (New York: Citadel Press, 2003), p. 28; *Memorie della vita e delle peregrinazioni del fiorentino Filippo Mazzei* (Lugano: Tipografia della Svizzera Italiana, 1846), Vol. 2, pp. 296, 299; *see also* Margherita Marchione, *Filippo Mazzei: Selected Writings and Correspondence* (Edizioni del Palazzo, 1983), p. 71 (referencing "Marchese Beccaria" and two copies of "*Dei delitti e delle pene*"); Margherita Marchione, *Philip Mazzei: World Citizen (Jefferson's "Zealous Whig")* (Lanham, MD: University Press of America, 1994), pp. 15, 24 (noting that "Cesare Beccaria's *Dei delitti e delle pene*" was undoubtedly "the subject of many discussions between Mazzei and Jefferson" and that, in England, Mazzei had "hailed Cesare Beccaria's treatise on crime and punishment and brought copies of it with him to Virginia").

25. Robert Aldrich & Garry Wotherspoon, eds., *Who's Who in Gay and Lesbian History: From Antiquity to World War II* (London: Routledge, 2002), p. 505; Margaretta Jolly, ed., *Encyclopedia of Life Writing: Autobiographical and Biographical Forms* (Chicago, IL: Fitzroy Dearborn Publishers, 2001), Vol. 1; Jonathan Israel, *Democratic Enlightenment: Philosophy, Revolution, and Human Rights 1750–1790* (Oxford: Oxford University Press, 2011), p. 359; Derek Beales, *Enlightenment and Reform in Eighteenth-Century Europe* (London: I.B. Tauris, 2005), pp. 52, 267.

26. Claudio Povolo, *The Novelist and the Archivist: Fiction and History in Alessandro Manzoni's The Betrothed* (New York: Palgrave Macmillan, Peter Mazur, trans. 2014), p. 81 n.17; Jonathan Israel, *Revolutionary Ideas: An Intellectual History of the French Revolution from The Rights of Man to Robespierre* (Princeton, NJ: Princeton University Press, 2014), p. 642.

27. Pierpaolo Polzonetti, *Italian Opera in the Age of the American Revolution* (Cambridge: Cambridge University Press, 2011), p. 27; Helen Zimmern, "Story of Mazzei," *New England Magazine: An Illustrated Monthly* (Oct. 1902), Vol. 27, pp. 198–202. Mazzei's London trading company is listed elsewhere as "Martin & Co." Ibid., p. 200; *Il Palazzo sul Potomac: The Embassy of Italy in Washington* (Colombo Duemila S.p.A., 2014), p. 7.

28. Margherita Marchione, ed., Filippo Mazzei, *My Life and Wanderings* (American Institute of Italian Studies, Samuel Scalia, trans. 1980), p. 99; Theresa Strouth Gaul & Sharon M. Harris, eds., *Letters and Cultural Transformations in the United States, 1760–1860* (Surrey, England: Ashgate Publishing Limited, 2009), pp. 20–21; Tommaso Tittoni, *Modern Italy: Its Intellectual, Cultural and Financial Aspects* (Williamstown, MA: The Institute of Politics Publications, Williams College, 1922), p. 70; Richard Garlick, *Philip Mazzei, Friend of Jefferson: His Life and Letters* (Baltimore, MD: Johns Hopkins Press, 1933), Vol. 7, pp. 22–23; Carlo Calisse, *A History of Italian Law* (Washington, DC: Beard Books, 2001), Vol. 2, p. 485; Kevin Jon Heller & Markus D. Dubber, eds., *The Handbook of Comparative Criminal Law* (Stanford, CA: Stanford Law Books, 2011), p. 13; Astolfo Di Amato, *Criminal Law in Italy* (The Netherlands: Kluwer Law International, 2011), p. 44; Francesco Carrara (jurist), http://en.academic.ru/dic.nsf/enwiki/6415274.

29. John Hostettler, *The Politics of Punishment* (Hampshire, UK: Waterside Press, 2016), p. 115; "American Revolution: 1764—John Wilkes expelled from Parliament," http://www.history.com/this-day-in-history/john-wilkes-expelled-from-parliament; Chiara Cillerai, " 'A continual and almost exclusive correspondence': Philip Mazzei's Transatlantic Citizenship," *in* Theresa Strouth Gaul and Sharon Harris, eds., *Letters and Cultural Transformations in the United States, 1760–1860* (New York: Routledge,

2016).

30. Margherita Marchione, *The Fighting Nun: My Story* (New York: Cornwall Books, 2000), pp. 111–12.

31. Lyons, *Foreign-Born American Patriots*, pp. 6–10; Howard R. Marraro, ed., *Philip Mazzei, Virginia's Agent in Europe: The Story of His Mission as Related in His Own Dispatches and Other Documents* (New York: The New York Public Library, 1935), pp. 5–6, 23 & n.18, 24; John David Smith & Thomas H. Appleton, Jr., eds., *A Mythic Land Apart: Reassessing Southerners and Their History* (Westport, CT: Greenwood Press, 1997), p. 9; *see also* Thomas Jefferson to Philip Mazzei, Apr. 4, 1780 ("Indeed you can form no conception how much our wants of European commodities are increased tho' the superiority of the French and Spanish fleets in Europe, and their equality here have reduced the risk of capture to be very moderate. Hearing of Mr. Bettoia's captivity and distress in New York, I wrote to him making a tender of any services I could render him. But I have since heard he had left that place before my letter could have got there.").

32. Marraro, *Philip Mazzei, Virginia's Agent in Europe*, p. 6; Lyon, *Foreign-Born American Patriots*, p. 11; Michael Kranish, *Flight from Monticello: Thomas Jefferson at War* (Oxford: Oxford University Press, 2010), p. 45 ("Jefferson and Mazzei together published anonymous letters in the *Virginia Gazette*. One such item, written in French by Mazzei and translated into English by Jefferson, told Virginians, 'All men are by nature equally free and independent. Such equality is necessary in order to create a free government. Every man must be the equal of any other in natural rights.' Later this would be cited by some as evidence that Mazzei had inspired 'All men are created equal.'").

33. Enrico Zucchi, "The Boundaries of Tolerance: Oppositions in 'Tolérantisme' in the Religious and Juridical Culture of the Late Eighteenth Century," *in* Paolo Scotton & Enrico Zucchi, eds., *Tracing the Path of Tolerance: History and Critique from the Early Modern Period to the Present Day* (Newcastle upon Tyne, UK: Cambridge Scholars Publishing, 2016), p. 97 n.10.

34. Katherine Ramsland, *Beating the Devil's Game: A History of Forensic Science and Criminal Investigation* (New York: Berkley Books, 2007), p. 23.

35. William Missouri Downs, Lou Anne Wright & Erik Ramsey, *The Art of Theatre: Then and Now* (Boston, MA: Wadsworth, 3d ed. 2013), p. 357.

36. U.S. Const., amend. I; "Jefferson's Letter to the Danbury Baptists," Jan. 1, 1802, https://www.loc.gov/loc/lcib/9806/danpre.html; "Thomas Jefferson and the Virginia Statute for Religious Freedom," Virginia Historical Society, http://www.vahistorical.org/collections-and-resources/virginia-history-explorer/thomas-jefferson.

37. "Edward Livingston, Report Made to the General Assembly of the State of Louisiana: On the Plan of a Penal Code for the Said State (New Orleans: Benjamin Levy, 1822); James Madison to Edward Livingston, July 10, 1822, https://founders.archives.gov/documents/Madison/04-02-02-0471.

38. John Hostettler, *Cesare Beccaria: The Genius of "On Crimes and Punishments"* (Hampshire, UK: Waterside Press, 2011), p. 216.

39. Mark Jones & Peter Johnstone, *History of Criminal Justice* (London: Routledge, 5th ed. 2012), p. 178; Dwight C. Kilbourn, *The Bench and Bar of Litchfield County, Connecticut 1709–1909* (Litchfield, CT, 1909), pp. 171–72; Carlton Hayes, *A Syllabus of Modern History* (New York: Columbia University, 1913); Eric H. Monkkonen, *Violence and Theft* (Munich: K. G. Saur, 1992), Part 2, p. 581.

40. Lyon, *Foreign-Born American Patriots*, pp. 11–14; *The Magazine of Ablemarle County History* (1982), Vols. 37–38, p. 45; Marraro, *Philip Mazzei, Virginia's Agent in Europe*, pp. 6–8. The second Italian to whom Jefferson likely referred was Carlo Bellini, a native of Florence whom Mazzei enticed to come to America. For 24 years, Bellini—a proficient language teacher—was a professor at the College of William and Mary, teaching French, German, Italian and Spanish. Ibid., pp. 8–12.

41. Bessler, *The Birth of American Law*, p. 116; Filippo Mazzei, *Recherches historiques et politiques sur les États-Unis de l'Amérique septentrionale* (1788), Vol. 1, pp. 114, 209, 212; Filippo Mazzei, *Recherches historiques et politiques sur les États-Unis de l'Amérique septentrionale* (1788), Vol. 2, pp. 116, 217; 3 Filippo Mazzei, *Recherches historiques et politiques sur les États-Unis de l'Amérique septentrionale* (1788), Vol. 3, pp. 15, 61; Filippo Mazzei, *Recherches historiques et politiques sur les États-Unis de l'Amérique septentrionale* (1788), Vol. 4, p. 353; Constance D. Sherman, ed. & trans., Philip Mazzei, *Researches on the United States* (Charlottesville, VA: University Press of Virginia, 1976), p. xv.

42. Sherman, Philip Mazzei, *Researches on the United States*, p. 91.

43. New Hampshire Const., Art. 18, *available at* https://www.nh.gov/constitution/oaths.html.

44. Lyon, *Foreign-Born American Patriots*, pp. 14–15; "Fabbroni, Giovanni Valentino Mattia, 1752–1822," Social Networks and Archival Context, http://socialarchive.iath.virginia.edu/ark:/99166/w66q2fj7.

45. Bessler, *The Birth of American Law*, pp. 79–80, 399, 585; Marco Fontani, Mary Virginia Orna & Mariagrazia Costa, *Chemistry and Chemists in Florence: From the Last of the Medici Family to European Magnetic Resonance Center* (Switzerland: Springer, 2016), p. 10.

46. John D. Bessler, *Cruel and Unusual: The American Death Penalty and the Founders' Eighth Amendment* (Boston: Northeastern University Press, 2012), p. 141.

47. Ibid., p. 130.

48. Ibid., pp. 130–31.

49. Bessler, *The Birth of American Law*, p. 151.

50. John S. Doskey, ed., *The European Journals of William Maclure* (Philadelphia: American Philosophical Society, 1988), p. 474 ("*Grand Duke Leopold* (1747–1792) ruled Tuscany between 1765 and 1790, and gave the former Medici territory 'perhaps the best government in Europe.' Although he was only eighteen years of age when he came to power, he gathered about him mature and respected Italians such as Cesare Beccaria (1738–1794), who were familiar with the people, their needs, and the possibilities of the duchy."). When Leopold, the Grand Duke of Tuscany and, later, the Emperor of Germany, died, it was also reported then that he had been influenced by Beccaria. "Emperor of Germany," *The Waterford Herald* (Waterford, Ireland), Mar. 27, 1792, p. 2 ("His Government was that of a philosophic Prince, who wished to secure the affections of his subjects by promoting their happiness."); ibid. ("Disgusted with the multiplicity of the penal statutes, which afforded so many pretences to a tyrannical sovereign, to disgrace, punish, and even cut off the most virtuous citizens, he formed and introduced a Criminal Code, no less celebrated for its justice than its humanity."); ibid. ("Beccaria, who had already distinguished himself by his celebrated treatise on crimes and punishments, was consulted and cherished by him. He drew that great man from the seclusion of private life, and enabled him to convert his theory into practice, by placing him at the head of one of the tribunals of justice."); *see also* "To the Legislatures of the Respective States," *Raleigh Register and North-Carolina State Gazette* (Raleigh, NC), Oct. 1, 1804, p. 1 (noting that the Grand Duke of Tuscany had "read and admired the marquis of Beccaria, and determined to try the effect of his plan"). During the 1790s, Beccaria's treatise continued to be cited and discussed throughout the world; often, Beccaria's name was spoken of with great admiration or praise, including in English-speaking countries. *E.g.,* "For the Northern Star," *The Northern Star* (Belfast, Northern Ireland), Apr. 18, 1792, p. 4 ("[t]he enlightened and amiable Beccaria"); *see also Raleigh Register and North-Carolina State Gazette* (Raleigh, NC), Feb. 9, 1807, p. 2 ("the learned and benevolent Beccaria"); *The Adams Sentinel* (Gettysburg, PA), Apr. 22, 1807, p. 3 ("the enlightened and humane Beccaria").

51. Edward Langworthy, ed., *Memoirs of the Life of the Late Charles Lee, Esq.* (London: J. S. Jordan, 1792), pp. 76–77, 80, 82.

52. Gordon S. Wood, *Empire of Liberty: A History of the Early Republic, 1789–1815* (Oxford: Oxford University Press, 2009), p. 492.

53. John Forrest Dillon, *The Laws and Jurisprudence of England and America: Being a Series of Lectures Delivered Before Yale University* (Boston: Little, Brown, and Co., 1894), p. 368.

54. Bruce Ackerman, *The Rise of World Constitutionalism*, 83 Va. L. Rev. 771, 771–72 (1997) ("The English had never indulged the Enlightenment conceit that a formal constitution was necessary for modern government. It was their culture of self-government, their common sense and decency, that distinguished their evolving commitment to democratic principles—not paper constitutions and institutional gimmicks like judicial review."); Markus Dirk Dubber, *The Pain of Punishments*, 44 Buff. L. Rev. 545, 593 (1996) ("Bentham ... along with every other enlightenment reformer of law at the time, sought to eliminate the discretion of judges and called for a strict literalism and formalism in the judicial application of codes. Judicial discretion to these reformers was an obstacle in the path of the enlightened modernization of the law through codification. As a result, enlightenment reformers of the law, from Montesquieu in France, Frederic II in Prussia, Beccaria in Italy, Feuerbach in Bavaria, to Bentham in England, thought it imperative to require literal application of their new codes and

to prohibit non-official commentaries.").

55. Bryan A. Garner, *Garner on Language and Writing: Selected Essays and Speeches of Bryan A. Garner* (Chicago, IL: American Bar Association, 2009), p. 441.

56. Stephen C. Thaman, *Should Criminal Juries Give Reasons for Their Verdicts?: The Spanish Experience and the Implications of the European Court of Human Rights Decision in* Taxquet v. Belgium, 86 Chi.-Kent L. Rev. 613, 615 n.18 (2011) ("In Italy, Enlightenment thinkers Cesare Beccaria and Gaetano Filangieri shared Montesquieu's views and sought to make the judge's role as mechanistic and automatic as possible.").

57. U.S. Const., amends. V & XIV.

58. U.S. Const., amend. XIV.

59. Giacinto della Cananea, *Due Process of Law Beyond the State: Requirements of Administrative Procedure* (Oxford: Oxford University Press, 2016), p. 140; Ronald Banaszak, Sr., *Fair Trial Rights of the Accused: A Documentary History* (Westport, CT: Greenwood Press, 2002), p. 79.

60. *See generally* John D. Bessler, *Tinkering Around the Edges: The Supreme Court's Death Penalty Jurisprudence*, 49 Am. Crim. L. Rev. 1913 (2012).

61. John D. Bessler, *The Inequality of America's Death Penalty: A Crossroads for Capital Punishment at the Intersection of the Eighth and Fourteenth Amendments*, 73 Wash. & Lee L. Rev. Online 487, 515 (2016), http://scholarlycommons.law.wlu.edu/cgi/viewcontent.cgi?article=1065&context=wlulr-online.

62. Bessler, *Cruel and Unusual*, p. 157.

63. Ibid.

64. Frank McLynn, *Crime and Punishment in Eighteenth-century England* (New York: Routledge, 2002), p. xi.

65. Paul O'Mahony, *Criminal Justice in Ireland* (Dublin: Institute of Public Administration, 2002), p. 22.

66. Marraro, *Philip Mazzei, Virginia's Agent in Europe*, pp. 6, 12–13; Thomas Jefferson to Philip Mazzei, Apr. 24, 1796; John Ferling, *Adams vs. Jefferson: The Tumultuous Election of 1800* (Oxford: Oxford University Press, 2004), pp. 64–67; Debra J. Allen, *Historical Dictionary of U.S. Diplomacy from the Revolution to Secession* (Lanham, MD: Scarecrow Press, 2012), p. 141.

67. Richard Buel Jr., *The A to Z of the Early American Republic* (Lanham, MD: Scarecrow Press, 2006), pp. 309–10.

68. Marraro, *Philip Mazzei, Virginia's Agent in Europe*, pp. 12–13.

69. *See, e.g.,* "From the Boston Gazette," *The Maryland Gazette* (Annapolis, MD), July 18, 1816, p. 2 ("Copy of a letter written by Thomas Jefferson, late President of the U.S. to Monsieur Philip Mazzei; published in the Paris Moniteur 25th Jan. 1797, during the administration of the immortal Washington. 'Our political situation is prodigiously changed since you left us. Instead of that noble love of liberty and that *republican* government which carried us through the revolution, an *anglo monarchic-aristocratic party* has arisen. Their avowed object is to impose on us the (*a*) Form of the British Government. Nevertheless the principal body of our citizens remain faithful to republican principles. We have against us the (*b*) Executive power, the Judiciary power (*two* out of three branches of our government) all the officers of the government, all who are seeking office, all *timid* men, who prefer the calm of Despotism to the tempestuous sea of liberty....."); *The Pittsburg Gazette* (Pittsburgh, PA), Aug. 10, 1833, p. 2 ("we asserted that Jefferson had written a letter to Mazzei, *a foreigner, residing in Italy,* slandering Washington"); "Reputation of Calumnies," *Public Ledger and Daily Transcript* (Philadelphia, PA), Feb. 15, 1850, p. 2 ("This letter to Mazzei is a signal proof of the malignity and dishonesty with which Jefferson has been pursued by some of his enemies. Signor Mazzei, an Italian republican, had resided for some years in Virginia, on intimate terms with Jefferson, and returned to Tuscany about 1791. Jefferson wrote to him in April 24, 1796, a letter which was afterwards translated into Italian, and published in Florence. From this Italian version it was translated into French, and published in Paris. From this French version it was translated into English, and published in the United States, to prove Jefferson's 'instinctive hatred of Washington!' ").

70. Randall E. Adkins, ed., *The Evolution of Political Parties, Campaigns, and Elections: Landmark Documents, 1787–2007* (Washington, DC: CQ Press, 2008), p. 37.

71. Joseph R. Conlin, *The American Past: A Survey of American History* (Boston, MA: Wadsworth, 9th ed. 2010), p. 196; "Thomas Jefferson, Aaron Burr and the Election of 1800," Smithsonian.com,

http://www.smithsonianmag.com/history/thomas-jefferson-aaron-burr-and-the-election-of-1800-131082359/.

72. Marraro, *Philip Mazzei, Virginia's Agent in Europe,* p. 14; Carlo Calisse, *A History of Italian Law* (Washington, D.C.: Beard Books, Layton B. Register, trans. 1928), Vol. II, p. 485.

73. Bessler, *The Birth of American Law,* pp. 182–195, 287.

74. Ibid., p. 174.

75. Ibid., pp. 131–32.

76. Ibid., pp. 17–18.

77. Cesare Beccaria, *On Crimes and Punishments* (Englewood Cliffs, NJ: Prentice Hall Henry Paolucci, trans. 1963), p. 11.

78. John Adams, *A Defence of the Constitutions of Government of the United States, Against the Attack of M. Turgot in His Letter to Dr. Price, Dated the Twenty-Second Day of March, 1778* (Philadelphia: William Cobbett, 3d ed. 1797), Vol. 1, p. 133.

79. Pierre Force, *Self-Interest Before Adam Smith: A Geneaology of Economic Science* (Cambridge: Cambridge University Press, 2003), p. 8.

80. Barry Alan Shain, *The Myth of American Individualism: The Protestant Origins of American Political Thought* (Princeton: Princeton University Press, 1994), p. 186.

81. George A. Peek, Jr., ed., *The Political Writings of John Adams* (Indianapolis, IN: Hackett Pub. Co., 1954), p. xiv.

82. Stephen L. Schechter, ed., *Roots of the Republic: American Founding Documents Interpreted* (Lanham, MD: Madison House Publishers, 1990), p. 123.

83. Richard Samuelson, "John Adams and the Republic of Laws," in Bryan-Paul Frost & Jeffrey Sikkenga, eds., *History of American Political Thought* (Lanham, MD: Lexington Books, 2003), p. 114.

84. James A. Gardner, ed., *State Expansion of Federal Constitutional Liberties: Individual Rights in a Dual Constitutional System* (New York: Psychology Press, 1999), Vol. 1, p. ix.

85. The Declaration of Rights of the 1780 Massachusetts Constitution envisioned "a government of laws and not of men." Constitution of the Commonwealth of Massachusetts (1780), Art. XXX.

86. Bessler, *The Birth of American Law,* p. 174.

87. Declaration of Independence (July 4, 1776).

88. John Adams, *A Defence of the Constitutions of Government of the United States, Against the Attack of M. Turgot in His Letter to Dr. Price, Dated the Twenty-Second Day of March, 1778* (Philadelphia: William Cobbett, 3d ed. 1797), Vol. 1, pp. 96, 99, 103, 108, 110–11, 120, 124.

89. Declaration of Independence (July 4, 1776).

90. Cesare Beccaria's influence would extend throughout the United States. *See generally* Bessler, *The Birth of American Law; see also* James W. Ely, Jr. & David J. Bodenhamer, *Regionalism and American Legal History: The Southern Experience,* 39 Vand. L. Rev. 539, 557 (1986) ("The tenets of revolutionary republicanism demanded a limitation on the power of the state, thus stimulating criminal law reform throughout the new nation, including the South. Heavily influenced by eighteenth century rationalism, the writings of Montesquieu and Cesare Beccaria, and the codification efforts of Edward Livingston, southern legislators by the 1820s had drafted criminal codes that rivaled those of northern jurisdictions.").

91. H. Jefferson Powell, *The Original Understanding of Original Intent,* 98 Harv. L. Rev. 885, 893 (1985).

92. Stephen L. Schechter, ed., *Roots of the Republic: American Founding Documents Interpreted* (Lanham, MD: Madison House, 1990), pp. 416–19.

93. U.S. Const., amend. XIII.

94. John Adams, *A Defence of the Constitutions of Government of the United States, Against the Attack of M. Turgot in His Letter to Dr. Price, Dated the Twenty-Second Day of March, 1778* (Philadelphia: William Cobbett, 3d ed. 1797), Vol. 1, pp. i–ii, xii, xxi, xxix–xxxii, 9, 57–58, 365; Paul A. Rahe, *Against Throne and Altar: Machiavelli and Political Theory under the English Republic* (Cambridge: Cambridge University Press, 2008), p. 354 & n.21.

95. Andrew Burnaby to George Washington, Apr. 19, 1765, *available at* www.founders.archives. gov. The Corsican Republic was a representative democracy led by a General Diet that met annually and by an executive committee, of which General Pasquale Paoli—the country's commander-in-

chief—was president. Paoli, the Corsican patriot who rose to power in 1755 after summoning islanders to proclaim a constitution, reportedly carried Montesquieu's works about with him. The Genose had long sought to control the island, but Paoli—who ruled from 1755 to 1769—sought to forge a permanent republic and new laws. He founded a college, instituted a system of public education, and encouraged agricultural production. He also drove the Geneose from every port except Bastia. Although the Genoese were unsuccessful in dislodging him, Paoli had been forced to take refuge in England in 1769 after his countrymen battled more powerful French forces, an army of 22,000 men, who seized control of Corsica and defeated Paoli's troops. The island—the home of many patriotic Corsicans— had been ceded to France by a frustrated and embattled Genoa in 1768, and the final battle, at Ponte Nuevo, was lost in 1769, leading to Paoli's exile in England. In England, Paoli became—as one scholar put it—"a part of the English-Irish-American radical movement." The Scottish writer James Boswell, who went to Corisca in the mid-1760s and befriended Paoli, authored *An Account of Corsica*, making General Paoli famous throughout the world. H. G. Koenigsberger, *Politicians and Virtuosi: Essays in Early Modern History* (London: The Hambledon Press, 1986), p. 61; Herbert Aptheker, *The American Revolution 1763–1783* (New York: International Publishers, 1960), p. 161; James Boswell, *An Account of Corsica, the Journal of a Tour to that Island, and Memoirs of Pascal Paoli* (London: Edward and Charles Dilly, 1768); "Corte of Corsica," *San Francisco Chronicle* (San Francisco, CA), Jan. 27, 1889, p. 1; "Glimpse of Corsica," *Akron Daily Democrat* (Akron, OH), Sept. 30, 1899, p. 8; "Corsica and De Paoli," *The Bucks County Gazette* (Briston, PA), Sept. 18, 1914, p. 4; A. W. Macy, "Curious Bits of History: A Great Corsican Patriot," *The Bedford Gazette* (Bedford, PA), May 5, 1916, p. 3; Editorial note 4, Committee of the Boston Sons of Liberty to John Wilkes, Nov. 4, 1769, *available at* www. founders.archives.gov.

96. To James Madison from Thomas Appleton (Abstract), 11 June 1805, *available at* www.founders. archives.gov.

97. Theodore N. Ferdinand & Helmut Kury, "Punitivity in the United States," *in* Helmut Kury & Theodore N. Ferdinand, eds., *International Perspectives on Punitivity* (Bochum: Universitätsverlag Brockmeyer, 2008), p. 88.

98. American Archives: Documents of the American Revolutionary Period, 1774–1776, http:// amarch.lib.niu.edu/islandora/object/niu-amarch%3A86601.

99. Lorenzo Sears, *John Hancock: The Picturesque Patriot* (Boston: Little, Brown, & Co., 1913), pp. 109, 228.

100. Brian Steele, *Thomas Jefferson and American Nationhood* (Cambridge: Cambridge University Press, 2012), p. 40 n.136.

101. Bessler, *The Birth of American Law*, pp. 66, 147; *see also Littell's Living Age* (Boston: Littell and Co., 1891), Vol. CLXXXIX, p. 709 (noting that "[d]uring the War of Independence impassioned appeals were made to the French of Canada to join the thirteen colonies against England" and "references were made to the writings of Beccaria and to the spirit of the 'immortal Montesquieu'").

102. Donald Fyson, Université Laval/CIEQ, La peine capitale au Québec (1760–1960): de l'adaptation coloniale au conservatisme provincial (Jan. 2016).

103. David W. Robson, *Educating Republicans: The College in the Era of the American Revolution, 1750–1800* (Westport, CT: Greenwood Press, 1985), p. 70.

104. "To the Inhabitants of the Province of Quebec," *The Pennsylvania Gazette* (Philadelphia, PA), Nov. 9, 1774, pp. 5–6.

105. Rebecca K. Kingston, ed., *Montesquieu and His Legacy* (Albany: State University of New York Press, 2009), p. 275.

106. "To the Inhabitants of the Province of Quebec," *The Pennsylvania Gazette* (Philadelphia, PA), Nov. 9, 1774, pp. 5–6; U.S. Const., art. 1, sec. 9 & amend. I; John Sergeant, *Eulogy on Charles Carroll of Carrollton: Delivered at the Request of the Select and Common Councils of the City of Philadelphia (Dec. 31, 1832)* (Philadelphia: Lydia R. Bailey, 1833), pp. 39, 42; Scott McDermott, *Charles Carroll of Carrollton: Faithful Revolutionary* (New York: Scepter Publishers, 2002), p. 68. Cesare Beccaria, who supported *certain* punishments rather than *severe* ones, also supported the right to trial by jury in *On Crimes and Punishments*. Bessler, *The Birth of American Law*, p. 36.

107. "To the Inhabitants of the Province of Quebec," *The Pennsylvania Gazette* (Philadelphia, PA), Nov. 9, 1774, pp. 5–6.

108. Ibid.

109. The Boston Tea Party took place in December 1773. Angered by the British Parliament's attempt to give a monopoly on the import of tea into America to the East India Company, colonists boarded ships in the harbor and threw more than 300 chests of tea overboard. Steven L. Danver, *Revolts, Protests, Demonstrations, and Rebellions in American History: An Encyclopedia* (Santa Barbara, CA: ABC-CLIO, 2011), Vol. 1, pp. 204–5.

110. The confederation of Canada, now more than 150 years old, did not occur until 1867. *The Canadian Times* (Canada: The Carswell Co., 1911), Vol. 30, p. 828.

111. "To the Inhabitants of the Province of Quebec," *The Pennsylvania Gazette* (Philadelphia, PA), Nov. 9, 1774, pp. 5–6. The October 26, 1774 letter of the Continental Congress, signed by its president Henry Middleton, concluded: "That Almighty God may incline your minds to approve our equitable and necessary measures, to add yourselves to us, to put your fate, whenever you suffer injuries which you are determined to oppose, not on the small influence of your single province, but on the consolidated powers of North-America, and may grant to our joint exertions an event as happy as our cause is just, is the fervent prayer of us, your sincere and affectionate friends and fellow-subjects." Ibid.

112. Alan B. Simmons, *Immigration and Canada: Global and Transnational Perspectives* (Toronto: Canadian Scholars' Press, 2010), p. 53; Rand Dyck, *Canadian Politics* (Toronto: Nelson Education, 5th ed. 2012), p. 106.

113. Bessler, *Cruel and Unusual*, pp. 86–87, 108.

114. Ibid., p. 49.

115. Ibid., p. 178.

116. Ibid., pp. 179–81.

117. Louis J. Palmer, Jr., *The Death Penalty: An American Citizen's Guide to Understanding Federal and State Laws* (Jefferson, NC: McFarland & Co., 1998), p. 14 ("Mandatory death penalty statutes existed in all of the original 13 colonies prior to the Revolutionary War. Offenses that carried mandatory death sentences included: murder, arson, rape, robbery, burglary, sodomy, piracy, and treason.").

118. Steven Wilf, *Law's Imagined Republic: Popular Politics and Criminal Justice in Revolutionary America* (Cambridge: Cambridge University Press, 2010), p. 139.

119. Bessler, *Cruel and Unusual*, pp. 188, 300.

120. Ibid., p. 141.

121. Ibid., pp. 141–42, 156–57. In fact, after it was published and translated into English in 1767, Beccaria's treatise—publicized by Blackstone and Voltaire, whose French-to-English commentary on it was regularly reprinted with *On Crimes and Punishments*—steadily grew in popularity on American soil. Ibid., pp. 39, 56.

122. Jordan M. Steiker, *The American Death Penalty: Constitutional Regulation as the Distinctive Feature of American Exceptionalism*, 67 U. Miami L. Rev. 329, 331 (2013).

123. Bessler, *Cruel and Unusual*, pp. 183–84.

124. Bessler, *The Birth of American Law*, pp. 226, 373–74.

125. Ibid., p. 157.

126. Ibid.

127. Todd R. Clear, George F. Cole & Michael D. Reisig, *American Corrections* (Belmont, CA: Wadsworth, 10th ed., 2013), p. 44.

128. Lawrence M. Friedman, *A History of American Law* (New York: Simon & Schuster, 1985), p. 281.

129. Norval Morris & David J. Rothman, eds., *The Oxford History of the Prison: The Practice of Punishment in Western Society* (Oxford: Oxford University Press, 1995), p. 103; Douglas Bradburn, *The Citizenship Revolution: Politics & the Creation of the American Union 1774–1804* (Charlottesville: University of Virginia Press, 2009), p. 196.

130. Louis P. Masur, *Rites of Execution: Capital Punishment and the Transformation of American Culture, 1776–1865* (Oxford: Oxford University Press, 1991), p. 71.

131. Charles Richmond Henderson, *Correction and Prevention* (New York: Russell Sage Foundation, 1910), p. 151; *The Complete Works of Edward Livingston on Criminal Jurisprudence: Consisting of Systems of Penal Law for the State of Louisiana and for the United States of America; with the Introductory*

Reports to the Same (New York: The National Prison Association of the United States of America, 1873), Vol. 1, pp. 31, 36–37, 56, 116.

132. Bessler, *Cruel and Unusual*, pp. 85–91.

133. Guyora Binder, *Felony Murder* (Stanford, CA: Stanford University Press, 2012), p. 128.

134. Mitchel P. Roth, *Prisons and Prison Systems: A Global Encyclopedia* (Westport, CT: Greenwood Press, 2006), p. 29.

135. Bessler, *Cruel and Unusual*, p. 85.

136. Bessler, *The Birth of American Law*, p. 43.

137. Bessler, *Cruel and Unusual*, pp. 47–55.

138. Ibid., p. 52; Maeva Marcus, ed., *The Documentary History of the Supreme Court of the United States, 1789–1800: The Justices on Circuit, 1790–1794* (New York: Columbia University Press, 1988), Vol. 2, pp. 189–90, 402; Robert Aitken & Marilyn Aitken, *Law Makers, Law Breakers and Uncommon Trials* (Chicago, IL: American Bar Association, 2007), p. 15.

139. Dagobert D. Runes, ed., *The Selected Writings of Benjamin Rush* (New York: The Philosophical Library 1947), p. 46.

140. Bessler, *Cruel and Unusual*, p. 53; *see also* "America," *The Pennsylvania Packet* (Philadelphia, PA), May 12, 1787, p. 2 (reprinting extract from Dr. Rush's "Inquiry into the Effects of public Punishments upon Criminals, and upon Society" that was presented "at the House of his Excellency Benjamin Franklin, Esq. in Philadelphia, March 9, 1787").

141. "Communication," *Raleigh Register and North Carolina Gazette* (Raleigh, NC), June 5, 1846, p. 2 ("The right of Government to punish offences arises from *necessity*. It is based on the principle of self-preservation, which is applicable to Governments as well as individuals. 'Every punishment,' says Baron Montesquieu, 'which does not arise from *absolute necessity*, is *tyrannical*'—and *Beccaria*, in his admirable work on crimes, remarks 'All punishment which oversteps *necessity* become *tyranny*.'"); ibid. ("When one enters the social compact he is presumed to consent to a surrender of so much of his personal or natural liberty as may be necessary for the protection or safety of the whole. It is under this that Government derives the power to deprive one of life—limb—or member—or to inflict upon him any bodily pain whatever. When the necessity for such punishment ceases, then the right to inflict it likewise ends. If a milder penalty will accomplish the purpose, and afford ample protection to Society, then Government is bound to dispense with the harsher, or it becomes tyrannical. We are told 'that whoso shedeth man's blood, by man *shall* his blood be shed,' but when there is no absolute *necessity* for it, what right has Government to take life for any other offence?").

142. "To the Editor of the Evening Post," *The Evening Post* (New York, NY), Aug. 3, 1802, p. 2 ("[B]ut, says the great Montesquieu, 'every penal regulation which does not arise from absolute necessity, is tyrannical'. The question now recurs, Does this law arise from absolute necessity? Are there no other means less oppressive by which the contemplated benefit may be effected?"); "The Death Penalty—Let us Rid Ourselves of this Relic of Barbarism," *The Brooklyn Daily Eagle* (Brooklyn, NY), Aug. 29, 1867, p. 2 ("'Every punishment which does not arise from absolute necessity,' says the great Montesquieu, 'is tyran[n]ical, or every act of authority of one man over another, or of a nation over a man, for which there is not an absolute necessity is tyrannical;' and if it is not a necessity to hang for any crime, and we believe it is not, the death penalty, therefore, is a war of a whole nation against one man.... It was said by Marquis Boccarin [sic], over one hundred years ago, 'that the punishment of death was pernicious to society, from the example of barbarity it affords,' 'and that it is absurd that the laws which detest and punish homicide should, in order to prevent murder, publicly commit murder themselves.'"); *compare* Charles E. Rice, *A Cultural Tour of the Legal Landscape: Reflections on Cardinal George's Law and Culture*, 1 Ave Maria L. Rev. 81, 85 (2003) ("The Catholic Church teaches ... that the use of the death penalty may not be justified for purposes of retribution, general deterrence, or generalized protection of society. Instead, the state may exercise capital punishment only where it is absolutely necessary to protect other lives from *that* criminal.").

143. "Communication," *Raleigh Register and North Carolina Gazette* (Raleigh, NC), June 5, 1846, p. 2.

144. *Memoir, Autobiography and Correspondence of Jeremiah Mason* (Kansas City, MO: Lawyers' International Pub. Co., 1917), p. 12.

145. Masur, *Rites of Execution*, p. 52.

146. *See generally* Bessler, *The Birth of American Law*; James R. Maxeiner, *A Government of Laws Not of Precedents 1776–1876: The Google Challenge to Common Law Myth*, 4 Br. J. Am. Leg. Studies 137, 158 (2015).

147. Rod Gragg, *Forged in Faith: How Faith Shaped the Birth of the Nation 1607–1776* (New York: Howard Books, 2010), pp. 22, 88, 185.

148. "A Bill for Proportioning Crimes and Punishments in Cases Heretofore Capital," *in* Julian P. Boyd et al., eds., *The Papers of Thomas Jefferson* (Princeton, NJ: Princeton University Press, 1950), Vol. 2.

149. Bessler, *Cruel and Unusual*, pp. 54–55.

150. John R. Shook, ed., *Dictionary of Early American Philosophers* (New York: Bloomsbury Academic, 2012), p. 882; W. Hamilton Bryson, *The History of Legal Education in Virginia*, 14 U. Rich. L. Rev. 155, 176 (1979); Mary Wood, "The First Law Professor," *UVA Lawyer* (Fall 2016), p. 56; Albert Ellery Bergh, ed., *The Writings of Thomas Jefferson* (Washington, DC: The Thomas Jefferson Memorial Association, 1907), Vol. 19, p. 494; Nancy Isenberg, *Fallen Founder: The Life of Aaron Burr* (London: Penguin Books, 2007), p. 509 n.21; Litchfield Historical Society, http://www.litchfieldhistoricalsociety. org/history/law_school.php; "A Brief Timeline of Our First Two Centuries," Harvard Law School, hls. harvard.edu/about/history/.

151. Bessler, *Cruel and Unusual*, p. 142.

152. Ibid., p. 54.

153. Bessler, *The Birth of American Law*, p. 185.

154. Bessler, *Cruel and Unusual*, p. 141; Henry S. Randall, *The Life of Thomas Jefferson* (Philadelphia: J. B. Lippincott, 1863), Vol. 1, p. 218.

155. Thomas Jefferson to Edmund Pendleton, Aug. 26, 1776, *available at* www.founders.archives.gov; Thomas Jefferson to Maria Cosway, Oct. 12, 1786 (Jefferson writes of "abolishing sanguinary punishments" and "reforming and improving our laws in general"), *available at* www.founders.archives.gov. In a draft bill to establish a government for the "territory of Columbia," Jefferson included this typical provision: "Excessive bail shall not be required, nor excessive fines imposed nor cruel & unusual punishment inflicted." Jefferson Papers, Draft Bill [Before 7 December 1801], *available at* www.founders.archives.gov.

156. Bessler, *The Birth of American Law*, p. 189; *see also* Jeffery K. Sawyer, *The Rhetoric and Reality of English Law in Colonial Maryland, Part I — 1632–1689*, 108 *Maryland Historical Magazine* 393, 393 (2013) ("The history of English law in Maryland produced such powerful elements in local political culture, that even as the British colonial regime collapsed (1774–1776), the right of the inhabitants to English common law and selected British statutes was enshrined and preserved in the state's first constitution."); Jeffrey K. Sawyer, *English Law and American Democracy in the Revolutionary Republic: Maryland, 1776–1822*, 108 *Maryland Historical Magazine* 261, 261 (2013) ("On the one hand, English law had been built into the basic fabric of American law through authorizing charters, governor's commissions, and like acts, as well as by decades of specific local legislation and judicial decisions in colonial courts. On the other hand, government based on the sovereignty of the people and common sense was a fundamental purpose of the fight for independence."); ibid., p. 263 ("Between 1776 and 1784, eleven of the original thirteen states made some provision for the continuing authority of the common law and British statutes."); ibid., p. 268 ("In 1776 the common law was understood almost universally in the English-speaking world as a body of ancient principles underpinning the fundamental rights of free Englishmen and as a vast repository of specific rules, substantive and procedural, that defined property rights, differentiated 'lawful' from 'unlawful' acts in everyday commerce, defined criminality and provided a system for dealing with criminals, and so on.").

157. Bessler, *The Birth of American Law*, pp. 183–84.

158. Francis D. Cogliano, *Thomas Jefferson: Reputation and Legacy* (Charlottesville: University of Virginia Press, 2006), p. 43 n.59; Peter S. Onuf, ed., *Jeffersonian Legacies* (Charlottesville: University of Virginia Press, 1993), p. 227; Thomas Jefferson to Skelton Jones, July 28, 1809, *available at* www.founders.archives.gov. In that letter, Jefferson described his involvement in the 1770s project to revise Virginia's laws, then applauds the adoption of the penitentiary system. As Jefferson wrote to Jones:

[A]fter settling our plan, Colo Mason declined undertaking the execution of any part of it, as not being sufficiently read in the law. mr Lee very soon afterwards died, & the work was distributed between Mr Wythe, mr Pendleton & myself. to me was assigned the Common law (so far as we thought of altering it), & the statutes down to the Reformation, or end of the reign of Elizabeth; to mr Wythe the subsequent body of the statutes, & to mr Pendleton the Virginia laws. this distribution threw into my part the laws concerning crimes & punishments, the law of descents, & the laws concerning religion. after completing our work separately, we met (mr W. mr P. & myself) in Williamsburg, and held a very long session, in which we went over the 1st & 2d parts in the order of time, weighing & correcting every word, & reducing them to the form in which they were afterwards reported. when we proceeded to the 3d part, we found that mr Pendleton had not exactly seised the intentions of the committee, which were to reform the language of the Virginia laws, and reduce the matter to a simple style & form. he had copied the acts verbatim, only omitting what was disapproved; and some family occurrence calling him indispensably home, he desired mr Wythe & myself to make it what we thought it ought to be, and authorised us to report him as concurring in the work. we accordingly divided the work, & reexecuted it entirely so as to assimilate it's plan & execution to the other parts, as well as the shortness of the time would admit, and we brought the whole body of British statutes, & laws of Virginia into 127. acts, most of them short. this is the history of that work as to it's execution. it's matter & the nature of the changes made will be a proper subject for the consideration of the historian. experience has convinced me that the change in the style of the laws was for the better, & it has sensibly reformed the style of our laws from that time downwards, insomuch that they have obtained in that respect the approbation of men of consideration on both sides of the Atlantick. whether the change in the stile & form of the criminal law, as introduced by mr Taylor, was for the better is not for me to judge. the digest of that act employed me longer than I believe all the rest of the work; for it rendered it necessary for me to go with great care over Bracton, Britton the Saxon statutes, & the works of authority on criminal law: & it gave me great satisfaction to find that in general I had only to reduce the law to it's antient Saxon condition, stripping it of all the innovations & rigorisms of subsequent times, to make it what it should be. the substitution of the Penitentiary instead of labor on the high road, & of some other punishments truly objectionable, is a just merit to be ascribed to mr Taylor's law. when our report was made, the idea of a Penitentiary had never been suggested: the happy experiment of Pensylvania we had not then the benefit of. Ibid.

159. Bessler, *Cruel and Unusual*, p. 145.

160. A. Owen Aldridge, *Thomas Paine's American Ideology* (Cranbury, NJ: Associated University Presses, 1984), p. 71; Jonathan I. Israel, *Democratic Enlightenment: Philosophy, Revolution, and Human Rights 1750–1790* (Oxford: Oxford University Press, 2011), p. 452.

161. Luigino Bruni, *The Genesis and Ethos of the Market* (New York: Palgrave Macmillan, 2012), pp. 137–40; R. H. Inglis Palgrave, ed., *Dictionary of Political Economy* (New York: Palgrave Macmillan, 1894), Vol. 1, p. 637; *see also* ibid., p. 127 (after noting the Beccaria's lecture notes "are very remarkable considering they were written before A. Smith's *Wealth of Nation*," the *Dictionary of Political Economy* emphasizes: "Beccaria treats political economy as an art to maximise the value of the produce of work, regarding labourers as engines whose *duty* has to be maximised. From this principle he deduces the necessity of a division of labour, a determination of the value of a labourer, and the nature and function of capital. His lectures are also remarkable for an exposition of the laws of growth of population in relation to subsistence, now known as Malthus's theory.").

162. Bruni, *The Genesis and Ethos of the Market*, pp. 137–39; Ferdinando Facchinei, *Note ed osservazioni sul libro intitolato Dei delitti e delle pene* (1765).

163. John P. Kaminski, ed., *Citizen Paine: Thomas Paine's Thoughts on Man, Government, Society, and Religion* (Lanham, MD: Madison House, 2002), p. 6; J. Thomas Scharf & Thompson Westcott, *History of Philadelphia 1609–1884* (Philadelphia: L. H. Everts & Co., 1884), Vol. 1, p. 310.

164. David Wootton, ed., *Republicanism, Liberty, and Commercial Society, 1649–1776* (Stanford, CA: Stanford University Press, 1994), p. 414 n.136.

165. Ibid., pp. 36–39.

166. Bessler, *The Birth of American Law*, p. 179.

167. Thomas Jefferson to John Adams, Dec. 10, 1819, *reprinted in* Joyce Appleby & Terence Ball, eds., *Jefferson: Political Writings* (Cambridge: Cambridge University Press, 1999), pp. 225–26.

168. Humbert S. Nelli, ed., *The United States and Italy: The First Two Hundred Years: Proceedings of the Ninth Annual Conference of the American Italian Historical Association (AIHA) Held at Georgetown University* (Washington, D.C., Oct. 8–10, 1976), p. 32.

169. Cecilia Miller, *Enlightenment and Political Fiction: The Everyday Intellectual* (New York: Routledge, 2016), pp. 215–20.

170. Bessler, *The Birth of American Law*, pp. 17, 107–8, 116, 118, 120, 124, 134–36, 175–79, 502.

171. *E.g.*, John Adams, *A Defence of the Constitutions of Government of the United States, Against the Attack of M. Turgot in His Letter to Dr. Price, Dated the Twenty-Second Day of March, 1778* (Philadelphia: William Cobbett, 3d ed. 1797).

172. John Adams Papers, June 1771 (entry for June 13, 1771) & John Adams to Nathanael Greene, May 24, 1777, *available at* www.founders.archives.gov; James Madison Papers, Report on Books for Congress, Jan. 23, 1783, *available at* www.founders.archives.gov.

173. Bessler, *The Birth of American Law*, p. 159.

174. Samuel Paterson to Alexander Hamilton, Feb. 16, 1793, *available at* www.founders.archives.gov (citing Gaetano Filangieri, *An Analysis of the Science of Legislation* (London: W. Kendall, trans. 1791)). William Kendall's translation, published in London in the early 1790s, was the first English translation of Filangieri's work. At that time, Kendall only translated the first book; the edition of 1806 covered books one and two. "Gaetano Filangieri and Benjamin Franklin: The Relationship Between the Italian Enlightenment and the U.S. Constitution," pp. 65–66, *available at* http://sedi2.esteri.it/sitiweb/ AmbWashington/Pubblicazioni/2_filangieri_interno.pdf. For further information on the influence of the Italian Enlightenment on the American Revolution, see John D. Bessler, *The Italian Enlightenment and the American Revolution: Cesare Beccaria's Forgotten Influence on American Law*, Mitchell Hamline L.J. Pub. Pol'y & Practice, Vol. 37, Iss. 1, Article 1.

175. Marrone, *Encyclopedia of Italian Literary*, p. 663.

176. Gaetano Filangieri, *An Analysis of the Science of Legislation, from the Italian of the Chevalier Filangieri* (London: G. G. J. & J. Robinson, William Kendall, trans., 1791), pp. 3–4; Cecilia Feilla, *The Sentimental Theater of the French Revolution* (New York: Routledge, 2013), p. 179.

177. David A.J. Richards, *Interpretation and Historiography*, 58 S. Cal. L. Rev. 489, 526 (1985).

178. John Adams, *A Defence of the Constitutions of Government of the United States, Against the Attack of M. Turgot in His Letter to Dr. Price, Dated the Twenty-Second Day of March, 1778* (Philadelphia: William Cobbett, 3d ed. 1797), Vol. 1, p. 128.

179. Joyce Appleby & Terence Ball, eds., *Jefferson: Political Writings* (Cambridge: Cambridge University Press, 1999), p. 74; S. J. Kleinberg, *Votes for Women: Women in the United States 1830–1945* (New Brunswick, NJ: Rutgers University Press, 1999), p. 91; Bessler, *The Birth of American Law*, pp. 306–9; "Jefferson's Views on Slavery," Thomas Jefferson's Poplar Forest, http://www.poplarforest.org/ jefferson/plantation-life/jeffersons-views-on-slavery/#.WKHTRTKZOjQ; William Frederick Poole, *Anti-Slavery Opinions Before the Year 1800: Read Before the Cincinnati Literary Club* (Bedford, MA: Applewood Books, 2008), pp. 42–45. The preamble to the organization's new constitution read:

> It having pleased the Creator of the world to make of one flesh all the children of men, it becomes them to consult and promote each other's happiness, as members of the same family, however diversified they may be by color, situation, religion, or different states of society. It is more especially the duty of those persons who profess to maintain for themselves the rights of human nature, and who acknowledge the obligations of Christianity, to use such means as are in their power to extend the blessings of freedom to every part of the human race; and in a more particular manner to such of their fellow-creatures as are entitled to freedom by the laws and constitutions of any of the United States, and who, notwithstanding, are detained in bondage by fraud or violence. From a full conviction of the truth and obligation of these principles; from a desire to diffuse them wherever the miseries and vices of slavery exist, and in humble confidence of the favor and support of the Father of mankind, the subscribers have associated themselves, under the title of 'The Pennsylvania

Society for promoting the Abolition of Slavery, and the Relief of Free Negroes unlawfully
held in Bondage, and for improving the condition of the African race.'
Ibid., pp. 45–46 n.*.

180. Israel, *Democratic Enlightenment*, pp. 359–61; *see also* Povolo, *The Novelist and the Archivist*, p. 81 n.17 ("The Milanese Gorani was familiar with Giulia Beccaria's circle, and he kept track of her even from his distant exile in Geneva.").

181. Israel, *Democratic Enlightenment*, p. 362; To George Washington from the National Assembly of France, Aug. 26, 1792 & To Alexander Hamilton from Jean Marie Roland, Oct. 10, 1792, *available at* www.founders.archives.gov.

182. Anthony Kenny, *Philosophy in the Modern World: A New History of Western Philosophy* (Oxford: Oxford University Press, 2007), Vol. 4, p. 2.

183. Lynn Hunt, *Inventing Human Rights: A History* (New York: W. W. Norton & Co., 2007), p. 254 n.43.

184. Catherine Elliott, "France," *in* Heller & Dubber, *The Handbook of Comparative Criminal Law*, p. 210.

185. Ibid.

186. Bonnie R. Nelson, *Criminal Justice Research in Libraries and on the Internet* (Westport, CT: Greenwood Press, 1997), p. x.

187. Declaration of Independence (July 4, 1776).

188. Pietro Verri's name is largely absent from early American newspapers. A search for his name on the database newspapers.com reveals that the first references to his name appear in September 1899 in various Kansas newspapers. Those newspapers take note of a letter that Pietro Verri wrote in 1780 on the subject of "English calmness." "An Italian on the English," *The Osage County Chronicle* (Burlingame, KS), Sept. 20, 1899, p. 3; "An Italian on the English," *The Advocate* (Lakin, KS), Sept. 21, 1899, p. 7; "An Italian on the English," *The Hoisington Dispatch* (Hoisington, KS), Sept. 21, 1899, p. 7; "An Italian on the English," *Garnett Journal* (Garnett, KS), Sept. 22, 1899, p. 7; "An Italian on the English," *The Valley Falls New Era* (Valley Falls, KS), Sept. 23, 1899, p. 7.

189. Gaetana Marrone, ed., *Encyclopedia of Italian Literary Studies* (New York: Routledge, 2007), p. 1980.

190. Ann Hallamore Caesar & Michael Caesar, *Modern Italian Literature* (Cambridge: Polity Press, 2007), p. 38.

191. Joseph A. Schumpeter, *History of Economic Analysis* (New York: Routledge, 1997), p. 178 ("Count Pietro Verri (1728–97), an officer in the Austrian administration of Milan—but not a teacher—would have to be included in any list of the greatest economists. But though it would be easy to survey his various recommendations as to policy—which for him were the important things; in the preface to his main work, he exclaimed: *potessi io dire qualche cosa di utile, potessi io farla* (how I wish to say something useful, nay, to do it!)—it is less easy to convey an idea of his purely scientific achievement; some aspects of it will be mentioned later. Here we need to mention only two of his many publicaitons, the *Elementi del commercio* (1760), which established him, and the *Meditazioni sull' economia politica* (1771; republ. in the Custodi collection; there are French and German translations) into which the former was expanded. Besides presenting a powerful synthesis, these works contain a number of original contributions (among them his constant-outlay demand curve). Among other things, he had a clear if undeveloped conception of economic equilibrium based, in the last instance, upon the 'calculus of pleasure and pain' (he anticipated Jevons' phrase) and was, as far as this goes, rather above than below A. Smith.").

192. Allen Jayne, *Jefferson's Declaration of Independence: Origins, Philosophy, and Theology* (Lexington, KY: The University Press of Kentucky, 1998), pp. 128–29.

193. Ibid., p. 129. "That we call *Good*," Locke wrote, is that "which *is apt to cause or increase Pleasure, or diminish Pain in us*. And on the contrary, we name that *Evil*, which *is apt to produce or increase any Pain, or diminish any Pleasure in us*." Ibid. Locke believed that "all Men desire Happiness," and that it was the "great end" of human beings, making men devoted to the "pursuit of happiness." Ibid., pp. 129–30.

194. Stephen D. Sowle, *A Regime of Social Death: Criminal Punishment in the Age of Prisons*, 21 N.Y.U. Rev. L. & Soc. Change 497, 524 (1995) ("Inspired by European writers such as Cesare Beccaria,

American reformers condemned the bodily punishments of the colonial period as inhumane and self-defeating. In Beccaria's words, 'the severity of punishment of itself emboldens men to commit the very wrongs it is supposed to prevent,' because they 'are driven to commit additional crimes' in order to avoid detection.").

195. Kevin J. Hayes, *The Road to Monticello: The Life and Mind of Thomas Jefferson* (Oxford: Oxford University Press, 2008), p. 338.

196. America's Founding Documents, National Archives, https://www.archives.gov/founding-docs.

197. Hayes, *The Road to Monticello*, pp. 157, 209, 219.

198. Bessler, *The Birth of American Law*, pp. 205–9, 344–47.

199. Calvin J. Larson & Gerald R. Garrett, *Crime, Justice, and Society* (Walnut Creek, CA: AltaMira Press, 2d ed. 1996), p. 180.

200. Samuel Walker, *Popular Justice: A History of American Criminal Justice* (Oxford: Oxford University Press, 1980), p. 40.

201. Clayton E. Cramer, *For the Defense of Themselves and the State: The Original Intent and Judicial Interpretation of the Right to Keep and Bear Arms* (Westport, CT: Praeger, 1994), p. 28; Brent L. Pickett, *Historical Dictionary of Homosexuality* (Lanham, MD: The Scarecrow Press, 2009), p. 78; Thomas F. X. Noble, Barry Strauss, Duane J. Osheim, Kristen B. Neuschel, Elinor A. Accampo, David D. Roberts & William B. Cohen, *Western Civilization Beyond Borders* (Boston, MA: Houghton Mifflin Co., 5th ed. 2008), Vol. 2, p. 567; *see also* V. A. C. Gatrell, *The Hanging Tree: Execution and the English People 1770–1868* (Oxford: Oxford University Press, 1994), p. 8 ("The Prussian code had restricted capital punishment as early as 1743, and after 1794 only murderers were executed."). "Until 1794 a Prussian Code dictated that those found guilty of 'unnatural acts' were to be burned at the stake...." Robert Aldrich & Garry Wotherspoon, eds., *Who's Who in Gay and Lesbian History: From Antiquity to World War II* (London: Routledge, 2002), p. 320.

202. Ellen Krefting, Aina Nøding & Mona Ringvej, ed., *Eighteenth-century Periodicals as Agents of Change: Perspectives on Northern Enlightenment* (Leiden, The Netherlands: Brill, 2015), pp. 31–32; *see also* Robert M. Bohm, *DeathQuest: An Introduction to the Theory and Practice of Capital Punishment in the United States* (Waltham, MA: Anderson Publishing, 4th ed., 2011), p. 174 n.113 ("Denmark, by an ordinance of December 18, 1767, deliberately abandoned the death penalty in cases where 'melancholy and other dismal persons (committed murder) for the exclusive purpose of losing their lives'").

203. Leon Radzinowicz & Marvin E. Wolfgang, *Crime and Justice: The Criminal in the Arms of the Law* (New York: Basic Books, 1977), p. 51 n. 5 ("In Dano-Norwegian legal history there is one remarkable example of the death penalty being abandoned because it defeated its purpose in a certain type of crime. The Ordinance of December 18, 1767, replaced the death penalty with penal servitude for life in cases where 'melancholy and other dismal persons [committed murder] for the exclusive purpose of losing their lives.'"); *see also* Mark Lindsay & David Lester, *Suicide by Cop: Committing Suicide by Provoking Police to Shoot You* (Amityville, NY: Baywood Publishing Co., 2004), p. 57 ("[T]he Danish government decided in 1767 to waive the death penalty in cases where the offender murdered in order to be executed.").

204. Tyge Krogh, *A Lutheran Plague: Murdering to Die in the Eighteenth Century* (Lieden, The Netherlands: Brill, 2012), pp. 149–50; *see also* ibid., p. 150 ("It could be assumed that the decree was an early consequence of Cesare Beccaria's *Dei delitti e delle pene* ('On Crimes and Punishments'), which was published in 1764. Beccaria's book, with its questioning of the rationality of the death penalty, quickly became well known all over Europe, including in Copenhagen."); ibid., p. 150 n.30 ("A Danish scientist informed Beccaria of the new decree a few weeks after it came out.") (citing Ditlev Tamm, 'Hvorfor læse Beccaria?,' in *Cesare Beccaria: Om forbrydelse og straf*, Copenhagen, 1998, p. 213).

205. Tamm, "Punishment in the Scandinavian Countries Since the 18th Century," p. 42.

206. J. Neville Figgis, *The Theory of the Divine Right of Kings* (Cambridge: Cambridge University Press, 1896, pp. 5–6.

207. Krogh, *A Lutheran Plague*, pp. 144–51; Krefting, Nøding & Ringvej, *Eighteenth-century Periodicals as Agents of Change*, p. 192.

208. Charles H. Ainsworth, ed., *Selected Readings for Introductory Sociology* (New York: MSS Information Corp., 1972), p. 74; *The Westminster Review* (London: Trübner & Co., 1882), pp. 356–57; "Execution of the State Criminals," *The Gentleman's Magazine and Historical Review*, Vol. 42 (May 1772); Almut Spalding, *Elise Reimarus (1735–1805), The Muse of Hamburg: A Woman of the German Enlightenment* (Würzburg, Königshausen & Neumann, 2005), pp. 146–47.

209. Krogh, *A Lutheran Plague*, p. 151; Carhart, *The Science of Culture in Enlightenment Germany*, pp. 65–66.

210. *Culture and Values: A Survey of the Humanities* (Clifton Park, NY: Cengage Learning, 2013), p. 556; Franck, *The Barbaric Punishment*, pp. 49–50.

211. *Cesare Beccaria and Modern Criminal Policy* (Milano: A. Giuffrè, 1990), p. 271; *see also* Ditlev Tamm, "Punishment in the Scandinavian Countries Since the 18th Century," *La Peine—Punishment* (Bruxelles: De Boeck Université, 1989), p. 34 ("During the late decades of the 18th century, King Gustaf III (1771–1792) worked for a reform of the penal law in Sweden. He was influenced by the ideas of the enlightenment and openly stated that punishment had other purposes than revenge. Inspired by the writings of Beccaria and the rational arguments against capital punishment, the king proposed restrictions in the use of death sentences."); John Boli, *New Citizens for a New Society: The Institutional Origins of Mass Schooling in Sweden* (Oxford: Pergamon Press, 1989), p. 98 ("Gustav III was also able to abolish the death penalty for a number of offenses: rape, dual adultery, fourth-conviction theft, and bigamy. Although the death penalty remained on the books for many crimes (68 in all at this time), all death sentences were subject to review by the king, and by the end of the 1780s actual execution of convicted criminals was quite rare.") (citations omitted); T. K. Derry, *A History of Scandinavia: Norway, Sweden, Denmark, Finland and Iceland* (Minneapolis: University of Minnesota Press, 1979), p. 186 (noting that Gustav III was "a king who admired the writings of Beccaria"); *compare* Tamm, "Punishment in the Scandinavian Countries Since the 18th Century," p. 35 ("When Gustaf III was murdered (1792) this rational and humanitarian reform period ended….").

212. Marcello Truzzi, *Sociology and Everyday Life* (Englewood Cliffs, NJ: Prentice-Hall, 1968), p. 128; Finn Hornum, "The Executioner: His Role and Status in Scandinavian Society," *in* Charles H. Ainsworth, ed., *Selected Readings for Introductory Sociology* (New York, NY: MSS Information Corp., 1972), p. 70.

213. Richard Volger, *A World View of Criminal Justice* (Aldershot: Ashgate, 2005), p. 47.

214. Carlo Calisse, *A History of Italian Law* (Washington, DC: Beard Books, 2001), Vol. 2, pp. 456, 460; *see also* ibid., pp. 460–61 ("The Society of Economics of Berne voted him a gold medal for the courage of his protest in aid of humanity against deep rooted prejudices. Even the Empress of Russia, who enjoyed corresponding with the French philosophers, learned through them of Beccaria and desired him at her Court. Though D'Alembert advised against it, he decided to accept the invitation and had already set out upon his journey when Lombardy, recognizing in him the trained mind capable of rendering a great service to his country, and fearing criticism should he be lost through the invitation of a foreign country, succeeded in holding him in Italy by creating for him in 1768 a professorship in the political sciences, later known as political economy.").

215. William Schabas, *The Abolition of the Death Penalty in International Law* (Cambridge: Cambridge University Press, 3d ed. 2002), p. 4; Corey Brettschneider, "Rights within the Social Contract: Rousseau on Punishment," *in* Austin Sarat, Lawrence Douglas & Martha Merrill Umphrey, *Law as Punishment/Law as Regulation* (Stanford, CA: Stanford Law Books, 2011), pp. 52, 59 (in speaking of "[t]he social treaty," Rousseau wrote: "Whoever wishes to preserve his life at the expense of others should also give it up for them when necessary…. The death penalty inflicted on criminals can be viewed from more or less the same point of view. It is in order to avoid being the victim of an assassin that person consents to die, were he to become one."); ibid., p. 60 (in another place, Rousseau wrote: "Frequency of physical punishment is always a sign of weakness or of torpor in the government. There is no wicked man who could not be made good for something. One has the right to put to death, even as an example, only someone who cannot be preserved without danger.").

Chapter 6

1. John D. Bessler, "The American Enlightenment: Eliminating Capital Punishment in the United States," *in* Lill Scherdin, ed., *Capital Punishment: A Hazard to a Sustainable Criminal Justice System?* (Surrey, England: Ashgate, 2014), p. 100; Kent S. Miller & Michael L. Radelet, *Executing the Mentally Ill: The Criminal Justice System and the Case of Alvin Ford* (Newbury Park, CA: Sage Publications, 1993), p. 111 n.5; John Ferling, *Adams vs. Jefferson: The Tumultuous Election of 1800* (Oxford: Oxford University Press, 2004), pp. xi–xii.

2. John D. Bessler, "Capital Punishment Law and Practices: History, Trends, and Developments," *in* James R. Acker, Robert M. Bohm and Charles S. Lanier, eds., *America's Experiment with Capital Punishment: Reflections on the Past, Present, and Future of the Ultimate Penal Sanction* (Durham, NC: Carolina Academic Press, 3d ed. 2014).

3. John D. Bessler, *Cruel and Unusual: The American Death Penalty and the Founders' Eighth Amendment* (Boston: Northeastern University Press, 2012), p. 51.

4. John D. Bessler, *The Birth of American Law: An Italian Philosopher and the American Revolution* (Durham, NC: Carolina Academic Press, 2014), pp. 3, 5, 34–35, 50, 65, 79–80, 147, 164, 166–67, 172, 192, 206, 270, 312, 331, 366, 369–70, 385, 396.

5. Ibid., pp. 9, 29, 48, 147, 180, 220, 333, 343, 366.

6. O. F. Lewis, *The Development of American Prisons and Prison Customs 1776–1845* (Albany, NY: Prison Association of New York, 1922), pp. 8–9, 11, 13–14, 46, 151, 257, 325, 342.

7. Ibid., pp. 25, 271, 293; Bessler, *The Birth of American Law*, pp. 317–20; Bernard E. Harcourt, *The Illusion of Free Markets: Punishment and the Myth of Natural Order* (Cambridge, MA: Harvard University Press, 2012), p. 214.

8. Mitchell P. Roth, *Prisons and Prison Systems: A Global Encyclopedia* (Westport, CT: Greenwood Press, 2006), p. 341.

9. *The Christian Examiner and Theological Review* (Boston: David Reed, 1826), Vol. 3, pp. 204–5.

10. Harry Ammon, *James Monroe: The Quest for National Identity* (Charlottesville: University of Virginia Press, 1990), p. 180.

11. Laurie Throness, *A Protestant Purgatory: Theological Origins of the Penitentiary Act, 1779* (Hampshire, UK: Ashgate Publishing, 1998), pp. 119–20; Tim Hitchcock & Robert Shoemaker, *London Lives: Poverty, Crime and the Making of a Modern City 1690–1800* (Cambridge: Cambridge University Press, 2015), p. 404; Penitentiary Act, 19 Geo. III, ch. 74 (1779).

12. A. Highmore, *Philanthropia Metropolitana: A View of the Charitable Institutions Established in and Near London, Chiefly during the Last Twelve Years* (London: Longman, Hurst, Rees, Orme, and Brown, 1822), pp. 555–56.

13. George E. Baker, ed., *The Works of William H. Seward* (New York: Redfield, 1853), p. 174; Gustave de Beaumont & Alexis de Tocqueville, *On the Penitentiary System in the United States and Its Application in France* (Carbondale, IL: Southern Illinois University Press, 1979) (1833), Vol. 2, pp. 39, 106, 119.

14. Shahid M. Shahidullah, *Crime Policy in America: Laws, Institutions, and Programs* (Lanham, MD: University Press of America, 2008), p. 61.

15. Wilbur R. Miller, ed., *The Social History of Crime and Punishment in America: An Encyclopedia* (Thousand Oaks, CA: Sage Publications, 2012), p. 1074.

16. John T. Whitehead, Mark Jones & Michael C. Braswell, *Exploring Corrections in America* (Newark, NJ: Matthew Bender & Co., 2008), pp. 46–47; Harcourt, *The Illusion of Free Markets*, pp. 214–15.

17. Daniel Bowen, *A History of Philadelphia* (Carlisle, MA: Applewood Books, 2009) (1839), p. 180.

18. J. A. C. Sykes, ed., *France in Eighteen Hundred and Two: Described in a Series of Contemporary Letters by Henry Redhead Yorke* (London: William Heinemann, 1906), pp. 251–52; Maestro, *Cesare Beccaria and the Origins of Penal Reform*, pp. 113–14, 121–22, 151–52.

19. Christopher Storrs, "The Savoyard State: Another Enlightened Despotism?," *in* Gabriel Paquette, ed., *Enlightened Reform in Southern Europe and Its Atlantic Colonies, c. 1750–1830* (Surrey, England:

Ashgate 2009), pp. 206, 210; Enciclopedia delle donne, http://translate.google.com/translate?hl=en&
sl=it&u=http://it.wikipedia.org/wiki/Giulia_Beccaria&prev=search (entry for Giulia Beccaria).

20. Claudio Povolo, *The Novelist and the Archivist: Fiction and History in Alessandro Manzoni's*
The Betrothed (Palgrave Macmillan, 2014), ch. 1, n.4.

21. 1 Helen Maria Williams, *A Tour in Switzerland; or, A View of the Present State of the Governments
and Manners of Those Cantons* (London: G. G. & J. Robinson, 1798), p. 227.

22. Lacy Collison-Morley, *Modern Italian Literature* (Boston: Little, Brown & Co., 1912), p. 180;
Ann Hallamore Caesar & Michael Caesar, *Modern Italian Literature* (Cambridge, UK: Polity Press,
2007), p. 87; Leon Radzinowicz, *A History of English Criminal Law and Its Administration from 1750:
The Movement for Reform, 1750–1833* (New York: Macmillan Co., 1948), Vol. 1, p. 277; Richard Bel-
lamy, Beccaria, On Crimes and Punishments *and Other Writings* (Cambridge: Cambridge University
Press, Richard Davies, trans. 1995), p. xxxix.

23. 9 Charles G. Herbermann, ed., *The Catholic Encyclopedia: An International Work of Reference
on the Constitution, Doctrine, Discipline, and History of the Catholic Church* (New York: Robert Appleton
Co., 1910), p. 634; Alessandro Manzoni (1785–1805), http://www.internetculturale.it/opencms/
directories/ViaggiNelTesto/manzoni/eng/a1.html.

24. 13 *The American Catholic Quarterly Review* 736–39 (1888).

25. James A. McCafferty, ed., *Capital Punishment* (New Brunswick, NJ: Aldine Transaction, 2010),
p. 14; *Pharmaceutical Journal and Transactions* (1864–65) (London: John Churchill and Sons, 1865),
Vol. VI, p. 31; John R. McKivigan, *Forgotten Firebrand: James Redpath and the Making of Nineteenth-
Century America* (Ithaca, NY: Cornell University Press, 2008), p. 94; John Cunningham, *The Quakers:
An International History* (Edinburgh: John Menzies & Co., 1868), p. 229; *The Chemist & Druggist: A
Monthly Trade Journal*, Vol. XXI, p. 325 (Aug. 15, 1879 issue); John Macrae Moir, *Capital Punishment,
Based on Professor Mittermaier's 'Todesstrafe'* (London: Smith, Elder and Co., 1865), p. 239; *see also*
James Langland, comp., *The Chicago Daily News Almanac and Year-Book for 1916* (1916), p. 135 (referring to the Chicago-based Anti-Capital Punishment Society of America); *see also* Irwin Isenberg,
ed., *The Death Penalty* (New York: The H. W. Wilson Co., 1977), p. 32 ("Anti-gallows societies came
into being in every state along the eastern seaboard, and in 1845 an American Society for the Abolition
of Capital Punishment was organized.").

26. Constitution of New Hampshire (June 2, 1784), Part I—The Bill of Rights, Art. XVIII.

27. Bessler, *The Birth of American Law*, p. 137.

28. Michael Tonry, ed., *The Oxford Handbook of Crime and Criminal Justice* (Oxford: Oxford University Press, 2011), p. 735; David Bruce, *The Life of Sir Thomas Fowell Buxton: Extraordinary Perseverance* (Lanham, MD: Lexington Books, 2014), p. 97 n.50; James Knowles, ed., *The Nineteenth
Century: A Monthly Review* (London: C. Kegan Paul & Co., 1878), Vol. 3, p. 803; Mrs. E. R. Pitman,
Elizabeth Fry (Boston: Roberts Brothers, 1886), pp. 109–11; *see also* Sara Malton, *Forgery in Nineteenth-Century Literature and Culture: Fictions of Finance from Dickens to Wilde* (New York: Palgrave
Macmillan, 2009), p. 149 n.2 ("In 1832 the Forgery Act and Coinage Offences Act abolished capital
punishment for all such offenses, except forgery of wills and powers of attorney to transfer stock;
capital punishment for these latter two offenses was abolished by the Forgery Act of 1837."); *compare*
ibid. ("[E]mbezzlement by servants of the Bank of England remained a capital crime until 1861,
when treason and murder alone remained statutory capital offenses. The last public execution took
place in 1868.").

29. Philip English MacKey, "Edward Livingston and the Origins of the Movement to Abolish
Capital Punishment in America," *Louisiana History: The Journal of the Louisiana Historical Association*,
Vol. 16, No. 2 (Spring 1975), pp. 145–66.

30. Victor Hugo, *The Last Day of a Condemned Man* (Surray, UK: Oneworld Classics, Christopher
Moncrieff, trans. 2009), pp. 5, 19, *available at* http://www.almaclassics.com/excerpts/lastday.pdf.

31. G. Larry Mays & L. Thomas Winfree, Jr., *Essentials of Corrections* (Belmont, CA: Wadsworth,
4th ed. 2009), pp. 39–40; Calvin J. Larson & Gerald R. Garrett, *Crime, Justice, and Society* (Lanham,
MD: AltaMira Press, 2d ed. 2003), p. 324.

32. Julius R. Ruff, *Violence in Early Modern Europe 1500–1800* (Cambridge: Cambridge University
Press, 2001), pp. 112–13; Patricia Ewick, Robert A. Kagan & Austin Sarat, eds., *Social Science, Social
Policy, and the Law* (New York: Russell Sage Foundation, 1999), pp. 47–48; W. David Lewis, *From*

Newgate to Dannemora: The Rise of the Penitentiary in New York, 1796–1848 (Ithaca, NY: Cornell University Press, 2009), pp. 15, 23–34, 58; Mark Jones & Peter Johnstone, *History of Criminal Justice* (Waltham, MA: Anderson Publishing, 5th ed. 2012), p. 151.

33. Todd R. Clear, George F. Cole & Michael D. Reisig, *American Corrections* (Belmont, CA: Wadsworth, 10th ed. 2013), p. 38; Mark Goldie & Robert Wokler, eds., *The Cambridge History of Eighteenth-Century Political Thought* (Cambridge: Cambridge University Press, 2006), p. 567; Marilyn McShane & Frank P. Williams III, *Criminal Justice: Contemporary Literature in Theory and Practice* (New York: Garland Publishing, 1997), p. 780 n.6.

34. Ronald R. Seagrave, *Dinwiddie County Virginia: A Brief History* (Charleston, SC: The History Press, 2012), p. 34.

35. Winfield Scott, *Memoirs of Lieut.-General Scott, LL.D.* (New York: Sheldon & Co., 1864), p. 26.

36. Povolo, *The Novelist and the Archivist*, p. 11.

37. As noted elsewhere, Alessandro Manzoni—the son of Cesare Beccaria's daughter Giulia—was, by most accounts, fathered by Giulia's lover Giovanni Verri, a brother of Pietro and Alessandro Verri. *See* Claudio Povolo, *The Novelist and the Archivist: Fiction and History in Alessandro Manzoni's* The Betrothed (New York: Palgrave Macmillan, 2014), p. 17 n.4 ("While Giulia's husband Pietro Manzoni—whom her father had forced her into marrying—recognized Alessandro as his son, Alessandro's biological father was Giovanni Verri, a musician and brother to Pietro and Alessandro Verri, both *philosophes* in Beccaria's circle. Giovanni Verri and Giulia Beccaria were lovers in the mid-1780s.").

38. Povolo, *The Novelist and the Archivist*, p. 11; *compare* Edward Peters, *Torture* (Philadelphia: University of Pennsylvania Press, 1985), p. 86 ("In 1842 Alessandro Manzoni published his epigonal indictment of the criminal procedure of the *ancien régime, The Story of the Column of Infamy*, an account of a famous trial in Milan in 1630, whose title referred to a column erected at the site of a demolished house of a criminal to remind the Milanese forever of the shame of the criminal."); *see also* Alessandro Manzoni (1785–1873), *I Promessi Sposi*, The Harvard Classics, 1909–14, Introductory Note, *available at* http://www.bartleby.com/21/1001.html (describing the history of Manzoni's historical novel); Povolo, *The Novelist and the Archivist*, p. 68 ("*Agostino Carli Rubbi was most likely the archivist from whom Manzoni came into possession of the 17th [century] trial records that inspired his novel. Carli Rubbi knew the Milanese cultural environment very well: in the 1760s [he] had been the favourite student of Cesare Beccaria, illustrious expert on criminal law and Manzoni's grandfather. Carli Rubbi first worked in the archive at San Teodoro and then in the Frari archive, where the documents of the former Venetian Republic had been transferred.*"); ibid., pp. 69–70 (noting that Agositino Carli Rubbi was born in Venice in 1748, studied law in Vienna, lived in Milan and was introduced to "men of letters" such as Giuseppe Gorani, Paolo Frisi and Pietro Verri; and further noting that Rubbi was Cesare Beccaria's student and friend who, according to one of Rubbi's own July 1770 letters, "[f]or the last fortnight" spent "each afternoon from one o'clock till after seven in enthusiasm and delight quite alone with my dear friend Beccaria, with never a dull moment, and completely unawares of the passage of time"). Even many decades after its first appearance, *On Crimes and Punishments* was still being read, thus influencing American and European policymakers. For instance, in New York, it is known that Lewis Lawes (1883–1947)—a prison warden at Sing Sing who bitterly opposed capital punishment but who oversaw more than 300 executions—read works by both Beccaria and Howard. Anthony James, *New Look at Capital Punishment* (New York: Belmont Tower Books 1977), p. 128; "Lewis E. Lawes, Former Sing Sing Warden, Succumbs," *The Evening Independent* (St. Petersburg, FL), April 23, 1947, p. 2.

39. Collison-Morley, *Modern Italian Literature*, p. 41.

40. Piers Beirne, "Inventing Criminology: The 'Science of Man' in Cesare Beccaria's *Dei delitti e delle pene* (1764)," *in* Marilyn McShane & Frank P. Williams III, *Criminal Justice: Contemporary Literature in Theory and Practice* (New York: Garland Publishing, 1997), pp. 21, 24, 32–38, 50–51, 53; Harcourt, *The Illusion of Free Markets*, p. 252 n.3; Online Library of Liberty, http://oll.libertyfund.org/pages/condillac-1714-1780?q=Beccaria# (citing *Commerce and Government Considered in their Mutual Relationship*, translated by Shelagh Eltis, with an Introduction to His Life and Contribution to Economics by Shelagh Eltis and Walter Eltis (Indianapolis: Liberty Fund, 2008)).

41. Bessler, *Cruel and Unusual*, p. 159.

42. G. F. H. Crockett, *An Address to the Legislature of Kentucky, on the Abolition of Capital Punishments, in the United States, and the Substitution of Exile for Life* (Georgetown, KY: N. L. Finnell, 1823).

43. Bessler, *Cruel and Unusual*, p. 158.

44. Ibid., p. 159.

45. Ibid., pp. 275–76.

46. Michael J. Pfeifer, *Rough Justice: Lynching and American Society 1874–1947* (Urbana, IL: University of Illinois Press, 2004), p. 114; 2 Richard N. Current, *The History of Wisconsin: The Civil War Era, 1848–1873* (Madison, WI: State Historical Society of Wisconsin, 1976), p. 191; "1851 Kenosha Hanging Led to Capital Punishment Ban," *The Milwaukee Sentinel*, Apr. 23, 1962, p. 4.

47. Martin Hintz, *Wisconsin Portraits: 55 People Who Made a Difference* (Black Earth, WI: Trails Books), pp. 20–21; Richard N. Current, *The Typewriter and the Men Who Made It* (Champaign, IL: University of Illinois Press, 1954), p. 2.

48. Bessler, *Cruel and Unusual*, pp. 276–77.

49. *Remarks of John L. Stevens, in the Senate of Maine, Feb. 11 and 12, 1869* (Kennebec, ME: Kennebec Journal Office, 1869).

50. Kenneth C. Haas & James A. Inciardi, *Challenging Capital Punishment: Legal and Social Science Approaches* (Thousand Oaks, CA: Sage Publications, 1988), p. 103; Jeffrey D. Merrill Sr., *Maine State Prison 1824–2002* (Charleston, SC: Arcadia Publishing, 2009), p. 116; John J. Pullen, *Joshua Chamberlain: A Hero's Life & Legacy* (Mechanicsburg, PA: Stackpole Books, 1999), pp. 37–48.

51. Marvin H. Bovee, *Reasons for Abolishing Capital Punishment* (Chicago, IL: A. J. Cox and Co., 1878), p. 196.

52. Antonio Pace, ed., *Luigi Castiglioni's Viaggio: Travels in the United States of North America 1785–1787* (Syracuse, NY: Syracuse University Press, 1983), pp. 313–14.

53. Bessler, *The Birth of American Law*, pp. 35–36.

54. Pace, *Luigi Castiglioni's Viaggio*, pp. xii, xxix–xxxiv.

55. Ibid., pp. 12–13, 34, 109–13, 127–32, 215–16; Antonio Pace, *Benjamin Franklin and Italy* (The American Philosophical Society, 1958), p. 88.

56. Bessler, *The Birth of American Law*, pp. 34–37, 127–28; Paolo Frisi to Benjamin Franklin, May 30, 1784 (letter sent in French from Paolo Frisi in Milan to Benjamin Franklin in Passy after Frisi had returned from London, where Frisi had gotten to know Franklin), *available at* www.franklinpapers.org.

57. Benjamin Franklin to "Count Castiglione," Oct. 14, 1787, *available at* www.franklinpapers.org.

58. Benjamin Franklin to Lorenzo Manini, Nov. 19, 1784 & Alphonse Pellegrini to Benjamin Franklin, June 26, 1785, *available at* www.franklinpapers.org; J. S. Ersch, *La France Littéraire Contenant Les Auteurs Français De 1771 à 1796* (Hambourg: B. G. Hoffmann, 1798), p. 33 (referencing Alphonse Pellegrini, described as "*Prof. en Langue italienne et en Cosmographie à Paris*"); A Norman Jeffares, *Images of Invention: Essays on Irish Writing* (Buckinghamshire: Colin Smythe Limited, 1996), p. 120 (referencing a "Dr. Alphonse Pelligrini, Professor of Italian at Trinity College, Dublin"); *see also* Theodore Ayrault Dodge, ed., *Ceremony Held in Paris to Commemorate the Bi-Centenary of the Birth of Benjamin Franklin April 27, 1906* (Paris: The Chairman of the Press Committee, 1906), p. 23 ("Lorenzo Manini created the Cis-Apline Republic and leaned upon the encouraging Franklin.").

59. Pace, *Luigi Castiglioni's Viaggio*, pp. 313–14; Bessler, *The Birth of American Law*, pp. 105, 108, 110, 170. William Bradford's pamphlet, *An Enquiry How Far the Punishment of Death Is Necessary in Pennsylvania*, was printed in Pennsylvania for the Journal of the Senate for January 5, 1793. William Bradford, *An Enquiry How Far the Punishment of Death Is Necessary in Pennsylvania*, 12 Am. J. Leg. Hist. 122 (Apr. 1968) (1793).

60. Pace, *Luigi Castiglioni's Viaggio*, pp. 313–14.

61. "A Republican," "To the People of Maryland," Number III, *The Maryland Gazette* (Annapolis, MD), Apr. 14, 1780, p. 1. The letter writer expressed this view: "For the crimes of murder, and high treason, the penalty of death is denounced; and, I think, in these cases the legislature has not exceeded its warrant. He that sheds man's blood, upon cool, deliberate malice, is guilty of a crime, which strikes at the very being of society." "High treason, as defined by our treason act," the writer continued, "is an offence tending to introduce every evil which society was instituted to guard against; it is a

crime of deeper malignity than simple murder." Ibid.

62. David Luban, *Liberalism, Torture, and the Ticking Bomb*, 91 Va. L. Rev. 1425, 1434 (2005).

63. "A Republican," "To the People of Maryland," Number III, *The Maryland Gazette* (Annapolis, MD), Apr. 14, 1780, p. 1. As "A Republican" argued: "[I]f a law were proposed, to punish simple fornication by death, there is not a man who would not reject it with anger and disdain; but appeal to a wealthy citizen for his sentiments, with respect to the punishment of a noctural thief, and he will tell you at once, that property can never be secure, unless such invaders are cut off from the face of the earth. Hence it is, that truth and justice, the feelings of humanity, and the indelible rights of nature, are so often violated by sanguinary laws." Ibid.

64. Ibid. "With due submission to an authority, so much revered by every humane, intelligent, mind," the letter writer asserted, referencing Beccaria and speaking of society's power to punish, is a right "derived from a higher source, from the universal principle of self-preservation, which directs us to secure our safety, by the death of that transgressor, who manifests a disposition, beyond the power of human correction, or the probability of amendment." "These reflections have, with difficulty, reconciled me to the idea of capital punishment," the writer editorialized, noting, "I am still shocked at the manner, directed by the terrible sentence in high treason; it may be milder than the wheel, or other infernal engines, invented in some countries in Europe, but every enlightened mind considers these as a disgrace among civilized nations." Ibid.

65. "Of the Obscurity of Laws," *The Pennsylvania Gazette* (Philadelphia, PA), Oct. 20, 1784, p. 2. A little over a month later, *The Pennsylvania Packet* published an "Extract of a letter from Paris, to a gentleman in New York, received by the last French Packet." The following extract pertaining to Beccaria is found in that letter:

> We understand from you with great pleasure, that the system of the *marquis de Beccaria*, is likely to be adopted by several of your legislative assemblies: — to your consideration, to the exalted honor of so many excellent heads may human nature owe the adoption of so useful a branch of legislation: may your bright example cross the atlantic to illuminate some kingdoms in Europe, and serve to expele the remaining shades of our Gothic darkness. We are very glad the states of Massachusetts and New York are likely to be the first to adopt it, and change the punishment of death for public works; I hope that in less than two or three years, your criminal laws will be corrected and amended by able Beccaria's; if I was with you I should most certainly enrol myself in that sect, and glory in the appellation.

The Pennsylvania Packet (Philadelphia, PA), Nov. 24, 1784, p. 3.

66. Pace, *Luigi Castiglioni's Viaggio*, p. 314; Franco Venturi & R. Burr Litchfield, *The End of the Old Regime in Europe, 1776–1789, Part I: The Great States of the West* (Princeton, NJ: Princeton Legacy Library, R. Burr Litchfield, trans., 1991), p. 79.

67. Pace, *Luigi Castiglioni's Viaggio*, pp. 1–269; Bessler, *Cruel and Unusual*, pp. 12, 14, 105, 109–12, 128–30.

68. Peter Bondanella & Julia Conaway Bondanella, eds., *Cassell Dictionary of Italian Literature* (London: Cassell, 2001), pp. 197–98; Sophus A. Reinert, "Patriotism, Cosmopolitanism and Political Economy in the *Accademia dei pugni* in Austrian Lombardy, 1760–1780" *in* Koen Stepelbroek & Jani Marjanen, eds., *The Rise of Economic Societies in the Eighteenth Century: Patriotic Reform in Europe and North America* (New York: Palgrave Macmillan, 2012), pp. 131–32.

69. Larry Wolff, *Paolina's Innocence: Child Abuse in Casanova's Venice* (Stanford, CA: Stanford University Press, 2012), p. 97.

70. Reinert, "Patriotism, Cosmopolitanism and Political Economy in the *Accademia dei pugni* in Austrian Lombardy, 1760–1780," in Stepelbroek & Marjanen, *The Rise of Economic Societies in the Eighteenth Century*, p. 132; Michel Delon, ed., *Encyclopedia of the Enlightenment* (London: Routledge, 2001), Vol. 1, pp. 292–94.

71. Marcello Maestro, "The Death Penalty Viewed as an Act of Self-Defense by Two Italian Jurists in the Eighteenth Century," *Proceedings of the American Philosophical Society*, Vol. 124, No. 1 (Feb. 29, 1980), p. 52.

72. Pace, *Luigi Castiglioni's Viaggio*, p. 314.

73. David Levinson, ed., *Encyclopedia of Crime and Punishment* (Thousand Oaks, CA: Sage Publications, 2002), Vol. 1, p. 153.

74. Bessler, *The Birth of American Law*, p. 12.

75. Ibid., p. 373.

76. "A Speech, intended to have been delivered in the House of Commons, in Support of the American Congress' Petition to the King," *The Pennsylvania Gazette* (Philadelphia, PA), Aug. 30, 1775, pp. 1–2 ("Under so shameful a violation of Parliamentary Faith, what confidence, what respect can you desire from America? What other bond of Government will be left you, but fear? And let me ask in the words of the sagacious Beccaria, 'What ought we to think of that Government which has no other means of managing the subject, but fear?'").

77. Stephen L. Schechter, ed., *Roots of the Republic: American Founding Documents Interpreted* (Madison, WI: Madison House, 1990), pp. 401–7, 416–18.

78. Thomas Katheder, *The Baylors of Newmarket: The Decline and Fall of a Virginia Planter Family* (Bloomington, IN: iUniverse, 2009), p. 118.

79. "For the Times," *The Times* (London, England), Nov. 3, 1790, p. 4. The U.S. Bill of Rights was ratified on December 15, 1791. Terence Ball, ed., *Hamilton, Madison, and Jay: The Federalist with Letters of "Brutus"* (Cambridge: Cambridge University Press, 2003), p. xxxvi.

80. *E.g.*, Kevin Jon Heller & Markus D. Dubber, eds., *The Handbook of Comparative Criminal Law* (Stanford, CA: Stanford University Press, 2011), p. 489 ("Modern Spanish criminal law was influenced by the humanist and utilitarian ideals of the Enlightenment and, more specifically, by Cesare Beccaria's *Dei delitti e delle pene* (1764).").

81. "The World Moves Towards Abolition," Amnesty International, International Death Penalty, http://www.amnestyusa.org/our-work/issues/death-penalty/international-death-penalty ("International death penalty trends are unmistakably towards abolition. Use of the death penalty worldwide has continued to shrink, and use of the death penalty has also been increasingly curtailed in international law.").

82. Bessler, *The Birth of American Law*, p. 66; Hanns Gross, *Rome in the Age of Enlightenment: The Post-Tridentine Syndrome and the Ancien Regime* (Cambrige: Cambridge University Press, 1990), p. 219; Hans Göran Franck, *The Barbaric Punishment: Abolishing the Death Penalty* (The Hague, The Netherlands: Martinus Nijhoff Publishers, William Schabas, rev. & ed. 2003), pp. 49–50; *see also* Thomas Banchoff & Robert Wuthnow, eds., *Religion and the Global Politics of Human Rights* (Oxford: Oxford University Press, 2011), p. 288.

83. Rebecca Gates-Coon, *The Charmed Circle: Joseph II and the "Five Princesses," 1765–1790* (West Lafayette, IN: Purdue University Press, 2015), p. 260; Theodore Ziolkowski, *Lure of the Arcane: The Literature of Cult and Conspiracy* (Baltimore, MD: The Johns Hopkins University Press, 2013), pp. 129–30; A. Lentin, *Enlightened Absolutism, 1760–1790: A Documentary Sourcebook* (Newcastle-upon-Tyne, England: Avero Publications, 1985), p. 119. "This abolitionist period was short," Robert Fico of the Ministry of Justice of Slovakia later wrote, "because soon after Joseph's death, Emperor Franz II issued a decree in 1796 by which the death penalty was restored. Robert Fico, "The Death Penalty in Slovakia," *in The Death Penalty: Abolition in Europe* (Strasbourg: Council of Europe Publishing, 1999), Vol. 285, p. 117.

84. Bessler, *Cruel and Unusual*, p. 33; R. R. Palmer, *The Age of the Democratic Revolution: The Challenge* (Princeton: Princeton University Press, 1959), p. 106; Maestro, *Cesare Beccaria and the Origins of Penal Reform*, p. 127; Barbara Becker-Cantarino, ed., *German Literature of the Eighteenth Century: The Enlightenment and Sensibility* (Rochester, NY: Camden House, 2005), Vol. 5, p. 251.

85. Richard S. Frase, *Limiting Excessive Prison Sentences Under Federal and State Constitutions*, 11 U. Pa. J. Const. L. 39, 45 n.22 (2008) (noting proportionality principles were endorsed in the French Declaration of the Rights of Man and Citizen of 26 August 1789, with Article 8 of the Declaration limiting punishments to those that are "strictly and obviously necessary").

86. Michel Foucault, *Abnormal: Lectures at the Collège de France 1974–1975* (New York: Picador, Valerio Marchetti & Antonella Salomoni, eds. & Graham Burchell, trans., 1999), p. 91 & 105 n.8; Abbe Smith & Monroe H. Freedman, eds., *How Can You Represent Those People?* (New York: Palgrave Macmillan, 2013), p. 198 n.7; Michael Tonry, ed., *Why Punish? How Much?: A Reader on Punishment* (Oxford: Oxford University Press, 2011), p. 46 ("The death penalty was retained in the French Penal Code of 1791, but only with restrictions and after a long and searching debate.").

87. Heller & Dubber, *The Handbook of Comparative Criminal Law*, p. 210; George A. Bermann

& Etienne Picard, *Introduction to French Law* (The Netherlands, Kluwer Law International, 2008), p. 104.

88. Peter Becker & Richard F. Wetzell, eds., *Criminals and Their Scientists: The History of Criminology in International Perspective* (Cambridge: Cambridge University Press, 2006), p. 34; *see also* John P. McKay, Bennett D. Hill, John Buckler, Clare Haru Crowston, Merry E. Wiesner-Hanks & Joe Perry, *A History of Western Society* (Boston, MA: Bedford/St. Martin's, 10th ed., 2011), Vol. 2, p. 637 ("[T]he Reign of Terror (1793–1794) solidified the home front. Special revolutionary courts responsible only to Robespierre's Committee of Public Safety tried 'enemies of the nation' for political crimes. Some forty thousand French men and women were executed or died in prison.").

89. Clifford Stevens Walton, *The Civil Law in Spain and Spanish-America, including Cuba, Puerto Rico and Philippine Islands, and the Spanish Civil Code in Force, Annotated and with References to the Civil Codes of Mexico, Central and South America* (Washington, DC: W. H. Lowdermilk & Co., 1900), p. 493 n.‡.

90. David Garland, *Peculiar Institution: America's Death Penalty in an Age of Abolition* (Cambridge: The Belknap Press of Harvard University Press, 2010), p. 136.

91. Hans Göran Franck, *The Barbaric Punishment: Abolishing the Death Penalty* (The Hague, The Netherlands: Martinus Nijhoff Publishers, William Schabas, rev. & ed. 2003), pp. 49–50 ("Beccaria's publication won him a considerable following among philosophers and political leaders. Both enlightened despots and political thinkers adopted his ideas. In 1767, Empress Catherine II of Russia appointed a commission to draw up a new penal code, which rejected capital punishment. Leopold II, Grand Duke of Tuscany, abolished the death penalty in 1786 and the following year the Emperor of Austria, Joseph II, followed suit, although in that case it was soon to be reintroduced."); ibid., p. 50 ("A letter sent to all the appeals courts in Sweden by King Gustav III in 1777 stipulated that no death sentence was to be carried out before it had been signed by him. In the same year the King also submitted a bill to Parliament, which limited the uses of the death penalty. In England, Sir Samuel Romilly started his campaign to reduce the number of capital offences. In London, an organization for the abolition of the death penalty was created in 1829, probably the first in the world.").

92. Charles W. Bergquist, *Coffee and Conflict in Columbia, 1886–1910* (Durham, NC: Duke University Press, 1986), p. 11.

93. Amnesty International, *When the State Kills … : The Death Penalty, A Human Rights Issue* (1989), pp. 72, 231; *see also* Donna Keyse Rudolph & G.A. Rudolph, *Historical Dictionary of Venezuela* (Metuchen, NJ: Scarecrow Press, 1971), p. 117 ("EL VENEZOLANO. The Liberal Party in 1840 established this newspaper to express their views. Its editor was Antonio Leocadio Guzman who from its pages demanded universal suffrage, immediate emancipation of the slaves, and abolition of capital punishment for political crimes.").

94. Joel Krieger, ed., *The Oxford Companion to Comparative Politics* (Oxford: Oxford University Press, 2012), p. 141; *see also* Banchoff & Wuthnow, *Religion and the Global Politics of Human Rights*, p. 288 ("Internationally, Venezuela abolished the death penalty in 1863, followed by several other Latin American republics.").

95. Robert J. Cottrol, *The Long, Lingering Shadow: Slavery, Race, and Law in the American Hemisphere* (Athens, GA: University of Georgia Press, 2013), pp. 60, 64.

96. *The Open Court: A Weekly Journal, Devoted to the Work of Conciliating Religion with Science* (Chicago: The Open Court Publishing Co., 1888–89), Vol. 2, p. iii (quoting Frederick Gerhard of New York).

97. Constance Brooks, *Antonio Panizzi: Scholar and Patriot* (Manchester University Press, 1931), p. 28; Maurizio Isabella, "Entangled Patriotisms: Italian Liberals and Spanish America in the 1820s," *in* Matthew Brown & Gabriel Paquette, eds., *Connections After Colonialism: Europe and Latin America in the 1820s* (Tuscaloosa: The University of Alabama Press, 2013), p. 94.

98. Isabella, *Risorgimento in Exile*, pp. 45, 48–49.

99. Marco Vitale, ed., *Carlo Cattaneo: Intelligence as a Principle of Public Economy* (Lanham, MD: Lexington Books, 2003), pp. 129, 131; Giuseppe Pecchio, *Semi-Serious Observations of an Italian Exile, During His Residence in England* (London: Effingham Wilson, 1833), pp. 229, 391; *The Foreign Review, and Continental Miscellany* (London: Black, Young, and Young, 1829), Vol. 4, p. 201; Thomas Sadler, ed., *Diary, Reminiscences, and Correspondence of Henry Crabb Robinson, Barrister-at-Law, F.S.A.*

(London: Macmillan and Co., 1869), Vol. 2, pp. 475–76.

100. John D. Bessler, *Legacy of Violence: Lynch Mobs and Executions in Minnesota* (Minneapolis: University of Minnesota Press, 2003), p. 174.

101. Donald P. Kommers, John E. Finn & Gary J. Jacobsohn, eds., *American Constitutional Law: Essays, Cases, and Comparative Notes* (Lanham, MD: Rowman & Littlefield, 3d ed. 2010), Vol. 2, pp. 130–31.

102. *Frommer's Nicaragua & El Salvador* (Mississauga, ON: John Wiley & Sons Canada, 2010), p. 16.

103. Thomas M. Leonard, ed., *Encyclopedia of U.S.-Latin American Relations* (Thousand Oaks, CA: CQ Press, 2012), Vol. 1, p. 982.

104. F. Garcia Calderon, *Latin America: Its Rise and Progress* (New York: Charles Scribner's Sons, 1915), p. 82.

105. Roger Hood & Carolyn Hoyle, *The Death Penalty: A Worldwide Perspective* (Oxford: Oxford University Press, 5th ed. 2015), pp. 70–71; ibid., p. 71 ("Argentina first abolished the death penalty for political offences in 1853 and for all crimes in 1921, five years after the last execution had been carried out in 1916. However, military governments in the post-Second World War period reintroduced the death penalty at various times for violent crimes and other acts associated with political objectives. On each occasion, such was the opposition from civil society that these laws were soon repealed, except under military law. The last such phase was under the military junta which was in power from 1976 to 1983. No one was judicially executed but large-scale extrajudicial executions and disappearances were rife. When the military junta fell and democracy was restored, the National Congress abolished the death penalty for all ordinary offences in 1984."); ibid. ("in 2008 … the Code of Military Justice was abolished and Argentina ratified the Second Optional Protocol to the ICCPR and the Protocol to the American Convention on Human Rights to Abolish the Death Penalty").

106. Mark Berman, "There Are 18 States Without the Death Penalty: A Third of Them Have Banned It Since 2007," *Washington Post*, April 30, 2014.

107. Inter-American Commission on Human Rights, *The Death Penalty in the Inter-American Human Rights System: From Restrictions to Abolition* (Organization of American States, 2011), p. 188.

108. Donald P. Kommers, John E. Finn & Gary J. Jacobsohn, eds., *American Constitutional Law: Essays, Cases, and Comparative Notes* (Lanham, MD: Rowman & Littlefield, 3d ed. 2010), Vol. 2, pp. 130–31.

109. Hood & Hoyle, *The Death Penalty*, pp. 73–74.

110. Christopher Hibbert, *Garibaldi: Hero of Italian Unification* (New York: St. Martin's Press, 2008), pp. 38–39, 120, 363; Paul Moses, *An Unlikely Union: The Love-Hate Story of New York's Irish and Italians* (New York: New York University Press, 2015), pp. 15–16; Alfonso Scirocco, *Garibaldi: Citizen of the World* (Princeton, NJ: Princeton University Press, 2007), p. 4; Litta-Visconti-Arese, *The Birth of Modern Italy: Posthumous Papers of Jessie White Mario* (London: T. Fisher Unwin, 1909), p. 183.

111. 58 *Political Science Quarterly* 241 (1943).

112. Karen Racine, *Francisco de Miranda: A Transatlantic Life in the Age of Revolution* (Wilmington, DE: Scholarly Resources, 2003), pp. 98, 101. Miranda's library included *On Crimes and Punishments*. Francisco de Miranda, *Los libros de Miranda* lii, lxix (Comisión Nacional del Cuatricentenario de la Fundación de Caracas, Comité de Obras Culturales, 1996); Vicente Dávila, ed., *Francisco de Miranda, Archivo del General Miranda* (Editorial Sur-América, 1930), Vol. 7, pp. 163, 183; Francisco de Miranda & Josefina Rodríguez de Alonso, *Colombeia: 1781–1783* (Ediciones de la Presidencia de la República, 1979), Vol. 2, pp. 25, 164, 373.

113. John MacDonell & Edward Manson, eds., *Great Jurists of the World* (Boston: Little, Brown & Co., 1914), Vol. 1, p. 540; ibid., p. 540 (noting of Bentham: "[E]very educated man studied his writings as those of another Lycurgus or Solon. Rivadavia, the legislator of Buenos Ayres, was his pupil; José del Valle, the President of Guatemala, was another pupil. They, as well as Andrade, the Brazilian Minister, corresponded with the sage regarding the legislation of their States. The constitutions and all of the laws of the new republics show traces of Bentham's influence. His works were used as textbooks in the schools; though, sad to relate, his earnest disciple, Bolivar, when he turned Dictator in 1826, forbade the use of his master's works in the public schools."); Louis E. Bumgartner, *José del*

Valle of Central America (Durham, NC: Duke University Press, 1963), p. 121 ("Valle sought answers for each of the many problems, and his views on public order and crime and punishment made the reference to the Marquis di Beccaria … in *El Amigo* more significant.").

114. John MacDonell & Edward Manson, eds., *Great Jurists of the World* (Boston: Little, Brown & Co., 1914), Vol. 1, p. 540.

115. Osvaldo Barreneche, *Crime and the Administration of Justice in Buenos Aires, 1785–1853* (Lincoln: University of Nebraska, 2006), pp. 72, 79–82.

116. Kristin Ruggiero, *Modernity in the Flesh: Medicine, Law, and Society in Turn-of-the-Century Argentina* (Stanford, CA: Stanford University Press, 2004), p. 9.

117. Hood & Hoyle, *The Death Penalty*, p. 71.

118. *An Introduction to the History of Mexican Law* (Dobbs Ferry, NY: Oceana Publications, 1983), pp. 165, 178.

119. Patrick Timmons, "Seed of Abolition: Experience and Culture in the Desire to End Capital Punishment in Mexico, 1841–1857," *in* Austin Sarat & Christian Boulanger, eds., *The Cultural Lives of Capital Punishment* (Stanford, CA: Stanford University Press, 2005), p. 73.

120. Lawrence S. Cunningham, John J. Reich & Lois Fichner-Rathus, *Culture & Values: A Survey of the Western Humanities* (Stamford, CT: Cengage Learning, 8th ed. 2015), p. 526.

121. Aniceto Masferrer, "The Liberal State and Criminal Law Reform in Spain," *in* Mortimer Sellers & Tadeusz Tomaszewski, eds., *The Rule of Law in Comparative Perspective* (Dordrecht: Springer, 2010), p. 35; Michel Delon, *Encyclopedia of the Enlightenment* (New York: Routledge, 2013), p. 1257; 8 *The English Review* 6 (Sept. 1847); Earl of Ilchester, ed., *The Spanish Journal of Elizabeth, Lady Holland (1791–1811)* (London: Longmans, Green & Co., 1910), p. 152.

122. Derek Beales & Eugenio F. Biagini, *The Risorgimento and the Unification of Italy* (New York: Routledge, 2d ed. 2013), p. 18.

123. *Crime, Histoire & Société* (Droz, 1998), p. 18.

124. 5 *Criminal Justice History: An International Annual* 50–52 (1984).

125. Joan Lynne Pataky Kosove, *The "Comedia Lacrimosa" and Spanish Romantic Drama (1773–1865)* (London: Tamesis Books, 1977), p. 49; *see also* Robert Hughes, *Goya* (New York: Knopf, 2003) (noting that Jovellanos "learned both Italian and English"; "corresponded fluently with friends abroad, intellectuals in Paris and such Englishmen as Lord Holland, the former ambassador to Madrid, with whom he was on warm terms of friendship"; was "[i]nspired by the writings of the eighteenth-century Italian liberal penologist Cesare Beccaria"; was "greatly concerned with penal reform" and "fought for the abolition of judicial torture"; and "[i]n his role as playwright, which he also was, he wrote a comedy about crime and punishment, *El delincuente honrado* (1774)").

126. Elzbieta Szoka, ed., *Fourteen Female Voices from Brazil: Interviews and Works* (Austin, TX: Host Publications, 2002), pp. 287–88.

127. Edward Peters, *Torture* (Philadelphia: University of Pennsylvania Press, 1999), p. 264.

128. Bessler, *The Birth of American Law*, pp. 436–37; Osvaldo Barreneche, *Crime and the Administration of Justice in Buenos Aires, 1785–1853* (Lincoln: University of Nebraska, 2006), p. 22; Ruth Pike, *Penal Servitude in Early Modern Spain* (Madison: University of Wisconsin Press, 1983), pp. 57, 64, 147; Manuel de Lardizábal y Uribe, *Discurso Sobra Las Penas Contrahido á Las Leyes Criminales de España, Para Facilitar su Reforma* (Madrid: Joachin Ibarra, 1782), pp. 76, 99, 100–2, 130–32, 167–68, 177, 181.

129. Robert M. Buffington, *Criminal and Citizen in Modern Mexico* (Lincoln: University of Nebraska Press, 2000), p. 13.

130. *Excerpta Criminologica* (Excerpta Criminologica Foundation, 1961), Vol. 1, p. 378; *Revista de Madrid* (Madrid: Imprenta de la Sociedad Literaria y Tipografica, 1844), Vol. III, p. 49.

131. Heller & Dubber, *The Handbook of Comparative Criminal Law*, p. 489.

132. Julio César Rivera, ed., *The Scope and Structure of Civil Codes* (Dordrecht: Springer, 2013), p. 333 n.8.

133. Gabriel Haslip-Viera, *Crime and Punishment in Late Colonial Mexico City, 1692–1810* (Albuquerque: University of New Mexico Press, 1999), p. 43.

134. Robert Buffington, *Criminal and Citizen in Modern Mexico* (Lincoln: University of Nebraska Press, 2000), p. 19.

135. Timmons, "Seed of Abolition," *in* Sarat & Boulanger, *The Cultural Lives of Capital Punishment*, pp. 78–82.

136. Ibid., p. 81.

137. Ibid.

138. Chris Frazer, *Bandit Nation: A History of Outlaws and Cultural Struggle in Mexico, 1810–1920* (Lincoln: University of Nebraska Press, 2006), p. 46; Mark Wasserman, *Everyday Life and Politics in Nineteenth Century Mexico: Men, Women, and War* (Albuquerque: University of New Mexico Press, 2000), p. 104; Timmons, "Seed of Abolition," *in* Sarat & Boulanger, *The Cultural Lives of Capital Punishment*, pp. 73–77, 83; *compare* Hood & Hoyle, *The Death Penalty*, p. 71 ("It is not clear why it took Mexico 150 years to abolish capital punishment. After the breakdown of the authoritarian and repressive dictatorship of Santa Anna in 1855 the liberal government prepared a new constitution which outlawed torture, illegal imprisonment, and the death penalty. However, the death penalty was only abolished for political crimes, with full abolition for ordinary crimes being contingent on the construction of a national penitentiary regime.").

139. Hood & Hoyle, *The Death Penalty*, p. 72 ("Although the Political Constitution of the United Mexican States of 1917 provided for the death penalty for several categories of murder, in fact it was abolished by the Federal Penal Code in 1930 and eventually by all Mexican states. The last execution took place in the state of Puebla in 1937. And while the Code of Military Justice provided for capital punishment for specific offences, in practice death sentences had always been commuted to long-term imprisonment. The death penalty was abolished in military criminal law in April 2005 and in June 2005 the Mexican House of Representatives approved, with only two abstentions, an amendment to Articles 14 and 22 of the Constitution of the United Mexican States, which abolished the death penalty for all crimes. It came into force on 9 December 2005.").

140. Gordon K. Lewis, *Main Currents in Caribbean Thought: The Historical Evolution of Caribbean Society in Its Ideological Aspects, 1492–1900* (Lincoln: University of Nebraska Press, 2004), p. 266.

141. *A Political Account of the Island of Trinidad, From Its Conquest by Sir Ralph Abercrombie, in the Year 1797, to the Present Time, in a Letter to His Grace the Duke of Portland* (London: Cadell and Davies, 1807), pp. 49, 54 (written "By a Gentleman of the Island"); *see also* Thomas Jones Howell, *A Complete Collection of State Trials and Proceedings for High Treason and Other Crimes and Misdemeanors from the Earliest Period to the Year 1783* (London: Longman, Hurst, Rees, Orme, & Brown, 1822), Vol. 30, p. 455 ("General Picton should have carried this with him to Trinidad, he should have born in mind the folly of supposing that an instrument of torture is an instrument to extract truth. The subject has been reduced by a foreign writer (Beccaria, chap. 16), quoted by Mr. Justice Blackstone into the form of a mathematical problem....").

142. Richard Davey, *Cuba Past and Present* (New York: Charles Scribner's Sons, 1898), p. 19.

143. Hood & Hoyle, *The Death Penalty*, p. 128 ("Even though executions in the Commonwealth Caribbean have become rare and its death rows sparsely populated (with the exception of Trinidad and Tobago) these countries remain an obstruction to the worldwide movement towards abolition.").

144. Donald P. Kommers, John E. Finn & Gary J. Jacobsohn, eds., *American Constitutional Law: Essays, Cases, and Comparative Notes* (Lanham, MD: Rowman & Littlefield, 3d ed. 2010), Vol. 2, p. 130.

145. Captain Maconochie, *Australiana: Thoughts on Convict Management, and Other Subjects Connected with the Australian Penal Colonies* (London: John W. Parker, 1839), p. 73 n.* (quoting Beccaria as follows: "To set a price on the head of a criminal ... is the strongest proof of a weak or unwise Government."); ibid., p. 75 n.* (quoting Beccaria as saying: "There is nothing more dangerous than the common axiom, *the spirit of the laws is to be considered*.").

146. John Gascoigne, *The Enlightenment and the Origins of European Australia* (Cambridge: Cambridge University Press, 2002), pp. 123–25; N. L. Kentish, *Essay on Capital Punishment: With an Earnest Appeal and Dutyful Petition to the Sovereign for the Abolition Throughout Her Majesty's Dominions of the Sanguary and Unholy Laws which Santion the Taking of Human Life* (Hobart Town: S.A. Tegg, 1842); N. L. Kentish, *Treatise on Penal Discipline* (Melbourne: J.J. Blundell, 1858); *see also* Gascoigne, *The Enlightenment and the Origins of European Australia*, p. 125 ("Beccaria's influence was also mediated through the widely read Cambridge textbook, *Principles of Morals and Political Philosophy* (1785), by William Paley."); *see also The Age* (Melbourne, Australia), July 6, 1968, p. 13 (publicizing a lecture

by Sivio Colloridi on Cesare Beccaria at the Instituto Italiano di Cultura (Italian Cultural Institute) in Melbourne, Australia).

147. Carsten Anckar, *Determinants of the Death Penalty: A Comparative Study of the World* (New York: Routledge, 2004), p. 17. In 1849 the Roman Republic banned capital punishment in its constitution, and the small city-state of San Marino did the same in 1865. Martin Collier, ed., *Italian Unification 1820–71*, at 43 (Oxford: Heinemann, 2003); Alan Felthous & Henning Sass, eds., *The International Handbook of Psychopathic Disorders and the Law* (West Sussex, England: John Wiley & Sons, 2007), Vol. 2, p. 344.

148. Robert J. Cottrol, *The Long, Lingering Shadow: Slavery, Race, and Law in the American Hemisphere* (Athens, GA: University of Georgia Press, 2013), p. 99.

149. Bessler, *The Birth of American Law*, p. 38.

150. Peter Oliver, *'Terror to Evil-doers': Prisons and Punishment in Nineteenth-century Ontario* (Toronto: University of Toronto Press, 1998), pp. 80, 95, 97–98, 104–5, 114, 520 (citing Upper Canada Statutes, c. 4 (1833)); *compare* Jeffrey L. McNairn, "'A just and obvious distinction': The Meaning of Imprisonment for Debt and the Criminal Law in Upper Canada's Age of Reform," *in* G. Blaine Baker & Donald Fyson, eds., *Quebec and the Canadas: Essays in the History of Canadian Law* (Toronto: University of Toronto Press/Osgoode Society for Canadian Legal History, 2013), p. 214 ("Leading Anglo-American legal reformers and their foundational statements, such as Henry Brougham or Cesare Beccaria's *On Crimes and Punishments*, concerned themselves with insolvency as well as crime, but in Upper Canada they were cited and their principles invoked primarily in a civil rather than criminal context.").

151. Jim Phillips, R. Roy McMurtry & John T. Saywell, eds., *Essays in the History of Canadian Law: A Tribute to Peter N. Oliver* (Toronto: Osgoode Society for Canadian Legal History, 2008), pp. 284–85; *compare* Donald Fyson, "Beccaria contre Howard? La réforme pénale au Québec, 1760–1841," *in Actes du colloque Césare Beccaria: réception et héritage. Du temps des Lumières à aujourd'hui* (Rennes: Presses de l'Université de Rennes, 2015).

152. Bonnie R. Nelson, *Criminal Justice Research in Libraries and on the Internet* (Westport, CT: Greenwood Press, 1997), p. x.

153. The 1824 Mexican Constitution provided in part: "No authority shall apply any form of torture, whatever may be the nature or state of the prosecution." Mexican Constitution (Oct. 4, 1824), sec. 7, ¶ 149.

154. Timmons, "Seed of Abolition," *in* Sarat & Boulanger, *The Cultural Lives of Capital Punishment*, pp. 73, 77.

155. Robert Buffington, "Looking Forward, Looking Back: Judicial Discretion and the Mexican Revolutionary State," *in Crime, History & Societies: International Association for the History of Crime and Criminal Justice* (Droz, 1998), Vol. 2, pp. 15, 18, 32; *see also* Marvin E. Wolfgang, ed., *Crime and Culture: Essays in Honor of Thorsten Sellin* (New York: John Wiley & Sons, 1968), p. 322 ("Lardizabal went further than Beccaria and Bentham in that, while accepting the utilitarian and intimidative purpose of the penalty, he put the emphasis on the correction of the offender, 'para hacerlo mejor, si puede ser, y para que no vuelva a perjudicar a la sociedad' (to make him better, if possible, and so that he should not damage society again).").

156. J. Robert Lilly, Francis T. Cullen & Richard A. Ball, *Criminological Theory: Context and Consequences* (Thousand Oaks, CA: Sage Publications, 6th ed. 2015), ch. 2.

157. 5 *Criminal Justice History: An International Annual* 51 (1984).

158. Alejandro Agüero and Marta Lorente, "Penal enlightenment in Spain: from Beccaria's reception to the first criminal code" (Nov. 2012), *available at* http://www.forhistiur.de/es/2012-11-aguero-lorente/?l=en; *compare* ibid.:

> In spite of this auspicious beginning, as Tomás y Valiente has shown, the reception of Beccaria in Spain was 'uneven and just moderately prolific in the short term'. The translation had been preceded by academic debate on the use of judicial torture, which was not aimed at achieving its abolishment but at adjusting its use to the ancient rules. It was followed not only by the publication of a profuse treatise by friar Fernando de Ceballos against 'the false philosophy or atheism, deism, materialism and other new sects convinced of the crime against the State and the Sovereigns', but by its subsequent inclusion in the Spanish Inqui-

sition's *index* of prohibited books in 1777. Even while these kinds of conservative reactions against Beccaria did not occur exclusively in Spain, they show the ideological gap between the two dominant political trends of the moment, clearly represented in the different attitudes adopted by the Royal Council, on the one hand, and by the Supreme Inquisition Council, on the other, both parts of the highest level of royal bureaucracy.

159. Harcourt, *The Illusion of Free Markets*, p. 57 ("Most recently, contemporary scholars of law and economics have embraced Beccaria as one of their own. Richard Posner traces his intellectual genealogy, in the area of penal law, specifically to Beccaria."); *see also* ibid., p. 56 ("*On Crimes and Punishments* is celebrated as the first economic analysis of crime and Beccaria is revered as the first economist to have applied rational choice theory to the field of crime and punishment."); Francesco Forte, *Principles of Public Economics: A Public Choice Approach* (Northampton, MA: Edward Elgar Publishing, 2010), p. 294 ("According to a theorem proposed by Cesare Beccaria and Gary Becker, the deterrence of massive sanctions is less effective tha[n] the deterrence of accurate enforcement. Thus for the offender, a sanction of 100 with a 50 percent likelihood of its application means a probability of paying 50, while a sanction of 80 with a 65 per cent likelihood of application means a probability of paying 52.").

160. Harcourt, *The Illusion of Free Markets*, p. 58. Beccaria's writings have thus framed the deterrence debate, as well as the arguments about the legitimacy of vengeance-seeking for past criminal transgressions, for more than two-and-a-half centuries. Ibid. ("The purpose of punishment is not to look backward, Beccaria emphasized—foreshadowing English utilitarianism. It will not undo a crime already committed. 'The wailings of a wretch,' Beccaria wrote, cannot 'undo what has been done and turn back the clock.' The purpose of punishment to Beccaria was 'nothing other than to prevent the offender from doing fresh harm to his fellows and to deter others from doing likewise.'").

161. Ibid. These two chairs, the one in Naples and the one in Milan, were later suppressed by Neapolitan and Austrian authorities. Ibid., pp. 18–19 ("But it is not in countries subject to arbitrary governments, and deprived of the freedom of the press, that lectures on Political Economy can be of any considerable service. The timid and jealous rulers of Naples and Austria speedily took fright at the existence of institutions which the enemies of improvement taught them to fear might have the effect to excite dissatisfaction; and the chairs founded by Intieri and Maria Theresa were in consequence suppressed.").

162. *Critical Memoirs of the Times: Containing a Summary View of the Popular Pursuits, Political Debates, and Literary Productions of the Present Age* (G. Kearsly, 1769), p. 267.

163. *The Monthly Review: or, Literary Journal* (London: R. Griffiths, 1795), Vol. XVI, pp. 501–4.

164. John Mason Good, Olinthus Gregory & Newton Bosworth, *Pantologia: A New Cyclopædia, Comprehending a Complete Series of Essays, Treatises, and Systems, Alphabetically Arranged* (London: G. Kearsley et al. 1813), Vol. VI (entry for kneading).

165. Denis Mack Smith, *The Making of Italy, 1796–1866* (New York: Palgrave, 1988); *Oxford Symposium on Food and Cookery, 1989: Staple Foods (Proceedings)* (London: Prospect Books, 1990), p. 136; Marco Beretta & Alessandro Tosi, eds., *Linnaeus in Italy: The Spread of a Revolution in Science* (Canton, MA: Science History Publications/USA, 2007); p. 163; Aldo Castellani & Albert Chalmers, *Manual of Tropical Medicine* (New York: William Wood and Co., 1920), p. 1702; Andrew Cunningham & Roger French, eds., *The Medical Enlightenment of the Eighteenth Century* (Cambridge: Cambridge University Press, 1990), pp. 292, 295; Maestro, *Cesare Beccaria and the Origins of Penal Reform*, pp. 90–91, 93, 102–3, 111–12; Giuliano Pancaldi, *Volta: Science and Culture in the Age of Enlightenment* (Princeton, NJ: Princeton University Press, 2003), p. 93; Venturi & Litchfield, *The End of the Old Regime in Europe, 1776–1789*, p. 614; Heinz Gärtner, *John Christian Bach: Mozart's Friend and Mentor* (Portland, OR: Amadeus Press, Reinhard G. Pauly, 1994), p. 156; "Transactions of the Patriotic Society of Milan, directed to the Advancement of Agriculture and the Arts, Vol. III" (Milan, 1793), *The Monthly Review; or, Literary Journal, Enlarged* (London: R. Griffiths, 1795), Vol. XVI, pp. 501–6; *The Analytical Review, or History of Literature, Domestic and Foreign, on an Enlarged Plan* (London: J. Johnson, 1797), Vol. XXV, p. 336; "Observations on the Use of Sithes for reaping Corn, &c. published by the Patriotic Society of Milan," *in The Repertory of Arts of Manufactures: Consisting of Original Communications, Specifications of Patent Inventions, and Selections on Useful Practical Papers from the

Transactions of the Philosophical Societies of All Nations, &c. &c. (London: The Proprietors, 1796), Vol. 5, p. 62; *The New Annual Register, or General Repository of History, Politics, and Literature, for the Year 1789* (London: G. G. J. and J. Robinson, 1790), p. 302.

166. Maestro, *Cesare Beccaria and the Origins of Penal Reform*, pp. 93–94.

167. Peter Groenewegen, *Eighteenth-century Economics: Turgot, Beccaria and Smith and Their Contemporaries* (London: Routledge, 2002), pp. 20–21 & Table 1.1 (listing Beccaria's writings).

168. Riccardo Faucci, *A History of Italian Economic Thought* (New York: Routledge, 2014), p. 53; Carlo Cattaneo, *Intelligence as a Principle of Public Economy* (Lanham, MD: Rowman & Littlefield, Marco Vitale, ed. & Ruggero di Palma Castiglione, trans. 2007), pp. 131, 137; Jomo K.S. & Erik S. Reinert, eds., *The Origins of Development Economics: How Schools of Economic Thought Have Addressed Development* (London: Zed Books, 2005), p. 38.

169. Groenewegen, *Eighteenth-century Economics*, Table 1.2.

170. Daniel P. Mannix, *The History of Torture* (Lake Oswego, OR: eNet Press Inc., 2014), p. 142; Maestro, *Cesare Beccaria and the Origins of Penal Reform*, pp. 88–90; T. R. Malthus, *An Essay on the Principle of Population* (Mineola, NY: Dover Publications, 2007); Francesco S. Nitti, *Population and the Social System* (London: Swan Sonnenschein & Co., 1894), p. 8; Mitchel P. Roth, *Prisons and Prison Systems: A Global Encyclopedia* (Westport, CT: Greenwood Press, 2006), p. 29; Maestro, *Cesare Beccaria and the Origins of Penal Reform*, pp. 118–20.

171. Garry Wills, *Inventing America: Jefferson's Declaration of Independence* (New York: Knopf Doubleday, 2017).

172. Lynn McDonald, *The Early Origins of the Social Sciences* (Montreal: McGill-Queen's University Press, 1993), p. 156.

173. John Bemelmans Marciano, *Whatever Happened to the Metric System? How America Kept Its Feet* (Bloomsbury Publishing, 2014).

174. Witold Kula, *Measures and Men* (Princeton, NJ: Princeton University Press, R. Szreter, trans. 1986), p. 269; Henry Alfred Todd & Raymond Weeks, eds., *The Romanic Review: A Quarterly Journal* (New York: Columbia University Press, 1922), Vol. XIII, p. 353; Maestro, *Cesare Beccaria and the Origins of Penal Reform*, pp. 107–108.

175. Kula, *Measures and Men*, pp. 4, 268–69.

176. *The Foreign Review, and Continental Miscellany* (London: Black, Young, and Young, 1829), Vol. IV, pp. 208–9.

177. O. M. Brack, Jr., ed., *Studies in Eighteenth-century Culture* (Madison: University of Wisconsin Press, 1984), Vol. 13, p. 275.

178. Maestro, *Cesare Beccaria and the Origins of Penal Reform*, p. 109; Prototype Meter of 36, Vaugirard Street, http://www.parisparcours.com/place/100070/22/prototype-meter-of-36-vaugirard-street.

179. John D. Bessler, *Cruel and Unusual: The American Death Penalty and the Founders' Eighth Amendment* (Boston: Northeastern University Press, 2012), p. 38; Maestro, *Cesare Beccaria and the Origins of Penal Reform*, pp. 122–24; John A. Davis & Paul Ginsborg, eds., *Society and Politics in the Age of the Risorgimento: Essays in Honour of Denis Mack Smith* (Cambridge: Cambridge University Press, 1991), p. 153; R. B. Bernstein, *Thomas Jefferson* (Oxford: Oxford University Press, 2003), p. 38; Maurizio Isabella, *Risorgimento in Exile: Italian Émigrés and the Liberal International in the Post-Napoleonic Era* (Oxford: Oxford University Press, 2009), p. 164.

180. Maestro, *Cesare Beccaria and the Origins of Penal Reform*, pp. 75–76; Clorinda Donato, "Illustrious Connections: The Premises and Practices of Knowledge Transfer between Switzerland and the Italian Peninsula," in André Holenstein, Hubert Steinke & Martin Stuber, eds., *Scholars in Action: The Practice of Knowledge and the Figure of the Savant in the 18th Century* (Lieden: Brill, 2013), Vol. 1, p. 554; Venturi & Litchfield, *The End of the Old Regime in Europe, 1776–1789*, Part II, p. 666 n.73; John C. Barentine, *The Lost Constellations: A History of Obsolete, Extinct, or Forgotten Star Lore* (Cham, Switzerland: Springer Praxis Books, 2016), p. 169; Martha Feldman, *Opera and Sovereignty: Transforming Myths in Eighteenth-Century Italy* (Chicago: The University of Chicago Press, 2007), p. 462.

181. Bessler, *The Birth of American Law*, p. 28; Maestro, *Cesare Beccaria and the Origins of Penal Reform*, pp. 77–79; Cesare Beccaria, *Recherches sur le style* (Paris: Molini, 1771), *available at* http://babel.hathitrust.org/cgi/pt?id=nyp.33433067364178;view=1up;seq=9.

182. Lynn McDonald, *The Early Origins of the Social Sciences* (Montreal: McGill-Queen's University Press, 1993), p. 197.

183. Groenewegen, *Eighteenth-century Economics*, Table 1.1 (listing Beccaria's writings).

184. Robert Panzarella & Daniel Vona, *Criminal Justice Masterworks: A History of Ideas About Crime, Law, Police, and Corrections* (Durham, NC: Carolina Academic Press, 2006), p. 9.

185. Bessler, *The Birth of American Law*, p. 431.

186. Nicholas Guyatt, *Providence and the Invention of the United States 1607–1876* (Cambridge: Cambridge University Press, 2007), p. 160; John Danforth Dunbar, *An Oration Pronounced on the 4th July, 1805, at Pembroke; at the Request of a Convention of Republicans, from Various Parts of the County of Plymouth* (Boston: True & Parks, 1805), pp. 4–7.

187. Dunbar, *An Oration Pronounced on the 4th July, 1805, at Pembroke*, pp. 7–8.

188. U.S. Const., Art. 1, sec. 9.

189. Brian Duignan, ed., *Forms of Government and the Rise of Democracy* (New York: Britannica Educational Publishing), p. 73.

190. Barry Nicholas, *An Introduction to Roman Law* (Oxford: Oxford University Press, 1975), p. 1.

191. Dunbar, *An Oration Pronounced on the 4th July, 1805, at Pembroke*, pp. 9–10.

192. Peter M. Tiersma & Lawrence M. Solan, eds., *The Oxford Handbook of Language and Law* (Oxford: Oxford University Press, 2012), pp. 14–15; Michael J. Romano & William Streitwieser, *Barron's Regents Exams and Answers: General History and Geography* (Hauppauge, NY: Barron's Educational Series, 2004), p. 239; Nicholas, *An Introduction to Roman Law*, pp. 15–16, 208–10; Kelly Rodgers, *Justinian I: Byzantine Emperor* (Huntington Beach, CA: Teacher Created Materials, 2013), p. 9.

193. Dunbar, *An Oration Pronounced on the 4th July, 1805, at Pembroke*, pp. 10–11.

194. Ibid., pp. 18–19, 22.

195. Washington's Farewell Address 1796, http://avalon.law.yale.edu/18th_century/washing.asp.

196. *Journal of the Senate of the State of Indiana, during the Twenty-Seventh Session of the General Assembly* (Indianapolis, IN: Dowling and Cole, 1842), pp. 4, 240.

197. "Publius" [Alexander Hamilton], "The Union as a Safeguard Against Domestic Faction and Insurrection," *available at* http://thomas.loc.gov/home/histdox/fed_09.html. " 'Publius' was the pseudonym under which Alexander Hamilton, James Madison, and John Jay authored *The Federalist Papers*. *The Federalist Papers* were published variously in three New York newspapers — the *Independent Journal*, the *New-York Packet*, and the *Daily Advertiser* — from October 27, 1787, through August 13, 1788." V. James Strickler, "Constitutional Cassandra: The Prophetic Fears of Brutus, the Anti-Federalist," *in* Anthony A. Peacock, ed., *Freedom and the Rule of Law* (Lanham, MD: Lexington Books, 2010), p. 93 n.2.

198. "Publius" [James Madison], "The Same Subject Continued: The Powers Conferred by the Constitution Further Considered," http://thomas.loc.gov/home/histdox/fed_43.html.

199. "Publius" [James Madison], "The Particular Structure of the New Government and the Distribution of Power Among Its Different Parts," http://thomas.loc.gov/home/histdox/fed_47.html.

200. "Publius" [Alexander Hamilton], "The Judiciary Department," http://thomas.loc.gov/home/histdox/fed_78.html.

201. Victor Hugo, *Claude Gueux: The Last Day of a Condemned Man* (New York: Carleton, 1869), p. 108.

202. The bulk of criminal-law adjudications took place then, as they do now, at the state level. Beccaria's proportionality principle shows up in various state constitutions. The U.S. Constitution, however, provided only limited enumerated federal authority with respect to the punishment of crime. In Article I, the U.S. Constitution provides that Congress "shall have Power ... To provide for the Punishment of counterfeiting the Securities and current Coin of the United States; ... To define and punish Piracies and Felonies committed on the high Seas, and Offences against the Laws of Nations; ... To provide for organizing, arming, and disciplining, the Militia...." U.S. Const., Art. I, sec. 8.

203. Alexander Hamilton, James Madison & John Jay, *The Federalist Papers* (New York: Bantam Dell, 2003), pp. 263–64. In *Federalist No. 43*, Madison was alluding to a clause in the Constitution that read: "The Congress shall have Power to declare the Punishment of Treason, but no Attainder of Treason shall work Corruption of Blood, or Forfeiture except during the Life of the Person attainted."

U.S. Const., art. III, sec. 3, cl. 2.

204. Alexander Hamilton, James Madison & John Jay, *The Federalist Papers* (New York: Bantam Dell, 2003), pp. 452–53. On another occasion, Hamilton took note of the fact that "[t]he temper of our country, is not a little opposed to the frequency of capital punishment." Bessler, *The Birth of American Law*, p. 238.

205. Gordon S. Wood, *The Radicalism of the American Revolution* (New York: Alfred A. Knopf, 1992), p. 193.

206. Bessler, *The Birth of American Law*, pp. 17–18, 21, 192, 256, 263, 373–75, 429.

207. Alexander Hamilton, James Madison & John Jay, *The Federalist Papers* (New York: Bantam Dell, 2003), p. 522. In *Federalist No. 15*, Hamilton—in addressing men "who object to the New Constitution"—also wrote of "a principle which has been found the bane of the old," then spoke of substituting "the violence and sanguinary agency of the sword to the mild influence of the Magistracy." Ibid., p. 84.

208. Rebecca M. McLennan, *The Crisis of Imprisonment: Protest, Politics, and the Making of the American Penal State, 1776–1941* (Cambridge: Cambridge University Press, 2008), pp. 17, 33–35.

209. John D. Bessler, *Death in the Dark: Midnight Executions in America* (Boston: Northeastern University Press, 1997), p. 31; McLennan, *The Crisis of Imprisonment*, p. 37.

210. Bessler, *The Birth of American Law*, p. 125. Beccaria's book would remain a popular title—and would continue to be discussed and debated in America and abroad—for decades to come. "Books," *Raleigh Register and North-Carolina State Gazette* (Raleigh, NC), Dec. 19, 1803, p. 4 (noting a donation of Beccaria's *On Crimes and Punishments* to the University of North Carolina "by the Citizens of Johnson County"); "Mr. Peel's Improvement of the Criminal Law," *The Times* (London, England), June 15, 1827, p. 8 (referencing Beccaria); *Raleigh Register and North-Carolina Gazette* (Raleigh, NC), Nov. 25, 1830, p. 4 (quoting Beccaria's views on pardons and clemency).

211. A. Owen Aldridge, "Thomas Jefferson and the Enlightenment: Reflections on Literary Influence," *in* William G. Shade, ed., *Revisioning the British Empire in the Eighteenth Century: Essays from Twenty-Five Years of the Lawrence Henry Gipson Institute for Eighteenth-Century Studies* (London: Lehigh University Press, 1998), p. 138.

212. Bessler, *The Birth of American Law*, pp. 564–67.

213. "To the People of America," *The Freeman's Journal; or, The North-American Intelligencer* (Philadelphia, PA), Jan. 16, 1788, p. 3; *see also The Independent Gazetteer* (Philadelphia, PA), Mar. 19, 1788, p. 2 ("The dangers of adopting the new constitution having been pointed out, I shall now proceed to consider, whether it would b[e] necessary and proper, and, whether Americans have any good reason to put more con[fi]dence in their rulers than Europeans.... 'In political arithmetic (says De Beccaria) it is necessary to substitute a calculation of probabilities, to mathematical exactness. That force which continually impels us to our own private interests, like gravity, acts incessantly, unless it meets an obstacle to oppose it.'").

214. Jack Stark, *Prohibited Government Acts: A Reference Guide to the United States Constitution* (Westport, CT: Praeger, 2002), p. 10.

215. Bessler, *The Birth of American Law*, pp. 151–218.

216. The Yale-educated and Massachusetts native St. John Honeywood wrote a whole poem titled "Crimes and Punishments," an homage to Beccaria's treatise. Bessler, *The Birth of American Law*, pp. 303–6 (reprinting a portion of St. John Honeywood's poem titled "Crimes and Punishments"); *see also The Evening Post* (New York, NY), Aug. 26, 1830, p. 2 ("The American poet Honeywood, more than thirty years ago, in putting the maxims of Beccaria into verse, said—(we quote from memory)—'Close to the gibbet's side the villain clings, / And pilfers while the hapless culprit swings'").

217. *See, e.g.*, "Does Capital Punishment Prevent Crime," *The Robesonian* (Lumberton, NC), Oct. 15, 1906, p. 7 ("Those laws, too, are passing away before the enduring eloquence of men like Beccaria, Montesquieu, Turgot, Franklin, Guizot, Augo, and John Bright and the inexorable logic of an experience that is teaching the world the folly of shedding human blood."); Benjamin F. New Hall, "Minority Report on Capital Punishment," *The Liberator* (Boston, MA), May 3, 1844, p. 4:

> Even the criminal is beginning to be recognized as a man, and to be treated in accordance
> with his spiritual dignity. The mitigation in our own criminal code, as well as that in many
> States in the Union, points firmly and directly at the entire abolition of the gallows. To be

sure, there may be some who may coldly sneer at this, as a matter of little consequence, if indeed worthy of engaging the attention of legislators at all; but to such it may be necessary only to say, that if this is a weak humanity, it is the weakness of Dr. Johnson, of Judge Blackstone, of Beccaria, and Montesquieu.

218. *See, e.g.* Pauline Maier, *Ratification: The People Debate the Constitution, 1787–1788* (New York: Simon & Schuster, 2010) (containing no index entry for Beccaria); Pauline Maier, *American Scripture: Making the Declaration of Independence* (New York: First Vintage Books, 1998) (same); Jack N. Ravoke, *Original Meanings: Politics and Ideas in the Making of the Constitution* (New York: First Vintage Books, 1997) (same); Richard Beeman, *Plain, Honest Men: The Making of the American Constitution* (New York: Random House, 2010) (same); Catherine Drinker Bowen, *Miracle at Philadelphia: The Story of the Constitutional Convention May to September 1787* (New York: Little, Brown & Co., 1986) (same). Only a few historians have paid proper attention to Beccaria's influence in the American colonies. *See, e.g.*, Bernard Bailyn, *The Ideological Origins of the American Revolution* (Cambridge: Harvard University Press, enlarged ed. 2012), p. 27:

> The ideas and writings of the leading secular thinkers of the European Enlightenment—reformers and social critics like Voltaire, Rousseau, and Beccaria as well as conservative analysts like Montesquieu—were quoted everyone in the colonies, by everyone who claimed a broad awareness. In pamphlet after pamphlet the American writers cited Locke on natural rights and on the social and government contract, Montesquieu and later Delolme on the character of British liberty and on the institutional requirements for its attainment, Voltaire on the evils of clerical oppression, Beccaria on the reform of criminal law, Grotius, Pufendorf, Burlamaqui, and Vattel on the laws of nature and of nations, and on the principles of civil government.

See also ibid. ("Josiah Quincy, Jr., referred with approval to a whole library of enlightened authors, among them Beccaria, Rousseau, Montesquieu, and the historian Roberson....").

219. Stuart Woolf, *A History of Italy, 1700–1860: The Social Constraints of Political Change* (London: Methuen & Co., 1999), p. 99; James Madison to John Henry Purviance, Dec. 24, 1804; John Adams Papers, Mar. 9, 1783, *available at* www.founders.archives.gov.

220. The *Illuminismo*, or *light*, has been described as distinct from the French Enlightenment and the English Enlightenment "in its determination not to lose sight of the psychic faculties and the social conditions out of which reason emerges." As that source summarizes the major aspects of the Italian Enlightenment.

> The figures of the Italian Enlightenment—in its two main centers, Naples and Milan—retain a close contact with civil society and practical life. The explicit refusal of metaphysics and of abstraction is exemplified by Antonio Genovesi (1712–69), the first person in Europe to be appointed to a chair in political economy (in 1754), and whose thought focused on the interwoven interests and aspirations of humankind, and on the struggle against privilege. The Enlightenment philosophy of Lombardy was more orientated toward law; it also found expression in the dynamic review *Il caffé* (1764–66), and its major representatives were Pietro Verri (1728–97) and Cesare Beccaria (1738–94). The Enlightenment project for them, on the one hand, developed in the direction of a modernization of society, facilitating the individual search for happiness, and, on the other, aimed at making the correctional system more humane through the abolition of torture, by humanizing punishment, and by making judgments more clear-cut and quicker. The light of a human reason (and no longer that of Providence) that tried hard to become more just, thus struggled to break through the darkness of social life.

Barbara Cassin, Emily Apter, Jacques Lezra & Michael Wood, eds., *Dictionary of Untranslatables: A Philosophical Lexicon* (Princeton, NJ: Princeton University Press, 2014), p. 521.

221. Anthony V. Baker, *"Through a Glass, Darkly ...": Christianity, Law and Capital Execution in Twenty-first Century America,"* 82 U. Det. Mercy L. Rev. 521, 521 n.2 (2005) (noting that Cesare Beccaria's *On Crimes and Punishments* "influenced American thinking" on capital punishment and "'elicited great interest and broad support among Enlightenment thinkers throughout Europe'" and was "'widely read in the United States as well'") (quoting *The Death Penalty in America: Current Controversies* (Oxford: Oxford University Press, Hugo Adam Bedau, ed., 1997), p. 4).

222. Bessler, *The Birth of American Law*, pp. 3–4, 75–149, 564–68; *see also* "Public Execution," *Columbian Repository* (Chapel Hill, NC), June 18, 1836, p. 3 ("take the sage and impressive remarks of Montesquieue [sic] and Beccaria").

223. *An Essay on Crimes and Punishments, Translated from the Italian; with a Commentary Attributed to Mons. De Voltaire, Translated from the French* (London: J. Almon, 1767); Simon Harvey, ed., *Voltaire: Treatise on Tolerance and Other Writings* (Cambridge: Cambridge University Press, 2000), pp. xxi, xxiv (taking note of Voltaire's dedication to Beccaria in Voltaire's *Account of the Death of the Chevalier de La Barre*).

224. Ullmann v. United States, 350 U.S. 422 (1956) (Douglas, J., dissenting) ("Beccaria, whose works were well known here and who was particularly well known to Jefferson, was the main voice against the use of infamy as punishment."); Solem v. Helm, 463 U.S. 277, 312 n.5 (1983) (Burger, C.J., dissenting) (Beccaria's name appears in the following comment cited by the Court: *The Eighth Amendment, Beccaria, and the Enlightenment: An Historical Justification for the* Weems v. United States *Excessive Punishment Doctrine*, 24 Buffalo L. Rev. 783 (1975)); Payne v. Tennessee, 501 U.S. 808, 820 (1991) ("Writing in the 18th century, the Italian criminologist Cesare Beccaria advocated the idea that 'the punishment should fit the crime.' He said that '[w]e have seen that the true measure of crimes is the injury done to society.'") (citing J. Farrer, *Crimes and Punishments* (1880), p. 199); Furman v. Georgia, 408 U.S. 238, 343 n.85 (1972) (Marshall, J., concurring) ("Punishment as retribution has been condemned by scholars for centuries....") (citing Cesare Beccaria, *On Crimes and Punishments* (H. Paolucci, trans., 1963)).

225. Bessler, *The Birth of American Law*, pp. 5–11.

226. *See generally* John D. Bessler, *The Death Penalty as Torture: From the Dark Ages to Abolition* (Durham, NC: Carolina Academic Press, 2017).

227. Ibid., pp. 88–89.

228. State of Connecticut v. Eduardo Santiago, Conn. Sup. Ct., SC 17413 (argued Apr. 23, 2013; officially released Aug. 25, 2015), *available at* https://www.jud.ct.gov/external/supapp/Cases/AROcr/CR318/318CR306.pdf.

229. Furman v. Georgia, 408 U.S. 238 (1972); Hugo Adam Bedau, ed., *The Death Penalty in America: Current Controversies* (New York: Oxford University Press, 1997), pp. 34–35.

230. S v Makwanyane and Another (CCT3/94) [1995] ZACC 3; 1995 (6) BCLR 665; 1995 (3) SA 391; [1996] 2 CHRLD 164; 1995 (2) SACR 1 (6 June 1995), paras. 6, 11, 26, & 33 & n.42, 146, 148; John Dugard, *Human Rights and the South African Legal Order* (Princeton, NJ: Princeton Legacy Library, 1978), p. 126.

231. *Encyclopedia of Violence, Peace, and Conflict* (San Diego, CA: Academic Press, 1999), Vol. 1, p. 478.

232. "Death Sentence: A Struggle for Abolition," International Seminar on Relevance of the Indian Penal Code in Controlling and Combating Crime in Modern Age (Commemorating the Hundred fiftieth Anniversary of the Indian Penal Code, 1860), Dec. 14–15, 2010, p. 47, *available at* http://www.rmlnlu.ac.in/pdf/international_souvenir.pdf.

233. Judgment (Sup. Ct. of India) of April 12, 2013 (G. S. Singhvi, J.), Devender Pal Singh Bhullar v State of N.C.T. of Delhi, Writ Petition (Criminal) D.No. 16039 of 2011, p. 7, *available at* http://www.sci.nic.in/outtoday/40266.pdf.

234. Somya Deshwal, "Death Penalty: Contemporary Issues," Indian National Bar Association, https://www.indianbarassociation.org/death-penalty-contemporary-issues/.

235. Bessler, *The Death Penalty as Torture*; Interim report of the Special Rapporteur on torture and other cruel, inhuman or degrading treatment or punishment, United Nations General Assembly, Sixty-seventh session, Item 70 (a) of the provisional agenda, A/67/279 (Aug. 9, 2012), *available at* http://antitorture.org/wp-content/uploads/2013/03/A67279_Death_Penalty.pdf.

236. "Designed to Break You: Human Rights Violations on Texas' Death Row," Human Rights Clinic, The University of Texas School of Law, https://law.utexas.edu/wp-content/uploads/sites/11/2017/04/2017-HRC-DesignedToBreakYou-Report.pdf, p. 7.

237. *See, e.g.*, Jianfu Chen, *Chinese Law: Context and Transformation* (Leiden, The Netherlands: Martinus Nijhoff Publishers, 2008), p. 272 (noting Beccaria's influence on the Chinese version of the principle of "proportionality").

238. Jianfu Chen, *Chinese Law: Towards an Understanding of Chinese Law, Its Nature and Development* (The Hague, The Netherlands: Kluwer Law International, 1999), p. 176; *see also* ibid., pp. 175–76 ("One of the guiding principles incorporated in the 1979 Criminal Law was the policy of combining punishment with leniency, which mean 'leniency to those who confess and severity to those who resist' in the determination of sentence."); ibid., p. 176 ("The incorporation of this principle [of proportionality], according to explanations given to the NPC [National People's Congress] by Wang Hanbin, is to make sure that serious crimes are punished heavily and light crimes leniently."). In 1935, compulsory rehabilitation also appeared in the "Temporary Rules" of the Criminal Law of the Republic of China, a document modeled—at least in part—after continental European legal codes that were, themselves, inspired by writers such as Montesquieu and Beccaria. Flora Sapio, *Sovereign Power and the Law in China* (Leiden, The Netherlands: Brill, 2010), p. 184.

239. Hong Lu & Terance D. Miethe, *China's Death Penalty: History, Law, and Contemporary Practices* (New York: Routledge, 2010), p. 49.

240. *See, e.g.*, Amnesty International, Death Sentences and Executions 2014 (London: Amnesty International, 2015).

241. Tom Rousseau, *Chinese Heroes: The Battle for Justice and Free Speech in the New Superpower* (New York: ME Publisher, 2014).

242. Michelle Miao, "Examining China's Responses to the Global Campaign Against the Death Penalty," *in* Roger Hood & Surya Deva, eds., *Confronting Capital Punishment in Asia: Human Rights, Politics, and Public Opinion* (Oxford: Oxford University Press, 2013), pp. 46, 48.

243. Jichun Shi, ed., *Renmin Chinese Law Review: Selected Papers of The Jurist* (Cheltenham, UK: Edward Elgar Publishing, 2017), Vol. 4, p. 138; *Contemporary Chinese Thought: Translations and Studies* (2004), Vol. 36, p. 34 (referencing 2002 edition published in Beijing by Zhongguo fazhi chubanshe); Dui Hua, Criminal Justice, http://duihua.org/wp/?page_id=136; Huang Feng, Beijing Normal University Law School, http://www.bnulaw.com/en/content/?143.html.

244. Schmidt, *Capital Punishment in Japan*, pp. 88–89.

245. Irokawa Daikichi, *The Culture of the Meiji Period* (Princeton, NJ: Princeton Library of Asian Translations, Marius B. Jansen, trans. 1988), p. 111; *see also* Shahid M. Shahidullah, *Comparative Criminal Justice Systems: Global and Local Perspectives* (Burlington, MA: Jones & Bartlett Learning, 2014), p. 138 ("In Japan, the medieval Tokugawa monarchy was overthrown and the Meiji emperor created the foundation of a modern state in 1868. The rise of Meiji rule disintegrated the basis of feudalism in Japan.").

246. Botsman, *Punishment and Power in the Making of Modern Japan*, pp. 167–68.

247. Schmidt, *Capital Punishment in Japan*, pp. 89–88.

248. Kuniji Shibahara, "The Influence of Cesare Beccaria's Thought on the Science of Criminal Law in Japan," *in Cesare Beccaria and Modern Criminal Policy* (Milano: A. Giuffrè, 1990), p. 344.

249. *An English and Chinese Standard Dictionary, Comprising 120,000 Words and Phrases, with Translations, Pronunciations, Definitions, Illustrations, Etc. Etc.* (Shanghai: The Commercial Press, 1908), p. 17.

250. Angelo Paratico, "500 Years of Italians in Macau and Hong Kong," Blog post of Feb. 14, 2014, https://beyondthirtynine.com/500-years-of-italians-in-macau-and-hong-kong/; Angelo Paratico, "Eugenio Zanoni Volpicelli—An Italian Sir Edmund Backhouse?", Blog post of Oct. 9, 2013, https://beyondthirtynine.com/eugenio-zanoni-volpicelli-an-italian-edward-backhouse/.

251. Devender Pal Singh Bhullar v. State of N.C.T. of Delhi, Petition (Criminal) D.NO. 16039 of 2011 (G. S. Singhvi, J.) (Apr. 12, 2013), p. 8 (citing another judge's opinion emphasizing that Beccaria "is supposed to be the intellectual progenitor of today's fixed sentencing movement"); *see also* 1 G.R. Madan, *Indian Social Problems: Social Disorganization and Reconstruction* (New Delhi: Allied Publishers, 1996), p. 121 (referring to Beccaria as "one of the foremost leaders of penal reforms").

252. Stephen C. Angle & Marina Svensson, eds., *The Chinese Human Rights Reader: Documents and Commentary 1900–2000* (London: Routledge, 2015), p. 146 ("The fundamental purpose of law is to protect human rights. Beccaria, a political theorist who based himself on jurisprudence, believed that the goal of law was to seek the greatest good for the greatest number."); *Philippine Law Journal*, Vol. 52 (1977), p. 62 ("Beccaria believed that the only justification of legal confinement was the protection of society by prevention of crime and that the principle of uniform maximum severity was

wrong and ineffective.").

253. Kuniji Shibahara, "The Influence of Cesare Beccaria's Thought on the Science of Criminal Law in Japan," *in Cesare Beccaria and Modern Criminal Policy* (Milano: A. Giuffrè, 1990), p. 344.

254. Marvin E. Wolfgang, "Of Crimes and Punishments," *in* Robert A. Silverman, Terence P. Thornberry, Bernard Cohen & Barry Krisberg, eds., *Crime and Justice at the Millennium: Essays by and in Honor of Marvin E. Wolfgang* (Dordrecht, The Netherlands: Springer Science+Business Media, 2002), p. 399; *see also* Mark F. Gilbert & K. Robert Nilsson, *Historical Dictionary of Modern Italy* (Lanham, MD: Scarecrow Press, 2007), p. 52 ("[T]he young jurist wrote *Dei delitti e delle pene* (*Of Crimes and Punishment*, 1764).... After translation into virtually every European language (the French edition bore a commentary by Voltaire), these ideas spread to the entire Western world and—with the eventual adoption of the civil law in Africa, Asia, South America, and the Middle East—to the rest of the world as well.").

255. Lidia De Michelis, "Letters from London: A 'Bridge' between Italy and Europe," *in* Frank O'Gorman & Lia Guerra, eds., *The Centre and the Margins in Eighteenth-Century British and Italian Cultures* (Newcastle upon Tyne, UK: Cambridge Scholars Publishing, 2013), pp. 50–51 n.18.

256. Tahir Wasti, *The Application of Islamic Criminal Law in Pakistan: Sharia in Practice* (Leiden: Brill, 2009), p. 11.

257. Angelo Del Boca, *Mohamed Fekini and the Fight to Free Libya* (New York: Palgrave Macmillan, Antony Shugaar, trans. 2011), p. 49.

258. George N. Sfeir, *The Place of Islamic Law in Modern Arab Legal Systems: A Brief for Researchers and Reference Librarians* (Law Library of Congress, 1999), p. 2.

259. Umberto Bacchi, "Execution Central: Saudi Arabia's Bloody Chop-Chop Square," *International Business Times*, Apr. 3, 2013, http://www.ibtimes.co.uk/saudi-arabia-chop-square-beheading-453240.

260. Marc Ancel, *The Collection of European Penal Codes and the Study of Comparative Law*, 106 Univ. Pa. L. Rev. P. 329, 340 (1958).

261. Ibid., p. 350.

262. Hugh Henry Brackenridge, *Law Miscellanies: Containing an Introduction to the Study of the Law* (Philadelphia: P. Byrne, 1814), p. 497.

263. James Madison to William Bradford, Jr., Jan. 24, 1774, *in The Writings of James Madison* (1900), Vol. 1, pp. 16–21.

264. *Catalogue of the Printed Books and Manuscripts in the John Rylands Library* (Manchester: J. E. Cornish, 1899), Vol. 1; William Godwin, *An Enquiry Concerning Political Justice* (Oxford: Oxford University Press, 2013), pp. 374, 492; Basil Montagu, *The Opinions of Different Authors upon the Punishment of Death* (London: Longman, Hurst, Rees, and Orme, 1809); John Bramsen, *Travels in Egypt, Syria, Cyprus, The Morea, Greece, Italy, &c. &c. in a Series of Letters Interspersed with Anecdotes of Distinguished Person, and Illustrations and Political Occurrences* (London: Henry Colburn and Co., 2d ed. 1820), Vol. 2, pp. 214–15.

Conclusion

1. Carlo Calisse, *A History of Italian Law* (Washington, DC: Beard Books, 2001), Vol. 2, pp. 456, 460.

2. Timothy Snyder, *On Tyranny: Twenty Lessons from the Twentieth Century* (New York: Tim Duggan Books, 2017), pp. 9–10.

3. *The Monthly Magazine, and British Register* (London: R. Phillips, 1798), Vol. VI, p. 260.

4. M. Valery, *Historical, Literary, and Artistical Travels in Italy: A Complete and Methodical Guide for Travellers and Artists* (Paris: Baudry's European Library, C. E. Clifton, trans. 1839), pp. 62–63.

5. M. Malte-Brun, *Universal Geography, or A Description of All the Parts of the World, on a New Plan, According to the Great Natural Divisions of the Globe* (Philadelphia: John Laval, 1832), Vol. V, p. 264.

6. Enrico Ferri, *The Positive School of Criminology: Three Lectures Given at the University of Naples, Italy on April 22, 23 and 24, 1901* (Chicago, IL: Charles H. Kerr & Co., Ernest Untermann, trans. 1913), p. 10; Victor H. Brombert, *The Romantic Prison: The French Tradition* (Princeton, NJ: Princeton

University Press, 1978), p. 40.

7. *Il Palazzo sul Potomac: The Embassy of Italy in Washington* (Colombo Duemila S.p.A., 2014), pp. 9–11.

8. Gilbert Faccarello & Heinz D. Kurz, eds., *Handbook on the History of Economic Analysis: Schools of Thought in Economics* (Cheltenham, UK: Edward Elgar Publishing, 2016), Vol. 2, p. 102; *The Universal Instructor or Self-Culture for All* (London: Ward, Lock, and Co. 1884), Vol. 3, p. 768; Sylvanus Urban, *The Gentleman's Magazine: and Historical Chronicle* (London: John Nichols and Son, 1824), p. 351.

9. William Stanley Jevons, *The Theory of Political Economy* (London: Macmillan and Co., 3d ed., 1888); *An Essay on the Theory of Money* (London: J. Almon, 1771) (attributed to Henry Lloyd).

10. *E.g., Catalogue of the London Library, established MDCCCXLI, at No. 49, Pall Mall* (London: M'Gowan and Co., 1842), p. 9 (listing a 1764 edition of "Dei Delitti e Delle Pene"); Cesare Beccaria, *Dei delitti e delle pene*, Library of Congress catalog listing, https://catalog.loc.gov/vwebv/holdings Info?searchId=27218&recCount=25&recPointer=1&bibId=3551865; *see also* Tiziana Fiorini, *La biblioteca di Vincenzo Dalberti* (Bellinzona: Edizioni Casagrande, 1991), p. 78.

11. Geoffrey Treasure, *The Making of Modern Europe, 1648–1780* (London: Routledge, 2003), p. 139.

12. Pennsylvania Prison Society, *The Journal of Prison Discipline and Philanthropy* (Philadelphia: The Philadelphia Society for Alleviating the Miseries of Public Prisons, 1886), p. 82; George F. Shrady, *Medical Record: A Weekly Journal of Medicine and Surgery* (New York: William Wood & Co., 1890), Vol. 37, p. 16; "A Penalogical Club," N.Y. Times, Dec. 19, 1889.

13. Marcello Maestro, *Cesare Beccaria and the Origins of Penal Reform* (Philadelphia: Temple University Press, 1973), p. 155.

14. Ibid., p. 152.

15. *The Encyclopædia Britannica: A Dictionary of Arts, Sciences, and General Literature* (Philadelphia: J. M. Stoddart Co., 9th ed. 1885), Vol. 19, p. 375.

16. *Milan: Guide de Agostini* (Istituto geografico de Agostini, 1990), p. 259; Cesare Beccaria, Turismo Milano, http://www.turismo.milano.it/wps/portal/tur/en/arteecultura/personaggi/artistieletterati/Cesare_Beccaria; Mojazza Cemetery, Turismo Milano, http://www.turismo.milano.it/wps/portal/tur/en/arteecultura/architetturaemonumenti/palazzivilleecastelli/cimitero_mojazza; Biography of Cesare Beccaria (Apr. 28, 2016), http://edukalife.blogspot.com/2016.

17. Maestro, *Cesare Beccaria and the Origins of Penal Reform*, p. 155.

18. Giuseppe Parini, Turismo Milano, http://www.turismo.milano.it/wps/portal/tur/en/arteecultura/personaggi/artistieletterati/giuseppe_parini.

19. Cliff Eisen, ed., Hermann Abert, *W. A. Mozart*, (New Haven, CT: Yale University Press, Stewart Spencer, trans. 2007), p. 1310; Rob Humphreys, *The Rough Guide to Vienna* (London: Rough Guides, 2001), p. 191; Lalla Fumagalli, ed., *An Open-Air Museum: The Monumental Cemetery of Milan* (Roma: Youcanprint Self-Publishing, 2014), pp. 7–8; E-mail of Carlo Scognamiglio Pasini (April 2, 2017); http://www.storiadimilano.it/citta/cimiteri/cimiteri_milanesi.htm.

20. Maestro, *Cesare Beccaria and the Origins of Penal Reform*, pp. 156–57; *see also* Jonathan Israel, *Revolutionary Ideas: An Intellectual History of the French Revolution from* The Rights of Man *to* Robespierre (Princeton: Princeton University Press, 2014), p. 649:

> During the summer of 1797, virtually on his own authority, Napoleon merged the Cispadane into the Cisalpine Republic, now covering much of the northern half of Italy, with its capital at Milan. The new republic comprised the Milanese, Mantua, Venetian Lombardy, and the Valteline area (which in October 1797 broke away from the Swiss federation). The Cisalpine Republic's constitution, proclaimed on 8 July 1797, again provided for two separate legislative chambers and a five-member Directoire, largely based, like its administration, on the current French model. Its territory was duly divided into departments, creating districts of equal population, with local assemblies of electors each representing, as in France, approximately two hundred people. The two chambers were called the Gran Consiglio, with around eighty members, and a smaller Consiglio dei Seniori. The "people's representatives" were mostly co-opted, comprising party Italian revolutionaries with reputations acquired abroad, partly local academics, and partly progressive local notables, including several former friends and

disciples of Beccaria, and occasionally also French supervisors. Alfonso Longo (1738–1804), one of Beccaria's and Pietro Verri's collaborators on the Milan journal *Il Caffè* in the 1760s, was among ten notables who signed the new constitution alongside Napoleon. "It is not without interest," observed Roederer, that it is the remaining friends and collaborators of Beccaria — Verri, Lambertenghi, and Longo — who "today occupy the chief places in the new republic, which indeed augurs well for its future."

21. Mario Ricciardi & Filippo Santoni de Sio, "Cesare Beccaria: Utilitarianism, Contractualism and Rights," *philinq II*, Feb. 2014, p. 84.

22. A. Mitchell Polinsky & Steven Shavell, eds., *Handbook of Law and Economics* (Amsterdam: Elsevier, 2007), Vol. 2, p. xi.

23. Henry Dunning Macleod, *A Dictionary of Political Economy* (London: Longman, Brown, Longmans, and Roberts, 1863), Vol. 1, pp. 252–59.

24. William Spalding, *Italy and the Italian Islands: From the Earliest Ages to the Present Time* (Edinburgh: Oliver & Boyd, 1841), Vol. 2, pp. 391–92.

25. *E.g.*, J. R. McCulloch, *A Discourse on the Rise, Progress, Peculiar Objects, and Importance, of Political Economy: Containing an Outline of a Course of Lectures on the Principles and Doctrines of that Science* (Edinburgh: Archibald Constable and Co., 1824), pp. 86–88 (noting that the lectures of Antonio Genovesi, who began teaching a course on political economy in Naples on November 5, 1754, "were very successful, were published in 1764, in two volumes octavo, under the title of *Lezioni di Commercio o sia di Economia Civile*," and that, "[i]n 1769, the Empress Maria Theresa founded a similar chair in the University of Milan, and appointed the justly celebrated Marquis Beccaria its first professor"); Sophus A. Reinert, *Translating Empire: Emulation and the Origins of Political Economy* (Cambridge, MA: Harvard University Press, 2011), pp. 230–31 (discussing the influence of Genovesi's lectures and how Genovesi was praised by both Pietro Verri and Cesare Beccaria, and noting that "[t]he Venetian *Giornale d'Italia*, one of the first journals on the peninsula to explicitly focus on economic matters, inaugurated its first issue with an extensive review of the 1764 Venetian edition of Genovesi's *History*").

26. *E.g.*, Donald A. Walker, ed., *Perspectives on the History of Economic Thought: Classical and Neoclassical Economic Thought — Selected Papers from the History of Economics Society Conference, 1987* (Hants, England: Edward Elgar, 1989), Vol. 1, pp. 62–63:

> In the course of the eighteenth century, by a process begun in Piedmont in 1715 and culminating in the period between 1750 and 1780, higher education was reformed fundamentally throughout Italy. The motivation for the reforms were: (1) the need to set up a high state bureaucracy; (2) the growing range and complexity of the new economic and social problems which needed to be kept under control; and (3) the increasing specialization of intellectual activity. The principal aims of the reformers were checking the seriousness of the studies, of centralizing in the hands of the state the feudal privileges of the religious bodies and professional colleges, and of spreading adequate knowledge and values for the economic and cultural progress of the citizens, within the framework of an enlightened despotism. The natural allies of the State were, at this time, the emerging speculating classes, the new professionals, and the enlightened nobility. The most important changes for the Italian universities concerned the Arts Faculty. Newly erected, it was normally subdivided into two two-year periods: the first, during which natural philosophy was taught, was compulsory for anyone aspiring to attend university; the second was devoted to training technicians.
>
> The first Italian chairs of Political Economy were found only within the Arts Faculties, namely technical schools destined for the new professionals whom the state was beginning to need in large numbers. The first Professors of Economics were Genovesi (Naples, 1754), Beccaria (Milan, 1769), Paradisi (Modena, 1772) and Sergio (Palermo, 1779). The most important of these were Genovesi and Beccaria, the former an exponent of the Neapolitan school, the latter of the Milanese. Of the two, Genovesi played a predominant role. His chair was founded on the wishes of a wealthy patron, Bartolomeo Intieri, who donated a large amount of capital to the state in order to finance the teaching. Thanks to this independent funding, the chair no longer risked being axed. The case was different in Northern

NOTES 413

Italy where teaching was paid for by the government and would be suspended and reopened according to political whims. Certainly the economic learning of Genovesi was initially stricter. He was attached to the same school as Ferdinando Galiani, namely to the discussion group of two Tuscans who had been transferred to Naples: Bartolomeo Intieri and Alessandro Rinuccini. Cultured, wealthy, very able businessmen, experts in international trade, moved by a great sense of civic pride and friends of some of the most important men of the Kingdom of Naples, such as the Prime Minister Tanucci and the Minister for Public Education Celestino Galiani, the uncle of Ferdinando. They were masters, in theory and in practice, of the problems of both economics and politics, and from their influential positions considered that the spread of science and of economic theory favoured the material and civil progress of the country.

In accordance with the wishes of the reforming authorities, the teaching should have a more technical and pragmatic orientation than theoretical. The great themes faced by the first teachers were subdivided according to the principal lines of the Genovesian example, into Political bodies, Population, Agriculture, Manufacturing, Business and Finance. The student intake was quite large. The students attending the courses at Beccaria's home numbered over one hundred in two years, coming from a broad spectrum of social classes: ecclesiastical, aristocratic and businessmen. The lectures were open to the public and given in the vernacular and not in Latin as in the other university courses.

27. *The Encyclopædia Britannica, or Dictionary of Arts, Sciences, and General Literature* (Edinburgh: Adam and Charles Black, 8th ed. 1854), Vol. 4, p. 558. Some of Cesare Beccaria's pupils ended up in important positions of power, and Beccaria also stayed in touch with some of those former students. Aaron Thomas, ed., Cesare Beccaria, On Crimes and Punishments *and Other Writings* (Toronto: University of Toronto Press, Aaron Thomas & Jeremy Parzon, trans. 2008), p. 178 n.1 (noting that Francesco Gallarati Scotti, a former pupil at Milan's *Scuole* Palatine, ended up as "a councillor in the ministry of justice"); Claudio Povolo, *The Novelist and the Archivist: Fiction and History in Alessandro Manzoni's* The Betrothed (New York: Palgrave Macmillan, Peter Mazur, trans. 2014), pp. 69–70 (noting that Agostino Carli Rubbi (1748–1803), the son of the aristocrat Gian Rinaldo Carli, returned to Millan after studying law in Vienna; "became a part of the enlightened intellectual milieu of the Societa' del Caffe,'" where he was "introduced to men of letters such as Giuseppe Gorani, Paolo Frisi and Pietro Verri"; and "[f]or years afterwards he corresponded with a number of these men on the questions of economics and mathematics, which had lately attracted his interest"; after attending Cesare Beccaria's "lessons on political economy," it is noted, Agostino Carli Rubbi stayed in close touch with his teacher and friend, reportedly spending—as one source reports—"each afternoon from one o'clock till after seven in enthusiasm and delight quite alone with my dear friend Beccaria, with never a dull moment, and completely unawares of the passage of time"; "He takes great pleasure in sharing his knowledge with me," Agostino Carli Rubbi wrote one correspondent of his interactions with Beccaria, "and I happily drink it in like a sponge."); ibid., p. 122 ("an old student of Cesare Beccaria, Agostino Carli Rubbi, who was assigned with the task of reorganising the archive of the State Inquisitors in 1813, was given almost unsupervised control over this collection of documents until 1820–1821").

The record shows that Cesare Beccaria in fact considered his pupil, Agostino Carli Rubbi, a student he took into his confidence, to be his potential successor at the Palatine School (a succession ultimately necessitated by Beccaria's realized aspiration to join Milan's Supreme Economic Council). As Agostino Carli Rubbi, speaking about Beccaria, wrote in a July 18, 1770 letter to his friend Giampaolo Polesini of Montana:

I am expecting any moment now the first part of the *Saggio sopra lo stile* (*Essay on Style*), his most beloved work, which should arrive from Livorno where it was printed by the Encyclopedists. I am waiting until his treatise on commerce has been copied, and you will be able to have all of this at some point in the future, because it would be too expensive to send it by post.... I confide in you as a particular friend, so if you refer to this in writing, be sure you send it separately in a sealed envelope: Beccaria has told my father that since he expects to have a place as member of the Council he truly cannot think of a person more qualified than I to replace him in the position of professor of administrative science. I have been told to write something, so I shall write a dissertation on a grand scale.... I'll write it and perhaps have it printed anonymously, and I can't accept the honor offered me, because I have no wish to remain in this country: This much I have already decided. It's now one o'clock, so I'm off to Beccaria, who is expecting me.

Another letter, written by Agostino, provided this additional information to his friend Giampaolo Polesini, explaining Beccaria's literary and professional activities in this way:

> Beccaria is going to send you his *Stile*, and I think he will also send you his complete works in the Naples edition. He is now councillor in the Royal Supreme Council of Political Economy, as you know.... He has written no more treatises based on his course, except for a rough draft of the one on commerce: but with corrections and additions he has completely transformed the first two parts of his course, the general principles and agricultural policy, and if he had found the time, he would have done the same with manufacturing. Now as for myself—I have refused the permanent chair of economics, which will continue to be occupied this year by Beccaria. Such a position would draw me more and more into a dependence on my domestic Excellency, and I'd like to see even his shadow fade to nothingness.

Ibid., pp. 70–71. The reference to his "domestic Excellency," a reference to his father Gian Rinaldo, alluded to the fact—as one modern commentator put it—that the apparently domineering father was continuing to "reprimand" the son for "his carefree and wasteful behaviuor." Ibid., p. 71.

28. Aaron Garrett, ed., *The Routledge Companion to Eighteenth Century Philosophy* (New York: Routledge, 2014), p. 51 ("British sources were important to two important groups of the Italian Enlightenment: in Milan, the journal *Il Caffé* was based on the example of the *Spectator*, and its contributors, Pietro and Alessandro Verri and Cesare Beccaria, quoted extensively from English and Scottish works. Of particular importance were Hume's philosophical and historical writings. In Naples, political economists often read Scottish works in French translations, and a highly significant process of reception ensued.").

29. The "School of Milan"—also called the "Milanese School" of economics or the "Italian economic school"—has been distinguished from that of the French physiocrats in terms of its focus on human happiness. *E.g.*, Pier Luigi Porta, "Italy," *in* Vincent Barnett, ed., *Routledge Handbook of the History of Global Economic Thought* (New York: Routledge, 2015), p. 63 (italics in original):

> The "School of Milan," as Voltaire called it, was established by Pietro Verri (1728–97). The notion of *felicità pubblica*, or public happiness, best conveys the meaning and the significance of the contribution of the Milanese School. Their concern was first of all about *happiness* and the utilitarian language becomes more explicit and richer in Milan. At the same time the *public* dimension becomes more prominent and intertwined with the practical needs for reform. Economists here are directly involved with the design and practical implementation of the Theresian Reforms in the Milanese territories. The predecessors of the generation of the Verris are Ludovico Antonio Muratori, who had put forward the ideal of public happiness and Pompeo Neri, the Tuscan economist and administrator who had worked on the practical side of the promotion of public happiness with his decisive contribution to the cadastral reform of the 1750s.
>
> Pietro Verri also founded the Accademia dei Pugni (the *punching academy*, a curious name) and the periodical *Il Caffè* (the *coffee house*), a kind of Italian *Spectator*. Cesare Beccaria (1738–94), by far the best known name of the Italian economic school of the time, was one of his younger associates. Four main themes emerge from Verri's work: 1) money; 2) free trade, especially in staples; 3) pain and pleasure scientifically considered in order to measure happiness and public happiness in particular; 4) quantitative tools to analyse the economy and draw policy conclusions. The Italian School worked in parallel with the physiocratic school, but with a difference. Italian authors took up mercantilist themes—trade, money, public and private finance—in the context of a different agenda in which real growth, based on a concept of real production and income, takes the lead together with an emphasis on *creativity* in a context of *trust* and *sociality*. The competitive drive, not without exception, becomes the symbol of the abolition of privileges and obstacles. *Money* and *trust*, thereby sociality, are naturally bound together. At the same time the Italians, while they follow physiocracy on free trade (with qualifications) do not confine positive economic

productivity to agriculture only....

The main follower of Verri certainly was Cesare Beccaria, by far the best known figure of the Italian Enlightenment, himself among the early Professors of Political Economy worldwide. Curiously he is sometimes *not* perceived as an economist, but more as a scholar on public law or a moral philosopher of a utilitarian breed. His reputation is almost entirely due to the pamphlet *Dei delitti e delle pene* (Of Crimes and Punishment) of 1764. In fact, Beccaria, ten years Verri's junior, had made his first significant contributions (published in *Il Caffè*) as a mathematical economist. He was still in his twenties when he acquired a world-wide reputation and his celebrated pamphlet on crimes and punishment became an explosive success. That is probably by far the best known works of the whole Italian Enlightenment. Beccaria, like Verri, was also a consultant administrator and a member of the Economic Council from 1771 in Milan. Both Beccaria and Verri contributed a number of reports, or *Consulte*, within the Council giving advice to the government. Beccaria also left a volume of his lectures in Milan at the Scuole Palatine: they were only published as *Elementi di Economia Pubblica* in Milano in the Custodi Collection in 1804.

See also R. H. Inglis Palgrave, ed., *Dictionary of Political Economy* (New York: Palgrave Macmillan, 1894), Vol. 1, p. 474:

CUSTODI, PIETRO (1771–1846), born near Novara. He was by profession a lawyer, but soon entered into journalism and directed the paper *Amico della libertà Italiana*. He became privy councilor and baron. The *History of Milan* by Pietro Verri was continued by Custodi; as an economist he is widely known as the editor of a collection of the principal Italian economists in fifty volumes.

30. Roger Middleton, "England," *in* Vincent Barnett, ed. *Routledge Handbook of the History of Global Economic Thought* (New York: Routledge, 2015), pp. 19–20 (noting that the East India Company, the world's first multi-national company, was formed in 1600; that the Bank of England was established in 1694; and that "seventeenth-century England has been described as an 'age of great intellectual vigour, scientific curiosity and inventiveness', with Hutchison claiming that leadership in what came to be the discipline of political economy lay with the English from 1662 to the early eighteenth century, with the work of William Petty (1623–87) the 'notable' advance from whom others followed.") (citations omitted); Renee Prendergast, "Ireland," *in* Vincent Barnett, ed., *Routledge Handbook of the History of Global Economic Thought* (New York: Routledge, 2015), p. 50 ("[W]hile Petty complained that Ireland being 'thinly peopled' was an impediment to its development, by the 1720s, unemployment and poverty had emerged as major problems, causing Jonathan Swift (1667–1745) to argue that (Petty's) maxim 'that people are the riches of a nation' did not apply in Ireland. Faced with the constraints placed by the British parliament on Irish trade, some, including Swift and George Berkeley (1685–1753), advocated the substitution of domestic products for imports as a means of developing domestic industry.") (citations omitted); Alexander Dow & Sheila Dow, "Scotland," in Vincent Barnett, ed., *Routledge Handbook of the History of Global Economic Thought* (New York: Routledge, 2015), pp. 40–41 (citations omitted):

The literature on the history of Scottish economic thought is dominated by attention to the work of Adam Smith. Yet Smith was influenced by a range of others, from his precursors Carmichael and Hutcheson to his contemporaries such as Hume and Anderson. Further, his ideas should be considered in relation to the range of economic ideas put forward by others within the Scottish tradition: Smith was not an author generous in giving credit to others. The key figures in the eighteenth and nineteenth centuries can be identified as Francis Hutcheson, David Hume, Adam Smith, Sir James Steuart, Adam Ferguson, Dugald Stewart, John Rae, Thomas Chalmers, W.S. Nicholson and William Smart.

Compare José Luís Cardoso & Luis Perdices de Blas, "Spain and Portugal," *in* Vincent Barnett, ed., *Routledge Handbook of the History of Global Economic Thought* (New York: Routledge, 2015), p. 81 ("Eighteenth-century Spanish economists were aware of the writings coming from Europe and some of these works were translated into Spanish...."); Erik Grimmer-Solem, "Germany: From Sciences of State to Modern Economics," *in* Vincent Barnett, ed., *Routledge Handbook of the History of Global Economic Thought* (New York: Routledge, 2015), p. 86:

In the eighteenth century German economics grew out of *Staatskunst* (statecraft) into

Staatswirtschaft (state economy), an administrative discipline that had evolved alongside the needs of enlightened absolutist rules, the political order that defined the courts of Austria, Prussia and many of the lesser German states following the catastrophe of the Thirty Years War (1618–48). As such, it was a field preoccupied with the practical administrative needs of the court, namely management of royal domain lands, forests, mines, and military and luxury industries, as well as royal finances. While many of the German states were open to new economic ideas coming from the French and Scottish Enlightenments, notably the ideas of Du Pont, Mirabeau, Quesnay, Turgot, and especially Adam Smith, the political, social, and economic conditions in Germany (estate order, guilds, remnants of serfdom) made their application difficult until the Napoleonic invasions and the modernizing reforms they forced on the German states, most prominently the Stein-Hardenberg reforms in Prussia after 1807.

Even as Adam Smith's ideas began to inform German understandings of the economy as an autonomous component of civil society, the administrative legacy of cameralistic Staatswirtschaft remained prominent in modern German conceptions of economics. As such the economy, even an ostensibly free economy, was conceived as something ordered by law and institutions and requiring administrative guidance. Inspired by Smithian ideas, Prussian civil servant reformers introduced a liberalization of customs and tolls (1818) and then the German Customs Unions (1834), which enabled a national division of labor among the German states for the first time and which would later spur the rapid industrial development of Germany in the 1850s and 1860s.

31. Daniel Coetzee & Lee W. Eysturlid, eds., *Philosophers of War: The Evolution of History's Greatest Military Thinkers* (Santa Barbara, CA: ABC-CLIO, 2013), pp. 96–97; Béla Kapossy, Isaac Nakhimovksy & Richard Whatmore, *Commerce and Peace in the Enlightenment* (Cambridge: Cambridge University Press, 2017), p. x. Major General Henry Lloyd (1729–1783), who lived in Italy during the late 1760s as a British secret agent, has been described as a "military *philosophe*." His writings, sought out by Pietro Verri and his fellow Italian *philosophes*, included two significant works, *An Essay on the English Constitution* (1770) and *An Essay on the Theory of Money* (1771), published by John Almon. As one source notes, Lloyd "aided Pasquale Paoli's failed Corsican revolt and mingled with Italy's literary elite." As that source further observes of Lloyd's activities in relation to John Wilkes (1727–1797), the co-founder of *The North Briton*, a journal that, in 1763, had attacked George III and his ministers: "In 1768, the 'Wilkes and Liberty' movement erupted in England, prompting him [Lloyd] to predict revolution. He returned to London in 1770 and published his first political treatise under the pseudonym 'Cato,' which launched his career as an enlightened thinker and reformer." "A Wilkes's partisan," that source points out, noting the influence of Montesquieu on the general's thinking, "Lloyd wrote this essay to condemn the unjust and unlawful use of Parliamentary power." The 1770 essay gave his views on "the Rights of the Subjects, so lately and wantonly violated," with Lloyd opposing "tyranny" and arbitrary punishments and writing of "the principles of equality, which we have shewn to be the basis, and foundation of all free governments." Patrick J. Speelman, ed., *War, Society and Enlightenment: The Works of General Lloyd* (Leiden: Brill, 2005), pp. xiv, 6, 189–92, 203, 214–15, 220, 262.

In *An Essay on the English Constitution*, Lloyd gave his positive, rather glowing views of English criminal *procedure* but then harshly critiqued English *punishments*, especially capital ones, showing his obvious familiarity with the ideas Beccaria had explored a few years earlier in *On Crimes and Punishments*. As Lloyd wrote in 1770:

No country upon earth, can boast of more humanity towards criminals than England, who knows neither tortures, perpetual imprisonments, gallies, or slavery. All processes must be finished in a few months. The witnesses are examined in public, and confronted with the accused, to whom the laws administer every means, that may contribute to his justification. Arbitrary power is excluded, as well in the form of his trial, as in the sentence which is determined by the laws. The jury, chose by lot, are alone his judges. I wish the same indulgence was found in the penalties imposed on criminals, which, in my opinion, are much too severe. The spirit of avarice, too natural in a commercial people, has carried the degree of punishments beyond the limits prescribed by humanity and natural equity. All ideas of distributive justice, are lost and confounded by the number and equality of punishment: death being almost a common penalty for all crimes, great and small. The manner of it makes little or no difference. The king's humanity has, indeed, saved many, but still the numbers which thus perish annually, is a real loss to a nation, and their example neither does nor will diminish the number of crimes.

These are essentially connected with the morals of the nation, which being generally corrupted, in great and opulent cities, it is in vain to attempt diminishing the number of crimes by any penalty whatever: for, while the causes remain, the effects become necessary consequences of them. Punishments therefore only destroy the inhabitants, without diminishing the evil. What then? no punishments? Yes, but such only as are necessary, to hinder any future evil from a criminal, and which may render him an useful example to deter others: while he lives, the example lives, and his life may be rendered useful to the state. An inanimate and dead being is useless, and soon forgot. The wants of man are immediate and strong. The fear of punishment is diminished by its distance and uncertainty, and must therefore cede to the first, unless you diminish the sources from which the crimes proceed, the number of laws and punishments will only prove their impotency.

Ibid., p. 225.

In *An Essay on the Theory of Money* (1771), Henry Lloyd defined *money* as the "Universal Merchandise," offered an equation of supply and demand, spoke of "[t]he love of liberty and independence" inherent in all people, wrote that an "inequality of riches" necessarily "produces an inequality of power," and stressed that "[i]n despotic governments the inequality of power and riches is extreme." "A great inequality of fortunes necessarily implies a national and general poverty," Lloyd observed in his essay, also expressing his desire—in line with Beccaria's previously expressed views—that "all princes would agree to fix the same proportion between their respective coins, because it would greatly contribute to facilitate trade between different nations, and prevent the coins being extracted by foreigners, or melted down by the subject." One reviewer, writing in January 1772 in *The Monthly Review*, observed that "the Author of this essay is an 'ingenious' and able writer, and that he has thrown out several observations, which merit the public attention." Ibid., pp. 257, 261–62 & n.1, 267, 287, 294, 304, 342. In *An Essay on the Theory of Money*, Lloyd invoked Montesquieu's name more than once and had a whole chapter titled "LIBERTY IS IN PROPORTION TO THE EQUALITY, AND DESPOTISM TO THE INEQUALITY OF CIRCULATION." "While few are rich, the number of the poor will be extreme," Lloyd wrote in that chapter. Ibid., pp. 276, 287–88, 316, 321. "Today," explains Patrick Speelman, the editor of General Lloyd's writings, "economic historians consider Lloyd an important link in the emergence of modern economic thought and a major influence on Pietro Verri (1728–97) and the Milanese Enlightenment." Ibid., p. 262. "Lloyd's definition of money as the 'universal merchandise,'" Speelman adds, "mirrors that found in Pietro Verri, *Meditazioni sulla economia politica* (1771)." "This similarity," Speelman reports, "led to a coolness of relations between the two friends," with Speelman emphasizing of the Verri-Lloyd dispute over pride of authorship: "For years the controversy so vexed Verri that in the end he credited the definition to Lloyd." Ibid., p. 267 n.1.

32. Sophus A. Reinert, "'One will make of political economy ... what the scholastics have done with philosophy': Henry Lloyd and the Mathematization of Economics," 39 *History of Political Economy* 643, 649–50 (2007); *see also* ibid., p. 646 ("Men, for Lloyd, were nothing but machines seeking pleasure and avoiding pain in a utilitarian world free from providential codes of morality. Nevertheless, he argued, their wiring catered to some forms of political organization more than to others. They might have been biological automata, but wealthy, egalitarian, and virtuous republics, he concluded, were their true habitat."); ibid., p. 653 ("In the end, for Lloyd, man was good or bad according to his 'circumstances' and nothing else. No more radical conclusion could be drawn from Enlightenment moral philosophy, and one should not be surprised that Lloyd never published his realization. From this insight, however, he derived the hedonistic notion, discussed widely since Hobbes, that all actions could be measured in 'Pleasure and Pain' and that the main spring of all man's actions was 'pain,' which 'solicits us to change our situation' and to assess 'the principle of utility.'"); ibid., p. 647 (noting of Lloyd and his connection to Milanese intellectuals: "The best account of his evolution as a person and political economist ... can be pieced together from his countless appearances in the intense correspondence between the Counts Pietro and Alessandro Verri. The Verri brothers were among the founding members of the *Accademia dei pugni* (literally, the 'Academy of Fists'), a coterie of young

upper-class Milanese aristocrats and reformers embodying the ideals of their age."); ibid., p. 648 ("Lloyd befriended Pietro Verri at Bautzen in 1759, while they served in the Austrian army during the Seven Years' War, and the two would repeatedly rendezvous in Milan in the decades to come. The first months they spent together after the siege of Dresden, surveying battlefields at dawn and browsing bookshops in the afternoons, were particularly formative in their respective intellectual developments."); ibid., p. 650 ("The economic methodology that developed in late-eighteenth-century Milan looked beyond the mere quantifications of political arithmeticians toward analytical formalization, toward uncovering underlying mechanisms by means of selective abstractions, which could be expressed in algebraic terms. 'The spirit of geometry,' Verri argued in the pages of *Il caffè*, 'saturates and perfects all sciences.'").

33. *E.g.*, Marcello T. Maestro, *Cesare Beccaria and the Origins of Penal Reform* (Philadelphia: Temple University Press, 1973), p. 49 (noting that Cesare Beccaria's "plumpness was certainly a consequence of his love for good food and good wine"); Stephen E. Brown, Finn-Aage Esbensen & Gilbert Geis, *Criminology: Explaining Crime and Its Context* (New York: Routledge, 9th ed. 2015), p. 159 (noting that Beccaria was "obese, as he was inordinately fond of fine food and wine"); John A. Rice, *Antonio Salieri and Viennese Opera* (Chicago: The University of Chicago Press, 1998), pp. 261, 266–67 (reprinting portions of letters from Pietro Verri to his brother, Alessandro, about a drama, *Europa*, the orchestra's overture, and the staging and actors of the performance); Martha Feldman, *The Castrato: Reflections on Natures and Kinds* (Oakland: University of California Press, 2015), p. 180 ("In Milan the poet and librettist Giuseppe Parini, who was central to the Milanese group centered around the opera-loving intellectual powerhouse Pietro Verri, who published the periodical *Il Caffè*, declared that the malevolence of castrating fathers was even more unnatural than the state of their sons."); Georges Vigarello, *The Metamorphoses of Fat: A History of Obesity* (New York: Columbia University Press, C. Jon Delogu, trans., 2013), p. 105 (reprinting a 1764 description by Pietro Verri of a table "filled with the most delicate foods possible," with Verri taking specific note of "chicken and other bird meat, herbs, and oranges and their juice" and then concluding: "This is our meal and we complete it with an excellent cup of coffee. One feels satisfied, full, but not stuffed or sleepy as one would from eating rough heavy foods."). For the views of Italian nobles, including Beccaria and the Verri brothers, on work and commercial activity by merchants, nobles and landowners, see Luca Mocarelli, "The Attitude of Milanese Society to Work and Commercial Activities: The Case of the Porters and the Case of the Elites," *in* Catharina Lis, *The Idea of Work in Europe from Antiquity to Modern Times* (New York: Routledge, 2016), ch. 4.

34. Jomo K.S. & Erik S. Reinert, eds., *The Origins of Development Economics: How Schools of Economic Thought Have Addressed Development* (London: Zed Books, 2005), p. 36; Agnar Sandmo, "Adam Smith and Modern Economics," *in* Ryan Patrick Hanley, ed., *Adam Smith: His Life, Thought, and Legacy* (Princeton, NJ: Princeton University Press, 2016), p. 239; Jerry Evensky, *Adam Smith's Moral Philosophy: A Historical and Contemporary Perspective on Markets, Law, Ethics, and Culture* (Cambridge: Cambridge University Press, 2005), p. 214; R. H. Campbell & A. S. Skinner, eds., Adam Smith, *An Inquiry into the Nature and Causes of the Wealth of Nations* (Indianapolis, IN: Liberty Classics, 1976), Vol. 1, pp. 12 & 21 n.5; Adam Smith, *An Inquiry into the Nature and Causes of the Wealth of Nations* (Basil: James Decker, 1801), Vol. 1, pp. 4, 92, 119, 221, 229, 395; Dennis C. Rasmussen, "The Problem with Inequality, According to Adam Smith," *The Atlantic*, June 9, 2006, https://www.google.com/amp/s/www.theatlantic.com/amp/article/486071/; *see also* Alessandro Roncaglia, *The Wealth of Ideas: A History of Economic Thought* (Cambridge: Cambridge University Press, 2006), p. 110:

> Both Verri and Beccaria adopted a subjective theory of value based on comparison between scarcity and utility; in general, they conceived the market as the point where buyers and sellers met (and this held true also for the rate of interest, determined by demand for and supply of loans). Moreover, both Verri and Beccaria took a wide interest in practical issues, from the fiscal and monetary situation to problems of customs duties, seasonal unemployment, and concession to private agents of monopolies for commodities such as salt and tobacco. On the latter issue, for instance, Verri, in his capacity as a high-ranking functionary in the Austro-Hungarian empire, succeeded in obtaining an important victory with abolition of the concessions in 1770.

Adam Smith, *An Inquiry into the Nature and Causes of the Wealth of Nations* (Basil: James Decker, 1801), Vol. 1, pp. 191–92 ("In England ... a charter from the king was likewise necessary [to start a corporation]. But this prerogative of the crown seems to have been reserved rather for extorting money from the subject, than for the defence of the common liberty against such oppressive monopolies."); *compare* Ernesto Screpanti & Stefano Zamagni, *An Outline of the History of Economic Thought* (Oxford: Oxford University Press, David Field & Lynn Kirby trans., 2d ed. rev. 2005), p. 62:

> Galiani accepted the Physiocrats' idea of natural order, which he reformulated in the view that the economy tends spontaneously towards equilibrium: nature 'settles everything in equilibrium', as if it were controlled by a 'supreme hand'; but he introduced an interesting dynamic consideration, by observing that any adjustment would be achieved only in the long run. In the short run, disorders and malfunctions could well manifest themselves. But the short run could also last a long time. Therefore, there would be ample leeway and excellent reasons to try to correct those disorders and malfunctions by law. *Laissez-faire* policy would not be justified in the short run. At all events, Galiani did not admit the possibility of establishing general criteria for state intervention in the economy. The most suitable measures would depend to a large extent on the time and place in which they were taken.
>
> This pragmatic attitude towards *laissez-faire* was also present in other Italian economists of the period. Genovesi, Beccaria, and Verri, for example, were in favour of economic freedom, which they considered from an illuminist point of view as a manifestation of the more general principle of human freedom. They justified this theoretically with the idea that nature tends to bring human things towards equilibrium if left free to do so—an idea that Genovesi supported with an argument similar to Hume's price-specie-flow mechanism. In practice, however, they limited this application of free trade to within national boundaries. In regard to foreign trade, they believed that the State had to guide and regulate the flows of imports and exports in the national interest, which might not coincide with the interests of the individual citizens....
>
> Filang[i]eri and Ortes were more extreme supporters of *laissez-faire*. The former took great steps forward in the construction of an illuminist normative system, and professed a strong faith in *laissez-faire*, justifying it with the observation that a reduction of imports would lead to reprisals by competing states and would therefore be followed by a reduction in exports. Ortes, on the other hand, justified his free-trade position with the argument that, in the absence of protectionist barriers, exports and imports of a country would tend to balance.

See also The Law Review, and Quarterly Journal of British and Foreign Jurisprudence (London: V. & R. Stevens, & G. S. Norton, 1855), Vol. XXII pp. 40–59 (discussing Gaetano Filangieri's views on law and economics); Stephen Copley & Kathryn Sutherland, eds., *Adam Smith's* Wealth of Nations: New Interdisciplinary Essays (Manchester, UK: Manchester University Press, 1995), pp. 9–10 (noting that Adam Smith himself did not actually use the term "laissez-faire" in his writings); John E. Hill, *Adam Smith's Equality and the Pursuit of Happiness* (New York: Palgrave Macmillan, 2016), p. 26 ("Smith never used laissez-faire explicitly, nor did he argue for its implicitly); Frank Solomon, *Capitalism: An Analysis and Summary of Adam Smith's* Wealth of Nations (Bloomington, IN: Archway Publishing, 2d ed. 2014), p. 208 (italics in original):

> Smith's idea of a marketplace was what would be produced *after* powerful, enforceable, and enforced laws went into effect against monopoly, price fixing (if possible), fraud, bribery, conflict of interest, violent threats, theft, murder, etc. The kind of economy should be left alone that would issue from these limitations. But there would still have to exist provisions for the introduction of temporary emergency measures in case the operation of his envisioned economy were to go very much awry and become a serious threat to Main Street or to the long term security and very existence of the nation. *But those exertions of the natural liberty of a few individuals, which might endanger the security of the whole society, are, and ought to be, restrained by the laws of all governments,* (*WN*, Bk. II, ch.ii, p. 308). It is seriously misleading to call such a system *laissez-faire. Smith never used this term* in any of his writings, and he disapproved of Quesnay's concept of an economy which would be ruled only by prescription and decree, not by laws.

35. Aaron Garrett, ed., *The Routledge Companion to Eighteenth Century Philosophy* (New York: Routledge, 2014), p. 468; Stuart K. Hayashi, *The Freedom of Peaceful Action: On the Origin of Individual Rights* (Lanham, MD: Lexington Books, 2014), p. 356 n.2; ibid. (noting that Francis Hutcheson "was the first philosopher during the Enlightenment to proclaim that the most moral option for individuals or governments to take is whichever provides the greatest happiness of the greatest number"); *see also* Neil Thin, "Social Planning Without Bentham or Aristotle: Towards Dignified and Socially Engaged Well-being," *in* Joar Vittersø, ed., *Handbook of Eudaimonic Well-Being* (Switzerland: Springer, 2016), p. 554 ("The single most important source of utilitarian philosophy, Hutcheson was also an arch-opponent of David Hume's hedonism, and was pretty close to Aristotle in seeing virtue as the cause of happiness: 'That action is best, which procures the greatest happiness of the greatest numbers'. Happiness matters in that it is the outcome of virtue. Happiness and virtue are inextricably linked—they are valued together."); Francis Hutcheson, *An Inquiry into the Original of Our Ideas of Beauty and Virtue; In Two Treatises* (London: J. & J. Knapton, et al., 3d ed. corr. 1729), pp. 102–3 (referring to "the Foundation of our greatest Happiness"); ibid., pp. 179–80 (italics in original):

> In comparing the *moral Qualitys* of Actions, in order to regulate our *Election* among various Actions propos'd, or to find which of them has the greatest *moral Excellency*, we are led by *our moral Sense* of *Virtue* to judge thus; that in *equal Degrees* of Happiness, expected to proceed from the Action, the *Virtue* is in proportion to the *Number* of Persons to whom the Happiness shall extend; (and here the *Dignity*, or *moral Importance* of Persons, may compensate Numbers) and in equal *Numbers*, the *Virtue* is as the *Quantity* of the Happiness, or natural Good; or that the *Virtue* is in a *compound Ratio* of the *Quantity* of Good, and *Number* of Enjoyers. In the same manner, the *moral Evil*, or *Vice*, is as the Degree of Misery, and *Number* of Sufferers; so that, *that Action* is best, which procures the *greatest Happiness* for the *greatest Numbers*; and *that, worst*, which, *in like manner*, occasions *Misery*.

Compare ibid., p. 196 (italics in original):

> I see no harm in supposing, "that Men are *naturally* dispos'd to *Virtue*, and not left *merely indifferent*, until some prospect of Interest allures them to it." Surely, the Supposition of a *benevolent universal Instinct*, would recommend *human Nature*, and its AUTHOR, more to the *Love* of a *good Man*, and leave room enough for the Exercise of our *Reason*, in contriving and settling *Rights*, *Laws*, *Constitutions*; in *inventing* Arts, and *practicing* them so as to gratify, in the most effectual manner, that generous Inclination. And if we must bring in *Self-Love* to make *Virtue rational*, a little Reflection will discover, as shall appear hereafter, that this *Benevolence* is our *greatest Happiness*; and thence we may resolve to cultivate, as much as possible, this *sweet Disposition*, and to despise every *opposite* Interest.

36. Sophus A. Reinert, "*Achtung! Banditi!* An Alternative Geneaology of the Market," *in* Philipp R. Rössner, *Economic Growth and the Origins of Modern Political Economy: Economic Reasons of State, 1500–2000* (New York: Routledge, 2016), p. 260. *Cameralism* has been called "[a]n approach to government and administration" that "originated in central Europe toward the end of the 17th century and developed over the 18th century." Harvey Chisick, *Historical Dictionary of the Enlightenment* (Lanham, MD: The Scarecrow Press, 2005), p. 99; *see also* Steven N. Durlauf & Lawrence E. Blume, eds., *The New Palgrave Dictionary of Economics* (New York: Palgrave Macmillan, 2d ed. 2008), Vol. 1, pp. 625–26:

> Cameralism is the specific version of mercantilism taught and practised in the German principalities (*Kleinstaaten*) in the 17th and 18th centuries. Becher (1635–82), von Justi (1717–71) and von Sonnenfels (1732–1817) are the principal figures who contributed to a vast cameralist literature of about 14,000 titles (Humpert, 1935). The subject matter of *Kameralismus* reflected the political and economic phenomena and problems in the German territorial states. As a branch of 'science' it is a fiscal *Kunstlehre*, that is, the practical art of how to govern an autonomous territory efficiently and justly via financial measures designed to fill the state's treasury. Its subject matter includes economic policy, legislation, administration and public finance. While there is no unifying analytical foundation of cameralism, it did develop in two distinct phases (a younger and an older branch) with varied emphasis on its different elements, and since the rising state was, in theory and reality, the focus and *Ultima Ratio* of political, economic and ethical (occasionally promotive) speculation, cam-

eralism takes on a unitary form (*Gestalt*) only when viewed in retrospect.

The term 'cameralism' itself originates in the management of the state's or prince's treasure (*Kammer, caisse, camera principis*), seen as the principal instrument of economic and political power. In the age of enlightened absolutism, German-Austrian cameralism, based on a somewhat obscure natural-law philosophy, emphasized the paternalistic character of the governments' centralized fiscal policy (not, as is sometimes mistakenly thought, a Keynesian short-run instrument but rather a regulator for development which was to serve the general happiness of the subjects (*Untertanen*), that is, an eudaemonistic utilitarianism). English and French mercantilism, on the other hand, stressed much more the wealth or 'riches' of the sovereign as an end.

The princely bureaucrats had been trained in their own universities (for example, Halle, Frankfurt/Oder, Vienna) in 'fiscal jurisprudence' (von Stein) — a mixture of both formal budget and tax 'principles' — and a highly pedantic and descriptive systematization of facts and definitions. Analytical economics, insights into the laws of the market and the study of the interaction between market and state (or even of the bureaucratic and political mechanism) are relatively unknown in the simple textbooks of the cameralists, which show otherwise sound common sense. Statistics, important for census and grasping foreign trade, became a new discipline of the cameral curriculum.

The *practical* policy of cameralism concentrated on the development of a country which had been devastated and depopulated in the Thirty Years' War and impoverished by the discovery of the sea route to India and the fall of Constantinople. Under these abnormal circumstances a political and bureaucratic monopoly attempted to reconstruct the economic foundations of the country by an active population policy, the establishment of state manufactures and banks, the extension of infrastructure (canals, bridges, harbours and roads) and the promotion of modernization. It strictly regulated the still important agriculture sector, as well as trade and commerce.

The state protected the trades (*Gewerbe*) by means of high tariffs to restrict imports of unnecessary raw materials and it facilitated exports of manufactures and import substitution. On the other hand, the government removed internal trade barriers by abolishing the medieval guild organization and by unifying the law for municipalities. Mercantilist efforts to augment the state treasure via trade surplus and money policy were, of course, another main cameralist aim.

Cf. Chisick, *Historical Dictionary of the Enlightenment*, p. 99 ("The term 'cameralism' derives from 'kammer,' the chamber, or exchequer, of the territorial lord. In its assumptions concerning the necessity of state control of economics, cameralism is close to mercantilism. However, unlike the mercantilists, cameralists tended to define their objective as the general well-being of the people rather than the power and prestige of the state."); ibid.:

Unlike the enlightened despotism of western Europe, cameralism had an established institutional base. In 1727 chairs of Administrative Science (*Cameralwissenschaft*) were established in the Universities of Halle and Frankfurt an der Oder. Another such chair in the University of Vienna was held by Johann H. G. von Justi, whose *Foundations of the Power and Happiness of States* (1760–1761) was one of the earliest authoritative texts of cameralism. Another occupant of this chair at the University of Vienna was Joseph von Sonnenfels, one of the leading figures of the Enlightenment in Austria, a counselor of Joseph II and author of the influential *Basic Principles of the Science of Administration, Business and Finance*, which appeared in three volumes between 1765 and 1776.

Mercantilism was "the economic policy of absolutism." Chisick, *Historical Dictionary of the Enlightenment*, p. 350. As one source reports of the system known as mercantilism:

It assumed that economics were an aspect of necessarily conflict-driven international relations, and required regulation as close as that in politics. Internally, old-regime economic policy assumed that both the production and the distribution of goods required corporate and government supervision. This is particularly clear in the grain trade. The government agreed that it had an obligation to assure that basic necessities were provided to the working population at manageable prices. To achieve this goal the government subsidized grain prices, imported grain and limited its circulation. The assumption here, as in the regulatory mentality generally, was that unless the authorities took appropriate measures to effect the desired objectives, these objectives would not be achieved.

Ibid.; *see also* ibid, p. 51:

> The absolutist state of the 17th century felt that it had the right and obligation to direct economic activity. The system of mercantilism, elaborated most notably by Colbert, set out to regulate production, prices, exports and imports according to the interests of the state. During the first half of the 18th century writers such as Jean François Melon and David Hume argued that the market functioned as a self-regulating mechanism that achieved maximal benefits by allowing free action to the self-interests of agents competing in the market. This view was adopted by the physiocrats in France and was most forcefully expressed by Adam Smith in *The Wealth of Nations*, which appeared in 1776.

Compare ibid. ("Economic liberals, who were usually responsible neither for public order nor for as-suring subsistence, favored the deregulation of the grain trade. They did so on the grounds that a deregulated market would in the long run increase production of grains, improve provisioning and reduce prices, thus benefiting all.").

In seventeenth- and eighteenth-century Italian locales, the concept of *sociability* (loosely connected with the profusion of European coffeehouses and salons) had a particular — if somewhat vague or ambiguous — meaning. The 1741 edition of the *Vocabolario* of the well-known Florentine academy, the *Accademia della Crusca* (Academy of the Bran), designed to defend the Italian language as derived from the Tuscan dialect, defined social as "*Who loves company*" and *sociable* as follows: "Man is the most sociable, or companionable animal of all.... Man, being a sociable animal that loves living with those of its own species, rejoices in the happiness of others." Sophus A. Reinert, "Enlightenment So-cialism: Cesare Beccaria and His Critics," *in* Kapossy, Nakhimovksy & Whatmore, eds., *Commerce and Peace in the Enlightenment*, p. 129; *see also* Brian Cowan, "Café or Coffeehouse? Transnational Histories of Coffee and Sociability," *in* Susanne Schmid & Barbara Schmidt-Haberkamp, eds., *Drink in the Eighteenth and Nineteenth Centuries* (New York: Routledge, 2016), ch. 3 ("The English coffee-house was clearly related to the French café or the Germanic *Kaffeehaus* and as such they can be un-derstood as individual parts of a broader, transnational and indeed global history of the discovery and rapid diffusion of coffee and the revolution in sociability that this brought about."); Scott Bre-uninger & David Burrow, eds., *Sociability and Cosmopolitanism: Social Bonds on the Fringes of the En-lightenment* (London: Routledge, 2016), p. 49 ("[E]ighteenth-century Italian states provided European travellers with a widespread diffusion of aristocratic and bourgeois female salons in cities such as Turin, Milan, Genoa, Bologna, Florence, Venice, Rome and Naples, only to cite the most internationally important.").

   37. The term *capitalism* appears to have first been used in the mid-nineteenth century. *See, e.g.*, William Batchelder Greene, *Equality* (West Brookfield, MA: O. S. Cooke & Co., 1849), pp. 3, 13, 59–61 (containing the following headings in discussing different socio-economic models: "COM-MUNISM — CAPITALISM — SOCIALISM" and "*Materialism — Capitalism — Plutocracy*"; defining *plutocracy* as "a government administered by, and for the advantage of, the more wealthy class of the community" and *socialism* as where "the government administers the wealth of the state"; emphasizing that "the capitalist buys what he desires to buy, while everything is cheap" and "sells what he has to sell, while prices are high" and that "[t]he capitalist and the laborer are mutually necessary to each other"); *compare* André Hakizimana, *Understanding Everyday Governments' Ways of Job Creation: Ideas and Governments' Sustainable Strategy to Facilitate Success in Job Creation* (Bloomington, IN: iUniverse, 2012), p. xii:

> According to the *Oxford English Dictionary* (Vol 2, p. 863), the world *capitalism* was first used in English by William Makepeace Thackeray in 1854, in his novel *The Newcomes* (1855, Vol 2, p. 45). In this context the word *capitalist* was first used in English in the 1780s by Arthur Young (*Travels in France*), and it was used by Turgot in his *Reflections on the Formation and Distribution of Riches* (LXIII–IV, 1770).

The term *capitalist* was not always used in a positive fashion as an extended excerpt from one mid-nineteenth century novel, about a seamstress and the dire circumstances faced by members of her poorly paid profession, makes clear:

Virginia's food consisted of coffee, tea, bread, and oatmeal. The Duke of Norfolk who so generously and humanely recommended the poor to use a pinch of currie power in a gallon of hot water "*to make an excellent soup,*" would doubtless tell us that "coffee, tea, bread, and oatmeal," constitute a perfect summary of luxuries! Malediction upon all aristocratic heartlessness! For, oh! how small—how infinitely small—how tiny were the quantities of tea and coffee which the poor girl was enabled to purchase at a time—and how frequently was the tea warmed up and the coffee boiled over and over again! Sugar she had completely broken herself of. And then, as for bread—judge, ye tyrant aristocrats! how much of *this* could poor Virginia afford to buy out of her three shillings a-week, after paying eighteen-pence for rent and sixpence for coal and candles! She could not even enjoy a penny roll a-day. Her principal food was therefore oatmeal;—and the fair, innocent, interesting girl, endowed with every virtue and every personal grace, was not a hundredth part so well fed as the Queen of England's lap-dog or the Duke of Norfolk's pigs!

As sure as there is a God in heaven, must a curse fall upon the land where such a system exists. The Almighty cannot—oh! no—he cannot, he cannot suffer such horrors to endure much longer. Neither will he permit them to go unpunished. What right has any set of men to make this country an earthly hell for all the rest? Bishops who preach patience to starving millions, are the vilest hypocrites that desecrate the human species: statesmen who bestow the name of "sedition" upon discontent, will have much to answer for when they stand before the throne of a just God, however successfully they may have ground down the masses in this world. Yes—truly, there must be a hell hereafter: or else where is the justice of the Eternal?

We have seen that Virginia was compelled to live upon three shillings a week. But this was a sum which she was not always sure of obtaining. Sometimes work was slack; at others she felt too ill to toil for eighteen hours a-day. Then, indeed, did she endure misery the most pinching—penury the most poignant: then, indeed, did she feel, and know, and experience all the horrors which must attend upon the lingering death of starvation. Her weekly struggle was to pay her rent: every sacrifice must be made to accomplish this object;—or else would she be turned adrift into the open streets—homeless, as she was already friendless! Poor girl—poor girl! she was perishing by inches—dying by slow famine—as so many thousands of British females are ever pining and fading away into early graves, while titled demireps and noble courtezans at the West End are revelling in all the luxuries and elegancies of life. Oh! if the thirty thousand pale, spectral, wasted needle-women of London were all to assemble and go down in a body to Buckingham Palace, and demand—yes, demand an interview with the Queen,—what would be the effect? Doubtless Victoria would be appalled by the aspect of that multitude of shadowy forms and wan faces: but she would refer them to her Ministers—and her Ministers would tell them to go quietly home, for fear their shocking appearance should excite the indignation of the people and thereby *endanger the security of property!*

"Ah! By all means protect the property of such establishments as that of Messrs. Aaron and Sons—no matter how many journeymen tailors may fashion their own funeral palls and how many seamstresses may work their own winding-sheets in the service of the wealthy slop-sellers! Besides, only consider—the City every now and then requires a Sheriff from that class of capitalists, competitors, and monopolists. What are a few thousands of starving tailors or famishing needlewomen, so long as the Government receives the duty upon the twenty thousand pounds sterling annually spent by Aaron and Sons in newspaper-advertisements? Why, there are pensioners, placemen, and sinecurists to be paid: and therefore the Government must have money—somehow or another! Raise that money, then, by taxing the tea and the coffee which the poor seamstress drinks: for again we ask, of what matter is it to the Government, the Aristocracy, the Bishops, or the Legislature, how many inoffensive, hard-working, miserable women are *starved to death* in the course of a year?

G. W. M. Reynolds, *The Seamstress; or, The White Slave of England* (London: John Dicks, 1853), p. 90.

38. Cesare Beccaria's early views on the right to property are somewhat unclear, with the language

Beccaria used in *Dei delitti e delle pene* about that right generating much debate and commentary. *See* Cesare Beccaria, *On Crimes and Punishments* (New York: Routledge, Graeme R. Newman & Pietro Marongiu, trans., 5th ed. 2017), chap. § XXII (Theft) n.2:

> It should be noted that Beccaria in the first edition of the *Treatise* (Livorno, 1764) wrote "terrible *but necessary right*,["] changing it to "terrible *and perhaps unnecessary right*" in the third edition (Lausanna, 1765). Elsewhere in this edition of the *Treatise*, he refers to the "sacred ownership of property," though stating, in the same chapter that "commerce and private property are not a goal of the social contract, but can be a means to obtain it" (see: Chapter XXXIV on Debtors). So it is difficult to establish his position on the right of property[.] According to Francioni (1984: 75, fn. 3) Beccaria's more radical view derives from Rousseau.

See also Matthias Reinhard-DeRoo, *Beneficial Ownership: Basic and Federal Indian Law Aspects of a Concept* (Sham, Switzerland: Springer, 2014), p. 89 & n.384 (in the context of discussing crime and punishment, "BECCARIA, the great Italian reformer whose ideas were highly influential on BENTHAM, was willing to consider property as a 'terrible, maybe even unnecessary right (terribile, e forse non necessario diritto').") (citing *Dei delitti e delle pene* and noting that Bentham disagreed with Beccaria's view, with Bentham seeing "the source of evil not in the law but in people's greed for possession"); J. R. McCulloch, *The Principles of Political Economy: With Some Inquiries Respecting Their Application, and a Sketch of the Rise and Progress of the Science* (Edinburgh: William Tait, new ed. 1843), pp. 87–88:

> [W]e may observe, that Rousseau and the Abbé Mably have made an object to the institution of private property, which has been, in some measure, sanctioned by Beccaria and others. They allow that this institution is advantageous for those who possess property; but they contend, that it is disadvantageous for those who are poor and destitute. It has condemned, they affirm, the great portion of mankind to a state of misery, and has provided for the exaltation of the few by the depression of the many! The sophistry of this reasoning is so apparent, as hardly to require being pointed out. The right of property has not made poverty, but it has powerfully contributed to make wealth. Previously to its establishment, the most civilized nations were sunk to the same level of wretchedness and misery as the savages of New Holland and Kamtchatska. All classes have benefited by the change; and it is mere error and delusion to suppose that the rich have been benefited at the expense of the poor.

In fact, Cesare Beccaria's assertion about the right to property in *Dei delitti e delle pene* (or, perhaps more accurately, his expression of doubt about it in the context of considering how thieves should be punished) led many Enlightenment thinkers to vigorously defend the right to property, arguing that property rights could benefit the poor as well as society's richest citizens. For example, Jeremy Bentham offered this spirited defense of the right to property:

> The laws in creating property have created wealth; but, with respect to poverty, it is not the work of the laws,—it is the primitive condition of the human races. The man who lives only from day to day is precisely the man in a state of nature. The savage, the poor in society, I acknowledge, obtain nothing but by painful labor; in a state of nature what could he obtain but at the price of his toil?.... Hence the laws, in creating property, have been benefactors to those who remain in their original poverty. They participate more or less in the pleasures, advantages, and resources of civilized society; their industry and labor place them among the candidates for fortune; they enjoy the pleasures of acquisition; hope mingles with their labors. The security which the law gives them, is this of little importance? Those who look from above at the inferior ranks see all objects less than they really are; but, at the base of the pyramid, it is the summit which disappears in its turn. So far from making these comparisons, they dream not of them; they are not tormented with impossibilities; so that, all things considered, the protection of the laws contributes as much to the happiness of the cottage as to the security of the palace. It is surprising that so judicious a writer as Beccaria should have inserted, in a work dictated by the soundest philosophy, a doubt subversive of the social order. "The right of property," says he, "is a terrible right, and may not, perhaps, be necessary." Upon this right tyrannical and sanguinary laws have been founded. It has been most frightfully abused; but the right itself presents only ideas of pleasure, of

abundance, and of security. It is this right which has overcome the natural aversion to labor—which has bestowed on man the empire of the earth—which has created a love of country and posterity. To enjoy quickly—to enjoy without punishment—this is the universal desire of man; this is the desire which is terrible, since it arms all those who possess nothing against those who possess anything. But the law which restrains this desire is the most splendid triumph of humanity over itself.

David J. Brewer, ed., *Crowned Masterpieces of Literature that Have Advanced Civilization: As Preserved and Presented by the World's Best Essays From the Earliest Period to the Present Time* (St. Louis, MO: Ferd. P. Kaiser Pub. Co., 1908), Vol. 2, pp. 438–39.

Ultimately, Cesare Beccaria, wrestling with how best to maximize the happiness of Italian society, expressed the view that the right to property (what he called a "sacred right" elsewhere in *Dei delitti e delle pene*) is a social right that should be subject to certain societal conditions. *See, e.g.,* Aaron Thomas, ed., Cesare Beccaria, On Crimes and Punishments *and Other Writings* (Toronto: University of Toronto Press, Aaron Thomas & Jeremy Parzen, trans. 2008), pp. xxxviii–xxxix:

> The urgent need for social justice is what gave rise to that passion that immediately struck readers of *On Crimes and Punishments*—and that may have rankled the rigorous and methodical mentality of the *philosophes*, or at least of the influential d'Alembert, whose support of the Abbé Morellet helped to steer the transformation of Beccaria's text into a more systematic treatise. Apart from the particular aspects of the theory, it is precisely the acute sensibility for the social question, however, that constitutes the most conspicuous legacy that united Beccaria with Rousseau. Take, for example, two crucial moments in Beccaria's argumentation that are both different and apparently unrelated: the recurring allusion to the social causes of crimes (an aspect of extraordinary modernity that seems to have been too rarely appreciated by readers of Beccaria) and the emphasis on the generality of law. The claim for social causes of delinquency leads even to a defence of theft (a crime born of poverty and desperation among those for whom the right to property has left them with nothing but the barest existence) and an aggressive call for social controls on property. As Beccaria argues in *Elementi di economia pubblica*, respect for the right to property is subject to two conditions: 'One is that everyone is equal in property, that is, that there is no property that is more or less subject to the laws, and thus that the laws that limit such property be universal, either against or in favour of everyone; the other is that the established laws do not impede or degrade the use of such property, which has been bestowed to each individual for the benefit of each.'

Beccaria—who, living in an age of enormous poverty and debtor's prisons, believed that an "innocent bankrupt" or debtor (as opposed to a fraudster) should not be "thrown into prison" and thus "deprived of his one poor remaining possession, bare liberty"—expressed the view in *Dei delitti e delle pene* that "[s]ecurity in one's own life is a natural right, while the protection of property is a social right." Ibid., p. 61; Cesare Beccaria, *On Crimes and Punishments* (Indianapolis, IN: Hackett Publishing Co., David Young, trans., 1986), p. 65; *see also* Lynn McDonald, *The Early Origins of the Social Sciences* (Montreal: McGill-Queen's University Press, 1993), p. 156:

> Beccaria's other social science work, *A Discourse on Public Economy and Commerce* (1769), was equally liberal but less influential. Except in his treatment of industry as well as agriculture as productive, Beccaria's political economy aligned with that of the physiocrats. He advocated free trade within the country and protective barriers against other countries. He proposed reforms in agriculture and forestry. He advocated public education and medicare. Property rights were to be limited in accordance with the common good, for property was the daughter of society, not the mother. The science of political economy was intended to increase the riches of the state for useful application.

The division between *natural rights* (*i.e.*, those inalienable or universal rights derived from nature) and *social rights* (*i.e.*, those derived from law, or a socially accepted mechanism for conferring rights, aimed at ensuring individuals specific rights or a particular standard of living, such as in old age) is one that has generated much discussion over time. *See, e.g.,* Kennedy M. Maranga, *Indigenous People and the Roles of Culture, Law and Globalization: Comparing the Americas, Asia-Pacific, and Africa* (Boca Raton, FL: Universal-Publishers, 2013), p. 144 (distinguishing between natural rights and social rights); Theo R.G. van Banning, *The Human Right to Property* (Antwerpen: Intersentia, 2001), p. 23 ("The term *social right* and the distinction between civil rights and social rights is not simple or articulate. All (human) rights connote relationships between an individual and a state or society. There is no international consensus as to the content of the term 'social' right."). There was certainly debate during the Enlightenment about the scope or content of particular rights, with some groups (*e.g.*, women and minorities) excluded entirely from the eighteenth-century social compacts that conferred individual or social rights in the first place. *E.g.*, Michael Dudley, Derrick Silove & Fran Gale, eds., *Mental Health and Human Rights: Vision, Praxis, and Courage* (Oxford: Oxford University Press, 2012), p. 57 ("Liberalism's 'father,' John Locke (1632–1704), conceived of individuals (by which he meant white, male, property-owning ones endowed with 'Life, Liberty and Estate') as the bearers of *pre-social* rights, that is, natural rights that precede and inform individuals' entry into political community.") (italics in original); Edward H. Crane & David Boaz, eds., *An American Vision: Policies for the '90s* (Washington, DC: Cato Institute, 1989), p. 327 & n.1 (noting that James Madison made the following statement in a speech in 1829 to the Virginia State Convention of 1829–1830: "It is sufficiently obvious, that persons and property are the two great subjects on which Governments are to act; and that the rights of persons, and the rights of property, are the objects, for the protection of which Government was instituted. These rights cannot be well separated. The personal right to acquire property, which is a natural right, gives to property, when acquired, a right to protection, as a social right."). *See also* Rodney P. Carlisle, ed., *The Encyclopedia of Politics: The Left and the Right* (Thousand Oaks, CA: Sage Publications, 2005), Vol. 1, p. 221:

> By the 17th century, some philosophers began to express the idea that all people are born free and equal and so have some natural rights, such as the right to life, liberty, and property. Thomas Hobbes (*Leviathan*, 1660) and later John Locke (*The Second Treatise of Government*, 1690) were the first of the natural rights theorists; for them, a person had rights by being human. In particular, Locke's formulation of rights constitutes the essence of the political and social thought of liberalism. For his formulation, each individual had some claims against both society and government, including the rights to life, liberty, property, and consent on how to be governed via a social contract. These rights were inalienable and needed to be protected by a proper political community.

39. *Compare* Andrew Zimbalist & Howard J. Sherman, *Comparing Economic Systems: A Political-Economic Approach* (Orlando, FL: Academic Press, 1984), p. 7 ("Pure *socialism* is defined as a system wherein all of the means of production are owned and run by the government and/or cooperative, nonprofit groups."). The term "obligatory social contract" has been used to describe situations where a population is *forced* into a social compact. Those types of social contracts are obviously not free. Michael A. Lebowitz, *The Contradictions of "Real Socialism": The Conductor and the Conducted* (New York: Monthly Review Press, 2012), p. 64. As a political theorist, Rousseau saw the *social contract* as an agreement between free and equal individuals, all consenting to put themselves under the general will. As Rousseau put it: "Each of us puts his person and all his power in common under the supreme direction of the general will, and, in our corporate capacity, we receive each member as an indivisible part of the whole." Lucien Goldmann, *The Philosophy of the Enlightenment: The Christian Burgess and the Enlightenment* (New York: Routledge: Henry Maas, trans. 2010), p. 14. The modern definition of *socialism* is "a political and economic theory of social organization that advocates that the means of production, distribution, and exchange should be owned or regulated by the community as a whole (meaning the government)." Dennis Machala, *A Different Look at the Business World* (New York: Page Publishing, 2017) (containing that definition and defining *capitalism*, by contrast, as "an economic and political system in which a country's trade and industry are controlled by private owners for profit, rather than by the state"). Many eighteenth- and nineteenth-century intellectuals looked to Beccaria's conception of the social contract, particularly in the context of thinking about the criminal justice system, for inspiration. *E.g.*, Mr. Russell (of Edinburgh), "The Abolition of Capital Punishments," *The Scottish Congregational Magazine* (Glasgow: James Maclehose, 1845), p. 520 (italics in original):

> Nations and states are composed of individuals, and have no power as nations to give up the life, over which as individuals they did not possess this right. The power assumed, therefore—to take away life—is as clearly a usurpation by government of a right they do not

possess, as that of the suicide who takes away his own life. They have no power *beyond* the source whence they derived their authority. In support of these views, I shall cite short extracts from the works of two eminent authorities—namely, the Marquis Beccaria, and Sir. W. Blackstone. The former says:—"Men have been compelled, upon entering into society, to sacrifice a portion of their liberty; *but it is the smallest portion possible.*"

There are, of course, many different types of social compacts; their number and variety are infinite and know no limits. Individual societies, for example, choose to set different rates of taxation, and there are rights that exist in some places that do not exist in others. Twenty-first century debates in the United States over the right to health care illustrate how individuals have very different views of what a well-ordered social compact is all about.

40. Reinert, "Enlightenment Socialism: Cesare Beccaria and His Critics," *in* Kapossy, Nakhimovsky & Whatmore, eds., *Commerce and Peace in the Enlightenment*, p. 148.

41. Eluggero Pii, "Republicanism and Commercial Society in Eighteenth-century Italy," *in* Martin van Gelderen & Quentin Skinner, eds., *Republicanism: A Shared European Heritage (The Values of Republicanism in Early Modern Europe)* (Cambridge: Cambridge University Press, 2002), Vol. 2, p. 271 (noting the Beccaria's appointment "to the Austrian administration of the Duchy of Milan from 1771 onwards" turned him into "the scrupulous executant of one of the many programmes of enlightened despotism"; "[b]eing a civil servant for Beccaria ... meant opting for silence").

42. Mary Vance Young, "Alessandro Manzoni-Beccaria, Romanticist," 13 *Romanic Review* 331, 353 n.85 (1922) ("Beccaria proposed the decimal system to the government of Milan in 1780, but the scheme was refused, largely for financial reasons.").

43. *The Penny Cyclopædia of the Society for the Diffusion of Useful Knowledge* (London: Charles Knight, 1835), Vol. 4, p. 127:

> In 1768 the Austrian government founded a professorship of political philosophy for him at Milan, which he filled with distinguished success. In 1769 he published a 'Discourse on Commerce and Public Administration,' which was translated into French by J. A. Comparet; and in 1781 a Report of a plan for producing uniformity in the weights and measures of Milan.... The lectures which he delivered as a professor were published at Milan in 1802, and they form a part of the series of 'Italian Economists,' published at Milan in 1804.

A reformation of Milan's system of weights and measures, as was equally true for other cities and locales, was long overdue. As one encyclopedia points out in the starkest of terms:

> The *Italian* measure is the bracchio, brace, or fathom. This obtains in the states of Modena, Venice, Florence, Lucca, Milan, Mantua, Bologna, &c. but is of different lengths. At Venice, it contains one Paris foot eleven inches three lines, or eight fif[t]eenths of the Paris ell. At Bologna, Modena, and Mantua, the brace is the same as at Venice. At Lucca it contains one Paris foot nine inches ten lines, or half a Paris ell. At Florence, it contains one foot nine inches four lines, or forty-nine hundredths of a Paris ell. At Milan, the brace for measuring of silks is one Paris foot seven inches four lines, or four-ninths of a Paris ell; for that woolen cloths is the same with the ell of Holland.

Encylopædia; or, A Dictionary of Arts, Sciences, and Miscellaneous Literature (Philadelphia: Thomas Dobson, 1798), Vol. 10, p. 716.

44. Reinert, "Enlightenment Socialism," *in* Kapossy, Nakhimovsky & Whatmore, eds., *Commerce and Peace in the Enlightenment*, p. 128. As Reinert explains in *Commerce and Peace in the Enlightenment*: " 'Socialists' were, in the final instances, those bold enough to believe that political economy trumped theology as a matrix for social organization." Ibid.; *see also* Sophus A. Reinert, "*Achtung! Banditi! An Alternative Genealogy of the Market,*" *in* Philipp R. Rössner, ed., *Economic Growth and the Origins of Modern Political Economy: Economic Reasons of State, 1500–2000* (New York: Routledge, 2016).

45. Pier Luigi Porta, "Free Trade and Protectionism in Primary Export Economies," *in* Mario Garcia-Molina & Hans-Michael Trautwein, ed., *Peripheral Visions of Economic Development: New Frontiers in Development Economics and the History of Economic Thought* (New York: Routledge, 2015), ch. 6, sec. 3; *On Character: Essays by James Q. Wilson* (Washington, DC: The AEI Press, 1995), pp. 139–40; *see also* Stuart Woolf, *A History of Italy, 1700–1860: The Social Constraints of Political Change* (London: Methuen & Co., 1979), p. 100 ("on Carli's advice, Beccaria was appointed to a chair of political economy at the Palatine Schools, 'to search for the surest and easiest method—taking into account the

situation, quality, produce and customs of the various nations—of spreading the greatest possible amount of goods among the greatest possible number of men'").

46. William Hamilton, ed., Dugald Stewart, *Lectures on Political Economy* (Edinburgh: T. & T. Clark, 1877), Vol. 1, p. 49; William Hamilton, ed., *The Collected Works of Dugald Stewart, Esq., F.R.S.S.* (Edinburgh: Thomas Constable and Co., 1855), Vol. VIII, p. 49 (same).

47. George W. Carey, ed., *The Political Writings of John Adams* (Washington, DC: Regnery Publishing, 2000), p. 159; Reinert, "Enlightenment Socialism: Cesare Beccaria and His Critics," *in* Kapossy, Nakhimovsky & Whatmore, eds., *Commerce and Peace in the Enlightenment*, p. 129 n.16 (noting that Pietro Verri discusses "luxury, which is never divorced from the universal culture and refinement [*ripulimento*] of nations"); *see also* Reinert, *"Achtung! Banditi!," in* Rössner, *Economic Growth and the Origins of Modern Political Economy.*

48. "Cesare Beccaria," Constitution Society, http://www.constitution.org/cb/beccaria_bio.htm; *compare* Luigino Bruni & Stefano Zamagni, "Economics and Theology in Italy since the Eighteenth Century," *in* Paul Oslington, ed., *The Oxford Handbook of Christianity and Economics* (Oxford: Oxford University Press, 2014), p. 63 (italics in original):

> Beccaria and others only mentioned the reward of virtue without exploring it further, whereas Dragonetti, inspired by a more radical and far-reaching approach, devoted his analysis entirely to this disregarded issue. Dragonetti envisioned an entire system of laws built around the idea of rewarding virtue ("political virtue" in particular): *a code of virtue* to go alongside the penal code.

49. Anthony J. Draper, *Cesare Beccaria's Influence on English Discussions of Punishment, 1764–1789*, 26 History of European Ideas 177, 179, 182 (2000); *see also* Mrs. Lincoln Phelps, *The Student, for Teachers, Parents and Daughters, or Fireside Friend, with an Appendix, on Moral and Religious Education* (New York: A. S. Barnes & Co., 1876), p. 119 ("Beccaria, an Italian writer on law, is still consulted by the legal practitioner.").

50. Dinah Birch, ed., *The Oxford Companion to English Literature* (Oxford: Oxford University Press, 7th ed. 2009), p. 108; *see also Harvard Law School Bulletin* (1962), Vols. 14–17, p. 74 ("Of equal revolutionary significance, though in a widely different sphere, is the little masterpiece, *Dei delitti e delle pene*, published exactly two centuries ago by Cesare Bonesana, Marchese di Beccaria, an obscure twenty-six-year old amateur in criminal law and penology."); André Klip & Göran Sluiter, *Annotated Leading Cases of International Criminal Tribunals: The International Criminal Tribunal for the Former Yugoslavia 2002–2003* (Intersentia, 1999), p. 73 n.11 ("The literature on the principle of legality of crimes is certainly immense. Definitely, Beccaria's masterpiece remains the milestone on this topic."); David J. Brewer, ed., *Crowned Masterpieces of Literature that Have Advanced Civilization* (St. Louis, MO: Ferd. P. Kaiser Pub. Co., 1908), Vol. 2, p. 419:

> It is only necessary to read a few clauses of anything the Marquis of Beccaria has written, to feel the commanding power of his great intellect. The reader accustomed to strive with other writers for the privilege of wresting their meaning from their words is so strongly compelled by Beccaria, that, unless he deliberately make up his mind to dissent at the beginning, he will be forced from one irresistible conclusion to another. It is doubtful if Italy since the time of Cicero, has produced Beccaria's equal as a master of style and as a thinker in his own field of the philosophy of human action…. [W]ithin fifty years after the publication of his great work, "Dei Delitti e Delle Pene" (On Crimes and Punishments), it had influenced for the better the whole course of government in every Caucasian nation of the world….

51. Mary Vance Young, "Alessandro Manzoni-Beccaria, Romanticist," 13 *Romanic Review* 331, 353 n.85 (1922) ("It will be remembered that the little book, *Dei delitti e delle pene*, was immediately hailed as a new Evangel, was translated into all European languages, and won for its author the highest honors…."); *see also The Starry Messenger and the Polar Star: Scientific Relations Between Italy and Sweden from 1500 to 1800: Catalogue of an Exhibition Held at the Naturhistoriska Riksmuseet—Stockholm* (Giunti, 1994), p. 146 (referencing a 1770 Swedish translation of Beccaria's *Dei delitti e delle pene*); John Cam Hobhouse, *Travels in Albania and Other Provinces of Turkey in 1809 & 1810* (Cambridge: Cambridge University Press, 2014), Vol. 1, p. 506 ("Mr. Corai, of Scio, has rendered himself well known by his French translation of Theophrastus's Characters, and of Hippocrates … and more par-

ticularly by a version of Beccaria in modern Greek, with a preliminary exhortation to his countrymen."); ibid., p. 508 (the author notes that on his travels he saw "one of Corai's Beccaria"); Anna Frangoudaki & Caglar Keyder, eds., *Ways to Modernity in Greece and Turkey: Encounters with Europe, 1850–1950* (New York: I.B. Tauris, 2007), pp. 101–2 ("[W]e may note that the Karamanli press of the Ottoman Empire was, among other things, a channel to transmit elements of European intellectual life. For example, at the end of the 1880s, a flourishing decade for the publication and translation of French novels into Turkish and Greek, the Karamanli newspaper *Terakki* (Progress) in 1888 listed among other names Victor Hugo, Balzac and Voltaire, Boccaccio and Beccaria.").

52. Thomas Rawling Bridgwater, "The Great Jurists of the World: Cæsar Bonesana, Marquis di Beccaria," *in* John MacDonell & Edward Mason, eds., *Journal of the Society of Comparative Legislation* (London: John Murray, 1908), pp. 219–28.

53. Daniel V. Botsman, *Punishment and Power in the Making of Modern Japan* (Princeton, NJ: Princeton University Press, 2005), p. 167; *see also* ibid., pp. 166–67 ("[T]he push to master Western-style 'civilization' in the early Meiji period was spearheaded by a small group of intellectuals known as the 'Meirokusha' or 'Meiji Six Society.' Named after the year it was founded (Meiji 6 = 1873), the group met regularly to discuss and debate key issues of the day, and from 1874 it also began to publish its famous 'journal of enlightenment,' the *Meiroku zasshi*. Western legal practices were a key concern of many members of the group, but the single most outspoken advocate of reform of the criminal justice and penal systems was Tsuda Mamichi (1829–1903)."); Alistair D. Swale, *The Meiji Restoration: Monarchism, Mass Communication and Conservative Revolution* (New York: Palgrave Macmillan, 2009), p. 105 & 191 n.48 (referencing Tsuda Mamichi's advocacy against the death penalty); Noel Williams, *The Right to Life in Japan* (London: Routledge, 1997) (citing Tsuda Mamichi's "On the Death Penalty"). In *Meiroku zasshi*, Tsuda Mamichi wrote in opposition to torture in 1874, and he attacked the death penalty's use the following year. Botsman, *Punishment and Power in the Making of Modern Japan*, p. 167; *see also* ibid., pp. 167–68 ("Tsuda went on to make an even more radical proposal in the August 1875 issue of the *Meiroku zasshi*, calling for nothing less than the abolition of all forms of death penalty. Citing passages from the Chinese classics in tandem with the example of Beccaria in Europe, he argued that the aim of punishment should be to reform and correct criminals, not to match one act of violence with another."); Petra Schmidt, *Capital Punishment in Japan* (Leiden: Brill, 2002), p. 88 ("Tsuda Mamichi, who at the end of the *Tokugawa* Period had studied in the Netherlands and brought his knowledge on Western legal science back to Japan, was the first Japanese who, based on Beccaria's ideas, openly demanded that the death penalty be replaced with penal servitude.").

54. *See, e.g.*, Luigino Bruni & Stefano Zamagni, *Civil Economy: Efficiency, Equity, Public Happiness* (Oxford: Peter Lang, 2007), pp. 70–71 (citation omitted):

> Historians of the nineteenth century commonly tend to contrast the "happy" Italian civil economy with the "wealthy" English political economy. Although we will observe that the positions were more shaded than that, this general view will be our departure point for analyzing the Italian and Scottish traditions' ideas on wealth and happiness.

> The 1710 book *Della vita civile* (On civil life), by Neapolitan philosopher Paolo Mattia Doria, had an influence on Genovesi's thought and on the Neapolitan School in general. The book with a clear-cut Civil Humanist title begins with the following words: "Without any doubt, the first object of our desire is human happiness."

> The word "happiness" appears in various titles of treatises by economists, not only in the Kingdom of Naples (as we'll see), but also in the book by the Tuscan physiocratic economist Ferdinando Paoletti, *I veri mezzi di render felici le società* (The true means to make societies happy) and in the many economic treatises circulating in Milan at the time. The public happiness tradition found a warm welcome in the Milan milieu. It soon became the central theme of the emerging Lombard School. Men like Pietro Verri, Cesare Beccaria and, in the nineteenth century, Gian Domenico Romagnosi and Carlo Cattaneo, made Milan one of the capitals of the European Enlightenment and of the economic civil tradition. According to the founder and leader of Milan's economic school, Pietro Verri, civil society held the central place in the social and economic dynamics. Civil society is an "industrious reunion of conspiring forces" that makes it possible to reach "the well-being of each one,

and which is resolved in public happiness, or at least the greatest happiness possible shared with the greatest equality possible. Every human law must tend to such an aim."

55. Philipp Blom, *A Wicked Company: The Forgotten Radicalism of the European Enlightenment* (New York: Basic Books, 2010), p. 221. Some of the French *philosophes*, whom Beccaria met at Parisian salons, were uncharacteristically dismissive of *On Crimes and Punishments* or found some of Cesare Beccaria's ideas to be impractical, lacking in intellectual rigor, or overhyped. Ian Cumming, *Helvetius: His Life and Place in the History of Educational Thought* (Abingdon, Oxon: Routledge, 1955), p. 57 (noting "Galiani and the marchese de Beccaria" as "illustrious men of letters" who attended the salon of Helvétius and his wife); Pier Francesco Asso, *From Economists to Economists: The International Spread of Italian Economic Thought, 1750–1950* (David Brown Book Co., 2001), p. 88 ("Sophie de Grouchy's salon, for example, was set up at the *Hôtel des Monnaies, quai de Conti*, in the official residence occupied by Condorcet since he was appointed *Inspecteur des Monnaies* by Turgot in 1775. Figures who frequented the salon included Adam Smith, who already knew Turgot and Condorcet, as well as Beccaria, Jefferson...."); Philipp Blom, *A Wicked Company: The Forgotten Radicalism of the European Enlightenment* (New York: Basic Books, 2010), p. 221 ("There is an offhand quality about his responses to Beccaria, and from Diderot's own handwritten notations to the Italian's book, it becomes clear that he thought the young man naïve: 'I am neither hard-hearted nor perverse,' the *philosophe* wrote in the margins of his copy. 'Nevertheless I am far from thinking that the work *Des délits et des peines* is as important, or its basic ideas as true, as is claimed for it.'"); ibid. ("There were other, even more critical voices about *Of Crimes and Punishments* in Holbach's salon."); ibid., p. 222 ("Both Diderot and Grimm had an ultimately pessimistic view of the progress of the Enlightenment, which, as Diderot had famously claimed, ended in the suburbs. Beccaria, they thought, had enjoyed a sheltered upbringing and seen no more of the world than the wealthier streets of Milan. The ambitious young man was simply too young, too unrealistic, to understand human nature."). Discussions at French and Italian salons, which helped to shape laws and public opinion, even revolutions, were always sure to be quite lively and entertaining. *E.g.*, Edith Sichel, *The Story of Two Salons* (London: Edward Arnold, 1895), pp. 133–34:

> At his side we see the Marquis of Beccaria, a zealous Italian, absorbed in his efforts to abolish capital punishment. His *Treatise on Pains and Penalties* was once, we hear, "on the mantelshelf of every salon," and nobody dreamed that his name would not live for ever. One day, at the Suards' supper-table, there arose a discussion as to the fitting punishment for a man who had just boiled and eaten a child. "Let us ask M. de Beccaria!" cried the rest of the company. "He should be compelled to be a vegetarian for the rest of his life," this authority replied.
>
> M. de Beccaria had a high-flown friendship for the Marquis de Véry, a politico-Economist of some standing. Three feelings were said to bind them together: their friendship for each other; their sentiment for women older than themselves; and their devotion to the rights and happiness of man. Suard and Morellet had more correspondence with them than with anybody else, and the Abbé and Véry indulged in *tête-à-tête* talks on economics, "for which eternity would have been too short."

Compare Annual Report of the American Historical Association for the Year 1914 (Washington, DC: U.S. Government Printing Office, 1916), Vol. 1, p. 82:

> Prof. Max P. Cushing, of Reed College, in a paper on "Holbach and the French Revolution," adopted the point of view that the French Revolution is one phase of a long struggle between radicalism and conservatism. Holbach, then, stands at one pole of thought at the end of a long development of thought. Among his associates and friends were not only Diderot and the French literary circle of his time, but also Wilkes, Hume, Lord Shelburne, Franklin, and Beccaria. His salon seems to have been the intellectual center of Paris. His philosophy was a very human one.

56. M. A. Ubicini, *Letters on Turkey: An Account of the Religious, Political, Social, and Commercial Condition of the Ottoman Empire; the Reformed Institutions, Army, Navy, &c. &c.* (London: John Murray, Lady Easthope, trans. 1856), pp. 83–84 (noting of Adamantios Coray (or Koraes or Korais) as his name is also often spelled: "His translation into Modern Greek (Romaic) of 'Beccaria's Treatise on Crimes and Punishments' (1802), which he dedicated to the young Republic of the Ionian Islands,

was the first work that attracted the notice of his countrymen. The style of the dedication, and the notes and other matter which he added to the text, left no doubt of the views of the writer, and conferred on his work almost the character of a political event.... [T]he translation of 'Beccaria' circulated rapidly, and made a vivid impression on the minds of its eager readers"); "Dr. Coray, and the Greek Church," *The American Quarterly Observer* (Boston: Perkins & Marvin, 1834), Vol. 2, No. IV, pp. 201, 203–204 (noting that Coray dedicated his translation of Beccaria's book to "the republic of the Seven Islands," a republic created in 1800, and that "Coray's modern Greek translation of Beccaria made him known to them as a man of letters and a patriot"); Heinz D. Kurz, Tamotsu Nishizawa & Keith Tribe, eds., *The Dissemination of Economic Ideas* (Cheltenham, UK: Edward Elgar, 2011), p. 166 ("The most important figure of the Greek Enlightenment, Adamantios Koraes, propagated *metakenosis*, the 'transfusion', or 'decanting', of Western ideas of rationalism and liberal humanism into Ottoman Greece 'through translation of European books into modern Greek, so as to awaken her from her Ottoman slumber, "resuscitate" memories of Classical Hellenism, and, essentially, synchronize it with contemporary European culture'. Koraes himself published a translation in 1802 of Cesare Beccaria's *Dei delitti e delle pene*."); *Adamantios Korais and the European Enlightenment* (Voltaire Foundation, 2010), pp. 13, 20 ("Korais worked from Abbé Morelet's French translation of Beccaria and appended long prolegomena and an extensive commentary to his edition, counselling his compatriots in the arts of liberty;" "[i]n 1823 Korais reissued his translation of Beccaria"); Olga Augustinos, "Philhellenic Promises and Hellenic Visions: Korais and the Discourses of the Enlightenment," *in* Katerina Zacharia, ed., *Hellenisms: Culture, Identity, and Ethnicity from Antiquity to Modernity* (New York: Routledge, 2016), ch. 7 n.15 ("Interestingly, although Korais encouraged the translation of works from European languages, he himself only translated one, namely Beccaria's *Dei delitti e delle pene* (Paris 1802)."); Richard Clogg, *Anatolica: Studies in the Greek East in the 18th and 19th Centuries* (Aldershot, Hampshire, Great Britain: Variorum, 1996), p. 308 ("It is interesting to find Korais writing in the introduction to his translation of Beccaria's *Dei delitti e delle pene*, published in Paris in the same year (1802) as the *Antifonisis*, 'glory and honour to those prudent (Greek) youths who travel through Europe, gathering like bees the beneficial flowers to braid the crown with which both their heads and their Fatherland are to be garlanded'....") (citation omitted).

57. Adamantios Koraes, Thomas Jefferson Foundation, https://www.monticello.org/site/jefferson/adamantios-koraes; *see also* Ioannis D. Evrigenis, "A Founder on Founding: Jefferson's Advice to Koraes," *The Historical Review*, Vol. I (Institute for Neohellenic Research, 2004) ("In 1823, shortly after the outbreak of the Greek Revolution, and in the context of a general attempt to gather support for the Greek cause, Adamantios Koraes wrote to Thomas Jefferson, whom he had met once in Paris, to request his advice on the founding of a Greek state.").

58. Allen C. Guelzo, *Fateful Lightning: A New History of the Civil War and Reconstruction* (Oxford: Oxford University Press, 2012) ("Enlightenment thought was the principal impulse behind the American Declaration of Independence in 1776, and it had its gospel in the writings of Montesquieu, Cesare Beccaria, James Harrington, Algernon Sidney, and above all John Locke, as well as in the classical examples of ancient Greece and Rome.").

59. Groenewegen, *Eighteenth-century Economics*, p. 20; Marco E.L. Guidi, The Division of Labour, Technical Change and the Firm: The Smithian Legacy in Italy from Melchiorre Gioia to Carlo Cattaneo, DSS Papers STO 1-02, https://www.unibs.it/sites/default/files/ricerca/allegati/1231Guidi02.pdf, p. 11; *see also* Marco E.L. Guidi & Daniela Parisi, eds., *The Changing Firm: Contributions from the History of Economic Thought: Selected Papers from the 7th Conference of Aispe Associazione Italiana per la Storia del Pensiero Economico* (Milano: FrancoAngeli s.r.l., 2005), p. 134 ("In his *Elementi di economia pubblica*, published in 1804 by Pietro Custodi, but drafted in 1769–1770 by a student who had attended his lectures at the Scuole Palatine of Milan (Bianchini 1988), Beccaria stated that 'everyone can prove by experience, that by constantly applying his hand and his understanding to the same kind of works and products, he will attain easier, more abundant and better results, than in the case in which everybody would produce in isolation all the things he needs.'") (citing Bianchini, M. (1988), "Una difficile gestazione: il contrastato inserimento dell'economia politica nelle università dell'Italia nord-orientale (1769–1866)). *A Discourse on Public Oeconomy and Commerce* (1769), by Cesare Beccaria, was printed for J. Dodsley and sold by T. and J. Merrill in Cambridge and Messrs. Kincad and Co. at Edinburgh. In *Gentleman's Magazine*, one item, "A Catalogue of New Publications," described Beccaria's 1769

work this way:

> A Discourse on public Oeconomy and Commerce ... Dodsley.—This discourse is translated from the Italian, written by the Marquis Beccaria, author of the celebrated Essay on Crimes and Punishments; and was pronounced by him on his being advanced last year to the new professorship instituted at Milan, for teaching the principles of Public Oeconomy. It contains a general account of the rise and progress of those sciences, which furnish the means of increasing the riches of a state, and applying them to the most useful purposes.

Sylvanus Urban, *The Gentleman's Magazine, and Historical Chronicle* (For the Year M.DCC.LXIX.), Vol. XXXIX, p. 310. At the time, the reviews of Beccaria's lecture were mixed, with praise and criticism intermingled. *E.g.*, *The Critical Review: or, Annals of Literature* (London: A. Hamilton, 1769), Vol. 28, p. 69 (containing the following review of *A Discourse on public Oeconomy and Commerce*: "The observations of this writer are plausible, and in some parts masterly, but, we are afraid, impracticable. To think of reducing public œconomy and commerce to a system, as he does, is a mere chimera.").

60. A summary of Cesare Beccaria's ideas on economics—and there were many of them, whether inspired by others or of his own making—can be found in Luigi Cossa's *An Introduction to the Study of Political Economy*. *See* Luigi Cossa, *An Introduction to the Study of Political Economy* (London: Macmillan and Co., Louis Dyer, trans. 1893), pp. 279–80 (citations omitted):

> The Marquis Cesare Beccaria (1738–94), famous as the author of the book *Dei delitti und* [sic] *delle pene* (Leghorn, 1764), published a *Prolusione* or "Prologue" in 1769, and wrote lectures on economics (1769–70), which remained unpublished until 1804: he also supported Verri and Carli in pushing though very necessary financial and economic reforms in Lombardy which affected the corn trade, the current coin of the realm, the standard weights and measures, and included the abolition of trades guilds (*corpi d'arte*) and of the practice of farming the taxes. Pascal Duprat, in the *Revue moderne* (1865), has shown himself too harsh a critic of Beccaria's *Elementi d' economia pubblica*, where the clearness of thought and expression is only equaled by the vigour and rigour of the logical processes applied. After this book no one should be surprised to find our author showing special gifts in applying mathematics to his subject, as in fact he did most expertly in an "Analytical Essay on Smuggling," published at Brescia (1764), in the periodical called *Caffè*. Inspired by this production, Guglielmo Silio, a Sicilian, produced something of the same kind in 1792. Upon the occasion of a journey to Paris where he made a short stay in 1766, Beccaria became personally acquainted with representative physiocrats, and substantially embraced their leading doctrines, but without breaking away entirely from the canons of mercantilism. Against corporations he declared war, and repudiated prohibitions of all kinds; as for the corn laws, he imitated Galiani in having no theory beyond eclecticism, but, unlike Galiani, he always leaned towards liberty in this matter. This did not, however, prevent him from defending, against Carli's vigorous opposition, bounties offered for the exportation of bread-stuffs, nor did it make him the less inclined to defend a protective tariff. No doubt Say has gone too far in lauding Beccaria's originality, so far as the analysis of the functions of capital goes, for on this topic he gives only what the physiocrats lent him; Pecchio and all the rest of those who made analogous claims for his treatment of the division of labour are equally mistaken, and so is Ingram in his similar commendation of Beccaria's account of the causes producing different rates of wages in different occupations, for Cantillon made all these points long before; but for all that Beccaria extorts praise from the most unwilling by his sound treatment of population, and still more by his masterly analysis of the law of normal value both in cases of monopoly and of open competition.

Luigi Cossa, a professor at the Royal University of Pavia, also gave an extended account of Pietro Verri's views on economics and compared Verri's work in that arena to Beccaria's writings on the subject. Here is what Cossa, as translated from the Italian by Louis Dyer at Balliol College, had to say about Pietro Verri in *An Introduction to the Study of Political Economy* (1893):

> Beccaria's contemporary, colleague, and personal friend, Count Pietro Verri, was also a Milanese, and lived from 1728–97. In genius as well as in literary culture and scientific attainments Verri was no match for Beccaria, but he outdid him in economics, for his writings are both more numerous and more solid. Verri was not deluded for a moment by the

glamour of the physiocratic dictim that all forms of manufacturing industry were barren. Mercantilism, however, had a certain power over his judgment; its prejudices lurk in various writings of his, particularly in his *Elementi del commercio* (1765). Nevertheless a whole chapter of liberalism may be gathered out of his "Reflections on hampering Laws, especially those imposed upon the Corn Trade," which were written in 1769 and printed in 1796. Elsewhere—as in his *Memorie sull' economia pubblica dello Stato di Milano* (1768), published in Custodi's *Raccolta* (vol. xviii.)—he shows an equal power of insight when describing the causes of the decay of Lombard trade and manufactures under Spanish rule.

In his *Meditations on Political Economy* (1771) Verri not only produced something far fuller and far clearer than Beccaria's *Elementi*, but the book is the best compendium published in Italy during the eighteenth century; in fact, but for Turgot's *Reflections*, which came after it, there would be nothing from any quarter to dispute its pre-eminence. In one respect certainly, if not in any other, Verri outdoes even Turgot, since his account of production is based upon a more accurate analysis and a more comprehensive survey of the facts. To begin with, he notes that man, whether engaged in agriculture or in manufactures, never creates new things, but only combines or separates what is under his hand. At this point curiously enough his insight fails him, and he repeats the old error of putting tradespeople into a special category of middle-men pure and simple, standing between producers on the one hand and consumers on the other. His *Meditations* deserve to be called a systematic treatise on economics, inasmuch as they are an investigation into the various causes at work for and against the accumulation of wealth in a given country, the causes allowing or hindering a surplus of production, which he says approaches the maximum only by continuous increase in population.

Here Verri parts company with Beccaria, and favours small holdings, making a vigorous onslaught upon the too great concentration of landed property in single hands, which he regards as just as much an infringement of lawful freedom as are direct restrictions imposed upon industries and trade. In fact, seeing that universal free trade is not attainable, our author allows protective tariffs, and thus—as Pierson has acutely perceived—he anticipates the views now current under the name of Fair Trade. Furthermore, he justifies such protective tariff duties by pointing out the practical impossibilities and the scientific fallacies involved in the physiocratic argument requiring one single tax upon land only. Taxation, as a matter of fact, falls upon the whole community more or less, and not upon landholders only; therefore, he argues, protective tariff duties must be combined with taxes directly imposed in any and every sound system of State finance. Finally, Verri attaches paramount importance to his theory of value, which materially diverges from Beccaria's. Almost confining himself to an account of current value, Verri makes it depend upon the law of supply and demand. This last he expounds in conspicuously infelicitous terms, going on at a great rate about the number of buyers and sellers, and landing himself in a formula, which has been ventilated, argued about, amended, and defended by Frisi, Gioja, Valeriani, and Rossi.

Luigi Cossa, *An Introduction to the Study of Political Economy* (London: Macmillan and Co., Louis Dyer, trans. 1893), pp. 280–81 (citations omitted).

61. *See* Ernesto Screpanti, ed., *The Fundamental Institutions of Capitalism* (London: Routledge, 2002).

62. Fernand Braudel, *Civilization and Capitalism: 15th–18th Century: The Perspective of the World* (Berkeley, CA: University of California Press, 1992), Vol. III, p. 592.

63. Reinert, "Enlightenment Socialism," *in* Kapossy, Nakhimovsky & Whatmore, eds., *Commerce and Peace in the Enlightenment*, p. 145 & n.90; *Scritti di argomento familiare e autobiografico* (Edizione Nazionale, Delle opera di Pietro Verri, 2003), Vol. 5, p. 213 n.38; *compare* Cesare Beccaria, *On Crimes and Punishments* (New York: Routledge, Graeme R. Newman & Pietro Marongiu, trans. 5th ed. 2017), A Note on the Text (citations omitted):

Some have argued that Pietro Verri exaggerated Beccaria's shortcomings out of envy for his growing international recognition and because Beccaria had not properly acknowledged his role in the creation of the book. Thus, Verri is a biased source. However, Beccaria's limited contribution to the production of the *Treatise* is generally acknowledged by his contemporaries. Marquis Freganeschi a very close friend of Pietro Verri, in another letter of January 18, 1783, for instance, made this caustic observation: "*Si ritiene il sig. Marchese Beccaria per autore del libro dei delitti e delle pene, quando sappiamo che quello che vi è di bouno non è suo e quello che vi è di suo non è buono*" ("Signor Marchese Beccaria is regarded as the author of the book on crimes and punishments, while we do know that what is good in it, is not his, and what is his, is not good"—our translation).

While the Verris always maintained that Beccaria's own manuscript was essentially not much more than a bunch of disorganized and virtually useless sheets or "scraps" of paper, Francioni doggedly tried to demonstate that this document, notwithstanding Beccaria's laziness and confusion in writing, showed an identifiable internal logic, which is quite different from the subsequent handwritten text of Verri. Francioni's basic assumption is that Beccaria's original intention was not to write a juridical treatise (acknowledging also his lack of specific background in the field), but rather a utilitarian styled pamphlet of moral and political philosophy about the role of the criminal justice system in fostering or impeding the progress of mankind towards "the greatest happiness for the greatest number." And being weak, Beccaria, could not resist Pietro Verri's tendency to turn the document into a more systematic juridical essay. This process can be understood in the context of the complex and very ambivalent relationship between Verris' dominant personalities and the passive Beccaria.

See also Cesare Beccaria, *On Crimes and Punishments* (Indianapolis, IN: Hackett Publishing Co., David Young, trans. 1986), p. xviii ("Beccaria was willing to put Pietro Verri's alterations into the book but seemed less willing to accept Morellet's.... For readers who wish to pursue textual questions further, the best recent scholarship on the subject is Gianni Francioni, *La prima redazione del "Dei delitti e delle pene"* (Naples, 1981).").

64. Pamela J. Schram & Stephen G. Tibbetts, *Introduction to Criminology* (Thousand Oaks, CA: Sage Publications, 2d ed. 2018), p. 66.

65. Steven A. Epstein, *Speaking of Slavery: Color, Ethnicity, and Human Bondage in Italy* (Ithaca, NY: Cornell University Press, 2001), p. 49.

66. Nadia Urbinati, *The Tyranny of the Moderns* (New Haven: Yale University Press, Martin Thom, trans. 2015), pp. 88–89.

67. Alex Körner, *America in Italy: The United States in the Political Thought and Imagination of the Risorgimento, 1763–1865* (Princeton, NJ: Princeton University Press, 2017), pp. 97–98.

68. Cesare Beccaria, *An Essay on Crimes and Punishments, Translated from the Italian; with a Commentary Attributed to Mons. De Voltaire, Translated from the French* (London: F. Newberry, 2d ed. 1769), p. 96.

69. *An Essay on the Constitutional Power of Great-Britain Over the Colonies in America; With the Resolves of the Committee for the Province of Pennsylvania, and Their Instructions to Their Representatives in Assembly* (Philadelphia: William and Thomas Bradford, 1774), pp. 350–51 & n.‡; *see also A New Essay [By the Pennsylvanian Farmer] on the Constitutional Power of Great-Britain Over the Colonies in America; With the Resolves of the Committee for the Province of Pennsylvania and Their Instructions to Their Representatives in Assembly* (Philadelphia/London: "Re-printed for J. Almon, opposite Burlington House, in Piccadilly," 1774), pp. 56–67 & n.†.

70. Robert Armitage, *The Penscellwood Papers: Comprising Essays on the Souls and Future Life of Animals; on Capital Punishments; on the Evangelical Alliance; on the Endowment of the Protestant and Roman Catholic Churches of Ireland; and on the Education of the People* (London: Richard Bentley, 1846), Vol. 1, p. 324; *see also* ibid. ("The whole was originally read, at different times, in the shape of lectures, to a society of learned men in the City of Milan, and published at their request. There is a Commentary appended to the Second Edition of the Translation, supposed to be written by Voltaire; and certainly it appears stamped with the characteristics of his flippant, indelicate, sceptical mind."). Even when readers did not fully agree with Cesare Beccaria's ideas, Beccaria's views—almost impossible to ignore in the intellectual milieu of the late eighteenth and early nineteenth centuries—were frequently taken into consideration. *E.g.*, James Kent, *Commentaries on American Law* (New York: O. Halsted, 2d ed. 1832), Vol. 1, p. 283.

The President has also the power to grant reprieves and pardons for offences against the

United States, except in cases of impeachment. The Marquis Beccaria has contended, that the power of pardon does not exist under a perfect administration of law, and that the admission of the power is a tacit acknowledgment of the infirmity of the course of justice. And where is the administration of justice, it may be asked, that is free from infirmity? Were it possible, in every instance, to maintain a just proportion between crime and the penalty, and were the rules of testimony, and the mode of trial, so perfect, as to preclude every possibility of mistake or injustice, there would be some colour for the admission of this plausible theory. But, even in that case, policy would sometimes require a remission of a punishment strictly due, for a crime certainly ascertained. The very notion of mercy implies the accuracy of the claims of justice.

71. *E.g.*, Anthony Page, *John Jebb and the Enlightenment Origins of British Radicalism* (Westport, CT: Praeger, 2003), p. 228 (noting that "Jebb read Montesquieu and Beccaria while at Cambridge, and in 1773 he began to prepare a course of 'political or constitutional lectures' (which he evidently failed to complete)"); *A New General Biographical Dictionary, Projected and Partly Arranged by the Late Rev. Hugh James Rose, B.D.* (London: B. Fellowes et al., 1848), Vol. 5, p. 60 (noting that Philip Briganti (1725-1804), "an Italian poet and writer on political economy," was "influenced by the writings of Montesquieu, Beccaria, and Vico"; published in 1780 his "Esame Economico del Istema Civile"; and wrote "a paper in defence of the doctrines of Beccaria"); Charles Sumner, *A Catalogue of the Law Library of Harvard University in Cambridge, Massachusetts* (Cambridge, MA: Charles Folsom, 1834), p. 6 (listing the 1766 "Harlem" edition of Beccaria's *Dei delitti e delle pene*, a 1766 French translation, and two English language translations, one from London (1770) and one from Philadelphia (1778)); *The Christian Union*, Aug. 27, 1879 (noting that "[a] copy of Beccaria's *Dei Delitti E Delle Pene* (Harlem and Paris: 1766)" had been "presented to Mr. Sumner by Sidney Smith"); *Catalogue of the Philological, Classical, and Law Library of the Late Hon. John Pickering* (Boston: Alfred Mudge, 1846), p. 161 (listing a 1785 London edition of *On Crimes and Punishments*). Oftentimes, Beccaria's treatise was elaborately bound. *E.g.*, *Autographs, Manuscripts and Broadsides from the Stock of the Late George D. Smith* (New York: The Anderson Galleries, 1921), p. 11 (noting a 1788 Edinburgh edition of *On Crimes and Punishments* and describing it as follows: "fine old calf binding, gilt back, the front cover containing an etched view of a Cathedral, and the back cover, one of a ruined castle, through the window of which is seen another church").

72. *E.g.*, Richard B. Sher, *The Enlightenment and the Book: Scottish Authors and Their Publishers in Eighteenth-century Britain, Ireland and America* (Chicago: The University of Chicago Press, 2006), p. 530 ("With rare exceptions, such as octavo editions of Beccaria's *Essay on Crimes and Punishments* and *Miscellanies by M. de Voltaire* (consisting of three philosophical tales), which appeared in 1778, Bell limited his Enlightenment publications during the early years of the war to smaller works."). Scottish publishers and booksellers actively promoted Enlightenment texts. *E.g.*, Stephen W. Brown & Warren McDougall, eds., *The Edinburgh History of the Book in Scotland: Enlightenment and Expansion 1707–1800* (Edinburgh: Edinburgh University Press, 2012), Vol. 2, p. 193. An understanding of Beccaria's *Dei delitti e delle pene* was, at one time, itself part of "an examination in law" to allow those reading law to qualify as Scottish barristers. Charles Knight, *The English Cyclopædia* (London: Bradbury, Evans, & Co., 1866), Vol. 1, p. 961.

73. Justin McHenry, "The Library of a Young, Country Lawyer: A Look at the Library of a Chambersburg Lawyer, William Chambers, from 1823," Franklin County, Pennsylvania, http://franklincountypa.gov/index.php?section=archives_blog/chambers_library; Adam Ferguson, *The History of the Progress and Termination of the Roman Republic* (Basil: J. J. Tourneisen, 1791); *The Edinburgh Monthly Review* (Jan.–June, 1821) (Edinburgh: Waugh & Innes, 1821), Vol. 5, p. 121 (discussing Sholto & Reuben Perry's *The Percy Anecdotes* and reprinting the excerpt about Beccaria), Sylvester Douglas, *Reports of Cases Argued and Determined in the Court of King's Bench in the Nineteenth, Twentieth, and Twenty-First Years of the Reign of George III* (London: A. Strahan & W. Woodfall, 3d ed. 1790).

74. *E.g.*, *A Catalogue of the Printed Books to Which Is Prefixed a Short Account of the Manuscripts, in the Library of Lincoln's Inn* (London: G. Davidson, 1835), p. 17 (listing a 1775 edition of Beccaria's *On Crimes and Punishments*); John A. Russell & W. Douthwaite, comps., *Catalogue of the Books in the Library of the Honorable Society of Gray's Inn: With an Index of Subjects* (London: C. Roworth &

Sons, 1872), p. 236 (listing a 1769 "Second edition" version of Beccaria's *On Crimes and Punishments*); James Mulligan & M. D. Severn, comps., *Catalogue of the Books in the Library of the Honourable Society of Gray's Inn: With an Index of Subjects* (London: Witherby & Co., 1906), pp. 855, 926 (listing a "2nd ed. 1769" version of Beccaria's book); *Catalogue of the Library of David Constable, Esq. Advocate* (Edinburgh, 1828), p. 9 (listing a 1769 edition of *On Crimes and Punishments*); *Catalogue of the Extensive and Valuable Library of the Late Thomas Rennell, D.D.*, Vol. 2, p. 16 (1840) (listing 1775 and 1778 editions of *On Crimes and Punishments* in the catalogue for the Dean of Winchester, a former Master of the Temple); *A Catalogue of the Law Books in the Advocates Library* (Edinburgh: Thomas Clark, 1831), p. 31 (listing a 1780 edition of *Dei delitti e delle pene*, a 1766 French translation, and an 1804 English translation of *On Crimes and Punishments* published in London); *Catalogue of the Printed Books in the Library of the Faculty of Advocates* (Edinburgh: William Blackwood and Sons, 1867), Vol. 1, p. 384 (listing under the entry for "BECCARIA (Cesare Bonesana, Marquis de)" a 1780 "Harlem" edition of *Dei delitti e delle pene*, a 1804 version of *On Crimes and Punishments*, and an edition of *Elementi di economia pubblica* published by Custodi); James Neild, *State of the Prisons in England, Scotland, and Wales, Extending to Various Places Therein Assigned, Not for the Debtor Only, But for Felons Also, and Other Less Criminal Offenders* (London: John Nichols and Son, 1812), pp. xlviii–xlix (citing Beccaria); George Tait, *A Treatise on the Law of Evidence in Scotland* (Edinburgh: Alex. Smellie, 1824), p. 439 n.3 (citing "Beccaria on Crimes"); J. J. S. Wharton, *The Police Law of the City of London and Metropolitan District* (London: E. Spettigue, 1841), pp. 9, 13, 18 (an attorney of Lincoln's Inn cites Beccaria); John Miller, *An Inquiry into the Present State of the Statute and Criminal Law of England* (London: John Murray, 1822), pp. 209–10, 221–22 (an attorney of Lincoln's Inn discussed Beccaria's treatise); M. Dawes, *An Essay on Crimes and Punishments with a View of, and Commentary Upon Beccaria, Rousseau, Voltaire, Montesquieu, Fielding, and Blackstone* (London: C. Dilly 1782) (citing Beccaria repeatedly and noting that Manasseh Dawes was "of the Inner Temple"); *The New Monthly Magazine and Literary Journal* (London: Henry Colburn & Richard Bentley, 1829), Pt. 3, p. 271 (discussing Manasseh Dawes, said to be "a gentleman of a very strong mind," and noting his association with the Inner Temple and his "great knowledge of the law"); John Foster Kirk, *A Supplement to Allibone's Critical Dictionary of English Literature and British and American Authors* (Philadelphia: J. B. Lippincott Co., 1902), Vol. 1 (entry for "Farrer, James Anson": noting that James Anson Farrer, born in London in 1849, an 1871 graduate of Oxford, and "called to the bar at the Inner Temple" shortly thereafter, did a new translation of Beccaria's *Dei delitti e delle pene* that was published in London in 1880); *The Philadelphia Register, and National Recorder* (Philadelphia: Littell & Henry, 1819), Vol. 1, p. 288 (noting that a newly translated version of Beccaria's *On Crimes and Punishments*, by Edward D. Ingraham, was "Just Published"). An online search of the library catalog of Trinity College in Dublin reveals multiple editions of Beccaria's work. Not only is there a copy of Beccaria's *A Discourse on Public Oeconomy and Commerce* (1769), but one finds a 1766 edition of *Dei delitti e delle pene*, numerous early English translations of *On Crimes and Punishments*, and a 1766 French edition of that work. The Library of Trinity College Dublin, http://stella.catalogue.tcd.ie/iii/encore/plus/C__SBeccaria__Orightresult__U__X0__Ks%401763e%401800?lang=eng&suite=cobalt.

75. *E.g.*, David Lieberman, *The Province of Legislation Determined: Legal Theory in Eighteenth-century Britain* (Cambridge: Cambridge University Press, 1989), pp. 206, 208 (noting that William Blackstone "regularly recorded his indebtedness to that 'ingenious writer,' Cesare Beccaria, who had 'well studied the springs of human action,' " and that England's penal reformers "most frequently and extensively embraced" the writings of "Cesare Beccaria, the celebrated Milanese aristocrat"); Ruth Paley, ed., William Blackstone, *Commentaries on the Laws of England: Book IV of Public Wrongs* (Oxford: Oxford University Press, 2016), p. ix (noting that Blackstone "made use of influential international texts of his own generation, some of which, such as Montesquieu's *Spirit of the Laws* and Beccaria's *On Crimes and Punishments*, we now regard as seminal," and that "[o]ne of Blackstone's stated motivations for publication was the circulation of manuscript copies of notes taken by students attending his lectures"); S. G. Goodrich, *One Thousand-and-One Lives, Their Beginning and Ending: Embracing the Most Eminent Characters of Every Age, Nation, and Profession, Including Painters, Poets, Philosophers, Politicians, Heroes, Warriors, Etc., Etc.* (New York: World Publishing House, 1876), p. 76 (noting in the entry for Cesare Beccaria, "an eminent Italian": "In 1764, appeared his Treatise on Crimes and Punishments, which was translated into several languages, and universally admired.");

Sidney Lee, ed., *Dictionary of National Biography* (New York: The Macmillan Co., 1909), Vol. 17, pp. 188–89 (noting that "Romilly, though much stimulated by Bentham, drew his original inspiration from Rousseau and Beccaria," and that before being called to the bar in 1783, he was a member of Gray's Inn where, during an illness and convalescence, "he learned Italian, and was soon deep in Machiavelli and Beccaria"); Lloyd C. Sanders, ed., *Celebrities of the Century: Being a Dictionary of Men and Women of the Nineteenth Century* (London: Cassell & Co., 1887), p. 122 (noting that Jeremy Bentham was called to the bar at Lincoln's Inn but that Bentham "promptly dashed the expectations of his father and his friends," but also emphasizing that, in 1769, "Montesquieu, Barrington, Beccaria, and Helvetius" awakened Bentham to "the principle of utility" and that Beccaria's phrase, "the greatest happiness of the greatest number," had delineated "for the first time" for him "a true standard for whatever is right or wrong"); Gregory Claeys, ed., *Encyclopedia of Modern Political Thought*, Vol. 1, p. 74 (noting of Jeremy Bentham: "Although admitted to the bar in 1769, he chose to devote his life to applying scientific principles to the reform of the England law. In later life, he remembered the year 1769 chiefly for his first reading of works by David Hume, Cesare Beccaria, and Claude Adrien Helvétius...."); Lester F. Ward, *The Psychic Factors of Civilization* (Boston, MA: Ginn & Co., 1893), p. 282 (quoting Jeremy Bentham as observing: "Priestley was the first (unless it was Beccaria) who taught my lips to pronounce this sacred truth: That the greatest happiness of the greatest number is the foundation of morals and legislation."); Edward Tagart, *Remarks on Bentham, His Obligations to Priestley, and His Early Studies* (London: Charles Green, 1844), p. 5 (calling *On Crimes and Punishments* "a small but admirable production, referred to and quoted by Priestley in terms of high admiration several times, as well in his remarks on Government as in the Lectures on History and General Policy"); *The Plough-Wright's Assistant: or, A Practical Treatise on Various Implements Employed in Agriculture* (Edinburgh: D. Willison, 1808), p. 10 (listing a "Fifth edition, revised and corrected" of Beccaria's *An Essay on Crimes and Punishments* as being published by "H. D. Symonds" at "*No. 20, Paternoster-Row, London*").

76. Anthony J. Draper, *Cesare Beccaria's Influence on English Discussions of Punishment, 1764–1789*, 26 History of European Ideas 177, 179, 187 (2000). Noting that English penal reformer William Eden, following Beccaria, thought that penal laws should encourage public virtue. Eden authored *Principles of Penal Law* (1771), which was published in London, and argued that lawmakers should have a "severe eye upon the offence" but a "merciful inclination towards the offender." Ibid., pp. 179, 188; *see also* ibid., p. 190:

> It has been found that during the period 1764–1765 Eden was in correspondence with Sir James Macdonald of Sleat, a close friend from his time at Oxford. Macdonald is believed not only to have reawoken Voltaire's interest in penal reform, by showing him a copy of Beccaria's book, but is also known to have corresponded with Eden just a few weeks before his contact with Voltaire. It is perfectly possible, therefore, that Eden received his first insights into Beccaria's work as early as 1765 ....

Cf. ibid., p. 191:

> Four editions of *Principles of Penal Law* were brought out within as many years, and with this success Eden very quickly came to the attention of those in Government. The publication of Eden's treatise in 1771 provoked yet another round of discussion in the London journals, and there can be little doubt that such eager approval of his position reflected much of the enthusiasm that had greeted Beccaria's work four years earlier.

The names of Sir James Macdonald and Cesare Beccaria show up in a compilation of Voltaire's correspondence. Voltaire, *Correspondence* (Gallimard, 1964), Vol. 8, pp. x, 754, 1273, 1280, 1421; *see also* William Eden, *Principles of Penal Law* (London: B. White & T. Cadell, 1771), pp. 235, 264, 296 (citing Beccaria). James Macdonald (1741–1766), who died in Rome, was a student at Eton and Oxford and, for his learning and intelligence, became known as "*The Scottish Marcellus*." The poet John MacCodrum was employed as a bard by James Macdonald. Archibald MacDonald, ed., *The Poems and Songs of John MacCodrum, Archibald MacDonald, and Some of the Minor Uist Bards* (Glasgow: Archibald Sinclair & Henry White, 1894), p. xliii; "James Macdonald—Marcellus of the North," http://www.jamesboswell.info/biography/james-macdonald-marcellus-north-8th-bart-sleat; *see also* Roderick Watson, *Literature of Scotland: The Middle Ages to the Nineteenth Century* (New York: Palgrave Macmillan, 2007) (noting that John MacCodrum was employed as a bard beginning in 1763).

77. Arthur Koestler, *Reflections on Hanging* (New York: Macmillan, 1957), p. 37; *see also* João Frederico Normano, *The Spirit of Russian Economics* (London: Dennis Dobson Limited, 1950), p. 29–31 (discussing P. I. Pestel, an economic thinker, and stating: "The regimental libraries contained works by Benjamin Franklin, Filangieri, Say, and so on. Pestel advised his associates to read Beccaria, Filangieri, Machiavelli, Voltaire, Helvetius, Adam Smith.").

78. *See* Anthony J. Draper, *Cesare Beccaria's Influence on English Discussions of Punishment, 1764–1789*, 26 History of European Ideas 177, 197 (2000) ("In England in particular, [Beccaria's] ideas were received with enthusiasm (or, as Bentham described it in 1776, 'as an Angel from heaven would be by the faithful')....").

79. "*A List of* BOOKS *and* PAMPHLETS *printed for* J. ALMON, *Bookseller and Stationer, opposite to* Burlington-house, *in* Piccadilly" does not say who did the actual translation of Beccaria's book into English. *The Tour of His Royal Highness Edward Duke of York, From England to Lisbon, Gibraltar, Minorca, Genoa, Alexandria, Asti, Turin, Milan, Parma, Florence, Leghorn, Pisa, Lucca, Pistoja, Sienna, Rome, Bologna, Mantua, Verona, Vicenza, Padua, Venice, &c. &c. &c.: With an Introduction and a Circumstantial and Historical Detail of Each Place Through Which He Passed* (Dublin: P. Wilson, S. Cotter, J. Potts & J. Williams, 1764), p. 25; *Grand Tour: The Lure of Italy in the Eighteenth Century* (London: Tate Gallery, 1996), pp. 35, 77; Jeremy Black, *George III: America's Last King* (New Haven: Yale University Press, 2006), p. 149; *see also The London Magazine: or, Gentleman's Monthly Intelligencer* (1764), Vol. XXXIII, p. 157:

> Turin, March 3. The duke of Modena, in his own name as such, and as administrator of Austrian Lombardy, and also by the order and on the part of the empress-queen, has sent tither the count Belgiojoso, a person of the first distinction of that country, to compliment his royal highness the duke of York, and to invite him to honour Milan with a visit, offering him an apartment in the Ducal Palace; or, upon his refusal of that, a hotel in the town. His royal highness made a suitable answer to these civilities, and proposes spending the three last days of the carnival at that place.

Cf. William Stewart, *Admirals of the World: A Biographical Dictionary, 1500 to the Present* (Jefferson, NC: McFarland & Co., 2009), p. 76 (noting that Prince Edward Augustus, Duke of York, took ill on his way to Genoa and died in the Palace of Honoré III, Prince of Monaco, on September 17, 1767).

80. John Almon, "*A List of* BOOKS *and* PAMPHLETS *printed for* J. ALMON, *Bookseller and Stationer, opposite to* Burlington-house, *in* Piccadilly" (1769); George Smith & Frank Benger, *The Oldest London Bookshop: A History of Two Hundred Years* (London: Ellis, 1928), p. 37; W. Roberts, *The Book-Hunter in London: Historical and Other Studies of Collectors and Collecting* (London: Elliot Stock, 1895), p. 249; *see also* Ralph Merritt Cox, *An English Ilustrado: The Reverend John Bowle* (Bern: Peter Lang, 1977), p. 56 ("By 1763 he had become conversant enough with Italian to order a list of Italian books from Mr. Peter Molini at the Smyrna Coffee-house in Pall-Mall, London."); Trevor Levere, Larry Stewart & Hugh Torrens (with Joseph Wachelder), *The Enlightenment of Thomas Beddoes: Science, Medicine, and Reform* (London: Routledge, 2017), p. 199 n.72 ("Murray told Beddoes that he obtained Italian books from Moline, presumably the London bookseller and publisher Pietro Molini (1729 or 1730–1806)."); Margherita Marchione, ed., *Philip Mazzei: 1788–1791, Agent for the King of Poland during the French Revolution* (Prato: Edizioni del Palazzo, 1983), p. 7 ("Signor Pietro Molini, London bookseller, will receive in four or six days two copies of my book, to be delivered, one to your Excellency and the other to Col. Smith."); Margherita Marchione, ed., Filippo Mazzei, *My Life and Wanderings* (American Institute of Italian Studies, 1980), p. 130 ("The Marquis, his heir, was advised to sell it in London, which was near and where he might expect to sell it more advantageously then elsewhere. He was referred to Signor Pietro Molini, a brother of Signor Claudio, Paris printer and bookseller, and of the Molini presently engaged in the same business in Florence. Signor Pietro had great talent, was a good mathematician...."); *cf. Atti della Società ligure di storia patria* (1988), Vol. 102, p.68 n.28 ("Pietro Molini risulta attivo a Londra, in Haymarket, almeno dal 1773 al 1795") (citing *The London Book Trades 1775–1800* and *A Dictionary of the Printers and Booksellers Who Were at Work in England, Scotland and Ireland from 1726 to 1775*).

81. Robert Panzarella & Daniel Vona, *Criminal Justice Masterworks: A History of Ideas About Crime, Law, Police, and Corrections* (Durham, NC: Carolina Academic Press, 2006), p. 7; William Spaggiari, *Geografie letterarie: Da Dante a Tabucchi* (LED Edizioni Universitarie di Lettere Economia Diritto,

2015), p. 97; William Spaggiari, "Scene ridicole e segrete malinconie: Cesare Beccaria alla moglie," *available at* http://www.e-periodica.ch/cntmng?pid=ver-001:2009:56::652; "Teresa Blasco," Post n 1496 pubblicato il 29 Dicembre 2011 da Odette.teresa1958, http://blog.libero.it/laviaggiatrice/10931297.html; *see also Annali D'italianistica* (1989), Vol. 7, p. 221 (noting that, in 1776, "Count Pietro Verri, the older and more remarkable of the two brothers founders of *Il caffè*, was ... a man of forty-eight [and] disappointed ... with the streak of love affairs with married ladies"); Antonella Cupillari, *A Biography of Maria Gaetana Agnesi, an Eighteenth-Century Woman Mathematician: With Translations of Some of Her Work into English* (Lewiston, NY: Edwin Mellen Press, 2007), p. 214 (noting that Pietro Verri, while in his twenties, "had a lengthy relationship with Maria Vittoria Ottoboni Boncompagni, who was married to the Duke Gabrio Serbelloni").

82. Joel Barlow, *The Hasty-Pudding: A Poem, in Three Cantos* (New Haven, CT: William Storer, 1838); Cecilia Miller, *Enlightenment and Political Fiction: The Everyday Intellectual* (New York: Routledge, 2016), p. 223 ("[Alessandro] Manzoni himself was a symbol of *il Risorgimento* in his own lifetime, mourned by the entire, young country when he died. Probably the greatest influence on his intellectual life was his maternal grandfather, Cesare Beccaria. Beccaria and Manzoni were not typical aristocrats, for they shared not only a commitment to abolishing torture and capital punishment but also the desire to reorganize Italian, and European, legal and political systems in ways that would benefit all people, regardless of birth."); ibid., p. 219 ("one of Manzoni's intellectual influences was his grandfather, even though his grandfather died when Alessandro was only nine years old"; "It was not necessary in the late eighteenth, early nineteenth century to have been a relative to have known of Beccaria's political contributions, now known as part of the fabric of classical liberalism."); ibid., p. 218 ("In 1861, at the time of the initial Unification [of Italy], there were 26 million Italians, almost 80 percent of whom were illiterate and almost 70 percent were agricultural workers. There was as well a sharp division of wealth between the North and South. *Il Risorgimento* represented a desire both for individual liberties and for a government that would support these rights and provide protection against both foreign enemies and domestic tyrants."); John MacCulloch, *The Highlands and Western Isles of Scotland, Containing Descriptions of Their Scenery and Antiquities, with an Account of the Political History and Ancient Manners, and of the Origin, Language, Agriculture, Economy, Music, Present Condition of the People, &c. &c. &c.* (London: Longman, Hurst, Rees, Orme, Brown, and Green, 1824), p. 160 (referencing "the humane Beccaria"); Seth Cotlar, *Tom Paine's America: The Rise and Fall of Transatlantic Radicalism in the Early Republic* (Charlottesville: University of Virginia Press, 2011), pp. 115 & 236 n.9; Carl H. Gross & Charles C. Chandler, eds., *The History of American Education Through Readings* (Boston, MA: D. C. Heath and Co., 1964) ("'When the clouds of ignorance are dispelled (says the Marquis of Beccaria) by the radiance of knowledge, power trembles, but the authority of laws remains immovable.'").

83. *The Political Writings of Joel Barlow* (New York: Mott & Lyon, new ed. corrected, 1796), p. 82 & n.*; Gail Stuart Rowe, The Transition of Joel Barlow's Political Thought: His Life and Writings, Stanford University, Dep't of History (1960), pp. 18, 75; Milton Cantor, "Joel Barlow: Lawyer and Legal Philosopher," 10 *American Quarterly* 165 (Summer 1958); *see also* Richard Buel Jr., *Joel Barlow: American Citizen in a Revolutionary World* (Baltimore, MD: The Johns Hopkins University Press, 2011), p. 208 (noting that Barlow found certain punishments in Algiers to be barbaric).

84. Jonathan Israel, *The Expanding Blaze: How the American Revolution Ignited the World, 1775–1848* (Princeton, NJ: Princeton University Press, 2017), pp. 19, 48, 54, 92, 100, 194, 260, 487; *see also* ibid., pp. 109–10 ("Quantitative analysis of American library holdings, readings habits, and editions in the 1790s and first decade of the new century reflects a market escalation of ideological conflict among academics and the student fraternity with radical works by Paine, Raynal, Rousseau, Volney, Beccaria, Condorcet, Godwin, and Wollstonecraft being read widely.").

85. Reinert, "Enlightenment Socialism," *in* Kapossy, Nakhimovsky & Whatmore, eds., *Commerce and Peace in the Enlightenment*, pp. 145–46; *see also* ibid., p. 148:

> Many of the preoccupations that had animated Beccaria's earliest writings would continue to inspire his more mature work, including the dangers of economic inequality in a polity, but he would never spell out the full spectrum of his ideas, nor the complex role he saw for private property in the history of human progress. But as fate would have it, and much to the satisfaction of the Verri brothers, Beccaria's project for the *Refinement of Nations*

never materialized. Overcome by practical duties, plausibly also a convenient excuse, Beccaria would instead channel his reformist impulse into his university lectures and practical work for the Habsburg administration. As Joseph A. Schumpeter would put it, 'Beccaria, almost certainly more richly endowed by nature, gave to the public service of the Milanese "state" what A[dam] Smith reserved for mankind'.

See also Elizabeth Boody Schumpeter, ed., Joseph A. Schumpeter, *History of Economic Analysis* (New York: Routledge, 1997), pp. 131–32, 179–81, 248, 258, 292, 306–307, 408, 510 (discussing the practical and intellectual contributions of Beccaria). Joseph Schumpeter, the economic historian, described the formulation, history, and operation of the *greatest happiness* principle in this way:

> The pleasures and pains of each individual are assumed to be measurable quantities capable of being (algebraically) added into a quantity called the individual's happiness (*felicità*); a frequently used German term was *Glückseligkeit*. These individual 'happinesses' are again summed up into a social total, *all of them being weighted equally*: 'everyone to count for one, nobody to count for more than one.' Finally, that social total is substituted for, or identified with, the common good or welfare of society, which is thus resolved into individual sensations of pleasure or pain, the only ultimate realities. This yields the normative principle of Utilitarianism, namely, the Greatest Happiness of the Greatest Number, which is chiefly associated, in recognition of ardent advocacy, careful elaboration, and extensive application, with the name of Bentham. If the idea was of ancient origin and grew so slowly as to defy dating, the slogan itself may be dated more precisely: so far as I know, it occurs first in Hutcheson (op cit. 1725), then in Beccaria (op cit. 1764, *la massima felicità divisa nel maggior numero*); after that in Priestley (op. cit. 1768), to whom Bentham gives the credit for what to him was a 'sacred truth.' Hume does not have the slogan, but should be included in this series all the same. The word Utilitarianism is Bentham's.

Ibid., pp. 131–32.

86. " 'That tremendous convulsion': January 1793 (A Charge delivered to the Grand Jury of the County of Dublin at the Quarter Sessions of the Peace held at Kilmainham on the 15th of January 1793 by Robert Day, Esq., M.P. Chairman," in Gerald O'Carroll, *Robert Day (1746–1841): The Diaries and the Addresses to Grand Juries 1793–1829* (Tralee, County Kerry, Ireland: Polymath Press, 2004), pp. 2, 5:

> The most dangerous and destructive Being in the Universe would be Man but for the restraints imposed upon him by divine and human institutions. Religion and Law are the chains which are thrown round Man in the Social state, and which fetter and bind him down to his good behaviour But in vain does the Legislature speak, if the Magistrate will not act; in vain do we boast of the best system of Criminal Jurisprudence in the world, if it be allowed to sleep in the Statute book, instead of being executed with vigour and inflexibility. It can not be denied that a general relaxation and imbecillity in the administration of Criminal Justice has long been the reproach and misfortune of Ireland. It is the observation of a humane Philosopher, 'that the greatest check to crimes is not the cruelty but the infallibility, not the severity but the certainty of punishment'. Let the Executive authority be liberal and mild, but let it be vigilant, firm and inflexible, and we shall seldom have occasion to resort to the severities of the Law. We know that the most likely means of human happiness are obedience to the Laws and the maintenance of established Order and well-regulated power.

Ireland—like England, France, Scotland and the Italian peninsula—had lots of writers who became animated by political, social and economic development. Indeed, the Beccaria-inspired quest for equality, economic justice and fairness—and for good laws that would serve the public welfare—helped to inspire various revolutions and republics and legal reforms. *See, e.g.*, James Livesey, ed., Arthur O'Connor, *The State of Ireland* (Dublin: The Lilliput Press, 1998), p. 1 ("The Irish Republic is one of the many daughters of the French Revolution. Its most obvious symbol, the tri-coloured flag, quotes the flag of the first French republic, and its central informing ideal—the nation as people who live together under laws they give to themselves—is the Jacobin definition of the nation."); ibid., p. 2 ("Arthur O'Connor (1763–1852) was the most important conduit between French republicanism and Irish political radicalism in the late 1790s.... O'Connor had been friendly with Lafayette and maintained his links with prominent French intellectuals, especially those in the circle around Sophie de Grouchy, translator of Adam Smith and widow of the philosopher Condorcet. He was later to marry Condorcet's daughter, Eliza.... His *State of Ireland*, published in 1798, created a distinctively Irish language of radical democracy out of the French sources, by fusing them with the local political tradition and Scottish political economy."). In *The State of Ireland*, Arthur O'Connor spoke of how the regulation of crime and punishment—the subject Cesare Beccaria had taken up more than three decades earlier—was central to the proper functioning of government. As O'Connor, channeling both Beccaria and the economics of Adam Smith, wrote in 1798:

> In the twofold objects of government, the first is the affording protection to every member of the community from the violence or injustice of his fellow citizens. The expense of defending citizen against citizen must ever depend on the degree of justice on which the constitution and laws are established. When they are such as to secure every member *equally*, the fullest enjoyment of his natural rights, the *freest* exercise of his industry, and the most *undisturbed* fruition of its produce—when they open to him every means of acquiring the most ample and liberal wages, by which he may procure the necessaries and comforts of life—when, by securing to his industry the most extensive markets for the work he has wrought, it ensures him constant employment—when he suffers no peculation—when no deductions are made from his earnings but what his own interest tells him he should readily and willingly grant—trust me, fellow citizens, a government founded on principles like these would require no expense to support it. In such a government, every citizen would find a protection for every blessing.

Ibid., p. 53.

87. Reinert, "Enlightenment Socialism," *in* Kapossy, Nakhimovsky & Whatmore, eds., *Commerce and Peace in the Enlightenment*, pp. 128–29, 146, 149–51; *see also* Reinert, *"Achtung! Banditi!,"* in Rössner, ed., *Economic Growth and the Origins of Modern Political Economy* ("In a discarded draft of his lectures, Beccaria similarly wrote of how the human condition itself, to escape the most primitive state of nature at the very beginning of civilization, required man's need 'to arm himself and defend himself against the assaults of ferocious beasts.'"); *compare* Axel Körner, *America in Italy: The United States in the Political Thought and Imagination of the Risorgimento, 1763–1865* (Princeton, NJ: Princeton University Press, 2017), p. 50 ("Beccaria, for his part, had shown little interest in the life of the American colonies; and his series of lectures *Elementi di economica pubblica* (published posthumously in 1804) did not refer to the colonial question at all.") *with* Jeremy Adelman, *Sovereignty and Revolution in the Iberian Atlantic* (Princeton, NJ: Princeton University Press, 2006), p. 25 ("The Asturian economist Pedro Rodríguez Campomanes, a follower of Campillo, warned his sovereign of what was at stake if he hung on to old ways. In 1762, as English forces stormed Spanish outposts, he finished a major treatise for the new Spanish ruler, Carlos III, called Reflexiones sobre el comercio español a Indias. 'The evil, Señor,' he wrote to the king, 'lies in the body of the Nation or in the rules that until now govern the Traffic with the Indies.' What ensued in the treatise was an extended analysis of the misbegotten rules that choked what should flow more freely: trade between the metropole and its possessions in the New World.").

88. Dugald Stewart, *Essays on Philosophical Subjects by the Late Adam Smith, LL. D., Fellow of the Royal Societies of London and Edinburgh, &c. &c. to Which is Prefixed, An Account of the Life and Writings of the Author* (Basil: James Decker, 1799), p. lxxix.

89. *E.g.*, Henry Shelton Sanford, *Penal Codes, Being a Report on the Different Codes of Penal Law in Europe* (Washington, DC: Beverly Tucker, 1854), p. 100 ("In Tuscany a project of a new penal code is prepared and published.... In this project it is worthy of remark that the influence exercised by the earlier Italian philosophers, and more especially the author of the celebrate work, 'Dei delitti e delle pene,' (Beccaria,) is particularly visible."); J. O'Byrne Croke, *Outlines of Italian Literature* (Dublin: E. Ponsonby, 1880), p. 92 ("Beccaria is chiefly known as the author of the celebrated work, *Dei Delitti e delle Pene* (1764)—a treatise on Crimes and Punishments which advocated great reforms in criminal legislation."); "Dal Pozzo's Happiness of Italy," in *The Westminster Review* (London: Simpkin and Marshall, 1834), Vol. 21, p. 130 ("It is forbidden in the public libraries to lend out, among other books, Beccaria's celebrated *Dei delitti et delle pene*.").

90. Reinert, "Enlightenment Socialism," *in* Kapossy, Nakhimovsky & Whatmore, eds., *Commerce*

and Peace in the Enlightenment, pp. 136, 139, 141–43 (noting, among other things, that "[t]he Tuscan jurist and philosopher Cosimo Amidei wrote to Beccaria that Facchinei 'deserves to be punished with infamy, as he already has been punished in the tribunal of reason', a statement which turned out to be remarkably prophetic."). Although Cesare Beccaria was depressed about the excesses of the French Revolution at the time of his death in 1794, his daughter, Giulia, who travelled in high-society circles in Paris, kept her father's legacy alive in her own way after his death—and until her own death in 1841. *E.g.*, Roy Sydney Porter, *Richard & Maria Cosway: Regency Artists of Taste and Fashion* (Scottish National Portrait Gallery, 1995), p. 91 (noting that Giulia Beccaria was "a friend of Maria Cosway," the two having met in Paris "during the Peace of Amiens, when Maria had portrayed Beccaria in a lively oil sketch"); John Goldworth Alger, *Napoleon's British Visitors and Captives 1801–1815* (Westminster: Archibald Constable and Co., 1904), p. 160 (noting that Italian visitors included "Bartolini, sculpter of a colossal bust of Napoleon, and a daughter of Beccaria, the Italian philosopher, who had inherited his intelligence and love of liberty, and possessed beauty into the bargain"; of Giulia Beccaria, that source further notes: "She had divorced her insane husband. Helen Williams in 1794–1795 had found her residing by the lake of Lugano. She seems to have settled in Paris in 1798, and Paine then made acquaintance with her. She presented Redhead Yorke with a portrait of her father, and Holcroft was now struck by her intelligence and affability. At her house he met Melzi, who had presented the keys of Milan to Napoleon on his entering that city, and who had scandalised lovers of liberty by accepting the vice-presidency of the so-called Cisalpine republic, though Napoleon soon superseded him by his step-son Eugène de Beauharnais."); Henry Redhead Yorke, *Letters from France, in 1802* (London: H. D. Symonds, 1804), Vol. II, pp. 390–91:

> I mention Madame *de Beccaria* in this place by way of a contrast. She is the daughter of the celebrated Marquis de Beccaria, author of the book on Crimes and Punishments. Elegant in her manners, and possessed of a pleasing person, she is modest, affable, and good natured. Though a rigid Catholic, she is not Saint, nor does she keep a *coterie*, or wish to take advantage of her father's great celebrity, to collect around her the fops of philosophy. On the contrary, she lives very retired, and I am sorry to add, appears oppressed with melancholy, as I imagine, from a disappointment in marriage, for which she is to be pitied. She has been divorced from her husband, Count———, an Italian nobleman, on account of his insanity. When any of his vassals approached him with the usual title of "My Lord," he made them down on their knees, and call him "My God." He is, of course, taken proper care of. Madame de Beccaria will go through London to Scotland in a few weeks for the pious purpose of having all her father's writings translated there, but she is greatly distressed at not being able to speak a word of the language. She made me a present of her father's portrait, which I shall keep as a treasure as long as I have breath, and she assured me that the Italian work, entitled *Saggio sopra la Politica e la Legislazione Romana*, which the French translator had the impudence to declare was written by the Marquis, is not his work.

See also K. R. L., "Alessandro Manzoni," *The American Catholic Quarterly Review* (Philadelphia: Hardy & Mahony, 1888), Vol. 13, pp. 737, 737 (noting that Alessandro Manzoni liked being called "Manzoni-Beccaria, or even Signor Beccaria," and that his mother "Donna Giulia herself had much family pride and joyed in the belief that through herself the virtues and the intellectual gifts of the Beccarias had been transmitted to her son"; that the Beccarias "had been for generations a typical Italian family of the rural nobility"; that Giulia (Beccaria) Manzoni was "infinitely benevolent in alms-giving, practically religious, full of tolerations for the follies and vices of all except for those who ignored her Alessandro's claims"; and that, "[o]ver her mortal remains, her son [Alessandro] inscribed this epitaph: 'To Giulia Manzoni, the daughter of Cesare Beccaria, a matron revered for her great intelligence, her liberality to the poor, her profound practical religion; who is committed by her inconsolable son and by all her afflicted family to the mercy of God and to the prayers of the faithful.'"); *cf.* Augustus Pallotta, *Alessandro Manzoni: A Critical Bibliography: 1950–2000* (Pisa: Fabrizio Serra, 2007).

91. John D. Bessler, *The Birth of American Law: An Italian Philosopher and the American Revolution* (Durham, NC: Carolina Academic Press, 2014), p. 259.

92. John Hostettler, *Champions of the Rule of Law* (Hampshire, UK: Waterside Press, 2011), pp. 75, 78.

93. Amanda Ruggeri, "The London Gallows Where Pirates Were Hanged," BBC.com, Dec. 16,

2016, http://www.bbc.com/autos/story/20161216-the-london-gallows-where-pirates-were-hanged; Charles Moore, Gyles Brandreth, Cherie Booth & George Weigel, *First Things: The Moral, Social and Religious Challenges of the Day* (London: Burns & Oates, 2005), p. 45; *see also* Alan Brooke & David Brandon, *Tyburn: London's Fatal Tree* (Gloucestershire: The History Press, 2013) (e-book); Nigel Cawthorne, *Public Executions: From Ancient Rome to the Present Day* (London: Arcturus Publishing, 2012).

94. Bessler, *The Birth of American Law*, p. xi; "The Busts in the Pincian Gardens: 228 Personalities Who Brought Prestige to Italy," *available at* http://roma.andreapollett.com/S1/roma-c23.htm.

95. David S. Clark, ed., *Encyclopedia of Law and Society: American and Global Perspectives* (Thousand Oaks, CA: Sage Publications, 2007), p. 585 (containing a biographical sketch of Gaetano Filangieri); Roy Palmer Domenico, *Remaking Italy in the Twentieth Century* (Lanham, MD: Rowman & Littlefield, 2002), p. 5 (noting Alfieri's dedication to George Washington); Charles Dudley Warner, ed., *Library of the World's Best Literature: Ancient and Modern* (New York: The International Society, 1896), Vol. 1, p. 373 (same); "Gaetano Filangieri and Benjamin Franklin: The Relationship Between the Italian Enlightenment and the U.S. Constitution," pp. 48–49, *available at* http://sedi2.esteri.it/sitiweb/AmbWashington/Pubblicazioni/2_filangieri_interno.pdf (noting the research project was directed by Counselor Giannicola Sinisi with research done by Dr. Monica D'Agostini with assistance from the Library of Congress, the American Philosophical Society of Philadelphia and the Museo Civico Gaetano Filangieri in Naples); Gaetana Marrone, ed., *Encyclopedia of Italian Literary Studies* (New York: Routledge, 2007), pp. 19–23, 1979–81 (containing biographical sketches of Pietro Verri and Vittorio Alfieri).

96. Gaetana Marrone, ed., *Encyclopedia of Italian Literary Studies* (New York: Routledge, 2007), p. 22.

97. Peter Adam Thrasher, *Pasquale Paoli: An Enlightened Hero, 1725–1807* (Hamden, CT: Archon Books, 1970), p. 3; Steven Epstein, *Speaking of Slavery: Color, Ethnicity, and Human Bondage in Italy* (Ithaca: Cornell University Press, 2001), p. 50; Harry Hearder, *Italy in the Age of the Risorgimento 1780–1870* (London: Routledge, 2013), p. 161; *Italy, Malta, and San Marino* (New York: Marshall Cavendish, 2010), p. 772; https://www.tuttocitta.it/mappa/roma/via-cesare-beccaria.

98. Mark F. Gilbert & K. Robert Nilsson, *Historical Dictionary of Modern Italy* (Lanham, MD: Scarecrow Press, 2007), p. 260.

99. *See, e.g.*, *Star and Banner* (Gettysburg, PA), June 1, 1835, p. 3 (taking note of "Manzoni's celebrated Italian novel").

100. Monument to Alessandro Manzoni, *available at* http://www.turismo.milano.it/wps/portal/tur/en/arteecultura/architetturaemonumenti/monumenti/monumento_alessandro_manzoni ("In front of the church of San Fedele, where today lies the headquarters of a bank, was palazzo Imbonati which was the premises of the Accademia dei Trasformati in the eighteenth century. It was owned by Carlo Imbonati, the Milanese nobleman with whom Giulia Beccaria, Manzoni's mother, decided to cohabit after abandoning her husband. In palazzo Imbonati in 1808—which in the meantime had been bought by the Blondel family—Alessandro Manzoni's wedding to his first wife, Enrichetta Blondel, was celebrated with a Calvinist ritual.").

101. *Milan: History, Map and Guide* (Firenze: Casa Editrice Bonechi, 2005), p. 28.

102. 36 *The Ladies' Repository* (J.F. Wright and L. Swormstedt, 1876), p. 128.

103. Cecilia Miller, *Enlightenment and Political Fiction: The Everyday Intellectual* (New York: Routledge, 2016), p. 215; "Alessandro Manzoni," NNDB, http://www.nndb.com/people/153/000085895/.

104. Sylvia Neely, *A Concise History of the French Revolution* (Lanham, MD: Rowman & Littlefield, 2008), p. 108.

105. Harry Hearder, *Italy in the Age of the Risorgimento, 1790–1870* (Essex: Longman, 1983), p. 261.

106. http://www.geocities.ws/imo146/maria_antonietta/det3_en.html.

107. Rinaldina Russell, *The Feminist Encyclopedia of Italian Literature*, p. 189.

108. Brian Hamnett, *The Historical Novel in Nineteenth-Century Europe: Representations of Reality in History and Fiction* (Oxford: Oxford University Press, 2011), p. 150; David Williams, *Condorcet and Modernity* (Cambridge: Cambridge University Press, 2004), pp. 1–4, 15, 43. For Cesare Beccaria's relationship with Voltaire, see Maria Laura Lanzillo, "*Des délits et des peines:* Beccaria et Voltaire,"

Corpus: revue de philosophie, No. 62 (2012), pp. 177–96. That review of philosophy also contains a series of articles about the death penalty and the views of Montaigne, Montesquieu, Giuseppe Pelli, Rousseau, Filangieri and Jeremy Bentham on that topic. *See, e.g.*, Jordi Bayod, "Montaigne, la peine de mort et la compassion," *Corpus: revue de philosophie*, No. 62 (2012), pp. 305–322; Francine Markovits, "Montesquieu et la peine de mort," *Corpus: revue de philosophie*, No. 62 (2012), pp. 107–134; Philippe Audegean, Le *Discorso della pena di morte* de Giuseppe Pelli (1760–1761)," *Corpus: revue de philosophie*, No. 62 (2012), pp. 135–56; Guillaume Coqui, "Rousseau et la peine de mort," *Corpus: revue de philosophie*, No. 62 (2012), pp. 157–76; Alessandro Tuccillo, "Filangieri et la peine de mort," *Corpus: revue de philosophie*, No. 62 (2012), pp. 231–44; Gilles Trimaille, "Le peine de mort dans la doctrine utilitariste de Jeremy Bentham," *Corpus: revue de philosophie*, No. 62 (2012), pp. 215–30. The correspondence with the Marquis de Condorcet can be accessed online at www.founders.archives.gov.

109. "Marie-Jean-Antoine-Nicolas de Caritat, marquis de Condorcet," https://www.britannica.com/biography/Marie-Jean-Antoine-Nicolas-de-Caritat-marquis-de-Condorcet#ref272130.

110. Ibid.

111. Steven Lukes & Nadia Urbinati, eds., *Condorcet: Political Writings* (Cambridge: Cambridge University Press, 2012), pp. ix–x, xviii–xix; Charles Coulston Gillispie, *Science and Polity in France: The Revolutionary and Napoleonic Years* (Princeton: Princeton University Press, 2004), p. 326; Groenewegen, *Eighteenth-century Economics*, p. 20.

112. Suzanne Desan, Lynn Hunt & William Max Nelson, eds., *The French Revolution in Global Perspective* (Ithaca, NY: Cornell University Press, 2013), p. 27.

113. 20 *The Romanic Review* 32 (1929).

114. 36 *The Ladies' Repository* (J.F. Wright and L. Swormstedt, 1876), p. 128. A photo of Giulia Manzoni Beccaria's tomb in Milan can be found here: Tomba_di_Giulia_Beccaria_e_di_Enrichetta_Blondel.

115. Carol Burnell, *Divided Affections: The Extraordinary Life of Maria Cosway—Celebrity Artist and Thomas Jefferson's Impossible Love* (Column House, 2007); Cynthia A. Kierner, *Martha Jefferson Randolph, Daughter of Monticello: Her Life and Times* (Chapel Hill: The University of North Carolina Press, 2012), p. 58 ("Not long after he returned to Paris, Jefferson enjoyed his famous flirtation with Maria Cosway, the beautiful and talented Italian-born wife of the English artist Richard Cosway and an accomplished artist in her own right. Jefferson and Maria Cosway enjoyed opera, theater, art, and each other's company during the early autumn of 1786, when she returned to London. In late February 1787, Jefferson left Paris for a tour of France and northern Italy that lasted three and a half months.").

116. Cynthia A. Kierner, *Martha Jefferson Randolph, Daughter of Monticello: Her Life and Times* (Chapel Hill: The University of North Carolina Press, 2012), p. 58.

117. Thomas Jefferson to Maria Cosway, Oct. 12, 1786.

118. "Treasury's Hamilton Bust," U.S. Department of the Treasury, https://www.treasury.gov/about/history/collections/Pages/Treasury's-Hamilton-Bust.aspx; "Small House Rotunda," Architect of the Capitol, https://www.aoc.gov/capitol-buildings/small-house-rotunda.

119. *Rome and the Environs: With a Plan of Rome and a Map of the Environs and 32 Engravings* (Milan: Fratelli Treves, 1906), p. 212.

120. Charles Knight, comp., *Biography: or, Third Division of "The English Cyclopædia"* (London: Bradbury, Evans, & Co., 1866), Vol. 1, pp. 649–50; Francis Claudon, *The Concise Encyclopedia of Romanticism* (Chartwell Books, 1980), p. 224; "Sardina," *The North American Review* (Oct. 1857), Vol. CLXXVII, p. 355; *Southern California Quarterly* (Spring 1977), p. 136; Mogens Trolle Larsen, *The Conquest of Assyria: Excavations in an Antique Lab 1840–1860* (New York: Routledge, 1996), p. 14.

121. "Italian Literature in the Nineteenth Century," in *The North American Review*, Vol. L, pp. 315–16 (Boston: Ferdinand Andrews, 1840); Bessler, *The Birth of American Law*, pp. 159–60.

122. Allen Walker Read, "The American Reception of Botta's Storia della Guerra dell' Independenza degli Stati Unita d'America," *Italica*, Vol. 14, No. 1 (Mar. 1937), pp. 5–8; *Proceedings of the Massachusetts Historical Society* (Boston, MA: Massachusetts Historical Society, 1879), Vol. 1 p. 333; Carlo Botta to Thomas Jefferson, Jan. 10, 1816; Thomas Jefferson to George Alexander Otis, July 8, 1820; Thomas Jefferson to George A. Otis, Dec. 25, 1820.

123. Rebecca Messbarger & Paula Findlen, eds. & trans., *The Contest for Knowledge: Debates over Women's Learning in Eighteenth-Century Italy* (Chicago: The University of Chicago Press, 2007), p. 12; U. M. Rose, "Beccaria and Law Reform," *The American Lawyer* (1900), Vol. 8, p. 302; Aaron Thomas, ed., Cesare Beccaria, On Crimes and Punishments *and Other Writings* (Toronto: University of Toronto Press, Aaron Thomas & Jeremy Parzen, trans. 2008), p. 27.

124. Bessler, *The Birth of American Law*, p. 279.

125. Robert K. Ax & Thomas J. Fagan, *Corrections, Mental Health, and Social Policy: International Perspectives* (Springfield, IL: Charles C. Thomas, 2007), pp. 16–17; William Hague, *William Wilberforce: The Life of the Great Anti-Slave Trade Campaigner* (Orlando, FL: Harcourt, 2007); *An Essay on the Slavery and Commerce of the Human Species, Particularly the African; Translated from a Latin Dissertation, Which Was Honoured with the First Prize in the University of Cambridge for the Year 1785* (London: J. Phillips, 2d rev. ed. 1788).

126. Epstein, *Speaking of Slavery*, pp. 49–50.

127. Richard R. Follett, *Evangelicalism, Penal Theory and the Politics of Criminal Law Reform in England, 1808–30* (New York: Palgrave, 2001), pp. 1, 9, 34, 53, 58, 139–40; David Bruce, *The Life of Sir Thomas Fowell Buxton: Extraordinary Perseverance* (Lanham, MD: Lexington Books, 2014), pp. 64, 83, 87, 89; Robert Adams, *The Abuses of Punishment* (London: Macmillan Press, 1998), p. 214; *Pharmaceutical Journal and Transactions (1864–65)* (London: John Churchill and Sons, 1865), Vol. VI, p. 31; William Tallack, *Peter Bedford, the Spitalfields Philanthropist* (London: S. W. Partridge, 1865), pp. 82–83, 87–88.

128. H. Bruce Franklin, "*Billy Budd* and Capital Punishment: A Tale of Four Centuries," *in* Katy Ryan, ed., *Demands of the Dead: Executions, Storytelling, and Activism in the United States* (Iowa City: University of Iowa Press, 2012), p. 144; James Raven, *London Booksellers and American Customers: Transatlantic Literary Community and the Charleston Library Society, 1748–1811* (Columbia: University of South Carolina Press, 2002), p. 214; *The American Magazine and Historical Chronicle* (1985), Vols. 1–2, p. 71.

129. Robert L. Gale, *A Henry Wadsworth Longfellow Companion* (Westport, CT: Greenwood Press, 2003), pp. 51, 96–98; Gaetana Marrone, ed., *Encyclopedia of Italian Literary Studies* (New York: Routledge, 2007), p. 1136.

130. Andrew Hilen, ed., *The Letters of Henry Wadsworth Longfellow* (Cambridge: Harvard University Press, 1972), Vol. 3, pp. 8, 217–18.

131. Thomas Dick, *The Philosophy of Religion, or, An Illustration of the Moral Laws of the Universe* (Philadelphia: E. C. & J. Biddle, 1847), Vol. 3, pp. 331–32 & n.*. Dick also listed the following under the rubric of "Punishments short of death": "Fine, pillory, imprisonment; compulsory labour at the mines, galleys, highways, or correction-house; whipping, bastonading; mutilation by cutting away the ears, the nose, the tongue, the breasts of women, the foot, the hand; squeezing the marrow from the bones with screws or wedges, castration, putting out the eyes; banishment, running the gauntlet, drumming, shaving off the hair, burning on the hand or forehead; and many others of a similar nature." Ibid., p. 332 n.*.

132. *The Brera Gallery: The Official Guide* (Milan: Touring Club Italiano, 1998), p. 10.

133. Gaetana Marrone, ed., *Encyclopedia of Italian Literary Studies* (New York: Routledge, 2007), Vol. 1, p. 148; Marcello Maestro, *Cesare Beccaria and the Origins of Penal Reform* (Philadelphia: Temple University Press, 1973), pp. 77–79.

134. Luisa Arrigoni, Emanuela Daffra & Pietro C. Marani, *The Brera Gallery: The Official Guide* (Milan: Touring Club Italiano, 1998), p. 10; *Milan: Guide de Agostini* (Instituto geografico de Agostini, 1990), p. 230; Franz Liszt, *Artist's Journey: Lettres d'un bachelier ès musique 1835–1841* (Chicago, IL: The University of Chicago Press, Charles Suttoni, trans. 1989), p. 94 n.13; Ashton Rollins Willard, *History of Modern Italian Art* (New York: Longmans, Green, and Co., 1898), pp. 54–56.

135. *The New Encyclopaedia Britannica* (1983), Vol. 2, p. 785; Cesare Beccaria, *Des Délits et Des Peines* (Paris: Deuxième edition 1823) (containing a French engraving of Beccaria on the title page); "Faucci, Carlo," *Dizionario Biografico degli Italiani*, Vol. 45 (1995), http://www.treccani.it/enciclopedia/carlo-faucci_(Dizionario-Biografico)/.

136. John Hostettler, *Cesare Beccaria: The Genius of 'On Crimes and Punishments'* (Hampshire, UK: Waterside Press, 2011), p. 33; D. Medina Lasansky, *The Renaissance Perfected: Architecture,*

Spectacle, and Tourism in Fascist Italy (University Park, PA: The Pennsylvania State University Press, 2004), p. 29; http://www.lombardiabeniculturali.it/opere-arte/schede/3n010-00069/.

137. "The Headsman's Widow: An Historical Scrap," *The World of Fashion, and Monthly Magazine of the Courts of London and Paris* (London, Sept. 1, 1841), No. 210, Vol. 18, p. 208.

138. Francis A. Hyett, *Florence: Her History and Art to the Fall of the Republic* (New York: E. P. Dutton & Co., 1903), p. 338; Robert Fletcher, *A Tragedy of the Great Plague of Milan in 1630* (Baltimore, MD: The Lord Baltimore Press, 1898), p. 13.

139. D. Medina Lasansky, *The Renaissance Perfected: Architecture, Spectacle, and Tourism in Fascist Italy* (University Park, PA: The Pennsylvania State University Press, 2004), p. 29.

140. Ashton Rollins Willard, *History of Modern Italian Art* (New York: Longmans, Green, and Co., 1898), p. 229.

141. *See, e.g.*, John D. Bessler, *Cruel and Unusual: The American Death Penalty and the Founders' Eighth Amendment* (Boston: Northeastern University Press, 2012); Michael Dow Burkhead, *A Life for a Life: The American Debate Over the Death Penalty* (Jefferson, NC: McFarland & Co., 2009), p. 5; James Anson Farrer, *Crimes and Punishments: Including a New Translation of Beccaria's 'Dei delitti e delle pene'* (London: Chatto & Windus, 1880), p. 170.

142. Paul Friedland, *Seeing Justice Done: The Age of Spectacular Capital Punishment in France* (Oxford: Oxford University Press 2012), p. 207.

143. John Hostettler, *Cesare Beccaria: The Genius of 'On Crimes and Punishments'* (Hampshire, UK: Waterside Press, 2011), p. 33; *Milan 360°* (OlliService Multimedia, 2014); Lasansky, *The Renaissance Perfected*, p. 29; *The Athenæum: Journal of Literature, Science, the Fine Arts, Music, and the Drama* (London: John Francis, 1871), p. 529.

144. T. Teighmouth Shore, ed., *Cassell's Biographical Dictionary* (London: Cassell, Petter, and Galpin, 1867), p. 267.

145. Piers Beirne, *Inventing Criminology: Essays on the Rise of 'Homo Criminalis'* (Albany: State University of New York Press, 1993), p. 61 n.134.

146. J. C. L. Simonde de Sismondi, *Historical View of the Literature of the South of Europe* (London: Henry G. Bohn, Thomas Roscoe, trans., 2d ed. 1846), Vol. 2, p. 61 ("About the same period flourished the celebrated Marquis Beccaria, who, in his Treatise on Crimes and Punishments, has defended with such animation the cause of humanity; and the Cavaliere Filangieri, the author of a valuable work on Legislation.").

147. Robert Boyd, *The Office, Powers, and Jurisdiction, of His Majesty's Justices of the Peace, and Commissioners of Supply, for Scotland* (Edinburgh: William Creech, 1794), Vol. 1, p. 413 ("The celebrated Marquis of Beccaria observes, that 'conjugal fidelity is always greater in proportion as marriages are more numerous, and less difficult; but, when the interest or pride of families, or paternal authority, not the inclination of the parties, unite the sexes, gallantry soon breaks the slender ties, in spite of common moralists, who exclaim against the effect, while they pardon the cause.'"); Andrew Boyle, ed., *The Everyman Encyclopædia* (J.M. Dent & Sons), Vol. 3, p. 294 (referring to "writings of the celebrated Marquis Beccaria").

148. *Florence: A Complete Guide to the Renaissance City, the Surrounding Countryside, and the Chianti Region* (Milano: Touring Club of Italy, 1999), p. 94.

149. Guido Zucconi & Pietro Ruschi, *Florence: An Architectural Guide* (Antique Collectors Club Limited, 1995), p. 122; Richard J. Goy, *Florence: A Walking Guide to Its Architecture* (New Haven, CT: Yale University Press, 2015), p. xxv.

150. *The Companion Guide to Florence* (New York: HarperCollins, 1991), p. 110; Larry J. Feinberg, *The Young Leonardo: Art and Life in Fifteenth-Century Florence* (Cambridge: Cambridge University Press, 2011), pp. 102–3.

151. Arnold Anthony Schmidt, *Byron and the Rhetoric of Italian Nationalism* (New York: Palgrave Macmillan, 2010), p. 18; A. L. Kroeber, *Configurations of Culture Growth* (Berkeley, CA: University of California Press, 1963), p. 302; "Herma of Cesare Beccaria," http://www.gettyimages.com/detail/photo/herma-of-cesare-beccaria-by-giuseppe-high-res-stock-photography/109267435.

152. https://en.wikipedia.org/wiki/Palazzo_Brentani; https://en.wikipedia.org/wiki/Neoclassical_architecture_in_Milan.

153. William Falconer, *Remarks on the Influence of Climate, Situation, Nature of Country, Population,*

Nature of Food, and Way of Life, on the Disposition and Temper, Manners and Behavior, Intellects, Laws and Customs, Form of Government, and Religion of Mankind (London: C. Dilly, 1781), pp. 26, 33, 98–103, 158, 459, 486, 488, 496.

154. Istvan Hont & Michael Ignatieff, *Wealth and Virtue: The Shaping of Political Economy in the Scottish Enlightenment* (Cambridge: Cambridge University Press, 1983), p. 348; James David Draper, "Thirty Famous People: Drawings by Sergent-Marceau and Bosio, Milan, 1815–1818," 13 *Metropolitan Museum Journal* (1979), pp. 113–30; *Poesie di Giovanni Fantoni fra gli Arcadi Labindo*, Tomo III (Italia 1823), p. 129; *Pinacoteca Ambrosiana* (Milano: Mondadori Electa S.p.A., 2008), pp. 364–65; *see also* Leader Scott, *Vincigliata and Maiano* 267 (Florence: G. Barbera, 1891) ("Giovanni Fantoni's Arcadian name was 'Labindo,' and under this appellation he put forth odes ... by the dozen...."); Peter Bondanella & Julia Conaway Bondanella, *Cassell Dictionary of Italian Literature* (Westport, CT: Greenwood Press, 1996), p. 205 ("Born in Fivizzano and educated in Rome, Fantoni joined the government of the Duchy of Tuscany in 1773 and entered the Accademia dell'Arcadia three years later as Labindo.").

155. Neal Zaslaw & William Cowdery, eds., *The Complete Mozart: A Guide to the Musical Works of Wolfgang Amadeus Mozart* (New York: W.W. Norton & Co., 1990), p. 322; Don Michael Randel, ed., *The Harvard Biographical Dictionary of Music* (Cambridge, MA: The Belknap Press of Harvard University Press, 1996), p. 616; Marchese Cesare Beccaria (1815–1818), http://www.nga.gov/content/ngaweb/Collection/art-object-page.159743.html (etching and stipple engraving; gift of John O'Brien).

156. John Hostettler, *Champions of the Rule of Law* (Hampshire, UK: Waterside Press, 2011), pp. 80, 142–44.

157. Hugh Henry Brackenridge, *Law Miscellanies: Containing an Introduction to the Study of the Law* (Philadelphia: P. Byrne, 1814), p. 497.

158. Sir John MacDonell & Edward Manson, eds., *Great Jurists of the World* (Boston: Little, Brown, and Co., 1914), Vol. 2, pp. 506–16.

159. Robert Badinter, *Abolition: One Man's Battle Against the Death Penalty* (Boston: Northeastern University Press, 2008); Bernard E. Harcourt, ed., Michel Foucault, *The Punitive Society: Lectures at the Collège de France 1972–1973* (New York: Palgrave Macmillan, Graham Burchell, trans. 2015), p. 20; Doreen Carvajal, "Paris Gawks Again at the Guillotine," N.Y. Times, May 7, 2010; Geoffrey Bennington, Marc Crépon & Thomas Dutoit, eds., Jacques Derrida, *The Death Penalty* (Chicago: The University of Chicago Press, Peggy Kamuf, trans., 2014), Vol. I, n. 33; "Standards for Awarding the Beccaria Award," http://www.justinian.org/cesare-beccaria-award.html; The Cesare Beccaria Award for Young Researchers: Call for Papers, https://www.h-net.org/announce/show.cgi?ID=157084; "International Society of Social Defence and Humane Criminal Policy — ISSD," www.cnpds.it/eng/index.php?link=organizzazioni2; "Judge James Charles Gulotta, noted as a compassionate juvenile and appellate jurist in New Orleans, is dead at 89," *The Times-Picayune*, Sept. 6, 2013, www.nola.com/crime/index.ssf.2013/09/judge_james_charles_gulotta_no.html.

160. http://www.lawschool.cornell.edu/faculty/bio_sandra_babcock.cfm; CV of Sandra L. Babcock, *available at* http://www.law.northwestern.edu/faculty/assets/documents/cv-BabcockSandraL_v2014-03-03;141621.pdf; Cornell Center on the Death Penalty Worldwide, http://www.deathpenaltyworldwide.org.

161. Dirk Verhofstadt, *Cesare Beccaria: 250 Years on Crimes and Punishments* (Lexington, KY, July 24, 2016), pp. 3, 5, 7.

162. Richard A. Posner, *The Economics of Justice* (Cambridge: Harvard University Press, 1983), p. 28 ("Beccaria's *Essay on Crimes and Punishments* was an elegant theoretical analysis of the principles of punishment. Blackstone took Beccaria's theoretical propositions and applied them to the actual system of criminal justice in England."); ibid., p. 29 (quoting from Blackstone):

> Blackstone's discussion of marginal deterrence, while derivative from Beccaria, indicates the way in which he related Beccaria's theoretical analysis to the actual laws of England (and other countries): 'It has been ... ingeniously proposed [by Beccaria], that in every state a scale of crimes should be formed, with a corresponding scale of punishments, descending from the greatest to the least: but, if that be too romantic an idea, yet at least a wise legislature will mark the principal divisions, and not assign penalties of the first degree to offences of an inferior rank. Where men see no distinction made in the nature and gradations of punishment, the generality will be led to conclude there is no distinction in the guilt.

See also ibid., p. 33:

> Bentham regarded himself not as a theoretical or academic thinker but as a legislative reformer. He got his ideas for legislative reform by deduction from the "greatest happiness," or utility, principle. Already stated clearly in the writings of Priestley, Beccaria, and others, this principle was that the test of sound social policy was whether it promoted the greatest happiness of the greatest number of people. Bentham translated the greatest-happiness principle into a host of specific public policies that he worked out in great detail. His best-known proposals were in the area of criminal justice, although, except for prison reform, he, like Blackstone, got most of his basic ideas in that area from Beccaria.

163. Ibid., pp. 49–50.

164. Richard A. Posner, *Frontiers of Legal Theory* (Cambridge, MA: Harvard University Press, 2004), p. 54; *see also* A. Mitchell Polinsky & Steven Shavell, eds., *Handbook of Law and Economics* (Amsterdam, The Netherlands: North-Holland, 2007), Vol. 2, p. xi ("The origins of law and economics may be traced to eighteenth century writings on crime by Beccaria (1767) and Bentham (1789).").

165. Bruni & Zamagni, *Civil Economy*, p. 111.

166. Bernard E. Harcourt, "Beccaria's *On Crimes and Punishments*: A Mirror on the History of the Foundations of Modern Criminal Law," *in* Markus D. Dubber, ed., *Foundational Texts in Modern Criminal Law* (Oxford: Oxford University Press, 2014), pp. 51–52.

167. MacDonell & Manson, *Great Jurists of the World*, Vol. 2, pp. 503–5.

168. Lawrence W. Sherman, "Enlightened Justice: Consequentialism and Empiricism from Beccaria to Braithwaite," *in* Erich Marks, Anja Meyer & Ruth Linssen, eds., *Quality in Crime Prevention* (Norderstedt, Germany: Books on Demand GmbH, 2005), p. 41; Marion Keim & Clemens Ley, eds., *International Dialogue: Exploring Potential Criteria for the Measurement of Safety and Crime Prevention* (Stellenbosch: Conference-RAP, 2010), p. 61; "Philadelphia Lawyer, and Advocate of Italian-American Advancement, Dies," The Legal Intelligencer Blog, Oct. 22, 2012, http://thelegalintelligencer.typepad.com/tli/2012/10/philadelphia-lawyer-and-advocate-of-italian-american-advancement-dies.html; "Beccaria Bust Ceremony June 28," http://www.philadelphiabar.org/page/NewsItem?appNum=3&newsItemID=1000649; *see also* "Beccaria Ceremony June 28," Philadelphia Bar Reporter Online, June 25, 2007, *available at* http://www.philadelphiabar.org/page/BRO062507?appNum=1#story6 (same).

169. "In Milan," art curator James Draper writes, "Bosio lived in the via Morigi," a locale named after another famous Milanese family. Yet another bust of Beccaria, sculpted by the late artist Lucille Drake of Atlanta, Georgia, was created much more recently and reportedly installed in December 2005 in the Hall of Justice in Washington, D.C. James David Draper, "Thirty Famous People: Drawings by Sergent-Marceau and Bosio, Milan, 1815–1818," 13 *Metropolitan Museum Journal* (1979), pp. 113–30; Obituary for Lucille Henry Drake (1/26/2006), http://www.genlookups.com/co/webbbs_config.pl/read/721; *Milan and the Lakes* (London: DK 2015), p. 85.

170. Joseph A. Schumpeter, *History of Economic Analysis* (New York: Routledge, 1997), pp. 130, 179–81; Christopher L. Tomlins, *Law, Labor, and Ideology in the Early American Republic* (Cambridge: Cambridge University Press, 1993), p. 43; *see also* Markus D. Dubber, ed., *Foundational Texts in Modern Criminal Law* (Oxford: Oxford University Press, 2014), p. 10 ("'THE word Economy, or OEconomy, is derived from oikos, a house, and nomos, law, and meant originally only the wise and legitimate government of the house for the common good of the whole family. The meaning of the term was then extended to the government of that great family, the State. To distinguish these two senses of the word, the latter is called general or political economy, and the former domestic or particular economy.'") (quoting Rousseau's *Discourse on Political Economy* published in 1755).

171. Ernesto Screpanti & Stefano Zamagni, *An Outline of the History of Economic Thought* (Oxford: Oxford University Press, 2d ed. rev. 2005), pp. 62–63.

172. Mario Ricciardi & Filippo Santoni de Sio, "Cesare Beccaria: Utilitarianism, Contractualism and Rights," 2 *Philosophical Inquiries* 79, 79–86 (2014).

173. https://fr.m.wikipedia.org/wiki/Rue_Beccaria.

174. Lewis Cass Aldrich, *History of Clearfield County, Pennsylvania* (Syracuse, NY: D. Mason & Co., 1887), p. 444; John F. Meginness, *History of the Great Island and William Dunn, Its Owner, and Founder of Dunnstown* (Williamsport, PA: Gazette and Bulletin Printing House, 1894), pp. 180–81.

175. "Preserving Area History," *The Progress* (Clearfield, Pennsylvania), Aug. 19, 1955, p. 12; "Dr.

J. G. Ricketts, Kin of County Pioneers, Dies," *The Progress* (Clearfield, Pennsylvania), Mar. 19, 1956, p. 1; "Just Received, And for Sale at the Office of the Journal, the Following new Books," *The North-Carolina Journal* (Halifax, North Carolina), July 6, 1807, p. 4; "Libels," *Raleigh Register, and North-Carolina State Gazette*, Feb. 9, 1807, pp. 1–2; "Report," *The Centinel* (Gettysburg, Pennsylvania), Apr. 22, 1807, pp. 1, 3; http://www.clearfieldco.org/Planning_Files/06Comp_plan/06Chapter_4_-_History__Resource_Invent___Preservation_Plan.pdf.

176. Sylvanus Urban, *The Gentleman's Magazine: And Historical Chronicle* (London: John Nichols, 1824), Vol. 94, p. 351.

177. George Ripley & Charles A. Dana, eds., *The American Cyclopædia: A Popular Dictionary of General Knowledge* (New York: D. Appleton and Co., 1881), Vol. 2, p. 437.

178. Paul Knepper, *Explaining Criminal Conduct: Theories and Systems in Criminology* (Durham, NC: Carolina Academic Press, 2001), p. 40.

179. George A. Scott, "The Clearfield Area," *The Progress* (Clearfield, Pennsylvania), Oct. 11, 1969, p. 12. The year before, one writer in *The Progress*—someone unfamiliar with the scope of Cesare Beccaria's influence in early America—had pondered aloud after taking note of townships named after well-known figures such as William Penn and Robert Morris: "I can understand place-namers of that era choosing any of these … but I should like to meet the person who decided to name a piece of Pennsylvania wilderness for Cesare Bonesana, Marquis de Beccaria. The Marquis was an Italian economist, jurist and philosopher who raised economic and religious shock waves for his advanced theories on fair wages and abolition of capital punishment. In the day when a serf had no reason to expect payment and the hint of divine disbelief was a matter of off with the head, [w]ho knew of de Beccaria when our townships were first named?" *The Progress* (Clearfield, Pennsylvania), Jan. 6, 1968, p. 4.

180. Lewis Cass Aldrich, ed., *History of Clearfield County, Pennsylvania: With Illustrations and Biographical Sketches of Some of Its Prominent Men and Pioneers* (Syracuse, NY: D. Mason & Co., 1887), p. 444.

181. E-mail from Carlo Scognamiglio Pasini to John Bessler (June 13, 2017); http://www.ambrosiana.eu/cms/progetti_in_corso-2305.html (referencing Cesare Beccaria's writings); Cesare Beccaria, *Dei delitti e delle pene* (Stenna UTET, 1965) (facsimile dell'edizione originale pubblicata anonima in Livorno nel 1764, con le aggiunte delle successive edizioni e degli autografi registrate in margine e su carte allegate dal Marchese Giulio Beccaria, figlio dell'autor; a cura di Luigi Firpo), *available at* http://bookstore.antrodiulisse.eu/libri/scienze-umane/scienze-sociali/cesare-beccaria-dei-delitti-e-delle-pene-utet-1965/.

182. Bessler, *The Birth of American Law*, p. 74; "Centennial of the Cabinet di Brera, Milan," *American Journal of Numismatics* (New York: The American Numismatic Society, 1907–8), p. 131; Villa Beccaria Lake Como, http://www.villaatlakecomo.com/villadetails/villa-beccaria-lake-como.html. Guilio's own coin collection ended up in the Royal Numismatic Cabinet di Brera in Milan.

183. Henry Wadsworth Longfellow, *The Poets and Poetry of Europe* (Boston: Houghton, Mifflin and Co., 1896), p. 613.

184. Alessandro Manzoni, *The Betrothed* (New York: D. Appleton & Co., 1845) (a new translation).

185. http://www.encyclopedia.com/article-1G2-2875900019/betrothed.html.

186. David Brooks, "Pope Francis, the Prince of the Person," *New York Times*, Sept. 22, 2015; Deacon Greg Kandra, "And Now, Some Advice for Engaged Couples from the Pope," Patheos.com, May 27, 2015, http://www.patheos.com/blogs/deaconsbench/2015/05/and-now-some-advice-for-engaged-couples-from-the-pope/.

187. Barry Jones, *Dictionary of World Biography* (Canberra: Australian National University Press, 2015), pp. 559, 879–80.

188. Robin Healey, *Italian Literature Before 1900 in English Translation: An Annotated Bibliography* (Toronto: University of Toronto Press, 2011), p. 253; Aaron Thomas, ed., Aaron Thomas & Jeremy Parzen, trans., Cesare Beccaria, On Crimes and Punishments *and Other Writings* (Toronto: University of Toronto Press, 2008), pp. 17, 26, 32–34, 51, 55–56.

189. Charles Botta, *History of the War of the Independence of the United States of America* (George Alexander Otis, trans., New Haven: Nathan Whiting, 8th ed. 1834); Don C. Seitz, *Paul Jones: His*

Exploits in English Seas During 1778–1780 (New York: E. P. Dutton and Co., 1917), p. 195 (listing Italian-to-English translated editions of Botta's book printed in Philadelphia, Boston, New Haven, and Cooperstown, New York).

190. Clifford Stevens Walton, *The Civil Law in Spain and Spanish-America, including Cuba, Puerto Rico and Philippine Islands, and the Spanish Civil Code in Force, Annotated and with References to the Civil Codes of Mexico, Central and South America* (Washington, DC: W. H. Lowdermilk & Co., 1900), p. 493 n.‡.

191. Nathaniel Chipman, *Sketches of the Principles of Government* (Rutland, VT: J. Lyon, 1793), p. 198 n.*.

192. Alexis de Tocqueville, *Democracy in America* (Stilwell, KS: Digireads, 2007), Vol. 2, p. 104.

193. Uriah Milton Rose (1834–1913), The Encyclopedia of Arkansas History & Culture, http:// www.encyclopediaofarkansas.net/encyclopedia/entry-detail.aspx?entryID=2271. Rose was also one of the original seventy-five founders of the American Bar Association. Ibid.

194. U. M. Rose, *Beccaria and Law Reform*, 8 *The American Lawyer: A Monthly Journal Serving the Business and Professional Interests of the American Bar* (New York: Stumpf & Steurer, 1900), pp. 298–99, 303 ("Being Portions of an Address Delivered as President of the Arkansas State Bar Association at Its Meeting held at Little Rock" on January 3, 1900).

195. Rev. Erasmus Perkins, *A Few Hints Relative to the Texture of Mind, and the Manufacture of Conscience*, p. v (London: T. Davison, 1820) ("Prefatory Address" to "Sir John Bailey, Knt.," "One of the Justices of the Court of King's Bench," "published for the Benefit of the Rev. R. Wedderburn, Now suffering Two Years Imprisonment in Dorchester Jail, for an alledged Blasphemous Libel" "with a Dedication to Judge Bailey who Passed that Sentence").

196. 3 David S. Clark, ed., *Encyclopedia of Law and Society: American and Global Perspectives* (Thousand Oaks, CA: Sage Publications, 2007), p. 117.

197. Larry Wolff, *Inventing Eastern Europe: The Map of Civilization on the Mind of the Enlightenment* (Stanford, CA: Stanford University Press, 1994), pp. 115–16.

198. Bernard E. Harcourt, *The Illusion of Free Markets: Punishment and the Myth of Natural Order* (Cambridge: Harvard University Press, 2012), p. 57.

199. Portrait of Giulio Bonesana Beccaria (1774–1856) by Eliseo Sala (1813–1879), http://www. gettyimages.com/detail/news-photo/portrait-of-giulio-bonesana-beccaria-son-of-cesare-beccaria-news-photo/122216111?#portrait-of-giulio-bonesana-beccaria-son-of-cesare-beccaria-painting-picture-id122216111; Giulia Beccaria, http://www.wikiwand.com/it/Giulia_Beccaria.

200. Universal Declaration of Human Rights, G.A. res. 217 A(III), U.N. Doc. A/810 at 71 (1948).

201. International Covenant on Civil and Political Rights, G.A. res. 2200A (XXI), 21 U.N. GAOR Supp. (No. 16) at 52, U.N. Doc. A/6316 (1966), 999 U.N.T.S. 171, *entered into force* Mar. 23, 1976 (Article 7).

202. Second Optional Protocol to the International Covenant on Civil and Political Rights, Aiming at Abolition of the Death Penalty, G.A. res. 44/128, 44 U.N. GAOR Supp. (No. 49) at 207, U.N. Doc. A/44/49, *entered into force* July 11, 1991 (Article 1).

203. Convention Against Torture and Other Cruel, Inhuman or Degrading Treatment or Punishment, G.A. res. 39/46, annex, 39 U.N. GAOR Supp. (No. 51) at 197, U.N. Doc. A/39/51 (1984), *entered into force* June 26, 1987.

204. André Klip & Göran Sluiter, *Annotated Leading Cases of International Criminal Tribunals: The International Criminal Tribunal for the Former Yugoslavia 2002–2003* (Intersentia, 1999), p. 73.

205. *The Death Penalty: Abolition in Europe* (Strasbourg: Council of Europe Publishing, 1999), p. 182.

206. Barry Latzer & David McCord, *Death Penalty Cases: Leading U.S. Supreme Court Cases on Capital Punishment* (Burlington, MA: Butterworth-Heinemann, 3d ed. 2011), p. 424.

207. Jeanmarie Fenrich, Paolo Galizzi & Tracy E. Higgins, eds., *The Future of African Customary Law* (Cambridge: Cambridge University Press, 2011), pp. 44–46, 402.

208. Vicki Schieber, Trudy D. Conway & David Matzko McCarthy, eds., *Where Justice and Mercy Meet: Catholic Opposition to the Death Penalty* (Collegeville, MN: Liturgical Press, 2013).

209. John D. Bessler, "Revisiting Beccaria's Vision: The Enlightenment, America's Death Penalty, and the Abolition Movement," 4 *Northwestern Journal of Law and Social Policy* 195, 316–28 (2009).

210. John H. Wigmore, *A Preliminary Bibliography of Modern Criminal Law and Criminology* (Chicago: Northwestern University Building, 1909), pp. ix–x.

211. Francis Fellowes, comp., "A Visit to the Count de Sellon, Founder and President of the Geneva Peace Society," *American Advocate of Peace* (Hartford: William Watson, 1836), Vol. II, No. X, pp. 81–83; "Death of Count de Sellon," *The Advocate of Peace* (1839), Vol. III, No. 4, p. 88; John Gittings, *The Glorious Art of Peace: From the* Iliad *to* Iraq (Oxford: Oxford University Press, 2012), p. 133; Cameron Muir, "On the Abolition of the Death Penalty," Inside Story, Mar. 5, 2015, http://insidestory. org.au/on-the-abolition-of-the-death-penalty.

John Howard (1726–1790), the English prison reformer and Beccaria disciple, had journeyed through Switzerland in the mid-1770s as he visited prisons in continental Europe. As one account described his trip: "In this journey Switzerland seemed to present a striking superiority to all other countries on the continent in her prison discipline. He saw not a single person in fetters. The scale of punishment was regulated by light. The greater the crime the darker the cell. In many of the cantons the gaols were quite empty." "Howard," that source emphasizes, "returned to England profoundly impressed with the superiority of the continental nations over his own, and with their more humane and enlightened view of the subject of imprisonment." Once back in England, Howard wrote *The State of the Prisons in England and Wales* (1777), with the account of Howard's 13,418-mile trip through Europe noting of the initial publication of that work on prisons (and of Howard's tremendous admiration for Cesare Beccaria): "On the first appearance of the work it excited great attention, for it had been long and anxiously expected. The biographer says that Beccaria's well known book on Crimes and Punishments was a great favourite with Howard; he studied it deeply, quoted it frequently, and appears to have concurred in almost every point with its humane and philanthropic principles, and it is, he says, highly probable that it had something to do with his assumption of his great mission." Sylvanus Urban, *The Gentleman's Magazine*, Vol. XXXIII, p. 12 (London: John Bowyer Nichols and Son, 1850). Cesare Beccaria's *On Crimes and Punishments* was, in fact, admired by a wide range of thinkers writing on various subjects, including economics. For example, one 1767 edition of Beccaria's book, recently sold as a rare book, bears the signature of Henry Lloyd Morgan (1801–1883), a financial scholar who authored works such as *Auditors of Accounts of Joint Stocks* (1857) and *Personal Liabilities of Directors of Joint Stock Companies* (1858). https://www.baumanrarebooks.com/rare-books/beccaria-cesare-bonsana-marchese-di/essay-on-crimes-and-punishments/79641.aspx.

Index

Abbeville, France, 81–82, 170, 307
Aberdeen, Scotland, 178
abolition (of corporal punishments): call for, 169, 254; and Cesare Beccaria, 69; in France, 226–27; John Hancock's call for, 15; in Massachusetts, 15; in Mexico, 255; in New York, 276; and substitution of imprisonment, 284
abolition (of death penalty): in Africa/African countries, 278, 326; in America(s), 15, 215, 248, 250–51, 256; in Argentina, 248, 250, 252; in Austria, 237, 247; and Benjamin Franklin, 215; Benjamin Rush's call for, 15, 215, 217–18, 233; best essay to promote, 315; in Brazil, 248, 250; Catherine II's call for, 169; in Central America, 248, 250–51; Cesare Beccaria's call for, 70, 86, 95, 169, 204, 217, 226, 244, 246, 252, 278, 286, 290, 294, 301, 315, 326–27; Charles Lee's call for, 202; in Colombia, 248, 250–51, 256; in Connecticut, 250; as contingent on construction of penitentiary system, 255; in Costa Rica, 248, 250, 256; in Denmark, 231; in Dominican Republic, 251; and early Anglo-American opposition, 68; and early Popes, 77; in Ecuador, 248, 250–51, 256; Edward Livingston's call for, 196, 216; and efforts in China, 279–80; and efforts in Japan, 279–81; and efforts in Louisiana, 237; and efforts in Mexico, 254; and efforts in Virginia, 216; and efforts to impose a moratorium on executions, 250–51, 279; in England, 237; in Europe, 22, 231, 237, 247–48, 318; in France, 247–48, 318; Gio-

vanni Carmignani's call for, 193, 206; in Guatemala, 248; in Haiti, 255; and "happiness of society," 217–18; in Honduras, 248; in Illinois, 250; and Inter-American human rights system, 250; in international conventions/treaties, 326; in Italy, 193, 315; James Madison's views on, 196, 215, 240; and Jean Calas' execution/torture as sparking "the beginning of the abolition movement," 79; leading advocates for, 318; in Maine, 241; in Maryland, 250; in Mexico/Mexican states, 250, 254–55; in Michigan, 241; in Minnesota, 250; and Montesquieu, 75; in New Jersey, 250; in New Mexico, 250; in New York, 250; in Nicaragua, 248; in Norway, 231; in Panama, 250–51; in peacetime, 248; in Pennsylvania, 216; for political crimes, 255; for property offenses, 230; in Rhode Island, 241; in Rwanda, 326; in Scandinavia, 231; for shoplifting, 237; for sodomy, 228; in South Africa, 278; in South America, 248, 250–51, 256; in Sweden, 231; as "the highest, holiest, most noble aim," 237; and Thomas Jefferson, 215; in Tuscany, 202, 216, 233, 237, 327; and United Nations, 279; in United States, 250; in Uruguay, 248, 250; in Venezuela, 248, 250, 256; in wartime, 202, 326; William Bradford's call for, 217, 242–43; in Wisconsin, 241. *See also* anti-death penalty movement/organizations; anti-gallows advocacy; anti-gallows societies; *specific countries, organizations, and states*